VIEWPOINTS

Paralleling of Gospels

by

Harold Dwight Henry

STAR BIBLE PUBLICATIONS
Fort Worth, Texas 76182

Acknowledgments

I express my appreciation to my wife, Averil, for her great patience during the many years I've worked to compare the four gospels and for her efforts in editing **Viewpoints**.

I have often supplicated God to grant me insight to understand why gospels emphasize different aspects of Jesus' life. I am confident I could never have fathomed their messages without God's help. With my thanks and praise I honor God and his mercy on those who call on him for help with a true heart.

#C-2469
ISBN 1-56794-133-8

Viewpoints
Preface

For many years I have wondered why gospel writers recorded different incidents in Jesus' life. Even when all four writers mentioned the same encounter some add details omitted by others. One major obstacle for me to answer for myself why these variations appear was the time required in turning from gospel to gospel to compare the variations. To minimize this problem, I thought it might benefit me to place all records about the same or similar event in columns side by side for easy comparison. **Viewpoints** attempts to copy all accounts of the same or similar event in side-by-side columns in the same book opening. Evaluating the similarities and differences, my best conclusion is that each gospel audience needed varying exhortations to help them solve problems they faced, particularly those of false teachers and discouraged brethren. As Paul's letters to the churches and young ministers usually centered on helping Christians in each locality overcome specific problems he knew they encountered, it appears to me that each gospel writer stressed in John's and Jesus' lives those events which helped his audience solve their problems. Need of the audience largely determined gospel content.

Each gospel writer viewed John and Jesus as fulfilling specific Old Testament (O.T.) prophecies. These viewpoints serve as the focal point or theme of the events they record. References to O.T. prophecies, John's, Jesus', apostles', and others' teaching and/or comments recorded all center on the central theme to benefit their gospel audience with God's help in mastering their difficulties. Seeing how John and Jesus served in God's hand to defeat Satan's control of peoples' lives, gospel audiences may trust in how God's hand aids them in thwarting Satan's domination in their personal lives, giving them hope, and strengthening them to trust in God's providence.

Present-day church situations and problems closely resemble situations and problems faced by churches to whom the gospels were addressed. As false teachers circulated among churches and changed the truth about the lives and doctrines of John the Baptist and Jesus then, so Christians today encounter similar strange doctrines which deter us from believing and doing God's truth. Faithful Christians may compare what teachers and ministers advocate with the true records contained in the gospels. If we detect alterations in what is taught, we must abandon the false teachings as Satan's influence to continue his practice of separating us from God and Christ.

I have found this comparative gospel study enlightening and strengthening for my personal faith as I encounter life's difficulties and false doctrines. I pray God may bless any who reads **Viewpoints** that it may encourage you, too, to seek God's and Christ's honor by how you live and associate with your families, friends, and colleagues.

Harold Dwight Henry May 1, 1997

Contents

Contents

Contents

Contents

Contents

Relationship of Four Gospels

Viewpoints discusses these questions:
1. Why are there four gospels?
2. What is the nature of the kingdom of heaven, its people, King, laws, and judges?
3. How does God's King and kingdom relate to kingdoms of this world?
4. How does God's King and kingdom interact with individuals who choose not to enter God's kingdom and those who consider themselves citizens of God's kingdom, but have never participated in God-authorized initiation into God's kingdom?
5. Do gospels record all God's ordinances to identify and regulate his kingdom?
6. How does God's righteousness manifest itself in his kingdom?
7. When did the kingdom of heaven begin?
8. What function has God designed for teaching, faith, repentance, confession, baptism, humility, mercy, prayer, and forgiveness to serve in his kingdom?
9. How does obeying the precepts of God's kingdom bless people's lives?
10. How and for what purposes does God discipline offenders in his kingdom?
11. What theme unites each gospel and how does it affect the narrative?
12. Are events in each gospel in chronological sequence?

If God inspired gospels, what God-given reasons account for variations? If each gospel writer showed Jesus fulfilled Messianic prophecies and Moses' law, each must provide examples showing Jesus fulfilled O.T. references. Since the O.T. records about 330 Messianic prophecies, it would take one very long gospel to record examples of how Jesus fulfilled every Messianic prophecy and all Moses' law. I suggest each gospel writer recorded features in Jesus' life that demonstrated he fulfilled particular prophecies which affected his intended audience. If Matthew desired to convince Jews Jesus fulfilled O.T. law and prophets, he would pick examples, centering on God's promises to Abraham and David. If Mark aimed to encourage Gentiles to grasp the good news of salvation available to every nation, he would include examples, explaining how the new covenant offers salvation to every person in all nations and every generation. If Luke desired to demonstrate how God's wisdom blesses all who do his will that fathers and sons might unite in spirit and deed to fulfill Malachi's prophecy, he would emphasize those features in Jesus' ministry. If John viewed Jesus as the Prophet like Moses who spoke all God's truth to Israel, he would stress this concept in Jesus' life. Author's purpose and audience's needs and background control gospel content.

Consider variations in accounts of Jesus' feeding 5000, an event recorded by all four gospels. Matthew recorded Jesus departed into a desert by ship, fed 5000; disciples collected uneaten food; Jesus sent the disciples away by ship, retired to a mountain, prayed, walked on water, invited Peter to walk on water to him; and disciples confirmed their belief Jesus was God's Son. (Math.14:1-33) Mark observed Herod beheaded John, and apostles returned from preaching repentance in Israel. After teaching the multitude, Jesus showed compassion for and fed them. Disciples collected uneaten food; Jesus sent them by boat to Bethsaida, sent away the multitude, went into a mountain, prayed, and walked on water to the disciples, but Mark said nothing of Peter walking on water. (Mk.6:14-25) Luke noted Jesus sent apostles to preach; Herod beheaded John the Baptist; apostles returned; a multitude gathered; Jesus healed, explained God's kingdom, and fed them; 12 baskets of food remained, but Luke omitted Jesus' walking on water. (Lk.9:2-17) John observed Jesus visited Jerusalem to attend a Jewish feast where he strengthened one impotent for 38 years; the Passover neared; in Galilee he fed 5000; disciples collected uneaten food; people commented Jesus must be that Prophet; people planned to make

Jesus king; Jesus retired to a mountain; disciples departed by boat; Jesus walked on water to the disciples who received him into the boat. The following day Jesus taught about heavenly bread, offending and alienating many of his disciples. (Jno.5:1-6:69)

Other examples illustrate gospel variations. Why did Matthew record Jesus' ancestry to Abraham through David, but Luke traced his genealogy to Adam? Why did Mark and John omit his physical genealogy? Why did John refer to Jesus as God's Son by whom God created all things? Why did Matthew include the coming of wise men from the East, but Luke recorded God's message to shepherds near Bethlehem? When Matthew, Mark, and Luke each record Jesus' temptation in the wilderness, why do Matthew and Luke include details, but Mark merely mentioned the incident? Why did John omit his forty-day temptation? Why did Luke name kings, governors, and priests at Jesus' birth? Matthew noted only that Herod ruled Judah, but Mark and John ignored the political and religious leaders at that time.

Four gospels state John the Baptist prepared the Lord's way. (Math.3:3; Mk.1:3; Lk.3:4; Jno.1:23) Matthew, Luke, and John say John's preaching fulfilled Isaiah's message; Mark stated he fulfilled prophets, not just Isaiah's prophecy. Gabriel told Zacharias John's mission fulfilled Malachi's prophecy. (Lk.1:17) Do introductions show writers' viewpoints or are they incidentals?

Matthew and Luke say Jesus will baptize with the Holy Spirit and fire (Math.3:11; Lk.3:16); Mark and John state he baptizes with God's Spirit. (Mk.1:8; Jno.1:33) What accounts for two mentioning both baptisms and two speaking of only one? Do these variations indicate different audiences?

Matthew and Luke record Jesus' Sermon on the Mount or its equivalent. Matthew indicated Jesus taught all this at one time, but Luke penned much of the same material in separated areas. Did Jesus teach the Sermon on the Mount all at one time and then parts of it at various other times as Luke has it recorded? Jesus did preach the same concepts many times in many places. Matthew compared doing good to your brethren or friends to a publican practice, but Luke likened it to sinners' deeds. (Math.5:46; Lk.6:33) Matthew noted Jesus promised blessings on people's godly attitudes, but Luke recorded God blessed those economicly poor and physically hungry. (Math.5:3; Lk.6:20) Neither Mark nor John mentioned the Sermon on the Mount. Matthew and Mark state Daniel foretold Jerusalem's destruction. Luke said Gentiles executed wrath on Jerusalem. John omitted Jesus' prophecy of Jerusalem's destruction. These gospel variations intrigue me, and provide evidences about why and to whom each gospel writer taught about Jesus' life and work. Daniel and the wise men lived in the East. Matthew wrote to Jews scattered by Assyrian and Babylonian captors. They needed proof Jesus sits on David's throne to restore Israel's glory. Matthew and Luke stress Jesus fulfilled all the law and Messianic prophecies. (Math.5:17; Lk.24:44)

Matthew and Luke record Jesus' physical birth. Mark narrates Jesus' life, beginning with his approaching John the Baptist for baptism. John's gospel stresses Jesus' eternal existence as Creator embodied in flesh who, by God's Spirit, identifies the true nature of Jesus' eternal Father who so loves his disobedient children he willingly sacrifices his only begotten Son to save every person who believes and submits to the truth Jesus taught. (Jno 3:16-36)

Luke recorded Jesus' genealogy to Adam. Theophilus, a Gentile ruler, desired a physical relationship to Christ, indicating God offered Gentiles salvation, as Matthew recorded Jesus' ancestry to Abraham for Jews to note their physical relationship to the Messiah. That Matthew mentioned only Herod ruled Judah at Jesus' birth indicates he wrote to Jews, but Luke's record of numerous leaders especially near Syria and Judah and Jewish priests indicates he wrote to Gentiles who desired a historical account of Jesus' life. Internal evidences provide insight about audiences and purposes.

Jesus' preaching in Nazareth illustrates how writers record much or little about an incident to emphasize their purpose. Matthew omits the substance of Jesus' message in Nazareth's synagogue. Fellow citizens marvelled at his wisdom and miracles, but discredited him because he was simply a hometown boy. (Math.13:1-58) Mark's gospel differs little from Matthew's. (Mk.6:1-6) Luke stressed what Jesus taught and placed the incident early in his gospel. Matthew and Mark placed it after Jesus' series of parables on God's kingdom, but John omitted Nazareth's visit. Luke related Jesus stood and read from Isaiah chapter sixty-one. Closing the book, he stated he fulfilled Isaiah's prophecy that day. Nazarenes wondered at his message, but minimized his words, saying he was only Joseph's son. Jesus remarked no prophet is honored in his own city. He compared Israelites to Syrians, riling his audience. He reminded Nazarenes God sent Elijah to a Syrian widow during the 3 1/2-year drought when Israel contained many widows. Many lepers remained unclean in Israel when Elisha cleansed a Syrian's leprosy. Jesus barely escaped death by the hands of his former neighbors. (Lk. 4:16-30)

What conclusions are warranted from gospel variations? Did Luke record how Jesus honored Syrians above Israelites because Luke addressed a Syrian ruler? Was John silent on this event because he emphasized events in Judah rather than Galilee and because Nazarenes failed to consider Jesus as the Prophet like Moses who taught Israel all God's truth? (Deu.18:15-19)

Why did John relate Jesus turned water to wine in Cana, Galilee, but synoptic gospels omitted the event though they recorded many of Jesus' Galilean miracles? (Jno.2:1-11) Jesus performed that wonder before Herod imprisoned John. It transpired before they began relating Jesus' Galilean ministry. (Math.4:12; Mk.1:14)

Each gospel centers around a theme, audience, and Messianic prophecies, showing Jesus fulfilled God's law and prophets. He is God's promised Christ, anointed King, Prince of peace, Lord of all peoples. Refusing to submit to him results in grave consequences in this life and that to come because we deny our Creator the right to control his creation. Would we be angered if someone restricted our right to use our property as we please? If we affirm our right to control our property, why disallow God's right to control his creation? For us to deny God his right to use his creatures would be like farm animals denying their owner the right to sell or use them as his pleases.

Tendency for God's people to allow Satan to turn God's truth into a lie repeats itself in every generation. Eve preferred Satan's lie that she would not die by eating of the tree of the knowledge of good and evil to God's truth. Satan insisted she would become wise as God, knowing good and evil. (Gen:3:1-7) After Israel endured Egyptian bondage for four generations, God's first command to Israel at Sinai restricted them from having other gods, for God in heaven alone is God (Ex.20::2-3), but within sixty days they made a golden calf for their god. (Ex.32:1-6) When God empowered Cyrus to release Jews from Babylon's 70-year exile to return to Jerusalem to rebuild God's temple (Ezra 1:1-6), sixteen years later they contended **"The time is not come, the time that the Lord's house should be built."** (Ha.1:2) Gentiles once knew God's truth but put it out of their minds, imagined vain things, professed themselves wise, worshiped creatures, not God, and changed God's truth into a lie. (Rom.1:19-25) Was it Satan's influence that diverted Israel's attention from God to a golden image and Judah's return from Babylon from rebuilding the temple?

Consequences of Christian Unbelief

Christians have proved for nearly 2000 years we prefer Satan's lies to God's truth. Before apostle John died, some affirmed Jesus came not in flesh. (1 Jno.4:2-3) Some denied a resurrection. (1 Cor.15:12-20) Others boldly railed on God's truth that Christ's return raises all the dead to stand before him to be judged for violating righteousness, at which time everything physical will melt with fervent heat. (2 Pet.3:3-12)

God chastised early Christians for turning his truth to lies as he chastened Eve, Israel, and Gentiles. God gave Christians into the hand of a cruel lord for more than a 1000 years. (Rev.11:2-3) When they cried to God because of their oppression, God sent reformers who challenged the authority and doctrines of their Christian lord. By God's grace, they tumbled that ungodly usurper from his lordly state, much as he humbled Pharaoh before Israel when they exited Egypt. (Gen.15:12-14; Ex.5:1-14:31)

After God severed Christians from their proud Christian lord's cruelty, did Christrians remember God's truth or prefer Satan's lies? Hardly had the millions of corpses decayed before Christians continued their desire for Satan's lies rather than cherish God's truth. Again God scuttled Reformers' choice for lies by sending the Restoration movement in the early 1800s, but by 1850, Satan's lies most Restorationists loved. In this century alone the world endured two global wars which prematurely killed tens of millions by frightful deaths; hundreds of millions suffered torture, lost body parts, cities were leveled, creatures became extinct, and families were shredded. How shall God humble us to repent of abandoning his truth that we perish not? (Lk.13:3,5) Are we too feeble in mind and body to distinguish God's truth from Satan's lies?

God's word always tells us truth, corrects errors, encourages faith, and shows us how to please God. Gospels record God's truth to keep Christians in the way of life. God included four accounts of Jesus' life, deeds, God's truth about his only begotten Son, his death, and resurrection. Notwithstanding, some present-day Christians contradict nearly every truth recorded in God's gospels. 1. Jesus was not born of a virgin. 2. He did not teach <u>all</u> God's truth. 3. He did not perform miracles such as restoring sight and raising Lazarus from death. 4. He did not pronounce condemnation on divorce and remarriage to another. 5. He did not teach God hates immoral acts as prostitution, murder, and homosexuality. 6. Jesus was not God's Son; he was only a renowned teacher. 7. God did not raise him from the dead. 8. He will not return and raise from the dead all who ever lived . 9. There is no day of eternal judgment. 10. God will not destroy this world with fire. 11. God did not create the world in six days, it evolved over a period of billions of years..

With many Christians believing and acting on Satan's lies, why claim to be Christians, attend church, perform acts of courtesy? Why not demand others serve me, do as I please, or refuse restriction on actions?

Gospels record God's true account of his Son as O.T. writers foretold. He fulfills every promise God made to Jewish fathers, relating to the Messiah and God's everlasting kingdom. Gospels record those things truly believed by early Christians and confirmed by Jesus' apostles. (Lk.1:1,4) Christians need to repent and believe the gospel. (Mk.1:15) Jesus is <u>that</u> <u>Prophet</u> Moses promised to speak <u>all</u> God's truth. (Jno. 1:21,25;4:25-26;6:14;7:40;15:15) Every miracle recorded in gospels serves as God's confirmation of the truth Jesus taught. Believing anything contradicting what gospels record amounts to accepting Satan's lie in preference to God's truth. Would we stand before a civil or criminal judge in the land and call him a liar? If not, why stand before the most supreme judge of heaven and earth and call him a liar? (1 Jno.5:10) Gospels record God's truth. Change it not!

If Christians disbelieve God's truth, does it diminish its effectiveness? Paul asked what advantage God gave Jews. Their chief benefit lay in possessing God's oracles. Yet some did not believe their Scriptures. (Rom.3:1-3) Did their unbelief nullify God's law? No, God fulfilled every promise recorded in their Scriptures, punishing their unbelief and disobedience. (Dan.9:2-19) If Christians follow the same example of unbelief of God's oracles, will our rejection of truth free us from suffering consequences of unbelief? God's wrath burns against all ungodliness of men who hold his truth in unrighteousness. (Rom.1:18) Christians, be wise, repent, and believe God's gospel lest God's wrath consume us.

Repentance: Central Theme of Gospels

Synoptic gospels focus on God's promised kingdom. They concentrate on John and Jesus preaching repentance to Satan-snared Israelites. John's gospel urges Israelites in Galilee and Judah to abandon their God-blaspheming ways and submit to God's truth to praise the living God.

Obedience to God's kingdom promised to remedy abuses, blighting Israelite lives. Isaiah prophesied of John the Baptist, **"The voice of him that crieth in the wilderness, Prepare ye the way of the Lord, make straight in the desert a highway for our God. Every valley shall be exalted, and every mountain and hill shall be made low: and the crooked shall be made straight, and the rough places plain."** (Is. 40:3-4) Malachi testified, **"Behold, I will send my messenger, and he shall prepare the way before me: and the Lord, whom ye seek, shall suddenly come to his temple, even the messenger of the covenant, whom ye delight in: behold, he shall come, saith the Lord of hosts. But who may abide the day of his coming? and who shall stand when he appeareth? for he is like a refiner's fire, and like a fuller's soap: And he shall sit as a refiner and purifier of silver: and he shall purify the sons of Levi, and purge them as gold and silver, that they may offer unto the Lord an offering in righteousness. Then shall the offering of Judah and Jerusalem be pleasant unto the Lord, as in the days of old, and as in former years. And I will come near to you to judgment; and I will be a swift witness against the sorcerers, and against the adulterers, and against false swearers, and against those that oppress the hireling in his wages, the widow, and the fatherless, and that turn aside the stranger from his right, and fear not me, saith the Lord of hosts. For I am the Lord, I change not; therefore ye sons of Jacob are not consumed. Even from the days of your fathers ye are gone away from mine ordinances, and have not kept them. Return unto me, and I will return unto you, saith the Lord of hosts. But ye said, Wherein shall we return?"** (Mal.3:1-7) If we disregard the purifying nature of John's and Jesus' preaching, we miss much of the urgency of their ministries. Israelites displeased God, and they must be taught how to honor their heavenly Father.

Isaiah's and Malachi's prophecies serve as a general foundation on which each gospel writer viewed activities of John the Baptist and Jesus. Both came to correct Israelite transgression against God's precepts Moses delivered to Israel. When the disciples asked Jesus why scribes taught Elijah must first precede Christ, Jesus replied, **"Elias truly shall first come, and restore all things. But I say unto you That Elias is already come, and they knew him not, but have done unto him whatsoever they listed. Likewise shall also the Son of man suffer of them."** (Math.17:11-12) God sent John and Jesus to remedy Israelite transgression, but most Jews chafed at their message. Rather than straighten the way for the Lord by repenting of their sins and performing righteousness, they chose to abuse and ultimately to destroy both preparer and messenger of the covenant. We need to ask ourselves if we allow God's messengers to purify our lives that we may produce fruits of righteousness, or do we reject and/or eliminate those God sends to purify us?

Only Mark seems to limit his view of John's and Jesus' preaching primarily to Isaiah's and Malachi's prophecies. He stressed people needed to repent and believe the good news of God's kingdom which opens to every person a close association with our eternal heavenly Father who loves us and grieves that we disregard his admonition to live respectfully before him and bless our own consciences with forgiveness of sins. (Mk.1:15)

Matthew and Luke provide details of how John and Jesus purified Israelites. Gabriel informed Zacharias that John shall turn many of the children of Israel to their God. (Lk.1:16) Mary noted God put down the mighty and exalted them of low degree, filling the hungry with good things, but sending the rich away empty. (Lk.1:52-53) Zacharius foretold how John must go before the Lord's face to prepare his way by giving his people knowledge of salvation by remission of their sins. (Lk.1:76-77) Simeon informed Mary that Jesus shall cause many in Israel to fall and rise again. (Lk.2:34) Matthew's and Luke's gospels stress the need for Israelites to abandon formal religion, devoid of justice and mercy. John insisted Israelites must make crooked ways straight, elevate valleys, and level mountains. (Lk. 3:4-5) Descending from Abraham amounts to nothing if you live as vipers. God demands fruits which demonstrate repentance. (Math.3:7-10) If you own two coats and possess plenty of food, share with those who need a coat or food. Tax collectors must collect only that which Rome authorized. Soldiers must do violence to none, falsely accuse none, and be content with their wages. (Lk.3:6-14) Jesus answered Satan's taunts to summarize what God requires: 1) Man truly lives by obeying every word of God, not by choosing to do what pleases himself; 2) One must worship and serve God, not power, riches, fame or pleasure; and 3) We must not tempt God by endangering our lives in risky ventures. (Math. 4:4-6; Lk.4:4-6) Good news of God's kingdom promises healing to the brokenhearted, deliverance to those Satan captivates by sin, recovery of spiritual sight to those blinded by Satan's lies, healing to those Satan bruised by godless living, and fellowship with our heavenly Father to those who draw near to God through obedience to his Son's commands. (Lk.4:18-19)

Why Four Gospels?

Why has God provided us with four accounts of the life, teaching, deeds, death, resurrection, and ascension of his only begotten Son Jesus? God established a foundation by which men may determine truth, **"at the mouth of three witnesses, shall the matter be established."** (Deu. 19:15) God set forth this rule to guide his people to distinguish truth from error. It offers security in man's affairs as well as God's. God applies it to his own testimony. Four witnesses testified to Jesus' birth, truth taught, service, death, resurrection, and ascension. For about forty days he appeared often to his followers to confirm his resurrection. If four witnesses agree to these truths, they must be true. For us to deny these evidences amounts to our calling gospel writers and God liars. (1 Jno.5:10)

God utilized this three-or-more-witness rule in the O.T. Five books of law testified to God's justice and order. Genesis records the orderly account of God's wonderful creation of heaven and earth, heavenly bodies, plants and animals with man as God's magnificent handiwork who resembles both God who is Spirit and his creation which dwell in physical bodies. Exodus records God's deliverance of his chosen people from Egyptian bondage and his life-enhancing statutes and judgments to guide Israel in proper conduct and decisions, based on mutual agreement between God and Israel. (Ex.19:5-8) Leviticus delineates how God's law applied to and directed the tribe of Levi as they served as priests and caretakers for God's house. Numbers explains how God's commands applied to all twelve tribes, how God selected the tribe of Levi to replace the firstborn in each family, how Israelites inherited Canaan, and how cities of refuge must be set aside for a haven to those who accidentally killed a person. Deuteronomy confirms God's covenant and law given at Sinai to the second generation who exited Egypt to receive God's promised land and to cause God's name to be honored in all nations.

God's three-or-more-witness law functioned in recording deeds of kings in Israel and Judah. Both books of Samuel record God granting Israel a king who must rule as God prescribed in his law. (Deu.17:14-20) When Saul, Israel's first visible king, refused to abide by God's law, God replaced him with David, a man after God's own heart who would keep all God's commands. (1 Sam.13:8-14) Though David sinned in defiling Bathsheba, killing her husband, and numbering Israel's warriors, his heart steadfastly rested on doing God's will. Because David humbled himself God cleansed his conscience and forgave him. God established his throne forever to rule over God's people. (2 Sam.7:12-16) First and second Kings trace the kings of Israel and Judah from Solomon to Judah's desolation and exile by Babylon, delineated from the Kingdom of Israel's perspective. Both books of Chronicles reiterate God's kings from David to Judah's desolation and exile by Babylon, from Judah's viewpoint. All six books of kings emphasize how God honored or rejected kings, based on how they submitted to or violated God's law.

Isaiah, Jeremiah, Ezekiel, and Daniel, God's four major prophets, served to reinforce God's three-or-more-witness rule. Each testified to Israel's transgression of God's law, pending disasters as God set forth in his covenant, and God's promise to restore them to their homeland when they repented and submitted to their covenant with God. (Lev.26:3-46; Deu. ch. 27-28)

Four gospels reinforce God's three-or-more-witness law. These four books testify God sent his only begotten Son to manifest God living with men, his proclaiming God's everlasting righteousness, rejection, condemnation, crucifixion, death, resurrection, and ascension. Are four witnesses trustworthy? Do they confirm Jesus to be God's Son, benefiting men by word and deed? If they do, why say some among us Jesus was not born of a virgin, did not teach <u>all</u> God's truth, did not die, rose not from the dead, ascended not to heaven, and shall not appear again to judge every person as to how he/she submitted to or rebelled against God's law? These truths apostolic Christians believed. (Lk.1:1) Will God bless or bring woes on Christians as he did to Israel and Judah with their kings for unbelief and transgression? (Rom.1:18)

Paul's, James', John's, and Jude's epistles to the churches also illustrate God's use of the three-or-more rule to determine truth.

Matthew's Gospel Theme

Matthew's gospel emphasizes how Jesus fulfilled every promise God made to Abraham and David, blessing all families and nations. Because Abraham commanded his children to keep the way of the Lord to do justice and judgment, God promised Abraham, **"In thee shall all families of the earth be blessed."** (Gen.12:3;18:18-19) David sang of God, **"Blessed is he whose transgression is forgiven, whose sin is covered.**

Blessed is the man unto whom the Lord imputeth not iniquity, and in whose spirit there is no guile." (Ps.32:1-2) Our heavenly Father is gracious to overlook our misdeeds if we believe in Jesus' cleansing blood and obey his God-given precepts.

After Jesus came into Galilee, preaching repentance for the kingdom of God neared (Math.4:17), Matthew recorded the Sermon on the Mount. Jesus instructed his audience how to participate in all the blessings God promised Abraham and David. He enumerated eight attitudes which, if incorporated into a person's life, produce genuine blessings God promised to Abraham and David. These attitudes lift a person above life's discouragements and ever offer hope in every situation. Matthew stressed the need to avoid guile by desiring to please God, not man, in prayer, giving, fasting, and accumulating wealth. (Math.6:1-23) Incorporating these purifying attitudes and eliminating guile, which seeks man's praise for religious actions, God will not charge us with iniquity when we falter through weakness. Keeping God's commands to perform justice and judgment assures us we receive the blessings God promised Abraham and David. (Math.7:21-27)

What is God's justice and judgment? Abraham practiced those qualities in his association with others. He pleased God. When Abraham's descendants dwelt in Egypt and endured Pharaoh's rigorous harshness, many lost sight of God's justice and judgment. To refresh their minds, God explained justice and judgment when Moses delivered the ten commandments. (Ex.20:1-23:33) Besides ten commands, Moses recorded forty-six penalties to chasten violators of justice. God's decrees and penalties gave Israel a jurisprudence far superior to any people of their day. (Deu. 4:8;32:31) Gentile nations persisted in deeds destructive to themselves and others. (Lev. 18:3-30;20:2-27) With the coming of God's eternal kingdom, God offers Jews and Gentiles his superior statutes of justice and judgment which never change. "**Behold my servant, whom I uphold; mine elect, in whom my soul delighteth; I have put my spirit upon him: he shall bring forth judgment to the Gentiles....He shall not fail nor be discouraged till he have set judgment in the earth: and the isles shall wait for his law.**" (Is.42:1,4) Only Matthew referred to Isaiah's promise. "**Behold my servant, whom I have chosen; my beloved, in whom my soul is well pleased: I will put my spirit upon him and he shall shew judgment to the Gentiles.**" (Math. 12:18) Jesus taught and demonstrated to Israelites and Gentiles God's judgment as recorded in the Sermon on the Mount. (Math.5:1-7:29) He <u>showed</u> (demonstrated) how to apply God's justice and judgment by healing sicknesses and infirmities, restoring limbs, casting out devils, restoring sight and hearing, feeding the hungry and restoring life to the deceased. (Math.8:1-9:38) Why? because he, like his heavenly Father, grieved because of Satan's hurts, afflicting his people. He showed God's truth, "**All things whatsoever ye would that men should do to you, do ye even so to them: for this is the law and the prophets.**" (Math.7:12) He selected and commissioned apostles to explain and show God's justice and judgment. (Math.10:1-42)

We often fail to comprehend benefits available to those who do God's justice and judgment. "**The law of the Lord is perfect, converting the soul: the testimony of the Lord is sure, making wise the simple. The statutes of the Lord are right, rejoicing the heart: the commandment of the Lord is pure, enlightening the eyes. The fear of the Lord is clean, enduring for ever: the judgments of the Lord are true and righteous altogether. More to be desired are they than gold, yea, than much fine gold: sweeter also than honey and the honeycomb. Moreover by them is thy servant warned: and in keeping of them**

there is great reward." (Ps.19:7-11) God's statutes always bless us. (Deu.6:24) They produce the greatest possible happiness in our lives. (Jno.10:10; 1 Tim.4:8) God's commands never deny anything that benefits our lives. (Ps.84:11)

To David, the faithful king, God promised a son to rule on his throne forever if his children kept God's commands. (2 Sam.7: 12-13; 1 Kin.9:4-9; Am.9:11; Zech.6:12-13; Act.15:16-17) Matthew's gospel shows how Jesus fulfilled the blessings and power promised to Abraham and David. Matthew referred to at least 37 prophecies and 36 passages recorded in Jewish Scriptures. Tracing Jesus' ancestry through David to Abraham, Matthew appealed to Jewish interest. Their nation produced the Christ, the savior of all nations. Matthew's ancestry of Jesus corresponds to how Holy Scripture recorded genealogy. (Gen.2:4;6;9; 10:1;11:10,27;25:12,19;36:1;37:2) His gospel addressed a Jewish audience.

How did Jesus extend Abraham's blessings to all people? God spoke of Abraham, **"Seeing that Abraham shall surely become a great and mighty nation, and all the nations of the earth shall be blessed in him? For I know him, that he will command his children and his household after him, and they shall keep the way of the LORD, to do justice and judgment; that the LORD may bring upon Abraham that which he hath spoken of him."** (Gen. 18:18-19) Jesus began his ministry, explaining that men's lives are blessed by manifesting the Beatitudes and in obeying God's instructions in the Sermon on the Mount. 1) Blessed are the poor in spirit; 2) Blessed are they that mourn; 3) Blessed are the meek; 4) Blessed are they who hunger and thirst after righteousness; 5) Blessed are the merciful; 6) Blessed are the pure in heart; 7) Blessed are the peacemakers; and 8) Blessed are those persecuted for righteousness' sake. (Math. 5:3-12) These attitudes guided Abraham's life. In every age people who maintain and act on these attitudes receive God's blessings promised Abraham and his children. They dwell in God's kingdom with Abraham, Isaac, and Jacob and manifest the Beatitudes in daily living, All who retain guile God excludes from the kingdom of heaven. (Math.8:11-12) Like Abraham, Jesus lived the Beatitudes. When the blind longed for sight, he restored his sight. If a leper sought cleansing, he healed his leprosy. When asked to eliminate devils, he cast out the evil spirits. If Jesus had been afflicted with one or more of these maladies, he would have desired relief. He helped others as he would like to have been helped. (Math.7:12) God blesses Abraham's children because they keep the way of the Lord to do justice and judgment: love God and man. (Math.22:37-40) Matthew narrated these deeds in Jesus' life. He taught with authority. If we desire blessings God promised Abraham, we perform all our Father's will: show justice, judgment, equity, and mercy.

Jesus, David's son, performs all God-authorized king duties: 1) Saves God's people from their enemies (1 Sam.9:16; 2 Sam.3: 18; Ezek.38:23-28; Math.1:21); 2) Judges his people (1 Sam.8:5; Math.9:12-13;11: 21-24;12:24-28;15:16-20;18:21-35;20:25-28;21:24-25,33-41;25:31-46); 3) Feeds God's people heavenly manna (2 Sam.5:2; Ezek.34:23-24; Math.14:14;15:32-38); 4) Leads his people in righteousness (1 Sam. 23:31-46;25:28; 2 Sam.5:2; Math.6:13); 5) Builds God's house (2 Sam.7:12-13; 1 Chr.28:5-6; Math.16:18); 6) Rules forever on David's throne in heaven (2 Sam.7:12-13; Act.2:30-36); and 7) Prophesies about Christ like David. Nearly every incident Matthew recorded relates to one or more of these regal activities God promised to Abraham and/or David.

Unlike man's choice of a king, God has provided us with a King who genuinely cares for each of us, provides for all our needs, rules righteously, and is not easily discouraged. (Is.9:6-7;42:1-4)

Mark's Gospel Theme

Mark's gospel centers on repenting and believing the good news of God's Son. Jesus taught and worked wonders to correct transgressions of God's law, blighting Jewish lives. John and Jesus promised forgiveness of sins to the obedient. John the Baptist introduced Jesus as Isaiah and Malachi indicated. (Is.40:3-5; Mal.3:1-6) To prepare for God's kingdom abandon your evil lifestyle and do righteousness. (Mk.1:2-3) John leveled mountains, elevated valleys, and straightened people's crooked lives. Common people rejoiced in John, but Pharisees, scribes, and priests, wishing to retain their formal religious practices, opposed John and reviled him and Jesus' miracles rather than produce fruits of God's righteousness.

As God-ordained King, Jesus manifested God's power and authority over nature, disease, evil spirits, doctrine, Sabbath, sin, death, and Satan. He comforted by healing and saying God's kingdom appeared during their lifetime. (9:1) Nearing Jerusalem for the last Passover before his death, Jesus added he restored David's kingdom as God intended, not as Jews expected. God's kingdom rules by revamping thinking and actions, not as a political power. Forgiveness of sins he offered to all nations. (16:15-16) Mark addressed Romans.

Jesus corrected Jews' and his disciples' crooked ways. Scribes asked who can forgive sins, but God? (2:7) Jesus demonstrated his power on earth to forgive sins. (2:10) Pharisees chided when Jesus ate with publicans and sinners. (2:16) God sent him not to call the righteous, but sinners to repentance. (2:17) John's disciples and Pharisees asked why Jesus' disciples didn't fast. (2:18) When the bridegroom is taken away, then they shall have reason to fast. (2:20) Pharisees fretted when his disciples picked grain on the Sabbath. (2:23) God made the Sabbath for man, not man for the Sabbath. (2:27) Pharisees wondered if he healed on the Sabbath. (3:2) Is it lawful to do good on the Sabbath? (3:4) Scribes accused him casting out devils by Satan's power. (3:22) Satan won't destroy himself. (3:23) People considered Jesus' fleshly relatives, but he explained spiritual relationships. (3:32-35) Nazarenes wondered how he gained his power. (5:2) A prophet has no honor in his own country. (5:4) John rebuked Herod because he married his brother's wife while his brother still lived. (6:17-18) Pharisees and scribes, thought Jesus' disciples should obey elders' traditions. (7:5) Isaiah prophesied of your hypocrisy. You lay aside God's commands to keep your traditions. (7:6-13) Pharisees asked if it were lawful to put away one's wife. (10:2) Whosoever puts away his wife and marries another commits adultery. (10:11-12) A Jew asked how to gain eternal life. (10:17) Keep God's commands. (10:18-19) Priests, scribes, and elders questioned his authority to cleanse the temple. (11:28) Was John's baptism from God or man? (11:29-30) Disciples desired a parable's meaning. (4:10) Four groups hear God's word, but only those who bear fruit are converted and have their sins forgiven. (4:11-20) Disciples asked why wind and sea obeyed Jesus. (4:41) Why be fearful? (4:40) Disciples wanted to send people to buy food for themselves. (6:36) You give them food. (6:37) Peter rebuked Jesus for saying he must die. (8:32) Get behind me, Satan, you seek the things of this world. (8:33) Disciples asked why Elijah must first come. (9:11) Elijah shall come first and restore all things. He came, and they killed him. (9:12-13) Why couldn't we cast out the devil? (9:28) This kind comes out only by prayer and fasting. (9:29) Disciples asked who should be greatest. (9:34) He who is servant of all is greatest. (9:35) James and John desired chief positions. (10:35-37) God gives that honor, not me. (10:38-40) Other disciples resented their seeking first honor. (10:41) Gentile lords rule; you serve. (10:42-45) Disciples admired the temple. (13:1,4)

It shall be destroyed. (13:2,5-37) Why not sell the ointment and give the money to the poor? (14:3-5) She did a good work, let her alone. (14:6-9) Who shall betray you? (14:18-19) He who dips in the dish with me. (14:18,20-21)

As God sent John and Jesus to correct attitudes and deeds, separating Jews from God, he sends ministers to us to correct our godless attitudes and deeds, keeping us from our heavenly Father. Christ benefits only those who obey him. (16:15-16)

Luke's Gospel Theme

False teachers spread doctrines, appealing to the flesh. Luke supplied Theophilus with an accurate account of what God wanted Christians to believe about John, Jesus, and God's kingdom. God sent John to prepare Israel to receive Christ and God's kingdom. They must abandon ungodliness and return to God's righteousness to enter his kingdom. Satan bound Israelites in his prison, but Jesus came to free them. In Nazareth, Jesus read from Isaiah, **"The Spirit of the Lord GOD is upon me; because the LORD hath anointed me to preach good tidings unto the meek; he hath sent me to bind up the brokenhearted, to proclaim liberty to the captives, and the opening of the prison to them that are bound. To proclaim the acceptable year of the Lord, and the day of vengeance of our God; to comfort all that mourn; to appoint unto them that mourn in Zion, to give unto them beauty for ashes, the oil of joy for mourning, the garment of praise for the spirit of heaviness; that they might be called trees of righteousness, the planting of the Lord, that he might be glorified."** (Is.61:1-3; Lk.4:18-19) Jesus provided God's light in man's spirit to all who obey God's commands. God liberates from Satan's sin-prison, but he punishes the disobedient.

Luke quoted Malachi, showing God's task for John the Baptist. **"Behold, I will send you Elijah the prophet before the coming of the great and dreadful day of the Lord: and he shall turn the heart of the fathers to the children, and the heart of the children to their fathers lest I come and smite the earth with a curse**." (Mal.4:5-6) Though Luke omitted part of Malachi's prophecy about joining the hearts of the children to their fathers, this becomes part of Luke's theme. Luke includes three concepts about returning fathers' and sons' hearts toward each other: 1) Zacharias', Joseph's, and others' hearts cared for their sons. (ch. 1,2,8,11,15; 2) Hearts of sons turned to their fathers; (ch. 2,5,11,15) 3) God and his children turn to each other when his children repent. (ch. 3,6,11,12,15) Luke leads us to evaluate our relationship to God's kingdom. We prepare Christ's way by returning our hearts to our children and our children's hearts to us. Otherwise, how shall God claim us as his children or we to look to God as our heavenly Father? Parable of two sons (ch. 15) summarizes this part of Luke's message. A father shared his goods with his sons. The younger son took his portion and journeyed into a far country where he chose a lifestyle radically alien to his father's, and wasted his inheritance in riotous living. During famine, this son fell into deep poverty and fed swine to supply his needs. He reflected on his distress, and he realized his father's servants prospered better than did he. He resolved to return to his father, admit his sin, and ask his father to receive him as a servant. As he neared home, his father recognized him before he arrived, ran, embraced, and kissed his son. Without hearing his son's confession and request, his father sent a servant to fetch the best robe for his son, put a ring on his finger, placed shoes on his feet, and prepare the fatted calf for a merry feast. His dead son now lived.

The elder son, returning from the field, heard the merry-making and asked a servant the reason for the rejoicing. Understanding his father rejoiced at the return of his younger son, his anger flamed, and he refused to join the party. His father went to him, entreating him to rejoice. You have served with me, and all I have is yours. It's proper to be glad that your dead brother lives again. The father's heart yearned for both his sons. The elder son's heart fretted because he felt his father withheld good from him to make merry with his friends. Though the younger son's heart once departed from his father, he now understood his father had treated him well, and he wanted that better life. This parable depicts God's faithfulness, but our hearts wander from our heavenly Father. Satan convinces us God deprives us of life's joys as he persuaded the younger son his father restricted him from the better things of life. Realizing God's way benefits us above Satan's sham, we devote our hearts to God. He rejoices greatly at our return and shares his blessings with us. He desires all his children love all God's children. (1 Jno. 4:7)

God assigned John to turn the disobedient to the wisdom of the just. Luke pursued this activity in John's and Jesus' ministries. Good fruits indicate the wisdom of the just. Luke recorded incidents, contrasting disobedient attitudes and deeds with wisdom of the just. (1:17) People asked John how to prepare for the Lord's coming. He answered that all who had two coats or extra food must give to those who lacked. (3:10-11) Publicans prepared for Christ by taxing only what Rome appointed. (3:12-13) Soldiers did violence no person; accused none falsely; and were content with their wages. (3:14) Jesus instructed Satan man needs every word of God, besides body food, to live. (4:4) We ought worship nothing but God. (4:8) We must not tempt God. (4:12) Jesus explained that being poor, hungry, weeping, or reproached for Christ's sake brings blessings. (6:20-23) Treating enemies kindly demonstrates wisdom of the just. Woes darken lives of all who live as if this world holds life's fullness. (6:27-36) Examples are: 1) When a Pharisee invited Jesus to dine with him, the Pharisee lacked wisdom by not providing water to wash Jesus' feet, gave no him no kiss, and anointed not his head. A woman the Pharisee despised as a sinner showed wisdom of the just by anointing Jesus' feet, washing his feet with tears, kissing, and wiping his feet with her hair. (7:36-50) 2) Jesus illustrated who's our neighbor by contrasting the disobedience of the priest and Levite with the kindness of the Samaritan. (10:25-37) 3) Example of the rich man and Lazarus contrast the rich man's satisfaction with his material wealth with Lazarus' patience in hunger and disease in this life to lay hold on wealth of eternal life. (16:19-31) 4) Jewish leaders' mock trial and Pilate's refusal to execute justice Luke contrasted with Jesus' submission to God's plan for his life. Jesus showed wisdom of the just. (22:66-23:25)

What is the wisdom of the just? Habakkuh stated the just live by faith. (Hab.2:4) Wisdom of the just strengthens us during trials to live to receive God's promised blessings. We overlook insults and privations now to gain eternal riches and our heavenly Father's honor later. We treat kindly those who act discourteously because we have great respect for God and his promise even though we presently suffer. (Heb.11:6,13,16,26,39-40)

Theme of John's Gospel

John corrects Jewish disobedience to God's law that their sacrifices might honor God. John combines a second thread in his gospel. Jesus is the Prophet like Moses. **"The LORD thy God will raise up unto thee a Prophet from the midst of thee, of thy brethren, like unto me; unto him ye shall hearken; According to all that thou desiredst of the LORD thy God in Horeb in the day of the assembly, saying, Let me**

not hear again the voice of the LORD my God, neither let me see this great fire any more, that I die not. And the LORD said unto me, They have well spoken that which they have spoken. I will raise them up a Prophet from among their brethren, like unto thee, and will put my words in his mouth; and he shall speak unto them all that I shall command him. And it shall come to pass, that whosoever will not hearken unto my words which he shall speak in my name, I will require it of him." (Deu.18:15-19) Only John's gospel mentions the or that Prophet. "**The law was given by Moses, but grace and truth came by Jesus Christ.**" (1:17) Jews and Samaritans awaited that Prophet. (Jno.1:21,25) He must tell them all things. (4:25-42) Feeding the 5000 convinced Galileans Jesus was that Prophet. (6:14) In Jerusalem, Jews believed Jesus was that Prophet (7:40), but they rejected God's word. They continued not in God's truth which proved they were Satan's children, not God's. (8: 30-47) Jesus taught all God's truth as Moses promised. (15:15) God cut off the disobedient from among his people for spurning his truth. (Act.3:22-23) Those who heard and received God's truth Jesus called friends. (Jno.17:6-8;15:14-16) As God sent Jesus to tell Israel all God commanded them, Jesus sent his disciples to spread that truth to all nations. As God provided Jesus with his Holy Spirit to know and do all God's will, Jesus granted God's Spirit to empower his apostles to know and do all the Father's will. (3:34;16:13) When apostles neared death, they recorded all God's truth that men of all nations and generations might believe Jesus to be the Prophet and God's Son to forgive sins. (20:30-31) Believing and continuing in God's truth we gain eternal life. Disbelieving or refusing to continue in his truth brings death. John addressed Gentiles.

God accepts us as obedient children only if we do what Jesus commanded. (Jno.8:31)

Summary of Gospel Themes

Examining each gospel's theme unifies the writer's record of Jesus' life and work. Each gospel is more than a collection of actions and teachings. Each carries a particular message, a point of view, showing how Jesus fulfilled one or more prophecies from God. Each incident, miracle, remark of friend or foe, adds to the culmination of the theme, carried throughout the epistle. This concept increases one's appreciation for each gospel. Matthew saw how Jesus brought Abraham's and David's blessings to fulfill the work of Emmanuel, God dwelling with man. Mark encouraged everyone to repent and believe the good news of salvation. After his resurrection and ascension, Jesus offers Emmanuel to every nation, family, and person, bringing Abraham's blessings to all who do Abraham's deeds. To Luke, Jesus frees Satan's captives, giving us God's light (wisdom of the just). John saw Jesus as The Prophet Moses promised who delivers God's complete truth to Israel. Disobeying that truth severed people from God's blessings. Each gospel shows how John and/or Jesus purified Jews who had abandoned God's truth. Believing themselves to be God's people without correcting their lives dishonors God. Gospels include much of the same material, but recording how John and Jesus fulfilled particular God-given promises, they stress different points. This accounts for variations.

To enjoy God's blessings today we must repent of our sins, purge our thoughts and deeds of Satan's lies, think about and do God's righteousness, and love our neighbors as we love ourselves. (Mk.12:33) Follow not the steps of Pharisees and scribes who stubbornly insisted that their traditions opened to them God's eternal rest. Man's pride offends God. He made us subject to vanity to keep us humble, and the humble God offers eternal life. (Rom.8:20-21)

Outline 1: Luke Identifies God's Kingdom

Luke's Summary of God's Kingdom

I. Nature of God's Kingdom
  A. God's Christ rules 9:20
  B. Son of Highest on David's throne 1:32; 18:28-29,38
  C. Horn of salvation 1:69-71,74-75
  D. Savior of all peoples 2:30; 4:18
  E. Mightier than
    1. John 3:16
    2. Satan 11:21-22
    3. Solomon 11:31
    4. Jonah 11:32;
    5. David 20:41-44
  F. Mighty power of God 9:11,43
    1. Lord of Sabbath 4:43;6:5
    2. Spoke word with power 4:32-36
    3. Wind & water obeyed him 8:25
    4 Relieved any ailment 9:6,11
    5. God delivered all things to Jesus 10:22;20:2-4
  G. King of Jews 23:2-3,37-38,42
  H. Undivided kingdom 11:17-20
  I. Shall come with power 21:27

II. Coming of Kingdom
  A. Before some there died 9:27
  B. Immediately? 19:11-27
  C. Nigh to you 10:9,11;11:20; 21:31
  C. Some tried to press into it 16:16
  D. Comes not with observation 17:20
  E. It's within a person 17:21
  F Some waited for it 22:51
  G. Comes in name of Lord 19:38

III. Citizens of Kingdom
  A. Poor enter 6:20
  B. Seek King's reward 6:46;14:14
  C. Least greater than John 7:28
  D. Seek 1st God's kingdom 12:31
  E. Disobedient thrust out 13:31
  F. Eat in Kingdom 14:15-24;22:16
  G. Like little children 18:16
  H. Strengthen brethren 22:32
  I. Understand mysteries 8:10;10:21
  J. Humble are exalted 1:52;18:17
  K. Delivered from enemies 1:74
  L. Are holy & righteous 1:75
  M. Love their enemies 6:27-36
  N. Judge not & forgive 6:37
  O. Have good-treasured hearts 6:45
  P. Possess great faith 7:9
  Q. Glorify God 7:16
  R. Not offended in Jesus 7:23
  S. Justify God in baptism 7:29
  T. Love much--forgiven much 7:47
  U. Turn back--unfit for K. 9:62
  V. Persecuted 21:12
  W. Choose good part 10:42
  X. Are taught of God 1:77;11:1
  Y. Ask of God 11:9-13
  Z. Satan can repossess 11:24-26
  AA. Repent 13:3,5
  BB. Forsake all & serve 14:33;22:25-32
  CC. Enter not temptation 22:40,46

IV. Mysteries of God's Kingdom
  A. Explained by parables 8:10
    1. Like mustard seed 13:19-21
    2. Like leaven 13:31
    3. Blind don't lead 6:39
    4. Good fruit 6:43
    5. Rock or sand foundation 6:47
    6. As children in market 7:32
    7. Two creditors 7:41-42
    8. Sowed seed 8:5-8
    9. Lighted candle 8:16;11:33-36
    10. Family relationships 8:21
    11. Small child 9:48
    12. Good Samaritan 10:30-37
    13. Importunity 11:5-8
    14. Sparrows 12:6
    15. Rich man--fool 12:16-21
    16. Barren fig tree 13:6-9;21:29-31
    17. Salt 14:34-35
    18. 100 sheep 15:4-7
    19. 10 silver pieces 15:8-10
    20. Prodigal son 15:11-32
    21. Unjust steward 16:1-12
    22. Rich man & Lazarus 16:19-31
    23. Lightning 17:24
    24. Noah & Lot 17:32-36
    25. Pharisee & publican 18:9-14
    26. Wicked husbandmen 20:9-18
    27. Fig tree 21:29-31
    28. Two gates 13:24

Matthew

1:1 The book of the generation of Jesus Christ, the son of David, the son of Abraham.

Audience Matthew addressed Jews dispersed by Assyrian and Babylonian exile. They lived in the eastern part of the Roman Empire from which the wise men (elite as opposed to shepherds from Luke's record) came looking for King of the Jews. (Math. 2:1) Daniel had dwelt in Babylon. He prophesied of Jewish return to Judah, rebuilding Jerusalem and their temple, coming of the Messiah, and another desolation of Jerusalem and God's temple. He noted God's kingdom must subdue all kingdoms. The King to rule God's kingdom appears before God to receive dominion. (Dan.2:44-45;7:13-14;9:24-27) Jesus referred to Daniel's prophecy (Math.24:15) These connections with the dispersed indicate Matthew wrote to dispersed Jews. Tradition states Matthew ministered to Eastern Jews.

Viewpoint Matthew viewed Jesus as fulfilling three major prophecies to Jewish fathers. Abraham's son extends God's blessings to every person in every nation. (Gen.12:3) David's son sits on David's throne forever and build God's house. (2 Sam.7:12-13) Emmanuel is God dwelling among men. (Math.1:23; Is.8:8-10) Matthew shows Jesus fulfilled all these promises. As king he taught attitudes that blessed and saved his people from their sins. He healed every kind of malady tormenting mankind, raised the dead, controlled nature, preached and authorized apostles to preach God's kingdom, exceeded the temple in glory, was Lord of the Sabbath, bound Satan to spoil his house, excelled Jonah in calling people to repentance, overshadowed Solomon in wisdom, built his church, outranked David who called him "Lord," and possessed all power in heaven and in earth. Truly he was God dwelling among men. (Math.1:21;2:1;4:17, 24;5:3-12;8:26;9:23-25;10:5;12:6,8,25-42; 16:18;22:43-45;27:29,37;28:18)

Mark

1:1 The beginning of the gospel of Jesus Christ, the Son of God;

Audience: Mark assisted Paul in Rome during Paul's imprisonment. He mentioned Rufus whom Paul named. (Mk.15:21; Rom. 16:13) He omitted Jesus' early life, rulers at his birth, Sermon on the Mount, and numerous parables which contained little meaning to Romans to whom Mark addressed his gospel. Romans personally knew Mark. He placed himself in his narrative as an eyewitness to Jesus' death, burial, resurrection, and ascension (Mk.14:51-52) Omitting Jesus' genealogy may have reduced Roman prejudice against Jesus.

Viewpoint: Good news of God's kingdom John the Baptist introduced and Jesus demonstrated by preaching that Jews, God's chosen people, needed to repent and show true righteousness in daily living. Hypocrisy God will not tolerate. Jesus informed Israel that God's kingdom with power appeared during the lifetime of those who heard him. (Mk.9:1) Twice Mark mentioned that Jesus shall destroy the temple made with hands and replace it with one made without hands. (Mk.14:58;15:29) Jesus authorized apostles to preach the gospel to all nations. All who believe and submit to baptism escape Satan's dominion to enter God's kingdom.. (Mk. 16:15-16)

Mark presented ongoing evidence demonstrating Jesus is God's Son. God acknowledged Jesus as his Son when John the Baptist baptized him. (Mk.1:9-11) His miracles proved he came from God to benefit all he met? Jesus showed God's power to rid lives of diseases, demons, leprosy, withered limbs, blindness, and death. If any of Satan's evils torment us, God's Son can cancel that terror. Jesus can deliver us from Satan's eternal punishment if we submit to his commands rather than Satan's. (Mk.9:42-49;1:21-27;16:15-16) Realizing Jesus can benefit each person's life, all should repent and believe God's gospel. (Mk.1:15)

Luke

1:1 Forasmuch as many have taken in hand to set forth in order a declaration of those things which are most surely believed among us, 2 Even as they delivered them unto us, which from the beginning were eyewitnesses, and ministers of the word; 3 It seemed good to me also, having had perfect understanding of all things from the very first, to write unto thee in order, most excellent Theophilus, 4 That thou mightest know the certainty of those things, wherein thou hast been instructed.

Audience: Luke addressed Theophilus, a Syrian Gentile ruler who loved God. He desired verified evidence of things he had heard about God's kingdom. Like Bereans, Theophilus wanted to search the Scriptures to determine if what he had heard about God's kingdom rested on sound evidence. (Act.17:11) False teacher could not change or deny God's truth.

Viewpoint: Using Moses' law, prophets, and Psalms to demonstrate Jesus fulfilled all things written in the O.T., Luke opened his gospel with births of John the Baptist and Jesus. When God sent John to restore God's righteousness in Israel, Jesus submitted to God's righteousness, being baptized of John. After tracing Jesus' ancestry to Adam, Luke noted Satan tempted Jesus in the wilderness, showing Theophilus that man defeats Satan by trusting all God's commands. (Lk.4:4,8, 12) Emphasizing that Jesus fulfilled the prophets, Luke placed Jesus' preaching in Nazareth first. After Jesus read from Isaiah, he closed the book, saying he fulfilled that prophecy that day. Near the close of his epistle, Luke again stressed Jesus fulfilled everything in the O.T. (Lk.24:25-27,44) Luke applied Malachi's prophecy to lives. The "Sun of righteousness" rises to heal Israel's afflictions, turning the hearts of the fathers to their sons and the simple to wisdom of the wise. (Mal.4:2-6; Lk.1:17) God's Son can unite parents and children to increase joys of family and daily life.

John

1:1 In the beginning was the Word, and the Word was with God, and the Word was God. 2 The same was in the beginning with God. 3 All things were made by him; and without him was not any thing made that was made. 4 In him was life; and the life was the light of men. 5 And the light shineth in darkness; and the darkness comprehended it not.

Audience: Like Mark, John interpreted many Jewish words, indicating his audience included Gentiles who needed an explanation of Jewish terms. Unlike synoptic gospels, John narrated Jesus teaching Samaritans, demonstrating he was the Christ who told them all things God desired of them. (Jno.4:3-42;15:15) Jewish antagonists in Jerusalem accused Jesus of being a Samaritan. (Jno.8:48) Revelation indicates John also ministered to Gentiles in Asia. His gospel addressed Gentiles, showing that Jesus explained all God's truth that all people may honor the living God of heaven, rather than man-made gods which God regards as devil worship. (Jno.4:22-24; 1 Cor.10:20)

Viewpoint: Showing Jesus to be **the Prophet** like Moses weaves John's gospel into a unit. **"The Lord thy God will raise up unto thee a Prophet form the midst of thee, of thy brethren, like unto me; unto him ye shall hearken; According to all that thou desiredst of the Lord thy God in Horeb in the day of the assembly, saying, Let me not hear again the voice of the Lord my God, neither let me see this great fire any more, that I die not, And the Lord said unto me, They have well spoken that which they have spoken. I will raise them up a Prophet from among their brethren, like unto thee, and will put my words in his mouth; and he shall speak unto them all that I shall command him. And it shall come to pass, that whosoever will not hearken unto my words which he shall speak in my name, I will require it of him."** (Deu.18:15-19)

Luke

1:5 There was in the days of Herod, the king of Judaea, a certain priest named Zacharias, of the course of Abia: and his wife was of the daughters of Aaron, and her name was Elisabeth. 6 And they were both righteous before God, walking in all the commandments and ordinances of the Lord blameless. 7 And they had no child, because that Elisabeth was barren, and they both were now well stricken in years. 8 And it came to pass, that while he executed the priest's office before God in the order of his course, 9 According to the custom of the priest's office, his lot was to burn incense when he went into the temple of the Lord. 10 And the whole multitude of the people were praying without at the time of incense. 11 And there appeared unto him an angel of the Lord standing on the right side of the altar of incense. 12 And when Zacharias saw him, he was troubled, and fear fell upon him. 13 But the angel said unto him, Fear not, Zacharias: for thy prayer is heard; and thy wife Elisabeth shall bear thee a son, and thou shalt call his name John. 14 And thou shalt have joy and gladness; and many shall rejoice at his birth. 15 For he shall be great in the sight of the Lord, and shall drink neither wine nor strong drink; and he shall be filled with the Holy Ghost, even from his mother's womb. 16 And many of the children of Israel shall he turn to the Lord their God. 17 And he shall go before him in the spirit and power of Elias, to turn the hearts of the fathers to the children, and the disobedient to the wisdom of the just; to make ready a people prepared for the Lord. 18 And Zacharias said unto the angel, Whereby shall I know this? for I am an old man, and my wife well stricken in years. 19 And the angel answering said unto him, I am Gabriel, that stand in the presence of God; and am sent to speak unto thee, and to shew thee these glad tidings. 20 And, behold, thou shalt be dumb, and not able to speak, until the day that these things shall be performed, because thou believest not my words, which shall be fulfilled in their season. 21 And the people waited for Zacharias, and marvelled that he tarried so long in the temple. 22 And when he came out, he could not speak unto them: and they perceived that he had seen a vision in the temple: for he beckoned unto them, and remained speechless. 23 And it came to pass, that, as soon as the days of his ministration were accomplished, he departed to his own house. 24 And after those days his wife Elisabeth conceived, and hid herself five months, saying, 25 Thus hath the Lord dealt with me in the days wherein he looked on me, to take away my reproach among men.

That Theophilus might check John's and Jesus' work against Moses' law and prophets, Luke showed how they fulfilled both. In Herod's reign, Zacharias burned incense on the golden altar in God's holy place as God ordained. Smoke rising before the veil, separating the most holy and holy places, signified prayers ascending to God on the mercy seat above the ark behind the veil in the most holy place. People in the court prayed as Zacharias burnt incense. At the same time, Gabriel appeared beside the golden altar. Soothing Zacharias' astonishment, Gabriel encouraged him, promising Elisabeth, his wife, would give birth to a son named John whose lifestyle must conform to that of a Nazarite by drinking no alcohol. John shall serve God as a prophet like Elijah to return Israel to God, fulfilling Malachi's prophecy, uniting sons and fathers in love. (Mal.4:5-6) Zacharias questioned Gabriel's promise because Zacharias and Elisabeth were aged. Wherefore, God gave Zacharias a sign. Zacharias would remain speechless until John's birth.

Luke's gospel includes several examples of parental concern besides that of Zacharias' prayer for a son. Elisabeth and Mary demonstrated love and concern before the births of John and Jesus. (Lk.1:26-56) Joseph and Mary worried about Jesus when he remained in Jerusalem after the Passover. (Lk.2:41-52) A father hesitated to rise and give bread to a friend after he and his children retired for the night. (Lk.11:7) A father refused to give a son a serpent if he asked for a fish. (Lk.11:11-13) Parents and children often divide as fathers and sons or mothers and daughters work contrary to one another. (Lk.12:52-53) Prodigal son, his brother, and father illustrate alienation in spite of a father's love for both his sons and how the younger son returned to his father when he realized his father treated him well in his early years. (Lk.15:11-32) This father-son love conveys God's love for his children in giving his only begotten Son, Jesus, to regain his wayward children's love.

God gave John a second responsibility of turning those disobedient to God to the wisdom of the just. John shall serve God as a restorationist. Jews strayed from God's commands which meant they abandoned the wisdom of the just.

What wisdom resides with the just, but eludes others? Does peace abide with the greedy? Will kindness dwell with the unkind? Do the proud find genuine friends? How often does overindulgence bring misery to the intemperate? Does true joy abide with evildoers? Why do people despise the selfish and him who must be always first? Wisdom of the just guides them to do to others as they wish others to do to them. If they need food, give food. If they are sick, visit and minister to them. When they sorrow, comfort them. As they rejoice, rejoice with them. Rewards of this wisdom surpass abundance of silver and gold. John counseled people to provide a coat to him who had none. Publicans, collect no more tax than you're appointed. Soldiers, do no violence, be content with your wages, and accuse none falsely. (Lk.3:10-14) If heeded, John's advice produced fruits of righteousness and showed wisdom of the just. In turn, it prepared the obedient to meet the King who reigns on David's throne and to abide in the kingdom of God whose dominion never ends. (Lk.1:32-33; Ps.36:3)

Did Israelites ready themselves for their Lord? Publicans, harlots, and soldiers asked John what they needed to do to prepare for David's son, but Pharisees, lawyers, priests, and rulers rejected John's invitation. (Lk.3:7-14;7:29-30;11:42-52;18:9-14;19:2-10) When Jesus began his ministry, Jewish leaders soon opposed his call for repentance. Jesus' story of the prodigal son illustrated this. The wayward son portrayed the publicans and harlots. The son who remained at home illustrated the Pharisees, lawyers, rulers, and priests.

Luke set the stage for sinners' acceptance of God's messenger, but rejection by the self-righteous leaders. Mary remarked that God put down the mighty and exalted the lowly. (Lk.1:52) God's mercy rests on all who fear him. (Lk.1:50) Sinners admitted straying from God, but Jewish elite maintained they adhered to God's righteousness. The truth that their righteousness violated God's righteousness they refused to concede. Therefore, when Jesus came preaching repentance, for the kingdom of heaven and God's righteousness approached, those who feared God, knowing their sins severed them from God, heard him gladly, but the mighty and proud ridiculed and destroyed him.

If our interest in reading the four accounts of the preaching of Jesus, his miracles, his concern for others, and his death and resurrection fails to generate repentance within our hearts and lives, we act the role of the Pharisees, lawyers, rulers, and priests. Will God need to bring great deprivation on us as he did to the prodigal son before we admit we need and seek God's blessings? or will our love for God and his Son lead us to repentance without having to endure the kinds of hardships Israel experienced?

Luke

1:26 And in the sixth month the angel Gabriel was sent from God unto a city of Galilee, named Nazareth, 27 To a virgin espoused to a man whose name was Joseph, of the house of David; and the virgin's name was Mary. 28 And the angel came in unto her, and said, Hail, thou that art highly favoured, the Lord is with thee: blessed art thou among women. 29 And when she saw him, she was troubled at his saying, and cast in her mind what manner of salutation this should be. 30 And the angel said unto her, Fear not, Mary: for thou hast found favour with God. 31 And, behold, thou shalt conceive in thy womb, and bring forth a son, and shalt call his name JESUS. 32 He shall be great, and shall be called the Son of the Highest: and the Lord God shall give unto him the throne of his father David: 33 And he shall reign over the house of Jacob for ever; and of his kingdom there shall be no end. 34 Then said Mary unto the angel, How shall this be, seeing I know not a man? 35 And the angel answered and said unto her, The Holy Ghost shall come upon thee, and the power of the Highest shall overshadow thee: therefore also that holy thing which shall be born of thee shall be called the Son of God. 36 And, behold, thy cousin Elisabeth, she hath also conceived a son in her old age: and this is the sixth month with her, who was called barren. 37 For with God nothing shall be impossible. 38 And Mary said, Behold the handmaid of the Lord; be it unto me according to thy word. And the angel departed from her. 39 And Mary arose in those days, and went into the hill country with haste, into a city of Juda; 40 And entered into the house of Zacharias, and saluted Elisabeth. 41 And it came to pass, that, when Elisabeth heard the salutation of Mary, the babe leaped in her womb; and Elisabeth was filled with the Holy Ghost: 42 And she spake out with a loud voice, and said, Blessed art thou among women, and blessed is the fruit of thy womb. 43 And whence is this to me, that the mother of my Lord should come to me? 44 For, lo, as soon as the voice of thy salutation sounded in mine ears, the babe leaped in my womb for joy. 45 And blessed is she that believed: for there shall be a performance of those things which were told her from the Lord.

In Elisabeth's sixth month, Gabriel appeared to Mary who descended through Judah and David. Gabriel promised Mary a son by the Holy Spirit though she remained a virgin. Being God's Son, Jesus shall reign endlessly in righteousness and justice on David's throne. Mary consented to God's plan. (Ps.2:1-12;110:1-7; Is.7:14;9:6-7)

Gabriel informed Mary of Elisabeth's conception, and she hastened to Judah to rejoice with Elisabeth. As Mary greeted Elisabeth, John leaped within Elisabeth's womb. By inspiration, Elisabeth encouraged Mary to believe Gabriel's promise.

Though Gabriel called Elisabeth Mary's cousin, about fifty-one generations separate them. Mary descended through Judah, but Elisabeth through Levi, both sons of Jacob. (See Genealogy of Jesus, pp. 35-36, listing the genealogy of Jesus from Genesis, 1 Chronicles, Matthew, and Luke.) Neither old age nor virginity deters God from providing women with children.

Luke's declaration to Theophilus accounts for the physical and miraculous conceptions and births of John the Baptist and Jesus, truths believed by Christians at that time. Some who consider themselves Christians today ridicule any such notion that God suspends the laws of nature to perform such wonders. Indeed, they believe not many of God's truths recorded concerning his great power to show men he is God. (Is.41:21-23;46:9-10) Why call God a liar if we claim to be his children? Are we unable to discern between God's and Satan's words?

**46 And Mary said, My soul doth magnify
the Lord, 47 And my spirit hath rejoiced
in God my Saviour. 48 For he hath regarded the low estate of his handmaiden:
for, behold, from henceforth all generations shall call me blessed. 49 For he that
is mighty hath done to me great things;
and holy is his name. 50 And his mercy is
on them that fear him from generation to
generation. 51 He hath shewed strength
with his arm; he hath scattered the proud
in the imagination of their hearts. 52 He
hath put down the mighty from their
seats, and exalted them of low degree. 53
He hath filled the hungry with good
things; and the rich he hath sent empty
away. 54 He hath holpen his servant
Israel, in remembrance of his mercy; 55
As he spake to our fathers, to Abraham,
and to his seed for ever. 56 And Mary
abode with her about three months, and
returned to her own house.**

When Mary realized Elisabeth confirmed Gabriel's promise, she glorified and rejoiced in God. He elevated Mary, a lowly maiden, to give birth to God's only begotten Son. As God showed her mercy, he shows mercy in every generation to all who fear and serve him faithfully. Strength of God's arm knows no limitations. The proud imagine they rule supreme by their own wisdom and power, but God scatters and deposes the proud and exalts the humble in their place. He unfolds a spiritual feast to the hungry, but the rich he famishes for want. God helps Israel, fulfilling ancient promises to Abraham and his children.

How did Mary's exultation and praise of God unify Luke's theme, declaring to Theophilus those things truly believed by Christians as opposed to errors promulgated in the churches by false teachers and prophets? 1. Mary believed Gabriel's message that she, a virgin, would conceive and give birth to God's Son as God promised by Isaiah. (Is.7:14) 2. As God confirmed Gabriel's message to Mary, God often encourages his faithful by others who restate God's message. "**In the mouth of two or three witnesses every word may be established.**" (Math. 18:16) 3. Contrary to unbelievers and the proud, God controls nations and their rulers, elevating and deposing as he pleases to accomplish his eternal plan to promote righteousness on earth. 4. Though you and I may seem insignificant in man's system, God honors those who retain humility before God as he honored Mary's humility. Her remembrance among all peoples shall remain as long as man teaches the love of God exemplified by Jesus' life. Isn't God's message a source of great comfort to those weary of violence so rampant among those who deny God's hand in man's activities? (Ps.22:28; Dan.4:17)

God helped Jacob, showing him mercy as he promised Abraham. This mercy refers to Christ, though lowly in men's eyes, God exalted him to supreme King over every nation to rule forever. Through Jesus, God supplies spiritual nourishment, denied to the mighty of this earth until they humble themselves before David's son who reigns eternally. Compare Mary's praise and exaltation of God with that of Hannah when she lent Samuel to the Lord in return for his mercy in granting her a son. (1 Sam.2:10)

What spiritual food awaits God's children through Jesus which he denies to unbelievers? Quoting Moses, Jesus taught, "**Man shall not live by bread alone, but by every word of God**." (Deu.8:2; Lk.4:4) Submitting to God's will, his children embrace all God's truth, but unbelievers consider it beneath them to let such lowly principles direct their lives. God instructs his faithful to love and treat with kindness every person, for as we deal with them, we do such to Jesus and to his heavenly Father. (Math.25:40) This spirit of brotherhood of God with man and man with man satisfies deep needs within everyone. Mercy destroys the barriers, dividing men and man from God. Why live with hate when it makes life bitter?

Luke

1:57 Now Elisabeth's full time came that she should be delivered; and she brought forth a son. 58 And her neighbours and her cousins heard how the Lord had shewed great mercy upon her; and they rejoiced with her. 59 And it came to pass, that on the eighth day they came to circumcise the child; and they called him Zacharias, after the name of his father. 60 And his mother answered and said, Not so; but he shall be called John. 61 And they said unto her, There is none of thy kindred that is called by this name. 62 And they made signs to his father, how he would have him called. 63 And he asked for a writing table, and wrote, saying, His name is John. And they marvelled all. 64 And his mouth was opened immediately, and his tongue loosed, and he spake, and praised God. 65 And fear came on all that dwelt round about them: and all these sayings were noised abroad throughout all the hill country of Judaea. 66 And all they that heard them laid them up in their hearts, saying, What manner of child shall this be! And the hand of the Lord was with him.

Imagine the great joy Zacharius, Elisabeth, and friends expressed with the birth of John. God promised them a son and fulfilled his promise with the birth of John as Gabriel had said. God restored Zacharius' speech as he named his son. All the wonders God performed in connection with John's birth amazed those who heard about the unusual events. Would John herald the coming of God's everlasting kingdom? Something great must be in the air. Would God soon send the Messiah to redeem them from sin to fulfill his promises of old? God's plans and works he broadcasts that men may recognize his activities among men. Though we often forget God and attempt to push him out of our minds, he never abandons those who obey him.

67 And his father Zacharias was filled with the Holy Ghost, and prophesied, saying, 68 Blessed be the Lord God of Israel; for he hath visited and redeemed his people, 69 And hath raised up an horn of salvation for us in the house of his servant David; 70 As he spake by the mouth of his holy prophets, which have been since the world began: 71 That we should be saved from our enemies, and from the hand of all that hate us; 72 To perform the mercy promised to our fathers, and to remember his holy covenant; 73 The oath which he sware to our father Abraham, 74 That he would grant unto us, that we being delivered out of the hand of our enemies might serve him without fear, 75 In holiness and righteousness before him, all the days of our life.

Being filled with the Holy Spirit, Zacharius praised God for fulfilling his promises made by all his prophets from creation. Zacharius explained John's God-given responsibility. He must introduce God's Messiah, foretold by God's prophets.

Theophilus, God spoke to Abraham and his children to encourage them. Endure the contradictions of unbelievers now. The day shall come when I provide you with deliverance from your enemies. A son of David shall rebuild David's kingdom. By vanquishing the enemies of righteousness, his glorious reign continues forever. You who labor in darkness of sin shall see light of life and freedom from man's ancient foe, Satan. The Messiah arises as the "horn" of salvation. (Am.9:11-12; Act.15:15-18)

God's prophets often used the term "horn" to denote a king. For example, Daniel wrote of the two horns of Media and Persia, the great horn of Grecia, and ten horns of a very destructive beast. (Dan.7:7,8,20-21,24;8:3, 5-9,20-25) To help his children understand his plans, God often identifies "horns" as he did for Media, Persia, and Greece. Jesus is David's "horn", king.

Luke

1:76 And thou, child, shalt be called the prophet of the Highest: for thou shalt go before the face of the Lord to prepare his ways; 77 To give knowledge of salvation unto his people by the remission of their sins, 78 Through the tender mercy of our God; whereby the dayspring from on high hath visited us, 79 To give light to them that sit in darkness and in the shadow of death, to guide our feet into the way of peace. 80 And the child grew, and waxed strong in spirit, and was in the deserts till the day of his shewing unto Israel.

Zacharius prophesied that his son John preceded the King of salvation to herald his coming. John, you shall go before the face of God's anointed to prepare his coming. Explain to Israel how to gain remission for their sins. Because of God's mercy, he forgives all our transgressions. Inform the people that the "Sun of Righteousness" arises to radiate the light of God into their hearts, to deliver them from sin's dark dungeon, and provide them peace within their souls. Truly, God has visited and redeemed his people. (Mal.4:2-3)

John remained relatively unknown until the time for God to initiate his plan. During this time, John matured physically. He lived in an area of Judah with few inhabitants. When God decided the time had come, he spoke to John and commanded him to speak to his people, telling them time has come for God's kingdom to appear. Return to God. Produce fruits of righteousness which he has sought in all ages. Though not yet identified, God's King of glory now stands among you. (Jno.1:29-33)

Why did Luke devote so much space to the birth of John the Baptist? Evidently, Theophilus desired an accurate account of John's origin and God's hand in preparing him to introduce Christ. When did God appoint him to this responsibility? What prophetic records foretold John's coming and work? How did God communicate to John the message he preached? How did he know when to begin preaching? Did John know that Jesus, the son of Joseph and Mary of Nazareth, as the Christ before the Spirit descended on him? Why did the common people listen to John's message and obey it, but the leaders of Israel refused to submit to his baptism of repentance for the remission of sins?

It's the responsibility of a ruler to search out such information on movements that capture the attention of many. **"It is the glory of God to conceal a thing: but the honour of kings to search out a matter."** (Prov.25:2) Using this material, Theophilus placed himself in position to consider the benefits and problems associated with Christianity. When asked for his opinion about the worthwhileness of the movement, he may respond with intelligence. For example, while David ruled as king over all Israel, a widow of Tekoah approached him with a problem. She had two sons who fought in the field. One killed the other. Her family demanded that she deliver her remaining son to be slain for killing his brother. If she complied with their demands, she would have no heir, and her life must end with no children. David perceived that Joab instructed this woman to present this problem that he might cause Absalom to return from hiding after slaying his brother Amnon. (2 Sam.14:1-20) Rulers need information in order to evaluate situations wisely.

Theophilus asked for as much information about the kingdom of God as Luke supplied him. Luke responded first in writing his gospel account of John and Jesus and later by recording the activities of some of the apostles who preached in Luke's area of the Roman Empire. From these records he could evaluate God's kingdom. Did it fulfill God's promises in the law of Moses and prophets? As Theophilus searched the Scriptures to determine if John and Jesus fulfilled God's promised, we must check, too.

Matthew

**1:18 Now the birth of Jesus Christ was on
this wise: When as his mother Mary was
espoused to Joseph, before they came
together, she was found with child of the
Holy Ghost. 19 Then Joseph her husband,
being a just man, and not willing to make
her a publick example, was minded to put
her away privily. 20 But while he thought
on these things, behold, the angel of the
Lord appeared unto him in a dream,
saying, Joseph, thou son of David, fear not
to take unto thee Mary thy wife: for that
which is conceived in her is of the Holy
Ghost. 21 And she shall bring forth a son,
and thou shalt call his name JESUS: for
he shall save his people from their sins. 22
Now all this was done, that it might be
fulfilled which was spoken of the Lord by
the prophet, saying, 23 Behold, a virgin
shall be with child, and shall bring forth a
son, and they shall call his name Emmanuel, which being interpreted is, God
with us. 24 Then Joseph being raised from
sleep did as the angel of the Lord had
bidden him, and took unto him his wife:
25 And knew her not till she had brought
forth her firstborn son: and he called his
name JESUS.**

God provided Jesus with a supernatural birth. Though a virgin, Mary carried a child in her womb. When she returned from visiting Elisabeth and showed evidence of being with child, her fiancé, Joseph, considered divorcing her. What should he do? As he contemplated, God's angel appeared to him in a dream and explained Mary had not committed fornication. God gives her a son by the Spirit of God. Proceed with your plan to take Mary for your wife. Name her son Jesus. He shall save his people from their sins. Jesus' birth fulfills Isaiah's words that a virgin gives birth to a son called Emmanuel, which interpreted is God with us. (Is.7:14; 8:8-10) Understanding God's plan, Joseph took Mary as his wife, but they remained sexually apart until Jesus' birth.

Luke's gospel seems to indicate Jesus' mission served more as a political salvation from their enemies who harassed them. (Lk.1:71,74) Luke stated that Jesus provided great joy to all people, not to Jews alone. (Lk.2:10) Gospels stress Jesus fulfilled God's O.T. law and prophets, providing four-fold evidence Jesus is Christ. All may examine the evidence themselves.

Matthew described Joseph as just before God, unwilling to make Mary a public example, and Luke stated that Zacharius and Elisabeth submitted to all God's precepts blamelessly. (Lk.1:5-6) Obeying God improves our poor relationships with one another and with God. If Joseph had chosen to make Mary miserable for committing fornication, would he have been just, for who is perfect and sins not? (1 Kin.8:46; 2 Chr.6:36; Prov.20:9; Ecc.7:20; Rom.3:23; 1 Jno.1:8,10) Extending mercy to those who wrong us makes us just, like our heavenly Father (Math.5:48) who also shows us mercy for our many transgressions against him and his law. Showing mercy, we partake of the divine nature. (2 Pet.1:4) Man's revenge shows no mercy and works not the righteousness of God. (Ja.1:20) As children of God, we willingly forgive, because God forgives as we forgive. If we from our hearts forgive not the offenses of others, God forgives not our transgressions. (Math. 6:2;18:35; Lk.11:4)

How often do we fetter ourselves by holding a grudge against someone who has offended us? Does not our unwillingness to forgive increase hostilities and separate us from family members and friends? Alienation serves Satan's cause; forgiveness and refusing to hold a grudge produce the peace of God. Even our own consciences tell us that bitterness toward others serves only to produce darkness within ourselves. God sent Jesus to expose darkness and introduce light of life into the lives of all whom Satan imprisons with hate. Those who love light forgive; those who love darkness don't.

Viewpoints

Matthew

2:1 Now when Jesus was born in Bethlehem of Judaea in the days of Herod the king, behold, there came wise men from the east to Jerusalem, 2 Saying, Where is he that is born King of the Jews? for we have seen his star in the east, and are come to worship him. 3 When Herod the king had heard these things, he was troubled, and all Jerusalem with him. 4 And when he had gathered all the chief priests and scribes of the people together, he demanded of them where Christ should be born. 5 And they said unto him, In Bethlehem of Judaea: for thus it is written by the prophet, 6 And thou Bethlehem, in the land of Juda, art not the least among the princes of Juda: for out of thee shall come a Governor, that shall rule my people Israel.

Using a star, God guided wise men from the East to find him whom God chose to rule as King of the Jews. Their arrival in Jerusalem generated a wave of excitement throughout the city. When King Herod heard of the wise men, he inquired of Jewish scholars where Christ should be born. They replied that God set Bethlehem, Judah for his birthplace. "**But thou, Bethlehem Ephratah, though thou be little among the thousands of Judah, yet out of thee shall he come forth unto me that is to be ruler in Israel; whose goings forth have been from of old, from everlasting.**" (Mi.5:2) As a father proud of his newborn son, God published the event abroad. He wanted all people to know about the birth of his only begotten Son who came to live on earth.

Matthew's record of the wise men from the east, approaching Jerusalem, searching for him born King of the Jews, opened a door to show all Jews how Jesus fulfilled the prophecy of Micah. It connected the dispersion in the East with Jesus' birth, providing them hope of God's mercy though they dwelt far from their homeland.

Luke

2:1 And it came to pass in those days, that there went out a decree from Caesar Augustus, that all the world should be taxed. 2 (And this taxing was first made when Cyrenius was governor of Syria.) 3 And all went to be taxed, every one into his own city. 4 And Joseph also went up from Galilee, out of the city of Nazareth, into Judaea, unto the city of David, which is called Bethlehem; (because he was of the house and lineage of David:) 5 To be taxed with Mary his espoused wife, being great with child. 6 And so it was, that, while they were there, the days were accomplished that she should be delivered. 7 And she brought forth her firstborn son, and wrapped him in swaddling clothes, and laid him in a manger; because there was no room for them in the inn. 8 And there were in the same country shepherds abiding in the field, keeping watch over their flock by night. 9 And, lo, the angel of the Lord came upon them, and the glory of the Lord shone round about them: and they were sore afraid. 10 And the angel said unto them, Fear not: for, behold, I bring you good tidings of great joy, which shall be to all people. 11 For unto you is born this day in the city of David a Saviour, which is Christ the Lord. 12 And this shall be a sign unto you; Ye shall find the babe wrapped in swaddling clothes, lying in a manger. 13 And suddenly there was with the angel a multitude of the heavenly host praising God, and saying, 14 Glory to God in the highest, and on earth peace, good will toward men.

Luke's gospel associated Jesus' birth with the Gentile rulers of the day: Augustus ruled the Roman Empire; Cyrenius governed Syria. Luke related Jesus' birth to history and Scripture. Jesus' birth is fact, not a myth. God notified shepherds like those in Syria that they might spread the joyous news.

Viewpoints

Matthew

2:7 Then Herod, when he had privily called the wise men, inquired of them diligently what time the star appeared. 8 And he sent them to Bethlehem, and said, Go and search diligently for the young child; and when ye have found him, bring me word again, that I may come and worship him also. 9 When they had heard the king, they departed; and, lo, the star, which they saw in the east, went before them, till it came and stood over where the young child was. 10 When they saw the star, they rejoiced with exceeding great joy. 11 And when they were come into the house, they saw the young child with Mary his mother, and fell down, and worshipped him: and when they had opened their treasures, they presented unto him gifts; gold, and frankincense, and myrrh. 12 And being warned of God in a dream that they should not return to Herod, they departed into their own country another way.

Herod viewed a Jewish king his rival. Before sending the wise men to Bethlehem, Herod inquired of the wise men when the star first appeared and of the scribes where Christ should be born. Then Herod directed the wise men to Bethlehem. He instructed them to bring him word when they found this king, indicating he, too, would worship Christ. The star led the wise men to Jesus where they worshiped him and presented him with precious gifts of gold, frankincense, and myrrh. God knew Herod intended to slay Jesus, so he directed the wise men to return to their own land by a different route. They followed God's instructions as they returned home.

The wise men found Jesus in a house, but shepherds in Luke's gospel found him in a manger because there was no room for Joseph, Mary, and Jesus in the inn. This suggests the shepherds arrived and possibly departed before the wise men found Jesus.

Luke

2:15 And it came to pass, as the angels were gone away from them into heaven, the shepherds said one to another, Let us now go even unto Bethlehem, and see this thing which is come to pass, which the Lord hath made known unto us. 16 And they came with haste, and found Mary, and Joseph, and the babe lying in a manger. 17 And when they had seen it, they made known abroad the saying which was told them concerning this child. 18 And all they that heard it wondered at those things which were told them by the shepherds. 19 But Mary kept all these things, and pondered them in her heart. 20 And the shepherds returned, glorifying and praising God for all the things that they had heard and seen, as it was told unto them.

Shepherds and wise men rejoiced upon finding Jesus. They understood God's redemption included all peoples. Departing from Jesus, shepherds spread the wonderful news angels revealed to them. A Savior is born today in Bethlehem. He brings peace and good will to all peoples, replacing hatred and war which divide or destroy families, neighbors, tribes, nations, and empires.

How can Jesus as Savior reorient the relationships between peoples to cancel constant bickering and hatred? Have we lost this peace and good will because we have forgotten God's instructions? What has God to offer that reestablishes peace and good will? Satan's lifestyle elevates each of us in our own minds above others and drives man by selfishness and pride, attitudes that produce ill will and war, dividing friends and families and destroying good relationships. God sent Jesus to teach us principles which redirect our attitudes and energies. Pray for and seek the best for others rather than seeking to elevate ourselves above others. Obeying Jesus, restores peace and harmony. (See Deu.12:8.)

Matthew

2:13 And when they were departed, behold, the angel of the Lord appeareth to Joseph in a dream, saying, Arise, and take the young child and his mother, and flee into Egypt, and be thou there until I bring thee word: for Herod will seek the young child to destroy him. 14 When he arose, he took the young child and his mother by night, and departed into Egypt: 15 And was there until the death of Herod: that it might be fulfilled which was spoken of the Lord by the prophet, saying, Out of Egypt have I called my son. 16 Then Herod, when he saw that he was mocked of the wise men, was exceeding wroth, and sent forth, and slew all the children that were in Bethlehem, and in all the coasts thereof, from two years old and under, according to the time which he had diligently inquired of the wise men. 17 Then was fulfilled that which was spoken by Jeremy the prophet, saying, 18 In Rama was there a voice heard, lamentation, and weeping, and great mourning, Rachel weeping for her children, and would not be comforted, because they are not.

Matthew didn't tell how many days lapsed after Jesus' birth before God warned Joseph to flee with Jesus to Egypt. Luke indicates at least a month lapsed before Joseph departed for Egypt that Mary might be purified as Moses taught. (Lev.12:2-4) God protects his obedient people. (Rev.3:10)

During Jesus' stay in Egypt, Herod waited for word from the wise men. When they failed to return, he vented his wrath on all the young male children, two years old and younger, near Bethlehem. Many families there grieved because of Herod's brutality and jealousy. Satan's influence in our lives encourages us to commit terrible deeds to protect our positions. If we trust God, he will provide and secure for us positions of honor without our rage and anger, which make our lives bitter and make us children of Satan, not God. (2 Sam.7:9)

Luke

2:21 And when eight days were accomplished for the circumcising of the child, his name was called JESUS, which was so named of the angel before he was conceived in the womb. 22 And when the days of her purification according to the law of Moses were accomplished, they brought him to Jerusalem, to present him to the Lord; 23 (As it is written in the law of the Lord, Every male that openeth the womb shall be called holy to the Lord;) 24 And to offer a sacrifice according to that which is said in the law of the Lord, A pair of turtledoves, or two young pigeons. 25 And, behold, there was a man in Jerusalem, whose name was Simeon; and the same man was just and devout, waiting for the consolation of Israel: and the Holy Ghost was upon him. 26 And it was revealed unto him by the Holy Ghost, that he should not see death, before he had seen the Lord's Christ. 27 And he came by the Spirit into the temple: and when the parents brought in the child Jesus, to do for him after the custom of the law, 28 Then took he him up in his arms, and blessed God, and said, 29 Lord, now lettest thou thy servant depart in peace, according to thy word: 30 For mine eyes have seen thy salvation, 31 Which thou hast prepared before the face of all people; 32 A light to lighten the Gentiles, and the glory of thy people Israel. 33 And Joseph and his mother marvelled at those things which were spoken of him. 34 And Simeon blessed them, and said unto Mary his mother, Behold, this child is set for the fall and rising again of many in Israel; and for a sign which shall be spoken against; 35 (Yea, a sword shall pierce through thy own soul also,) that the thoughts of many hearts may be revealed. 36 And there was one Anna, a prophetess, the daughter of Phanuel, of the tribe of Aser: she was of a great age, and had lived with an husband seven years from

her virginity; 37 And she was a widow of about fourscore and four years, which departed not from the temple, but served God with fastings and prayers night and day. 38 And she coming in that instant gave thanks likewise unto the Lord, and spake of him to all them that looked for redemption in Jerusalem.

When Joseph, Mary, and Jesus arrived at the temple to purify Mary and to present Jesus to the Lord (Ex.13:1-2; Lev.12:1-8), Simeon, an elderly prophet, met them and confirmed God's word to Mary that Jesus fulfilled God's promise to Abraham and all the fathers. Jesus is the Christ. Anna, an elderly prophetess, added yet another voice to assure Mary and Joseph that Jesus was the Messiah. It seems people need frequent reassurance that God directs the affairs of men as he has promised. (Heb.3:13)

Men must first fall before they rise to enter God's kingdom. (Lk.2:24) Mary testified to this. God put down the mighty from their seats and exalted them of low degree. (Lk.1:52) Isaiah indicated likewise when he wrote that every mountain and hill shall be brought low. (Is.40:3) Jesus preached it. (Lk.3:5) "**Whosoever shall not receive the kingdom of God as a little child shall in no wise enter therein.**" (Lk.18:17) Satan counters God's message. He tutors us to be great and wise. (Gen.3:1-6) God advises us to be humble. Until we distinguish God's wisdom from Satan's deceptions, God's kingdom remains closed to us.

Apostles continued to struggle with the problem of desiring greatness in God's kingdom during much of their association with Jesus. (Math.18:1,4;20:20;23:11; Mk. 9:34; Lk.9:46;22:24) Explaining to the apostles the true nature of the kingdom of heaven, Jesus approached the attitude of humility from several angles. He asked if they were able to endure the suffering he must endure to complete God's plan of redemption. (Math.20:20-22) At another time he set a small child among them to explain that one needed to become as a small child to enter God's kingdom. (Lk.18: 16-17) Contrasting God's kingdom with Gentile government, Jesus noted that the most exalted Gentile lords exercised the greatest power and forced subjects to do their bidding. Among God's people, he who serves most shall be considered the greatest. (Math.20:20-28)

Struggling with the desire for greatness continues to distract God's people. Preachers feel Satan's hand, nudging them to seek renown among their peers. Song leaders strive for the apex position. Elders desire preeminence within their ranks. Should it seem strange when we loathe ourselves for wanting man's praise? It requires constant vigilance for us to thwart the devil's influence within each of us to seek stardom among brethren. Is it degrading to be equal? God provides each of us with abilities to edify the whole body of Christ. (Eph.4:10-14) Can't we be content with using our talents to build God's praise instead of our own? If we serve God faithfully, he shall elevate us to positions of honor as he chooses. (Eph.2:6) Did not God elevate David to be honored among the kings of his day? (2 Sam.5:12) Solomon's wealth and wisdom spread his fame among many peoples. (1 Kin.4:29-24) After Hezekiah purged Judah of idols, God destroyed Assyria's army which threatened Jerusalem, and Hezekiah became known even in Babylon. (Is.36:1-39:2) Though Paul sought no honor among men, he commented that he was well known even by those who tried not to recognize his influence. (2 Cor.6:9) "**God forbid that I should glory, save in the cross of our Lord Jesus Christ, by whom the world is crucified unto me, and I unto the world.**" (Gal.6:14) O humility, how art thou found? Faith in God's plan will develop humility within each of us, and people of the world shall glorify our heavenly Father for working through our lives as he worked through Paul and others. (Math.5:16)

Matthew

2:19 But when Herod was dead, behold, an angel of the Lord appeareth in a dream to Joseph in Egypt, 20 Saying, Arise, and take the young child and his mother, and go into the land of Israel: for they are dead which sought the young child's life. 21 And he arose, and took the young child and his mother, and came into the land of Israel. 22 But when he heard that Archelaus did reign in Judaea in the room of his father Herod, he was afraid to go thither: notwithstanding, being warned of God in a dream, he turned aside into the parts of Galilee: 23 And he came and dwelt in a city called Nazareth: that it might be fulfilled which was spoken by the prophets, He shall be called a Nazarene.

Joseph, Mary, and Jesus continued in Egypt about two years (based on the time Herod waited for the wise men to give him word that they had found the King of the Jews and when Herod killed all the male children two years and under.) After Herod died, God instructed Joseph to return to Israel with Mary and her young son, for Herod no longer sought to kill Jesus.

As we see how God protected Jesus then, we need to ask ourselves if God cares for his people today and protects us. Today many tend not to trust God to deliver us from the wicked as we try to do his will. From the days of Noah, and all through the Old Testament, God thwarted evil schemes to destroy his faithful. This does not mean none of God's people perished by wicked hands, but are we to believe God has abandoned us today and gives us no protection? Did not Jesus promise the apostles to be with them to the end? (Math.28:20) Remember, "Emmanuel" means God with us. (Math.1:23) Trusting that God watches over and protects us gives us security during the trying times which tarnish life's joy. (Rom.8:18-39; Heb.13:5)

Luke

2:39 And when they had performed all things according to the law of the Lord, they returned into Galilee, to their own city Nazareth. 40 And the child grew, and waxed strong in spirit, filled with wisdom: and the grace of God was upon him. 41 Now his parents went to Jerusalem every year at the feast of the passover. 42 And when he was twelve years old, they went up to Jerusalem after the custom of the feast. 43 And when they had fulfilled the days, as they returned, the child Jesus tarried behind in Jerusalem; and Joseph and his mother knew not of it. 44 But they, supposing him to have been in the company, went a day's journey; and they sought him among their kinsfolk and acquaintance. 45 And when they found him not, they turned back again to Jerusalem, seeking him. 46 And it came to pass, that after three days they found him in the temple, sitting in the midst of the doctors, both hearing them, and asking them questions. 47 And all that heard him were astonished at his understanding and answers. 48 And when they saw him, they were amazed: and his mother said unto him, Son, why hast thou thus dealt with us? behold, thy father and I have sought thee sorrowing. 49 And he said unto them, How is it that ye sought me? wist ye not that I must be about my Father's business? 50 And they understood not the saying which he spake unto them. 51 And he went down with them, and came to Nazareth, and was subject unto them: but his mother kept all these sayings in her heart. 52 And Jesus increased in wisdom and stature, and in favour with God and man.

Returning to Nazareth with Mary and Joseph, Jesus grew to manhood, being subject to his parents. Joseph, Mary, and Jesus regularly attended Jewish feasts in Jerusalem. Luke stressed Jesus fulfilled all God's law and prophets. (Lk.24:44)

Matthew

3:1 In those days came John the Baptist, preaching in the wilderness of Judaea, 2 And saying, Repent ye: for the kingdom of heaven is at hand. 3 For this is he that was spoken of by the prophet Esaias, saying, The voice of one crying in the wilderness, Prepare ye the way of the Lord, make his paths straight. 4 And the same John had his raiment of camel's hair, and a leathern girdle about his loins; and his meat was locusts and wild honey. 5 Then went out to him Jerusalem, and all Judaea, and all the region round about Jordan, 6 And were baptized of him in Jordan, confessing their sins.

When Matthew first viewed John's ministry, he looked at it only from Isaiah's prophecy. He prepared for the Lord's coming by commanding the people to repent and turn from transgressing God's law. (Is.40:3-5) Not until Jesus explained John's mission to his disciples did Matthew include Malachi's perspective of John's work as a refiner's fire to purge the impurities within Israelite lives. (Mal.3:1-3; Math.17:10-13; 21:32) John instructed Israelites to produce fruits of righteousness which honor God. Pharisees and Sadducees, Israel's spiritual leaders, rejected John's message, refusing to believe God sent him. John warned them not to think they shall enter the kingdom of God because their father Abraham pleased God. In God's eyes you are vipers who poison the minds of God's people against the truth of God's commands and replace them with your human-conceived precepts. Each person prepares to enter God's kingdom by living righteously before God and by submitting to God's commands, not man's. Common people heard John gladly, believed John's message, and repented.

In contrast to Matthew's approach, Mark opened his gospel by referring to all God's prophets who mentioned John's coming to encourage Israelites to amend their ways and prepare for God's kingdom. (Mk.1:2)

Mark

1:2 As it is written in the prophets, Behold, I send my messenger before thy face, which shall prepare thy way before thee. 3 The voice of one crying in the wilderness, Prepare ye the way of the Lord, make his paths straight. 4 John did baptize in the wilderness, and preach the baptism of repentance for the remission of sins. 5 And there went out unto him all the land of Judaea, and they of Jerusalem, and were all baptized of him in the river of Jordan, confessing their sins. 6 And John was clothed with camel's hair, and with a girdle of a skin about his loins; and he did eat locusts and wild honey; 7 And preached, saying, There cometh one mightier than I after me, the latchet of whose shoes I am not worthy to stoop down and unloose.

Mark emphasized forgiveness of sins for those John baptized. He opened and closed his gospel, promising forgiveness of sins to those who obeyed God. (Mk.1:4;16:15-16) One might wonder why Matthew stressed Pharisees and Sadducees rejected John's message, but Mark indicated all Judaea and Jerusalem submitted to John's baptism. I suggest that Matthew explained to his own people how their leaders turned deaf ears to John, but Mark encouraged sinners to gain relief from sin by submitting to John's baptism. How would Matthew's record encourage Jews to obey Jesus when they understood their leaders refused John who introduced Jesus? If unprejudiced Jews considered John's testimony, the prophecies of their own Scriptures, and the wonders Jesus performed, hopefully they might turn to Jesus as Christ, seeing how blindly their leaders acted. Mark encouraged Gentiles to accept Jesus as God's anointed by showing that common people submitted to John to gain remission of their sins and because John introduced Jesus. John and O.T. scriptures told of Christ's coming to introduce everlasting righteousness to all nations. (Is.9:6-7)

Viewpoints

Luke

3:1 Now in the fifteenth year of the reign of Tiberius Caesar, Pontius Pilate being governor of Judaea, and Herod being tetrarch of Galilee, and his brother Philip tetrarch of Ituraea and of the region of Trachonitis, and Lysanias the tetrarch of Abilene, 2 Annas and Caiaphas being the high priests, the word of God came unto John the son of Zacharias in the wilderness. 3 And he came into all the country about Jordan, preaching the baptism of repentance for the remission of sins; 4 As it is written in the book of the words of Esaias the prophet, saying, The voice of one crying in the wilderness, Prepare ye the way of the Lord, make his paths straight. 5 Every valley shall be filled, and every mountain and hill shall be brought low; and the crooked shall be made straight, and the rough ways shall be made smooth; 6 And all flesh shall see the salvation of God.

As a ruler, Theophilus desired to know which rulers controlled areas near Judaea when John began his preaching. Luke quoted more of Isaiah's prophecy. (Is.40:3-4) John and Jesus leveled mountains and hills (rulers) and elevated valleys (common people), so rulers and common people stood equal before God. Crooked lives they straightened, and rough lives became smooth before Jesus. All nations God invited to partake of this great hope of peace and good will. This included the Syrians, the people of Luke and Theophilus. In ages past they fought Israel, but with the coming of the Lord and his glorious kingdom, all peoples consider themselves equal partakers of the salvation of God whose kingdom rises as the protector of all who love God and live godly. (Is.11:1-9)

Luke's gospel appeals to Gentiles. God invites all to join in partaking of the blessings afforded to peoples in every nation. If you long for fellowship with your Creator, come to Christ.

John

1:6 There was a man sent from God, whose name was John. 7 The same came for a witness, to bear witness of the Light, that all men through him might believe. 8 He was not that Light, but was sent to bear witness of that Light. 9 That was the true Light, which lighteth every man that cometh into the world. 10 He was in the world, and the world was made by him, and the world knew him not. 11 He came unto his own, and his own received him not. 12 But as many as received him, to them gave he power to become the sons of God, even to them that believe on his name: 13 Which were born, not of blood, nor of the will of the flesh, nor of the will of man, but of God. 14 And the Word was made flesh, and dwelt among us, (and we beheld his glory, the glory as of the only begotten of the Father,) full of grace and truth. 15 John bare witness of him, and cried, saying, This was he of whom I spake, He that cometh after me is preferred before me: for he was before me. 16 And of his fulness have all we received, and grace for grace. 17 For the law was given by Moses, but grace and truth came by Jesus Christ. 18 No man hath seen God at any time; the only begotten Son, which is in the bosom of the Father, he hath declared him.

God sent John the Baptist to identify Jesus, the true Light from heaven. Only by him light illuminates the spirit within man. Jesus came to his own people to provide them that spiritual enlightening, but most of them rejected his truth. Those who believed Jesus to be God's Son gained power to become God's children (1:12-13), but they must be born again of water and Spirit. (Jno.3:3,5,7) Though many believed Jesus performed miracles, they refused rebirth, and God severed them from among his people. (Deu.18:15-19; Act.3:22-23) Sinners preferred darkness to spiritual light. (Jno. 3:20-21)

Matthew

3:7 But when he saw many of the Pharisees and Sadducees come to his baptism, he said unto them, O generation of vipers, who hath warned you to flee from the wrath to come? 8 Bring forth therefore fruits meet for repentance: 9 And think not to say within yourselves, We have Abraham to our father: for I say unto you, that God is able of these stones to raise up children unto Abraham. 10 And now also the axe is laid unto the root of the trees: therefore every tree which bringeth not forth good fruit is hewn down, and cast into the fire. 11 I indeed baptize you with water unto repentance: but he that cometh after me is mightier than I, whose shoes I am not worthy to bear: he shall baptize you with the Holy Ghost, and with fire: 12 Whose fan is in his hand, and he will throughly purge his floor, and gather his wheat into the garner; but he will burn up the chaff with unquenchable fire.

John contrasted himself with Jesus. I am unfit even to wear or untie his shoes. I baptize with water; he baptizes with God's Spirit and fire. John the Baptist accepted his limitations. (Jno.3:22;4:1-2) Jesus' disciples baptized with water to prepare people for God's kingdom, but Jesus possessed complete power to strengthen believers with God's Spirit or to destroy unbelievers. As a farmer threshes his harvest to separate chaff from grain, Christ severs the fruitless from the fruitful. Farmers store grain to preserve it; God translates his faithful into his everlasting kingdom. Chaff a farmer consumes in flames; God destroys the wicked with everlasting fire. Whether Jesus baptizes with God's Spirit or fire, the one baptized is completely immersed therewith.

Israelites prepared for Christ by repenting of fruitless lives before God. Those with extra coats, food, money, etc. shared with those who lacked. Tax collectors collected only authorized tax. Soldiers abandoned violence and accepted their wages. Mercy and wholesome acts identify those in God's kingdom. All who grieved because of their sins repented, but many leaders repented not. (Math.21:23-45)

Mark

1:8 I indeed have baptized you with water: but he shall baptize you with the Holy Ghost.

Why did Mark and John record Jesus baptizes with God's Spirit, but Matthew and Luke noted he baptized with God's Spirit and fire? If Mark and John addressed Christians, and Matthew and Luke addressed unbelievers, one may understand why Matthew and Luke taught Jesus baptized with the Holy Spirit, but those who reject him he baptizes with fire. Mark and John stated Jesus baptizes with God's Spirit. Their audiences believed, but desired written record of Jesus' life, doctrine, and deeds. God's Spirit strengthens us against Satan's temptations. (Lk.11:13; Act.2:38;5:32; Eph.3:16; Col.1:11; See Jno.1:33.)

God's wrath burns obstinate sinners. Every unrepentant offender shall be cast into unquenchable fire. (Math.5:30;18:8; Mk.9:42-48) Unbelievers and professed believers deny God punishes the unrighteous. Closing our minds to part of God's message shall not change his truth. Priests, scribes, Pharisees, and Sadducees turned deaf ears to truth, but their obstinance reaped destruction of their glorious city, Jerusalem, and eternal damnation. David sang, **"The fool saith in his heart, There is no God. They are corrupt, they have done abominable works, there is none that doeth good."** (Ps.14:1)

Vain religion demands no change in life style. God sent Jesus to help us enjoy life fully. (Jno10:10) Mistreating others produces conflict, not a good life. Heeding God's truth produces joyful life and a clean conscience. (Heb.9:14) Satan's ministers in churches then and today contradict God's truth as Satan did to Eve in Eden. If we desire a full life we will abandon Satan.

Viewpoints

Luke

3:7 Then said he to the multitude that came forth to be baptized of him, O generation of vipers, who hath warned you to flee from the wrath to come? 8 Bring forth therefore fruits worthy of repentance, and begin not to say within yourselves, We have Abraham to our father: for I say unto you, That God is able of these stones to raise up children unto Abraham. 9 And now also the axe is laid unto the root of the trees: every tree therefore which bringeth not forth good fruit is hewn down, and cast into the fire. 10 And the people asked him, saying, What shall we do then? 11 He answereth and saith unto them, He that hath two coats, let him impart to him that hath none; and he that hath meat, let him do likewise. 12 Then came also publicans to be baptized, and said unto him, Master, what shall we do? 13 And he said unto them, Exact no more than that which is appointed you. 14 And the soldiers likewise demanded of him, saying, And what shall we do? And he said unto them, Do violence to no man, neither accuse any falsely; and be content with your wages. 15 And as the people were in expectation, and all men mused in their hearts of John, whether he were the Christ, or not; 16 John answered, saying unto them all, I indeed baptize you with water; but one mightier than I cometh, the latchet of whose shoes I am not worthy to unloose: he shall baptize you with the Holy Ghost and with fire: 17 Whose fan is in his hand, and he will throughly purge his floor, and will gather the wheat into his garner; but the chaff he will burn with fire unquenchable. 18 And many other things in his exhortation preached he unto the people.

John and Jesus preached to Jews whose lives needed change. Sin cursed their lives. God grieved for his children whom Satan deceived with lies. (Gen.6:6)

John

1:19 And this is the record of John, when the Jews sent priests and Levites from Jerusalem to ask him, Who art thou? 20 And he confessed, and denied not; but confessed, I am not the Christ. 21 And they asked him, What then? Art thou Elias? And he saith, I am not. Art thou that prophet? And he answered, No. 22 Then said they unto him, Who art thou? that we may give an answer to them that sent us. What sayest thou of thyself? 23 He said, I am the voice of one crying in the wilderness, Make straight the way of the Lord, as said the prophet Esaias. 24 And they which were sent were of the Pharisees. 25 And they asked him, and said unto him, Why baptizest thou then, if thou be not that Christ, nor Elias, neither that prophet? 26 John answered them, saying, I baptize with water: but there standeth one among you, whom ye know not; 27 He it is, who coming after me is preferred before me, whose shoe's latchet I am not worthy to unloose. 28 These things were done in Bethabara beyond Jordan, where John was baptizing.

John's gospel compares Moses and Jesus. As Moses delivered all God's commandments to Israel; Jesus is **the Prophet** like Moses who delivers God's complete new covenant from God to all nations. (Deu. 18:15-19; Jno.1:17;9:28-33; Act.3:22-23) Though John didn't view himself as fulfilling Malachi's prophecy about Elijah, he considered himself as demonstrating Isaiah's forerunner to introduce the Lord's anointed. When apostles commented to Jesus they expected Elijah to precede Christ, Jesus identified John as Elijah who restores all God's things among God's people. (Is.40:3-5; Mal.4:5-6; Math.11:14;17:10-13) Thus, John and Jesus viewed their missions as ordained of God to lead God's people back to their heavenly Father. God's word will lead our generation back to God today.

Viewpoints

Matthew

**1:2 Abraham begat Isaac; and Isaac be-
gat Jacob; and Jacob begat Judas and his
brethren; 3 And Judas begat Phares and
Zara of Thamar; and Phares begat Esrom; and Esrom begat Aram; 4 And
Aram begat Aminadab; and Aminadab
begat Naasson; and Naasson begat Salmon; 5 And Salmon begat Booz of
Rachab; and Booz begat Obed of Ruth;
and Obed begat Jesse; 6 And Jesse begat
David the king; and David the king begat
Solomon of her that had been the wife of
Urias; 7 And Solomon begat Roboam; and
Roboam begat Abia; and Abia begat Asa;
8 And Asa begat Josaphat; and Josaphat
begat Joram; and Joram begat Ozias; 9
And Ozias begat Joatham; and Joatham
begat Achaz; and Achaz begat Ezekias; 10
And Ezekias begat Manasses; and Manasses begat Amon; and Amon begat Josias;
11 And Josias begat Jechonias and his
brethren, about the time they were carried away to Babylon: 12 And after they
were brought to Babylon, Jechonias begat
Salathiel; and Salathiel begat Zorobabel;
13 And Zorobabel begat Abiud; and Abiud begat Eliakim; and Eliakim begat
Azor; 14 And Azor begat Sadoc; and
Sadoc begat Achim; and Achim begat
Eliud; 15 And Eliud begat Eleazar; and
Eleazar begat Matthan; and Matthan
begat Jacob; 16 And Jacob begat Joseph
the husband of Mary, of whom was born
Jesus, who is called Christ. 17 So all the
generations from Abraham to David are
fourteen generations; and from David
until the carrying away into Babylon are
fourteen generations; and from the
carrying away into Babylon unto Christ
are fourteen generations.**

Jesus' genealogies recorded in Genesis, Ruth, 1 Chronicles, Matthew, and Luke show variations. Matthew recorded three groups of fourteen generations: 1) Abraham to David; 2) David to Jechonias, and 3) Jechonias to Jesus, making a total of forty-two generations. Kings and Chronicles record eighteen kings from David to Jechonias, but three of the last four were Josiah's sons, not generations. Luke follows 1 Chronicles' record, except his gospel contains an additional Cainan in the thirteenth generation. Matthew's marginal reading includes Jakim or Jehoiakim between Josias and Jechonias as indicated by 1 Chronicles. Matthew may have omitted purposely Jehoiakim's name to group by fourteens. A scribe's error following Luke probably included an extra Cainan. (See pp. 35-36.)

Bible critics capitalize on these differences to persuade others the Bible is not accurate and therefore not inspired. Some claim that Luke's extra Cainan indicates many other generations may be omitted in the Sacred Scriptures. They utilize this to propagate their doctrine of evolution and the billions of years they insist earth's life needs to evolve to present forms. This view appeals to geologists and evolutionists, but calls God a liar. This influence now persuades most Bible publishers to omit dates which many Bible publishers once included in margins. From my own study of Genesis through Malachi when checked against history, I've found no more that four years' variation between Bible records of events and Ussher's chronology. Neither Genesis nor Exodus supports the theory that earth's creation precedes B.C. 4004 by billions of years. **"For in six days the Lord made heaven and earth, the sea, and all that in them is."** (Ex.20:11) Jude confirms that Enoch was the seventh, not thousands of generations, from Adam. (Jude 14) Joshua's exhortation encourages each person to choose whom he trusts. (Josh.24:14-15) Will it be the godless evolutionists who revel in sin and claim we are in beasts' image, or will it be God who testifies he made man in his own image? (Gen.1:26-28) Our bodies conform to the structures of beasts, but our inner person God created in his own image. He made us both physical and spiritual.

Viewpoints

Luke

**3:23 And Jesus himself began to be about
thirty years of age, being (as was supposed) the son of Joseph, which was the
son of Heli, 24 Which was the son of
Matthat, which was the son of Levi, which
was the son of Melchi, which was the son
of Janna, which was the son of Joseph, 25
Which was the son of Mattathias, which
was the son of Amos, which was the son of
Naum, which was the son of Esli, which
was the son of Nagge, 26 Which was the
son of Maath, which was the son of
Mattathias, which was the son of Semei,
which was the son of Joseph, which was
the son of Juda, 27 Which was the son of
Joanna, which was the son of Rhesa,
which was the son of Zorobabel, which
was the son of Salathiel, which was the
son of Neri, 28 Which was the son of
Melchi, which was the son of Addi, which
was the son of Cosam, which was the son
of Elmodam, which was the son of Er, 29
Which was the son of Jose, which was the
son of Eliezer, which was the son of
Jorim, which was the son of Matthat,
which was the son of Levi, 30 Which was
the son of Simeon, which was the son of
Juda, which was the son of Joseph, which
was the son of Jonan, which was the son
of Eliakim, 31 Which was the son of
Melea, which was the son of Menan,
which was the son of Mattatha, which was
the son of Nathan, which was the son of
David, 32 Which was the son of Jesse,
which was the son of Obed, which was the
son of Booz, which was the son of Salmon,
which was the son of Naasson, 33 Which
was the son of Aminadab, which was the
son of Aram, which was the son of Esrom,
which was the son of Phares, which was
the son of Juda, 34 Which was the son of
Jacob, which was the son of Isaac, which
was the son of Abraham, which was the
son of Thara, which was the son of
Nachor, 35 Which was the son of Saruch,
which was the son of Ragau, which was
the son of Phalec, which was the son of
Heber, which was the son of Sala, 36
Which was the son of Cainan, which was
the son of Arphaxad, which was the son of
Sem, which was the son of Noe, which was
the son of Lamech, 37 Which was the son
of Mathusala, which was the son of
Enoch, which was the son of Jared, which
was the son of Maleleel, which was the son
of Cainan, 38 Which was the son of Enos,
which was the son of Seth, which was the
son of Adam, which was the son of God.**

Matthew recorded Jesus' genealogy to Abraham through Joseph, Mary's husband, but Luke traced Jesus' genealogy to Adam through Mary. From Abraham to David, Matthew and Luke show the same ancestry for Jesus. From David to Jesus their genealogies differ because Joseph descended through Solomon, but Mary through Nathan, both being David's sons. (See genealogies on pages 35-36.)

Why did Matthew trace Jesus' ancestry to Abraham, but Luke to Adam? I suggest that both show the relationship of their audiences to God. Jews claimed to be God's children through Abraham. Gentiles traced their ancestry to God through Adam. Using these viewpoints, Matthew and Luke appealed to their audiences as being related to God. Both Jews and Gentiles, being God's offspring, ought to consider God their Father and respect his laws. (Mal.1:6) Matthew and Luke appealed to their own peoples to honor their most ancient Father. God loves all his children, but sin alienates us from his presence. God has opened to us an avenue whereby all his children may now return to him. If we are willing by faith to be cleansed from sin by the blood of his Son Jesus, God will dwell with us while we live on earth, and we can dwell with in heaven after death.

Luke's genealogy seems to show it's the seed of the woman that bruises the serpent's head. (Gen.3:15) Matthew may show this by identifying five women in Jesus' genealogy. (1:3,5,6,16)

Viewpoints
Table 1: Genealogy of Jesus

Name	Reference	Name	Reference
	Genesis		1 Chronicles
1. Adam	5:3	1. Adam	1:1
2. Seth	5:4	2. Sheth	1:1
3. Enos	5:6	3. Enosh	1:1
4. Cainan	5:9	4. Kenan	1:2
5. Mahalaleel	5:15	5. Mahalaleel	1:2
6. Jared	5:18	6. Jered	1:2
7. Enoch	5:21	7. Henoch	1:3
8. Methuselah	5:26	8. Methuselah	1:3
9. Lomech	5:28	9. Lamech	1:3
10. Noah	5:32	10. Noah	1:4
11. Shem	10:22	11. Shem	1:17,24
12. Arphaxad	10:24	12. Arphaxad	1:17
13. Salah	10:24	13. Shelah	1:18
14. Eber	10:25	14. Eber	1:18
15. Peleg	10:25	15. Peleg	1:19
16. Reu	11:21	16. Reu	1:15
17. Serug	11:22	17. Serug	1:26
18. Nahor	11:22	18. Nahor	1:26
19. Terah	11:26	19. Terah	1:26
20. Abram (Abraham)	11:26	20. Abram (Abraham)	1:27
21. Issac	25:8-9	21. Issac	1:28
22. Jacob	25:19-26	22. Jacob (Israel)	2:1
23. Judah	46:8-27	23. Judah	2:3
24. Pharez	46:12	24. Pharez	2:4
25. Hezron	46:12	25. Hezron	2:5
26. Ram	Ruth 4:18	26. Ram	2:9
27. Amminadab	Ruth 4:19	27. Amminadab	2:10
28. Nahshon	Ruth 4:20	28. Nahshon	2:10
29. Salmon	Ruth 4:20	29. Salma	2:11
30. Boaz	Ruth 4:21	30. Boaz	2:11
31. Obed	Ruth 4:21	31. Obed	2:12
32. Jesse	Ruth 4:22	32. Jesse	2:13
33. David	Ruth 4:22	33. David	2:15
34.		34. Solomon	3:5
35.		35. Rehoboam	3:10
36.		36. Abia	3:10
37.		37. Asa	3:10
38.		38. Jehoshaphat	3:10
39.		39. Joram	3:11
40.		40. Ahaziah	3:11
41.		41. Joash	3:11
42.		42. Amaziah	3:12
43.		43. Azariah	3:12
44.		44. Jotham	3:12
45.		45. Ahaz	3:13
46.		46. Hezekiah	3:13
47.		47. Manasseh	3:13
48.		48. Amon	3:14
49.		49. Josiah	3:14
50.		50. Jehoikim	3:15
51.		51. Jeconiah	3:16
52.		52. Salathiel	3:17
53.		53. Zerubbabel	3:19

Viewpoints
Table 1: Genealogy of Jesus continued

Name	Reference Matthew	Name	Reference Luke
1.		1. Adam	3:38
2.		2. Seth	3:38
3.		3. Enos	3:38
4.		4. Cainan	3:37
5.		5. Maleleel	3:37
6.		6. Jared	3:37
7.		7. Enoch	3:37
8.		8. Mathusala	3:37
9.		9. Lamech	3:36
10.		10. Noe	3:36
11.		11. Sem	3:36
12.		12. Arphaxad	3:36
13.		13. Sala (Cainan exclu.)	3:35
14.		14. Heber	3:35
15.		15. Phalec	3:35
16.		16. Ragau	3:35
17.		17. Saruch	3:35
18.		18. Nachor	3:34
19.		19. Thara	3:34
20. Abraham	1:2	20. Abraham	3:34
21. Issac	1:2	21. Isaac	3:34
22. Jacob	1:2	22. Jacob	3:34
23. Judas	1:2	23. Juda	3:33
24. Phares	1:3	24. Phares	3:33
25. Esrom	1:3	25. Esrom	3:33
26. Aram	1:3	26. Aram	3:33
27. Aminadab	1:4	27. Aminadab	3:32
28. Naasson	1:4	28. Naason	3:32
29. Salmon	1:4	29. Salmon	3:32
30. Booz	1:5	30. Booz	3:32
31. Obed	1:5	31. Obed	3:32
32. Jesse	1:5	32. Jesse	3:32
33. David	1:6	33. David	3:32
34. Solomon	1:6	34. Nathan	3:31
35. Roboam	1:7	35. Mattatha	3:31
36. Abia	1:7	36. Menen	3:31
37. Asa	1:7	37. Melea	3:30
38. Josaphat	1:8	38. Eliakim	3:30
39. Joram	1:8	39. Jonan	3:30
40. Ozias (Ahaziah)	1:8	40. Joseph	3:30
41. Joash	omitted	41. Juda	3:30
42. Amaziah	omitted	42. Simeon	3:30
43. Azariah	omitted	43. Levi	3:29
44. Joatham	1:9	44. Matthat	3:29
45. Achaz	1:9	45. Jorim	3:29
46. Ezekias	1:9	46. Eliezer	3:29
47. Manasses	1:10	47. Jose	3:29
48. Amon	1:10	48. Er	3:28
49. Josias	1:10	49. Elmodam	3;28
50. Jakim	margin	50. Cosam	3:28
51. Jechonias	1:11	51. Addi	3:28
52.		52. Melchi	3:28
53.		53. Neri	3:27
54. Salathiel	1:12	54. Salathiel	3:27
55. Zorobabel	1:12	55. Zorobabel	3:27
56.		56. Resa	3:27
57.		57. Joanna	3:27
58. Abiud	1:12	58. Juda	3:27
59.		59. Joseph	3:26
60. Eliakim	1:13	60. Semei	3:26
61.		61. Mattathias	3:26
62. Azor	1:14	62. Maath	3:26
63.		63. Nagge	3:25
64. Sadoc	1:14	64. Esli	3:25
65.		65. Naum	3:25
66. Achim	1:14	66. Amos	3:25
67.		67. Mattathias	3:25
68. Eliud	1;14	68. Joseph	3:24
69.		69. Janna	3:24
70. Eleazar	1:15	70. Melchi	3:24
71.		71. Levi	3:24
72. Matthan	1:15	72. Matthat	3:24
73. Jacob	1:15	73. Heli	3:23
74. Joseph	1:16	74. Joseph	3:23
75. Jesus	1:16	75. Jesus	3:24

Matthew

3:13 Then cometh Jesus from Galilee to Jordan unto John, to be baptized of him. 14 But John forbad him, saying, I have need to be baptized of thee, and comest thou to me? 15 And Jesus answering said unto him, Suffer it to be so now: for thus it becometh us to fulfil all righteousness. Then he suffered him. 16 And Jesus, when he was baptized, went up straightway out of the water: and, lo, the heavens were opened unto him, and he saw the Spirit of God descending like a dove, and lighting upon him: 17 And lo a voice from heaven, saying, This is my beloved Son, in whom I am well pleased.

God sent John the Baptist to prepare Israel for God's kingdom and to identify Christ. John testified he did not know Christ. God promised to identify Christ to John by God's Spirit descending and abiding on him. When John baptized Jesus, he testified God's Spirit as a dove descended and abode on Jesus. He shall reign on David's throne in heaven forever. (Ps.110:1-7; Act.3:20-21)

As God anointed David king over Israel and gave him his Spirit, God gave his Holy Spirit to Jesus when he anointed him King of Israel. (1 Sam.16:1-13; Act.10:38) As God called David's son, Solomon, his son, God called Jesus his beloved Son. He reigns on David's throne. (2 Sam.7:13; 1 Chr.17:11,12) God makes us kings to reign with Jesus by anointing us with his Spirit. (Rev.3:21)

Did God's Holy Spirit alight on Jesus before or after John baptized him? God anointed Jesus with his Spirit after Jesus submitted to all God's righteousness. Is this pattern our example? Does God's Spirit come to dwell in us today before or after we submit to baptism which symbolizes rebirth? When did God audibly confessed Jesus to be his Son. Was it before or after John baptized Jesus? Gospels show God confessed Jesus to be his Son after he submitted to all his Father's righteousness. Is this God's pattern for us today? For example, on Pentecost, when Peter addressed Jews who asked what they should do, he commanded them to be baptized for forgiveness of sins and to receive the Holy Spirit. (Act.2:38) Does God recognize us as his faithful children before or after we have submitted to all his commands to believe and be baptized? (Mk.16:15-16)

Mark

1:9 And it came to pass in those days, that Jesus came from Nazareth of Galilee, and was baptized of John in Jordan. 10 And straightway coming up out of the water, he saw the heavens opened, and the Spirit like a dove descending upon him: 11 And there came a voice from heaven, saying, Thou art my beloved Son, in whom I am well pleased.

John the Baptist viewed Jesus as the mighty King of Israel and indicated his inferiority in that he needed to be baptized by Jesus. In God's humble manner, Jesus never humiliated John as one of the world might. Instead, he came to demonstrate God to Israel and to all men. If it was God's plan to make him supreme ruler of all nations, he would begin by complying with all God's righteousness. (Ps.40:6-8; Heb.10:5-9) He honored others as he wished others to honor him. (Math.7:12) Thereby he showed to all mankind that though he become King of kings and Lord of lords, he subjected himself to his Father to do his will always. (Jno. 8:29) If we honor our heavenly Father, we, too, will do always those things which please him, not ourselves. We begin by first submitting to God's will by believing Jesus to be God's Son and by being born again in water baptism which symbolizes rebirth. Then we enter God's kingdom. (1 Cor.12:13; Gal. 3:26-27; Col.1:13; 1 Pet.3:21) Trying to enter God's kingdom any other way than the door, we act like thieves. (Jno.10:1) Only by obedience to our heavenly Father will he open to us the door leading to the kingdom of heaven. Shall we submit to God's plan, or rebel as Israel of old? (Deu.9:24; Act.7:51)

Luke

3:19 But Herod the tetrarch, being reproved by him for Herodias his brother Philip's wife, and for all the evils which Herod had done, 20 Added yet this above all, that he shut up John in prison. 21 Now when all the people were baptized, it came to pass, that Jesus also being baptized, and praying, the heaven was opened, 22 And the Holy Ghost descended in a bodily shape like a dove upon him, and a voice came from heaven, which said, Thou art my beloved Son; in thee I am well pleased.

Luke indicates that shortly after John baptized Jesus Herod imprisoned John for rebuking him because he transgressed God's law by marrying his brother's wife while his brother still lived and for other indecencies. Being jailed suggests that John completed his mission though he lived until Herod beheaded him.

Notice how Luke related rulers of the day to events he recorded. This permitted Theophilus to relate rulers to Luke's gospel. Herod ruled a fourth of the region, (tetrarch = a ruler of a fourth part.) (Lk.3:1,19)

All four gospels direct their attention to Jesus' activities after Herod jailed John. Though John the Baptist's name appears several times, Jesus is the central figure. John himself conceded that his ministry must wane while that of Jesus should expand. (Jno.3:25-36) Jesus referred to John as a great prophet, the one of whom Isaiah and Malachi prophesied should prepare Israel for the Lord's coming. John the Baptist and Jesus honored one another's labor for God and the common good of Israel. Satan urges God's people to consider themselves better than others. Selfishness and pride identifies Satan's people, not God's. (2 Pet.2:9-10; Jude 7-8)

John's gospel indicates John the Baptist and Jesus baptized disciples at the same time, but more turned to Jesus as John's ministry closed. (Jno.3:22-24)

Synoptic gospels all record God audibly

John

1:29 The next day John seeth Jesus coming unto him, and saith, Behold the Lamb of God, which taketh away the sin of the world. 30 This is he of whom I said, After me cometh a man which is preferred before me: for he was before me. 31 And I knew him not: but that he should be made manifest to Israel, therefore am I come baptizing with water. 32 And John bare record, saying, I saw the Spirit descending from heaven like a dove, and it abode upon him. 33 And I knew him not: but he that sent me to baptize with water, the same said unto me, Upon whom thou shalt see the Spirit descending, and remaining on him, the same is he which baptizeth with the Holy Ghost. 34 And I saw, and bare record that this is the Son of God.

confessed Jesus to be his beloved Son. Here John's gospel omits God's acknowledgment of Jesus as his Son. Instead, John the Baptist testified Jesus is God's Son. His testimony he justified on grounds that he who sent him to baptize instructed him that the one who received the Holy Spirit to dwell on him would be he of whom all Israel sought, the Son of God. John's gospel dwells more on John as the one to introduce Jesus to Israel rather than to prepare his way. For this reason John announced Jesus as God's Son. John the Baptist's message as recorded by John's gospel deals more with Jesus as the one to explain to Israel the complete message of God to his people. (Jno.15:15) Like Moses, Jesus spoke face to face with God to receive that message and came to the earth to deliver it to people. **"I said therefore unto you, that ye shall die in your sins: for if ye believe not that I am he, ye shall die in your sins."** (Jno.8:24) Jesus is our only hope to stand justified before God. Shall we submit to **that Prophet**, or rebel and reap God's wrath by being separated from among God's people as Moses and Peter taught? (Deu.18:15-19; Act.3:22-23)

John

1:35 Again the next day after John stood, and two of his disciples; 36 And looking upon Jesus as he walked, he saith, Behold the Lamb of God! 37 And the two disciples heard him speak, and they followed Jesus. 38 Then Jesus turned, and saw them following, and saith unto them, What seek ye? They said unto him, Rabbi, (which is to say, being interpreted, Master,) where dwellest thou? 39 He saith unto them, Come and see. They came and saw where he dwelt, and abode with him that day: for it was about the tenth hour. 40 One of the two which heard John speak, and followed him, was Andrew, Simon Peter's brother. 41 He first findeth his own brother Simon, and saith unto him, We have found the Messias, which is, being interpreted, the Christ. 42 And he brought him to Jesus. And when Jesus beheld him, he said, Thou art Simon the son of Jona: thou shalt be called Cephas, which is by interpretation, A stone. 43 The day following Jesus would go forth into Galilee, and findeth Philip, and saith unto him, Follow me. 44 Now Philip was of Bethsaida, the city of Andrew and Peter. 45 Philip findeth Nathanael, and saith unto him, We have found him, of whom Moses in the law, and the prophets, did write, Jesus of Nazareth, the son of Joseph. 46 And Nathanael said unto him, Can there any good thing come out of Nazareth? Philip saith unto him, Come and see. 47 Jesus saw Nathanael coming to him, and saith of him, Behold an Israelite indeed, in whom is no guile! 48 Nathanael saith unto him, Whence knowest thou me? Jesus answered and said unto him, Before that Philip called thee, when thou wast under the fig tree, I saw thee. 49 Nathanael answered and saith unto him, Rabbi, thou art the Son of God; thou art the King of Israel. 50 Jesus answered and said unto him, Because I said unto thee, I saw thee under the fig tree, believest thou? thou shalt see greater things than these. 51 And he saith unto him, Verily, verily, I say unto you, Hereafter ye shall see heaven open, and the angels of God ascending and descending upon the Son of man.

Only John's gospel tells us that Jesus gathered disciples the day after his baptism. Matthew, Mark, and Luke say nothing about his disciples until after Herod imprisoned John, and Jesus walked by the sea of Galilee. John recorded the true "beginning" of Jesus gathering his disciples. When John the Baptist identified Jesus as the Lamb of God who takes away the sin of the world, Andrew became the first disciple named to follow Jesus. He first found his brother, Peter, and informed him he had found the Messiah. Andrew brought Peter to Jesus.

John interpreted Jewish names and titles: Rabbi = master; Messias = Christ, Cephas = stone, Siloam = sent, Gabbatha = pavement, Golgotha = place of a skull, and Passover = high Sabbath (Jno.1:41,49;4:25;9:7;19:13, 19;20:16) If John had written to Jews, he had no need to interpret Jewish words. He probably addressed Samaritans or Gentiles near Ephesus. Strangers from the customs of Israel needed explanations of Jewish terms to understand John's gospel. His interpretations benefits Gentiles for all generations.

Notice how John's gospel recorded a day-by-day account of Jesus' activities for the first few days after John baptized Jesus. His record shows clearly that Jesus' temptation in the wilderness did not begin until after he attended the marriage in Cana of Galilee. This being the correct order of events, Mark's use of "straightway" must mean the next event he recorded. Philip saw Jesus as fulfilling Moses' promise of a Prophet like Moses. (Jno.1:45) He speaks all God's truth which Israel must obey or God severs them from among his people. (Deu.18:15-19; Act.3:22-23) If we Gentiles refuse to obey all Jesus commanded, God rejects us that we may not enter God's heavenly kingdom.

John

2:1 And the third day there was a marriage in Cana of Galilee; and the mother of Jesus was there: 2 And both Jesus was called, and his disciples, to the marriage. 3 And when they wanted wine, the mother of Jesus saith unto him, They have no wine. 4 Jesus saith unto her, Woman, what have I to do with thee? mine hour is not yet come. 5 His mother saith unto the servants, Whatsoever he saith unto you, do it. 6 And there were set there six waterpots of stone, after the manner of the purifying of the Jews, containing two or three firkins apiece. 7 Jesus saith unto them, Fill the waterpots with water. And they filled them up to the brim. 8 And he saith unto them, Draw out now, and bear unto the governor of the feast. And they bare it. 9 When the ruler of the feast had tasted the water that was made wine, and knew not whence it was: (but the servants which drew the water knew;) the governor of the feast called the bridegroom, 10 And saith unto him, Every man at the beginning doth set forth good wine; and when men have well drunk, then that which is worse: but thou hast kept the good wine until now. 11 This beginning of miracles did Jesus in Cana of Galilee, and manifested forth his glory; and his disciples believed on him. 12 After this he went down to Capernaum, he, and his mother, and his brethren, and his disciples: and they continued there not many days.

Jesus performed his first miracle at Cana in Galilee. He, his disciples, mother, and brothers attended a marriage feast there. Before the feast ended, guests consumed all the wine. Jesus' mother informed him no wine remained. He replied his time to do wonders hadn't arrived, but he directed the servants to fill the water containers for Jews to purify themselves then give a drink to the feast's governor. Taste of this wine surprised the governor so much he called the bridegroom and remarked that his actions differed from other gatherings. Hosts usually serve the best wine first and the poor quality after guests have consumed the best. You have reserved the best till last.

God sent his Son, to reveal God's true attitude toward man. God always gives man his best. In creation, God gave man heaven, studded with celestial gems: sun, moon, stars, planets, and galaxies that we may gaze on their beauty and enjoy their benefits. All peoples and generations wonder at God's handiwork. God provided man with amazing varieties of birds to fly upon the air and filled the waters with an array of creatures that continue to fascinate us. On earth he presented us with such a mixture of plants and animals, we often wonder how God formed such diversity. Not only has God's creation appealed to our eyes and mind, he endowed us with five senses to enjoy all God's wonders. These physical blessings God gave us to satisfy our needs and for our enjoyment.

God also offers us manifold wonders for the spirit within each of us. Because we so often overlook God's spiritual blessings, God gave us his most precious gift, his only begotten Son, to enlighten us about his spiritual wonders. As God demonstrated in the beginning his giving, Jesus taught and showed that giving out of love and compassion for others blesses far more than receiving. (Act.20:35) Proper attitude is a spiritual gift from God. (Phil.2:5,13;4:6-8)

Was Jesus' ability to turn water to wine sufficient to convince his disciples he was God's Son? Yes. Did it convince his brothers who also witnessed the wonder? No, John later explained that his brothers did not believe on him. (Jno.7:5) Had we been there, would we have been convinced Jesus performed a genuine miracle? If we read the narrative and disbelieve, witnessing the miracle would not convince us. Belief is our view of evidence. (Heb.11:1) We choose to believe or disbelieve evidence.

Matthew

4:1 Then was Jesus led up of the Spirit into the wilderness to be tempted of the devil. 2 And when he had fasted forty days and forty nights, he was afterward an hungred. 3 And when the tempter came to him, he said, If thou be the Son of God, command that these stones be made bread. 4 But he answered and said, It is written, Man shall not live by bread alone, but by every word that proceedeth out of the mouth of God. 5 Then the devil taketh him up into the holy city, and setteth him on a pinnacle of the temple, 6 And saith unto him, If thou be the Son of God, cast thyself down: for it is written, He shall give his angels charge concerning thee: and in their hands they shall bear thee up, lest at any time thou dash thy foot against a stone. 7 Jesus said unto him, It is written again, Thou shalt not tempt the Lord thy God. 8 Again, the devil taketh him up into an exceeding high mountain, and sheweth him all the kingdoms of the world, and the glory of them; 9 And saith unto him, All these things will I give thee, if thou wilt fall down and worship me. 10 Then saith Jesus unto him, Get thee hence, Satan: for it is written, Thou shalt worship the Lord thy God, and him only shalt thou serve. 11 Then the devil leaveth him, and, behold, angels came and ministered unto him.

Why do Matthew and Luke include details of Jesus' temptation, but Mark only mentioned Satan tempted him, but John excluded this event? Author's purpose and audience determines material included. Satan's tempting Jesus was a key issue to Matthew and Luke and those they addressed. Mark considered it of some importance, but it didn't apply to John's theme of showing Jesus is **the Prophet** like Moses. (Jno.1:21) Trusting God's word helps us overcome Satan's temptations as it helped Jesus defeat Satan in the wilderness. (Ps. 119:9-16)

Mark

1:12 And immediately the Spirit driveth him into the wilderness. 13 And he was there in the wilderness forty days, tempted of Satan; and was with the wild beasts; and the angels ministered unto him.

Satan tempted Jesus from four sources: 1) others; 2) satisfying body needs; 3) desire for power; and 4) tempting God. These sources of tempting Jesus resurface often in gospels. Scribes, Pharisees, and Sadducees harassed Jesus, calling him Beelzebub (Math.10:25;12:24), accusing him of breaking the Sabbath, and blasphemy. (Math. 9:3;12:2,10) They arraigned him before the council, beat, and killed him. These indecencies deterred not Jesus from steadfastness to his Father. Others tempt us by persecution, tribulation, exclusion, and etc. Jesus taught God's children to expect any or all these contradictions from unbelievers. Trusting God, intimidation or persecution will not estrange us from God. (Rom.8:35-39)

Satan suggested Jesus turn stones to bread to satisfy hunger. Jesus replied body food alone fails to satisfy a craving within the human heart. Satan utilizes various avenues to convince God's children to look to the needs of the body and disregard God's food for the spirit. (3 Jno.2)

Satan also tempted Jesus with the desire to rule, but he resisted. When Satan dangled this morsel before James and John, they desired chief places in God's kingdom. (Math.20:20-28; Mk.9:33-35;10:35-45; Lk. 9:46;22:24-27) Satan even encouraged Jesus to tempt God by placing himself in danger and asking God to protect him from harm. (Math.4:5-7; Lk.4:9-12) We must resist sin that we may honor our heavenly Father and overcome. (Eph.1:6,12)

Jesus' trials taught him obedience and perfected him. (Heb.5:8-9) We are perfected by overcoming our temptations. (Math.5:48; Ja.1:2-4)

Luke

**4:1 And Jesus being full of the Holy Ghost
returned from Jordan, and was led by the
Spirit into the wilderness, 2 Being forty
days tempted of the devil. And in those
days he did eat nothing: and when they
were ended, he afterward hungered. 3
And the devil said unto him, If thou be the
Son of God, command this stone that it be
made bread. 4 And Jesus answered him,
saying, It is written, That man shall not
live by bread alone, but by every word of
God. 5 And the devil, taking him up into
an high mountain, shewed unto him all
the kingdoms of the world in a moment of
time. 6 And the devil said unto him, All
this power will I give thee, and the glory
of them: for that is delivered unto me;
and to whomsoever I will I give it. 7 If
thou therefore wilt worship me, all shall
be thine. 8 And Jesus answered and said
unto him, Get thee behind me, Satan: for
it is written, Thou shalt worship the Lord
thy God, and him only shalt thou serve. 9
And he brought him to Jerusalem, and set
him on a pinnacle of the temple, and said
unto him, If thou be the Son of God, cast
thyself down from hence: 10 For it is
written, He shall give his angels charge
over thee, to keep thee: 11 And in their
hands they shall bear thee up, lest at any
time thou dash thy foot against a stone. 12
And Jesus answering said unto him, It is
said, Thou shalt not tempt the Lord thy
God. 13 And when the devil had ended all
the temptation, he departed from him for
a season.**

What helped Jesus overcome sin? Knowledge of and trust in God's word assisted Jesus to resist Satan's temptations. Each time the Evil One set some appealing lure before Jesus, he responded by what God spoke concerning the situation. How can we expect to thwart the devil's tests if we do not know and believe what our heavenly Father tells us about sin and disobedience?

Most of us remember how our parents' instructions prevented us from engaging in some activity which might have cost us our lives. When around swift or riled streams, they taught us to stay out of the water. Don't play in the street where automobiles might crush you. Avoid playing with matches or electrical circuits if you are wet. We may have recalled their reminders too late and suffered some harm. (Prov.2:1-9)

Our heavenly Father also forewarns us of spiritual dangers which, if disregarded, will end in serious consequences. God instructed his Son Jesus to show and explain to people in every family and nation that forgetting our heavenly Father's cautions endangers us physically and spiritually. Though Satan and his children try to convince us that God prevents us from enjoying life's benefits, their words are lies. Our heavenly Father looks down and beholds with grief how Satan prevents us from enjoying the truly good things of life. Many trouble themselves by desiring riches, but end in bitterness, disappointment, and devoid of true friends. What of those who seek pleasure with men and women because they lust for them? Do they find more than they expect? Do they endure a smiting conscience, contract some loathsome disease, and feel dirty? God's instructions produce only good. (Deu. 6:24; Ps.84:11) If we really want to discover a great life, submit to our heavenly Father's guidance, and he will assure us that pleasant life. (Jno.10:10; 1 Tim.4:8;6:6)

Looking at Jesus' example of overcoming Satan's enticements strengthens us during our adversities. We cease to look on persecution and difficulties as things out of control. We know God abides with us and will make all things turn for our good if we will submit to what our Father in heaven teaches us. (Rom.8:28; Heb.13:5) Let's not grieve our heavenly Father. (Gen.6:6) Every instruction God gives us prevents us from engaging in something harmful to us and those with whom we associate.

Matthew

4:18 And Jesus, walking by the sea of Galilee, saw two brethren, Simon called Peter, and Andrew his brother, casting a net into the sea: for they were fishers. 19 And he saith unto them, Follow me, and I will make you fishers of men. 20 And they straightway left their nets, and followed him. 21 And going on from thence, he saw other two brethren, James the son of Zebedee, and John his brother, in a ship with Zebedee their father, mending their nets; and he called them. 22 And they immediately left the ship and their father, and followed him.

For many years, I wondered how the calling of Peter, Andrew, James, and John as recorded in the synoptic gospels harmonized with John's account which indicates Peter, Andrew, Philip, and Nathanael followed Jesus the first or second day after his baptism. (Jno.1:35-51; Act.1:21-22) Sequence of events remain unclear, but I offer this explanation: Peter, Andrew, Philip, Nathanael and perhaps other disciples followed Jesus to Cana in Galilee on the third day after his baptism. (Jno.2:1-11) After the marriage, Jesus, his mother, brothers, and disciples descended to Capernaum. (Jno.2:12) Jesus separated from his disciples and entered the wilderness where Satan tempted him. During those forty days, his disciples probably remained near Capernaum and worked at their former occupations. When Jesus returned from his bout with Satan, he called Peter, Andrew, James and John who promptly abandoned fishing to work with Jesus to advance God's kingdom. Jesus and his disciples soon attended the Passover in Jerusalem. (Jno.2:13-4:3)

Why do synoptic gospels omit Jesus' first calling of disciples, but John excluded his second? Matthew, Mark, and Luke began their Galilean narratives after Herod imprisoned John. John stressed Jesus' Judean ministry, beginning with Jesus' baptism. Synoptic gospels focus on Galilee and God's

Mark

1:16 Now as he walked by the sea of Galilee, he saw Simon and Andrew his brother casting a net into the sea: for they were fishers. 17 And Jesus said unto them, Come ye after me, and I will make you to become fishers of men. 18 And straightway they forsook their nets, and followed him. 19 And when he had gone a little further thence, he saw James the son of Zebedee, and John his brother, who also were in the ship mending their nets. 20 And straightway he called them: and they left their father Zebedee in the ship with the hired servants, and went after him.

approaching kingdom, fulfilling promises to Abraham and David. Within it people of every nation may bask in the spiritual sunshine promised to Abraham and David. (Gen.12:3; 2 Sam.7:12-14; Ps.32:1-2; Math. 1:23;12:24; Rom.4:6-8)

John's gospel stresses Jesus as **the** or **that Prophet** like Moses who speaks all God's truth. (Deu.18:15-19; Jno.1:21,25,45;15:15) Moses delivered all God's law to Israel, but grace and truth came by Jesus Christ. (Jno. 1:17) Most Jews rejected Jesus because he taught with great authority things they didn't expect. (Jno.3:10-11;6:53-60) Rejecting his message severed them from promises God made to Abraham and their fathers. (Act. 3:22-23) Those who grasped and obeyed what Jesus taught experienced rebirth and great joy. (Jno.1:11,13;3:3,5,7)

Synoptic gospels place more emphasis on the approaching kingdom of God and how people must change their attitudes and conduct to dwell therein. Justice, mercy, truth, and honest judgment form the bedrock for God's kingdom. To dwell therein and enjoy all the blessings God offers his faithful children we must be born again of God's truth, show mercy, and do justice and judgment to others. (Gen.18:19; Deu.33:20-21; Ps.89:14;119:121; Is.9:6-7;56:1; Jer:23:5; Math.4:12;9:13;12:7;23:23)

Luke

**5:1 And it came to pass, that, as the people
pressed upon him to hear the word of
God, he stood by the lake of Gennesaret, 2
And saw two ships standing by the lake:
but the fishermen were gone out of them,
and were washing their nets. 3 And he
entered into one of the ships, which was
Simon's, and prayed him that he would
thrust out a little from the land. And he
sat down, and taught the people out of the
ship. 4 Now when he had left speaking, he
said unto Simon, Launch out into the
deep, and let down your nets for a
draught. 5 And Simon answering said
unto him, Master, we have toiled all the
night, and have taken nothing: nevertheless at thy word I will let down the net.
6 And when they had this done, they
inclosed a great multitude of fishes: and
their net brake. 7 And they beckoned unto
their partners, which were in the other
ship, that they should come and help
them. And they came, and filled both the
ships, so that they began to sink. 8 When
Simon Peter saw it, he fell down at Jesus'
knees, saying, Depart from me; for I am a
sinful man, O Lord. 9 For he was
astonished, and all that were with him, at
the draught of the fishes which they had
taken: 10 And so was also James, and
John, the sons of Zebedee, which were
partners with Simon. And Jesus said unto
Simon, Fear not; from henceforth thou
shalt catch men. 11 And when they had
brought their ships to land, they forsook
all, and followed him.**

Before Luke noted Jesus called his disciples, he recorded Jesus going to Nazareth to preach in their synagogue. His friends there wondered at his teaching, but since he was a hometown boy, they refused to honor him. Jesus reminded them that God sent Elijah to a widow in Sidon (a Syrian city) during the 3 1/2-year drought though many widows then lived in Israel. If that were not enough to irritate Nazarenes, he added how Elisha healed Naaman's (a Syrian's) leprosy though many in Israel suffered from leprosy during Elisha's lifetime. Angered beyond limits, his countrymen tried to cast him off a cliff near their city for these aggravations. (Lk.4:16-30)

Jesus' preaching in Nazareth obviously occurred after calling his disciples. Why did Luke record this first? One might suppose that calling his disciples should take precedence over preaching in his hometown. Luke's purpose in writing his gospel explained to Theophilus that God included Gentiles in his plan of salvation. More particularly, since the widow and Naaman both had lived in the region controlled by Syria, the incident proved Jesus honored people of Syria where Theophilus lived and ruled. In Luke's gospel, chronological order takes second place to God's eternal plan and the truth Jesus taught. Sequence of events in the synoptic gospels gives way to importance of God's message. This explains why events do not appear in the same order and why each writer includes or omits parts of the narrative recorded in other gospels.

Realizing writers maintain a specific theme, one begins to analyze the narrative of each gospel to grasp that central theme. For me, this adds greater meaning to each. It ties all the story into a cohesive unit, not just a series of events taken at random.

All three synoptic gospels recorded how Jesus called Peter, Andrew, James, and John at the sea of Galilee. Luke included two ideas not mentioned by others. A multitude gathered to listen to Jesus preach, and Jesus assisted Simon to enclose a large catch of fish, showing Theophilus that God helps those who attempt to make a living as well as those who gather to hear his truth. Theophilus needed to know how our eternal Father cares for and provides spiritual and physical feasts for all his children in every nation even when we are not too attentive to his messengers. (Act.17:22-25) God demonstrates his great love for us.

John

2:13 And the Jews' passover was at hand, and Jesus went up to Jerusalem, 14 And found in the temple those that sold oxen and sheep and doves, and the changers of money sitting: 15 And when he had made a scourge of small cords, he drove them all out of the temple, and the sheep, and the oxen; and poured out the changers' money, and overthrew the tables; 16 And said unto them that sold doves, Take these things hence; make not my Father's house an house of merchandise. 17 And his disciples remembered that it was written, The zeal of thine house hath eaten me up. 18 Then answered the Jews and said unto him, What sign shewest thou unto us, seeing that thou doest these things? 19 Jesus answered and said unto them, Destroy this temple, and in three days I will raise it up. 20 Then said the Jews, Forty and six years was this temple in building, and wilt thou rear it up in three days? 21 But he spake of the temple of his body. 22 When therefore he was risen from the dead, his disciples remembered that he had said this unto them; and they believed the scripture, and the word which Jesus had said. 23 Now when he was in Jerusalem at the passover, in the feast day, many believed in his name, when they saw the miracles which he did. 24 But Jesus did not commit himself unto them, because he knew all men, 25 And needed not that any should testify of man: for he knew what was in man.

Reading the synoptic gospels, it appears Jesus called the future apostles after Herod jailed John the Baptist. (Math.4:12-22; Mk. 1:14-20; Lk.5:1-11) John's gospel shows the apostles followed Jesus to the first Passover after his baptism. They baptized for Jesus before Herod imprisoned John the Baptist. Jesus evidently enlisted them between his temptation and John's imprisonment. (Jno.2: 12;3:22-24;4:1-3) This suggests that none of the synoptic gospels follow a chronological sequence, or they omitted most of the incidents between Jesus' baptism and the day Herod jailed John.

Is John's gospel in chronological sequence? It appears to be. For example, John relates events to major Jewish feasts. The first Passover neared as Jesus descended to Capernaum. (Jno.2:13-23) A second feast (probably Pentecost) brought Jesus to Jerusalem. (Jno.5:1) A second Passover neared just prior to the feeding of the 5000. (Jno.6:4) Jesus' brothers taunted him to attend the feast of Tabernacles. (Jno.7:2) For feast of the dedication during the winter Jesus trekked to Jerusalem again. (Jno.10:22) He rode the ass colt triumphantly into Jerusalem for the third and final Passover prior to his crucifixion. (Jno.11: 55;12:1;13:1) Since John related events to Jewish feasts, it appears he placed events in their correct sequence.

Why have all four gospel writers recorded Jesus calling some disciples? Notice synoptic gospels named Peter, Andrew, James, John, and Matthew, while John named Andrew, Peter, Philip, and Nathanael. Those named appear as principle characters in the gospel where Jesus called them. I suggest the intended audience of each gospel knew these apostles personally, having been taught by them. Except for Judas who betrayed him, they demonstrated a complete trust that Jesus' miracles and deeds proved him to be the Son of the living God. Consider these examples: Andrew approached Peter with the declaration, "**We have found the Messias**." (Jno.1:41) Philip searched for Nathanael to share the news, "**We have found him, of whom Moses in the law, and the prophets, did write, Jesus of Nazareth, the son of Joseph**." (Jno.1:45) When Jesus explained to Nathanael, he saw him before Philip brought him the glad tidings, Nathanael confessed, "**Rabbi, thou art the Son of God; thou art the King of Israel.**" (Jno.1:49) Later, Peter stated, "**Thou art the Christ, the Son of the living**

God." (Math.16:16) Again Peter declared, "**Lord, to whom shall we go: thou hast the words of eternal life. And we believe and are sure that thou art that Christ, the Son of the living God**." (Jno.6:68-69) Their devotion to Jesus rested solidly on evidence demonstrated often by wonders, words, deeds, and Scripture. Jesus is God's true Son.

All four gospel writers recorded Jesus cleansing the temple of commercial activities. (Math.19:45-46; Mk.11:15-17; Lk.19: 45-46; Jno.2:14-16) Context of the cleansing in the synoptic gospels indicates that all three referred to the cleansing within a week of Jesus' crucifixion. They all record the temple cleansing near the end of their gospels. John noted its cleansing near the beginning of his gospel. This suggests that Jesus cleansed the temple at least twice. Since all four writers noted that Jesus cleansed the temple during a Passover feast, it would seem they all described the same event. However, John noted that certain events followed the cleansing he described. First, Jesus discoursed with Nicodemus. (Jno.3:1-21) Second, Jesus baptized in Judaea. (Jno. 3:22;4:1-2) Third, Herod had not yet jailed John the Baptist. (Jno.3:22-24) Fourth, Jesus departed from Judaea to Galilee. (Jno. 4:3) If we understand John correctly, the temple cleansing he recorded must have been at the first Passover after John baptized Jesus. (Jno.2:13,23,6.4,11.55,12:1;13:1)

Why do gospel writers record two cleansings of God's temple, one at the beginning of Jesus' ministry and the other at the end? Didn't God approve of their worship? It wasn't the buying and selling that displeased God. Merchants preyed on worshipers to become rich This reflected poorly on God. People saw this as a money-making scheme, whereas God intended his house be considered by all nations as a house of prayer, a place where people could truly approach God with concerns pressing heavily on their hearts. Why did Mark alone mention the temple was a house of prayer for all nations? (Mk.11:17; Is.56:7) I suggest that this supports the idea that Mark wrote to Gentiles to confirm God shows concern for people of every nation, not Jews alone.

Assuming there were at least two temple cleansings, how long had God's house endured merchandising for profit? Perhaps it had existed before Jesus' birth, for God allowed Jews who lived far from Jerusalem to sell their goods at home and buy the things they needed for the feast when they arrived at his house. (Deu.14:26) Even Gentiles may have purchased their needs after they arrived at God's house.

Temple authorities questioned how Jesus had authority to drive merchants from the temple. Speaking by parable, he replied that if they destroyed this temple, he would raise it up again in three days. (Jno.2:19) Jews replied that it required forty-six years to construct the temple, how could he reconstruct in three days? (Jno.2:20) John remarked that Jesus spoke of his rising from the dead. (Jno.2:21) Jesus knew from Scripture his countrymen would condemn him to death, but his Father would raise him the third day. This sign indicated his authority from God to cleanse the temple.

At this Passover feast Jesus amazed the populace with miracles. Surely these wonders proved he came from God, and many believed on him. However, believing on Jesus did not mean they believed what he taught, and it's the word which Jesus preached that enlightens the spirit within man. (Ps.119:105,130; Jno.6:63) As John's gospel shows, those who believed on Jesus often rejected his message. (Jno.8:30-47) All must confirm belief in Jesus by obedience to his commands to gain rebirth and enter God's eternal kingdom. (Rom.10:16; Ja.1:22-25) Most Jews in Jesus' day and most people today are offended in Jesus because his message requires complete submission to everything he taught as being God's message to his wayward children.

John

**3:1 There was a man of the Pharisees,
named Nicodemus, a ruler of the Jews: 2
The same came to Jesus by night, and said
unto him, Rabbi, we know that thou art a
teacher come from God: for no man can
do these miracles that thou doest, except
God be with him. 3 Jesus answered and
said unto him, Verily, verily, I say unto
thee, Except a man be born again, he
cannot see the kingdom of God. 4 Nicodemus saith unto him, How can a man be
born when he is old? can he enter the
second time into his mother's womb, and
be born? 5 Jesus answered, Verily, verily,
I say unto thee, Except a man be born of
water and of the Spirit, he cannot enter
into the kingdom of God. 6 That which is
born of the flesh is flesh; and that which is
born of the Spirit is spirit. 7 Marvel not
that I said unto thee, Ye must be born
again. 8 The wind bloweth where it
listeth, and thou hearest the sound
thereof, but canst not tell whence it
cometh, and whither it goeth: so is every
one that is born of the Spirit. 9 Nicodemus answered and said unto him, How
can these things be? 10 Jesus answered
and said unto him, Art thou a master of
Israel, and knowest not these things? 11
Verily, verily, I say unto thee, We speak
that we do know, and testify that we have
seen; and ye receive not our witness. 12 If
I have told you earthly things, and ye
believe not, how shall ye believe, if I tell
you of heavenly things? 13 And no man
hath ascended up to heaven, but he that
came down from heaven, even the Son of
man which is in heaven. 14 And as Moses
lifted up the serpent in the wilderness,
even so must the Son of man be lifted up:
15 That whosoever believeth in him
should not perish, but have eternal life. 16
For God so loved the world, that he gave
his only begotten Son, that whosoever
believeth in him should not perish, but
have everlasting life. 17 For God sent not
his Son into the world to condemn the
world; but that the world through him
might be saved. 18 He that believeth on
him is not condemned: but he that believeth not is condemned already, because
he hath not believed in the name of the
only begotten Son of God. 19 And this is
the condemnation, that light is come into
the world, and men loved darkness rather
than light, because their deeds were evil.
20 For every one that doeth evil hateth the
light, neither cometh to the light, lest his
deeds should be reproved. 21 But he that
doeth truth cometh to the light, that his
deeds may be made manifest, that they
are wrought in God.**

Jesus generated considerable excitement in Jerusalem during this Passover feast. Amazed Jews recognized God's hand in Jesus' wonders. Nicodemus served as an example. Approaching Jesus by night, Nicodemus admitted Jesus must be a teacher sent from God. No person could perform these miracles unless God sent him. Acknowledging that Jesus' wonders manifested God's power, one might expect Nicodemus to have accepted all that Jesus taught him, but he didn't. When Jesus explained that no one enters God's kingdom without rebirth, Nicodemus questioned how one can be reborn. Can one re-enter his mother's womb and be reborn? No, he must be born again of water and God's Spirit (by the word of God's Spirit). Nicodemus replied again, "**How can these things be**?" Jesus interpreted Nicodemus' query as a rejection of God's truth. I've told you God's truth, but you won't receive it. (Jno.3:11)

In light of John's introduction, "**He came to his own, and his own received him not**" (Jno.1:11), it appears that rejecting what Jesus taught meant that a person didn't receive Jesus. Rejecting Jesus' words that a man must be reborn of water and God's Spirit excludes him from God's kingdom and his people. This fulfilled Moses' promise of God's wrath on those who refused to hear the words of **the Prophet** who would be like Moses whom God would send to his people. (Deu.18:15-19; Act.3:22-23) Nicodemus severed himself from God's people and kingdom by refusing to believe the words Jesus spoke to him. Later, Jesus taught, "**Ye shall die in your sins if ye believe not that I am he.**" (Jno.8:24)

Will our refusal to hear and obey Jesus be any less damning? If we express an interest in things of God, but submit not to what Jesus taught, are we excluded from God's kingdom and people? If a Jew who had covenant relationship with God through circumcision was severed from God's people and blessings because he refused the truth Jesus taught, do we Gentiles suppose God shows us more favor than he did to his own people? The truth God gave to Jesus applies equally to people of all nations and all generations. We must be born again of water and God's Spirit. Being born of good parents is insufficient. John the Baptist cautioned Jews who listened to him, "**Begin not to say within yourselves, We have Abraham to our father: for I say unto you, That God is able of these stones to raise up children to Abraham.**" (Lk.3:8) If you and I anticipate enjoying the blessings of heaven, we must submit to the rebirth by water and Spirit.

How does one gain a new birth by water and Spirit? It begins with being taught of God. "**No man can come to me, except the Father which hath sent me draw him: and I will raise him up at the last day. It is written in the prophets, And they shall be all taught of God. Every man therefore that hath heard, and hath learned of the Father, cometh unto me.**" (Jno.6:44-45) To learn God's truth, one comes to Jesus, for he has the words of life. "**It is the spirit that quickeneth; the flesh profiteth nothing: the words that I speak unto you, they are spirit, and they are life.**" (Jno.6:63) Jesus commissioned his apostles to preach the gospel to all nations. "**He that believeth and is baptized shall be saved.**" (Mk16:16) Paul explained that new birth must be preceded by dying with Christ. "**Know ye not, that so many of us as were baptized into Jesus Christ were baptized into his death? Therefore we are buried with him by baptism into death: that like as Christ was raised up from the dead by the glory of the Father, even so we also should walk in newness of life. For if we have been planted together in the likeness of his death, we shall be also in the likeness of his resurrection: Knowing this, that our old man is crucified with him, that the body of sin might be destroyed, that henceforth we should not serve sin. For he that is dead is freed from sin. Now if we be dead with Christ, we believe that we shall also live with him: knowing that Christ being raised from the dead dieth not more; death hath no more dominion over him. For in that he died, he died unto sin once; but in that he liveth, he liveth unto God. Likewise reckon ye also yourselves to be dead indeed unto sin, but alive unto God through Jesus Christ our Lord.**" (Rom. 6:3-11)

Those who judge themselves worthy of salvation did as Jesus and his apostles instructed to be born of water and Spirit. They believed Jesus to be God's Son and were buried with him in baptism. As they rose from spiritual death in the watery grave of baptism with Jesus, they experience the new birth from water, and they are born of God's Spirit by having believed and submitted to what Jesus taught by the Spirit of God.

As Israel journeyed through the wilderness from Egyptian bondage to possess their promised land of Canaan, many of them sinned. Their chiding Moses and God for their hardships provoked God who sent deadly serpents among them. Those bitten God offered one remedy. They must look to the brazen serpent God instructed Moses to elevate on a pole. (Num.21:8-9)

Satan, the deadly serpent of all mankind, stings us with the venom of sin which produces spiritual death. (Rom.1:32;6:23) Unless we look to Jesus whom God lifted up as our only hope of life, Satan's poison destroys us as the venom of the deadly serpents did those Jews in the wilderness who refused to look on the brazen serpent which Moses set up for their hope of life. God didn't send Jesus into the world to condemn us, but to provide life. Why? because he loves his wayward children and wishes to spare our lives. If we believe Jesus to be God's only begotten Son and obey him, his blood spares us from the penalty of sin. Refusing to trust him and obey his words allows Satan's poison (lies) to condemn us to eternal death. (Rom.5:1-6:23)

Jesus identifies two kinds of responses to his message. Honest people like light; evil people prefer darkness because it hides their evil deeds. They who seek a good life prefer God's truth which provides the light of life. Unrighteous people hate the light of God's word because it tells their deeds are evil. Each of us may know clearly whether we are children of light or darkness by how we react to the message of God's truth. If we come to God through Jesus' truth, we show to ourselves and the world that we are of God. Avoiding God's way declares to us and the world that we prefer the fellowship with our father, Satan. (Jno.8:39-47) This message Jesus spoke to Nicodemus, but he did not choose the light of life at that time. (Jno. 3:12) God extends mercy. He holds the door of life open, hoping we will enter.

Manasseh, king of Judah serves as an example of God's mercy. Manasseh probably transgressed God's law given by Moses worse than all the kings of Judah. He erected idols to and worshiped nearly every god he knew. When he refused to listen to God's prophets who exhorted him to repent, God sent the king of Assyria who punished Judah and carried Manasseh captive to Babylon. When Manasseh finally humbled himself before God, God allowed him to return to serve as king of Judah again. Then Manasseh destroyed all the idols he had worshiped before God's chastening. (2 Kin. 21:1-18; 2 Chr.33:1-20)

How severely shall God chasten Israel and us before we will obey Jesus as our King and savior? After Jews killed Jesus and persecuted his apostles, God sent the Roman army to destroy Jerusalem and to carry Jews away from the land God promised them by Abraham. Have Germany's atrocities during W.W.II when Hitler burned six million of them to death in gas chambers subdued their resistance to God's plan? Will God execute a more severe plan to break Jewish resistance to God's will? God assures all men that the day shall come when all will bow to King Jesus, even the Jews and we Gentiles. (Is.45:22-25; Rom.14:11; Phil.2:10-11) Moses testified to Israel that even in the latter days (Christian age) they would refuse to submit to God who would continue to curse them for their rebellion. (Lev.26:14-39; Deu. 31:29)

Nicodemus' rejection of the new birth was but a continuation of the rebellious conduct of Israel. Moses testified, **"Remember, and forget not, how thou provokedst the Lord thy God to wrath in the wilderness: from the day that thou didst depart out of the land of Egypt, until ye came unto this place, ye have been rebellious against the Lord."** (Deu.9:7) That same day he wrote, **"Ye have been rebellious against the Lord from the day that I knew you."** (Deu.9:24) Later, Moses penned, **"For I know thy rebellion, and thy stiff neck: behold, while I am yet alive with you this day, ye have been rebellious against the Lord; and how much more after my death?"** (Deu.31:27) Isaiah stated, **"I have spread out my hands all the day unto a rebellious people, which walked in a way that was not good, after their own thoughts; A people that provoketh me to anger continually to my face; that sacri-**

ficeth in gardens, and burneth incense upon altars of brick." (Is.65:2-3) God informed Jeremiah concerning Judah, "**But this people hath a revolting and a rebellious heart; they are revolted and gone.**" (Jer.5:23) Ezekiel remarked, "**And he said unto me, Son of man, I send thee to the children of Israel, to a rebellious nation that hath rebelled against me: they and their fathers have transgressed against me, even unto this very day.**" (Ezek.2:3) Daniel included himself in the great rebellion, "**We have sinned, and have committed iniquity, and have done wickedly, and have rebelled, even by departing from thy precepts and from thy judgments: Neither have we hearkened unto thy servants the prophets, which spake in thy name to our kings, our princes, and our fathers, and to all the people of the land.**" (Dan.9:5-6) Paul added, "**The Jews: Who both killed the Lord Jesus, and their own prophets, and have persecuted us; and they please not God, and are contrary to all men: Forbidding us to speak to the Gentiles that they might be saved, to fill up their sins alway: for the wrath is come upon them to the uttermost.**" (1 Thes.2:14-16)

Does God also chasten Gentiles for not submitting to the words of **that Prophet**? Daniel foretold of a time when many would forsake the holy covenant by doing wickedly. God responds by giving his people into the hands of a wicked lord who eliminates the daily sacrifice and casts down God's sanctuary for 2300 years. (Dan.8:9-14;11:21-24,30-39) Did Daniel speak of Jewish or Christian transgression? Did God send this cruel lord to punish Christians by eliminating our daily sacrifice (Christ) and by casting down God's sanctuary (the church)? Did God remove his sanctuary from among Christians because we, like Israel, turned deaf ears to his commands? (Lev.26:3-39) Paul spoke clearly to the church at Thessalonica, foretelling of a time when Christians would no longer retain a love of God's truth that we might be saved. Then God would send us a strong delusion that we might believe a lie and be damned because we delight in unrighteousness rather than in God's righteousness. (2 Thes.2:3-13)

That Christians today respond to the words of Jesus as rebelliously as did Israel to Moses should be apparent. Jesus prayed to his Father that all his followers might be one, even as Jesus and his Father were one in purpose and action. (Jno.17:20-21) Christians at Corinth divided on numerous points: over leaders, use of spiritual gifts, as they met to eat together, over the resurrection, etc. (1 Cor.1:10-13;11:18-22;12:1-31;14:23-33;15:12-20) At Thessalonica some refused to work because they anticipated the immediate return of Jesus. (2 Thes.3:6-12) James understood Jewish Christians showed partiality to the rich, but despised the poor, stirred up resentment among themselves by desiring positions of great honor, fighting among themselves because of physical lusts, and the rich cheated their poor laborers. Jude deplored how some Christians turned the grace of Christ into lasciviousness. (Jude 3-4) Each of these abuses of God's truth delivered to us by God's Son Christians today transgress, but what seems more deplorable, we dismiss ministers who call us to repentance to save our souls from eternal destruction. Let us not think God will overlook our rebellion! God blesses his obedient children, not disobedient. Old and New testament writers pleaded that we submit to our heavenly Father or perish. We choose eternal blessings or everlasting torment, depending on how we respond to truth. God sent Jesus to plead for our repentance. If we reciprocated God's genuine love in giving us his only begotten Son to demonstrate his love and concern for our hardships, we would confess our rebellion like Daniel and return to God by submitting to the truth Jesus taught.

John

3:22 After these things came Jesus and his disciples into the land of Judaea; and there he tarried with them, and baptized. 23 And John also was baptizing in Aenon near to Salim, because there was much water there: and they came, and were baptized. 24 For John was not yet cast into prison. 25 Then there arose a question between some of John's disciples and the Jews about purifying. 26 And they came unto John, and said unto him, Rabbi, he that was with thee beyond Jordan, to whom thou barest witness, behold, the same baptizeth, and all men come to him. 27 John answered and said, A man can receive nothing, except it be given him from heaven. 28 Ye yourselves bear me witness, that I said, I am not the Christ, but that I am sent before him. 29 He that hath the bride is the bridegroom: but the friend of the bridegroom, which standeth and heareth him, rejoiceth greatly because of the bridegroom's voice: this my joy therefore is fulfilled. 30 He must increase, but I must decrease. 31 He that cometh from above is above all: he that is of the earth is earthly, and speaketh of the earth: he that cometh from heaven is above all. 32 And what he hath seen and heard, that he testifieth; and no man receiveth his testimony. 33 He that hath received his testimony hath set to his seal that God is true. 34 For he whom God hath sent speaketh the words of God: for God giveth not the Spirit by measure unto him. 35 The Father loveth the Son, and hath given all things into his hand. 36 He that believeth on the Son hath everlasting life: and he that believeth not the Son shall not see life; but the wrath of God abideth on him.

After attending the Passover feast, Jesus and his disciples descended to the Jordan to baptize disciples. John the Baptist continued to baptize near the same area, for Herod had not yet put him in prison. Jews and John's disciples approached John about Jesus baptizing and large numbers coming to him rather than to John. At that time John commented that he had explained earlier that God gives blessings to each person as he chooses. John received his charge to preach repentance and baptism and to introduce Christ. God has given to Jesus his responsibility. As the friend of the bridegroom rejoices to see the groom, so John the Baptist rejoiced to see Jesus. He marries the bride. Jesus shall increase, but since John had fulfilled his charge, he shall lose followers. Jesus came from heaven and reigns supreme. John originated on earth and held a less important position. Having been in God's presence, Jesus came to earth to speak to men what God showed and commanded him to teach. Though few received his message, God sent him as the messenger of the new covenant which Moses, Jeremiah, and Malachi promised. (Deu.18:15-19; Jer.31:31-34; Mal.3:1) Though Israel rejected God's message, Jesus testified it shall not reduce its validity. They only call God a liar. (1 Jno. 5:10) Those who accept Jesus' words agree that God sent Jesus to tell men truth. Jesus spoke God's words by God's Spirit that we may know all God's truth. As the Father of all men, God loved Jesus, his only begotten Son, and committed to him everything created in the beginning. He possesses all power in heaven and earth. (Math.28:18; Heb.2:8;10:12) He reigns at God's right hand until he subdues all who oppose him. (Ps.110:1-7; Act.2:34-35;3:21) All who believe the Son gain eternal life. All who reject and disobey the words of the Son shall never see eternal life. God's wrath rests on them. Eternal life begins with knowing God and Jesus. (Jno.17:3) Those who refuse to hear Jesus spurn their only way to gain everlasting life. Jesus informed his people, **"I said therefore unto you, that ye shall die in your sins: for if ye believe not that I am he, ye shall die in your sins."** (Jno.8:24)

Many recreation activities require reserve tickets to attend. If we arrive at the specified location at the proper time and expect to see the performance without reserve tickets, what happens? Doorkeepers or gatekeepers refuse us entrance. This common illustration should convince us that God requires reservations for all who seek to enter heaven. He provides us with a reserve ticket. Hear Paul, "**Now he which stablisheth us with you in Christ, and hath anointed us, is God; who hath also sealed us, and given the earnest of the Spirit in our hearts.**" (2 Cor.1:21-22) "**In whom ye also trusted, after that ye heard the word of truth, the gospel of your salvation: in whom also after that ye believed, ye were sealed with that holy Spirit of promise which is the earnest of our inheritance.**" (Eph.1:13-14) Our reserve ticket to heaven is God's Spirit, received after obedience to God's commands. (Act.5:32)

Many in our generation ridicule the idea that a loving God punishes offenders. Did God's wrath manifest itself in the days of Noah when wise, renowned, and giant men roamed the earth? Genesis and Jesus attest that God destroyed everything that breathed which entered not the ark before the deluge. (Gen.7:17-24; Math.24:37-39; 2 Pet.3:5-7) He spared only Lot and his daughters when he rained fire and brimstone on Sodom and Gomorrah because of their wickedness. (Gen.19:1-29) All Israel's (603,550) chosen men of war, except for Joshua and Caleb, who exited Egypt perished in the wilderness because of their disobedience. (Num.2:32; 14:1-39;26:63-65) These examples demonstrate that God spares those who do his will, but destroys all who refuse to submit to his commandments. God sent Jesus to inform people of every nation and every generation that those who refuse to believe Jesus to be God's messenger of the new covenant and refuse to enter his spiritual body by the new birth, God denies them the only place of safety when he melts with fervent heat all his creation. (2 Pet.3:3-12) Denying or scoffing at God's warning will not diminish its truth and consequences. You and I shall stand before God to give account of how we receive or reject Jesus' truth. (Math.25:31-46; Jno.5:21-29; Rom.14:10-12; 2 Cor.5:9-11)

Knowing God places Jesus as our only hope of standing before him in judgment uncondemned, it behooves each of us to examine carefully our options. God offers but two: eternity with the devil and his angels or eternity with God, Jesus, and the redeemed. (Math.25:46; Jno.5:28-29; 1 Cor.15:52-57; 1 Thes.4:13-17; 2 Pet.2:4-22)

Jesus explained the torment of the unrighteous. One who languished in terrible anguish begged for water to cool his parched tongue. Being denied his request, he pleaded that one from the dead might go to his brothers and warn them to avoid the place where he suffered. He certainly hoped his relatives might escape the suffering he endured. He believed they would listen to one who rose from the dead. God raised Jesus from the dead, but those who love the pleasures of sin reject his warning. Even if God sends someone from hell itself to warn people to change their lives, God knows they will not listen. This request God denied. If people refuse to believe the record God provides in the Bible, the voice of one returned from perdition will not persuade them to repent. (Lk.16:19-31)

God has no desire to punish us for our rebellious lives. His whole biblical record shows that he, as a loving father, cares for all his children's well-being. God wants us to enjoy life's good things. Those of us who have reared children see firsthand that our children and even we ourselves often choose the path of sin which leads to misery. When love and kindness fail to melt our resistance to good living and proper conduct to escape a disastrous life, the threat of punishment may remain God's only choice to deter wayward lives. Honest thinking ought to show us that those who travel the path of sin and unrighteousness reap misery. Why do we choose to live as rebels? Satan convinces us that the good life comes only from denying God's way. At first, the pleasures of sin please, but bitterness follows. (See Ps. 1:1-6.)

If we concede that God's wrath rests heavily on Israel in this present age, we ought to ask why? In former ages, God explained how and why his wrath burned against his people. (Lev.26:14-39) Does God continue to chasten Israel for their rebellion? Why did Rome destroy Jerusalem and exile Jews in 70 A.D.? When God sent Babylon to level Jerusalem, he informed Isaiah and Jeremiah that Judah must serve the Babylonians 70 years, then they would return and inhabit Judah, rebuild Jerusalem and God's temple. (Isa.13:1-22; 43:14;44:26-45:1-4;47:1-16;48:9-20;52:1-12; Jer.25:11;29:10-14) Isaiah informed Judah that Cyrus, king of Persia, would release Jews from Babylonian captivity and command them to rebuild Jerusalem and God's temple. (Is.44:21-45:4) Cyrus issued that decree. (Ez.1:1-4) God sent Babylon to punish Judah for transgressing God's law Moses gave them. (2 Chr.36:14-21) What Jewish transgression caused God to send Rome to destroy Jerusalem and exile the Jews in 70 A.D.? This exile lasted above 1800 years. Like Isaiah and Jeremiah, Daniel and Jesus warned Jews that God would desolate Jerusalem and God's temple again. (Dan. 9:24-27; Math.24:1-35; Mk.13:1-31; Lk.21: 5-36) Why did God for over 1800 years take Jews off the land he promised Abraham? God sent Rome to punish Jews for another rebellion: rejecting and disobeying **that Prophet's** words. Was it not for their rejection of Jesus whom God sent to save them from their sins? (Math.1:21) God promised Jews he would send them a **Prophet** like Moses. God would put in his mouth all God's truth. If any man refused to hear **that Prophet**, God would require it of him. (Deu.18:15-19; Act.3:22-23) Jewish rejection of Jesus resulted in their calamity at the hands of Rome. God has not ceased to chasten after the pattern Moses described. Hear Moses, "**For I know that after my death ye will utterly corrupt yourselves, and turn aside from the way which I have commanded you; and evil will befall you in the latter days; because ye will do evil in the sight of the Lord, to provoke him to anger through the work of your hands.**" (Deu.31:29) Did Moses indicate that God's pattern of blessing and cursing Israel would end with the coming of Christ, or would it continue in the latter days (after the coming of Christ)? Since the **latter days** began with Christ's death and resurrection, (Act.2:16-17; Heb.1:1-2) and since Moses promised Israel blessing or cursing even in latter days, how can any person honestly contend God doesn't bless obedience and curse disobedience today? Why did Hitler roast millions of Jews? Were Hitler's atrocities without God's hand? (Is.45:7; Am.3:6) Were these God's chastenings because Jews rejected **that Prophet** like Moses who came to explain all God's truth, which if rejected resulted in God requiring it of them? (Deu.18:15-19)

Understanding that God continues to bless and curse Israel even today, depending on whether they obey or disobey, what about Christians? Does God bless and curse us also, depending on whether we obey or disobey? How do you explain why Islam overran the region of Asia and Africa where Christianity once prevailed? Why did Europe experience the wandering Asiatic warriors that swamped and destroyed the Roman Empire during the 300s-400s A.D.? By the fifth century Christianity had converted most of the peoples of southern Europe. Why would God direct these hordes to enslave Christians if they obeyed him? Why did Europe's cities, highways, and harvests suffer such desolation with the coming of the Asiatic hordes? Was this from God's hand or coincidence? Why has the world witnessed two world wars, maiming millions, killing millions, laying waste cities, and bringing such suffering to humanity? Has God forsaken the earth as deists claim, or is God chastening his rebellious children? God testified that neither good or ill affects mankind without his hand. (Is.45:7; Am.3:6) Does God lie, or do we disbelieve his testimony? Why claim belief in God then call him a liar? Why refuse to hear God and suffer his wrath now and in the hereafter, too?

Has not God recorded the lives of all the men and women in both Old and New testaments to serve as examples of how God blesses those who submit to his commands, but chastens those who rebel? (Rom.15:4; 1 Cor.10:1-11; Heb.11:1-12:1; 2 Pet.2:6; Jude 5) How can their lives serve as examples if God discontinues to bless and chasten after the same pattern he has used since creation? Do we honestly charge God with double-mindedness after the manner of ourselves? or are we trying desperately to find some means to justify our sins? Has not God testified that he changes not? (Mal.3:6) Furthermore Jesus changes not. (Heb.13:8)

Moses, Jesus, and the apostles John, Peter, and Paul confirm God's testimony. God sent Jesus into this world to deliver to all men the message of God's grace to those who submit to Jesus' message, but he chastises those who rebel. (Deu.18:15-19; Jno. 1:11-17;21,5;3:32-36;4:25;6:6:14;7:40; Act. 3:22-23; Rom.1:18-19; Tit.2:11-12) Are testimonies of two or three witnesses insufficient to establish God's truth? (Deu.19:15; 1 Tim.5:19)

Christian rebellion so closely resembles Israel's I shudder when I read God's truth. God sent Isaiah to persuade Israel to repent, promising great affliction if they persisted in their sins. (Is.8:11-22) They responded, **"We have made a covenant with death, and with hell are we at agreement; when the overflowing scourge shall pass through, it shall not come unto us: for we have made lies our refuge, and under falsehood have we hid ourselves."** (Is. 28:15) Judah responded to Jeremiah's call to repentance, contending they possessed God's temple. God called these lying words. (Jer.3:12-14;7:3-4) Later, Jeremiah asked, **"How do ye say, We are wise, and the law of the Lord is with us? Lo, certainly in vain made he it; the pen of the scribes is in vain."** (Jer.8:8) Jews retaliated, **"Then said they, Come, and let us devise devises against Jeremiah; for the law shall not perish from the priest, nor counsel from the wise, nor the word from the prophet. Come, and let us smite him with the tongue, and let us not give heed to any of his words."** (Jer.18:18) Ezekiel warned, **"Mischief shall come upon mischief, and rumour shall be upon rumour; then shall they seek a vision of the prophet; but the law shall perish from the priest, and counsel from the ancients."** (Ezek.7:26)

Christians insist God's word resides with our ministers. We have the Bible. No terror shall overtake us, we have God's everlasting spiritual temple abiding with us. God assures us that it's not knowing God's will that shields us, but doing his word. (Ja.1:22-25) God's word benefits only those who mix faith with what they hear. (Heb.4:2) Do we believe Jesus and do his commands? (Jno. 15:10,14) If not, we need to repent and obey him. Otherwise, God will chastise severely until we submit to God's truth Jesus taught and receive his mercy. (Rom.1:18-32) Did not Paul inform Corinthians Jesus shall rule till he hath put all enemies under his feet? (1 Cor.15:25) Who are Jesus' enemies? Are they not those who reject and disobey his commands which God gave him to deliver to all nations? Jesus remarked, **"Not everyone that saith unto me, Lord, Lord, shall enter into the kingdom of heaven; but he that doeth the will of my Father which is in heaven."** (Math.7:21) Why tempt God by denying he means what he says? **"In vain the net is spread in the sight of any bird."** (Prov.1:17)

John

4:1 When therefore the Lord knew how the Pharisees had heard that Jesus made and baptized more disciples than John, 2 (Though Jesus himself baptized not, but his disciples,) 3 He left Judaea, and departed again into Galilee. 4 And he must needs go through Samaria. 5 Then cometh he to a city of Samaria, which is called Sychar, near to the parcel of ground that Jacob gave to his son Joseph. 6 Now Jacob's well was there. Jesus therefore, being wearied with his journey, sat thus on the well: and it was about the sixth hour. 7 There cometh a woman of Samaria to draw water: Jesus saith unto her, Give me to drink. 8 (For his disciples were gone away unto the city to buy meat.) 9 Then saith the woman of Samaria unto him, How is it that thou, being a Jew, askest drink of me, which am a woman of Samaria? for the Jews have no dealings with the Samaritans. 10 Jesus answered and said unto her, If thou knewest the gift of God, and who it is that saith to thee, Give me to drink; thou wouldest have asked of him, and he would have given thee living water. 11 The woman saith unto him, Sir, thou hast nothing to draw with, and the well is deep: from whence then hast thou that living water? 12 Art thou greater than our father Jacob, which gave us the well, and drank thereof himself, and his children, and his cattle? 13 Jesus answered and said unto her, Whosoever drinketh of this water shall thirst again: 14 But whosoever drinketh of the water that I shall give him shall never thirst; but the water that I shall give him shall be in him a well of water springing up into everlasting life. 15 The woman saith unto him, Sir, give me this water, that I thirst not, neither come hither to draw. 16 Jesus saith unto her, Go, call thy husband, and come hither. 17 The woman answered and said, I have no husband. Jesus said unto her, Thou hast well said, I have no husband: 18 For thou hast had five husbands; and he whom thou now hast is not thy husband: in that saidst thou truly. 19 The woman saith unto him, Sir, I perceive that thou art a prophet. 20 Our fathers worshipped in this mountain; and ye say, that in Jerusalem is the place where men ought to worship. 21 Jesus saith unto her, Woman, believe me, the hour cometh, when ye shall neither in this mountain, nor yet at Jerusalem, worship the Father. 22 Ye worship ye know not what: we know what we worship: for salvation is of the Jews. 23 But the hour cometh, and now is, when the true worshippers shall worship the Father in spirit and in truth: for the Father seeketh such to worship him. 24 God is a Spirit: and they that worship him must worship him in spirit and in truth. 25 The woman saith unto him, I know that Messias cometh, which is called Christ: when he is come, he will tell us all things. 26 Jesus saith unto her, I that speak unto thee am he.

Jesus and his disciples departed Judaea for Galilee after Herod cast John into prison for informing Herod he violated Moses' law by marrying his brother's wife while his brother, Philip, still lived. (Math.4:12; Mk. 1:14; Lk.3:19-20;4:14) Passing through Samaria, Jesus came to Sychar where Jacob, centuries before, had dug a well. Samaria's culture diverged from Jewish customs. John focused on two alien and two common practices in Jesus' dialogue with the Samaritan woman. God's seventh command forbade adultery. Six times this woman violated God's marriage law, but Jesus opened conversation with the Samaritan woman, not by challenging her immorality, but by asking from her a drink of water, a common need in any culture. She asked why a Jew would ask water of a Samaritan when their peoples have no common dealings. Rather than discuss their alienations, Jesus changed the subject, saying, if she had asked a drink from him, he would supply her with living water. Jesus chose to discuss kindness and common needs, not differences. Living water appealed to her, but how could Jesus supply water when he lacked water-drawing instruments? Was he greater than Jacob, a common ancestor? Again Jesus redirected. All who drink from Jacob's well thirst again. Water Jesus offered allows the one who drinks thereof to thirst no more. Its springing water produces everlasting life. She desired that water so she need never thirst again nor return to Jacob's well to draw water. Jesus redirects again. He asked her to bring her husband for that water. She admitted she had no husband. Jesus responded that she replied truthfully. She had had five husbands and now lived with another man. She perceived Jesus could know this only if he were a prophet. She desired to know if Samaria or Jerusalem were the proper place to worship. Again Jesus redirected, explaining that where one worships was not as important as worshiping God in spirit and in truth. She knew the Messiah would come who would tell her all things. Jesus informed her he was that Christ. Only John's gospel narrates **the Prophet's** aspect of Christ's ministry. Like Moses before, Jesus stands as the law-giver and mediator between God and man.

How does one worship God in spirit and in truth? Have you participated in a game, but you showed little interest in it? You say you aren't really in the game. This lack of interest is a lack of spirit. In religion one may attend worship, but not actually put himself into drawing near to God. God seeks people who have a deep desire to draw close to God. He wants to be a part of your every activity. This constitutes worshiping God in spirit. Worship in truth comes only by serving God as he instructs. (Deu.4:2)

Consider how the Samaritans worshiped. Beginning with Jeroboam's rise to power in the ten tribes, he instituted worship places and practices similar to, but different from those God ordained in Jerusalem. Fearing his people might return to serve Rehoboam if they assembled to worship in Jerusalem as God instructed, Jeroboam established places of worship in Dan and Bethel. He changed priesthoods, too. Instead of using Aaron's sons, he ordained common people priests. He set feast days similar to, but different from God's. He sacrificed, but not where God instructed. These changes in worship God regarded as sin. (Deu.12:11-14; 1 Kin. 12:26-33; 2 Kin.17:24-41) Samaritans continued this imitation worship to the day Jesus came to Sychar. No wonder Jesus commented that you know not what you worship. They may have served with fervor or spirit, but not according to truth or as God taught. God seeks people who worship him zealously (in spirit) and in truth (as God commands). If you and I truly search for a closer walk with our heavenly Father, we will earnestly put ourselves into the worship to praise God and perform every service as he prescribes for honoring him.

Is Christian worship today in spirit and truth? If we all worship in truth, how do we account for the vast differences in patterns of worship? Have Christians imitated Jeroboam's practice of instituting patterns of worship which please us rather than God? From the day Jeroboam made his golden calves and determined that Israel should frequent Bethel and Dan to worship rather than Jerusalem as God instructed, God testified that Jeroboam caused Israel to sin. (1 Kin.12:26-33;13:1-3;14:7-16)

Do Christians sin today by participating in worship which modifies God's worship pattern? Has God testified against us that our worship is sinful? Moses instructed Israel, **"Ye shall not do after all the things that we do here this day, every man whatsoever is right in his own eyes.**" (Deu.12:8) Do we please ourselves or God when we worship? If we attend with a mind to honor and please God, half our worship pleases God. True worship must also comply with God's worship pattern to worship in spirit.

John

4:27 And upon this came his disciples, and marvelled that he talked with the woman: yet no man said, What seekest thou? or, Why talkest thou with her? 28 The woman then left her waterpot, and went her way into the city, and saith to the men, 29 Come, see a man, which told me all things that ever I did: is not this the Christ? 30 Then they went out of the city, and came unto him. 31 In the mean while his disciples prayed him, saying, Master, eat. 32 But he said unto them, I have meat to eat that ye know not of. 33 Therefore said the disciples one to another, Hath any man brought him ought to eat? 34 Jesus saith unto them, My meat is to do the will of him that sent me, and to finish his work. 35 Say not ye, There are yet four months, and then cometh harvest? behold, I say unto you, Lift up your eyes, and look on the fields; for they are white already to harvest. 36 And he that reapeth receiveth wages, and gathereth fruit unto life eternal: that both he that soweth and he that reapeth may rejoice together. 37 And herein is that saying true, One soweth, and another reapeth. 38 I sent you to reap that whereon ye bestowed no labour: other men laboured, and ye are entered into their labours. 39 And many of the Samaritans of that city believed on him for the saying of the woman, which testified, He told me all that ever I did. 40 So when the Samaritans were come unto him, they besought him that he would tarry with them: and he abode there two days. 41 And many more believed because of his own word; 42 And said unto the woman, Now we believe, not because of thy saying: for we have heard him ourselves, and know that this is indeed the Christ, the Saviour of the world.

After the Samaritan woman hastened to spread the news that she had found Christ, the disciples encouraged Jesus to eat. He responded that he had food they failed to notice. Had someone else brought him something to eat? No, his food consisted of completing the task God assigned him. Disciples ought not think that harvest didn't arrive for four months. Visualize clearly, for God provides harvest today. In grain harvest, those who sow and those who reap rejoice together. Similarly, harvest time for eternal life has those who sow and those who reap. You are reapers for God. Others before you broadcast the seed of God's kingdom. You reap from their labor that you and our Father in heaven may rejoice together.

Why did Jesus speak this parable at that time? Who had spread God's word to the Samaritans that Christ must come to save the world? Who had explained to them that he would tell them all God desired of them? Since hostility had divided the Jews and Samaritans for centuries, the message must have been handed down after Moses from generation to generation among the Samaritans themselves. Yet Jesus and the disciples benefited from that teaching which had been kept alive all those centuries. (Deu. 18:15-19)

When the Samaritan woman challenged the men of Sychar to come see a man that told her everything she had done, even she helped prepare the field for harvest of eternal life. They, too, held a hope that Christ would come to deliver them. She suggested this all-knowing stranger must be Christ. They responded by following her to meet the man and evaluate his message for themselves. What Jesus explained to them convinced many Jesus was truly Christ.

Seed of the kingdom of God may lie dormant for ages only to spring into life when time and interest coordinate. None need feel that sowing the seed of God's kingdom accomplishes nothing if the response is not immediate. Who knows? Gospel of God's kingdom may lie dormant until men thirst for God's righteousness.

Jesus spoke of gathering fruit of eternal life and receiving wages. Farmers and/or laborers in harvest gather grain or fruit to sustain physical life for themselves and others. Using this annual activity, Jesus impressed his disciples with a significant truth of the kingdom of heaven. As it requires work to harvest grain or fruit, so considerable effort in teaching and preaching the truth of God prepares men and women to be harvested for God's kingdom.

Perhaps the apostles needed this lesson on gathering fruit unto eternal life. When they returned from purchasing food in Sychar, they marveled that Jesus talked with the Samaritan woman. They saw her as an enemy of Israel. Jesus viewed her as one of God's lost daughters, needing revitalization from God. The apostles gathered food for the body. Jesus encouraged them to gather fruit for eternal life.

In pursuit of business, it's easy to lose sight of God's objective. Frustrations and weariness gnaw at one's patience and strength, influencing farmers and ministers of God alike to forget the rewards of their labors. Could it be that the twelve, weary of their journey from Jerusalem and hungry, considered the Samaritan woman a hindrance to their immediate interest in eating? Jesus, sensing the apostles' nearsightedness, considered it appropriate to redirect the disciples' goals. Don't say to yourselves there are yet four months before harvest. Fruit in Sychar is ripe now and needs gathering. It's in this activity that I've enlisted your assistance. Be ready to direct your efforts toward harvesting for eternal life each time you meet a person. Do not allow yourselves to bypass an opportunity because you suppose the person wouldn't listen. Nationality, occupation, friend, enemy, or however you perceived a person in the past, you now need to view each as a fruit ripe for harvest of everlasting life. Timidity, stranger, or whatever must not dampen your zeal for harvesting for our eternal Father in heaven. No person can return to God unless he hears the message of God's love and mercy.

As the apostles needed encouragement to see with their mind's eye the potential harvest of eternal life, so Christians need to awaken to how we visualize those we meet each day. (2 Cor.4:18) Whether people are skeptics, infidels, deceived religionists, or servants of some strange sect, each person longs for God though he/she may not realize it. Any word from God we speak may plant seed of God's kingdom to germinate in the heart and awaken the desire to return to our heavenly Father. God counts on his faithful to spread the hope of eternal life.

In this decaying society, we urgently need to pray to God for faith and words to interest each person we meet to obey God. He assures us that his word spoken will accomplish the purpose for which it is given. (Is.55:11) We labor together with God to gather fruit unto eternal life. (1 Cor.3:9) Unless each person hears the words of life, he/she cannot respond to it. The apostles then and we now need to rejuvenate our spiritual eyesight. Harvest of eternal life may be ripe, but unless we see it, we will respond as the apostles at Sychar or as farmers who say the fields are too wet, we can't harvest.

God provides when we believe and obey. This includes harvesting for eternal life. Abraham instructed Isaac, God shall provide the lamb for sacrifice. (Gen.22:7-8) Abraham believed God would provide a wife for his son Isaac. (Gen.24:1-60) Paul believed God would provide material needs to Corinthians if they gave as God prospered them. (2 Cor.9:8) When we act on God's promises, we demonstrate our faith in God's truth. (Ja.2:16-18) We must complete the work Jesus has assigned us. (1 Pet.4:10) Then we can rejoice with Jesus, our heavenly Father, and the angels in heaven. There is joy in heaven over one sinner that repents, more than over ninety-nine just persons who need no repentance. (Lk.15:7)

Matthew

4:12 Now when Jesus had heard that John was cast into prison, he departed into Galilee; 13 And leaving Nazareth, he came and dwelt in Capernaum, which is upon the sea coast, in the borders of Zabulon and Nephthalim: 14 That it might be fulfilled which was spoken by Esaias the prophet, saying, 15 The land of Zabulon, and the land of Nephthalim, by the way of the sea, beyond Jordan, Galilee of the Gentiles; 16 The people which sat in darkness saw great light; and to them which sat in the region and shadow of death light is sprung up. 17 From that time Jesus began to preach, and to say, Repent: for the kingdom of heaven is at hand.

Matthew referred to Galilee as of the Gentiles. He based this on Isaiah's writings. (Is.9:1) Isaiah continued, saying that Galileans who walked in darkness saw great light. Matthew also noted that Galileans walked in darkness, but they witnessed great light by the coming of Jesus and by the word of God he explained provided they listened and did it. (Math.7:21-27)

Did Jesus produce light in Galilee? Did he lighten the nobleman's household when he healed his son? The nobleman must have rejoiced to hear his son recovered, but is this the only light Jesus caused to shine in Galilee? Truth of God's word introduces spiritual light into the lives of those who hear and trust it. When Jesus taught the Beatitudes, Jesus turned on the light of everlasting life. (Math.5:14-16) Bitterness, anger, and hate lingering in people's minds produce darkness. Jesus promised that if his audience changed their outlook on life by doing the Father's will, their dark attitude would be replaced with the brilliance of God's light. If you seek true joy in life, think about all the wonders God provides. It enlightens the lives of his children, giving them hope for despair and courage to face opposition. (Tit.1:15-16)

Mark

1:14 Now after that John was put in prison, Jesus came into Galilee, preaching the gospel of the kingdom of God, 15 And saying, The time is fulfilled, and the kingdom of God is at hand: repent ye, and believe the gospel.

Evil thoughts fill the mind with darkness. Dwelling on life's good generates light. Paul recommended, "**Be careful for nothing; but in everything by prayer and supplication with thanksgiving let your requests be made known unto God. And the peace of God, which passeth all understanding, shall keep your hearts and minds through Christ Jesus. Finally, brethren, whatsoever things are true, whatsoever things are honest, whatsoever things are just, whatsoever things are pure, whatsoever things are lovely, whatsoever things are of good report; if there be any virtue, and if there be any praise, think on these things. Those things, which ye have both learned, and received, and heard, and see in me, do: and the God of peace shall be with you.**" (Phil.4:6-8) How we think determines our attitude toward the world. Solomon remarked that as a man thinks in his heart, so is he. (Prov.23:7) Jesus explained, "**those things which proceed out of the mouth come forth from the heart; and they defile the man. For out of the heart proceed evil thoughts, murders, adulteries, fornications, thefts, false witness, blasphemies: These are the things which defile a man: but to eat with unwashen hands defileth not a man.**" (Math. 15:17-20) Solomon concluded, "**Keep thy heart with all diligence; for out of it are the issues of life.**" (Prov.4:23) Good thoughts brighten life. Evil thoughts permeate life with darkness. Jesus brings the light of life to all who obey him. (Jno.12:46)

Jesus' second Galilean miracle after Herod jailed John the Baptist healed a nobleman's son. Capernaum heard Jesus came to Cana. A nobleman hurried to Cana to secure the

Luke

3:19 But Herod the tetrarch, being reproved by him for Herodias his brother Philip's wife, and for all the evil which Herod had done, 20 Added yet this above all, that he shut up John in prison.

4:14 And Jesus returned in the power of the Spirit into Galilee: and there went out a fame of him through all the region round about. 15 And he taught in their synagogues, being glorified of all.

great physician. He appealed to Jesus to come heal his son. Jesus suggested he would not believe unless he saw a miracle. The nobleman urged Jesus to come before his son died. Sensing the father's deep plea for help, Jesus assured him that his son lived. He trusted Jesus and started home. Before reaching Capernaum, his servant met and refreshed him with glad tidings. His son had recovered suddenly about 1:00 P.M. the day before. The nobleman realized that was when Jesus told him that his son lived. Then he truly believed Jesus.

Will Jesus' coming into communities today displace Satan's darkness? Most communities in the United States know about Jesus, yet darkness remains in most communities and in individual lives. If Jesus dispels darkness, why do we see darkness rather than light? Knowing about Jesus differs greatly from knowing him personally. Understanding principles Jesus taught benefits only those who incorporate God's words to experience productive and self-fulfilling lives. Bibles in homes fail to enrich those who live in the homes unless they read, hear, and abide by the truths the Bible teaches. Even attending church regularly and admitting the minister delivers excellent words of wisdom will not improve hearers' lives unless we set our minds to incorporate the words of wisdom into our daily associations with family members, friends and colleagues. Only a fool hears Jesus' teaching and refrains from doing it. (Math.7:26) "**Ye are my friends, if ye do whatsoever I command you.**" (Jno.15:14) Knowing what to do and obeying blesses. Christianity is a performance religion. James admonished, "**But be ye doers of the word, not hearers only, deceiving your own selves.**" (Ja.1:22) Even Moses impressed on Israelites that they keep God's commands that they may live and that it may be well with them, even prolonging their lives in the good land God had given them. (Deu.5:33)

John

4:43 Now after two days he departed thence, and went into Galilee. 44 For Jesus himself testified, that a prophet hath no honour in his own country. 45 Then when he was come into Galilee, the Galilaeans received him, having seen all the things that he did at Jerusalem at the feast: for they also went unto the feast. 46 So Jesus came again into Cana of Galilee, where he made the water wine. And there was a certain nobleman, whose son was sick at Capernaum. 47 When he heard that Jesus was come out of Judaea into Galilee, he went unto him, and besought him that he would come down, and heal his son: for he was at the point of death. 48 Then said Jesus unto him, Except ye see signs and wonders, ye will not believe. 49 The nobleman saith unto him, Sir, come down ere my child die. 50 Jesus saith unto him, Go thy way; thy son liveth. And the man believed the word that Jesus had spoken unto him, and he went his way. 51 And as he was now going down, his servants met him, and told him, saying, Thy son liveth. 52 Then inquired he of them the hour when he began to amend. And they said unto him, Yesterday at the seventh hour the fever left him. 53 So the father knew that it was at the same hour, in the which Jesus said unto him, Thy son liveth: and himself believed, and his whole house. 54 This is again the second miracle that Jesus did, when he was come out of Judaea into Galilee.

Mark

1:21 And they went into Capernaum; and straightway on the sabbath day he entered into the synagogue, and taught. 22 And they were astonished at his doctrine: for he taught them as one that had authority, and not as the scribes. 23 And there was in their synagogue a man with an unclean spirit; and he cried out, 24 Saying, Let us alone; what have we to do with thee, thou Jesus of Nazareth? art thou come to destroy us? I know thee who thou art, the Holy One of God. 25 And Jesus rebuked him, saying, Hold thy peace, and come out of him. 26 And when the unclean spirit had torn him, and cried with a loud voice, he came out of him. 27 And they were all amazed, insomuch that they questioned among themselves, saying, What thing is this? what new doctrine is this? for with authority commandeth he even the unclean spirits, and they do obey him. 28 And immediately his fame spread abroad throughout all the region round about Galilee.

Only Mark and Luke record Jesus' third Galilean miracle. What significance did they see in casting out a devil? God's kingdom subdues Satan, individuals, and nations. Casting out the devil showed God granted Jesus King to deliver his people from Satan's power. Since devils obey him, it should be evident that God's kingdom neared. For those seeking the kingdom of God, it's time to listen. Everyone entering God's kingdom must be taught of God. (Is.2:1-4;54:13; Jno.6:44-45) Coupling authoritative teaching with power to cast out demons demonstrated God made Jesus King and empowered him to depose his foes, including Satan. By God's decree, Jesus shall cast down and scatter all rebellion against God and rule in righteousness until God ends time on earth. (1 Cor.15:25) Preaching and working miracles, Jesus encouraged hearers to repent and believe the gospel which offers forgiveness of sins and eternal salvation.

Luke

4:31 And came down to Capernaum, a city of Galilee, and taught them on the sabbath days. 32 And they were astonished at his doctrine: for his word was with power. 33 And in the synagogue there was a man, which had a spirit of an unclean devil, and cried out with a loud voice, 34 Saying, Let us alone; what have we to do with thee, thou Jesus of Nazareth? art thou come to destroy us? I know thee who thou art; the Holy One of God. 35 And Jesus rebuked him, saying, Hold thy peace, and come out of him. And when the devil had thrown him in the midst, he came out of him, and hurt him not. 36 And they were all amazed, and spake among themselves, saying, What a word is this! for with authority and power he commandeth the unclean spirits, and they come out. 37 And the fame of him went out into every place of the country round about.

Under Moses' law Jews lived in sin's darkness. (Gal.4:1-5) Jesus, preaching the light-giving truth of God's gospel, offered them liberty. Believers who submitted to God's truth escaped darkness. Disobedient hearers continued to reside in sin and Satan's dark kingdom. (Col.1:12-14) **"The word preached did not profit them, not being mixed with faith in them that heard it."** (Heb.4:2) God's promises to Jews or Gentiles benefit only those who obey his commands. (Math.7:21,24-27; Lk.6:46;11:28; Rom.2:13; Ja.1:22; 1 Jno.3:7; Rev.22:14; See Rom.6:17-18; Heb.12:28.) Priests, Pharisees, scribes, and Jewish leaders Satan enslaved in sin. Rather than submit to God's righteousness by repenting of their vain devotions which lacked love and respect for others, they denied John and Jesus fulfilled God's promises to their fathers. Neither John's exhortation, nor Jesus' miracles and references to their Scriptures convinced them that God sent John and Jesus to deliver Israel from Satan's evil way. God demands a changed lifestyle for those entering his kingdom. Show justice, judgment, equity, and mercy, not outward signs of devotion. (Math. 9:13;12:7;23:23) God demands obedience with all one's heart, soul, mind, and strength. (Deu.6:5;10:12;11,13) Moses taught this, but Israel did not respond obediently. Limiting religion to assemblies, observing feasts, learning about God, or claiming godly parents rejected God's new birth and excluded them from God's kingdom.

Jesus embodied God who grieves because Satan works havoc in our lives. The Evil One curses us with physical ills: leprosy, typhoid, cholera, and physical death, and with social and spiritual curses by dividing friends, neighbors, relatives, peoples, and nations, and separates all people from our heavenly Father. Jesus descended to destroy Satan's burdens. (Is.42:1-4;59:1-8;61:1-3; Math.9:18-31)

Physical relief, though great, brings only a fleeting benefit. Jesus came also to heal Satan's spiritual blights. Guilt darkens as completely as physical illness. **"Unto the pure all things are pure: but unto them that are defiled and unbelieving is nothing pure; but even their mind and conscience is defiled."** (Tit.1:15)

When did Jesus become King, and did he receive power and authority at his coronation? Comparing when God anointed Jesus with how and when God elevated other Israelite kings may answer these questions. God chose Saul as Israel's first visible king. Samuel anointed Saul and informed him God anointed him captain over God's inheritance. (1 Sam.10:1) God gave Saul his Spirit when he anointed him king. (1 Sam.10:9-10) When Ammonites threatened Israel, Saul summoned Israelite warriors to save his people. (1 Sam.11:1-15)

After God rejected Saul as king for disobedience, Samuel anointed David king, and God gave David his Holy Spirit. (1 Sam.16:13) After ten years Saul died, and David gained power in Judah. (2 Sam.2:4) Anointing and giving a man his Holy Spirit symbolized God made one king over his people, but exercising power followed some time later. God continued this pattern with Jesus. John the Baptist baptized Jesus, and God anointed Jesus with his Holy Spirit. (Math.3:16; Mk.1:10; Lk.3:22; Jno.1:32; Act.10:38) God made Jesus King at his baptism. Three years later Jesus exercised his power on Pentecost. Jesus declared, **"All power is given unto me in heaven and in earth."** (Math.28:18)

Where and when does Jesus sit on David's throne to exercise authority? Peter quoted David, **"Being a prophet, and knowing that God had sworn with an oath to him, that of the fruit of his loins, according to the flesh, he would raise up Christ to sit on his throne; He seeing this before spake of the resurrection of Christ, that his soul was not left in hell, neither his flesh did see corruption, This Jesus hath God raised up, whereof we all are witnesses. Therefore being by the right hand of God exalted, and having received of the Father the promise of the Holy Ghost, he hath shed forth this, which ye now see and hear."** (Act.2:30-33) Christ's throne remains at God's right hand. His regal power first manifested itself on Pentecost, 33 A.D. when God gave the apostles the Holy Spirit, and they spoke in the various languages of all the Jews who came to worship. (Ps.110:1-7; Lk. 24:49; Act.1:4-5;2:1-47;3:20-21) Jesus instructed his apostles, **"And behold, I send the promise of my Father upon you: but tarry ye in the city of Jerusalem, until ye be endued with power from on high."** (Lk.24:49) On Pentecost, apostles gathered, and God's Spirit descended upon them as a flame. They began to speak in the various languages, and the multitude gathered. Jews assembled to behold this unusual event. Acts records Peter's discourse. He explained that what they witnessed fulfilled Joel's prophecy. God's Spirit causes your sons, daughters, and aged to prophesy. Call on God, and ye shall be saved. Peter recalled God's promise to raise up Christ to sit on David's throne. What ye see today fulfills God's promise. You killed Jesus, God's and David's son, but God raised him from the dead and set him on David's throne in heaven at God's right hand. He now demonstrates his power by granting us his Spirit. God has made this Jesus whom you crucified both Lord (king) and Christ (anointed).

Peter instructed believers to repent and be baptized. The obedient entered God's kingdom which began on earth that day. Being born again of water and Spirit, God translated them into his kingdom, the church. (Act.2:47; Col.1:13-14)

Jewish kings and priests served as judges to settle differences between brethren. (1 Sam.8:5; Deu.19:16-21) David judged the young man who claimed he killed Saul, killing the man because he killed God's anointed. (2 Sam.1:2-6) Solomon judged between two women, each claiming a baby. (1 Kin.3:16-28) Difficult decisions God laid on priests who approach God who used the Urim and Thummim to cast the final lot. (Ex.18:13-26;28:30; Num.27:21; Deu.1:9-17;17:8-18;33:8-10; Prov.16:33)

Judging in God's kingdom shows similarity to Jewish kings and priests as judges. God utilizes Christian judges to settle differences plaguing fellowship between brethren. Jesus spoke to apostles, **"Verily I say unto you, That ye which have followed me, in the regeneration when the Son of man shall sit in the throne of his glory, ye also shall sit upon twelve thrones, judging the twelve tribes of Israel."** (Math.19:28; See Lk.22:30.)

Did apostolic decisions rest on God's commands as God required of O.T. judges, or were they free to decide from human wisdom? The first recorded apostolic decision included apostles best choice, but finally God decided. After Judas vacated his apostolic position by choosing to betray Jesus and by hanging himself, surviving apostles separated Barsabas and Matthias as potential replacements for Judas. By lot, God chose Matthias. (Act.1:15-26)

Apostles and elders in Jerusalem faced a difficult doctrinal decision after Gentiles entered God's kingdom. Had Peter acted alone in baptizing Cornelius into God's kingdom, or had God included Gentiles? Peter explained his and Cornelius' visions, and presented six Jewish brethren who witnessed the event. Evaluating the evidence, church leaders concluded God offered salvation to Gentiles. (Act.11:1-18)

Soon some Jewish believers affirmed Gentiles must submit to circumcision and keep Moses' law to be saved. In Antioch, Paul and Barnabas disputed the Jewish contention. Failing to convince them of error, they came to Jerusalem to determine if apostles and elders held this belief. Peter, James, Paul, and Barnabas spoke about the issue and concluded God's Spirit did not require Gentiles to keep Moses' law and submit to circumcision to be saved. They must refrain from idolatry, fornication, eating blood, and things strangled. (Act.15:1-31) God's truth, not man's, settled the issue.

God's pattern of anointing kings and providing them with his Spirit applies to Christians. Each person who submits to God's righteousness, God anoints with his Spirit to become a king and priest before God. (2 Cor.1:21-22; Eph.1:13; 1 Pet.3:21;2:9; 1 Jno. 2:27; Rev.1:6) Each reigns on earth while Jesus reigns in heaven at his Father's right hand. (Eph.2:6; Rev.2:26-27;3:26-27;5:10; 12:5;20:4-5) As we judge issues, do we judge according to God's truth?

Has Satan convinced us that what God foretold in Jewish Scriptures, confirmed by the preaching of John the Baptist, Jesus, his apostles, and later recorded in the New Testament is not God's truth? Is Satan continuing his lies as in the beginning? (Gen.3:1-6; Jno.8:44) Has he infiltrated churches with his lying children to convince God's people to believe a lie and be damned?

(2 Thes.2:11-12) Satan persuades us not to continue in the doctrine of Christ. (Jno.15:1-10; Rom.11:22; 2 Cor.11:1-15; Gal.2:4-55) Each assembly needs to decide differences between brethren. A Corinthian brother lived with his father's wife, and brethren went to court before unbelievers to resolve differences. Paul directed them to submit to God's truth in settling differences. As kings and priests before God, Christian decisions are God's, not man's, and must be just. (1 Cor. ch. 5-6; Deu.1:9-18) Accept God's decision and function as judges to settle matters of disagreement among yourselves. Don't ask those in Satan's kingdom to sit as judges to resolve differences in God's kingdom of light.

Gospels emphasize four points concerning Jesus' return to Galilee after Herod imprisoned John the Baptist. 1. Matthew stressed Jesus fulfilled Isaiah's prophecy, related to Galilee. Before Jesus' coming, Galileans sat in darkness, but Jesus offered them great light if they would listen to God's truth, believe and act on its principles. 2. Mark stressed God's set time had arrived to introduce his everlasting kingdom. Galileans, repent and believe God's good news. 3. Luke contrasted nations' military might with power of God's Spirit by which God conquers and reigns. Nations use military might; Jesus employs power of God's Spirit. 4. Narrating a nobleman's plea to come heal his dying son, John emphasized Jesus spoke a healing command in Cana which instantly cured the son in Capernaum, some fifteen miles distant. Believing Jesus' word effected the healing. Synthesizing these four concepts, God sent Jesus into Galilee to speak God's light-giving and life-giving word which demonstrated time had arrived for God to initiate his kingdom, powered by God's Spirit whose word effects wonders when trusted by ordinary people accustomed to social and spiritual darkness.

Synoptic gospels utilize central themes to identify Jesus' Galilean ministry. Matthew conveyed God's view of Galilee's populous before Jesus launched his amazing wonders and illuminating teaching. Disregarding how Galileans saw themselves, God viewed them as prisoners, sitting in gloomy, cold dungeons with no hope of release. To their amazement, sunlight streamed into their cells, offering them light, warmth, and hope of release. Mark encouraged these captives to change their outlook. Repent and believe God's message. Time has arrived for God's kingdom to conquer darkness. Luke noted how Jesus' words with power of God's Spirit and miracles offered hope to those accustomed to darkness. Wherever the need exists, John capitalized on the fact that distance and lack of Jesus' physical presence does not limit God's Spirit's power to correct the wrong. Believing Jesus' word, John observed, heals across space and disregards time.

God's gospel message proves timeless and disregards political, social, and economic circumstance. Age, nationality, social status, ethnic background, every individual without God sits in Satan's prison cell chained in sin, without hope until he/she hears the Spirit's light-giving message. Each may declare there is no hope, but for those seeking release, you need to repent, and obey. Release is assured. Eternal light will fill your soul. God provides freedom from Satan's dungeon if you seek release.

God is loving and gracious. All ought to trust him through Jesus' God-given words. Like loving earthly fathers, our heavenly Father explains what opens the door to the best life offers, but warns against those things which bring bondage and sorrow. If we are too arrogant to listen to our earthly parents, we set snares for our lives. Refusing to listen to our heavenly Father snares in this life and that to come. (Prov.10:8,17;12:1; 14:9;15:5) God sent Jesus into Galilee, preaching, **"Time is fulfilled, and the kingdom of God is at hand: Repent ye, and believe the gospel."**

Viewpoints

Matthew

**8:14 And when Jesus was come into
Peter's house, he saw his wife's mother
laid, and sick of a fever. 15 And he
touched her hand, and the fever left her:
and she arose, and ministered unto them.
16 When the even was come, they brought
unto him many that were possessed with
devils: and he cast out the spirits with his
word, and healed all that were sick: 17
That it might be fulfilled which was
spoken by Esaias the prophet, saying,
Himself took our infirmities, and bare our
sicknesses.**

**4:23 And Jesus went about all Galilee,
teaching in their synagogues, and preaching the gospel of the kingdom, and healing
all manner of sickness and all manner of
disease among the people. 24 And his
fame went throughout all Syria: and they
brought unto him all sick people that were
taken with divers diseases and torments,
and those which were possessed with
devils, and those which were lunatick, and
those that had the palsy; and he healed
them. 25 And there followed him great
multitudes of people from Galilee, and
from Decapolis, and from Jerusalem, and
from Judaea, and from beyond Jordan.**

Mark

**1:29 And forthwith, when they were come
out of the synagogue, they entered into the
house of Simon and Andrew, with James
and John. 30 But Simon's wife's mother
lay sick of a fever, and anon they tell him
of her. 31 And he came and took her by
the hand, and lifted her up; and
immediately the fever left her, and she
ministered unto them. 32 And at even,
when the sun did set, they brought unto
him all that were diseased, and them that
were possessed with devils. 33 And all the
city was gathered together at the door. 34
And he healed many that were sick of
divers diseases, and cast out many devils;
and suffered not the devils to speak,
because they knew him. 35 And in the
morning, rising up a great while before
day, he went out, and departed into a
solitary place, and there prayed. 36 And
Simon and they that were with him
followed after him. 37 And when they had
found him, they said unto him, All men
seek for thee. 38 And he said unto them,
Let us go into the next towns, that I may
preach there also: for therefore came I
forth. 39 And he preached in their synagogues throughout all Galilee, and cast
out devils.**

Apostles' family members experienced Satan's heavy hand. Peter's mother-in-law lay fevered in bed. Jesus' word canceled her fever and raised her up to help others. God gives his children a desire to serve.

Peter's house never had so many visitors at one time as gathered there the night Jesus came. As the word flashed from house to house in Capernaum that a man named Jesus that day cast out a devil and cured a debilitating fever, the reply must have been, "Where is this Jesus? Maybe he will heal our diseases, too."

"He's at Peter's house!" As the news spread, loved ones with diseases, devils, and all ills were hastened to Peter's house. Jesus embodied God. He shows how sorrowfully our heavenly Father looks down on the havoc Satan works among men. He casts the burden of guilt for sin on the race. Sin darkens our lives. Each of us consists of two persons, blended into one body and spirit. Both parts need daily food. As we eat and drink to sustain the physical body, the spiritual being needs spiritual food and water, issuing from God's throne. Without Jesus' life-giving words, our spirits become malnourished, diseased by sin, and hover at the brink of death. (Math.4:4) Jesus beheld his people's spirits starving and bound in sin by Satan. Jesus demonstrated the compassion of our heavenly Father by relieving spiritual and body burdens. Jesus benefits only those who accept his healing.

Luke

4:38 And he arose out of the synagogue, and entered into Simon's house. And Simon's wife's mother was taken with a great fever; and they besought him for her. 39 And he stood over her, and rebuked the fever; and it left her: and immediately she arose and ministered unto them. 40 Now when the sun was setting, all they that had any sick with divers diseases brought them unto him; and he laid his hands on every one of them, and healed them. 41 And devils also came out of many, crying out, and saying, Thou art Christ the Son of God. And he rebuking them suffered them not to speak: for they knew that he was Christ. 42 And when it was day, he departed and went into a desert place: and the people sought him, and came unto him, and stayed him, that he should not depart from them. 43 And he said unto them, I must preach the kingdom of God to other cities also: for therefore am I sent. 44 And he preached in the synagogues of Galilee.

Unless we listen to the words of Jesus, God cannot free us from our captor's dungeon. As Adam and Eve listened to the advice of the serpent in Eden and entered into his prison of sin, none of us can escape Satan's death hold unless we listen to the truth of God Jesus explained. Satan lied to our progenitors. We do die the day we transgress God's law. (Gen.2:15-3:11) Jesus informs us we can live again if we turn deaf ears to the father of lies and open our ears to the Father of truth and life, even God. Man does not live by bread alone. Our spirits must feast on every word of God to abound in health. (Math.4:4)

Doctors confirm that a baby left unloved will not survive even if fed. It is not good for man to remain alone. (Gen.2:18) This should help us to understand that fellowship with God sustains our spiritual health. Even as we seek friendship on earth, our inner being seeks for fellowship with our Creator. Without companionship for the body and for the inner being, we only partially experience life. (Jno.10:10)

God commissioned his Son Jesus to enter the realm of physical life to portray visibly our heavenly Father. Compassion, love, kindness, and mercy feeds the spirit of man as meat, bread, and water sustains the physical body. Even the most vile person senses how mercy shown to him or her relieves stress and generates an attitude of good will to others. It's this spirit of wanting to benefit others that reaches the most inner parts of our soul to feed that which longs for love. As one comprehends this satisfying process of exchanging kindness and mercy with others, he realizes that God provides an avenue for us to have life more abundantly. (Jno.10:10) It is true, man does not live by bread alone. Every word of God explains to us how to interact with every man, woman, child, and God to behold the fullness of life.

If God had withheld his Son Jesus from living among us and showing us by example and word the true life, we most likely would have continued to follow the wisdom of the Evil One who contends that each person should look out for himself and forget about the hardships inflicting others. We witness this manner of life about us continually. We seek to get ahead. Get ahead of what? Get ahead of others? By what means? Is the desire to succeed providing a full life if it abandons a sincere consideration of the welfare of those about us? Emptiness of life stalks every one of us who follows this vain life style. Collecting more wealth, honor, wisdom, etc. leaves us empty without the mercy and love others and God bestow on us. If we need that kindness to experience a full life, we must share love and mercy with others that they too may understand the fullness of life. No wonder God is love. (1 Jno.4:8) He offers this love to all his children even after we have offended him and injured his other children.

John

5:1 After this there was a feast of the
Jews; and Jesus went up to Jerusalem. 2
Now there is at Jerusalem by the sheep
market a pool, which is called in the Hebrew tongue Bethesda, having five porch-
es. 3 In these lay a great multitude of
impotent folk, of blind, halt, withered,
waiting for the moving of the water. 4 For
an angel went down at a certain season
into the pool, and troubled the water:
whosoever then first after the troubling of
the water stepped in was made whole of
whatsoever disease he had. 5 And a certain man was there, which had an infirmity thirty and eight years. 6 When Jesus
saw him lie, and knew that he had been
now a long time in that case, he saith unto
him, Wilt thou be made whole? 7 The
impotent man answered him, Sir, I have
no man, when the water is troubled, to
put me into the pool: but while I am coming, another steppeth down before me. 8
Jesus saith unto him, Rise, take up thy
bed, and walk. 9 And immediately the
man was made whole, and took up his
bed, and walked: and on the same day
was the sabbath. 10 The Jews therefore
said unto him that was cured, It is the
sabbath day: it is not lawful for thee to
carry thy bed. 11 He answered them, He
that made me whole, the same said unto
me, Take up thy bed, and walk. 12 Then
asked they him, What man is that which
said unto thee, Take up thy bed, and
walk? 13 And he that was healed wist not
who it was: for Jesus had conveyed himself away, a multitude being in that place.
14 Afterward Jesus findeth him in the
temple, and said unto him, Behold, thou
art made whole: sin no more, lest a worse
thing come unto thee. 15 The man departed, and told the Jews that it was
Jesus, which had made him whole. 16 And
therefore did the Jews persecute Jesus,
and sought to slay him, because he had
done these things on the sabbath day. 17
But Jesus answered them, My Father
worketh hitherto, and I work. 18 Therefore the Jews sought the more to kill him,
because he not only had broken the
sabbath, but said also that God was his
Father, making himself equal with God.
19 Then answered Jesus and said unto
them, Verily, verily, I say unto you, The
Son can do nothing of himself, but what
he seeth the Father do: for what things
soever he doeth, these also doeth the Son
likewise. 20 For the Father loveth the Son,
and sheweth him all things that himself
doeth: and he will shew him greater
works than these, that ye may marvel. 21
For as the Father raiseth up the dead, and
quickeneth them; even so the Son
quickeneth whom he will. 22 For the
Father judgeth no man, but hath committed all judgment unto the Son: 23 That
all men should honour the Son, even as
they honour the Father. He that honoureth not the Son honoureth not the
Father which hath sent him. 24 Verily,
verily, I say unto you, He that heareth my
word, and believeth on him that sent me,
hath everlasting life, and shall not come
into condemnation; but is passed from
death unto life. 25 Verily, verily, I say unto you, The hour is coming, and now is,
when the dead shall hear the voice of the
Son of God: and they that hear shall live.
26 For as the Father hath life in himself;
so hath he given to the Son to have life in
himself; 27 And hath given him authority
to execute judgment also, because he is the
Son of man. 28 Marvel not at this: for the
hour is coming, in the which all that are in
the graves shall hear his voice, 29 And
shall come forth; they that have done
good, unto the resurrection of life; and
they that have done evil, unto the
resurrection of damnation. 30 I can of
mine own self do nothing: as I hear, I
judge: and my judgment is just; because I
seek not mine own will, but the will of the
Father which hath sent me. 31 If I bear

witness of myself, my witness is not true. 32 There is another that beareth witness of me; and I know that the witness which he witnesseth of me is true. 33 Ye sent unto John, and he bare witness unto the truth. 34 But I receive not testimony from man: but these things I say, that ye might be saved. 35 He was a burning and a shining light: and ye were willing for a season to rejoice in his light. 36 But I have greater witness than that of John: for the works which the Father hath given me to finish, the same works that I do, bear witness of me, that the Father hath sent me. 37 And the Father himself, which hath sent me, hath borne witness of me. Ye have neither heard his voice at any time, nor seen his shape. 38 And ye have not his word abiding in you: for whom he hath sent, him ye believe not. 39 Search the scriptures; for in them ye think ye have eternal life: and they are they which testify of me. 40 And ye will not come to me, that ye might have life. 41 I receive not honour from men. 42 But I know you, that ye have not the love of God in you. 43 I am come in my Father's name, and ye receive me not: if another shall come in his own name, him ye will receive. 44 How can ye believe, which receive honour one of another, and seek not the honour that cometh from God only? 45 Do not think that I will accuse you to the Father: there is one that accuseth you, even Moses, in whom ye trust. 46 For had ye believed Moses, ye would have believed me: for he wrote of me. 47 But if ye believe not his writings, how shall ye believe my words?

Returning from his Galilean ministry to Jerusalem for a feast (probably Pentecost). (Deu.16:16), Jesus kept Moses' law so none could convict him of sin. (Jno.8:46)

Jerusalem abounded with bodies and spirits Satan blighted. Relieving physical afflictions, Jesus demonstrated God's love for man and his power to destroy the works of the Evil One. Jesus captured people's attention that he may impart God's message, which believed and obeyed, alleviates their spiritual defects. His word offered God's blessings promised to Abraham. (Gen.12:3)

At this feast, Jesus saw a man with a thirty-eight-year-old disability. Jesus asked him if he desired to be healed. He had tried to avail himself of the healing in the pool near the sheep market, but had not succeeded. Jesus commanded him to arise, lift up his bed, and walk. Immediately he walked away, carrying his bed.

Jewish watchdogs halted the man whom Jesus gave strength to walk and questioned why he carried his bed on the Sabbath. He replied the man who healed him told him to take up my bed and walk.

Later, Jesus found the man in the temple and advised him to sin no more lest a more dreadful affliction overtake him. Willing to justify himself with the Jewish officials, he explained that Jesus had commanded him to carry his bed. Jewish leaders harassed Jesus for healing on the Sabbath. (Jno.5:16)

Why did Jesus heal on the Sabbath? Each Jewish feast lasted seven days. Had he healed on any other day, rulers might not have taunted him. Conflicts urge people to evaluate positions. What is important in religion? Jewish officials regarded keeping their law's details as a sign of righteousness. Does God regard keeping details of law above helping those whom Satan wounds? Jesus asked his countrymen what their Scriptures meant, **"I will have mercy, and not sacrifice."** (Math.9:13;12:7)

Did Jesus intentionally heal on the Sabbath to encourage law-keepers to reconsider religion? Is strictness of law supreme over humane deeds? Are both equal? Does brotherly kindness outweigh law-keeping? Is law without mercy religion? Is mercy without law religion? Jesus chastised Pharisees and scribes, **"Woe unto you, scribes and Pharisees, hypocrites! for ye pay tithe of mint and anise and cummin, and have omitted the weightier matters of the law,**

judgment, mercy, and faith: these ought ye to have done, and not to leave the other undone." (Math.23:23; Lk.11:42) Law and mercy God counts equal. Truth and spirit stand high before God. (Jno.4:23-24) In final judgment we give account to our Creator for both.

Could Jesus modify the Jews' view of their law? He blessed the impotent man by restoring his ability to walk. Leaders looked upon the miracle as a violation of their law. Jesus utilized other means to correct his rulers' view. He asked who denies water to his ox or ass on the Sabbath? You serve animals' needs on the Sabbath. Why deny me the right to supply man's needs on the Sabbath? Are animals more important than people? On the Sabbath I relieved a man of Satan's curses (Lk.13:11-16;14:1-6), and you accuse me of violating the Sabbath. Do you judge fairly? If you relieve animal's needs on the Sabbath without transgressing God's law, why do I break the Sabbath when I relieve a man's needs on the Sabbath?

Did Jesus purposely heal on the Sabbath to stress God's love for man? John's gospel identifies Jesus as the only mediator between man and God. Moses stood as mediator between Israel and God during his lifetime. High priests replaced Moses as go-betweens. Jesus healed on the Sabbath to explain God chose him as the only one through whom God reaches to man. Jesus identified sixteen issues in which God exalted him: 1) God and Jesus do the same works (5:17); 2) The Son imitates his Father (5:19); 3) The Father shows his Son all things the Father does (5:20); 4) The Father will show the Son greater things that you may marvel (5:20); 5) Both Father and Son raise the dead (5:21); 6) The Father grants his Son authority to execute judgment (5: 22); 7) The Father desires all men honor his Son as they honor the Father (5:23); 8) Father and Son possess life within themselves (5:26,40); 9) All who hear and obey my words gain eternal life (5:27-29); 10) The dead shall hear the Son's voice and rise from the dead to appear for judgment (5:28-29); 11) I judge as my Father instructs (5:30); 12) My judgment is just because I do the Father's will (5:30); 13) Others bear witness of me (5:32-47); 14) God's word and love doesn't abide in you because you refuse to believe the Son whom he has sent (5:30,42); 15) I come in my Father's name, but you won't receive me (5:43); and 16) Moses, not I, shall accuse you to the Father because you don't believe Moses. (5:45-57)

Jesus and God worked together to heal the impotent man. (Jno.5:17) As a father explains to his son how to accomplish life's activities, so my Father shows me how to accomplish God's works. Jews hated Jesus because he made himself equal with God. (Jno.5:18) John's gospel shows Jesus is God in flesh! (Jno.1:1,14) What Jesus observed God do, he does. (Jno.5:19) God showed Jesus how to do everything God does. (Jno.5:20) For this reason, Jesus performed all the deeds of his Father. You know God has given me power to give strength to the impotent man. This astounded you, but my Father has showed me how to perform deeds greater than restoring strength to useless limbs that you may marvel. (Jno.5:20) My Father transferred all judgment to me. His purpose is that all may honor the Son as they honor God. (Jno.5:23) My Father possesses power to make men live forever. I now speak those words which give everlasting life, but you must believe what I say to pass from death to life. (Jno.5:24-26) Because my Father granted me authority to execute judgment, I will speak, and every person in the grave will hear and exit. (Jno.5:27-28) All who live righteously shall rise to live with me and my Father forever. Unrighteous lives bring a resurrection of damnation. (Jno. 5:29) I accomplish all this because God gives me this power. I do his will to glorify my Father. (Jno.5:30) Jews prepared to kill Jesus for making himself equal with God.

(Jno.5:18) They claimed he glorified himself. (Jno.8:13)

Jesus' miracles and message should have convinced his countrymen he was God's Son, but they refused to let God's truth dwell in their thinking. Rejecting God's truth, they could not receive Jesus as God's **Prophet** like Moses, sent to tell them all God required of them. (Deu.18:15-19)

People today may examine both Old and New testaments without trusting God or Jesus. If we think about and examine the Bible honestly, we come to trust God's truths. Then God's word blesses us now and provides a hope for the hereafter when God fulfills his promise for us to dwell with him and his Son. God's message proves Jesus is God's Son. He exercises all the power of his Father. (Math.28:18)

God's word executed power in the beginning. His words created all things. Words Jesus uttered raised the dead. When the Father instructs the Son time ends, Jesus will speak, and all in the tomb shall awake to life. Jesus speaks a double truth. All who sin die spiritually. (Rom.1:32:5:12;6:23) Jesus' words produce spiritual life to those dead in sin. They who hear and do his words rise from spiritual death to spiritual life now. (Jno.3:31-36; Col.2:12-13)

Did Jesus demonstrate his power to empty graves? Only John's gospel recorded how Jesus spoke to Lazarus, calling him from the grave. In Bethany, Jesus found Lazarus had lain in the grave four days. When they arrived at the sepulcher, Jesus prayed in the audience of all the people who comforted Mary and Martha. Jesus asked God to hear him that the people may believe God sent him. He cried in a loud voice, "**Lazarus, come forth.**" (Jno.11:43) Lazarus emerged from the tomb, bound hand and foot. Jesus commanded them to loose him from the grave clothes. Realizing Jesus had actually raised a decaying Lazarus, many Jews believed Jesus must show God's power. (Jno.11:1-53)

Did raising Lazarus from the dead convince his adversaries that God and Jesus worked together to raise people from the grave? They admitted he performed many miracles, but they counseled to put him to death. Eyewitnesses to Lazarus' resurrection could not change rulers' minds. What will convince people that Jesus is God's Son? Giving strength to an impotent man failed to convince Jews. Restoring Lazarus' life didn't faze them. God provides solid evidence whereby we can check Jesus' testimony. Moses and Jewish scrolls provide about 330 criteria whereby we can identify Christ. If we don't believe Moses or prophets, how can we expect to believe God's record of his Son? (Math.3:17; Mk.1:11; Lk.3:22; 1 Jno. 5:10) Are five witnesses insufficient to convince people that Jesus is Christ? "**At the mouth of two witnesses, or three witnesses, shall he that is worthy of death be put to death; but at the mouth of one witness he shall not be put to death.**" (Deu.17:6; See Math.18:16; 1 Tim.5:19.) "**Ye will not come to me, that ye might have life.**" (Jno.5:40) "**I go my way, and ye shall seek me, and shall die in your sins: whither I go, ye cannot come.**" (Jno.8:21) "**I said therefore unto you, that ye shall die in your sins: for if ye believe not that I am he, ye shall die in your sins.**" (Jno.8:24) "**O Jerusalem, Jerusalem, thou that killest the prophets, and stonest them which are sent unto thee, how often would I have gathered thy children together, even as a hen gathereth her chickens under her wings, and ye would not! Behold, your house is left unto you desolate. For I say unto you, Ye shall not see me henceforth, till ye shall say, Blessed is he that cometh in the name of the Lord.**" (Math.23:37-39)

When Jesus stated he knew they had not the love of God, he judged. Is not this what Moses said concerning **that Prophet** whom God would send? (Deu.18:15-19)

Viewpoints

Matthew

5:1 And seeing the multitudes, he went up into a mountain: and when he was set, his disciples came unto him: 2 And he opened his mouth, and taught them, saying, 3 Blessed are the poor in spirit: for theirs is the kingdom of heaven. 4 Blessed are they that mourn: for they shall be comforted. 5 Blessed are the meek: for they shall inherit the earth. 6 Blessed are they which do hunger and thirst after righteousness: for they shall be filled. 7 Blessed are the merciful: for they shall obtain mercy. 8 Blessed are the pure in heart: for they shall see God. 9 Blessed are the peace-makers: for they shall be called the children of God. 10 Blessed are they which are persecuted for righteousness' sake: for theirs is the kingdom of heaven. 11 Blessed are ye, when men shall revile you, and persecute you, and shall say all manner of evil against you falsely, for my sake. 12 Rejoice, and be exceeding glad: for great is your reward in heaven: for so persecuted they the prophets which were before you.

Matthew and Luke record similar information about Jesus' Sermon on the Mount or Jesus' Doctrine. (Math.5:1-7:29: Lk.6:20-49; 11:1-13,33-36;12:22-40,58-59;14:34-35) From these references, you can tell Matthew recorded Jesus' message all in one place, much as Moses recorded the law of God, given at Sinai (Ex.20:1-23:33), but Luke intermingled similar doctrine in several chapters in the first half of his treatise. This may indicate a Jewish preference for their law to be in a single block. The Beatitudes Matthew penned call attention to attitudes which result in blessings for those who maintain these attitudes. Luke noted how Jesus pronounced blessings on those poor, hungry, hated, or separated from others. They need not think being poor or outcasts on earth separates them from God who ever remains faithful to his obedient children. Our Father considers all people equal.

Luke

6:20 And he lifted up his eyes on his disciples, and said, Blessed be ye poor: for yours is the kingdom of God. 21 Blessed are ye that hunger now: for ye shall be filled. Blessed are ye that weep now: for ye shall laugh. 22 Blessed are ye, when men shall hate you, and when they shall separate you from their company, and shall reproach you, and cast out your name as evil, for the Son of man's sake. 23 Rejoice ye in that day, and leap for joy: for, behold, your reward is great in heaven: for in the like manner did their fathers unto the prophets. 24 But woe unto you that are rich! for ye have received your consolation. 25 Woe unto you that are full! for ye shall hunger. Woe unto you that laugh now! for ye shall mourn and weep. 26 Woe unto you, when all men shall speak well of you! for so did their fathers to the false prophets.

Jesus explained that children of God must follow the examples of their heavenly Father. In creation when God made light, he looked on it and said it was good. (Gen.1:4) He made dry land, gathered the waters together as seas, and remarked that these were good. (Gen.1:10) He looked upon the grass, flowering shrubs, and trees he made, and stated that they were good. (Gen.1:12) Viewing the sun, moon, and stars he created, he said that they were good. (Gen.1:18) His water creatures he regarded as good. (Gen. 1:21) Gazing on land animals, he considered them with pleasure. (Gen.1:31) Even man he created good, as in his own image. (Gen.1:31)

By first example, God demonstrated a good attitude toward all his surroundings. Since one's outlook on his environment determines how he evaluates the various parts of his habitat, he must maintain a good view of his surroundings to find them pleasant. A bad consideration of them produces darkness in his life. (Math.15:17-20; Phil.4:8; Tit.1:15-16) God provides us with wonders of nature for our enjoyment. Do we view them as good? Attitude sets the stage of life for light or darkness.

Desiring to be rich, well fed, find pleasure, and have others speak well of me, I concede that my surroundings control my happiness. God appoints a superior way. Think on the good, and you enjoy the good. Think about the evil, and the world looks evil. (Tit.1:15-16) I control my outlook.

Luke included woes pronounced on individuals who view life after Satan's example. He maintains that everything must make me look great. Desiring to be rich produces woes. When I cherish to accumulate great wealth, I seldom become satisfied with possessions God put under my control. Being thankful to God for my blessings produces light in life. Desiring abundance results in woes. Having all I want brings complacency. Being concerned for those who need seldom matters. Laughing in this life also results in woe. Pleasure-seeking individuals regard neither man nor God. That which brings pleasure becomes their god. Desiring to receive a pat on the back by all my peers results in another woe. All base deeds known to man are committed by those who feel a need to gain praise of peers. Our society falls apart because most people seek for their own welfare and disregard the plight of the less fortunate. Others engage in immoral acts and take drugs because they don't want to be called "chicken". Desire to gain the praise of others leads to unending demands of worldly-minded people who demand I participate in their ungodly acts. This is basically the reason Jewish leaders rejected Christ. They desired the praise of men. (Jno.12:42-43)

Seeking honor from God brings peace. Worldly people say cutting remarks which often weigh heavily on a person, but God will not abandon his own. (Heb.13:5-6)

Eight attitudes characterize children of the kingdom of heaven: 1) They are poor in spirit such as the centurion who considered himself unworthy for Jesus to enter his house (Math.8:5-13); 2) Those who mourn for tragedies befalling their children or others. Other examples include Jarius who grieved for his daughter, a woman with an issue of blood, Canaanite woman pleading for her daughter, and a father grieving for his lunatic son (Math.9:18;10:20-26;15:22-28;17:15-19); 3) God blesses the meek who submit their will to others as Jesus who chose to let God's will be done rather than his own (Math.26:39); 4) They hunger and thirst after righteousness, illustrated, in part, by the rich young ruler (Math.19:16-22); 5) They show mercy as demonstrated by God's love for man in sending Jesus, or as when forgiving others, rescuing a sheep on the Sabbath (Math.9:13;10:42;12:7,11-12;18:21-35) and by the good Samaritan who cared for the man robbers left half dead (Lk.10:30-35); 6) Being pure in heart as Jesus in all his actions and teaching; 7) Are peacemakers as when one attempts to reconcile differences (Math.18:15-35); 8) Those persecuted for righteousness as the Jewish leaders did Jesus and would act toward the apostles for preaching the resurrection of Jesus and the kingdom of God. (Math.10:16-36)

Luke noted how Jesus pronounced blessings on the poor, those who hunger now, those who weep, and those hated. If you experience hardships in life, you may find hope in God's kingdom. Though poor financially, you can be rich spiritually. Sorrowing because of hardships God turns to joy in Christ because of the hope to dwell with Jesus, God, and the redeemed in paradise. Your neighbors and relatives may hate your now, but in God's kingdom, you have fellowship with God and his children. God turns weeping to joy in Christ. God comforts his faithful children in life's problems. (2 Cor.1:3-4) Does God's love encourage you to love by showing obedience to God and kindness to others?

Matthew

5:13 Ye are the salt of the earth: but if the salt have lost his savour, wherewith shall it be salted? it is thenceforth good for nothing, but to be cast out, and to be trodden under foot of men. 14 Ye are the light of the world. A city that is set on an hill cannot be hid. 15 Neither do men light a candle, and put it under a bushel, but on a candlestick; and it giveth light unto all that are in the house. 16 Let your light so shine before men, that they may see your good works, and glorify your Father which is in heaven.

Attitude is an important factor in honoring God and entering his kingdom. I must be confident God placed me on earth to manifest God dwelling with men to improve life, then I demonstrate God's spice to life. As salt preserves food, my life exemplifies God's constant care, preserving me as I submit to his will. (Job 1:9-10; Ps.34:7; Math.18:10) I am light to those who grope in sin's night. As a city on a hill gleams in the sun and adds hope to a wayfarer, God's goodness in my life lends hope to those who watch me. I must not hide God's radiance, but set God's light humbly as a beacon to the sailor tossed on life's raging ocean. Friends praise God for my encouragement when life's tragedies engulf them. As God sent Jesus to be the light of men (Jno.9:1), God gives me the task of carrying life's torch to show wanderers the way to God, Jesus, and heaven. Attitude powerfully directs my life when I keep in mind that I'm God's, and he cherishes to have me dwell in his house. Without this uplifting attitude, I wander in darkness which Satan draws over the lives of those who recognize not the hand of our Creator and sustainer of life. Attitude toward life creates or destroys. Once salt's seasoning ability ceases, it's useless. Men discard it. If my walk with God is replaced by Satan's fool's treasure people soon abandon me as light as I have abandoned God as my giver of light.

Mark

4:21 And he said unto them, Is a candle brought to be put under a bushel, or under a bed? and not to be set on a candlestick? 22 For there is nothing hid, which shall not be manifested; neither was any thing kept secret, but that it should come abroad.

When the prophet Isaiah told of the coming Christ and his death, he asked a question, "**He was taken from prison and from judgment: and who shall declare his generation? for he was cut off out of the land of the living: for the transgression of my people was he stricken.**" (Is.53:8) Pilate judged Jesus unworthy of death, for he committed no acts worthy of death. Notwithstanding, Jesus' own people cried for his crucifixion. Pilate disregarded his own judgment and gave Jesus to be scourged and crucified. (Math.27:11-50; Mk.14:15; Lk. 23:13-22) Obedient Christians carry on the generation of this righteous man, Jesus. He had no children of the flesh. God calls on those who regard Jesus as the Son of God to perpetuate his life on earth.

How shall I accomplish this? I must live as Jesus lived. He came not to do his own will, but the will of his Father who sent him. (Jno.6:38) Jesus preached God's truth for others to serve God. As David and Jesus served their generations by God's grace, I must carry on Jesus' generation by serving as God says. (Act.13:36)

In the Sermon on the Mount, Jesus addressed Jews who knew the law of Moses. They might compare what Jesus taught with God's ten commandments. The first nine statutes of Moses' law were designed to modify behavior, but the tenth God designed to modify attitude or thought. "**Thou shalt not covet.**" All who subscribed to God's law delivered by Moses must have no other gods, neither bow to any idol. None must swear falsely by God's name. The Sabbath day became a day to follow God's example to rest from labor. Children should honor

Luke

14:34 Salt is good: but if the salt have lost his savour, wherewith shall it be seasoned?

11:33 No man, when he hath lighted a candle, putteth it in a secret place, neither under a bushel, but on a candlestick, that they which come in may see the light. 34 The light of the body is the eye: therefore when thine eye is single, thy whole body also is full of light; but when thine eye is evil, thy body also is full of darkness. 35 Take heed therefore that the light which is in thee be not darkness. 36 If thy whole body therefore be full of light, having no part dark, the whole shall be full of light, as when the bright shining of a candle doth give thee light.

Matthew

5:17 Think not that I am come to destroy the law, or the prophets: I am not come to destroy, but to fulfill. 18 For verily I say unto you, Till heaven and earth pass, one jot or one tittle shall in no wise pass from the law, till all be fulfilled. 19 Whosoever therefore shall break one of these least commandments, and shall teach men so, he shall be called the least in the kingdom of heaven: but whosoever shall do and teach them, the same shall be called great in the kingdom of heaven. 20 For I say unto you, That except your righteousness shall exceed the righteousness of the scribes and Pharisees, ye shall in no case enter into the kingdom of heaven.

their parents. No person shall murder another, commit adultery, steal, or testify as a false witness. Fifteen centuries these commands directed Jewish life. Now Jesus taught that one's attitude played as important role in pleasing God as did their deeds. Thoughts determine who enters or is excluded from the kingdom of heaven. Did Jesus intend to banish their law? No, he insisted none of their law would perish until all was fulfilled. God's tenth command disallowed coveting. Is not desire an attitude, not action? The Sermon on the Mount might be considered as an elaboration of the tenth commandment. Doctors of Moses' law regarded the tenth commandment of little importance. God maintains mind guides deeds. If one thinks evil, he does evil. If he meditates on good ideas, his actions will honor God and benefit man. (Math.15:17-20)

Jesus' doctrine fulfills Moses' law, not destroys it. God commissioned Jesus to explain the intent of their law. Keeping God's ten commandments, they must fulfill even the least important as well as great precepts. It involved a distinct alteration of mind and emotion. Man desires to be great, but God smiles with approval on those who have captured truth. Humility pleases God, but a haughty spirit God despises. (Prov.6:16-17; Math.5:3) God honors and constantly watches over those who, by faith, forget not their Maker. (Ecc.7:2; Math.5:3) Willingness to relinquish my aspirations in favor of God's assures me that I'll rejoice with those who inherit the earth. (Ps.27:11,22; Math.5:3) Searching for righteousness as for sparkling water and pleasant food delights the Father of spirits. Show mercy as God shows mercy. (Math.18:23-35) Maintain a pure heart. It allows us to catch a lasting glimpse of our Creator. (Math.5:8) Wars and strife have plagued nations and individuals since God banished the race from Eden. Search for and maintain proper attitudes of honoring others' interests. Seek peace and ensue it, and you shall find peace. (Ja.4:1-11; 1 Pet.3:8-11)

Beatitudes stand as cherubims and flaming sword east of Eden, excluding all from our Father's heavenly kingdom who cherish evil thoughts and refuse to think on good things before God. (Gen.3:24) Don't covet evil things. (Ex.20:17) God may provide you with more than you wish and add sorrows which accompany them. (Ezek.20:24-26)

Matthew

**5:21 Ye have heard that it was said by
them of old time, Thou shalt not kill; and
whosoever shall kill shall be in danger of
the judgment: 22 But I say unto you, That
whosoever is angry with his brother
without a cause shall be in danger of the
judgment: and whosoever shall say to his
brother, Raca, shall be in danger of the
council: but whosoever shall say, Thou
fool, shall be in danger of hell fire. 23
Therefore if thou bring thy gift to the
altar, and there rememberest that thy
brother hath ought against thee; 24 Leave
there thy gift before the altar, and go thy
way; first be reconciled to thy brother,
and then come and offer thy gift. 25 Agree
with thine adversary quickly, whiles thou
art in the way with him; lest at any time
the adversary deliver thee to the judge,
and the judge deliver thee to the officer,
and thou be cast into prison. 26 Verily I
say unto thee, Thou shalt by no means
come out thence, till thou hast paid the
uttermost farthing. 27 Ye have heard that
it was said by them of old time, Thou shalt
not commit adultery: 28 But I say unto
you, That whosoever looketh on a woman
to lust after her hath committed adultery
with her already in his heart. 29 And if
thy right eye offend thee, pluck it out, and
cast it from thee: for it is profitable for
thee that one of thy members should
perish, and not that thy whole body
should be cast into hell. 30 And if thy
right hand offend thee, cut it off, and cast
it from thee: for it is profitable for thee
that one of thy members should perish,
and not that thy whole body should be
cast into hell. 31 It hath been said,
Whosoever shall put away his wife, let
him give her a writing of divorcement: 32
But I say unto you, That whosoever shall
put away his wife, saving for the cause of
fornication, causeth her to commit adultery: and whosoever shall marry her that
is divorced committeth adultery.**

Luke

**12:58 When thou goest with thine
adversary to the magistrate, as thou art in
the way, give diligence that thou mayest
be delivered from him; lest he hale thee to
the judge, and the judge deliver thee to
the officer, and the officer cast thee into
prison. 59 I tell thee, thou shalt not depart
thence, till thou hast paid the very last
mite.**

If the ten commandments were statutes which must not be changed (Ex.20:1-17), then God's judgments Moses delivered to Israel (Ex.21:1-23:33) explained how to apply the statutes in living situations. Similarly, the Beatitudes became the statutes of attitude. Their application (judgments) Jesus demonstrated by comparing the ten commandments and the attitudes God desires. (Math.5:21-7:27) Even the length of judgments of the ten commandments compare closely to the length of the judgments of the Beatitudes.

Jesus first showed how attitude preceded murder (sixth commandment). "**Thou shalt not kill**." (Ex.20:13) Jesus' doctrine taught that unprovoked anger leads to judgment. Harboring anger to call another a fool brings one to the edge of hell.

Moses commanded restitution of damage plus additional goods to placate the one offended's anger. (Lev.6:5) Jesus taught not restitution, but reconciliation before offering sacrifice to God to forgive transgression. Make peace with your fellow before asking peace with God. Peacemaking applies in litigation also. If someone threatens to take you to court to settle a dispute, approach that person humbly. Attempt to make an agreement. Failing to resolve the conflict before going to law may result in your being condemned, fined, and jailed. Court actions rarely, if ever, make friends. Hostilities usually deepen. Jesus explained how to convert a potentially offending situation into one of friendship and goodwill. This blessing God promised Abraham that through him and his seed all nations could be blessed. (Gal.3:8) If we have faith to do as Jesus explained, God truly blesses us. Jesus concluded his Sermon on the Mount, saying that hearing his sayings and doing them makes one wise as a person who builds his house securely on solid rock. Hearing, but not applying them to life, one builds on sand. Floods and storms of life erode the sand, and the house collapses. (Math.7:21-27)

Jesus noted relationship between the tenth commandment and the seventh. God said, "**Thou shalt not commit adultery**." (Ex. 20:14) God's tenth command forbade coveting or desiring. Jewish doctors of the law emphasized the seventh command, but apparently made little connection between desiring a woman and committing adultery with her. Jesus encouraged his countrymen to fulfill all the seventh command. If you lust after a woman, you commit adultery with her in your heart. You violate the tenth statute.

To illustrate the urgency of avoiding lust, Jesus spoke a parable. Pluck out your eye if looking on a woman prompts you to lust for her. If your right hand violates a woman, cut it off and thrust it from you. Losing your right eye or hand is far more profitable than losing your body and spirit in hell. Jesus did not intend for us to destroy body parts, but rather to abandon lust. Thus, "**Blessed are the pure in heart, for they shall see God**." (Math.5:8) With Abraham, God blesses all who keep the seventh command by preserving the tenth.

Divorce and remarriage curses every nation and people. Attitude of mind generates the problem. Whether it's a man or woman, Satan convinces the person that a different companion becomes more appealing. Once this attitude takes root, the person seeks for a reason to divorce his/her mate. God allowed profane Jews to divorce and remarry because of "uncleanness." (Deu.24:1-2) If the person later realized that the first companion had been the better choice, God did not allow the person to return to the first companion after remarriage. (Deu.24:3-4) Dissolving a marriage and remarrying another God forbade to priests, for he considered priests holy, not profane. (Lev.21:1,6-8; Ezek.44:15,22-23) Some profane Jews in Jesus' day justified divorce for any cause, not for "uncleanness" alone. Moses explained "uncleanness" as unfaithfulness. (Num.5:11-20) In that same place God explained God's procedure for a man to follow to confirm a wife's suspected uncleanness. Jesus explained God's truth in Moses' law. If you divorce and remarry for any cause other than fornication, you commit adultery. (Math.5:32) Unless people understand Jesus taught the truth of Moses' law to the Jews, many attempt to justify Christian divorce and remarriage by using Moses' law. Jesus did not condone divorce and remarriage for Christians. If we are priests of God, then we are holy, not profane. (1 Pet. 2:9; Rev.1:6) Even by Moses' law God allowed no just cause for Christians to divorce and marry another. Luke's and Mark's gospels, being addressed to Christians, never recorded a God-given reason for divorce to marry another. (Mk.10:2-12; Lk.16:18)

Once we understand divorce and remarriage for Jews applied only to the profane Jews, it's clear why not one letter written to the churches allowed divorce and remarriage to another. Apostles always confirmed marriage binds for the lifetime of husband and wife. (Rom.7:1-4; 1 Cor.7:10-11,39)

God instituted marriage for people's benefit. Only the worldly and Satan advocate the advantage of divorce and marriage to another. God blesses all who submit to his plan for marriage, but heaps woes on those who depart from his precept. Even their children and other relatives suffer. Children learn how to bond to others by first bonding with parents. If parents shatter God's bonding process, they make it nearly impossible for children to assimilate solid bonding to others. They undermine perhaps God's most crucial bonding factor.

Matthew

5:33 Again, ye have heard that it hath been said by them of old time, Thou shalt not forswear thyself, but shalt perform unto the Lord thine oaths: 34 But I say unto you, Swear not at all; neither by heaven; for it is God's throne: 35 Nor by the earth; for it is his footstool: neither by Jerusalem; for it is the city of the great King. 36 Neither shalt thou swear by thy head, because thou canst not make one hair white or black. 37 But let your communication be, Yea, yea; Nay, nay: for whatsoever is more than these cometh of evil.

Satan curses men by influencing one man to lie to another. In Sacred Scriptures, God's people fell prey to this device of Satan. Abimelech approached Abraham and asked him to swear by God that Abraham would not deal falsely with him or his sons. Abraham swore to do as Abimelech requested. (Gen.21:22-24) Later, Abraham asked his servant to swear by the Lord, God of heaven and earth, not to take a wife for Isaac of the daughters of Canaan, but take him a wife of Abraham's father's house. His servant swore he would. (Gen.24:27-41)

Some 400 years later when God gave the law to Israel at Sinai, he commanded them not to swear falsely by God's name. (Ex. 20:7) By then man's word was not trustworthy. One couldn't even be sure that if he promised by an oath to God he would stand by his word. Jonathan and David swore to fulfill their promises to each other. (1 Sam. 20:11-17) Saul pleaded with David not to destroy his family after David became king. (1 Sam.24:16-22) Honest and godly men and women feel obligated before God to keep their promises, but by the time Jesus lived, he rebuked Jews for swearing and not keeping their oaths. (Math.23:16-22) If people are ever to trust one another's word, God's truth, not Satan's deception, must control our thoughts and words. Wouldn't this world be improved if yes meant yes?

Matthew

5:38 Ye have heard that it hath been said, An eye for an eye, and a tooth for a tooth: 39 But I say unto you, That ye resist not evil: but whosoever shall smite thee on thy right cheek, turn to him the other also. 40 And if any man will sue thee at the law, and take away thy coat, let him have thy cloke also. 41 And whosoever shall compel thee to go a mile, go with him twain. 42 Give to him that asketh thee, and from him that would borrow of thee turn not thou away.

Jesus laid the foundation to destroy Satan's speech deceptions. He taught his disciples to mean yes when they said yes, and to mean no when they said no. Faithful followers of Christ keep their word in daily associations with friends, neighbors, in business, government, and between governments. Even marriage vows will mean "till death do us part." Promises made will be honored even when it proves hurtful to keep them. (Ps.15:1,4) It will be an age of great blessing. All nations will experience Abraham's and his seed's blessings. (Gen. 12:3; Gal.3:8-9)

Even after the kingdom of God began to spread over the nations, it became necessary for the apostles to remind believers in Christ to speak the truth to one another. (Eph.4:25; Col.3:9) When each person lived as the world, men expected others to lie. After we die with Christ in baptism and rise with him to a new life, we must speak the truth to each other to glorify our heavenly Father. (Col. 3:1-3)

In Solomon's days, some vowed to God, but failed to keep their vows. The wise man Solomon observed that it is far better not to vow to God than to say it was an error after changing his mind, once he departed from the house of God. (Ecc.5:1-7)

Jewish leaders of Jesus' day and in this age say, "An eye for an eye, and a tooth for a tooth." When a group or nation attacks Jews, they plan retribution and justify their plan by repeating that phrase. When God instituted this expression, he spoke of securing justice by law within the Jewish community. By law, administer like punishment to one who intentionally inflicted damage to another. (Ex.21:22-25) You may feel that justice would be served by inflicting blow for blow by retaliating, but does this produce peace? If God's goal for peoples and nations to learn the arts of war no more is ever to come to fruition, will retaliation produce it? When Isaiah envisioned a time that God's kingdom reigned above the nations, he noted that many nations come to God and learn his ways. Nations would beat their swords into plowshares and their spears into pruning hooks. Nations would no longer lift sword against one another. They would no longer learn war. Individuals and nations walk in God's light. (Is.2:2-5) Jesus invited individuals and nations to come to the mount of God to learn his ways. Will this quiet the violence of mankind? Will offering the left cheek to him who slaps your right cheek humble an offender? Often it will make a deep impression, especially to a right-thinking person. However, the chief advantage is to the one offended. God gives grace to the humble and considers him righteous. (Ja.5:1-6)

Jesus provided four examples to illustrate how not to resist evil: 1) Turn the second cheek; 2) Give more than is required by a lawsuit; 3) Go the second mile, and 4) refuse not a borrower. (Math.5:39-42) Applying these truths of God to our lives produces God's righteousness in us.

Are we to consider these examples of resisting not evil to be all inclusive? Are parents not to restrain their children's tendencies to live after the flesh? God pronounced curses on the house of Eli because he failed to restrain his sons' adultery. (1 Sam.3:11-14) Are communities to allow crimes of murder to go unpunished? No. God demanded that Israel cleanse the land of blood by putting a murderer to death. (Num. 35:16-21,30-31) When Jesus advised his disciples not to resist evil, he referred to personal attacks on them while they worked God's righteousness. God authorizes civil authorities to punish evil doers according to law. (Rom.13:1-7) Don't deny or resist law officers in fulfilling their responsibilities to punish evil doers. Doing so adds to your frustration and that of the offender. Submission helps make peace. **"Blessed are the meek: for they shall inherit the earth."** (Ps.37:11; Math.5:5)

God asks for those who enter his kingdom to change life styles. Before turning to God, resisting evil prevailed. Change must come to the life of one entering God's kingdom, otherwise, there will be no difference between Satan's dominion and God's. God desires his children to perform justice, judgment, and equity. (Gen.18:19; Prov.1:3;2:9; Is.59:14) Such radical change may not become part of my life without genuine effort, but God's children must have faith in God's commands and promises in order to accomplish God's justice and equity.

The law of God given to Jews restricted both evil deeds and evil desires. Many teachers of their system in Jesus' day worked to restrict evil deeds visible to the eye, but overlooked evil thoughts in the mind. Jesus explained to his audience that depraved deeds originate in evil minds. If you seek to enter God's kingdom over which David's son reigns as King, you must fulfill the tenth commandment. Replace evil thoughts with good thoughts because evil minds generate evil deeds. To enter God's blessed kingdom, the heart must think on good and honest actions and reactions. (Phil.4:6-8)

Has God empowered citizens in his kingdom to change thinking patterns? Yes, believing God's truth and asking God in prayer to overcome evil thoughts, God assists his children to cast aside those thoughts which degrade ourselves and attribute evil designs to others' actions. Before turning to God we lacked strength, but now God strengthens us. (Rom.5:6; Eph.3:16; Col.1:11)

Matthew

5:43 Ye have heard that it hath been said, Thou shalt love thy neighbour, and hate thine enemy. 44 But I say unto you, Love your enemies, bless them that curse you, do good to them that hate you, and pray for them which despitefully use you, and persecute you; 45 That ye may be the children of your Father which is in heaven: for he maketh his sun to rise on the evil and on the good, and sendeth rain on the just and on the unjust. 46 For if ye love them which love you, what reward have ye? do not even the publicans the same? 47 And if ye salute your brethren only, what do ye more than others? do not even the publicans so? 48 Be ye therefore perfect, even as your Father which is in heaven is perfect.

Courtesy to others, whether friends or enemies, pleases God. Matthew and Luke record statements of Jesus which explain God's instruction for treating others with all due respect. These two writers address different audiences and employ different examples of comparison to illustrate why one should respect others. Matthew's audience followed a precept to love their neighbors, but hate their enemies. Even publicans subscribe to this conduct code, yet you consider publicans as disobedient to God. If you follow their examples, are you better than they? Luke contrasted his audience with sinners. If Christians love only those who love them, are you better than sinners?

Whether Jew or Gentile, Jesus instructs us to imitate our heavenly Father. He shows mercy to just and unjust alike. (Eph.2:2-4) He gives rain to the upright and to the wicked. He provides harvest to obedient and disobedient. (Act.17:25) God desires his children to live on a higher level than Satan's children who honor only those who honor them. Only those who show kindness to the just and unjust populate God's kingdom of heaven. (Math.8:11-12) God will help us learn if we determine to do his will.

Luke

6:27 But I say unto you which hear, Love your enemies, do good to them which hate you, 28 Bless them that curse you, and pray for them which despitefully use you. 29 And unto him that smiteth thee on the one cheek offer also the other; and him that taketh away thy cloke forbid not to take thy coat also. 30 Give to every man that asketh of thee; and of him that taketh away thy goods ask them not again. 31 And as ye would that men should do to you, do ye also to them likewise. 32 For if ye love them which love you, what thank have ye? for sinners also love those that love them. 33 And if ye do good to them which do good to you, what thank have ye? for sinners also do even the same. 34 And if ye lend to them of whom ye hope to receive, what thank have ye? for sinners also lend to sinners, to receive as much again. 35 But love ye your enemies, and do good, and lend, hoping for nothing again; and your reward shall be great, and ye shall be the children of the Highest: for he is kind unto the unthankful and to the evil. 36 Be ye therefore merciful, as your Father also is merciful.

Obeying God makes your life happier, and you will enrich the lives of all who experience your favor. Your life will show you believe the Father's promises by doing well to all you meet. This love demonstrates that you are a child of the kingdom of God though you live among those who know not the Father. You show mercy, and God extends mercy to you. (Math.6:14-15;18:33-35; Lk11:4) Like the faithful of old, you confess that this world is not your home. Our citizenship resides in heaven with Jesus and our Father. (Heb.11:13-16) God pleads with his children to manifest to all our Father's love Unless one makes a complete break with the world's outlook toward life and replaces its standards of conduct with God's, we are not his. We will not receive and inheritance with his children.

Viewpoints

Matthew

6:1 Take heed that ye do not your alms before men, to be seen of them: otherwise ye have no reward of your Father which is in heaven. 2 Therefore when thou doest thine alms, do not sound a trumpet before thee, as the hypocrites do in the synagogues and in the streets, that they may have glory of men. Verily I say unto you, They have their reward. 3 But when thou doest alms, let not thy left hand know what thy right hand doeth: 4 That thine alms may be in secret: and thy Father which seeth in secret himself shall reward thee openly. 5 And when thou prayest, thou shalt not be as the hypocrites are: for they love to pray standing in the synagogues and in the corners of the streets, that they may be seen of men. Verily I say unto you, They have their reward. 6 But thou, when thou prayest, enter into thy closet, and when thou hast shut thy door, pray to thy Father which is in secret; and thy Father which seeth in secret shall reward thee openly. 7 But when ye pray, use not vain repetitions, as the heathen do: for they think that they shall be heard for their much speaking. 8 Be not ye therefore like unto them: for your Father knoweth what things ye have need of, before ye ask him.

With man and God, purpose determines benefits. If our reason for demonstrating mercy seeks to gain respect of men, God gives no reward. Don't seek man's attention for benevolent deeds and kindness. God will note our efforts to demonstrate the kindness of God and will reward. When we forget that God observes how we show kindness, and we look to men for respect, God knows we want approval in men's sight, and God considers not that our efforts glorify him and his righteousness. It behooves us to keep in mind that God sees and blesses us for doing his will. Let our acts of kindness and mercy be done in secret between us and God. Others may come to know and approve of what we do, but we have not desired their respect. God rewards those who seek to please him.

Matthew also contrasts true prayer to God with how hypocrites and heathen pray. Hypocrites desire praise of peers when they pray. Heathen believe God honors the prayers of the eloquent and those who speak long. Approaching prayer from this perspective they become repetitious and feel God respects us because of our great speech. God, however, looks at the heart of the one who calls on him. If we speak to God, asking for mercy for our shortcomings with an honest and sincere heart, God listens and honors our petition. When we realize our weaknesses in dealing with life's situations and admit that we need help, God sees a contrite heart and blesses. (Ps.34:18) We and God walk and talk together. We ask for God's help when we can't see our way. God then guides and helps make decisions. When the humble man needs wisdom, he calls on God for help. Man's attention he neither seeks nor regards as he petitions God. Conversely, if we approach God's throne with an attitude of superiority, God sees only haughtiness which he despises in men. (Prov.16:18)

God knows our needs before we ask, but he, like earthly parents, likes for his children to state our wishes and thank him for his ongoing blessings. (Phil.4:6-8)

Having lived among hypocrites and heathen, the disciples and we ourselves need to examine our lives continuously, for we may have tendencies to become hypocritical in our alms, prayers, and other deeds of kindness. (2 Cor.13:5) Examples of our peers too often influence our actions. Therefore, we need to direct our desire for respect to God rather than men. In all probability the struggle to please only God will be ongoing. None of us completely disdains man's respect and recognition. Satan uses such subtle schemes to modify our goals we may slip into his life style unaware of it.

Matthew

6:9 After this manner therefore pray ye: Our Father which art in heaven, Hallowed be thy name. 10 Thy kingdom come. Thy will be done in earth, as it is in heaven. 11 Give us this day our daily bread. 12 And forgive us our debts, as we forgive our debtors. 13 And lead us not into temptation, but deliver us from evil: For thine is the kingdom, and the power, and the glory, for ever. Amen. 14 For if ye forgive men their trespasses, your heavenly Father will also forgive you: 15 But if ye forgive not men their trespasses, neither will your Father forgive your trespasses.

Apostles needed and desired instruction on how to pray properly to God. First, address and reverence our Father's name. He desires that his children recognize him as the heavenly Father of all and call on him as "our Father."

On earth, we observe many kingdoms or nations, varying in forms of government. Leaders of these principalities too often disregard God's right and power to direct their nations. God's plan of peace for nations shall prevail. When God subdues nations, peace and brotherhood of all men shall come to pass. We will genuinely demonstrate caring for one another. Christians await and pray that God's long-awaited kingdom shall prevail to guide all nations, cities, families and individuals. Then God's will shall be done on earth even as it is in heaven.

Jesus taught his followers to realize that God provides us with daily food to sustain our bodies. He asks us to thank him for his kindness and ask him to forgive misdeeds done to us. Then ask God to overlook our transgressions against him and those with whom we associate. Even people of the world appreciate our thanking them.

Unless we realize our susceptibility to fall into Satan's traps, we most certainly fall as his prey. Jesus instructed his disciples to

Luke

11:1 And it came to pass, that, as he was praying in a certain place, when he ceased, one of his disciples said unto him, Lord, teach us to pray, as John also taught his disciples. 2 And he said unto them, When ye pray, say, Our Father which art in heaven, Hallowed be thy name. Thy kingdom come. Thy will be done, as in heaven, so in earth. 3 Give us day by day our daily bread. 4 And forgive us our sins; for we also forgive every one that is indebted to us. And lead us not into temptation; but deliver us from evil. 5 And he said unto them, Which of you shall have a friend, and shall go unto him at midnight, and say unto him, Friend, lend me three loaves; 6 For a friend of mine in his journey is come to me, and I have nothing to set before him? 7 And he from within shall answer and say, Trouble me not: the door is now shut, and my children are with me in bed; I cannot rise and give thee. 8 I say unto you, Though he will not rise and give him, because he is his friend, yet because of his importunity he will rise and give him as many as he needeth.

petition our Father not to lead us into temptation, but to deliver us from the tempter's snares. Those of us who are fathers refuse to give our children a viper when our children ask for a fish or give them rocks when they plead for bread. If we know how to give our children good gifts when they ask of us, shall not our heavenly Father supply us with good things when we ask of him? God shall not grant us hurtful lives when we seek from him good days. If we ask for his Holy Spirit, he shall provide as one who furnishes what his friend needs. Knowing this, God instructs us to ask of him those things we need. If we believe God's promises, he will supply what we request. He shall grant our wishes one day at a time if we will humble ourselves to submit to his kingdom' rules. (Ja.1:5-8)

A genuine loving relationship develops between us and our heavenly Father when we regard him as our concerned and loving heavenly Father who truly cares about our discouragements, hurts, disappointments, and ravages of sin. Satan encourages us to participate in that which results in a defiled conscience. We grieve because we have offended a friend or another of our Father's children, and we feel shame before our Father in heaven. When we realize God's mercy to forgive us for our errors when we repent and seek help, we gladly call on him.

Summarizing Jesus' instruction on how to pray properly to God: seek only God's recognition, not for man's praise. Humility, not pride, before God pleases him as when our children willingly do what we ask of them. Ask for his continued guidance to escape the hurtful temptations of life. Forgive others, then our heavenly Father shall forgive us. Ask him for all the good things of life, even for his Holy Spirit which strengthens us in life to do our Father's will. If we trust that we can prevail against Satan's wiles by our own wisdom and power, the archenemy shall trip us. Seek for God's kingdom to spread over all the earth that his will be done on earth as it is done in heaven. Honor our heavenly Father's name as we honor our parents who have sustained and guided us in our youth. Such submission to God enriches our lives on earth and assures us we shall dwell in the kingdom of heaven on earth and in his eternal mansion in heaven which Jesus now prepares for all those who submit to the Father's will on earth.

As one reflects on the abundant blessings our heavenly Father bestows on his faithful children, can there be any doubt that God seeks our best interest at all times from before our birth unto the end of our fleshly lives on this planet? Truly, we are both flesh and spirit as both our progenitors. Recognition of our duel nature helps us to care for both parts of our being every day.

Matthew

6:16 Moreover when ye fast, be not, as the hypocrites, of a sad countenance: for they disfigure their faces, that they may appear unto men to fast. Verily I say unto you, They have their reward. 17 But thou, when thou fastest, anoint thine head, and wash thy face; 18 That thou appear not unto men to fast, but unto thy Father which is in secret: and thy Father, which seeth in secret, shall reward thee openly.

Fasting to convince our friends of our piety forfeits God's favor. If we seek God's praise through fasting, let him alone take knowledge of our fast. Informing others of how often or how long we fast may gain men's respect, but it forfeits God's approval. Our purpose determines our reward. Seeking to gain man's attention by fasting gains only man's respect. Letting God alone see our fast attracts only his attention. Seeking to show men our devotion to God by fasting makes us a hypocrite before God.

The prophet Isaiah identified a more perfect fast in God's sight. Rather than depriving ourselves of food, God prefers that we give to those in need. Do we think God regards our fast when we continue to find pleasure in fasting? Afflicting the body and continuing in strife with our neighbors, debating, and fighting negate any benefits which might be derived from fasting. Do we call it fasting when we spread ashes on our faces and refuse to eat? This fails to secure God's attention when we deal unjustly with our fellows. Bring the outcast to our houses; clothe the naked, and care for the needy, widows, and fatherless. This shows God a true fast and inclines his ear to attend to our requests. (Is.58:3-10)

God regards people as hypocrites and vain those who perform religious devotions to convince others they're devout. Religion that seeks man's honor offends our heavenly Father. He will not regard our prayers, fasts, or giving as honorable. (Is.58:3-14) Even the poor resent gifts without love.

Matthew

6:19 Lay not up for yourselves treasures upon earth, where moth and rust doth corrupt, and where thieves break through and steal: 20 But lay up for yourselves treasures in heaven, where neither moth nor rust doth corrupt, and where thieves do not break through nor steal: 21 For where your treasure is, there will your heart be also. 22 The light of the body is the eye: if therefore thine eye be single, thy whole body shall be full of light. 23 But if thine eye be evil, thy whole body shall be full of darkness. If therefore the light that is in thee be darkness, how great is that darkness!

In his Sermon on the Mount, Jesus contrasts Satan's kingdom with God's kingdom four ways: alms, prayer, fasting, and storing treasure. Satan's children seek rewards by giving alms, praying, fasting, or accumulating material wealth to gain man's respect. God's children give alms, pray, fast, and store treasure to please God.

Darkness fills the lives of Satan's children. Their rewards center on themselves and this life. Heavenly light illuminates God's children. Our aspirations and rewards center on glorifying God, not our selfish interests. Jesus illustrated the differences by contrasting eyes. An evil eye sees self-honor, but a righteous eye sees the heavenly Father who smiles on his faithful children who unselfishly supply others' needs. In the parable of the sower, light of God's truth shines on those by the wayside, stony ground, thorns, and productive ground. Each hears the words of God's kingdom. Only the fertile ground, signifying receptive hearts, casts off Satan's darkness worked by an evil eye. The pure eye sees good in God's creation and his providence. Once experiencing the illuminating effects of God's word, we gladly receive and cling to that which gives light to man's spirit. We ask God for help to avoid having an evil eye which loses sight of God and heaven, for God dwells with us on earth. (Math1:23).

The candlestick parable portrays Satan's kingdom as those who light a candle and place it under a bed or barrel, hiding God's light from others. People in God's kingdom place the candlestick so all within the house benefit or as a beacon to ships on a stormy sea. God's children place great confidence in God's promise that heavenly light, when tested, produces a more enjoyable life on earth and everlasting life to come. (Math. 19:27-30; Jno.10:10; 1 Pet.3:10)

Being physical creatures first, we tend to trust what we feel, see, taste, smell, and hear. Physical surroundings tend to influence us to rely on our senses. Others tell us about what they have seen. We believe evidence about what we have not seen. Once we enter the kingdom of heaven, "**We look not at the things which are seen, but at the things which are not seen: for the things which are seen are temporal; but the things which are not seen are eternal.**" (2 Cor. 4:18) When Moses and Israel exited Egypt, none of them had seen Canaan with their physical eyes. "**By faith he** [Moses] **forsook Egypt, not fearing the wrath of the king: for he endured, as seeing him who is invisible.**" (Heb.11:27) Their fathers told them of Canaan and God's promise to return them there. (Gen.15:13-16;50:24-25; Act.7: 17) God and Jesus tell us of a better life, a place we can't now see, feel, smell, taste, or hear, but we believe it exists because of God's word. If we desire God's gift, we will submit to God that we may inherit it. Faith in God's word sustains our belief in his promises. God invites all to share in his glorious kingdom, but he allows no unbeliever therein. Pharisees presented a great show of devotion to God, but inwardly their minds and affections rested on man's praise and worldly wealth. Faith in God's truth and promises famished in their lives. Jesus encouraged his disciples to avoid the pitfalls of those walking dead. Be assured that God,

Luke

12:32 Fear not, little flock; for it is your Father's good pleasure to give you the kingdom. 33 Sell that ye have, and give alms; provide yourselves bags which wax not old, a treasure in the heavens that faileth not, where no thief approacheth, neither moth corrupteth. 34 For where your treasure is, there will your heart be also.

our heavenly Father, desires to entrust us with the kingdom promised to David. To be worthy of that charge, we must "buy" into his kingdom. Demonstrate God's love by supplying the needs of the poor, widows, fatherless, and strangers. This invests in indestructible, heavenly, God-secured treasure. (Ps.112:1-9)

Faith to ask God in prayer and expecting God to provide, hearing the truth and wisdom Jesus taught, and doing it places the light of God on a candlestick. Praying to God, beholding his wonders, and hearing his message of love, but believing not that God hears our prayers, accusing Jesus of working miracles by Satan's power, or asking for signs, rather than believing God's truth indicates we have an evil eye. It fills our whole life with darkness. Paul explained, **"Unto the pure all things are pure: but unto them that are defiled and unbelieving is nothing pure; but even their mind and conscience is defiled. They profess that they know God; but in works they deny him, being abominable, and disobedient, and unto every good work reprobate**." (Tit.1:15-16) Which holds the hope of a better life, the pure or evil eye?

People whose hopes rest only on this world recognize darkness in their lives. Lyrics of popular songs show many sorrows fill the hearts of our generation because a lover abandoned him or her for someone else. Others sing of "blues", how their whole life falls apart, and there seems to be nothing or no person worthy of trust. Blackness of night fills their hearts and minds. They have an evil eye. God offers a whole changed outlook on life. Instead of looking on the bad, God instructs his children to understand that evil abounds, but you need not dwell on it. Consider what is good. Are there no admirable traits in people? When children are born into a family, joy usually fills the lives of the parents, grandparents, and others. When does darkness draw its shades over our lives? It's when we ponder difficulties rather than blessings which God provides. Darkness deepens as we advance farther into the night of gloom. God offers a light to those who will consider his principles. What do we see in people and life? Is it good or evil? Both are apparent, but which elevates our attitude about life? Looking at the good helps us see the beauty of nature, not the grime and trash of the city. Thinking about God's promises adds beauty and light to life.

How did Jesus avoid an evil eye when Pharisees, Sadducees, priests, and rulers chided and sought to kill him? Morning, noon, and night he kept his mind's eye on his heavenly Father, his promise of returning to sit at his Father's side in heaven when he completed his task on earth, and that God would fulfill his promise of subduing everything under him. Matthew quoted Isaiah, saying, Jesus would not be discouraged until he had showed judgment to the Gentiles. (Math.12;18; Is.42:1-4)

An evil eye considers only present events: how to satisfy the body's needs, to achieve recognition among peers, and to grasp the fleeting success of this life. God sent Jesus to open our eyes to more than grasping for the wind. Though not visible to the physical eye, it's indestructible, eternal, always living where God, Jesus, angels, and the redeemed reside.

Do God's promises appeal to you? Do they appear worth sacrificing personal whims to gain? If they do, stretch out your hand and heart to God by believing in Jesus and keeping his statutes.

Matthew

6:24 No man can serve two masters: for either he will hate the one, and love the other; or else he will hold to the one, and despise the other. Ye cannot serve God and mammon. 25 Therefore I say unto you, Take no thought for your life, what ye shall eat, or what ye shall drink; nor yet for your body, what ye shall put on. Is not the life more than meat, and the body than raiment? 26 Behold the fowls of the air: for they sow not, neither do they reap, nor gather into barns; yet your heavenly Father feedeth them. Are ye not much better than they?

What attitude does God desire his children to maintain toward material wealth? Did God supply it, or did I accumulate it by my own wisdom? Did God make it possible for me to accumulate it, or did he exercise no influence in my gathering material wealth? (Deu.8:17-18)

Jesus explained to listeners that God creates and supplies the needs of sparrows and ravens. Man places little value on these creatures of God, but they represent a small bit of his magnificent wisdom and power. He cares for them, providing their food, water, and habitat necessary for them to live and rear their young. You and I, being also part of God's wondrous creation, he values above sparrows and ravens. He created us in his own likeness. God cares for our physical needs as he does for the most insignificant fowls. More importantly, God sent his only begotten Son to supply our spiritual needs. With this bounty, God commissioned Jesus to explain and demonstrate how to trust God with our whole hearts and minds. Fret not about life's problems. God rules over nature, governments, and man, taking care of his faithful children. To show our appreciation, he asks that we supply others' needs. Doing God's will, we serve as instruments in God's hands to provide for others' needs. God makes us caretakers of his creation as he entrusted Eden to Adam.

Luke

12:22 And he said unto his disciples, Therefore I say unto you, Take no thought for your life, what ye shall eat; neither for the body, what ye shall put on. 23 The life is more than meat, and the body is more than raiment. 24 Consider the ravens: for they neither sow nor reap; which neither have storehouse nor barn; and God feedeth them: how much more are ye better than the fowls?

Luke included the term "storehouses" as well as barns. Why did he include a parable of a rich man and his barns (12:16-21)? Is there something about his audience that this parable speaks to particularly? This suggests Luke's audience engaged in both farming and commerce, perhaps traders or businessmen. Tyre and Zidon, cities of Syria, prophets called marts of the nations. (Is. 23:3) Ezekiel enumerated many items of their commerce and nations with whom Tyre traded. (Ezek.27:1-36) Luke mentioned incidents about people who lived in Tyre and Sidon.

Paul first contacted Luke in Syria, and it probably represented his homeland. When Luke penned his gospel, he included material that seemed pertinent to his people even when other gospel writers omitted such information. Luke seems to address his gospel to his people in Syria.

Mariners and traders might be more likely to identify with Luke's use of "storehouses" than by using "barns" alone. This shows that even businessmen and those who worked in fairs need to trust God's constant care equally with farmers or herders. They need not worry that their ships, camels, or storehouses are entirely at the mercy of the raiders, sea, or storms. God also protects their possessions even as he cares for sparrows and ravens. Worry not about your business enterprises. It distracts from life's joy and deprives from the abundant life which God provides. (Jno.10:10) Does worry enhance or dull life?

Luke

**12:13 And one of the company said unto
him, Master, speak to my brother, that he
divide the inheritance with me. 14 And he
said unto him, Man, who made me a judge
or a divider over you? 15 And he said
unto them, Take heed, and beware of
covetousness: for a man's life consisteth
not in the abundance of the things which
he possesseth. 16 And he spake a parable
unto them, saying, The ground of a certain rich man brought forth plentifully:
17 And he thought within himself, saying,
What shall I do, because I have no room
where to bestow my fruits? 18 And he
said, This will I do: I will pull down my
barns, and build greater; and there will I
bestow all my fruits and my goods. 19
And I will say to my soul, Soul, thou hast
much goods laid up for many years; take
thine ease, eat, drink, and be merry. 20
But God said unto him, Thou fool, this
night thy soul shall be required of thee:
then whose shall those things be, which
thou hast provided? 21 So is he that layeth
up treasure for himself, and is not rich
toward God.**

How we regard our possession distinguishes Satan's children from God's faithful children. When our affections entrench too deeply with material things, relationship with God and others suffers. God promises to supply body needs. As we use God's blessings to meet our needs, God instructs us to consider how others fare. The good life God couples with caring for others. Viewing our wealth as ours alone results in emptiness and contention as when this man approached Jesus to persuade his brother to share his inheritance. Covetousness comes from Satan, but willingness to share what God gives us with others originates with God's righteousness. Willingly sharing with others demonstrates God's love working within us and shows wisdom of the wise. (Phil.2:13; Lk.1:17) If men call us wise, wouldn't it be great for God to consider us wise?

God provides a complete life for those who live in and abide by the principles which guide his kingdom. They don't worry about whether they will have sufficient to carry them to life's end. They trust God's promise. Excess becomes an opportunity to help others and glorify God.

Some refuse to trust God because they receive not as much of this world's goods as they desire. Psalm seventy-three tells of one of God's people who considered how ungodly men prospered. He envied them when he thought on how they seemed to escape troubles which disquiet others. Even the steps of the godly nearly slip when they see life through the eyes of Satan's children. Not until the psalmist entered God's sanctuary did he understand the end of the ungodly. Then his heart grieved for thinking so foolishly about the wealthy who forget God. God provides his people fruitful, not vain, lives when we draw near to our heavenly Father to do his will.

Strong nations provide many benefits for their citizens. God's kingdom supplies amazing benefits to those in his kingdom while his people live by the laws which govern his domain. Citizens who violate the laws of their nation lose the benefits of being citizens within their country. If they are sentenced to jail or death, what benefits they might otherwise have enjoyed, they lose. Allow not Satan to influence you to depart from the precepts of God's kingdom and lose its rewards. Maintain a proper attitude toward this world's wealth.

How does one decide how much wealth to use for himself and how much to give to benefit others? Jesus instructed his followers to lay up treasure in heaven. If we think on his admonition, we gladly share our blessings with others that God and his kingdom receive honor. It then becomes a question of how much do I invest in heavenly treasure and how much in earthly. Am I storing treasure in heaven for later life as well as providing for this life's closing days?

Matthew

6:27 Which of you by taking thought can add one cubit unto his stature? 28 And why take ye thought for raiment? Consider the lilies of the field, how they grow; they toil not, neither do they spin: 29 And yet I say unto you, That even Solomon in all his glory was not arrayed like one of these. 30 Wherefore, if God so clothe the grass of the field, which to day is, and to morrow is cast into the oven, shall he not much more clothe you, O ye of little faith? 31 Therefore take no thought, saying, What shall we eat? or, What shall we drink? or, Wherewithal shall we be clothed? 32 (For after all these things do the Gentiles seek:) for your heavenly Father knoweth that ye have need of all these things. 33 But seek ye first the kingdom of God, and his righteousness; and all these things shall be added unto you. 34 Take therefore no thought for the morrow: for the morrow shall take thought for the things of itself. Sufficient unto the day is the evil thereof.

Jesus assures us God cares for all his creatures. Doesn't grass sprout and grow after severe drought? Don't flowers of the field blossom and seed? God provides for his handiwork. Are we who are in the image of our Creator beyond his consideration? Who ever heard of man securing a variety of either plants or animals that didn't care for them, especially those he prizes most? Will not our heavenly Father protect and supply the needs of the apex of his handiwork? Do what you can, but leave the rest to God. Worry only distracts from that which God provides for us to enjoy. God asks us to show faith and trust his promises. Demonstrating trust in God's promises becomes part of the fellowship between man and God, much as we trust the promises of our friends in this life. Without this trust, how can Jesus be Emmanuel, God with us? (Is.8:8-10; Math.1:23) God seeks our companionship and asks for us to seek his.

Luke

12:25 And which of you with taking thought can add to his stature one cubit? 26 If ye then be not able to do that thing which is least, why take ye thought for the rest? 27 Consider the lilies how they grow: they toil not, they spin not; and yet I say unto you, that Solomon in all his glory was not arrayed like one of these. 28 If then God so clothe the grass, which is to day in the field, and to morrow is cast into the oven; how much more will he clothe you, O ye of little faith? 29 And seek not ye what ye shall eat, or what ye shall drink, neither be ye of doubtful mind. 30 For all these things do the nations of the world seek after: and your Father knoweth that ye have need of these things. 31 But rather seek ye the kingdom of God; and all these things shall be added unto you.

Why did Matthew say Gentiles study how to meet body needs, but Luke states that the nations of the world follow this path? Matthew contrasted Jews with Gentiles who have lost sight of God's providence. Luke contrasted Gentile Christians with the nations of the world or peoples who live according to the world's life style. They see not the hand of God supplying their daily needs. In either case, God seeks children who trust him to provide all needs of the body in addition to man's spiritual requirements. Look to God in faith. He supplies the necessities of body and spirit. Fretting about how we're going to secure food or clothing, we lose sight of God's love. Trusting God to grant us all needs of the body and spirit relieves our minds of worry, so we may use that energy in some productive manner. As small children trust their parents to provide what they need, Jesus admonishes us to imitate God's Son in attitude and action. Is not this the wisdom of the wise, turning children's hearts to our heavenly Father? (Lk. 1:17) Have you tried trusting God as children do their parents?

Matthew

7:1 Judge not, that ye be not judged. 2 For with what judgment ye judge, ye shall be judged: and with what measure ye mete, it shall be measured to you again. 3 And why beholdest thou the mote that is in thy brother's eye, but considerest not the beam that is in thine own eye? 4 Or how wilt thou say to thy brother, Let me pull out the mote out of thine eye; and, behold, a beam is in thine own eye? 5 Thou hypocrite, first cast out the beam out of thine own eye; and then shalt thou see clearly to cast out the mote out of thy brother's eye. 6 Give not that which is holy unto the dogs, neither cast ye your pearls before swine, lest they trample them under their feet, and turn again and rend you.

Paul chastised Jews for condemning ungodly Gentiles when Jews also transgressed truth. (Rom.2:1) Jesus informs me to correct wrongs in my life before correcting others. One makes himself a hypocrite who overlooks his own faults, but freely identifies others' bad deeds. God seeks children who desire perfection. (Math.5:48)

Blind people aren't reliable leaders. Being too blind to see and change my own errors, I cannot see to guide others to modify their lives. Trees and plants we identify by their fruits. Figs aren't gathered from thorns, nor grapes from brambles. Men gather good fruit from good trees or vines. If my life bears unjust fruit, I am not an honorable child before God, and he will not work with me to help others eliminate evil fruits from their lives.

Finding fault generates like attitude in others toward me. Observing others' good, they look for blessings in my life. How I give to others determines what I receive. (Math.7:12) God shows us truth and wisdom to enrich and open our lives for God to dwell with us. "**Can two walk together, except they be agreed?**" (Am.3:3) Do you agree that God speaks wisdom of the wise?

Luke

6:37 Judge not, and ye shall not be judged: condemn not, and ye shall not be condemned: forgive, and ye shall be forgiven: 38 Give, and it shall be given unto you; good measure, pressed down, and shaken together, and running over, shall men give into your bosom. For with the same measure that ye mete withal it shall be measured to you again. 39 And he spake a parable unto them, Can the blind lead the blind? shall they not both fall into the ditch? 40 The disciple is not above his master: but every one that is perfect shall be as his master. 41 And why beholdest thou the mote that is in thy brother's eye, but perceivest not the beam that is in thine own eye? 42 Either how canst thou say to thy brother, Brother, let me pull out the mote that is in thine eye, when thou thyself beholdest not the beam that is in thine own eye? Thou hypocrite, cast out first the beam out of thine own eye, and then shalt thou see clearly to pull out the mote that is in thy brother's eye. 43 For a good tree bringeth not forth corrupt fruit; neither doth a corrupt tree bring forth good fruit. 44 For every tree is known by his own fruit. For of thorns men do not gather figs, nor of a bramble bush gather they grapes. 45 A good man out of the good treasure of his heart bringeth forth that which is good; and an evil man out of the evil treasure of his heart bringeth forth that which is evil: for of the abundance of the heart his mouth speaketh.

The disciple is not above his master. A teacher must correct his own life to prepare to eliminate errors in another's life. Otherwise, his disciple follows his teacher and resists correcting his faults. God desires that light fills our lives and the lives of all we instruct. We become doers before becoming teachers. (Act.1:1) One prepares to become a good teacher by developing a heart which thinks on good, not evil.

Matthew

7:7 Ask, and it shall be given you; seek, and ye shall find; knock, and it shall be opened unto you: 8 For every one that asketh receiveth; and he that seeketh findeth; and to him that knocketh it shall be opened. 9 Or what man is there of you, whom if his son ask bread, will he give him a stone? 10 Or if he ask a fish, will he give him a serpent? 11 If ye then, being evil, know how to give good gifts unto your children, how much more shall your Father which is in heaven give good things to them that ask him? 12 Therefore all things whatsoever ye would that men should do to you, do ye even so to them: for this is the law and the prophets.

Jesus explained our relationship to God by comparing it with good relationships between children and their fathers. How better could God convey his concern for his wayward children than to remind us of our associations as family members? Matthew and Luke encouraged us to ask God for bread or fish. Would a father supply his son a stone when he requested bread, or would he give a viper for a fish? Luke included asking for an egg. Would a father give a scorpion if his child asked for an egg? Therefore our heavenly Father gives good gifts to those who ask of him. When a person asks for a gift, he hopes to receive. God assures us that if we ask of him in faith, he will provide what is good for us.

Luke's closing statement follows the beginning idea of asking of God who gives the Holy Spirit to those who ask. This applies to Jew and Gentile equally, but doesn't single out followers of Moses like Matthew. Possessing God's Holy Spirit strengthens us against Satan's temptations as it did Jesus in the wilderness. (Math.4:4-11; Lk.4:4-13) We ought to supplicate God for his Spirit that we might abide by God's teaching and receive his blessings. (Eph. 3:16; Col.1:11) As a parent, do you enjoy giving to your children what they request?

Luke

11:9 And I say unto you, Ask, and it shall be given you; seek, and ye shall find; knock, and it shall be opened unto you. 10 For every one that asketh receiveth; and he that seeketh findeth; and to him that knocketh it shall be opened. 11 If a son shall ask bread of any of you that is a father, will he give him a stone? or if he ask a fish, will he for a fish give him a serpent? 12 Or if he shall ask an egg, will he offer him a scorpion? 13 If ye then, being evil, know how to give good gifts unto your children: how much more shall your heavenly Father give the Holy Spirit to them that ask him?

Matthew concluded his thought with the generalization that anything I hope others would do for me, I should eagerly do for others. This fulfills the law of Moses and the prophets. Matthew's remark indicates he addressed his Jewish people. Jesus assured his audience he had no intention of contradicting or destroying their law from God. None of it would be canceled until all should be fulfilled. What Jesus explained to his people might be summed by saying that you have God's great law, but you are failing to live by your wonderful law. (Jno.7:19) He is showing you how to fulfill what God asked of you when your fathers made their covenant with God at Sinai.

How would Jesus' audience react to his message? Would they rebel as had their fathers all through the Old Testament, or would they humble themselves before God? In rare instances Jewish fathers had repented and returned to God. Now God has sent his only begotten Son to speak to his people, pleading with them to listen to his truth. Leaders of the Jews, for the most part, turned deaf ears and harassed Jesus for encouraging them to repent and return to God. They anticipated Christ, but when he came, they turned deaf ears. They could not endure hearing God's truth. Can you and I listen to God or do we rebel, too?

Matthew

7:13 Enter ye in at the strait gate: for wide is the gate, and broad is the way, that leadeth to destruction, and many there be which go in thereat: 14 Because strait is the gate, and narrow is the way, which leadeth unto life, and few there be that find it.

It ought to be apparent few live properly with their associates in work, home, and recreation. Jesus capitalized on this fact by saying most people walk the broad path of disobedience and ultimate destruction. Few maintain admirable associations with their peers or God. Living as enemies of your neighbors and family God likens to living in darkness. Being courteous toward both friend and foe produces light in one's life.

Matthew pointed out two paths of life, but Luke mentioned only the strait way. The broad way ends in destruction. The strait way leads to eternal life. Matthew's narrow gate and Luke's strait way lead to the kingdom where Abraham, Isaac, and Jacob reside. Failure to enter the narrow gate or strait way excludes one from God's kingdom, and from associating with the three patriarchs. Luke adds that strangers from the four corners of the earth enter the strait gate. Luke appeals to Gentiles to enter God's pathway of life and gain the blessings offered to Abraham, Isaac, and Jacob.

Matthew included this concept later when he honored a centurion who demonstrated faith. (8:11-12) Jews who first enjoyed the blessing of being called God's people now faced the threat of losing that high honor. (Ex.19:5-6) Gentiles who, ages long gone, strayed from God now became first to receive Christ and the kingdom of God. Rather than accepting the truth of losing their privileged relationship, Jewish leaders refused to hear what Jesus taught. This rebellion Jesus likened to those who chose to walk the wide path to eternal banishment from God, Christ, patriarchs, and the redeemed of all ages.

Luke

13:23 Then said one unto him, Lord, are there few that be saved? And he said unto them, 24 Strive to enter in at the strait gate: for many, I say unto you, will seek to enter in, and shall not be able. 25 When once the master of the house is risen up, and hath shut to the door, and ye begin to stand without, and to knock at the door, saying, Lord, Lord, open unto us; and he shall answer and say unto you, I know you not whence ye are: 26 Then shall ye begin to say, We have eaten and drunk in thy presence, and thou hast taught in our streets. 27 But he shall say, I tell you, I know you not whence ye are; depart from me, all ye workers of iniquity. 28 There shall be weeping and gnashing of teeth, when ye shall see Abraham, and Isaac, and Jacob, and all the prophets, in the kingdom of God, and you yourselves thrust out. 29 And they shall come from the east, and from the west, and from the north, and from the south, and shall sit down in the kingdom of God. 30 And, behold, there are last which shall be first, and there are first which shall be last.

Being Abraham's children, Jews thought they automatically entered God's kingdom when it appeared. Their refusal to repent for sinful thinking and misdeeds barred them from entering the way of blessed Abraham their forefathers anticipated for 1500 years. Many Gentiles would admit their disgraceful ways, repent, and turn to Christ for mercy. God guided them to enter that strait way that leads to life. Unrepentant Jews would weep and gnash their teeth as they witnessed hated Gentiles gain what they hoped to receive, but lost through disobedience. God shows mercy to the humble, but turns the high-minded into the broad way of destruction. (Rom.11:19-22; 2 Chr.15:2) Paul admonished Gentiles not to be high-minded, for it caused Jews to fall. (Rom.11:18-22) If we Gentiles consider ourselves blessed above Jews by our own goodness, we err.

Matthew

**7:15 Beware of false prophets, which
come to you in sheep's clothing, but
inwardly they are ravening wolves. 16 Ye
shall know them by their fruits. Do men
gather grapes of thorns, or figs of thistles?
17 Even so every good tree bringeth forth
good fruit; but a corrupt tree bringeth
forth evil fruit. 18 A good tree cannot
bring forth evil fruit, neither can a
corrupt tree bring forth good fruit. 19
Every tree that bringeth not forth good
fruit is hewn down, and cast into the fire.
20 Wherefore by their fruits ye shall
know them.**

Luke

**6:43 For a good tree bringeth not forth
corrupt fruit; neither doth a corrupt tree
bring forth good fruit. 44 For every tree is
known by his own fruit. For of thorns
men do not gather figs, nor of a bramble
bush gather they grapes. 45 A good man
out of the good treasure of his heart
bringeth forth that which is good; and an
evil man out of the evil treasure of his
heart bringeth forth that which is evil:
for of the abundance of the heart his
mouth speaketh.**

False prophets plagued God's people from the days of Moses who cautioned Israel that false prophets shall arise to influence you to serve strange gods. Among their arsenal of tricks they utilize miracles to convince people that what they say God approves. Why will God permit false prophets to dupe his people? God answered this clearly. I want to prove you to determine if you submit to my commands or if you follow your own will by doing that which seems right in your own eyes. Even if the false prophet turns out to be a member of your own family such as your wife, son, daughter, father, mother, or a close friend, you must turn away from whoever encourages you to turn away from the commands of God. (Deu.12:8;13:1-18)

False prophets deceive as Satan beguiled Eve in the garden of Eden. He boldly approached Eve to ask if God permitted her to eat of all the fruits of the garden. She replied God allowed her to eat anything except fruit of the tree of the knowledge of good and evil. Eating of it results in death. The Deceiver then replied that God knows you won't die if you eat of that tree. On the contrary, your ability to know good and evil awakens, and you shall become as wise as God. False prophets deceive by changing the truth of God into a lie. That which appeals to the eye, mind, and flesh false prophets praise as good. Since we find these promises very appealing to the flesh, we desire to test their reality only to find we enslaved ourselves to sin. Is it any wonder Jesus warned his hearers to beware of false prophets? They will convince Christians to consider God a liar. (I Jno.5:10)

Are people today encountering these messengers of Satan? Unless you and I possess a genuine love of God's truth and a thorough and continuing desire to submit to God, Satan has already dispatched his deceivers to visit us. They contradict any or all that God recorded in the Bible. They contend that God's love won't let him condemn any person to hell; heaven and hell don't exist; this life is all there is, and you should get all you can to enjoy life while you live; divorce serves a good purpose and permits you to find a mate you can enjoy; abandon the extinct morality of your parents, they only defeat you from finding the fulfillment of life; get ahead in this world to attain a high standing in the community regardless of how it affects others; homosexuality is a natural style of life for some people even when God affirmed that he allowed no whore of the daughters of Israel or sodomite of the sons of Israel. (Deu.23:17) No law of God goes unchallenged by Satan and his emissaries who pose as guides of the great and the small.

Why did God send Jesus into this world? Was it not to expose the futility of Satan's lies and to save us from our enemies' lies?

Matthew

**7:21 Not every one that saith unto me,
Lord, Lord, shall enter into the kingdom
of heaven; but he that doeth the will of my
Father which is in heaven. 22 Many will
say to me in that day, Lord, Lord, have
we not prophesied in thy name? and in
thy name have cast out devils? and in thy
name done many wonderful works? 23
And then will I profess unto them, I never
knew you: depart from me, ye that work
iniquity. 24 Therefore whosoever heareth
these sayings of mine, and doeth them, I
will liken him unto a wise man, which
built his house upon a rock: 25 And the
rain descended, and the floods came, and
the winds blew, and beat upon that house;
and it fell not: for it was founded upon a
rock. 26 And every one that heareth these
sayings of mine, and doeth them not, shall
be likened unto a foolish man, which built
his house upon the sand: 27 And the rain
descended, and the floods came, and the
winds blew, and beat upon that house;
and it fell: and great was the fall of it. 28
And it came to pass, when Jesus had
ended these sayings, the people were
astonished at his doctrine: 29 For he
taught them as one having authority, and
not as the scribes.**

Luke

**6:46 And why call ye me, Lord, Lord, and
do not the things which I say? 47
Whosoever cometh to me, and heareth my
sayings, and doeth them, I will shew you
to whom he is like: 48 He is like a man
which built an house, and digged deep,
and laid the foundation on a rock: and
when the flood arose, the stream beat
vehemently upon that house, and could
not shake it: for it was founded upon a
rock. 49 But he that heareth, and doeth
not, is like a man that without a
foundation built an house upon the earth;
against which the stream did beat
vehemently, and immediately it fell; and
the ruin of that house was great.**

Life promised by false prophets and teachers resembles gathering the wind. When you think you have it, there is nothing. God and Jesus explain true life: bow to the or-dinances of God, for they alone supply the good life to enjoy. (Deu.6:24; Ps.84:11; Is.55:1-13; Jno.10:10; 1 Pet.3:10) You find the blessings God promised to Abraham. (Gen.12:3)

Knowing what Jesus taught, but failing to do it excludes people from God's kingdom and blessings. Many deceived by Satan's ambassadors believe that having godly progenitors or performing some spectacular deed opens that gate. Jesus explained that nothing short of a changed life--only doing God's will-- will open the door of life. Doing God's will to others in love will swing open heaven's portals. To reinforce this truth, Matthew and Luke observed that Jesus taught the parable of houses. One house erected on solid rock withstood lashing winds and torrential floods, but the house founded on sand or earth collapsed under the onslaught of high winds and gushing floods of Satan's children who deceive. Trials to lives resting solidly on the foundation of God's whole truth show little deterioration. By faith in God, their lives stand unscathed.

God's plan shows no favoritism to Jew or Gentile. Either abandon self to do God's will or no blessing awaits you in heaven with God, Christ, or all who submit to the Father's will. If you call Jesus Lord, act as he is your sovereign. Jesus' firm message then and now startles many. Jesus knew in the final day many would plead with him. They call to his attention great deeds they performed in his name by casting out demons and many other good works. God demands a changed life style. You die to sin and live unto God if you expect his blessings. Even Judas possessed power to cast out devils, but Satan dwelt in him and persuaded him to betray Jesus for thirty pieces of silver only to cast them away. Judas lost both lives. What will we lose if we listen to Satan?

Matthew

8:1 When he was come down from the mountain, great multitudes followed him. 2 And, behold, there came a leper and worshipped him, saying, Lord, if thou wilt, thou canst make me clean. 3 And Jesus put forth his hand, and touched him, saying, I will; be thou clean. And immediately his leprosy was cleansed. 4 And Jesus saith unto him, See thou tell no man; but go thy way, shew thyself to the priest, and offer the gift that Moses commanded, for a testimony unto them.

According to Matthew's gospel, Jesus healed all manner of diseases before preaching the Sermon on the Mount. (Math. 4:23-24) Matthew, Mark and Luke seem not to place the cleansing the leper in the same order chronologically. Therefore, I will consider not the time order of the event, but the importance of healing the leper in relation to what Jesus taught in the Sermon on the Mount and how Isaiah portrayed Christ.

Two important points present themselves in connection with Jesus cleansing the leper. First, Jesus taught in his sermon that every detail of Moses' law needed to be obeyed in attitude of mind and action. Doing to others as you would have them do to you if you were in their shoes Jesus must fulfill himself to be our example. The leper asked for Jesus to cleanse him. Desiring to convey God's compassion on men whom Satan tormented, Jesus showed God's and his own love. At the same time he did to others as he would have others do to him. Second, when Jesus directed the cleansed leper to show himself to the priest, he encouraged him to fulfill God's law to the Jews which commanded anyone cleansed of leprosy to obey. After a priest confirmed him a leper, Moses' law isolated the leper. Once the priest pronounced a leper clean, he regained liberty to circulate freely among the people as if he had never been afflicted with that still-incurable disease. (Lev. 13:1-14:57)

Mark

1:40 And there came a leper to him, beseeching him, and kneeling down to him, and saying unto him, If thou wilt, thou canst make me clean. 41 And Jesus, moved with compassion, put forth his hand, and touched him, and saith unto him, I will; be thou clean. 42 And as soon as he had spoken, immediately the leprosy departed from him, and he was cleansed. 43 And he straitly charged him, and forthwith sent him away; 44 And saith unto him, See thou say nothing to any man: but go thy way, shew thyself to the priest, and offer for thy cleansing those things which Moses commanded, for a testimony unto them. 45 But he went out, and began to publish it much, and to blaze abroad the matter, insomuch that Jesus could no more openly enter into the city, but was without in desert places: and they came to him from every quarter.

A third factor may be evident in that Jesus asked the leper not to publish the miracle. Isaiah spoke of Christ that he would not cause his voice to be heard in the streets, which seems to indicate he refused to seek praise of men. (Is.42:3) By spreading news of his wonderful healing, the leper's message worked contrary to Isaiah's picture of Christ. Later, Matthew quoted Isaiah's prophecy when Jesus charged the multitude who followed him not to make him known. (Math.12:15-20)

Had this leper listened to Jesus as he taught on the mountain? Had he witnessed Jesus healing others? What convinced him Jesus possessed power to cleanse him of leprosy? Whatever he had heard or seen, he believed this man Jesus could relieve him of his loathsome illness. Furthermore, his desire for relief prompted him to humbly approach Jesus and plead for God's mercy to heal him. We must want God's healing and mercy before God will work his wonders for us. This includes cleansing our sins. If sin weighs heavily on you, ask for God's mercy.

Luke

5:12 And it came to pass, when he was in a certain city, behold a man full of leprosy: who seeing Jesus fell on his face, and besought him, saying, Lord, if thou wilt, thou canst make me clean. 13 And he put forth his hand, and touched him, saying, I will: be thou clean. And immediately the leprosy departed from him. 14 And he charged him to tell no man: but go, and shew thyself to the priest, and offer for thy cleansing, according as Moses commanded, for a testimony unto them. 15 But so much the more went there a fame abroad of him: and great multitudes came together to hear, and to be healed by him of their infirmities.

Recognizing need and that there exists a means to relieve the need encourages us to visit physicians, psychiatrists, AA, and other support groups. God trained his Son in physical and spiritual healing and supplied him with both words and God's Spirit to heal every physical and spiritual ailment. Until each person perceives a need for that spiritual invigoration, he will not approach Jesus for assistance.

Were there factors which deterred the leper from seeking help from Jesus? Leaders among the Jews (Pharisees, Sadducees, and priests) discouraged the people from following this man Jesus. Notwithstanding, the leper's need persuaded him to seek help. Today, many forces dissuade those spiritually needy from coming to Jesus for relief. Ungodly ministers and church members turn more away from Christ than all other deterrents. Christianity must not be viewed as a pageant, a ritual, or a cloak to deceive. It's either a means of drawing near to God, our Creator, or it's spurious like other religions. Each of us determines within himself if he needs God, and whether Jesus can help him find and live with God.

During times of prosperity, Satan convinces men we have little or no need of God. When devastating circumstances overwhelm us, then we look to God for help. God seeks people who rely on him in good and bad conditions. How shall God ever subdue our inclination to forsake him when all goes well, but plead for help when destruction surrounds us? God spelled out in plain language how he worked with his people under the law of Moses. Leviticus chapter twenty-six and repeated numerous times throughout the Old Testament, God specified four means of humbling Jews to persuade them to trust him at all times. Famine, sword, disease, and wild beasts in groups of seven God utilized to subdue their stubborn hearts. Ezekiel included all four woes in one verse. (Ezek.14:21) Fifteen times in the book of *Judges* alone, God applied one or more of these sore judgments to return Israel to serve him faithfully. Even during David's reign, Absalom attempted to overthrow his father by force of arms because of David's adultery with Bathsheba. After the wise Solomon allowed his foreign wives to turn his heart from God to build places of worship to idols, God raised up Jeroboam to sever ten tribes from following Solomon's son. Rehoboam's sins brought Egypt's armies to plunder Jerusalem. Until Hezekiah cleansed Judah of idols, God planned to humble Judah by Assyria. God finally called Babylon to devastate Judah and Jerusalem. Is God today utilizing these four sore judgments to humble us for our transgressions? or are such tragedies incidental? Be assured, God destines his kingdom to subdue all resistance and to rule in righteousness. Christ reigns till he prevails against all his foes whether we follow godless religion or haughty political leaders. (1 Cor.15:25-26) Plead with God to spare us from his sore judgments because we humble ourselves before God through Jesus to obey his truth.

Matthew

8:5 And when Jesus was entered into Capernaum, there came unto him a centurion, beseeching him, 6 And saying, Lord, my servant lieth at home sick of the palsy, grievously tormented. 7 And Jesus saith unto him, I will come and heal him. 8 The centurion answered and said, Lord, I am not worthy that thou shouldest come under my roof: but speak the word only, and my servant shall be healed. 9 For I am a man under authority, having soldiers under me: and I say to this man, Go, and he goeth; and to another, Come, and he cometh; and to my servant, Do this, and he doeth it. 10 When Jesus heard it, he marvelled, and said to them that followed, Verily I say unto you, I have not found so great faith, no, not in Israel. 11 And I say unto you, That many shall come from the east and west, and shall sit down with Abraham, and Isaac, and Jacob, in the kingdom of heaven. 12 But the children of the kingdom shall be cast out into outer darkness: there shall be weeping and gnashing of teeth. 13 And Jesus said unto the centurion, Go thy way; and as thou hast believed, so be it done unto thee. And his servant was healed in the selfsame hour.

Matthew and Luke show how a humble Gentile centurion manifested remarkable faith, for which Jesus commended him. Jews who sought Jesus' healing appear to have considered it necessary to bring their sick to Jesus for him to heal. This centurion understood the power of delegated authority. He understood God delegated Jesus to demonstrate his power by relieving ailments. Luke stated the centurion commissioned (delegated) Jewish elders to approach Jesus on behalf of his sick servant. God had sent many prophets to Israel, but they rarely understood delegated authority, and few submitted to the commands of Moses or the word of their prophets. Their lack of faith in God' servants hindered their obedience.

Luke

7:1 Now when he had ended all his sayings in the audience of the people, he entered into Capernaum. 2 And a certain centurion's servant, who was dear unto him, was sick, and ready to die. 3 And when he heard of Jesus, he sent unto him the elders of the Jews, beseeching him that he would come and heal his servant. 4 And when they came to Jesus, they besought him instantly, saying, That he was worthy for whom he should do this: 5 For he loveth our nation, and he hath built us a synagogue. 6 Then Jesus went with them. And when he was now not far from the house, the centurion sent friends to him, saying unto him, Lord, trouble not thyself: for I am not worthy that thou shouldest enter under my roof: 7 Wherefore neither thought I myself worthy to come unto thee: but say in a word, and my servant shall be healed. 8 For I also am a man set under authority, having under me soldiers, and I say unto one, Go, and he goeth; and to another, Come, and he cometh; and to my servant, Do this, and he doeth it. 9 When Jesus heard these things, he marvelled at him, and turned him about, and said unto the people that followed him, I say unto you, I have not found so great faith, no, not in Israel. 10 And they that were sent, returning to the house, found the servant whole that had been sick.

Luke seems to indicate that healing the centurion's servant followed the Sermon on the Mount which teaching Luke recorded in parts in several chapters. It's quite likely Jesus taught the main parts of the Sermon on the Mount numerous times which may account for Luke's recording parts of it in separate places.

Since Jesus' ascension, he continues to solve our problems remotely as the centurion comprehended. God's wisdom demands that Jesus rule remotely from heaven until he subdues all his foes. (Ps.110:1)

As Jesus' teaching the Sermon on the Mount demonstrated his authority, he shows God delegated him power to subdue forces Satan controls. The Evil One curses men's lives. He subjected a man by one of his evil spirits. Jesus illustrated unquestionably God granted him power to destroy the works of Satan by casting the devil out of the man in the synagogue. (Mk.1:21-27)

When the synagogue audience realized Jesus had disenfranchised Satan's power in that devil-ridden man, they sat wide-eyed. How had this man received such power? Since John the Baptist had preached the kingdom of God neared, some probably realized Jesus must portray power of God's kingdom to overthrow Satan's dominion over men.

Departing from the synagogue, people spread abroad the news that they witnessed a great miracle that day. Hearing of this great wonder, multitudes sought Jesus to see for themselves this great power from God. Perhaps he would cast out Satan's destructive forces in their lives, too.

We need not despair that we cannot go to Jesus today like the people of that age. Though at God's right hand in heaven, Jesus continues to display God's power to overthrow Satan's influence in our lives. Healing our physical ills, as important as it is, must be considered of lesser importance to casting out Satan's power to destroy our relationships with families, friends, neighbors, and our heavenly Father. How often we regret saying cutting words to husband, wife, children, relatives, or friends. If we acknowledge our weakness to thwart Satan, Jesus shows how to destroy Satan's power in our lives today. Let us use his power. (Eph.3:16) It begins with knowing, believing, and applying God's truth as Jesus did when Satan tempted him.

Jesus does possesses authority to destroy Satan's works in our lives today. Do we struggle with ourselves, trying to overcome some bad habit? Jesus is willing to help, but we must rely on his power, not our own strength. Paul cautioned Corinthians, **"Wherefore let him that thinketh he standeth take heed lest he fall, There hath no temptation taken you but such as is common to man: but God is faithful, who will not suffer you to be tempted above that ye are able; but will with the temptation also make a way to escape, that ye may be able to bear it."** (1 Cor. 10:12-13) Do we trust God will provide help if we sincerely ask for his assistance against Satan. Isaiah pleaded with his people, **"Behold, the Lord's hand is not shortened, that it cannot save; neither his ear heavy, that it cannot hear: But your iniquities have separated between you and your God, and your sins have hid his face from you, that he will not hear."** (Is.59:1-2) In the following verses, Isaiah identified many of Judah's transgressions committed against God's law. God wants to aid us to defeat Satan's rule in our lives, but we must truly repent and call on God for his help before God grants our needed help.

David asked how a young man could cleanse his way before God. His first answer taught the young man to take heed to God's word with his whole heart. Don't wander from God's precepts. Hide God's truth in your heart that you might not sin against God. This involved God teaching him his statutes. He must rejoice in God's way as one rejoices in great riches, not consider it burdensome. Meditate on God's precepts, and respect his ways, even delight in them, not forgetting or fretting against his word. (Ps.119:9-16)

In humility call on God to teach us his truth. Be willing to relinquish habits, imaginations, and other hindrances that blind our eyes to what God desires of us. When God sees we truly desire to abandon Satan's lies and see the living God and his Son Jesus, God's grace supplies our needs. Don't endure Satan's burden, submit to God who loves to ease our loads.

Matthew

8:18 Now when Jesus saw great multitudes about him, he gave commandment to depart unto the other side. 19 And a certain scribe came, and said unto him, Master, I will follow thee whithersoever thou goest. 20 And Jesus saith unto him, The foxes have holes, and the birds of the air have nests; but the Son of man hath not where to lay his head. 21 And another of his disciples said unto him, Lord, suffer me first to go and bury my father. 22 But Jesus said unto him, Follow me; and let the dead bury their dead.

While near Capernaum, multitudes gathered to hear Jesus and to be healed. He purposed to cross the sea of Galilee to preach to other communities. As he commanded to cross the sea, a scribe offered to follow Jesus, but he reminded the scribe birds and foxes have homes, but Jesus had no home. Then a disciple begged permission to delay following him until he buried his father. Jesus explained there are two kinds of death: physical and spiritual. Let the spiritual dead bury your father, but now I've awakened you spiritually, follow me and preach God's gospel.

If Jesus walked among us today, would he comment the same? Those spiritually quickened need to teach God's message to those who consider themselves alive, but are spiritually deceased before God. Permit people whose love centers on material things to bury the physical dead. We may visualize ourselves as spry and spiritually potent, but unless we obey the revealed will of our Father in heaven, we are but walking spiritual corpses. This grieves our heavenly Father who wants all his children to gain fullness of life here and hereafter. (1 Tim. 4:8) While we continue spiritually dead, we realize not our condition. Like the angel of the church in Laodicea, we may feel we are rich and need nothing. (Rev.3:17) God can restore spiritual eyesight if we let him.

Luke

9:57 And it came to pass, that, as they went in the way, a certain man said unto him, Lord, I will follow thee whithersoever thou goest. 58 And Jesus said unto him, Foxes have holes, and birds of the air have nests; but the Son of man hath not where to lay his head. 59 And he said unto another, Follow me. But he said, Lord, suffer me first to go and bury my father. 60 Jesus said unto him, Let the dead bury their dead: but go thou and preach the kingdom of God. 61 And another also said, Lord, I will follow thee; but let me first go bid them farewell, which are at home at my house. 62 And Jesus said unto him, No man, having put his hand to the plough, and looking back, is fit for the kingdom of God.

Three followers of Jesus illustrate attitudes of people who learn about Christ. Many are willing to do the will of God, but show reservations. Comforts of home, families, friends, etc. beckon so strongly that they consider the cost too dear. Maybe at a later time things will be more favorable. King Agrippa refused to respond to Paul's exhortation to become a Christian on similar grounds. (Act.26:1-27) Satan utilizes all earthly interests to prevent his children from submitting to God. Even those of us who have declared allegiance to God and Christ often struggle with Satan's lures. (1 Cor.9:27)

Once Jesus awakens us to the fullness of life offered to those who know and believe God's truth, he encourages us to continue in that fuller life. Even so, Satan and his children continue to call us to return to his life of darkness. They promise liberty, but deceive. (2 Pet.2:18-20) Returning to that lifestyle results only in slavery to sin which produces bitterness, anger, wantonness, not life. Satan holds out lures to satisfy desires of the flesh which never satisfy. We always sense a void without God in our lives.

Why did Jesus reject the scribe as a companion in spreading the gospel of the kingdom of heaven? It would seem that a person well trained in the Scriptures might have been an asset in teaching people the correct use of their law. Instead, Jesus appears to have rejected him. Rather than choosing men well trained in the law of Moses, Jesus selected fishermen, farmers, tax collectors, and men of other common occupations. Looking back on those whom Jesus called to be apostles, we may well ask why choose these untrained individuals? Did Jesus see something in those he chose apostles that scribes and lawyers lacked? Today, some prefer to train their own business colleagues because they don't have to undo concepts that run counter to the philosophy of the enterprise. For example, Pharisees and disciples of John the Baptist fasted regularly as part of their devotion to God. Pharisees tithed even smallest parts of their income, washed cups and pots as service to God. All such activities Moses commanded, but mercy, judgment, and love to fellow men Pharisees deemed of little importance. Notwithstanding, God considered mercy, judgment, and love far more important than tithing meticulously and washing pots and cups. If Jesus had selected disciples who practiced details of their law, but overlooked its wieghtier matters, he might have encountered difficulty eradicating their lack of concern for others This he must accomplish if he were to teach his followers to truly become children of their heavenly Father.

Pitfalls that diverted the religious leaders in the days of Jesus still snag churchmen. As Satan convinced lawyers, scribes, and Pharisees that details of religion satisfied God, so Satan has blinded successfully Christian leaders' hearts to the gospel. Love your enemies and friends as you love yourselves. This love when coupled with the desire to do the whole will of our heavenly Father satisfies God. Thereby his children imitate their Father in heaven.

Consider the state of Christianity today. Do details of doctrine weigh more than love for others? Has the Evil father lured us into the same trap which snared religious leaders of Jesus's day? Daniel prophesied of a divided kingdom which must rule nations before the kingdom of God reigns supreme. (Dan.2:36-45) Are Christians now part of that divided kingdom of darkness? Jews who lived when John the Baptist came preaching repentance knew the curses of division. Pharisees believed in angels and the resurrection. Their counter part, the Sadducees, rejected any consideration of either angel or the resurrection. Any Jewish assembly which mentioned either spirit, angel, or resurrection immediately divided the assembly into opposing factions of Pharisees and Sadducees. (Act.23:6-8)

Certain topics today divide Christians. Paul taught that division signifies immaturity and worldliness. (1 Cor.3:3-4) Does Christian division indicate God's or Satan's kingdom? Are we equally carnal and need to correct our outlook toward the teaching of Christ and his kingdom? A genuine problem exists. How can divided Christianity stand against Satan? (Math.12:25-30) Jesus asked if Satan be divided against himself, how could his kingdom stand? If Christians be divided against one another, how shall Christianity prevail over other religions? We need to take a long look at what Paul wrote to the church at Corinth. Placing men above Jesus and his apostles generated their division. (1 Cor.3:3-4) Hope to eliminate Christian antagonism lays in loving God and man, not by elevating men above Jesus whom God anointed as head of the church. (Eph.1:19-23; Col.1:18) Reformers assisted us greatly to restore Christianity, but don't elevate them as kings. God chose Jesus to be head of the church and King of kings. Shall we sever him as head and elevate one of our own choice to replace Jesus?

Luke
7:11 And it came to pass the day after,
that he went into a city called Nain; and
many of his disciples went with him, and
much people. 12 Now when he came nigh
to the gate of the city, behold, there was a
dead man carried out, the only son of his
mother, and she was a widow: and much
people of the city was with her. 13 And
when the Lord saw her, he had com-
passion on her, and said unto her, Weep
not. 14 And he came and touched the bier:
and they that bare him stood still. And he
said, Young man, I say unto thee, Arise. 15
And he that was dead sat up, and began to
speak. And he delivered him to his
mother. 16 And there came a fear on all:
and they glorified God, saying, That a
great prophet is risen up among us; and,
That God hath visited his people. 17 And
this rumour of him went forth throughout
all Judaea, and throughout all the region
round about.

Journeying about twenty miles southwest from Capernaum, Jesus neared Nain as a funeral procession exited the city to bury the only son of a widow of the city. Jesus approached the pallbearers, halting the procession. As the mother and friends grieved over the young man's death, Jesus called him from death and presented him to his mother. Amazed and overjoyed, those who witnessed the event abandoned their burial and published abroad the wonder God manifested before their very eyes.

God's heart sorrows that Satan brought death into this world. God's plan promised eternal life before creation. (Tit.1:2) How can God convince men that death emanates from the Evil One, not God? He commissioned his Son Jesus to demonstrate to mankind that death need not seem natural.

Restoring life to those physically deceased, though marvelous, still leaves one subject to death again. God sent Jesus to earth to prove eternal life remains available to all who choose it. As Jesus returned the widow's son at Nain to physical life, he provides a spiritual resurrection no less spectacular, yet far more rewarding. Eternal life you and I may experience from the day we submit to die to the worldly life with Jesus and rise with him in the new birth associated with baptism. (Rom.6:3-7) No longer driven by customs of this world, we visualize a life, which, though on earth, corresponds to the life God intended for man in creation. This abundant life proves more joyous, more satisfying, more lasting than what those without God ever experience. Trusting God to supply every good offered in life, we submit to his will. (Ps.84:11) God fulfills his promise, giving an inner joy and rejoicing that those of this life fail to perceive. As they search for something to satisfy their fleshly nature, it flees their grasp just when they think they have attained. Ever searching, but always thwarted, their expectations never seem to meet their wants. God testifies that true satisfaction never comes by seeking to satisfy the longings of the flesh alone, but by every word of God. (Deu.8:3; Math.4:4; Lk.4:4) True life and joy comes not from being served; only serving others produces that satisfaction. How often have saints returned from visiting appreciative shut-ins, sick or fatherless only to discover we ourselves benefited more than they whom we visited. Inner satisfaction from service to others, including service to God, is a treasure God awards his children, but he deprives from those who believe him not. As a child attempts to please a parent and receives the parent's love therefrom, so God awards his children his love for submitting to his will. Life! yes, true life, not that spurious flesh-satisfying life Satan and his children herald. That life produces only bondage, want, dissatisfaction, hurt, discontentment, and a grasping for vapor. (Prov. 23:29-35) If God's promise of true life appeals to you, ask God in faith to understand his truth and then willingly obey the words God sent Jesus to explain how to gain eternal life.

Luke

12:1 In the mean time, when there were gathered together an innumerable multitude of people, insomuch that they trode one upon another, he began to say unto his disciples first of all, Beware ye of the leaven of the Pharisees, which is hypocrisy. 2 For there is nothing covered, that shall not be revealed; neither hid, that shall not be known. 3 Therefore whatsoever ye have spoken in darkness shall be heard in the light; and that which ye have spoken in the ear in closets shall be proclaimed upon the housetops. 4 And I say unto you my friends, Be not afraid of them that kill the body, and after that have no more that they can do. 5 But I will forewarn you whom ye shall fear: Fear him, which after he hath killed hath power to cast into hell; yea, I say unto you, Fear him. 6 Are not five sparrows sold for two farthings, and not one of them is forgotten before God? 7 But even the very hairs of your head are all numbered. Fear not therefore: ye are of more value than many sparrows. 8 Also I say unto you, Whosoever shall confess me before men, him shall the Son of man also confess before the angels of God: 9 But he that denieth me before men shall be denied before the angels of God.

In those days many priests believed Jesus fulfilled all the Jewish prophecies and that his miracles proved to them he must be Christ, but influence of those who believed not prevented them from confessing his name before their rulers. Jesus warned that if we refuse to confess him before men, he will not confess our names before his Father and his holy angels. (Math.10:32-33) Unless the priests admitted their belief in Jesus that he is the Christ, promised to Abraham and David, their belief provided them no respect from God. Desiring to please God more than gaining honor from friends divides us from influences of this world. Believing but not confessing is hypocricy.

Luke

12:49 I am come to send fire on the earth; and what will I, if it be already kindled? 50 But I have a baptism to be baptized with; and how am I straitened till it be accomplished! 51 Suppose ye that I am come to give peace on earth? I tell you, Nay; but rather division: 52 For from henceforth there shall be five in one house divided, three against two, and two against three. 53 The father shall be divided against the son, and the son against the father; the mother against the daughter, and the daughter against the mother; the mother in law against her daughter in law, and the daughter in law against her mother in law.

If I am willing to sever relationships on earth to please God, it proves I seek God's approval, not man's. Parents, brothers, sisters, children, friends, or neighbors who trust in this life's rewards employ every art to persuade those who would turn to God not to obey him. If we persist in listening to God's call to obey him, those who attempt to dissuade us find offense and often turn to become our enemies. Thus, resolution to return to God divides families and erects intense barriers of conflict. Jesus described this as igniting a fire on earth, burning paths which might return us to full fellowship with former patterns of society. Being unwilling to take this step to please God, we admit to ourselves and to God that retaining praises of men controls our lives. God will not accept nor reward such a choice. Either we serve God with all our hearts, or we serve him not. We must decide which we value more. Is it God who offers all or man who offers little?

Gospels record how some in the Iscariot family turned to Jesus, but others steadfastly stood with the Pharisees and rulers. This may have been a door which Satan used to influence Judas to betray Jesus. (See pp. 256-257.) Satan uses strong family ties to persuade some not to obey God.

Matthew

8:23 And when he was entered into a ship, his disciples followed him. 24 And, behold, there arose a great tempest in the sea, insomuch that the ship was covered with the waves: but he was asleep. 25 And his disciples came to him, and awoke him, saying, Lord, save us: we perish. 26 And he saith unto them, Why are ye fearful, O ye of little faith? Then he arose, and rebuked the winds and the sea; and there was a great calm. 27 But the men marvelled, saying, What manner of man is this, that even the winds and the sea obey him!

Those who have witnessed the lashing fierce winds and mountainous waves of a roily sea know fear, especially if they're in a small boat as were Jesus and his disciples. They beheld the winds whip a calm lake into raging waves which swamped their boat. Their fear mounted. Jesus seemed their only hope of survival. They awakened him suddenly, expressing their fear. Their lack of faith, not the storm, concerned Jesus. Didn't they believe he possessed all power from God? Had he not restored limbs and life? Surely they knew he could conquer this roily sea and save them from drowning. Look to God for help in all your distresses! He lends help if we ask.

Mark

4:35 And the same day, when the even was come, he saith unto them, Let us pass over unto the other side. 36 And when they had sent away the multitude, they took him even as he was in the ship. And there were also with him other little ships. 37 And there arose a great storm of wind, and the waves beat into the ship, so that it was now full. 38 And he was in the hinder part of the ship, asleep on a pillow: and they awake him, and say unto him, Master, carest thou not that we perish? 39 And he arose, and rebuked the wind, and said unto the sea, Peace, be still. And the wind ceased, and there was a great calm. 40 And he said unto them, Why are ye so fearful? how is it that ye have no faith? 41 And they feared exceedingly, and said one to another, What manner of man is this, that even the wind and the sea obey him?

Jesus demonstrated God's power to control nature, governments, and individuals. He allows each person the right of choice to serve God or self, but chastens disobedience, hoping we will submit to God and come to understand the love of God which passes understanding. Obeying God rewards us now and in the hereafter.

Luke

8:22 Now it came to pass on a certain day, that he went into a ship with his disciples: and he said unto them, Let us go over unto the other side of the lake. And they launched forth. 23 But as they sailed he fell asleep: and there came down a storm of wind on the lake; and they were filled with water, and were in jeopardy. 24 And they came to him, and awoke him, saying, Master, master, we perish. Then he arose, and rebuked the wind and the raging of the water: and they ceased, and there was a calm. 25 And he said unto them, Where is your faith? And they being afraid wondered, saying one to another, What manner of man is this! for he commandeth even the winds and water, and they obey him.

People desire a king they trust to deliver them from difficulties. This narrative illustrates Jesus' power to deliver. He needed only to speak, and forces of nature obeyed. Gospels record evidences of Jesus' power to control every aspect of creation. Only man possesses the opportunity to serve or disobey God. King Jesus remains faithful to deliver from the great oppressor, Satan, if we obey him. Animate and inanimate creation obeyed Jesus.

How are we to consider nature's wrath? Does God control storms or are they so powerful they're beyond control? Restated, the question asks does God's hand determine what's destroyed or spared and who suffers or escapes nature's ravages? As the disciples witnessed winds lash the sea of Galilee into mountainous, engulfing waves, their eyes focused on danger, not on God's care. Water swamped their boat. Their drowning seemed eminent. Could Jesus deliver them from this crisis? Did he care? Rushing to Jesus, they wakened him, asking, **"Master, carest thou not that we perish?"**

Does God care about our plights? If he cares, why does he allow us to suffer loss of property and life in storms and earthquakes? Does God bring massive destruction and death to help us see we need God's help? In the daily activities of life we tend to lose sight of God and go on as if we don't need him. Does God bring life's crises to sober us, to help us realize that without God's help we find no mercy from ravages of disease, storms, earthquakes, etc.?

Lack of faith in God and Jesus precipitated Jesus' rebuke to the disciples after he calmed the boisterous wind and churning sea. Failure to think on God's power and mercy prompted them to look on what they could see with the physical eye. The carnal or immature look on the visible, not the eternal things of God. **"While we look not at the things which are seen, but at the things which are not seen: for the things which are seen are temporal; but the things which are not seen are eternal."** (2 Cor.4:18) **"(For we walk by faith, not by sight:)"** (2 Cor.5:7) **"Yea, though I walk through the valley of the shadow of death, I will fear no evil: for thou art with me; thy rod and thy staff they comfort me."** (Ps.23:4) **"I say unto you my friends, Be not afraid of them that kill the body, and after that have no more that they can do. But I will forewarn you whom ye shall fear: Fear him, which after he hath killed hath power to cast into hell; yea I say unto you, Fear him."** (Lk.12:4-5) **"Hearken unto me, ye that know righteousness, the people in whose heart is my law; fear ye not the reproach of men, neither be ye afraid of their revilings. For the moth shall eat them up like a garment, and the worm shall eat them like wool: but my righteousness shall be for ever, and my salvation from generation to generation....I, even I, am he that comforteth you: who art thou, that thou shouldest be afraid of man that shall die, and of the son of man which shall be made as grass; And forgettest the Lord thy maker, that hath stretched forth the heavens, and laid the foundations of the earth; and hast feared continually every day because of the fury of the oppressor, as if he were ready to destroy? and where is the fury of the oppressor?"** (Is.51:7-8,12-13)

Jesus responded as God. **"Where is your faith?"** If you trust God, does it really matter whether you lose property or life? Are they not only temporary? If God guides us to submit to him by faith, he will supply our needs on earth and bring us to himself in heaven when our life here ceases. Yes, God controls and utilizes disasters to humble us before him and to regard his constant care and guidance. (Lev.26:14-39)

Why does God provide refuge from man and nature to his faithful, but often withholds it from sinners? David noted that children of faith dwell in the secret place of God, and his truth shields them from evil. (Ps.91:1-4) Without abiding in Jesus' and God's commands which Jesus taught, God casts aside unbelievers for destruction. (Jno.15:1-7) Honoring others as you wish others would deal with you obeys God and befriends man. The faithful no longer maintains his life is his own to do with it as he pleases. (Ps.12:4; 1 Cor.1:19-20) Yes, Jesus encouraged disciples to trust God's way on land, in sea, in cities, among friends or enemies, when famine threatens, or war prevails.

Viewpoints

Matthew

8:28 And when he was come to the other side into the country of the Gergesenes, there met him two possessed with devils, coming out of the tombs, exceeding fierce, so that no man might pass by that way. 29 And, behold, they cried out, saying, What have we to do with thee, Jesus, thou Son of God? art thou come hither to torment us before the time? 30 And there was a good way off from them an herd of many swine feeding. 31 So the devils besought him, saying, If thou cast us out, suffer us to go away into the herd of swine. 32 And he said unto them, Go. And when they were come out, they went into the herd of swine: and, behold, the whole herd of swine ran violently down a steep place into the sea, and perished in the waters. 33 And they that kept them fled, and went their ways into the city, and told every thing, and what was befallen to the possessed of the devils. 34 And, behold, the whole city came out to meet Jesus: and when they saw him, they besought him that he would depart out of their coasts.

Satan introduces misery into the lives of people. God sent Jesus to destroy Satan's work and to return peace to people's lives. (1 Jno.3:8; Jno.14:33) These two demon-possessed men must have been lonely and miserable, dwelling among the dead. Others had tried to improve their lives. Even swine fared better than the demon-possessed.

As Jesus neared, the demons asked if he came to torment them before the appointed time. To end Satan's control of these lives, Jesus commanded the demons to leave the men. As they did, they entered the swine and drove them to perish in the sea. Those who had been demon-possessed now rested peacefully, clothed, sane, and relieved. This incident dramatizes how Satan burdens lives, but Christ restores peace.

Others, aware of their financial loss and power of Jesus, asked him to leave. Fear of God and amazed by the change he produced induced many to shy away from God. After they observed beneficial changes in the men's lives, they willingly received Jesus when he returned. God produces wonderful improvements in all lives if we receive him and his Son Jesus and obey God's truth.

Backgrounds of the writers appear vividly here. Matthew and Mark referred to the sea of Galilee, but Luke called it a lake. Matthew and Mark referred to the boat as a ship, but Luke named it a boat. They also called the area by different names. Each writer employed terms common to his culture to encourage his audience to submit to Jesus as God's only begotten Son as savior.

Mark

5:1 And they came over unto the other side of the sea, into the country of the Gadarenes. 2 And when he was come out of the ship, immediately there met him out of the tombs a man with an unclean spirit, 3 Who had his dwelling among the tombs; and no man could bind him, no, not with chains: 4 Because that he had been often bound with fetters and chains, and the chains had been plucked asunder by him, and the fetters broken in pieces: neither could any man tame him. 5 And always, night and day, he was in the mountains, and in the tombs, crying, and cutting himself with stones. 6 But when he saw Jesus afar off, he ran and worshipped him, 7 And cried with a loud voice, and said, What have I to do with thee, Jesus, thou Son of the most high God? I adjure thee by God, that thou torment me not. 8 For he said unto him, Come out of the man, thou unclean spirit. 9 And he asked him, What is thy name? And he answered, saying, My name is Legion: for we are many. 10 And he besought him much that he would not send them away out of the country. 11 Now there was there nigh unto the mountains a great herd of swine feeding. 12 And all the devils besought him, saying, Send us into the swine, that we may enter into them. 13 And forthwith Jesus gave them leave. And the unclean spirits went out, and entered into the swine: and the herd ran violently down a steep place into the sea, (they were about two thousand;) and were choked in the sea. 14 And they that fed the swine fled, and told it in the city, and in the country. And they went out to see what it was that was done. 15 And they come to Jesus, and see him that was possessed with the devil, and had the legion, sitting, and clothed, and in his right mind: and they were afraid. 16 And they that saw it told them how it befell to him that was possessed with the devil, and also concerning the swine. 17 And they began to pray him to depart out of their coasts. 18 And when he was come into the ship, he that had been possessed with the devil prayed him that he might be with him. 19 Howbeit Jesus suffered him not, but saith unto him, Go home to thy friends, and tell them how great things the Lord hath done for thee, and hath had compassion on thee. 20 And he departed, and began to publish in Decapolis how great things Jesus had done for him: and all men did marvel.

Jesus relieved the demon-possessed, but deprived Gadarenes of their property. Was this a wise choice?

Luke

8:26 And they arrived at the country of
the Gadarenes, which is over against
Galilee. 27 And when he went forth to
land, there met him out of the city a
certain man, which had devils long time,
and ware no clothes, neither abode in any
house, but in the tombs. 28 When he saw
Jesus, he cried out, and fell down before
him, and with a loud voice said, What
have I to do with thee, Jesus, thou Son of
God most high? I beseech thee, torment
me not. 29 (For he had commanded the
unclean spirit to come out of the man. For
oftentimes it had caught him: and he was
kept bound with chains and in fetters; and
he brake the bands, and was driven of the
devil into the wilderness.) 30 And Jesus
asked him, saying, What is thy name?
And he said, Legion: because many devils
were entered into him. 31 And they
besought him that he would not command
them to go out into the deep. 32 And there
was there an herd of many swine feeding
on the mountain: and they besought him
that he would suffer them to enter into
them. And he suffered them. 33 Then
went the devils out of the man, and
entered into the swine: and the herd ran
violently down a steep place into the lake,
and were choked. 34 When they that fed
them saw what was done, they fled, and
went and told it in the city and in the
country. 35 Then they went out to see
what was done; and came to Jesus, and
found the man, out of whom the devils
were departed, sitting at the feet of Jesus,
clothed, and in his right mind: and they
were afraid. 36 They also which saw it
told them by what means he that was
possessed of the devils was healed. 37
Then the whole multitude of the country
of the Gadarenes round about besought
him to depart from them; for they were
taken with great fear: and he went up into
the ship, and returned back again. 38 Now
the man out of whom the devils were
departed besought him that he might be
with him: but Jesus sent him away,
saying, 39 Return to thine own house, and
shew how great things God hath done
unto thee. And he went his way, and
published throughout the whole city how
great things Jesus had done unto him. 40
And it came to pass, that, when Jesus was
returned, the people gladly received him:
for they were all waiting for him.

While Satan dominated these two men, they avoided people. After Satan departed, they wanted to stay with Jesus. When the bystanders recognized what God did, they wanted Jesus to come again. When we know God, we want to be near him.

Consider how Mark and Luke called Jesus the Son of the most high God. (Mk.5:7; Lk.8:28) Gentiles who recognized many gods commonly used "the most high God" to refer to the Creator, suggesting Mark and Luke addressed Gentiles. (Dan.3:26;4:2, 34;6:26) Writer's subtle comments become indicators of both the author's and their audiences' backgrounds.

Can God and Jesus drive Satan out of our lives today? If you contend Satan doesn't control men's lives today, perhaps you haven't considered how those usually calm and well-adjusted suddenly commit violent crimes. Why? and why are any of us driven to deprive others of courtesies, property, respect, etc. Jesus informed his people that whosoever commits sin becomes a servant of sin and demonstrates they recognize Satan as their father. (Jno.8:34,44) They who do the will of God as Jesus taught discover the only means to prevent Satan from driving them to commit sins against God and man. Unless husbands, wives, children, neighbors, nations, and the world turns to God through Christ, social structure deteriorates until it collapses. Are we destroying ourselves today by our abandoning Jesus, God's truth, and the basic principle of doing to others as we wish to be treated? (Math.7:12) Do Satan's or God's rules influence our actions?

Matthew

9:1 And he entered into a ship, and passed over, and came into his own city. 2 And, behold, they brought to him a man sick of the palsy, lying on a bed: and Jesus seeing their faith said unto the sick of the palsy; Son, be of good cheer; thy sins be forgiven thee. 3 And, behold, certain of the scribes said within themselves, This man blasphemeth. 4 And Jesus knowing their thoughts said, Wherefore think ye evil in your hearts? 5 For whether is easier, to say, Thy sins be forgiven thee; or to say, Arise, and walk? 6 But that ye may know that the Son of man hath power on earth to forgive sins, (then saith he to the sick of the palsy,) Arise, take up thy bed, and go unto thine house. 7 And he arose, and departed to his house. 8 But when the multitudes saw it, they marvelled, and glorified God, which had given such power unto men.

Four attitudes manifest themselves in this narrative. 1. Those who brought the palsied man to Jesus showed their faith in his power to heal. 2. Jesus knew God granted him authority to forgive sins. 3. Scribes and Pharisees regarded Jesus a blasphemer because he claimed power to forgive sins. 4. Multitude praised God who gave Jesus authority to show wonders and help men.

Who benefited from this encounter? Those who brought the palsied man realized their hope of helping their friend. Jesus glorified God. Common people believed in and honored God and Jesus. Pharisees and scribes, charging Jesus with blasphemy, gained no benefit because they refused to reevaluate their view of forgiveness of sin. Today people short-change themselves by how they regard others. Feeling threatened and defensive, we may deny ourselves uplifting associations with family members, friends, neighbors, etc. Viewing others as gifted by God's grace to enrich our lives, there remains no place for insecurity and defensiveness.

Mark

2:1 And again he entered into Capernaum, after some days; and it was noised that he was in the house. 2 And straightway many were gathered together, insomuch that there was no room to receive them, no, not so much as about the door: and he preached the word unto them. 3 And they come unto him, bringing one sick of the palsy, which was borne of four. 4 And when they could not come nigh unto him for the press, they uncovered the roof where he was: and when they had broken it up, they let down the bed wherein the sick of the palsy lay. 5 When Jesus saw their faith, he said unto the sick of the palsy, Son, thy sins be forgiven thee. 6 But there were certain of the scribes sitting there, and reasoning in their hearts, 7 Why doth this man thus speak blasphemies? who can forgive sins but God only? 8 And immediately when Jesus perceived in his spirit that they so reasoned within themselves, he said unto them, Why reason ye these things in your hearts? 9 Whether is it easier to say to the sick of the palsy, Thy sins be forgiven thee; or to say, Arise, and take up thy bed, and walk? 10 But that ye may know that the Son of man hath power on earth to forgive sins, (he saith to the sick of the palsy,) 11 I say unto thee, Arise, and take up thy bed, and go thy way into thine house. 12 And immediately he arose, took up the bed, and went forth before them all; insomuch that they were all amazed, and glorified God, saying, We never saw it on this fashion.

How would you feel if a preacher spoke to you in public and called you a sinner? This man showed no embarrassment. He rejoiced because he now walked and believed Jesus had forgiven his sins. When we cease trying to defend ourselves and admit our sins, God blesses our lives. Pride prevents us from coming to God for his blessings. Those who come to God must humble themselves.

Luke

**5:16 And he withdrew himself into the
wilderness, and prayed. 17 And it came to
pass on a certain day, as he was teaching,
that there were Pharisees and doctors of
the law sitting by, which were come out of
every town of Galilee, and Judaea, and
Jerusalem: and the power of the Lord was
present to heal them. 18 And, behold, men
brought in a bed a man which was taken
with a palsy: and they sought means to
bring him in, and to lay him before him.
19 And when they could not find by what
way they might bring him in because of
the multitude, they went upon the
housetop, and let him down through the
tiling with his couch into the midst before
Jesus. 20 And when he saw their faith, he
said unto him, Man, thy sins are forgiven
thee. 21 And the scribes and the Pharisees
began to reason, saying, Who is this which
speaketh blasphemies? Who can forgive
sins, but God alone? 22 But when Jesus
perceived their thoughts, he answering
said unto them, What reason ye in your
hearts? 23 Whether is easier, to say, Thy
sins be forgiven thee; or to say, Rise up
and walk? 24 But that ye may know that
the Son of man hath power upon earth to
forgive sins, (he said unto the sick of the
palsy,) I say unto thee, Arise, and take up
thy couch, and go into thine house. 25 And
immediately he rose up before them, and
took up that whereon he lay, and
departed to his own house, glorifying
God. 26 And they were all amazed, and
they glorified God, and were filled with
fear, saying, We have seen strange things
to day.**

God chose Jesus to be king over God's kingdom. He empowered him with his Spirit and limitless authority. Gospels explain how Jesus performed miracles which astounded those who witnessed them. His miracles benefited men and demonstrated the power God granted to the son of David whom God chose to reign on David's throne. Not one person ever called on Jesus for relief but what Jesus proved himself capable to fulfill the request. He didn't attribute his miracles to his own ability, but thanked his Father for what he empowered him to accomplish. He and God worked together to convince men that God cared for the ills that befall us. As Jesus explained, disobedience to the Father results in body ailments, sorrow of heart, and separation from God.

Gospel translated means good news. What story among men captures a more intense interest than that God cares for his children even when we have defied his right to instruct us in proper paths of life? Men tell fairy tales to show how wonders beyond the power of men have delivered people from situations they knew not how to manage. Perhaps man's tales are patterned after stories they have heard of how God has helped men. In the gospels, God recorded amazing wonders to convince us that God is, that he cares for our hurts, and that he provides a complete system whereby we may be delivered from the power of the Evil One who traps us by all sorts of things which appeal to our fleshly nature. God tells us that submitting to every truth of God empowers us to escape the toils and sorrows which befall us. His precepts allow us to enjoy a peace on earth not known to God's defiant children. God elevates us to reign as kings on earth. Our lordship authorizes us to subdue our own bodies. God frees our spirit from subjection to desires of the flesh which have beguiled our consciences and subjected us to the power of Satan. Now our spirit enslaves the body. We live with clean consciences. In addition, God promises life beyond the grave in which faithful children of God dwell as angels with God, Jesus, all God's prophets, and the redeemed of all ages. If God's promise appeals to you, obey him and experience the wonders God can perform in your life. If you haven't submitted to God with all your heart, you miss a great part of life.

Matthew

9:9 And as Jesus passed forth from thence, he saw a man, named Matthew, sitting at the receipt of custom: and he saith unto him, Follow me. And he arose, and followed him. 10 And it came to pass, as Jesus sat at meat in the house, behold, many publicans and sinners came and sat down with him and his disciples. 11 And when the Pharisees saw it, they said unto his disciples, Why eateth your Master with publicans and sinners? 12 But when Jesus heard that, he said unto them, They that be whole need not a physician, but they that are sick. 13 But go ye and learn what that meaneth, I will have mercy, and not sacrifice: for I am not come to call the righteous, but sinners to repentance.

Satan has mastered the art of dividing mankind; whereas God offers to heal differences. Here scribes and Pharisees disdain publicans and sinners. Jesus shows mercy, but scribes and Pharisees show contempt. How can any Jew condescend to respect one who gathers taxes for Rome?

God sent Jesus to show us all Satan's deceptions. Who among us remains guiltless? If I look down on a tax collector, what deed of mine prompts another to despise me?

Mark

2:13 And he went forth again by the sea side; and all the multitude resorted unto him, and he taught them. 14 And as he passed by, he saw Levi the son of Alphaeus sitting at the receipt of custom, and said unto him, Follow me. And he arose and followed him. 15 And it came to pass, that, as Jesus sat at meat in his house, many publicans and sinners sat also together with Jesus and his disciples: for there were many, and they followed him. 16 And when the scribes and Pharisees saw him eat with publicans and sinners, they said unto his disciples, How is it that he eateth and drinketh with publicans and sinners? 17 When Jesus heard it, he saith unto them, They that are whole have no need of the physician, but they that are sick: I came not to call the righteous, but sinners to repentance.

Matthew stated the issue more succinctly. God desires mercy, not sacrifice. Does mercy heal broken bonds of friendship? or is contempt the refresher? If I frown on others' offenses, does that make friends? No, all of us discern that forgiveness abolishes faults. Satan encourages us to maintain dignity and an air of superiority. We must appear wise and great in men's eyes.

Luke

5:27 And after these things he went forth, and saw a publican, named Levi, sitting at the receipt of custom: and he said unto him, Follow me. 28 And he left all, rose up, and followed him. 29 And Levi made him a great feast in his own house: and there was a great company of publicans and of others that sat down with them. 30 But their scribes and Pharisees murmured against his disciples, saying, Why do ye eat and drink with publicans and sinners? 31 And Jesus answering said unto them, They that are whole need not a physician; but they that are sick. 32 I came not to call the righteous, but sinners to repentance.

Our heavenly Father sent Jesus to show humility toward others. It shatters self-righteousness which hinders friendship.

Matthew or Levi as Luke and Mark called him performed a task essential to any government. Without taxes no nation performs services. Law and order gives way to anarchy, and social structures collapse. Were scribes and Pharisees willing to sacrifice the secure society Rome provided them? Were they considering the alternative? About thirty-five years later this proud Jewish attitude led them to rebel against Rome.

Matthew's invitation to follow Jesus refers to Hosea's prophecy, missing in Mark's and Luke's records, **"I will have mercy, and not sacrifice."** (Ho.6:6) What did God mean, and why did Mark and Luke omit this message? Jewish scribes and Pharisees interpreted God's instruction legally and regarded compassion or mercy as a least commandment. (Math.5:19) They failed to learn God's view of mercy, but regarded sacrifice of major significance in showing devotion to God. When scribes and Pharisees scowled at Jesus' eating with publicans and sinners, Jesus remarked they needed to learn God's view of mercy and sacrifice. (Math.12:7;23:23) All of us desire mercy for our faults. If I want mercy, show mercy. This fulfills God's law and prophets. (Math.7:12) Pharisee criticism of Jesus' eating with publicans and sinners, in effect, chided Jesus' choice of Matthew as an apostle. Why do you pick a hated publican rather than a scribe or Pharisee? Not only did Jesus' preference for a publican rile their resentment, it rebuffed their whole religious outlook. Their pride of righteousness Jesus disregarded as vain in God's eyes.

Consider Jesus' calling of Matthew as when children choose players for a game. Each person present hopes to be chosen. As captains choose, they usually pick first the ones they believe most capable of playing the game to win. The last chosen often feel inferior to the first chosen and may resent how the captain chose his team. Those remaining unchosen feel slighted. They harbor jealousy and anger, often saying to themselves, "I'm as good or a better player than certain ones chosen." Scribes and Pharisees remained after Jesus selected his team. They reacted as children rejected. Chiding Jesus by asking why he ate with publicans and sinners, they, in effect, let Jesus know they believed they were better candidates as teachers of God's kingdom.

All three synoptic gospels record Jesus' response to Pharisee and scribe taunting. Only the sick seek a physician. Those who feel well ask no help from a doctor. Transferring this parable into spiritual setting, Jesus meant those who believe they enjoy spiritual pertness seek not God, but those whose consciences smart for sin, look to God for mercy to gain forgiveness, and a cleansed conscience.

What did Matthew, Mark, and Luke see in their audiences that persuaded them to record this event? Did Matthew perceive his Jewish audience as viewing Jesus as a spiritual physician? Rulers thought they did not need him. They identified no spiritual blemish in themselves, but others admitted to themselves Satan's wiles infected them. Mark's Roman audience and Luke's Syrian audience, like you and me today, perceived they needed or didn't need God in their lives. It's not just now that we need God. If we gain great wealth and honor, but prepare not to meet God in judgment, what will we do when God casts us with Satan in eternity? Will we plead innocence because our parents failed to teach us about God? Denying God today will not change God's sentence. We either prepare to face God now or face him with embarrassment later.

God provides us with but one life to determine our eternal destiny. Hastening through life without preparing for hereafter resembles squandering income in youth and living in poverty in old age when physical strength and perhaps health suffer us not to earn our support. Such a decision one regrets in old age, but eternity seems a very long time to regret having never laid up treasure in heaven.

All four gospels present their audiences with making a clear choice. Will I serve self now and accept God's wrath later, or will I obey his Son now and gladly anticipate dwelling with God and Christ?

God directed gospel writers to record the truth about his Son. Are we convinced Jesus manifested God and his merciful love for all his children whom Satan binds in sin?

Luke

15:1 Then drew near unto him all the
publicans and sinners for to hear him. 2
And the Pharisees and scribes murmured,
saying, This man receiveth sinners, and
eateth with them. 3 And he spake this
parable unto them, saying, 4 What man of
you, having an hundred sheep, if he lose
one of them, doth not leave the ninety and
nine in the wilderness, and go after that
which is lost, until he find it? 5 And when
he hath found it, he layeth it on his
shoulders, rejoicing. 6 And when he
cometh home, he calleth together his
friends and neighbours, saying unto them,
Rejoice with me; for I have found my
sheep which was lost. 7 I say unto you,
that likewise joy shall be in heaven over
one sinner that repenteth, more than over
ninety and nine just persons, which need
no repentance. 8 Either what woman
having ten pieces of silver, if she lose one
piece, doth not light a candle, and sweep
the house, and seek diligently till she find
it? 9 And when she hath found it, she
calleth her friends and her neighbours
together, saying, Rejoice with me; for I
have found the piece which I had lost. 10
Likewise, I say unto you, there is joy in
the presence of the angels of God over one
sinner that repenteth. 11 And he said, A
certain man had two sons: 12 And the
younger of them said to his father, Father,
give me the portion of goods that falleth to
me. And he divided unto them his living.
13 And not many days after the younger
son gathered all together, and took his
journey into a far country, and there
wasted his substance with riotous living.
14 And when he had spent all, there arose
a mighty famine in that land; and he
began to be in want. 15 And he went and
joined himself to a citizen of that country;
and he sent him into his fields to feed
swine. 16 And he would fain have filled
his belly with the husks that the swine did
eat: and no man gave unto him. 17 And
when he came to himself, he said, How
many hired servants of my father's have
bread enough and to spare, and I perish
with hunger! 18 I will arise and go to my
father, and will say unto him, Father, I
have sinned against heaven, and before
thee, 19 And am no more worthy to be
called thy son: make me as one of thy
hired servants. 20 And he arose, and came
to his father. But when he was yet a great
way off, his father saw him, and had
compassion, and ran, and fell on his neck,
and kissed him. 21 And the son said unto
him, Father, I have sinned against heaven,
and in thy sight, and am no more worthy
to be called thy son. 22 But the father said
to his servants, Bring forth the best robe,
and put it on him; and put a ring on his
hand, and shoes on his feet: 23 And bring
hither the fatted calf, and kill it; and let us
eat, and be merry: 24 For this my son was
dead, and is alive again; he was lost, and
is found. And they began to be merry. 25
Now his elder son was in the field: and as
he came and drew nigh to the house, he
heard musick and dancing. 26 And he
called one of the servants, and asked what
these things meant. 27 And he said unto
him, Thy brother is come; and thy father
hath killed the fatted calf, because he hath
received him safe and sound. 28 And he
was angry, and would not go in: therefore
came his father out, and intreated him. 29
And he answering said to his father, Lo,
these many years do I serve thee, neither
transgressed I at any time thy commandment: and yet thou never gavest me a kid,
that I might make merry with my friends:
30 But as soon as this thy son was come,
which hath devoured thy living with
harlots, thou hast killed for him the fatted
calf. 31 And he said unto him, Son, thou
art ever with me, and all that I have is
thine. 32 It was meet that we should make
merry, and be glad: for this thy brother
was dead, and is alive again; and was lost,
and is found.

Luke introduced his gospel by quoting Malachi's prophecy, showing how John should turn the hearts of the fathers to their sons and the son's hearts to their fathers. Luke recorded an incident missing from other gospels, illustrating this point. When Jesus called Matthew, Jesus accepted Matthew's invitation to dine with him. Pharisees and scribes murmured because Jesus entered in to eat with a publican. To show his ad-versaries that God came to call sinners to re-pentance, Jesus taught parables of lost sheep and coins and how their owners rejoiced when they found that which they lost. He further illustrated that God rejoices when sinners repent by narrating the story of the father of two sons. The younger son portrayed publicans and sinners who departed from God, but the elder son who remained at home depicted scribes and Pharisees who contended they served God faithfully. When the younger son spent all his inheritance and realized how even his father's servants fared superior to him when he lived in want, he repented and determined to return to his father and confess his sins. Maybe his father would accept him as a hired servant. Having so resolved, the younger son returned home. As he neared, his father saw him coming and ran to embrace him. Being overjoyed, the father commanded his servants to fetch the best robe to clothe his lost son, kill the fatted calf, and prepare a great feast. After the festivities commenced, the elder son returned from the field and heard the music and excitement. He inquired of a servant what prompted all this rejoicing. When the servant informed him that his brother had returned, and his father had clothed him in the best robe and prepared this great party, his anger flamed, and he refused to join the festivities. When the father understood the older son balked at joining the father's feast for his lost son, he went to his son and explained how the feast expressed the father's great joy that his lost son returned home. You, too, should rejoice. Instead the elder son expressed his resentment that his father expended all this time and money to honor his son who had not only rejected his lifestyle but also wasted his living with sinners and harlots. Furthermore, I have remained home and served you as a faithful son, but you gave me not even a kid with which I might rejoice with my friends. Yet, when this rebellious son of yours returned home, you kill the fatted calf for him and celebrate his return. Though the father tried to console his elder son, his mind remained adamant. Bitterness vanquished love.

The younger son portrayed publicans and sinners whom scribes and Pharisees disdained. In their minds Pharisees served God faithfully, but publicans and sinners abandoned God. Now Jesus came receiving these transgressors and fellowshipping with them. Incised by Jesus' receiving publicans and sinners, scribes and Pharisees refused to participate in God's heavenly feast Jesus taught. Though Jesus explained how grateful they should be that their Jewish brethren repented and returned to God, they showed no concern for the spiritual welfare of their brethren.

Consider how Luke's use of this incident adds to Luke's theme that God sent John and Jesus to reconcile fathers to sons and sons to their fathers. The father of the two sons longed for both of his sons. He hoped to provide each of them with the best he had to offer. Notwithstanding, both sons' minds alienated toward their father. Even before the younger son returned, the older son chafed at how his father provided him nothing for him and his friends. Not until people reflect on how gracious God blesses us do our hearts desire to thank and honor our heavenly Father.

Are our thoughts toward our heavenly Father similar to the repentant younger son or as the elder son whose anger continued to flame against his father? Do we rejoice when sinners repent, or are we jealous like the Pharisees? Do we love God and man?

Matthew

9:14 Then came to him the disciples of John, saying, Why do we and the Pharisees fast oft, but thy disciples fast not? 15 And Jesus said unto them, Can the children of the bridechamber mourn, as long as the bridegroom is with them? but the days will come, when the bridegroom shall be taken from them, and then shall they fast. 16 No man putteth a piece of new cloth unto an old garment, for that which is put in to fill it up taketh from the garment, and the rent is made worse. 17 Neither do men put new wine into old bottles: else the bottles break, and the wine runneth out, and the bottles perish: but they put new wine into new bottles, and both are preserved.

Following tradition hinders improvement. Pharisees' and John the Baptist's disciples followed the custom of fasting, not so much for sorrow as for tradition. When they understood that Jesus and his disciples didn't keep their custom, they inquired why. Children do not fast when all the family gathers at home. Times of sadness or distress prompts one to fast. During times of joy one ought not fast. This explanation Jesus provided to explain proper times for fasting to honor God and draw near to him.

Mark

2:18 And the disciples of John and of the Pharisees used to fast: and they come and say unto him, Why do the disciples of John and of the Pharisees fast, but thy disciples fast not? 19 And Jesus said unto them, Can the children of the bridechamber fast, while the bridegroom is with them? as long as they have the bridegroom with them, they cannot fast. 20 But the days will come, when the bridegroom shall be taken away from them, and then shall they fast in those days. 21 No man also seweth a piece of new cloth on an old garment: else the new piece that filled it up taketh away from the old, and the rent is made worse. 22 And no man putteth new wine into old bottles: else the new wine doth burst the bottles, and the wine is spilled, and the bottles will be marred: but new wine must be put into new bottles.

Sadness or crises prompts people to fast. While I'm with my disciples they have no reason to fast. When I'm taken from them, they will have cause to fast.

What reasons might Pharisees give for fasting? In the Sermon on the Mount, Jesus suggested they fasted to appear righteous to men. Such fasts God hates. It's hypocrisy, feigning piety. God seeks true actions.

Luke

5:33 And they said unto him, Why do the disciples of John fast often, and make prayers, and likewise the disciples of the Pharisees; but thine eat and drink? 34 And he said unto them, Can ye make the children of the bridechamber fast, while the bridegroom is with them? 35 But the days will come, when the bridegroom shall be taken away from them, and then shall they fast in those days. 36 And he spake also a parable unto them; No man putteth a piece of a new garment upon an old; if otherwise, then both the new maketh a rent, and the piece that was taken out of the new agreeth not with the old. 37 And no man putteth new wine into old bottles; else the new wine will burst the bottles, and be spilled, and the bottles shall perish. 38 But new wine must be put into new bottles; and both are preserved. 39 No man also having drunk old wine straightway desireth new: for he saith, The old is better.

Those seeking to please God let their fasts for grief appear only to their Father in heaven. If their hearts bow to the Father's will, he looks on with pleasure, but he regards no fast which seeks man's honor. Isaiah identified perfect fasting. (Is.58)

Since many Christians fast in service to God, we should consider God's view of fasting that we might truly honor him if we choose to fast. In the Sermon on the Mount, Jesus contrasted a fast to impress man with one to honor God. If we fast to show men our righteousness, God regards it hypocrisy. Such a fast dishonors God. (Math.6:16-18) If we fast to please God, let not others observe our fasting.

In Isaiah's days Jews fasted unacceptably before God who explained why he disregarded their fasts. When Jews asked why God disregarded their fasts, he replied that their actions negated any benefits from God. They fasted, pleasing themselves, not God. In addition, they fasted for strife and debate, and fought with others. If you seek God's attention by fasting, you must change your association with those about you. Moses taught you to love your neighbors as you love yourself. If someone transgresses against you, rebuke him and not allow sin to abide on one another. I'm showing you how to be holy, for I am holy. (Lev.19:2,17-18) Don't hate and revenge yourself when wronged. Straighten out your differences before bitterness and hate cloud your life and the one who mistreated you.

Disregarding Moses' instruction, Jews in Isaiah's days manifested an attitude similar to that of Pharisees in Jesus' day. They believed how they interacted with others had no effect on their devotion to God. If they offered sacrifices for their sins and fasted, they believed God forgave their offenses to others. God spoke through Isaiah to correct their view. God chose not sacrifice, but mercy as the way to honor God. (Ho.6:6) The fast God observes looses the bands of wickedness, undoes heavy burdens, frees the oppressed, and breaks every yoke. Distribute bread to the hungry; bring the poor to your house, clothe the naked, hide not yourself from either friend or family when they need. If you will show compassion on the downtrodden, light will break forth as at sunrise or noon time; your health shall speedily improve; your righteousness shall precede you, and God shall speedily hear your prayers, and regard your fasts. He shall guide you continually, and fatten your bones. You shall be called a repairer of the breaches, a restorer of the ancient paths. If you abandon using the Sabbath and holy days to do your pleasure and delight in God's holy days, not speaking your words to replace God's and delight in God, rather than acting as if it is burdensome to serve God (Mal.1:12-13), then he will elevate and feed you with the heritage of your father Jacob. (Is.58:2-14)

Christians need to look within ourselves. Has our oppression and lack of compassion on others turned God's ear from hearing our prayers and caused him to disregard our fasts? Do our practices of using God's holy days to do what pleases us draw sin's gloom over our lives? Are we allowing transgression to go unresolved to abscess and putrefy our relationships with family members and associates? Is it drudgery to keep the Lord's day, to study his word, to approach God in prayer, to praise God in song in the assembly where Jesus assembles to lift his voice also in praise to his and our heavenly Father (Ps.22:22; Heb.2:11-12), and to remember the death of God's only begotten Son who purged our sins by his life's blood? (1 Cor.11:17-31; Heb.1:2-3) Have we developed an attitude that sacrifice will cover a multitude of wrongs to others, and that we let the poor suffer in the situation they brought on themselves by their laziness? Do we use our own words to teach the way to approach God? Let us humble ourselves before our heavenly Father as the prodigal son, admit our sins, and return to our God. He will receive us with open arms and rejoice as the prodigal son's father at his son's return. (Lk.15:11-32)

Our heavenly Father is gracious, abundant in mercy, forgiving transgressions of his truth if we transform our attitudes and deeds to be like his and that of his blessed Son Jesus.

Matthew

9:18 While he spake these things unto them, behold, there came a certain ruler, and worshipped him, saying, My daughter is even now dead: but come and lay thy hand upon her, and she shall live. 19 And Jesus arose, and followed him, and so did his disciples. 20 And, behold, a woman, which was diseased with an issue of blood twelve years, came behind him, and touched the hem of his garment: 21 For she said within herself, If I may but touch his garment, I shall be whole. 22 But Jesus turned him about, and when he saw her, he said, Daughter, be of good comfort; thy faith hath made thee whole. And the woman was made whole from that hour. 23 And when Jesus came into the ruler's house, and saw the minstrels and the people making a noise, 24 He said unto them, Give place: for the maid is not dead, but sleepeth. And they laughed him to scorn. 25 But when the people were put forth, he went in, and took her by the hand, and the maid arose. 26 And the fame hereof went abroad into all that land.

Jesus demonstrated his God-given power to heal any physical ailment and raise the dead. Do these abilities convince men Jesus must be God's Son? Only God's ancient prophets and Jesus' apostles performed such wonders. Jesus must possess power from God. Would God allow any man who claimed to be the Son of God to use these powers to convince men of a lie? If we answer no, Jesus must be God's Son and these miracles attest to this fact.

Mark adds more detail than either Matthew or Luke. Matthew's method appears to record many concise evidences, showing Jesus to be David's and God's Son who was God in the flesh, dwelling with man. Mark recorded the Hebrew words Jesus spoke when he raised Jairus' daughter from the dead. Then he explained their meaning, suggesting he did not write to Jews. (5:4)

Mark

5:21 And when Jesus was passed over again by ship unto the other side, much people gathered unto him: and he was nigh unto the sea. 22 And, behold, there cometh one of the rulers of the synagogue, Jairus by name; and when he saw him, he fell at his feet, 23 And besought him greatly, saying, My little daughter lieth at the point of death: I pray thee, come and lay thy hands on her, that she may be healed; and she shall live. 24 And Jesus went with him; and much people followed him, and thronged him. 25 And a certain woman, which had an issue of blood twelve years, 26 And had suffered many things of many physicians, and had spent all that she had, and was nothing bettered, but rather grew worse, 27 When she had heard of Jesus, came in the press behind, and touched his garment. 28 For she said, If I may touch but his clothes, I shall be whole. 29 And straightway the fountain of her blood was dried up; and she felt in her body that she was healed of that plague. 30 And Jesus, immediately knowing in himself that virtue had gone out of him, turned him about in the press, and said, Who touched my clothes? 31 And his disciples said unto him, Thou seest the multitude thronging thee, and sayest thou, Who touched me? 32 And he looked round about to see her that had done this thing. 33 But the woman fearing and trembling, knowing what was done in her, came and fell down before him, and told him all the truth. 34 And he said unto her, Daughter, thy faith hath made thee whole; go in peace, and be whole of thy plague. 35 While he yet spake, there came from the ruler of the synagogue's house certain which said, Thy daughter is dead: why troublest thou the Master any further? 36 As soon as Jesus heard the word that was spoken, he saith unto the ruler of the synagogue, Be not afraid, only believe. 37 And he suffered no man to

follow him, save Peter, and James, and
John the brother of James. 38 And he
cometh to the house of the ruler of the
synagogue, and seeth the tumult, and
them that wept and wailed greatly. 39
And when he was come in, he saith unto
them, Why make ye this ado, and weep?
the damsel is not dead, but sleepeth. 40
And they laughed him to scorn. But when
he had put them all out, he taketh the
father and the mother of the damsel, and
them that were with him, and entereth in
where the damsel was lying. 41 And he
took the damsel by the hand, and said
unto her, Talitha cumi; which is, being
interpreted, Damsel, I say unto thee, arise.
42 And straightway the damsel arose, and
walked; for she was of the age of twelve
years. And they were astonished with a
great astonishment. 43 And he charged
them straitly that no man should know it;
and commanded that something should be
given her to eat.

Why did Mark and Luke include details of how Jesus allowed the woman to confess her faith and problem before the multitude? It helped her and us realize another power of Jesus. Being God's Son, he must know all and be compassionate. Sensing that power issued from him to heal the woman points to Jesus' power. When Jesus asked who touched him, he provided the woman with an opportunity to explain her faith in Jesus' power to heal. For twelve years she sought healing from doctors who gave her no relief. She believed that touching Jesus' garment her issue of blood would end. Jesus didn't want her to feel he knew nothing of her healing, and he didn't care about her difficulty. He gave her opportunity to express her faith. It's another example of God's caring. This narrative shows us that Jesus and God care about our physical and spiritual needs. How could any child not love a parent who demonstrated such concern for him/her? God and his Son care about each of us and desire to help when Satan obscures hope.

Luke

8:41 And, behold, there came a man named
Jairus, and he was a ruler of the synagogue:
and he fell down at Jesus' feet, and
besought him that he would come into his
house: 42 For he had one only daughter,
about twelve years of age, and she lay a
dying. But as he went the people thronged
him. 43 And a woman having an issue of
blood twelve years, which had spent all her
living upon physicians, neither could be
healed of any, 44 Came behind him, and
touched the border of his garment: and
immediately her issue of blood stanched. 45
And Jesus said, Who touched me? When all
denied, Peter and they that were with him
said, Master, the multitude throng thee and
press thee, and sayest thou, Who touched
me? 46 And Jesus said, Somebody hath
touched me: for I perceive that virtue is
gone out of me. 47 And when the woman
saw that she was not hid, she came
trembling, and falling down before him, she
declared unto him before all the people for
what cause she had touched him, and how
she was healed immediately. 48 And he said
unto her, Daughter, be of good comfort: thy
faith hath made thee whole; go in peace. 49
While he yet spake, there cometh one from
the ruler of the synagogue's house, saying to
him, Thy daughter is dead; trouble not the
Master. 50 But when Jesus heard it, he
answered him, saying, Fear not: believe
only, and she shall be made whole. 51 And
when he came into the house, he suffered no
man to go in, save Peter, and James, and
John, and the father and the mother of the
maiden. 52 And all wept, and bewailed her:
but he said, Weep not; she is not dead, but
sleepeth. 53 And they laughed him to scorn,
knowing that she was dead. 54 And he put
them all out, and took her by the hand, and
called, saying, Maid, arise. 55 And her spirit
came again, and she arose straightway: and
he commanded to give her meat. 56 And her
parents were astonished: but he charged
them that they should tell no man what was
done.

Matthew

**9:27 And when Jesus departed thence,
two blind men followed him, crying, and
saying, Thou Son of David, have mercy on
us. 28 And when he was come into the
house, the blind men came to him: and
Jesus saith unto them, Believe ye that I
am able to do this? They said unto him,
Yea, Lord. 29 Then touched he their eyes,
saying, According to your faith be it unto
you. 30 And their eyes were opened; and
Jesus straitly charged them, saying, See
that no man know it. 31 But they, when
they were departed, spread abroad his
fame in all that country. 32 As they went
out, behold, they brought to him a dumb
man possessed with a devil. 33 And when
the devil was cast out, the dumb spake:
and the multitudes marvelled, saying, It
was never so seen in Israel. 34 But the
Pharisees said, He casteth out devils
through the prince of the devils. 35 And
Jesus went about all the cities and
villages, teaching in their synagogues, and
preaching the gospel of the kingdom, and
healing every sickness and every disease
among the people. 36 But when he saw the
multitudes, he was moved with compassion on them, because they fainted,
and were scattered abroad, as sheep
having no shepherd. 37 Then saith he unto
his disciples, The harvest truly is
plenteous, but the labourers are few; 38
Pray ye therefore the Lord of the harvest,
that he will send forth labourers into his
harvest.**

Matthew stresses Jesus as David's son. (1:1,9;9:27;12:23;15:22;20:30-31;21:9,15; 22:42) Twice two blind men called on Jesus as David's son. God promised David a son to reign on his throne forever. Being king on David's throne hailed the return of the Jewish kingdom. (Act.1:6) News spread throughout Galilee and surrounding peoples that Jesus fulfilled God's promise to David. Later, as he rode the colt into Jerusalem, the multitude hailed him as David's son.

Pharisees opposed the news that Jesus should reign on David's throne. They accused him of performing every wonder by Satan's power. (9:34;12:23-24) Envy motivated their accusations. Even Governor Pilate recognized that Jewish leaderes delivered Jesus to him for envy. (Math.27:18) Satan's children flock to every opportunity to discredit God's plan to benefit man.

To the blind men, Jesus, as the son of David, provided them with a hope to regain their sight. The dumb man possessed with a devil hoped Jesus might restore his speech and relieve him of the domination of the evil spirit. These men received of Jesus what they expected. Besides, he showed them compassion which many then and now have not received of their fellow sojourners on earth. May God help us show compassion on others' hardships. It will dissolve much of the envy that curses our lives.

As David's son, what benefit do we anticipate? Will he instantly cleanse, heal, or restore physical deficiencies? Do you expect great glory as James and John who desired to sit at his right and left hands in his kingdom? (20:20-24) What the people expected they didn't always attain. However, if you look to Jesus as David's son to introduce everlasting life and righteousness, forgiveness of sin, and a home with our heavenly Father, these Jesus provides to those of faith and obedience.

Jesus viewed the multitude as sheep with no shepherd and as a harvest without laborers. He entreated his disciples to pray the lord of the harvest to send laborers into the fields to gather wayfarers into the kingdom of God. It grieved him that so many of his countrymen needed vast amounts and kinds of assistance, but so few were willing to lend a hand to help. Isaiah remarked that he would not be discouraged until he had set judgment in the earth. Gentiles waited for his law. (Is.42:4) Do we really wait for his law, or do we hide ourselves from it to justify ourselves?

Matthew

10:1 And when he had called unto him his twelve disciples, he gave them power against unclean spirits, to cast them out, and to heal all manner of sickness and all manner of disease. 2 Now the names of the twelve apostles are these; The first, Simon, who is called Peter, and Andrew his brother; James the son of Zebedee, and John his brother; 3 Philip, and Bartholomew; Thomas, and Matthew the publican; James the son of Alphaeus, and Lebbaeus, whose surname was Thaddaeus; 4 Simon the Canaanite, and Judas Iscariot, who also betrayed him.

Eleven of the twelve apostles lived in Galilee. (Act. 2:7) Judas of Bethany, Judah, turned traitor for thirty pieces of silver. (Jno. 6:71;12:4;13:2; Math.26:15) It seems strange gospel writers include more about Judas' family than for other apostles. Lazarus, whom Jesus raised from the dead, Mary who anointed Jesus before his crucifixion, Martha who complained to Jesus that Mary failed to help prepare dinner, and a Pharisee named Simon, a leper, composed Judas' family. (Lk.7:36-50;10:38-42; Math. 26:6-13; Jno.11:1-12:11) Of these, only Mary and Martha showed faith in Jesus as the Son of God. Simon the Canaanite was not Israelite.

Mark

3:13 And he goeth up into a mountain, and calleth unto him whom he would: and they came unto him. 14 And he ordained twelve, that they should be with him, and that he might send them forth to preach, 15 And to have power to heal sicknesses, and to cast out devils: 16 And Simon he surnamed Peter; 17 And James the son of Zebedee, and John the brother of James; and he surnamed them Boanerges, which is, The sons of thunder: 18 And Andrew, and Philip, and Bartholomew, and Matthew, and Thomas, and James the son of Alphaeus, and Thaddaeus, and Simon the Canaanite, 19 And Judas Iscariot, which also betrayed him: and they went into an house.

Jesus prepared to select apostles by asking followers to pray the lord to send laborers into the harvest of God's kingdom. Only synoptic gospels name the twelve Jesus called apostles. Giving them the Holy Spirit, he sent them by twos. Jesus chose Galileans as apostles to send them among Jews scattered among the Gentiles. Their being accustomed to Gentile ways prepared them to go to Gentiles.

Luke

6:13 And when it was day, he called unto him his disciples: and of them he chose twelve, whom also he named apostles; 14 Simon, (whom he also named Peter,) and Andrew his brother, James and John, Philip and Bartholomew, 15 Matthew and Thomas, James the son of Alphaeus, and Simon called Zelotes, 16 And Judas the brother of James, and Judas Iscariot, which also was the traitor. 17 And he came down with them, and stood in the plain, and the company of his disciples, and a great multitude of people out of all Judaea and Jerusalem, and from the sea coast of Tyre and Sidon, which came to hear him, and to be healed of their diseases; 18 And they that were vexed with unclean spirits: and they were healed. 19 And the whole multitude sought to touch him: for there went virtue out of him, and healed them all.

Jesus commissioned apostles to preach God's kingdom's gospel in all the cities Jesus planned to visit. He limited their preaching to Jews, though Jesus visited Sidon, a Gentile city, and preached in Samaria. After Jesus' resurrection, God invited Gentiles to enter his kingdom. (Act. ch. 10,11)

Matthew

10:5 These twelve Jesus sent forth, and commanded them, saying, Go not into the way of the Gentiles, and into any city of the Samaritans enter ye not: 6 But go rather to the lost sheep of the house of Israel. 7 And as ye go, preach, saying, The kingdom of heaven is at hand. 8 Heal the sick, cleanse the lepers, raise the dead, cast out devils: freely ye have received, freely give. 9 Provide neither gold, nor silver, nor brass in your purses, 10 Nor scrip for your journey, neither two coats, neither shoes, nor yet staves: for the workman is worthy of his meat. 11 And into whatsoever city or town ye shall enter, inquire who in it is worthy; and there abide till ye go thence. 12 And when ye come into an house, salute it. 13 And if the house be worthy, let your peace come upon it: but if it be not worthy, let your peace return to you. 14 And whosoever shall not receive you, nor hear your words, when ye depart out of that house or city, shake off the dust of your feet. 15 Verily I say unto you, It shall be more tolerable for the land of Sodom and Gomorrha in the day of judgment, than for that city.

Matthew pleased Jews by noting Jesus restricted apostles from preaching to Gentiles and Samaritans. They took no extra food, clothing, or money, but depended on hearers for their needs. Expect many to reject your message. Jewish leaders rejected Jesus, and they will bring you before councils, beat, and persecute you too, but God will judge your oppressors who reject your message or harm you. Luke added that God shows greater mercy on Tyre and Sidon than to Bethsaida, Chorazin, and Capernaum. (Lk.10:13-15) Luke wrote to Syrians and honored their cities. Why might Gentile cities receive more mercy than Galileans? Israel's cities believed not on Jesus, but Gentile cities would hear and obey him. Israelites often promised faithfully to obey all God's commands, but they soon turned from God's precepts and refused to repent.

Mark

6:7 And he called unto him the twelve, and began to send them forth by two and two; and gave them power over unclean spirits; 8 And commanded them that they should take nothing for their journey, save a staff only; no scrip, no bread, no money in their purse: 9 But be shod with sandals; and not put on two coats. 10 And he said unto them, In what place soever ye enter into an house, there abide till ye depart from that place. 11 And whosoever shall not receive you, nor hear you, when ye depart thence, shake off the dust under your feet for a testimony against them. Verily I say unto you, It shall be more tolerable for Sodom and Gomorrha in the day of judgment, than for that city. 12 And they went out, and preached that men should repent. 13 And they cast out many devils, and anointed with oil many that were sick, and healed them.

Luke

9:1 Then he called his twelve disciples together, and gave them power and authority over all devils, and to cure diseases. 2 And he sent them to preach the kingdom of God, and to heal the sick. 3 And he said unto them, Take nothing for your journey, neither staves, nor scrip, neither bread, neither money; neither have two coats apiece. 4 And whatsoever house ye enter into, there abide, and thence depart. 5 And whosoever will not receive you, when ye go out of that city, shake off the very dust from your feet for a testimony against them. 6 And they departed, and went through the towns, preaching the gospel, and healing every where.

Matthew

**10:16 Behold, I send you forth as sheep in
the midst of wolves: be ye therefore wise
as serpents, and harmless as doves. 17
But beware of men: for they will deliver
you up to the councils, and they will
scourge you in their synagogues; 18 And
ye shall be brought before governors and
kings for my sake, for a testimony against
them and the Gentiles. 19 But when they
deliver you up, take no thought how or
what ye shall speak: for it shall be given
you in that same hour what ye shall speak.
20 For it is not ye that speak, but the
Spirit of your Father which speaketh in
you. 21 And the brother shall deliver up
the brother to death, and the father the
child: and the children shall rise up
against their parents, and cause them to
be put to death. 22 And ye shall be hated
of all men for my name's sake: but he that
endureth to the end shall be saved. 23 But
when they persecute you in this city, flee
ye into another: for verily I say unto you,
Ye shall not have gone over the cities of
Israel, till the Son of man be come.**

Moses remarked Jews rebelled as soon as promises issued from their mouths. (Deu. 9:7,24) Not only will your countrymen reject and persecute you, some will urge you to cease preaching the truth of God's gospel. Even so, God's testimony shall witness against them as it did against ancient Israel. Jesus also pleads with Christians to live faithfully before God.

Don't worry about what to say before their councils, governors, or kings. God's Spirit directs you to speak his truth. As the kingdom of God struggles to deliver men from Satan's grasp, brothers and families divide. Parents and children deliver one another to death. They hate you for preaching words that separate families and turn the people away from old customs. When they persecute you in one city, flee to another city to turn people to God's kingdom.

Preach God's kingdom and repentance.

Luke

**10:1 After these things the Lord ap-
pointed other seventy also, and sent them
two and two before his face into every city
and place, whither he himself would
come. 2 Therefore said he unto them, The
harvest truly is great, but the labourers
are few: pray ye therefore the Lord of the
harvest, that he would send forth
labourers into his harvest. 3 Go your
ways: behold, I send you forth as lambs
among wolves. 4 Carry neither purse, nor
scrip, nor shoes: and salute no man by the
way. 5 And into whatsoever house ye
enter, first say, Peace be to this house. 6
And if the son of peace be there, your
peace shall rest upon it: if not, it shall turn
to you again. 7 And in the same house
remain, eating and drinking such things
as they give: for the labourer is worthy of
his hire. Go not from house to house. 8
And into whatsoever city ye enter, and
they receive you, eat such things as are set
before you: 9 And heal the sick that are
therein, and say unto them, The kingdom
of God is come nigh unto you. 10 But into
whatsoever city ye enter, and they receive
you not, go your ways out into the streets
of the same, and say, 11 Even the very
dust of your city, which cleaveth on us, we
do wipe off against you: notwithstanding
be ye sure of this, that the kingdom of
God is come nigh unto you. 12 But I say
unto you, that it shall be more tolerable in
that day for Sodom, than for that city. 13
Woe unto thee, Chorazin! woe unto thee,
Bethsaida! for if the mighty works had
been done in Tyre and Sidon, which have
been done in you, they had a great while
ago repented, sitting in sackcloth and
ashes.**

Endure to the end, and God will reward you. My kingdom arrives before you cover Israel's cities. Only Luke shows Jesus sent seventy others to preach God's kingdom as he passed through Samaria.

Matthew

**10:24 The disciple is not above his mas-
ter, nor the servant above his lord. 25 It is
enough for the disciple that he be as his
master, and the servant as his lord. If they
have called the master of the house
Beelzebub, how much more shall they call
them of his household? 26 Fear them not
therefore: for there is nothing covered,
that shall not be revealed; and hid, that
shall not be known. 27 What I tell you in
darkness, that speak ye in light: and what
ye hear in the ear, that preach ye upon the
housetops. 28 And fear not them which
kill the body, but are not able to kill the
soul: but rather fear him which is able to
destroy both soul and body in hell. 29 Are
not two sparrows sold for a farthing? and
one of them shall not fall on the ground
without your Father. 30 But the very
hairs of your head are all numbered. 31
Fear ye not therefore, ye are of more
value than many sparrows. 32 Whosoever
therefore shall confess me before men,
him will I confess also before my Father
which is in heaven. 33 But whosoever
shall deny me before men, him will I also
deny before my Father which is in heaven.
34 Think not that I am come to send peace
on earth: I came not to send peace, but a
sword. 35 For I am come to set a man at
variance against his father, and the
daughter against her mother, and the
daughter in law against her mother in
law. 36 And a man's foes shall be they of
his own household. 37 He that loveth
father or mother more than me is not
worthy of me: and he that loveth son or
daughter more than me is not worthy of
me. 38 And he that taketh not his cross,
and followeth after me, is not worthy of
me. 39 He that findeth his life shall lose it:
and he that loseth his life for my sake
shall find it. 40 He that receiveth you
receiveth me, and he that receiveth me
receiveth him that sent me. 41 He that
receiveth a prophet in the name of a
prophet shall receive a prophet's reward;
and he that receiveth a righteous man in
the name of a righteous man shall receive
a righteous man's reward. 42 And whosoever shall give to drink unto one of these
little ones a cup of cold water only in the
name of a disciple, verily I say unto you,
he shall in no wise lose his reward.**

Master and disciple may expect equal acceptance or rejection. As some gladly heard and obeyed Jesus, some rejoice and return to God when you bring God's good news to them. To the opposite extreme, those like scribes, Pharisees, priests, and Sadducees chafed at what Jesus taught. They searched for a convenient way to justify disposing of Jesus. These examine every legal way to discredit God's truth you preach and ruin you. Others may listen, but ignore your message.

Your responsibility remains to explain to Israel what I told you. Don't fear rulers or lawless men. They may destroy your body, but God testifies that they remain powerless to slay your soul. Only God controls the destiny of both body and soul. He cares for sparrows and for you. Not a hair of your head may they touch without God's consent. Expect persecution, but be faithful, and God's blessings shall shower on you. He goes with you as you do his will.

Jesus charged the seventy with equal responsibilities with the twelve. Heal the sick, cast out devils, and inform the people God's kingdom nears. Stay with and bless those who receive you. Shake off dust of your feet against those who reject your message from God. Sodom and Gomorrah obtain more mercy than obstinate Israelite cities like Chorazin, Capernaum, and Bethsaida. Even Tyre and Sidon would have repented and accepted God's kingdom if they had heard and seen what these cities in Israel heard and observed, but rejected. Take courage and extend to all cities in Israel the opportunity to repent and return to our Father in heaven. Remember, God goes with you to help and strengthen you, so that no man may treat you wrongly without incurring his wrath.

For people today to read Jesus' exhortations and agree with them, but never respond obediently, be indifferent, or outright contradict, God promises condemnation. Though many consider America a Christian nation, most people continue to turn deaf ears to God's way of a better life. Rejection of God's plea for repentance tends to dampen our zeal to proclaim the good news of God's everlasting kingdom, but God and Jesus encourage us to faithfulness..

From creation, God offered man opportunity to chose. To Adam and Eve he commanded clearly what he desired of them. Even so, he opened a possibility for them to choose a different path. Eating of the tree of the knowledge of good and evil, though forbidden of God, still presented them a way to direct their own lives. They knew that eating the fruit of that tree resulted in death, but Satan presented what seemed a wiser plan. If they chose to eat of that tree to make them wise, then they could distinguish between good and evil. They chose Satan's message. As God said, it resulted in spiritual death that day by separating them from God and ultimately physical death when God severed them from the tree of life. (Gen.3:22-24)

We today continue making choices of food, clothing, style of clothes and houses, companions, and to serve or reject God's commands. Each opportunity to choose provides us with blessings if we obey God's instructions, but his curses if we disregard his ways. Choosing unwisely one's companion for life probably brings more disappointments than any other. Whether man or woman, we tend to look for the attractive or handsome individual. Considering only the person who pleases the eye for a life-long companion God's scribes call unwise. (Prov.12:4;14:1;21:9,19;31:10,30) Since Solomon addressed his son, he spoke of choosing a wife with whom his son could live peacefully and enjoyably all his days without regret. Disregarding whether that person possesses a genuine faith in God's promises, we may soon discover that our companion seeks selfish life patterns. Desiring to have his or her own way strains the relationship, often beyond our limit to endure, and we choose divorce to remedy an intolerable situation. Shortly after separation, we encounter loneliness and seek companionship. More times than not, a second marriage fails to solve our problems. Will we never learn that God's instructions, when followed, produce a much better way of life, but when disobeyed, sorrow follows?

We constantly face other choices. Do we choose friends who honor God, or change our standards to gain respect of our peers? Do we pray to God in Jesus' name and offend Jews, or omit his name to gain their respect? Serving pork offends Jews and Moslems, but pleases Germans. To confess Jesus as God's Son offends Jews, but denying him offends God. Our choices produce reactions in others. If we regard their opinions above God's, we may gain approval of some, but rejection of others. Even within our own families certain choices please some, but aggravate others. Refraining from making choices results in making a choice and makes us indecisive and without backbone. Asking God's council and being willing to submit to his instruction, brings true life. Let's not follow the example of Jews in Jeremiah's day after Nebuchadnezzar destroyed Jerusalem, and carried most of the Jews captive to Babylon. The few poor he allowed to reside in Judah with a few warriors who returned after fighting subsided approached Jeremiah, asking him to seek God's council, but they rebelled against it. (Jer.40:7-43:4) If we call on God for his direction, submit to his counsel without reservations. Would you be insulted if someone asked your advice, but rejected it to do as he pleased? Don't mock God by calling on him, then forsake his way.

Matthew

11:1 And it came to pass, when Jesus had made an end of commanding his twelve disciples, he departed thence to teach and to preach in their cities. 2 Now when John had heard in the prison the works of Christ, he sent two of his disciples, 3 And said unto him, Art thou he that should come, or do we look for another? 4 Jesus answered and said unto them, Go and shew John again those things which ye do hear and see: 5 The blind receive their sight, and the lame walk, the lepers are cleansed, and the deaf hear, the dead are raised up, and the poor have the gospel preached to them. 6 And blessed is he, whosoever shall not be offended in me.

Forgetfulness or uncertainty, a common problem for many of us, afflicted John the Baptist. Had not he identified Jesus as the Lamb of God to take away our sins? (Jno.1:36) Had he not proclaimed Jesus as the bridegroom, and that Jesus spoke words the Father gave him? (Jno.3:28-34) Had not John seen God's Spirit like a dove alight and remain on Jesus, identifying him as God's Son? (Jno.1:33) Notwithstanding, after Herod imprisoned John, he began to wonder if Jesus were Christ. To ease his mind, John sent two disciples to Jesus, asking if Jesus fulfilled God's promise to Israel. Are you the Christ to build again the kingdom of David and to reign for ever? Will you deliver us from our enemies? In the presence of John's disciples, Jesus healed plagues, restored sight and hearing, cleansed lepers, raised the dead, and preached the good news of God's kingdom to the poor. After performing all these manifestations of God's power and mercy, Jesus instructed John's disciples to return to John in prison and inform him of what they witnessed and heard. John might then answer his own question. In a sense, Matthew and Luke recorded this encounter with John's disciples to help their readers believe in Jesus. He is the Messiah God promised.

Luke

7:18 And the disciples of John shewed him of all these things. 19 And John calling unto him two of his disciples sent them to Jesus, saying, Art thou he that should come? or look we for another? 20 When the men were come unto him, they said, John Baptist hath sent us unto thee, saying, Art thou he that should come? or look we for another? 21 And in that same hour he cured many of their infirmities and plagues, and of evil spirits; and unto many that were blind he gave sight. 22 Then Jesus answering said unto them, Go your way, and tell John what things ye have seen and heard; how that the blind see, the lame walk, the lepers are cleansed, the deaf hear, the dead are raised, to the poor the gospel is preached. 23 And blessed is he, whosoever shall not be offended in me.

We, too, must evaluate the evidence. If this man Jesus healed every manner of malady Satan cast on men, including death, what reason could one have to question his claim of being Christ? Furthermore, Jesus promised Israel that God readied them to receive the kingdom of heaven. No longer need they await him whom God must send to deliver them from the bondage of the Evil One. (Rom.11:26-27) God now fulfills his promise. Enter God's place of refuge now.

Jesus added a second comment, "**Blessed is he, whosoever shall not be offended in me.**" While all goes well, most followers of Christ continue faithful, but when trials and hardships arise, as John experienced in prison, we often question whether the reward outweighs our difficulties. Being offended for Jesus prompts many to abandon God's Son. Jesus informed his followers often that trying times awaited those who trusted him. Enduring to the end brings God's promised reward. Don't count the cost too great. Be good soldiers of God. Endure hardships. (2 Tim.2:3) Faithfulness God awards with all his promises; unfaithfulness loses them all.

Matthew

11:7 And as they departed, Jesus began to say unto the multitudes concerning John, What went ye out into the wilderness to see? A reed shaken with the wind? 8 But what went ye out for to see? A man clothed in soft raiment? behold, they that wear soft clothing are in kings' houses. 9 But what went ye out for to see? A prophet? yea, I say unto you, and more than a prophet. 10 For this is he, of whom it is written, Behold, I send my messenger before thy face, which shall prepare thy way before thee. 11 Verily I say unto you, Among them that are born of women there hath not risen a greater than John the Baptist: notwithstanding he that is least in the kingdom of heaven is greater than he. 12 And from the days of John the Baptist until now the kingdom of heaven suffereth violence, and the violent take it by force. 13 For all the prophets and the law prophesied until John. 14 And if ye will receive it, this is Elias, which was for to come. 15 He that hath ears to hear, let him hear. 16 But whereunto shall I liken this generation? It is like unto children sitting in the markets, and calling unto their fellows, 17 And saying, We have piped unto you, and ye have not danced; we have mourned unto you, and ye have not lamented. 18 For John came neither eating nor drinking, and they say, He hath a devil. 19 The Son of man came eating and drinking, and they say, Behold a man gluttonous, and a winebibber, a friend of publicans and sinners. But wisdom is justified of her children.

John the Baptist identified Jesus as Christ, and Jesus testified John was Elijah sent to prepare Christ's way. (Is.40:3-5; Mal.3:1;4: 5-6) John approached you as a Nazarite who refused strong drink and ate locusts and wild honey. I came eating and drinking, but you rejected both of us. God justifies those who obey his will faithfully. (Rom.5:1-5)

Luke

7:24 And when the messengers of John were departed, he began to speak unto the people concerning John, What went ye out into the wilderness for to see? A reed shaken with the wind? 25 But what went ye out for to see? A man clothed in soft raiment? Behold, they which are gorgeously apparelled, and live delicately, are in kings' courts. 26 But what went ye out for to see? A prophet? Yea, I say unto you, and much more than a prophet. 27 This is he, of whom it is written, Behold, I send my messenger before thy face, which shall prepare thy way before thee. 28 For I say unto you, Among those that are born of women there is not a greater prophet than John the Baptist: but he that is least in the kingdom of God is greater than he. 29 And all the people that heard him, and the publicans, justified God, being baptized with the baptism of John. 30 But the Pharisees and lawyers rejected the counsel of God against themselves, being not baptized of him. 31 And the Lord said, Whereunto then shall I liken the men of this generation? and to what are they like? 32 They are like unto children sitting in the marketplace, and calling one to another, and saying, We have piped unto you, and ye have not danced; we have mourned to you, and ye have not wept. 33 For John the Baptist came neither eating bread nor drinking wine; and ye say, He hath a devil. 34 The Son of man is come eating and drinking; and ye say, Behold a gluttonous man, and a winebibber, a friend of publicans and sinners! 35 But wisdom is justified of all her children.

If Jews' refusal to submit to John's baptism rejected God's counsel against them, will God count our refusal to submit to Jesus' baptism be rejecting God's counsel for us? Will this cause God to deny us as his children and cost us eternal life? (Act. 13:46)

Matthew

11:20 Then began he to upbraid the cities wherein most of his mighty works were done, because they repented not: 21 Woe unto thee, Chorazin! woe unto thee, Bethsaida! for if the mighty works, which were done in you, had been done in Tyre and Sidon, they would have repented long ago in sackcloth and ashes. 22 But I say unto you, It shall be more tolerable for Tyre and Sidon at the day of judgment, than for you. 23 And thou, Capernaum, which art exalted unto heaven, shalt be brought down to hell: for if the mighty works, which have been done in thee, had been done in Sodom, it would have remained until this day. 24 But I say unto you, That it shall be more tolerable for the land of Sodom in the day of judgment, than for thee.

Repentance demands a change of attitude. Pride too often will not allow us to admit error. Pharisees and lawyers listened to John's preaching, **"Repent, ye: for the kingdom of heaven is at hand."** (Math.3:2) Rather than change, they found fault with John's eating habits. God restricted him from drinking wine (Lk.1:15), but they criticized him for refusing strong drink, claiming he was demon-possessed, (Math.11:18) When Jesus appeared, demanding repentance, they criticized him for eating and drinking wine. (Math.11:19) Without becoming poor in spirit (Math.5:3), we view others as inferior. This allows us to judge what they say or do as unacceptable. We justify ourselves by condemning others.

As individuals manifest an air of superiority, cities and even nations fall into the same Satanic trap. Chorazin, Bethsaida, and Capernaum characterized such attitudes. Jesus pronounced woe on all three cities for their mighty mind set. Compared to Gentile and sinful cities such as Tyre, Sidon, or Sodom, the three Israelite cities remained contemptible before God. Had Gentile cities witnessed John's preaching and Jesus' mir-

Luke

10:13 Woe unto thee, Chorazin! woe unto thee, Bethsaida! for if the mighty works had been done in Tyre and Sidon, which have been done in you, they had a great while ago repented, sitting in sackcloth and ashes. 14 But it shall be more tolerable for Tyre and Sidon at the judgment, than for you. 15 And thou, Capernaum, which art exalted to heaven, shalt be thrust down to hell. 16 He that heareth you heareth me; and he that despiseth you despiseth me; and he that despiseth me despiseth him that sent me. 17 And the seventy returned again with joy, saying, Lord, even the devils are subject unto us through thy name. 18 And he said unto them, I beheld Satan as lightning fall from heaven. 19 Behold, I give unto you power to tread on serpents and scorpions, and over all the power of the enemy: and nothing shall by any means hurt you. 20 Notwithstanding in this rejoice not, that the spirits are subject unto you; but rather rejoice, because your names are written in heaven.

acles, they would have abandoned their sinful paths, but Israelite cities Jesus frequented refused to repent. They saw and heard both John and Jesus, yet continued their God-condemned lifestyles.

Criticizing ungodly Israelite cities for impenitence to minimize our impenitent hearts today fails to persuade God that we are righteous. Multitudes of ministers today broadcast the message of repentance by radio, literature, television, and in person. Do we heed their call to repent any more readily than Pharisees, lawyers, or mighty cities in Israel? Rather than repent, we justify ourselves by finding fault with ministers' dress, mannerisms, inability to capture us with appealing stories, etc. Jesus remarked that if we received his ministers, we received him and God. Refusing to receive his ministers who encourage our repentance signifies we reject God.

Matthew

11:25 At that time Jesus answered and said, I thank thee, O Father, Lord of heaven and earth, because thou hast hid these things from the wise and prudent, and hast revealed them unto babes. 26 Even so, Father: for so it seemed good in thy sight. 27 All things are delivered unto me of my Father: and no man knoweth the Son, but the Father; neither knoweth any man the Father, save the Son, and he to whomsoever the Son will reveal him. 28 Come unto me, all ye that labour and are heavy laden, and I will give you rest. 29 Take my yoke upon you, and learn of me; for I am meek and lowly in heart: and ye shall find rest unto your souls. 30 For my yoke is easy, and my burden is light.

Explaining to the twelve and seventy how some received and others rejected John the Baptist, Jesus, and the twelve, Jesus thanked his Father for his wise plan which distinguishes God's children from Satan's. Men who pride themselves in their wisdom, abilities, or trust this life's patterns populate Satan's dominion. God's children humbly hear and do God's truths. We see through Satan's sham and submit to God's law, but Satan's children submit neither in mind nor deed to God's law. (Rom.8:9; 1 Jno.4:6) Good life and pleasant, long-lasting relationships emerge from courtesies. Serving, not being served, produces joy. Worldly minded people never comprehend God's life pattern. Maintaining humility, not pride, admitting weaknesses, not claiming perfection show evidences that we understand God, Jesus, and the way of truth. Children of this world consider this lifestyle foolishness. God's children perceive clearly at times, obscurely at others, but believe confidently that God's system produces a sense of worthwhileness lacking in Satan's life patterns. Denying true weaknesses blinds the eyes of those who refuse to submit to God's truth. (Is.6:9-10)

Luke

10:21 In that hour Jesus rejoiced in spirit, and said, I thank thee, O Father, Lord of heaven and earth, that thou hast hid these things from the wise and prudent, and hast revealed them unto babes: even so, Father; for so it seemed good in thy sight. 22 All things are delivered to me of my Father: and no man knoweth who the Son is, but the Father; and who the Father is, but the Son, and he to whom the Son will reveal him. 23 And he turned him unto his disciples, and said privately, Blessed are the eyes which see the things that ye see: 24 For I tell you, that many prophets and kings have desired to see those things which ye see, and have not seen them; and to hear those things which ye hear, and have not heard them.

Willingness to admit our faults to ourselves and to others prepares us to know God and his Son Jesus. With this attitude, we listen to God's plan of life. God reveals to us Jesus as his Son who demonstrates the pattern of wholesome life. As we see God's glimmer of light, it casts darkness from our lives. Jesus reveals God to us. Light of eternal life gleams more brilliantly for us as we meditate on God's truth to understand God and his way of life.

Jesus blessed the twelve and seventy, for they had seen and believed truths which ancients had longed to see and hear, but God reserved these glad tidings to the coming of his Son and to the obedient.

Is it any wonder Jesus invites all who find Satan's system a heavy burden to come to him? He promises and will deliver us from the bondage of the Evil One where we must hide our faults. God provides everlasting peace and rest, blessings, not rigor. When we comprehend how God relieves life's burdens, we ask ourselves why we resisted God's truth and how Satan convinces us God deprives of life's enjoyable experiences. (Ps.84:11)

Matthew

12:1 At that time Jesus went on the sabbath day through the corn; and his disciples were an hungred, and began to pluck the ears of corn, and to eat. 2 But when the Pharisees saw it, they said unto him, Behold, thy disciples do that which is not lawful to do upon the sabbath day. 3 But he said unto them, Have ye not read what David did, when he was an hungred, and they that were with him; 4 How he entered into the house of God, and did eat the shewbread, which was not lawful for him to eat, neither for them which were with him, but only for the priests? 5 Or have ye not read in the law, how that on the sabbath days the priests in the temple profane the sabbath, and are blameless? 6 But I say unto you, That in this place is one greater than the temple. 7 But if ye had known what this meaneth, I will have mercy, and not sacrifice, ye would not have condemned the guiltless. 8 For the Son of man is Lord even of the sabbath day.

Looking for faults consumed the Pharisees. They observed Jesus' disciples picking and eating grain on the Sabbath. They complained to Jesus, contending his disciples violated the law by picking grain to eat on the Sabbath. Jesus asked if

Mark

2:23 And it came to pass, that he went through the corn fields on the sabbath day; and his disciples began, as they went, to pluck the ears of corn. 24 And the Pharisees said unto him, Behold, why do they on the sabbath day that which is not lawful? 25 And he said unto them, Have ye never read what David did, when he had need, and was an hungred, he, and they that were with him? 26 How he went into the house of God in the days of Abiathar the high priest, and did eat the shewbread, which is not lawful to eat but for the priests, and gave also to them which were with him? 27 And he said unto them, The sabbath was made for man, and not man for the sabbath: 28 Therefore the Son of man is Lord also of the sabbath.

they had forgotten how David and his followers ate the shewbread when they needed food, though they knew God allowed only priests to eat it. Priests transgress the Sabbath by offering sacrifices, but God does not charge them with sin. God made the Sabbath to benefit man, not man to serve the Sabbath. God seeks mercy from those who draw close to him, but you show my disciples no mercy. Your lack of mercy annuls your devotion to God.

Luke

6:1 And it came to pass on the second sabbath after the first, that he went through the corn fields; and his disciples plucked the ears of corn, and did eat, rubbing them in their hands. 2 And certain of the Pharisees said unto them, Why do ye that which is not lawful to do on the sabbath days? 3 And Jesus answering them said, Have ye not read so much as this, what David did, when himself was an hungred, and they which were with him; 4 How he went into the house of God, and did take and eat the shewbread, and gave also to them that were with him; which it is not lawful to eat but for the priests alone? 5 And he said unto them, That the Son of man is Lord also of the sabbath.

As Creator, God made Jesus Lord of the Sabbath. He charged him to judge all men righteously. (Is.11:1-5) His disciples were quite hungry. Was keeping the Sabbath more righteous than depriving the hungry of food? God asks his children to show mercy, but rulers understood not God's mercy. (Mi.6:6-8; Math.9:12) They offered sacrifices, but showed not mercy. Did they fulfill God's law, or had Satan blinded their eyes to truth and mercy? (Math. 23:23) Do Christians replace mercy with sacrifice?

Matthew

12:9 And when he was departed thence, he went into their synagogue: 10 And, behold, there was a man which had his hand withered. And they asked him, saying, Is it lawful to heal on the sabbath days? that they might accuse him. 11 And he said unto them, What man shall there be among you, that shall have one sheep, and if it fall into a pit on the sabbath day, will he not lay hold on it, and lift it out? 12 How much then is a man better than a sheep? Wherefore it is lawful to do well on the sabbath days. 13 Then saith he to the man, Stretch forth thine hand. And he stretched it forth; and it was restored whole, like as the other. 14 Then the Pharisees went out, and held a council against him, how they might destroy him.

Performing miracles on the Sabbath irritated scribes and Pharisees, but Jesus looked for opportunities to relieve those whom Satan afflicted, even on the Sabbath. He appealed to their compassion to help them realize God valued mercy above their legal interpretation of their law. When he restored the man's hand, he hoped they also might consider compassion to man and beast more rewarding than keeping details of their law.

Mark

3:1 And he entered again into the synagogue; and there was a man there which had a withered hand. 2 And they watched him, whether he would heal him on the sabbath day; that they might accuse him. 3 And he saith unto the man which had the withered hand, Stand forth. 4 And he saith unto them, Is it lawful to do good on the sabbath days, or to do evil? to save life, or to kill? But they held their peace. 5 And when he had looked round about on them with anger, being grieved for the hardness of their hearts, he saith unto the man, Stretch forth thine hand. And he stretched it out: and his hand was restored whole as the other. 6 And the Pharisees went forth, and straightway took counsel with the Herodians against him, how they might destroy him.

God seeks love to guide the deeds of his children. Their righteousness must surpass what scribes and Pharisees regarded as righteousness. (Math.5:20) Submitting to Moses' law God regarded as righteousness. Moses' law required showing mercy to relieve others' suffering in addition to offering sacrifices for one's sins. Even Pharisees cared for their cattle on the Sabbath. Learn also to show mercy to people on the Sabbath to honor God.

Luke

6:6 And it came to pass also on another sabbath, that he entered into the synagogue and taught: and there was a man whose right hand was withered. 7 And the scribes and Pharisees watched him, whether he would heal on the sabbath day; that they might find an accusation against him. 8 But he knew their thoughts, and said to the man which had the withered hand, Rise up, and stand forth in the midst. And he arose and stood forth. 9 Then said Jesus unto them, I will ask you one thing; Is it lawful on the sabbath days to do good, or to do evil? to save life, or to destroy it? 10 And looking round about upon them all, he said unto the man, Stretch forth thy hand. And he did so: and his hand was restored whole as the other. 11 And they were filled with madness; and communed one with another what they might do to Jesus. 12 And it came to pass in those days, that he went out into a mountain to pray, and continued all night in prayer to God.

God gave Jesus authority over all creation. (Ps.8:3-8; Math.28:18; Heb.2:5-9) How shall Jesus convince you and me to submit to God's anointed or perish?

Matthew

**12:15 But when Jesus knew it, he with-
drew himself from thence: and great
multitudes followed him, and he healed
them all; 16 And charged them that they
should not make him known: 17 That it
might be fulfilled which was spoken by
Esaias the prophet, saying, 18 Behold my
servant, whom I have chosen; my beloved,
in whom my soul is well pleased: I will put
my spirit upon him, and he shall shew
judgment to the Gentiles. 19 He shall not
strive, nor cry; neither shall any man hear
his voice in the streets. 20 A bruised reed
shall he not break, and smoking flax shall
he not quench, till he send forth judgment
unto victory. 21 And in his name shall the
Gentiles trust.**

Mark

**3:7 But Jesus withdrew himself with his
disciples to the sea: and a great multitude
from Galilee followed him, and from
Judaea, 8 And from Jerusalem, and from
Idumaea, and from beyond Jordan; and
they about Tyre and Sidon, a great
multitude, when they had heard what
great things he did, came unto him. 9 And
he spake to his disciples, that a small ship
should wait on him because of the
multitude, lest they should throng him. 10
For he had healed many; insomuch that
they pressed upon him for to touch him,
as many as had plagues. 11 And unclean
spirits, when they saw him, fell down
before him, and cried, saying, Thou art
the Son of God. 12 And he straitly
charged them that they should not make
him known.**

Avoiding scribes and Pharisees who planned to destroy him, Jesus withdrew. Matthew quoted Isaiah to help convey Jesus' mild nature. He refrained from stirring up confrontations, but when his opponents sought encounters, he met them and confounded their arguments. God has no plan to upheave or confuse man's social structures violently. Changes must come, but only as individuals renounce the kingdom of darkness and turn to the light of God's truth. Men of the world operate differently. They arouse emotions among their kind and stir up convulsions and tumults. By force of numbers they overwhelm, hoping to squelch what they dislike. When Pharisees and their cohorts planned to destroy Jesus, he simply withdrew.

God's plan seeks to wrest every man and woman from Satan's slavery to sin. It includes Gentiles as well as Jews. Isaiah foresaw Jesus bringing God's judgments to Gentiles as he first did the Jews by Moses' law. God's judgments encompass all good interactions between individuals, families, companies, and nations to submit to God's commands to honor him, not Satan. (Is.2:2-5;54:13; Mi.4:1-3; Jno.6:44-45) Each individual must learn how to distinguish Satan's warlike system from God's path of peace. As each person chooses for himself to abandon Satan's self-seeking and considers how to benefit others in submission to God's kingdom's law in attitude and deed, God's kingdom conquers. In this sense only does Jesus war against the forces of evil. (Math.10:34; Eph.6:12-18)

When apostles introduced God's kingdom to Jews on the day of Pentecost, 33 A.D., Jews within Satan's realm continued to harass and rile up the masses. They threatened, imprisoned, or killed apostles and ministers to forestall the encroachment of God's kingdom. (Act.4:16-22;7:54-60; 12:1-4) Quoting David's psalm, apostles encouraged one another to engage Satan's followers to conquer for Jesus. (Act.4:23-26; Ps.2:1-12)

Only Matthew referred to Isaiah's prophecy of extending God's judgments to Gentiles, indicating to his Jewish audience how Jesus fulfilled their prophets and law. God also accepts Gentiles in his kingdom.

Viewpoints

Matthew

12:22 Then was brought unto him one possessed with a devil, blind, and dumb: and he healed him, insomuch that the blind and dumb both spake and saw. 23 And all the people were amazed, and said, Is not this the son of David? 24 But when the Pharisees heard it, they said, This fellow doth not cast out devils, but by Beelzebub the prince of the devils. 25 And Jesus knew their thoughts, and said unto them, Every kingdom divided against itself is brought to desolation; and every city or house divided against itself shall not stand: 26 And if Satan cast out Satan, he is divided against himself; how shall then his kingdom stand? 27 And if I by Beelzebub cast out devils, by whom do your children cast them out? therefore they shall be your judges. 28 But if I cast out devils by the Spirit of God, then the kingdom of God is come unto you. 29 Or else how can one enter into a strong man's house, and spoil his goods, except he first bind the strong man? and then he will spoil his house.

Removing devils by God's Spirit declares two important features of Jesus' ministry: 1) Jesus spoiled Satan's kingdom; 2) God's kingdom neared. Jesus confounded his adversaries when he asked

Mark

3:20 And the multitude cometh together again, so that they could not so much as eat bread. 21 And when his friends heard of it, they went out to lay hold on him: for they said, He is beside himself. 22 And the scribes which came down from Jerusalem said, He hath Beelzebub, and by the prince of the devils casteth he out devils. 23 And he called them unto him, and said unto them in parables, How can Satan cast out Satan? 24 And if a kingdom be divided against itself, that kingdom cannot stand. 25 And if a house be divided against itself, that house cannot stand. 26 And if Satan rise up against himself, and be divided, he cannot stand, but hath an end. 27 No man can enter into a strong man's house, and spoil his goods, except he will first bind the strong man; and then he will spoil his house.

them by whose power their children cast out devils. If they cast them out by God's Spirit, then I also cast them out by God's Spirit. If I cast out devils by Satan's power, Satan's kingdom destroys itself and must come to an end. If I cast out devils by God's Spirit, God's kingdom nears to overthrow Satan's realm. I overpower Satan and spoil his house.

Luke

11:14 And he was casting out a devil, and it was dumb. And it came to pass, when the devil was gone out, the dumb spake; and the people wondered. 15 But some of them said, He casteth out devils through Beelzebub the chief of the devils. 16 And others, tempting him, sought of him a sign from heaven. 17 But he, knowing their thoughts, said unto them, Every kingdom divided against itself is brought to desolation; and a house divided against a house falleth. 18 If Satan also be divided against himself, how shall his kingdom stand? because ye say that I cast out devils through Beelzebub. 19 And if I by Beelzebub cast out devils, by whom do your sons cast them out? therefore shall they be your judges. 20 But if I by the finger of God cast out devils, no doubt the kingdom of God is come upon you. 21 When a strong man armed keepeth his palace, his goods are in peace: 22 But when a stronger than he shall come upon him, and overcome him, he taketh from him all his armour wherein he trusted, and divideth his spoils. 23 He that is not with me is against me: and he that gathereth not with me scattereth.

Help Jesus defeat Satan.

Matthew

12:30 He that is not with me is against me; and he that gathereth not with me scattereth abroad. 31 Wherefore I say unto you, All manner of sin and blasphemy shall be forgiven unto men: but the blasphemy against the Holy Ghost shall not be forgiven unto men. 32 And whosoever speaketh a word against the Son of man, it shall be forgiven him: but whosoever speaketh against the Holy Ghost, it shall not be forgiven him, neither in this world, neither in the world to come. 33 Either make the tree good, and his fruit good; or else make the tree corrupt, and his fruit corrupt: for the tree is known by his fruit. 34 O generation of vipers, how can ye, being evil, speak good things? for out of the abundance of the heart the mouth speaketh. 35 A good man out of the good treasure of the heart bringeth forth good things: and an evil man out of the evil treasure bringeth forth evil things. 36 But I say unto you, That every idle word that men shall speak, they shall give account thereof in the day of judgment. 37 For by thy words thou shalt be justified, and by thy words thou shalt be condemned.

From God's perspective, men commit two types of sins: 1) forgivable and 2) unforgivable. God directed Moses to pen these two categories. Hear Moses. **"Ye shall have one law for him that sinneth through ignorance, both for him that is born among the children of Israel, and for the stranger that sojourneth among them. But the soul that doeth ought presumptuously, whether he be born in the land, or a stranger, the same reproacheth the Lord, and that soul shall be cut off from among his people. Because he hath despised the word of the Lord, and hath broken his commandment, that soul shall utterly be cut off; his iniquity shall be upon him."** (Num.15:29-31) Sin of ignorance God offered forgiveness, but not for

Mark

3:28 Verily I say unto you, All sins shall be forgiven unto the sons of men, and blasphemies wherewith soever they shall blaspheme: 29 But he that shall blaspheme against the Holy Ghost hath never forgiveness, but is in danger of eternal damnation. 30 Because they said, he hath an unclean spirit."

the sin of presumption. God severs a person from his people for presumptuous sin. (Num.15:31-32)

New Testament writers describe two kinds of sin. **"For it is impossible for those who were once enlightened, and have tasted of the heavenly gift, and were made partakers of the Holy Ghost, and have tasted the good word of God, and the powers of the world to come, if they fall away, to renew them again unto repentance: seeing they crucify to themselves the Son of God afresh, and put him to an open shame."** Heb.6:4-6). **"For if we sin wilfully after that we have received the knowledge of the truth, there remaineth no more sacrifice for sins, but a certain fearful looking for of judgment and fiery indignation, which shall devour the adversaries. He that despised Moses' law died without mercy under two or three witnesses: Of how much sorer punishment, suppose ye, shall he be thought worthy, who hath trodden under foot the Son of God, and hath counted the blood of the covenant, wherewith he was sanctified, an unholy thing, and hath done despite unto the Spirit of grace?"** (Heb. 10:26-29) **"Now the just shall live by faith: but if any man draw back, my soul shall have no pleasure in him."** (Heb. 10:38) **"If any man see his brother sin a sin which is not unto death, he shall ask, and he shall give him life for them that sin not unto death."** (1 Jno.5:16-17) **"For if after they have escaped the pollutions of the world through the knowledge of the**

Luke
12:10 And whosoever shall speak a word against the Son of man, it shall be forgiven him: but unto him that blasphemeth against the Holy Ghost it shall not be forgiven. 11 And when they bring you unto the synagogues, and unto magistrates, and powers, take ye no thought how or what thing ye shall answer, or what ye shall say: 12 For the Holy Ghost shall teach you in the same hour what ye ought to say.
Lord and Savior Jesus Christ; they are again entangled therein, and overcome, the latter end is worse with them than the beginning. For it had been better for them not to have known the way of righteousness, than, after they have known it, to turn from the holy commandment delivered unto them. But it is happened unto them according to the true proverb, The dog is turned to his own vomit again; and the sow that was washed to her wallowing in the mire." (2 Pet.2:20-22) **"But, beloved, remember ye the words which were spoke before of the apostles of our Lord Jesus Christ; how that they told you there should be mockers in the last time, who should walk after their own ungodly lusts. These be they who separate themselves, sensual, having not the Spirit....Keep yourselves in the love of God, looking for the mercy of our Lord Jesus Christ unto eternal life. And of some have compassion, and others save with fear, pulling them out of the fire; hating even the garment spotted by the flesh."** (Jude 17-23)

Those who covenant to obey God and try to please him in all of their activities of life have assurance that God will show mercy and forgive their transgressions. (Jer.31:31-34; Rom.4:6-8; Heb.8:10-12;10:15-24) People who turn to God through Christ, but later rebel and choose to live in the world again commit the presumptuous sin of blasphemy of the Holy Spirit. God will never show them mercy. They ceased to believe God's promises. Since we are saved by faith, when we disbelieve, God no longer shows us mercy. (Rom.11:18-23)

Why did Jesus refer to blasphemy of the Holy Spirit when the Pharisees accused him of casting out devils by the power of Satan? Were they not Jews, people who covenanted with God to do all Moses commanded? (Ex.19:5-8) Moses promised a new covenant by a special prophet. (Deu. 18:15-19) All Jews who rejected that prophet must be cut off from among God's people. (Act.3:22-23) Pharisees despised Jesus and the truth he taught which he received from God. They pulled back from obeying the word of their covenant. They blasphemed the Holy Spirit of God after they once covenanted with the living God. He shows people no mercy for this sin.

In summary, blasphemy of the Holy Ghost occurs when a believer turns to unbelief and refuses to submit to God's truth. (Rom. 11:22-23) Choosing to live in Satan's kingdom again God will not forgive. For this reason, God encourages believers to encourage one another daily to follow the way of the living God, lest some become hardened through discouragements or offenses and turn from God. (Heb.10:24-31)

Though John's gospel omits discussing the topic of blasphemy of the Holy Spirit, he traces how Jews rejected the words of Jesus, **that Prophet** Moses promised. For Jews to spurn the words of **that Prophet** severed them from among God's people. (Deu.18:15-19; Act.3:22-23) Thus, rejecting Jesus' words spoken by God's Spirit cut them off from the promise of forgiveness of sins. Whether one calls it rejecting **that Prophet's** words or blasphemy against the Holy Ghost, both result in one facing God condemned to eternal destruction. Rejecting God's truth is the one sin with no forgiveness. (Heb.10:28-29) Blasphemy against God's Spirit is an intentional rebellion against God's commands, never accidental.

Matthew

12:38 Then certain of the scribes and of the Pharisees answered, saying, Master, we would see a sign from thee. 39 But he answered and said unto them, An evil and adulterous generation seeketh after a sign; and there shall no sign be given to it, but the sign of the prophet Jonas: 40 For as Jonas was three days and three nights in the whale's belly; so shall the Son of man be three days and three nights in the heart of the earth. 41 The men of Nineveh shall rise in judgment with this generation, and shall condemn it: because they repented at the preaching of Jonas; and, behold, a greater than Jonas is here. 42 The queen of the south shall rise up in the judgment with this generation, and shall condemn it: for she came from the uttermost parts of the earth to hear the wisdom of Solomon; and, behold, a greater than Solomon is here.

Jesus compared himself to Jonah and Solomon. You seek from me a sign, but I give you no sign, but that of Jonah. As he spent three days in the whale's belly, I shall remain three days within the earth. People of Nineveh repented when Jonah preached to them repentance, but you rejected God's message to you to repent

Mark

8:10 And straightway he entered into a ship with his disciples, and came into the parts of Dalmanutha. 11 And the Pharisees came forth, and began to question with him, seeking of him a sign from heaven, tempting him. 12 And he sighed deeply in his spirit, and saith, Why doth this generation seek after a sign? verily I say unto you, There shall no sign be given unto this generation. 13 And he left them, and entering into the ship again departed to the other side.

when I came, preaching to you repentance. Ninevehvites shall condemn you in judgment. They repented when Jonah preached, but you reject God's message. God placed me above Jonah. The queen of Sheba journeyed long to listen to Solomon's wisdom, but God gives me wisdom above Solomon's. You despise my God-given wisdom which heals your spirits.

God would have destroyed Nineveh had they not repented. He shall destroy your system for refusing to repent. God sent prophets to Israel, telling them to repent. Did God abandon the woes he promised? No, he sent Assyria who destroyed Samaria and carried Israel captive when they rebelled against God's law, refusing to repent.

Luke

11:29 And when the people were gathered thick together, he began to say, This is an evil generation: they seek a sign; and there shall no sign be given it, but the sign of Jonas the prophet. 30 For as Jonas was a sign unto the Ninevites, so shall also the Son of man be to this generation. 31 The queen of the south shall rise up in the judgment with the men of this generation, and condemn them: for she came from the utmost parts of the earth to hear the wisdom of Solomon; and, behold, a greater than Solomon is here. 32 The men of Nineve shall rise up in the judgment with this generation, and shall condemn it: for they repented at the preaching of Jonas; and, behold, a greater than Jonas is here.

God sent Isaiah, Jeremiah, and Ezekiel to Judah, saying, turn from your evil ways, or I shall call Babylon to destroy Jerusalem, set fire to my sanctuary, and carry captive those who survive the carnage. Did Jehoiakim, Jehoiachin, or Zedekiah repent? No, they disbelieved and asked God to hasten his word that they may see what would happen. Daniel prophesied God would destroy Jerusalem again if they refused to keep God's covenant. (Is.5:19; Jer.17:15; Dan.9:27)

Matthew

12:43 When the unclean spirit is gone out of a man, he walketh through dry places, seeking rest, and findeth none. 44 Then he saith, I will return into my house from whence I came out; and when he is come, he findeth it empty, swept, and garnished. 45 Then goeth he, and taketh with himself seven other spirits more wicked than himself, and they enter in and dwell there: and the last state of that man is worse than the first. Even so shall it be also unto this wicked generation.

Luke

11:20 But if I with the finger of God cast out devils, no doubt the kingdom of God is come upon you. 21 When a strong man armed keepeth his palace, his goods are in peace: 22 But when a stronger than he shall come upon him, and overcome him, he taketh from him all his armour wherein he trusted, and divideth his spoils. 23 He that is not with me is against me: and he that gathereth not with me scattereth. 24 When the unclean spirit is gone out of a man, he walketh through dry places, seeking rest; and finding none, he saith, I will return unto my house whence I came out. 25 And when he cometh, he findeth it swept and garnished. 26 Then goeth he, and taketh to him seven other spirits more wicked than himself; and they enter in, and dwell there: and the last state of that man is worse than the first. 27 And it came to pass, as he spake these things, a certain woman of the company lifted up her voice, and said unto him, Blessed is the womb that bare thee, and the paps which thou hast sucked. 28 But he said, Yea rather, blessed are they that hear the word of God, and keep it.

After God drives Satan from one's life, is it possible for Satan to dominate that person's life again? God instructed his Son Jesus to tell us the truth that the Evil One, once defeated, continues to use the appetites of the flesh to entice us to engage in his life style again. Though Jesus himself vanquished Satan's wiles in the wilderness, Satan departed from him only for a season. Later he utilized his ambassadors and even Jesus' disciples to tempt Jesus to abandon God's plan. Pharisees tempted Jesus to moderate God's truth on marriage, divorce, and remarriage. (Math.19:3,7) At that time Jesus faced Satan's system which encourages God's children to challenge God's way. Unlike many ministers today, Jesus refused to abandon God's truth on the matter of marriage, divorce, and remarriage. Neither leaders of his own people who questioned God's marriage-for-life truth, nor his disciples who remarked it's better not to marry if God's law requires a man and his wife to be joined together as long as they both shall live. "**The natural man receiveth not the things of the Spirit of God: for they are foolishness unto him**." (1 Cor.2:14) Only they who are willing to put to death the desires of the flesh and submit to God's law in mind and deed shall receive God's truth. (Rom.8:7-11)

When Jesus began to explain to his disciples he must go to Jerusalem to be rejected by Jewish council, be condemned to die, but rise from the dead on the third day, Peter stood as Satan's messenger, declaring this would never happen. Jesus rebuked Peter as Satan himself. (Math.16:21-23)

After Jesus' death, burial, resurrection, and ascension, Peter encountered brethren who advocated the impossibility of apostasy. Without diminishing God's truth, Peter identified these brethren as scoffers who walked after their own lusts. (2 Pet.2:1-3:7) Jude identified them as sensual, having not God's Spirit, and those who separate themselves from God. (Jude 3-19)

Does Satan today undermine God's new creation to divert us from the narrow path leading to everlasting life? Does he modify God's truth as he did in the garden of Eden, persuading Eve God did not tell her the truth about the forbidden tree of the knowledge of good and evil? Is it possible for one reborn to God to return to the wide gate, leading to the broad way which ends in destruction? What did Jesus mean by the evil spirit returning to his house with seven evil spirits more wicked than himself? Did Jesus tell his audience God's truth that Satan can reconquer his children after God translates us into the kingdom of God? If this is God's true message, why do many present-day ministers affirm that once saved, always saved? Is it impossible for a child of the living God to fall from God's grace in the Christian age so as to be eternally lost? Who tells the truth? Did Jesus whom God sent into the earth to give the light and life tell the truth, or is it our ministers who contradict Jesus?

Does Satan utilize our preachers to cause us to believe a lie and be damned? (2 Thes.2:3-12) Is this his tactic to deceive by what appears innocent? How could ministers allow Satan to use their mouths and reputation to convince us to trust a lie and suffer eternally for trusting them to feed us heavenly manna? Could they be deceived, or are their hearts hardened by greed like Balaam? (Num.22:2-24:25;31:13-16; Jude 11; Rev.2:14)

How are we to distinguish truth from lies? Writers of the gospels penned their epistles to aid their audiences to distinguish the truth about what Jesus did and taught. Their audiences, like we today, encountered ministers who contradicted God's truth Jesus taught. Only by reading and believing the true gospel accounts could they determine whether their teachers taught truth or lies.

Do all people desire truth and want to serve God honestly and faithfully? If this were true, why do people avoid ministers and talking about God? Does our fleshly nature fight against God's way? (Rom.7:14-24; Gal.5:16-17; Ja.4:4-6) Is there a tendency for ministers to preach what appeals to man's fleshly nature rather than preach God's truth which gives life to man's spirit? We must read and distinguish God's truth from Satan's lies.

How does God deal with his children when we refuse to submit to his truth? Does he give us up to go our own way with little or no consequences or does he provide justice for disobedience? Consider what God spoke to Judah by Ezekiel. "**Because they had not executed my judgments, but had despised my statutes, and had polluted my sabbaths, and their eyes were after their fathers' idols. Wherefore I gave them also statutes that were not good, and judgments whereby they should not live; And I polluted them in their own gifts, in that they caused to pass through the fire all that openeth the womb, that I might make them desolate, to the end that they might know that I am the LORD**." (Ezek.20:24-26)

Does God chastise Christian rebellion as he did Jewish contempt for his law? While teaching Thessalonian Christians, Paul wrote about the great departure from Christ. "**And for this cause God shall send them strong delusion, that they should believe a lie: That they all might be damned who believed not the truth, but had pleasure in unrighteousness. But we are bound to give thanks alway to God for you, brethren beloved of the Lord, because God hath from the beginning chosen you to salvation through sanctification of the Spirit and belief of the truth:**" (2 Thes. 2:11-13) In both Old and New testaments God punished rebellion by raising up false teachers who propagated degrading lies. For Judah their leaders convinced them to sacrifice their firstborn. Christian false teachers convinced our foreparents and us our children are born in sin and must be baptized or christened to cleanse them of Adam's sin. Christians, trust God's truth. If we fail to read and meditate on the word of God, how are we to distinguish Satan's lies from God's truth? If we believe a lie we will be condemned with Satan and his angels.

Matthew

12:46 While he yet talked to the people, behold, his mother and his brethren stood without, desiring to speak with him. 47 Then one said unto him, Behold, thy mother and thy brethren stand without, desiring to speak with thee. 48 But he answered and said unto him that told him, Who is my mother? and who are my brethren? 49 And he stretched forth his hand toward his disciples, and said, Behold my mother and my brethren! 50 For whosoever shall do the will of my Father which is in heaven, the same is my brother, and sister, and mother.

When Jesus commissioned the twelve to preach the kingdom of God to the cities of Israel, he explained that God's word separated families. Now Jesus shows that since his brothers refused to believe him, in a sense, they were not his family, the children of God. (Jno.7:2-5) Being tempted in every manner as we, Jesus must have felt hurt by his own brothers considering him a deceiver. When his mother and brothers came asking for him, he asked who were his brethren. Then he answered, saying, whoever does the will of God, they become his brethern and mother. God's family obeys God's truth before Jesus calls them his family.

Mark

3:31 There came then his brethren and his mother, and, standing without, sent unto him, calling him. 32 And the multitude sat about him, and they said unto him, Behold, thy mother and thy brethren without seek for thee. 33 And he answered them, saying, Who is my mother, or my brethren? 34 And he looked round about on them which sat about him, and said, Behold my mother and my brethren! 35 For whosoever shall do the will of God, the same is my brother, and my sister, and mother.

Whether Jews, Gentiles, or his own family, all must submit to God's true pattern of life, or Jesus and his Father claim no family ties to them. Furthermore, Jesus opened to generations of all time a means to be referred to as his brethren or sisters. Though you and I live some 60 to 7000 generations after Jesus died, he makes available to each of us that spiritual relationship. However, knowing how to partake of his family membership, but not completing the Father's will excludes us from his and God's family. (Ps.22:30)

It might be interesting to know how his brothers felt when they realized Jesus counted his disciples closer family than he did each of them. Yet, in the final

Luke

8:18 Take heed therefore how ye hear: for whosoever hath, to him shall be given; and whosoever hath not, from him shall be taken even that which he seemeth to have. 19 Then came to him his mother and his brethren, and could not come at him for the press. 20 And it was told him by certain which said, Thy mother and thy brethren stand without, desiring to see thee. 21 And he answered and said unto them, My mother and my brethren are these which hear the word of God, and do it.

analysis, Jesus must say before his Father to each of us, "He/she is my brother or sister," or, "Depart from me, you worker of iniquity. I never knew you." Then how will you or I feel?

Now's the time to gain membership in God's family. Doing God's will completes the adoption. Continuing to do the Father's will sustains that relationship. Failing to abide in the Father's will severs that family relationship. Jesus denied disobedient Jews who believed they rightly called God their Father, but continued not in his commands. To them he said, **"Ye are of your father the devil, and the lusts of your father ye will do."** (Jno.8:44) Continue in God's truth to dwell with the Father and Son. (Jno.15:1-7)

Matthew

13:1 The same day went Jesus out of the house, and sat by the sea side. 2 And great multitudes were gathered together unto him, so that he went into a ship, and sat; and the whole multitude stood on the shore. 3 And he spake many things unto them in parables, saying, Behold, a sower went forth to sow; 4 And when he sowed, some seeds fell by the way side, and the fowls came and devoured them up: 5 Some fell upon stony places, where they had not much earth: and forthwith they sprung up, because they had no deepness of earth: 6 And when the sun was up, they were scorched; and because they had no root, they withered away. 7 And some fell among thorns; and the thorns sprung up, and choked them: 8 But other fell into good ground, and brought forth fruit, some an hundredfold, some sixtyfold, some thirtyfold. 9 Who hath ears to hear, let him hear.

Mark

4:1 And he began again to teach by the sea side: and there was gathered unto him a great multitude, so that he entered into a ship, and sat in the sea; and the whole multitude was by the sea on the land. 2 And he taught them many things by parables, and said unto them in his doctrine, 3 Hearken; Behold, there went out a sower to sow: 4 And it came to pass, as he sowed, some fell by the way side, and the fowls of the air came and devoured it up. 5 And some fell on stony ground, where it had not much earth; and immediately it sprang up, because it had no depth of earth: 6 But when the sun was up, it was scorched; and because it had no root, it withered away. 7 And some fell among thorns, and the thorns grew up, and choked it, and it yielded no fruit. 8 And other fell on good ground, and did yield fruit that sprang up and increased; and brought forth, some thirty, and some sixty, and some an hundred. 9 And he said unto them, He that hath ears to hear, let him hear.

Jesus compared God's kingdom to situations common to daily life. Planting and harvesting grain he used to explain how God's word planted in people's minds may produce or not produce, depending on condition of one's heart. Seed scattered on pavement or hard-packed soil has little chance of sprouting, growing, or producing grain. Birds or animals feed on the grain. In God's kingdom birds resemble Satan removing God's word from the heart before it produces fruit to God.

Grain scattered in rocky fields may sprout, grow, and produce, but if rainfall comes too late, the plants wither and die. Rocky soil portrays how people hear God's word and receive it gladly. Trials and temptations of life diminish their zeal for God, and they abandon God.

If farmers, either by neglect or lack of time, fail to cultivate the ground to kill the weeds, grain planted in weedy soil produces no harvest because weeds and grass choke the plants by consuming too much of soil's nutrients and grow more rapidly than the grain, and this soil produces little grain for harvest. Seed sown among thorns portrays how people hear God's truth and gladly accept it, but in time cares and riches of this world take more time and interest than God's kingdom. Helping others to please our heavenly Father diminishes. Influence of God's truth in our lives fades.

Fields well cultivated and watered produce plentiful harvest, depending on the fertility of the soil. Productive soil illustrates how people hear the word of God, use it to guide their lives, and produce abundant fruit to honor their heavenly Father. As some fields produce more abundantly than others, so the word of God activates some lives more than others, depending on abilities each possesses.

Luke included the names of women who accompanied and ministered to Jesus from

Luke

8:1 And it came to pass afterward, that he
went throughout every city and village,
preaching and shewing the glad tidings of
the kingdom of God: and the twelve were
with him, 2 And certain women, which
had been healed of evil spirits and
infirmities, Mary called Magdalene, out of
whom went seven devils, 3 And Joanna
the wife of Chuza Herod's steward, and
Susanna, and many others, which
ministered unto him of their substance. 4
And when much people were gathered
together, and were come to him out of
every city, he spake by a parable: 5 A
sower went out to sow his seed: and as he
sowed, some fell by the way side; and it
was trodden down, and the fowls of the
air devoured it. 6 And some fell upon a
rock; and as soon as it was sprung up, it
withered away, because it lacked
moisture. 7 And some fell among thorns;
and the thorns sprang up with it, and
choked it. 8 And other fell on good
ground, and sprang up, and bare fruit an
hundredfold. And when he had said these
things, he cried, He that hath ears to hear,
let him hear.

their own money. Theophilus evidently knew some of these people. Including their names made it possible for Theophilus to associate what Luke penned with what he knew, making a personal connection with the activities of Jesus.

Closing the parable of the sower, Jesus stressed the need to listen to the parable and heed it. Throughout Old Testament times, God instructed priests and prophets to call his people to repentance. Rarely did they respond to God. When they did, repentance lasted briefly. More likely, God's people ignored their teachers or persecuted them. Multitudes who came to hear Jesus acted similarly to their forefathers. They appeared to appreciate hearing the message of God as Jesus taught, but their hearts continued to long for the affairs of this life. Seed sown by the wayside signified them. They listened to the glad tidings that the kingdom of God neared, but to change lifestyle to prepare to enter that kingdom they refused. Seed sown on rocky soil typified many of his hearers. They chose to enter the kingdom, but frowns of Pharisees and their threats to cast them out of the synagogues curtailed their interest in the kingdom of God. Others interested in God's kingdom soon chose to return to seeking material gain, rather that the heavenly treasures. They demonstrated the seed sown among thorns. Cares and riches of this life choked the fruit of God out of their lives. Those disciples of Jesus who held fast to God's truth and changed their goals of life to honor God characterized the seed planted in good soil. Realizing how his audience would respond to his parable, Jesus pleaded with them to evaluate what he taught and picture their own lives to see clearly which kind of soil they depicted.

Today we hear ministers retell this parable and seem willing to evaluate it for others, but so often fail to see that even we ourselves portray one of the soils in the parable. God's kingdom opens only to those of us who hear the truth of God and produce fruit, honoring God.

Will God's word ever change this pattern of outward devotion to God which lacks depth? Will individuals some day learn that doing good to others rather than pushing them down blesses our lives and those we help? Can we expect nations to some day cease practicing war against one another? May we anticipate the time that rulers cease to rule for power, honor, and enriching their own pockets at the expense of the people? Will rulers some day find people obedient to the laws of the land? Does God really intend Jesus to rule on David's throne until he subdues rebellion in the lives of most people? Yes, but at present it looks as though that time must be centuries away.

Matthew

13:10 And the disciples came, and said unto him, Why speakest thou unto them in parables? 11 He answered and said unto them, Because it is given unto you to know the mysteries of the kingdom of heaven, but to them it is not given. 12 For whosoever hath, to him shall be given, and he shall have more abundance: but whosoever hath not, from him shall be taken away even that he hath. 13 Therefore speak I to them in parables: because they seeing see not; and hearing they hear not, neither do they understand. 14 And in them is fulfilled the prophecy of Esaias, which saith, By hearing ye shall hear, and shall not understand; and seeing ye shall see, and shall not perceive: 15 For this people's heart is waxed gross, and their ears are dull of hearing, and their eyes they have closed; lest at any time they should see with their eyes, and hear with their ears, and should understand with their heart, and should be converted, and I should heal them. 16 But blessed are your eyes, for they see: and your ears, for they hear. 17 For verily I say unto you, That many prophets and righteous men have desired to see those things which ye see, and have not seen them; and to hear those things which ye hear, and have not heard them.

Jesus illustrates seed sowed by wayside. Understanding parables proves difficult for those who cherish this world's ways. Why did Jesus speak to the multitude by parables? He explained some have not the love of God. When they hear God speak to them in parables, they have not sufficient interest to meditate on what God meant and dismiss the information, proceeding with their customary activities.

God's kingdom receives people who diligently desire to seek God and be subject to his law of righteousness. Righteous men throughout all ages have awaited the promised kingdom of God. Every word

Mark

4:10 And when he was alone, they that were about him with the twelve asked of him the parable. 11 And he said unto them, Unto you it is given to know the mystery of the kingdom of God: but unto them that are without, all these things are done in parables: 12 That seeing they may see, and not perceive; and hearing they may hear, and not understand; lest at any time they should be converted, and their sins should be forgiven them.

spoken to them meant a message from their living Father in heaven whom they wanted to meet and with whom they hoped to live forever. Gates of heaven remain closed to men who have little interest in anything beyond this life. How shall God separate the righteous from the unrighteous? Parables prove effective. Righteous men search for parable's meaning; the unrighteous soon dismiss them from their minds as unimportant. God opens the minds of those who meditate on God's words to fathom the meaning of parables. Since the unrighteous cared so little about understanding the mysteries of the kingdom of heaven, God withholds understanding. Ezra illustrates the issue. **"For Ezra had prepared his heart to seek the law of the Lord, and to do it, and to teach in Israel statutes and judgments."** (Ez.7:10) Unless we prepare our hearts to do and teach God's statutes and judgments more than we desire this world, God withholds understanding mysteries of his kingdom. God's ways are beyond us without his guidance. Either we truly desire to live in God's kingdom and search for it as a man searches for gold or God will not open our hearts to fathom the parables he uses to teach us. God instructed Isaiah to go to Israel and instruct them, but they would not understand. Their eyes and ears were closed that they perceived not what God said. (Is.6:9-10) We determine our destiny by holding or abandoning God's truth.

Luke

8:9 And his disciples asked him, saying, What might this parable be? 10 And he said, Unto you it is given to know the mysteries of the kingdom of God: but to others in parables; that seeing they might not see, and hearing they might not understand.

Consider the difference in how much of this encounter each gospel writer recorded. Matthew included details of Isaiah's prophecy whereas Mark and Luke omitted Isaiah's words. Why? I suggest that Matthew's audience, being Jews, knew Isaiah's prophecy. He referred to it to explain why Jesus spoke in parables. Mark and Luke addressed people whose background lacked knowledge of Isaiah and other Old Testament prophets. Referring to Isaiah, Matthew not only bolstered his position with Jews, he also documented his gospel with information which they accepted as reliable.

Jesus expected his disciples to understand all parables. Did he know the hearts of those he chose apostles? Were their hearts righteous so that they would seek the meaning of all parables? Consider their question. They asked for Jesus to explain the parable of the sower. Desire to understand God's word sets the stage to understand whether one was in the presence of Jesus then or in the presence of God today. If you and I apply our minds and hearts to know the will of God, he will provide that understanding. Unrighteous men care little about God, and he closes their minds to what they see and what they hear. Is not Judas an example? He followed Jesus during his personal ministry. He listened to those parables and saw overwhelming miracles, but he betrayed Jesus for thirty pieces of silver. Which did he value more: God or this life? Jesus testified of Judas, "**Have not I chosen you twelve, and one of you is a devil? He spoke of Judas Iscariot the son of Simon, being one of the twelve.**" (Jno.6:70-71)

If Judas who followed Jesus retained the unrighteous mind, what about those who consider themselves Christians and attend church frequently? Is it possible for the devil to deceive us, making us think we are righteous? Is not this the way Satan retained his control over scribes and Pharisees? Didn't they consider themselves righteous? The Pharisee who thanked God he wasn't like other men and publicans prided himself that he, in his eyes, pleased God. (Lk.18:9-14) Jesus cleared away the chaff and explained that the humble publican God justified, but not the self-righteous Pharisee. God's ways astound us. Affairs of this life obscure our spiritual vision. Without a heart set on loving God and his truth more than we love family, wealth, or life itself, God closes our ears and hearts to his truth. We never come to the knowledge of the way of the living Father in heaven.

How does one prepare his heart to seek the law of the Lord that God may reveal to him the mysteries of the kingdom of heaven? Paul penned, "**Set your affection on things above, not on things on the earth.**" (Col.3:2) Affections, not intellect alone, control the process. Studying about God without loving God with all our heart and mind, God remains remote. He draws nigh to those who truly draw near to him. (2 Chr.15:1-2) "**Draw nigh to God, and he will draw nigh to you.**" (Ja.4:8)

Does God work this way only with parables, or will God close the minds of all people that they understand not any of his truths if they set not their hearts to know and do his commands? Paul implies God works this way with all his word. "**Consider what I say; and the Lord give thee understanding in all things.**" (2 Tim.2:7) Whatever God commands, we must desire to do it, or he blocks our understanding.

When you and I read or hear God's word and think about what God asks us to do, God opens our minds. Without evaluating his word God closes our minds.

Matthew

13:18 Hear ye therefore the parable of the sower. 19 When any one heareth the word of the kingdom, and understandeth it not, then cometh the wicked one, and catcheth away that which was sown in his heart. This is he which received seed by the way side. 20 But he that received the seed into stony places, the same is he that heareth the word, and anon with joy receiveth it; 21 Yet hath he not root in himself, but dureth for a while: for when tribulation or persecution ariseth because of the word, by and by he is offended. 22 He also that received seed among the thorns is he that heareth the word; and the care of this world, and the deceitfulness of riches, choke the word, and he becometh unfruitful. 23 But he that received seed into the good ground is he that heareth the word, and understandeth it; which also beareth fruit, and bringeth forth, some an hundredfold, some sixty, some thirty.

Four groups hear good news about God's kingdom. Three respond: one fell away; one longed for the world; and one produced fruit faithfully. If God offers a better way of life, why do so few obey and continue faithful to God? Is this life that powerful?

Mark

4:13 And he said unto them, Know ye not this parable? and how then will ye know all parables? 14 The sower soweth the word. 15 And these are they by the way side, where the word is sown; but when they have heard, Satan cometh immediately, and taketh away the word that was sown in their hearts. 16 And these are they likewise which are sown on stony ground; who, when they have heard the word, immediately receive it with gladness; 17 And have no root in themselves, and so endure but for a time: afterward, when affliction or persecution ariseth for the word's sake, immediately they are offended. 18 And these are they which are sown among thorns; such as hear the word, 19 And the cares of this world, and the deceitfulness of riches, and the lusts of other things entering in, choke the word, and it becometh unfruitful. 20 And these are they which are sown on good ground; such as hear the word, and receive it, and bring forth fruit, some thirtyfold, some sixty, and some an hundred.

Satan's influence on men continues to produce evil fruits even after God's words enter our hearts.

As with Adam and Eve,

Luke

8:11 Now the parable is this: The seed is the word of God. 12 Those by the way side are they that hear; then cometh the devil, and taketh away the word out of their hearts, lest they should believe and be saved. 13 They on the rock are they, which, when they hear, receive the word with joy; and these have no root, which for a while believe, and in time of temptation fall away. 14 And that which fell among thorns are they, which, when they have heard, go forth, and are choked with cares and riches and pleasures of this life, and bring no fruit to perfection. 15 But that on the good ground are they, which in an honest and good heart, having heard the word, keep it, and bring forth fruit with patience.

Satan subverts God's truth. By convincing us God doesn't mean what he said; by filling minds with searching for aspirations of this world; or by persecution he diverts men from acting on God's truth. Instead, we follow Satan's way. This prevents us from entering the kingdom of God and producing fruit which honor God. Satan convinces us that his plan of life satisfies more than the complete life God offers. We must not believe or try his lies.

Mark

4:21 And he said unto them, Is a candle brought to be put under a bushel, or under a bed? and not to be set on a candlestick? 22 For there is nothing hid, which shall not be manifested; neither was any thing kept secret, but that it should come abroad. 23 If any man have ears to hear, let him hear. 24 And he said unto them, Take heed what ye hear: with what measure ye mete, it shall be measured to you: and unto you that hear shall more be given. 25 For he that hath, to him shall be given: and he that hath not, from him shall be taken even that which he hath.

Jesus employed the candle parable to encourage his followers to evaluate the parable of the sower and to examine their lives. Determine your condition before God. I brought to you the candle lighted by the Father himself. Don't hide it under a bed or bushel. Let God's light illuminate your life. His light may reveal to your friends deeds in your life you wish to hide, but they aren't secrets before God. Not one dark spot in your life remains concealed in judgment. Everyone will know. Show wisdom. Admit sin. Humble yourself before God; plead for God's mercy.

Jesus said hear what I've spoken to you. Retain it in your hearts and consider it day and night. Evaluate your status before God. He opens understanding. If you dismiss God's truth from your minds, even what knowledge of God you think you have shall vanish, leaving you in greater darkness of sin. God requires every person to give account to him for how he uses life. None of us must give account to Satan or his followers for serving God. If we live to please God, he shall fulfill his promises of a fuller life on earth and to dwell with him, his Son, and the redeemed of all ages. Wrath rests on all ungodliness and unrighteousness of men.

Paul echoed the same message to saints in

Luke

8:16 No man, when he hath lighted a candle, covereth it with a vessel, or putteth it under a bed; but setteth it on a candlestick, that they which enter in may see the light. 17 For nothing is secret, that shall not be made manifest; neither any thing hid, that shall not be known and come abroad. 18 Take heed therefore how ye hear: for whosoever hath, to him shall be given; and whosoever hath not, from him shall be taken even that which he seemeth to have.

Rome. Just men live by faith, but God's wrath rests on all who know God's truth, but deny its influence. God made known his majesty in creation, but men turned their thoughts from God's wonders and became unthankful for the beauty he made available for man's use. They exchanged a living God for idols and worshiped creatures instead of the Creator. Thrusting God from their minds, he abandoned them to fulfill their lusts. Men and women whom God created to become companions in life to populate the earth abandoned God's plan for lust, even becoming homosexuals. Every degrading activity imaginable drove men to hate and destroy one another. God looked on the chaos, but allowed us to reap the futility of our rejection of God. Though we know we'll face God in judgment, we try to cast this idea behind us. (Rom.1:17-32)

God, Jesus, apostles, and faithful ministers plead with us to place God's candle on a candlestick and examine what havoc Satan works in our lives and world. Those with wealth horde it and consider not the plight of the poor and needy. Once some gain power, they use it to coerce subordinates to comply or suffer. Husbands and wives fight and divorce and consider not their children's needs. God's light provides a better way of life to all who hear and do what he commands. If Satan's ugly deeds have darkened light of God's truth for you, repent and correct your life to honor God and Jesus.

Matthew

**13:24 Another parable put he forth unto
them, saying, The kingdom of heaven is
likened unto a man which sowed good
seed in his field: 25 But while men slept,
his enemy came and sowed tares among
the wheat, and went his way. 26 But when
the blade was sprung up, and brought
forth fruit, then appeared the tares also.
27 So the servants of the householder
came and said unto him, Sir, didst not
thou sow good seed in thy field? from
whence then hath it tares? 28 He said
unto them, An enemy hath done this. The
servants said unto him, Wilt thou then
that we go and gather them up? 29 But he
said, Nay; lest while ye gather up the
tares, ye root up also the wheat with them.
30 Let both grow together until the
harvest: and in the time of harvest I will
say to the reapers, Gather ye together
first the tares, and bind them in bundles
to burn them: but gather the wheat into
my barn.**

Matthew

**13:36 Then Jesus sent the multitude away,
and went into the house: and his disciples
came unto him, saying, Declare unto us
the parable of the tares of the field. 37 He
answered and said unto them, He that
soweth the good seed is the Son of man; 38
The field is the world; the good seed are
the children of the kingdom; but the tares
are the children of the wicked one; 39 The
enemy that sowed them is the devil; the
harvest is the end of the world; and the
reapers are the angels. 40 As therefore the
tares are gathered and burned in the fire;
so shall it be in the end of this world. 41
The Son of man shall send forth his
angels, and they shall gather out of his
kingdom all things that offend, and them
which do iniquity; 42 And shall cast them
into a furnace of fire: there shall be
wailing and gnashing of teeth. 43 Then
shall the righteous shine forth as the sun
in the kingdom of their Father. Who hath
ears to hear, let him hear.**

Jesus explained by parable a second mystery of the kingdom of God. How can God's kingdom encompass wicked people on earth? Jesus planted the good seed of the kingdom of God, but Satan's servants followed, scattering their propaganda of this life, persuading God's children that they need not adhere to all God's instructions. This message appeals to those who long for the flesh pots of spiritual Egypt. They mix the light of life with the night of death.

As God's children recognize Satan's children among them, they ask if they need to uproot and rid all Satan's followers from the kingdom of heaven. No, let them alone. In the day of reckoning, God plans to sever from his family all who practice unrighteousness and ungodliness.

Only those destitute of light fail to perceive today's state of the kingdom of heaven on earth. Not one decree of Satan fails to be propagandized by those who claim citizenship in God's kingdom. Every statute God decreed to organize his kingdom Satan's servants modify or delete. Presbyters or elders whom God decreed to be married, godly men Satan has changed to include unmarried men, women, and homosexuals. Ordinances explaining how men enter the kingdom of light by believing the gospel of Jesus Christ and being buried with him in the watery grave of baptism they replace with sprinkling unbelieving infants and/or believing without burial baptism. Daily godly living Satan changed to occasional church attendance with little restriction on how one lies, cheats, or degrades his fellow sojourners. Assemblies God ordained to promote fellowship with God and man Satan altered to become social gatherings to display man's pride which dishonors the poor. Worship to draw close to God through teaching, singing spiritual songs, prayer, weekly partaking the Lord' supper, and giving as one prospers Satan modifies to become assemblies to discuss social issues, band concerts, and

Mark

4:26 And he said, So is the kingdom of God, as if a man should cast seed into the ground; 27 And should sleep, and rise night and day, and the seed should spring and grow up, he knoweth not how. 28 For the earth bringeth forth fruit of herself; first the blade, then the ear, after that the full corn in the ear. 29 But when the fruit is brought forth, immediately he putteth in the sickle, because the harvest is come.

choirs which excite the fleshly emotions of participants and/or audiences, quarterly half communions of the Lord's supper where laity eats the bread, but priests drink the wine, and church fundraising bazaars instead of willful giving as God ordained. Have we fallen to the bottom of Satan's dungeon, or is the worst yet to come?

Jesus advised, "Let them grow together. God's angels shall sever and destroy the tares in the final day. Then shall the righteous shine brilliantly in the Father's kingdom." Will of the Father they have not changed. Organization of his church they honored by keeping it as given by his apostles. Assemblies remained gatherings to heal the heartaches caused by Satan's disrespectful children. They humbled themselves and encouraged the poor and persecuted. Reading the word of God and searching for how to improve their lives they gladly hear. Singing songs of heaven and dwelling with Jesus and God encouraged them to anticipate that heavenly abode and disregard the taunts Satan's servants cast at them for being so old fashioned and unprogressive. Communing with God and Jesus weekly remains a highlight with which to begin each week. Genuine prayers in which each child of God approaches God through his Son continues to be an often, more than daily, fellowship with our heavenly Father. Laying up treasure in heaven by visiting fatherless, widows, needy and giving willingly blesses their lives more than receiving this life's wealth. They experience the blessings God promised to the patriarch Abraham centuries long gone. David's throne makes available to them the promise that God remembered their sins and iniquities no more. Their consciences God cleanses and makes their offenses void before God and man because the blood of Christ ever cleanses them of sin.

Let us think sanely. If our lives fail to prosper in the ways of God today, reflect on the words of Jesus. Perhaps we, too, partake of Satan's tares. God blesses the lives of his children in this life and in that to come, only if we submit to all his will. Don't be deceived by Satan's modifications of the truth of the living God. He delivered to his Son Jesus all he desired of us. Not one decree of the Father did Jesus fail to explain to his apostles. (Jno.15:15) As Paul noted, we don't need to ask how we can know his will today. We have <u>all</u> of it. (Rom.10:6-8) Do we have faith to perform what God says?

Time has come that God's children must distinguish between the good seed of the kingdom of heaven and the tares of the Evil One. As Isaiah advised Judah centuries ago, don't look to those who point you to wizards and familiar spirits who mutter and peep. They who instruct you to seek unto the dead to intercede to God for you turn you from God. To the law and the testimony. If they speak not according to this word, it is because there is no light in them. (Is.8:19-20) If someone attempts to instruct you in searching for God by some other means than through what Jesus taught, they turn you from the living Father. Though they show ever so much piety and devotion to God, they know not God if they stray from the precepts delivered unto us through Jesus and his apostles.

What about whole assemblies that practice Satan's modifications of God's pattern for his holy sanctuary? Shall we change to become like them? If we do, we become part of the tares which God permits to exist until harvest, then they shall be destroyed. Ask God's for help to distinguish truth from error.

Matthew

13:31 Another parable put he forth unto them, saying, The kingdom of heaven is like to a grain of mustard seed, which a man took, and sowed in his field: 32 Which indeed is the least of all seeds: but when it is grown, it is the greatest among herbs, and becometh a tree, so that the birds of the air come and lodge in the branches thereof. 33 Another parable spake he unto them; The kingdom of heaven is like unto leaven, which a woman took, and hid in three measures of meal, till the whole was leavened. 34 All these things spake Jesus unto the multitude in parables; and without a parable spake he not unto them: 35 That it might be fulfilled which was spoken by the prophet, saying, I will open my mouth in parables; I will utter things which have been kept secret from the foundation of the world.

Parables of mustard seed and leaven each illustrate one feature of God's kingdom. Mustard seed, being one of the smallest garden seeds, germinates and grows to a magnificent plant, on which birds roost. Small amounts of leaven produce carbon dioxide sufficient to inflate great quantities of dough. God's kingdom originates as an insignificant small kingdom

Mark

4:30 And he said, Whereunto shall we liken the kingdom of God? or with what comparison shall we compare it? 31 It is like a grain of mustard seed, which, when it is sown in the earth, is less than all the seeds that be in the earth: 32 But when it is sown, it groweth up, and becometh greater than all herbs, and shooteth out great branches; so that the fowls of the air may lodge under the shadow of it. 33 And with many such parables spake he the word unto them, as they were able to hear it. 34 But without a parable spake he not unto them: and when they were alone, he expounded all things to his disciples.

among the nations, but it spreads to control people in every nation under heaven. Daniel compared its beginning to a stone quarried which grows to a mountain, filling the whole earth. (Dan.2:34-35,44-45)

At its inception on the day of Pentecost, 33 A.D., in Jerusalem, about 120 souls comprised God's kingdom on earth. (Act.1:15) By 450 A.D., it affected every corner of the Roman Empire, stretching from India to the Atlantic Ocean. Today, most nations feel the impact of God's kingdom, though not always in a wholesome form.

Luke

13:18 Then said he, Unto what is the kingdom of God like? and whereunto shall I resemble it? 19 It is like a grain of mustard seed, which a man took, and cast into his garden; and it grew, and waxed a great tree; and the fowls of the air lodged in the branches of it. 20 And again he said, Whereunto shall I liken the kingdom of God? 21 It is like leaven, which a woman took and hid in three measures of meal, till the whole was leavened.

What does the future hold for God's eternal kingdom on earth? God's decree destines it to control every nation and individual under heaven. Jesus shall rule till he subdues every enemy.

Will this super form of God's kingdom prove beneficial to individuals, families, and nations? Through it, God promised to Abraham that he would bless every family on earth. (Gen.12:3)

What aspect of God's kingdom produces benefits? From its beginning God designed it not to compete with civil governments. Instead, he plans it to bring honest leaders, obedient populace, and a consideration of the welfare of every person in all nations, and eternal life only to the obedient. In time, his kingdom will prevail.

Matthew

**13:44 Again, the kingdom of heaven is like
unto treasure hid in a field; the which
when a man hath found, he hideth, and
for joy thereof goeth and selleth all that
he hath, and buyeth that field. 45 Again,
the kingdom of heaven is like unto a
merchant man, seeking goodly pearls: 46
Who, when he had found one pearl of
great price, went and sold all that he had,
and bought it. 47 Again, the kingdom of
heaven is like unto a net, that was cast
into the sea, and gathered of every kind:
48 Which, when it was full, they drew to
shore, and sat down, and gathered the
good into vessels, but cast the bad away.
49 So shall it be at the end of the world:
the angels shall come forth, and sever the
wicked from among the just, 50 And shall
cast them into the furnace of fire: there
shall be wailing and gnashing of teeth. 51
Jesus saith unto them, Have ye
understood all these things? They say
unto him, Yea, Lord. 52 Then said he unto
them, Therefore every scribe which is
instructed unto the kingdom of heaven is
like unto a man that is an householder,
which bringeth forth out of his treasure
things new and old.**

Parables of a prized treasure and goodly pearl portray one significant characteristic of God's kingdom. Those who choose to enter value it so highly they willingly sell all they own to purchase a place therein. If you or I do not place unlimited value in the kingdom of God, sometime Satan will discover the correct combination to push us into sacrificing our place in God's kingdom to preserve whatever we treasure greater. Maybe it will be prestige, money, husband, wife, children, friends, etc. Until I place greater value on God's way, something shall influence me to sell God for part of this world.

Parables of net and tares convey equivalent messages. Kingdom of God encompasses a variety of spirits, many ungodly as well as righteous. Until the end of time, good and bad claim membership in God's kingdom. When the angel sounds the trumpet, heralding Christ's return, those yet alive rise to meet Christ in the air. All entombed hear the trumpet and exit their graves. (1 Thes.4:13-18) At that time God severs the tares from the wheat and the desirable fish from the offensive, illustrating God's separation of the wicked from the just. Then the righteous go with Jesus to his place of rest to dwell eternally. (Heb.4:8-11) Wicked souls God casts into eternal fire with the devil and his angels. (Math.25:41) In a sense, we make the judgment by our choices in life. Valuing material objects or favor of men above God's favor, we judge ourselves unworthy of God's rest. (Act.13:46)

Jesus asked the apostles if they understood these parables. They affirmed they did. In response, Jesus compared them to scribes. Parable of a scribe instructed the twelve to use the Old Testament to teach God's truth in addition to that which Jesus taught. Applying the Holy Scriptures to show Jesus fulfilled all Old Testament promises concerning him and to encourage godly living divides truth correctly. Compelling people to keep ceremonies of Moses' law as necessary for salvation violates both Old and New testaments. (1 Tim.1:2-11) Any scribe today or to the end of time who binds the yoke of bondage on people, fails to be a scribe of Jesus or God. (Act.15:1-29) Uninformed scribes divide God's kingdom today.

Summarizing Jesus' parables, it becomes obvious he utilized situations common to the lives of those whom he taught to explain how the kingdom of God functions, extent of its sphere of influence, how people who enter the kingdom value it, why God allows ungodly people to claim citizenship therein, but how God severs the wicked from among his people. Perceiving God's truth, it behooves each person to examine his/her value of God's kingdom. Is it genuine?

Matthew

13:53 And it came to pass, that when Jesus had finished these parables, he departed thence. 54 And when he was come into his own country, he taught them in their synagogue, insomuch that they were astonished, and said, Whence hath this man this wisdom, and these mighty works? 55 Is not this the carpenter's son? is not his mother called Mary? and his brethren, James, and Joses, and Simon, and Judas? 56 And his sisters, are they not all with us? Whence then hath this man all these things? 57 And they were offended in him. But Jesus said unto them, A prophet is not without honour, save in his own country, and in his own house. 58 And he did not many mighty works there because of their unbelief.

Matthew, Mark, and Luke record that Jesus preached in his hometown, Nazareth. All three tell how his acquaintances marveled and wondered how he gained his understanding and fluency in the Scriptures. He's but a carpenter's son. His mother, brothers, and sisters we know. Why is he different? They discredited him and his miracles. Jesus understood that even a prophet receives no honor in his own land.

Luke detailed that Jesus first read Isaiah 61:1-3 while in their synagogue. He explained that God anointed him to fulfill that day the deliverance Isaiah promised. Your rejection of God's deliverance resembles Israel's refusal of God's word in Elijah's day. During the forty-two-month drought and famine, God sent Elijah to a widow in Sidon. She received Elijah, and God blessed her and her son with food, while Israel perished. Furthermore, Elisha cleansed Naaman, the Syrian, of his leprosy, but left lepers in Israel to rot. These words of praise for hated Syrians chafed his neighbors. They prepared to cast him off the cliff near Nazareth, but God spared him as he had Elijah and Elisha.

Mark

6:1 And he went out from thence, and came into his own country; and his disciples follow him. 2 And when the sabbath day was come, he began to teach in the synagogue: and many hearing him were astonished, saying, From whence hath this man these things? and what wisdom is this which is given unto him, that even such mighty works are wrought by his hands? 3 Is not this the carpenter, the son of Mary, the brother of James, and Joses, and of Juda, and Simon? and are not his sisters here with us? And they were offended at him. 4 But Jesus said unto them, A prophet is not without honour, but in his own country, and among his own kin, and in his own house. 5 And he could there do no mighty work, save that he laid his hands upon a few sick folk, and healed them. 6 And he marvelled because of their unbelief. And he went round about the villages, teaching.

Why did Luke alone record praise for Syrians, but denunciation for people of Nazareth? I suggest that Luke came from Syria and wrote his gospel for Syrians. Seeing that Jesus honored their forefathers for believing God's prophets, he hoped the Syrians of his day might be encouraged to follow the examples of faith of the Sidon widow and their military leader, Naaman. When they read his gospel and noted that Jesus praised their fathers, perhaps they might realize that God opened the kingdom of heaven to them also.

What evidence documents Luke as having originated in Syria? As Paul confirmed the churches in Syria and Cilicia, he prepared to cross from Asia Minor to Macedonia. (Act.15:41-16:10) Luke first recorded his accompanying Paul at this time, using the term "we" as Paul prepared to cross over into Macedonia. Thus, Luke joined Paul's company while he preached in the area Syria controlled for centuries.

Luke

4:16 And he came to Nazareth, where he had been brought up: and, as his custom was, he went into the synagogue on the sabbath day, and stood up for to read. 17 And there was delivered unto him the book of the prophet Esaias. And when he had opened the book, he found the place where it was written, 18 The Spirit of the Lord is upon me, because he hath anointed me to preach the gospel to the poor; he hath sent me to heal the brokenhearted, to preach deliverance to the captives, and recovering of sight to the blind, to set at liberty them that are bruised, 19 To preach the acceptable year of the Lord. 20 And he closed the book, and he gave it again to the minister, and sat down. And the eyes of all them that were in the synagogue were fastened on him. 21 And he began to say unto them, This day is this scripture fulfilled in your ears. 22 And all bare him witness, and wondered at the gracious words which proceeded out of his mouth. And they said, Is not this Joseph's son? 23 And he said unto them, Ye will surely say unto me this proverb, Physician, heal thyself: whatsoever we have heard done in Capernaum, do also here in thy country. 24 And he said, Verily I say unto you, No prophet is accepted in his own country. 25 But I tell you of a truth, many widows were in Israel in the days of Elias, when the heaven was shut up three years and six months, when great famine was throughout all the land; 26 But unto none of them was Elias sent, save unto Sarepta, a city of Sidon, unto a woman that was a widow. 27 And many lepers were in Israel in the time of Eliseus the prophet; and none of them was cleansed, saving Naaman the Syrian. 28 And all they in the synagogue, when they heard these things, were filled with wrath, 29 And rose up, and thrust him out of the city, and led him unto the brow of the hill whereon their city was built, that they might cast him down headlong. 30 But he passing through the midst of them went his way,

A major question rises in my mind about Luke's record. Why did he mention first that Jesus preached in Nazareth? Even from his own account, he indicated Jesus preached and performed miracles in Capernaum before going to Nazareth. Luke's detail of John the Baptist's preaching tells how he explained to the people, publicans, and soldiers what they needed to do to prepare for the kingdom of God. This prepared his hearers for God's gospel. At Nazareth, only Luke mentioned Jesus as Joseph's son. How did he learn his message and gain the ability to work wonders? Receiving God's Spirit empowered him with unusual abilities. Reflecting on the people of old, it's evident that as God's Spirit joins with men, he empowers them to accomplish deeds impossible to others. Samson's strength rivaled all men's, but when God's Spirit departed, Samson's God-given power vanished. (Jud. 13:25;14:5-6;15:14-15;16:17,20)

Luke alone encouraged people to ask God for his Holy Spirit. (Lk.11:13) He alone noted that Jesus promised his apostles power when the Holy Spirit came to them. (Lk.24:49) Before receiving the gift of God's Spirit, they feared to acknowledge knowing Jesus. (Math.26:56-74) After God's Spirit visited them, they gained confidence to boldly preach Jesus in the face of seemingly insurmountable odds and oppositions. It seems Luke impressed on his readers that God gladly provides his Holy Spirit to his children, not necessarily to work wonders so much as to give them power to resist the forces of the Evil One. Today God grants his Holy Spirit to all who obey his commands. (Act.5:32) As his Spirit empowered Samson to withstand the forces of the Philistines, it strengthens us to overcome Satan's wiles. (Eph.3:16;6:10) Let us all have faith to ask for God's Spirit to strengthen us.

Luke

13:1 There were present at that season some that told him of the Galilaeans, whose blood Pilate had mingled with their sacrifices. 2 And Jesus answering said unto them, Suppose ye that these Galilaeans were sinners above all the Galilaeans, because they suffered such things? 3 I tell you, Nay: but, except ye repent, ye shall all likewise perish. 4 Or those eighteen, upon whom the tower in Siloam fell, and slew them, think ye that they were sinners above all men that dwelt in Jerusalem? 5 I tell you, Nay: but, except ye repent, ye shall all likewise perish.

Relating how bad others act or telling of some terrible catastrophe occupies conversations and thoughts of many. Some complained to Jesus how Governor Pilate degraded Galileans by mingling their blood with sacrifices. Jesus inquired if those Galileans committed more horrible sins than other Galileans which brought such dishonor to them. What about the eighteen on whom the tower of Siloam fell? Were they worse sinners than others in Jerusalem? We tend to think gross sinners suffer terribly, but God spares us because we are righteous. Jesus redirected their thinking. Unless all of you repent, you also shall all perish. (See Job 9:22; Ecc.9:11.)

Are all of us sinful before God? Why hasn't he destroyed us too? God isn't vengeful. He desires every person to correct relations with others and God. (2 Pet.3:9) Without repentance God promises that all shall perish. Parents need to correct their children's misdeeds. Often children persist in disobedience. After repeated correction, parents must apply some physical punishment, hoping to encourage a changed life pattern in their children. God uses this same procedure to produce repentance in his children. (Heb.12:4-11)

Luke's entry proposes to direct our attention away from how bad others act and influence us to consider our transgressions. Sin deserves death. (Rom.1:32;6:23) God demands that I cease living in sin, or he must use corrective measures to humble me. If I persist in rebellion, God utilizes more stringent chastening to produce repentance. Without repentance and submission to God's commands, I leave God no choice but to destroy me with Satan and all his followers. (Math.25:31-46)

How can this message be good news? It begins to banish barriers we build when we sin against others and God. (Col.1:21) God shows how to restore friendship and peace. It begins with humility. When I admit my faults and ask for help to change my relationships with God and others, then God opens a gateway to rebuilding proper associations.

If God is truly our heavenly Father who cares for all his children, the obedient and rebellious, will he not use every means available to correct his children lest we destroy ourselves by greed and selfishness? Would any of us as parents allow our children to proceed with activities which we know will destroy them? Don't we attempt to teach each of them better choices, hoping to save them from miseries they bring on themselves? Seeing we seek to spare our children unnecessary hardships, do we really expect our heavenly Father to sit by and allow us to go headlong into destruction without intervening?

God sent Jesus to inform Israelites their deeds were destroying themselves and those with whom they associated, but many disregarded Jesus' admonitions. He therefore warned them that unless they all repented, they likewise would perish in some catastrophic tragedy, or worse yet, die in rebellion to God and suffer eternally. His words must be regarded as applying to me, you, and every person who lives since Jesus uttered those words. Unless you and I repent, we all shall perish with all those we consider wicked.

Matthew

14:1 At that time Herod the tetrarch heard of the fame of Jesus, 2 And said unto his servants, This is John the Baptist; he is risen from the dead; and therefore mighty works do shew forth themselves in him. 3 For Herod had laid hold on John, and bound him, and put him in prison for Herodias' sake, his brother Philip's wife. 4 For John said unto him, It is not lawful for thee to have her. 5 And when he would have put him to death, he feared the multitude, because they counted him as a prophet. 6 But when Herod's birthday was kept, the daughter of Herodias danced before them, and pleased Herod. 7 Whereupon he promised with an oath to give her whatsoever she would ask.

Synoptic gospels turn their attention again to John the Baptist. They now explain why Herod jailed John. Not fearing Herod's wrath or that of Herodias, John faced Herod with God's truth. You sinned by marrying your brother Philip's wife while he lived. Fearing a tumult from the Galileans, Herod delayed killing John until Herodias' daughter danced for Herod and his friends. With an oath Herod promised to give the damsel what she desired. Her mother instructed her to ask that John's head be delivered

Mark

6:14 And king Herod heard of him; (for his name was spread abroad:) and he said, That John the Baptist was risen from the dead, and therefore mighty works do shew forth themselves in him. 15 Others said, That it is Elias. And others said, That it is a prophet, or as one of the prophets. 16 But when Herod heard thereof, he said, It is John, whom I beheaded: he is risen from the dead. 17 For Herod himself had sent forth and laid hold upon John, and bound him in prison for Herodias' sake, his brother Philip's wife: for he had married her. 18 For John had said unto Herod, It is not lawful for thee to have thy brother's wife. 19 Therefore Herodias had a quarrel against him, and would have killed him; but she could not:

to her on a platter. This provided Herod with an excuse to silence John forever. He sent an executioner to behead John while he remained in prison. Then he delivered John's head to the damsel, and she presented it to her mother.

Satan pushes us to commit violent atrocities when we allow him to enter and control our lives. God helps us to resist Satan if it's our desire to abandon the path of the wicked and honor God whose we are by creation.

Luke

9:7 Now Herod the tetrarch heard of all that was done by him: and he was perplexed, because that it was said of some, that John was risen from the dead; 8 And of some, that Elias had appeared; and of others, that one of the old prophets was risen again. 9 And Herod said, John have I beheaded: but who is this, of whom I hear such things? And he desired to see him.

When Herod heard of Jesus preaching and working miracles, he desired to see Jesus and witness for himself that Jesus actually performed these wonders. Jesus reminded Herod of his unjust slaying of John. God has ways of plaguing us for our sins until we repent and return to him. Sin haunts us as long as we try to hide it. Confessing and abandoning our sins has the effect of cleansing the conscience of guilt when we trust Christ's blood to cleanse us from sin. Any minister of God who fails to point out sin in the lives of those who hear him cannot please God who requires of us to face those whom we have injured. Facing our sins acts as a miniature day of judgment. God requires each of us to account for how we treat others. It's better to face our sins now than in final judgment when God shows no mercy.

Matthew

14:8 And she, being before instructed of her mother, said, Give me here John Baptist's head in a charger. 9 And the king was sorry: nevertheless for the oath's sake, and them which sat with him at meat, he commanded it to be given her. 10 And he sent, and beheaded John in the prison. 11 And his head was brought in a charger, and given to the damsel: and she brought it to her mother. 12 And his disciples came, and took up the body, and buried it, and went and told Jesus.

Mark portrayed Herod as having some decency. Herod regarded John as just and holy, and he gladly listened to him. Maybe he hoped John might soften his position and overlook his sin. I wonder if Mark included this better side of Herod to encourage Romans to see Christ favorably since Herod ruled for Rome.

How does this narrative of Herod, Herodias, and John benefit present-day readers? God's ministers must help us face our sins. Whatever our response, sin will haunt us until we die unless we abandon it and do the will of our heavenly Father. God endows each of us with a conscience that we might know when we displease him. He gives us a clean conscience when we submit. (Rom. 2:14-16; Heb.9:14) Though Herod suffered with a smiting conscience for adultery and murder, you and I need not endure an objecting conscience. Christ will purify our hearts if we die to sin and submit to be buried with Jesus in the spiritual grave of baptism. Then we rise a new creature, reborn to God. (Rom.6:2-7; Heb.9: 14;10: 22) God offers us a new start on life even though we made a terrible beginning when Satan directed our lives to fulfill the desires of the flesh and mind. (Eph.2:1-3,10) This new life creates us in the image of God as Adam and Eve in the beginning. (Eph.4:24) If Satan has defiled your life, and you would like to start again, obey God's commands he delivered to Jesus. (Mk. 16:15-16)

Mark

6:20 For Herod feared John, knowing that he was a just man and an holy, and observed him; and when he heard him, he did many things, and heard him gladly. 21 And when a convenient day was come, that Herod on his birthday made a supper to his lords, high captains, and chief estates of Galilee; 22 And when the daughter of the said Herodias came in, and danced, and pleased Herod and them that sat with him, the king said unto the damsel, Ask of me whatsoever thou wilt, and I will give it thee. 23 And he sware unto her, Whatsoever thou shalt ask of me, I will give it thee, unto the half of my kingdom. 24 And she went forth, and said unto her mother, What shall I ask? And she said, The head of John the Baptist. 25 And she came in straightway with haste unto the king, and asked, saying, I will that thou give me by and by in a charger the head of John the Baptist. 26 And the king was exceeding sorry; yet for his oath's sake, and for their sakes which sat with him, he would not reject her. 27 And immediately the king sent an executioner, and commanded his head to be brought: and he went and beheaded him in the prison, 28 And brought his head in a charger, and gave it to the damsel: and the damsel gave it to her mother. 29 And when his disciples heard of it, they came and took up his corpse, and laid it in a tomb.

John's life pleased God. He fulfilled his God-given charge to introduce Jesus as the Lamb of God who takes away our sins. Jews who listened to their ancient prophets anticipated the coming Messiah for about fifteen centuries. John explained to his audiences how they needed to repent and prepare for the coming of the Messiah and the kingdom of God. Ancestry alone provided no place in God's house. John refused to modify God's truth to gain man's respect.

As John the Baptist steadfastly sought to please God, so Jesus worked always to please his Father. (Jno.8:29) He continued in his Father's love, keeping his commandments. (Jno.15:10) Everything Jesus taught, the miracles he performed, and the compassion he displayed manifested his Father. When Nicodemus came to him by night, Jesus explained to him he must be born again, or he could not enter God's kingdom. When scribes and Pharisees gathered to hear, Jesus rebuked them for their visible signs of devotion to God, but they continued to defile their spirits with ungodly deeds. They preferred to purge their transgressions by sacrifices rather than show mercy and kindness to others. Jesus testified to them that zealously teaching others their system of devotions made their converts two-fold more children of hell than themselves. You swear by gold of the temple, but ignor God's decree that the temple sanctifies the gold therein. You cheat widows out of their livelihood, and claim innocence. Standing in public places, you look devout by your long prayers, but God knows your wickedness within. Did not God seek for you to show mercy more than sacrifice, and obedience more than tithing? In coming days you shall persecute and slay those God sends to turn you from your corrupt life. As you paint the prophets' graves white and declare that you would not have been party to those who killed the prophets, you actually show you approve your forefathers' killing their prophets. You are whited graves full of dead men's bones. (Math.23:2-36)

Would John and Jesus speak less harshly to Christians today? Are we whited sepulchres full of dead men's bones? Do others commend our outward devotions, but God finds our souls charred by sin? It's time we examine our state before God!

Are charities sufficient to influence God to close his eyes to how we mistreat family, friends, and acquaintances? Hear Paul! **"Though I bestow all my goods to feed the poor, and though I give my body to be burned, and have not charity, it profiteth me nothing. Charity suffereth long, and is kind; charity envieth not; charity vaunteth not itself, is not puffed up, Doth not behave itself unseemly, seeketh not her own, is not easily provoked, thinketh no evil; rejoiceth not in iniquity, but rejoiceth in the truth; beareth all things, believeth all things, hopeth all things, endureth all things. Charity never faileth."** (1 Cor.13:3-8)

Did Paul pen God's truth? Do good daily associations with others lay up treasures in heaven? If my pride makes me think I'm superior to others, does this degrade me before God? Does my impatience demonstrate disobedience? What are the effects of unseemly conduct, seeking me first, envying others, refusing to suffer, and thinking evil of others to my relationship with God? Do they defile me before God? or does God turn his eyes from such conduct in me?

Christian friends, let each realistically examine himself. Does my life cause others to praise God, or do I dishonor him? Is God's name magnified by how I treat others and control myself, or is he blasphemed? Jesus admonished, **"Let your light so shine before men, that they may see your good works, and glorify your Father which is in heaven."** (Math.5:16; See Is.43:7,21.)

Does God see me as an obedient or disobedient child? Am I submissive to his will, or do I please myself? Have I continued in God's light, or do I walk in darkness? Has Satan trapped me in his dungeon of darkness and sin, or do I walk in the glorious light of eternal life. Have I consented to die to this world and to be buried with Jesus in water baptism and raised with him to walk in the radiant light of God? (Rom.6:3-6) Man lives by keeping every command of God, not by keeping the ones which please me. Thinking God will be pleased by obeying a few commands is Satan's will, not God's.

Matthew

14:13 When Jesus heard of it, he departed thence by ship into a desert place apart: and when the people had heard thereof, they followed him on foot out of the cities. 14 And Jesus went forth, and saw a great multitude, and was moved with compassion toward them, and he healed their sick. 15 And when it was evening, his disciples came to him, saying, This is a desert place, and the time is now past; send the multitude away, that they may go into the villages, and buy themselves victuals. 16 But Jesus said unto them, They need not depart; give ye them to eat. 17 And they say unto him, We have here but five loaves, and two fishes. 18 He said, Bring them hither to me. 19 And he commanded the multitude to sit down on the grass, and took the five loaves, and the two fishes, and looking up to heaven, he blessed, and brake, and gave the loaves to his disciples, and the disciples to the multitude. 20 And they did all eat, and were filled: and they took up of the fragments that remained twelve baskets full. 21 And they that had eaten were about five thousand men, beside women and children. 22 And straightway Jesus constrained his disciples to get into a ship, and to go before him unto the other side, while he sent the multitudes away. 23 And when he had sent the multitudes away, he went up into a mountain apart to pray: and when the evening was come, he was there alone.

Jesus fed five thousand after the twelve apostles returned from preaching God's kingdom. To give the twelve an opportunity to rest and review the wonders God accomplished through them, Jesus retreated to a deserted region near Bethsaida. People recognized him and followed his boat. Coming ashore, Jesus encountered a large crowd. He healed their sick and explained the gospel of God's kingdom. At evening disciples encouraged Jesus to dismiss the people that they might go to villages for food and shelter. Instead, Jesus fed the 5000 with five barley loaves of bread and two small fish. For this compassion and kindness one might have expected those people to have been devoted to Jesus. John informs us that the same people forgot Jesus' compassion and turned away from him the next day. Satan influences people to be ungrateful for what God does for us.

Mark

6:30 And the apostles gathered themselves together unto Jesus, and told him all things, both what they had done, and what they had taught. 31 And he said unto them, Come ye yourselves apart into a desert place, and rest a while: for there were many coming and going, and they had no leisure so much as to eat. 32 And they departed into a desert place by ship privately. 33 And the people saw them departing, and many knew him, and ran afoot thither out of all cities, and outwent them, and came together unto him. 34 And Jesus, when he came out, saw much people, and was moved with compassion toward them, because they were as sheep not having a shepherd: and he began to teach them many things. 35 And when the day was now far spent, his disciples came unto him, and said, This is a desert place, and now the time is far passed: 36 Send them away, that they may go into the country round about, and into the villages, and buy themselves bread: for they have nothing to eat. 37 He answered and said unto them, Give ye them to eat. And they say unto him, Shall we go and buy two hundred pennyworth of bread, and give them to eat? 38 He saith unto them, How many loaves have ye? go and see. And when they knew, they say, Five, and two fishes. 39 And he commanded them to make all sit down by companies upon the green grass. 40 And they sat down in ranks, by hundreds, and by fifties. 41 And when he had taken the five loaves and the two fishes, he looked up to heaven, and blessed, and brake the loaves, and gave them to his disciples to set before them; and the two fishes divided he among them all. 42 And they did all eat, and were filled. 43 And they took up twelve baskets full of the fragments, and of the fishes. 44 And they that did eat of the loaves were about five thousand men. 45 And straightway he constrained his disciples to get into the ship, and to go to the other side before unto Bethsaida, while he sent away the people. 46 And when he had sent them away, he departed into a mountain to pray. 47 And when even was come, the ship was in the midst of the sea, and he alone on the land.
Though our heavenly Father manifests his everlasting love, people rarely seem to show

Luke

9:10 And the apostles, when they were
returned, told him all that they had done. And
he took them, and went aside privately into a
desert place belonging to the city called
Bethsaida. 11 And the people, when they
knew it, followed him: and he received them,
and spake unto them of the kingdom of God,
and healed them that had need of healing. 12
And when the day began to wear away, then
came the twelve, and said unto him, Send the
multitude away, that they may go into the
towns and country round about, and lodge,
and get victuals: for we are here in a desert
place. 13 But he said unto them, Give ye them
to eat. And they said, We have no more but
five loaves and two fishes; except we should
go and buy meat for all this people. 14 For
they were about five thousand men. And he
said to his disciples, Make them sit down by
fifties in a company. 15 And they did so, and
made them all sit down. 16 Then he took the
five loaves and the two fishes, and looking up
to heaven, he blessed them, and brake, and
gave to the disciples to set before the
multitude. 17 And they did eat, and were all
filled: and there was taken up of fragments
that remained to them twelve baskets.

John

6:1 After these things Jesus went over the sea
of Galilee, which is the sea of Tiberias. 2 And
a great multitude followed him, because they
saw his miracles which he did on them that
were diseased. 3 And Jesus went up into a
mountain, and there he sat with his disciples.
4 And the passover, a feast of the Jews, was
nigh. 5 When Jesus then lifted up his eyes,
and saw a great company come unto him, he
saith unto Philip, Whence shall we buy bread,
that these may eat? 6 And this he said to
prove him: for he himself knew what he
would do. 7 Philip answered him, Two
hundred pennyworth of bread is not sufficient
for them, that every one of them may take a
little. 8 One of his disciples, Andrew, Simon
Peter's brother, saith unto him, 9 There is a
lad here, which hath five barley loaves, and
two small fishes: but what are they among so
many? 10 And Jesus said, Make the men sit
down. Now there was much grass in the place.
So the men sat down, in number about five
thousand. 11 And Jesus took the loaves; and
when he had given thanks, he distributed to
the disciples, and the disciples to them that
were set down; and likewise of the fishes as
much as they would. 12 When they were
filled, he said unto his disciples, Gather up the
fragments that remain, that nothing be lost.
13 Therefore they gathered them together,
and filled twelve baskets with the fragments
of the five barley loaves, which remained over
and above unto them that had eaten. 14 Then
those men, when they had seen the miracle
that Jesus did, said, This is of a truth that
prophet that should come into the world. 15
When Jesus therefore perceived that they
would come and take him by force, to make
him a king, he departed again into a mountain
himself alone. 16 And when even was now
come, his disciples went down unto the sea, 17
And entered into a ship, and went over the sea
toward Capernaum. And it was now dark,
and Jesus was not come to them.

appreciation for all his kindness. This ungratefulness spills over into human relationships, too.

Though all four gospels recorded the feeding of the five thousand, John stressed points differing from those of the synoptic gospels. That Jesus met the physical and spiritual needs of the people occupied the center of the synoptic gospels, but John pursued the idea that Jesus fulfilled Moses' prophecy of **the prophet** which was to be like Moses. (Jno.6:14) Once the people perceived Jesus to be **that Prophet**, they desired to make him king. To avoid this, he retired into the mountain where Mark noted he prayed. Perhaps this constituted a temptation for Jesus. Many of us might have accepted the invitation to be elevated to king, but Jesus knew this corresponded not to God's plan. He therefore avoided them. God's plan called for Jesus to reign as King of kings and Lord of lords who rules in heaven, not on earth in the city of Jerusalem. (Ps.110:1-7; Act.2:32-36;3:21)

Many who claim to follow Jesus today continue to desire Jesus to sit on David's throne in the city of Jerusalem. Their expectation of his return to earth to occupy that position corresponds to the same desire the Jews manifested the day Jesus separated himself from those who intended to proclaim him king. Would to God that we might, without dissension, let God accomplish his own plan. Christ can't be our priest on earth. (Heb.8:4)

Matthew

14:24 But the ship was now in the midst of the sea, tossed with waves: for the wind was contrary. 25 And in the fourth watch of the night Jesus went unto them, walking on the sea. 26 And when the disciples saw him walking on the sea, they were troubled, saying, It is a spirit; and they cried out for fear. 27 But straightway Jesus spake unto them, saying, Be of good cheer; it is I; be not afraid. 28 And Peter answered him and said, Lord, if it be thou, bid me come unto thee on the water. 29 And he said, Come. And when Peter was come down out of the ship, he walked on the water, to go to Jesus. 30 But when he saw the wind boisterous, he was afraid; and beginning to sink, he cried, saying, Lord, save me. 31 And immediately Jesus stretched forth his hand, and caught him, and said unto him, O thou of little faith, wherefore didst thou doubt? 32 And when they were come into the ship, the wind ceased. 33 Then they that were in the ship came and worshipped him, saying, Of a truth thou art the Son of God.

Mark

6:48 And he saw them toiling in rowing; for the wind was contrary unto them: and about the fourth watch of the night he cometh unto them, walking upon the sea, and would have passed by them. 49 But when they saw him walking upon the sea, they supposed it had been a spirit, and cried out: 50 For they all saw him, and were troubled. And immediately he talked with them, and saith unto them, Be of good cheer: it is I; be not afraid. 51 And he went up unto them into the ship; and the wind ceased: and they were sore amazed in themselves beyond measure, and wondered. 52 For they considered not the miracle of the loaves: for their heart was hardened.

John

6:18 And the sea arose by reason of a great wind that blew. 19 So when they had rowed about five and twenty or thirty furlongs, they see Jesus walking on the sea, and drawing nigh unto the ship: and they were afraid. 20 But he saith unto them, It is I; be not afraid. 21 Then they willingly received him into the ship: and immediately the ship was at the land whither they went.

As the disciples beheld Jesus walking on the water and lifting Peter from perishing in the roiled sea, it convinced them Jesus must be God's Son. Why were they unimpressed by his feeding 5000? Mark observed that they considered not the feeding of the multitude. Without reflecting seriously on the many miracles Jesus worked to alleviate the ills of his people, none of us view Jesus as God's only begotten Son. Importance of meditating on God's word after we hear or read it becomes the one crucial issue which separates believers from unbelievers in the truth of God. As one reflects on God's truth, God opens our understanding to perceive his truth. Not thinking about what God says allows Satan to steal God's word from our minds. God's word fails to profit us without faith in what he says. (Heb.4:2)

Mark stated the issue succinctly when he wrote that Jesus instructed Israel to repent and believe the gospel. (Mk.1:15) From the days of Moses, Israel showed reluctance in believing what God's messengers taught. Time had now come for them to alter their response to God. They must repent of their indifference. If you and I ever reach the heavenly abode of God, we must listen intently to God's message and meditate thereon. Otherwise, God never operates on our minds and hearts to fathom his truth. Even the twelve apostles fell short by not always considering God's truth and Jesus' miracles.

Matthew

14:34 And when they were gone over, they came into the land of Gennesaret. 35 And when the men of that place had knowledge of him, they sent out into all that country round about, and brought unto him all that were diseased; 36 And besought him that they might only touch the hem of his garment: and as many as touched were made perfectly whole.

Crossing the sea of Galilee, Jesus and his disciples encountered people eager to have their sick healed. Not wishing to impose themselves on Jesus, they courteously asked him to relieve their diseased and impotent family members and friends. God commissioned Jesus to correct the hardships Satan had cast on his people. He sorrowed to see how they suffered terrible afflictions and hardships. Showing them compassion by relieving their loved ones' ailments, God hoped his people might consider how their heavenly Father watched over and blessed them even when they departed from his commandments.

Gospel writers recorded these manifestations of God's love, that people of all nations and generations might behold how God blesses people and willingly sent his only begotten Son to deliver them from the ills the Evil One cast upon the race. Seeing this, they might love God and return unto him as children separated from their father eagerly seek him. God and his children rejoice together when sinners repent of their disobedience to submit to their heavenly Father's commands. Jesus willingly gave his life to reunite God and his children. Many continue to look upon God as angry and spiteful rather than forgiving. He manifests his wrath on his children only when we rebel and spitefully mistreat his messengers. As our parents needed to correct us, sometimes harshly to keep us safe, God, too, chastens, not for vengeance, but of love. He earnestly seeks to show us the better life.

Mark

6:53 And when they had passed over, they came into the land of Gennesaret, and drew to the shore. 54 And when they were come out of the ship, straightway they knew him, 55 And ran through that whole region round about, and began to carry about in beds those that were sick, where they heard he was. 56 And whithersoever he entered, into villages, or cities, or country, they laid the sick in the streets, and besought him that they might touch if it were but the border of his garment: and as many as touched him were made whole.

Mark penned his message of love to Gentiles, perhaps those in Rome, that they might come to the knowledge and love of the will of the Lord of heaven and earth. Knowledge of God's great love and sacrifice alone will not benefit a person. Sin at first destroyed the friendship between God and man. To restore that comradeship, each person must abandon self-will which declares he/she has the right to live as he/she pleases, regardless of how it may affect his family, friends, and God. Others care about each of us and grieve to see us destroy ourselves by listening to the absurd promises of Satan and his followers who declare that a riotous life of indulgence fulfills the whole wants of a person. God rightly advises that bread or even pleasure alone will not sustain man's life. It takes bread, every word of God, and obedience to God's word to provide a complete life. Without each, an emptiness nags at a person which drives him/her to seek satisfaction from every possible source, except from God. Still unsatisfied, we often lose hope and resign ourselves to the uselessness of life. If gloom or depression creeps into your life or those about you, turning to God offers a certain brightness to all who seek him sincerely out of a pure heart. God will fulfill his promises and prove what is truly good in life.

John

6:22 The day following, when the people which stood on the other side of the sea saw that there was none other boat there, save that one whereinto his disciples were entered, and that Jesus went not with his disciples into the boat, but that his disciples were gone away alone; 23 (Howbeit there came other boats from Tiberias nigh unto the place where they did eat bread, after that the Lord had given thanks:) 24 When the people therefore saw that Jesus was not there, neither his disciples, they also took shipping, and came to Capernaum, seeking for Jesus. 25 And when they had found him on the other side of the sea, they said unto him, Rabbi, when camest thou hither? 26 Jesus answered them and said, Verily, verily, I say unto you, Ye seek me, not because ye saw the miracles, but because ye did eat of the loaves, and were filled. 27 Labour not for the meat which perisheth, but for that meat which endureth unto everlasting life, which the Son of man shall give unto you: for him hath God the Father sealed. 28 Then said they unto him, What shall we do, that we might work the works of God? 29 Jesus answered and said unto them, This is the work of God, that ye believe on him whom he hath sent. 30 They said therefore unto him, What sign shewest thou then, that we may see, and believe thee? what dost thou work? 31 Our fathers did eat manna in the desert; as it is written, He gave them bread from heaven to eat. 32 Then Jesus said unto them, Verily, verily, I say unto you, Moses gave you not that bread from heaven; but my Father giveth you the true bread from heaven. 33 For the bread of God is he which cometh down from heaven, and giveth life unto the world. 34 Then said they unto him, Lord, evermore give us this bread. 35 And Jesus said unto them, I am the bread of life: he that cometh to me shall never hunger; and he that believeth on me shall never thirst. 36 But I said unto you, That ye also have seen me, and believe not. 37 All that the Father giveth me shall come to me; and him that cometh to me I will in no wise cast out. 38 For I came down from heaven, not to do mine own will, but the will of him that sent me. 39 And this is the Father's will which hath sent me, that of all which he hath given me I should lose nothing, but should raise it up again at the last day. 40 And this is the will of him that sent me, that every one which seeth the Son, and believeth on him, may have everlasting life: and I will raise him up at the last day. 41 The Jews then murmured at him, because he said, I am the bread which came down from heaven. 42 And they said, Is not this Jesus, the son of Joseph, whose father and mother we know? how is it then that he saith, I came down from heaven? 43 Jesus therefore answered and said unto them, Murmur not among yourselves. 44 No man can come to me, except the Father which hath sent me draw him: and I will raise him up at the last day. 45 It is written in the prophets, And they shall be all taught of God. Every man therefore that hath heard, and hath learned of the Father, cometh unto me. 46 Not that any man hath seen the Father, save he which is of God, he hath seen the Father. 47 Verily, verily, I say unto you, He that believeth on me hath everlasting life. 48 I am that bread of life. 49 Your fathers did eat manna in the wilderness, and are dead. 50 This is the bread which cometh down from heaven, that a man may eat thereof, and not die. 51 I am the living bread which came down from heaven: if any man eat of this bread, he shall live for ever: and the bread that I will give is my flesh, which I will give for the life of the world. 52 The Jews therefore strove among themselves, saying, How can this man give us his flesh to eat? 53 Then

**Jesus said unto them, Verily, verily, I say
unto you, Except ye eat the flesh of the
Son of man, and drink his blood, ye have
no life in you. 54 Whoso eateth my flesh,
and drinketh my blood, hath eternal life;
and I will raise him up at the last day. 55
For my flesh is meat indeed, and my blood
is drink indeed. 56 He that eateth my
flesh, and drinketh my blood, dwelleth in
me, and I in him. 57 As the living Father
hath sent me, and I live by the Father: so
he that eateth me, even he shall live by
me. 58 This is that bread which came
down from heaven: not as your fathers
did eat manna, and are dead: he that
eateth of this bread shall live for ever. 59
These things said he in the synagogue, as
he taught in Capernaum. 60 Many
therefore of his disciples, when they had
heard this, said, This is an hard saying;
who can hear it? 61 When Jesus knew in
himself that his disciples murmured at it,
he said unto them, Doth this offend you?
62 What and if ye shall see the Son of man
ascend up where he was before? 63 It is
the spirit that quickeneth; the flesh
profiteth nothing: the words that I speak
unto you, they are spirit, and they are life.
64 But there are some of you that believe
not. For Jesus knew from the beginning
who they were that believed not, and who
should betray him. 65 And he said,
Therefore said I unto you, that no man
can come unto me, except it were given
unto him of my Father. 66 From that time
many of his disciples went back, and
walked no more with him. 67 Then said
Jesus unto the twelve, Will ye also go
away? 68 Then Simon Peter answered
him, Lord, to whom shall we go? thou
hast the words of eternal life. 69 And we
believe and are sure that thou art that
Christ, the Son of the living God. 70 Jesus
answered them, Have not I chosen you
twelve, and one of you is a devil? 71 He
spake of Judas Iscariot the son of Simon:
for he it was that should betray him, being
one of the twelve.**

Being **the Prophet** Moses promised, Jesus explained God's whole truth to them. Laboring to gain food to nourish the body God commanded. Equally necessary, the truth of God sustains man's spiritual life. They asked for a sign to prove he came from God. Hadn't they seen the miracle which fed them? They asked for another sign to give them food as Moses fed their fathers 40 years in the wilderness. God gave your fathers bread from heaven, not Moses. Jesus explained he came from God as the true bread of heaven. If they believed his truth, they would never die. They reminded him they knew his father and mother. You didn't come from heaven. They rejected words of **the Prophet**. (Deu.18:15-19)

How can people be taught of God, unless God sends a person to teach them? God sent Jesus to explain how to gain eternal and abundant life on earth. If one believes what Jesus taught, he is taught of God and comes to Jesus. His parable of bread and his body being bread from heaven indicates one must accept the truth he taught, or he has not eternal life. Believing the words of Jesus causes us to eat of his flesh. Rejecting the words God gave him might be likened to Israel in the wilderness. When they asked for food and God provided them manna, if they had refused to eat the manna, their actions would have compared to those who listened to Jesus, but refused to feast on the words of eternal life. Rejecting what God provided most certainly meant death: one physical and the other spiritual.

This comparison Jesus taught applies equally to all generations. Whether in the first century, twentieth, or thirtieth, rejecting the words of Jesus brings spiritual starvation which certainly results in death. Jesus reminded Satan, **"Man doth not live by bread only, but by every word that proceedeth out of the mouth of the Lord."** (Deu.8:3; Math.4:4; see Lk.4:4.)

Matthew

15:1 Then came to Jesus scribes and Pharisees, which were of Jerusalem, saying, 2 Why do thy disciples transgress the tradition of the elders? for they wash not their hands when they eat bread. 3 But he answered and said unto them, Why do ye also transgress the commandment of God by your tradition? 4 For God commanded, saying, Honour thy father and mother: and, He that curseth father or mother, let him die the death. 5 But ye say, Whosoever shall say to his father or his mother, It is a gift, by whatsoever thou mightest be profited by me; 6 And honour not his father or his mother, he shall be free. Thus have ye made the commandment of God of none effect by your tradition. 7 Ye hypocrites, well did Esaias prophesy of you, saying, 8 This people draweth nigh unto me with their mouth, and honoureth me with their lips; but their heart is far from me. 9 But in vain they do worship me, teaching for doctrines the commandments of men.

Man's tradition often conflicts with God's commands. God utilizes teachers, war, famine, or other disasters to encourage men to reevaluate their actions. During these difficult times some humble themselves, repent, and return to keep God's precepts. Many, however, persist in their traditions and reap serious consequences in this lifetime and eternal suffering. (Rom.1:18)

God sent Jesus to his people to explain that though they sacrificed and assembled as God commanded, their daily lives drifted far from justice, judgment, and equity which God taught. If they were to enter the approaching kingdom of God which Israel had expected for nearly 1500 years, they must change their manner of life and practice judgment, justice, and equity. Strictness of doctrine without loving your neighbor shuts the gates of the kingdom of heaven that you cannot enter. Christians today need to ponder this truth of God, lest he exclude us from the promised blessings. God desires obedience to God's commands and mercy toward all with whom we associate. (Math.5:7;9:13;12:7)

Mark

7:1 Then came together unto him the Pharisees, and certain of the scribes, which came from Jerusalem. 2 And when they saw some of his disciples eat bread with defiled, that is to say, with unwashen, hands, they found fault. 3 For the Pharisees, and all the Jews, except they wash their hands oft, eat not, holding the tradition of the elders. 4 And when they come from the market, except they wash, they eat not. And many other things there be, which they have received to hold, as the washing of cups, and pots, brasen vessels, and of tables. 5 Then the Pharisees and scribes asked him, Why walk not thy disciples according to the tradition of the elders, but eat bread with unwashen hands? 6 He answered and said unto them, Well hath Esaias prophesied of you hypocrites, as it is written, This people honoureth me with their lips, but their heart is far from me. 7 Howbeit in vain do they worship me, teaching for doctrines the commandments of men. 8 For laying aside the commandment of God, ye hold the tradition of men, as the washing of pots and cups: and many other such like things ye do. 9 And he said unto them, Full well ye reject the commandment of God, that ye may keep your own tradition. 10 For Moses said, Honour thy father and thy mother; and, Whoso curseth father or mother, let him die the death: 11 But ye say, If a man shall say to his father or mother, It is Corban, that is to say, a gift, by whatsoever thou mightest be profited by me; he shall be free. 12 And ye suffer him no more to do ought for his father or his mother; 13 Making the word of God of none effect through your tradition, which ye have delivered: and many such like things do ye.

Luke

11:37 And as he spake, a certain Pharisee besought him to dine with him: and he went in, and sat down to meat. 38 And when the Pharisee saw it, he marvelled that he had not first washed before dinner. 39 And the Lord said unto him, Now do ye Pharisees make clean the outside of the cup and the platter; but your inward part is full of ravening and wickedness. 40 Ye fools, did not he that made that which is without make that which is within also? 41 But rather give alms of such things as ye have; and, behold, all things are clean unto you. 42 But woe unto you, Pharisees! for ye tithe mint and rue and all manner of herbs, and pass over judgment and the love of God: these ought ye to have done, and not to leave the other undone. 43 Woe unto you, Pharisees! for ye love the uppermost seats in the synagogues, and greetings in the markets. 44 Woe unto you, scribes and Pharisees, hypocrites! for ye are as graves which appear not, and the men that walk over them are not aware of them.

These incidents seem to have transpired while Jesus attended one of the feasts in Jerusalem.

Manifesting outward signs of devotion to God without also changing the inward man makes a person a hypocrite in the eyes of God. He made us a visible body and a spiritual one visible only by our deeds and attitudes which resemble our heavenly Father when we keep his commandments, but portrays the Evil One when we forget God's truth. Throughout time, man deceives himself by thinking his pious actions make him religious, but at the same time he retains an evil attitude. God desires the inner person to show God's likeness in thought and action. God loves man and shows mercy though we sin. He wants his children to learn mercy which controls both the inner and outer man. Hating one's fellows and wishing them evil while we demonstrate all the outward signs of devotion to God lives a lie. We aren't what we claim. (1 Jno.4:7-8,20)

Scribes and Pharisees in the days of Jesus valued praise of men. Manifesting an outward show of devotion to God gained Jews' respect, but caused others to blaspheme God's name. Showing love toward the unfortunate, fatherless, widows, strangers, and even to those who hate us characterizes God's mercy. Doesn't God provide rain and harvest to righteous and unrighteous, to the thankful and unthankful? He desires us to learn the same mind that overlooks what others do to us that we may show them kindness in spite of their desire that evil overtake us. When the Pharisees found fault with Jesus and his disciples because they failed to wash before eating, they displayed an evil attitude: if you don't do as I do, you're not acceptable. This exclusive attitude divides men, hurts the poor, sick, fatherless, widows, and strangers. Regarding not the feelings of others and not treating them as we would like to be treated falls short of God's plan for his creatures made in his own image. God desires mercy, not sacrifice. (Math.9:13;12:7) We have learned the traditions of our earthly relatives who customarily look down on others in order to make themselves look superior. Our heavenly Father wants us to learn and practice his ways if we are to enter the kingdom of heaven and gain everlasting life. We show honor to our heavenly Father by living in his image of righteousness and loving his children.

It seems strange that many continue to look on Jews as God's chosen people when they have been disobedient, rebellious, stiff-necked, and hardhearted since the day Moses led them from their bondage in Egypt. (Deu.9:6-7,24) Jesus testified to them they continued to rebel even in his day, rejecting God's truth he taught. Is this age so blind we cannot see how cantankerous Jews continue to act, yet many consider them God's people.

John

**7:1 After these things Jesus walked in
Galilee: for he would not walk in Jewry,
because the Jews sought to kill him. 2
Now the Jews' feast of tabernacles was at
hand. 3 His brethren therefore said unto
him, Depart hence, and go into Judaea,
that thy disciples also may see the works
that thou doest. 4 For there is no man that
doeth any thing in secret, and he himself
seeketh to be known openly. If thou do
these things, shew thyself to the world. 5
For neither did his brethren believe in
him. 6 Then Jesus said unto them, My
time is not yet come: but your time is
alway ready. 7 The world cannot hate
you; but me it hateth, because I testify of
it, that the works thereof are evil. 8 Go ye
up unto this feast: I go not up yet unto this
feast; for my time is not yet full come. 9
When he had said these words unto them,
he abode still in Galilee. 10 But when his
brethren were gone up, then went he also
up unto the feast, not openly, but as it
were in secret. 11 Then the Jews sought
him at the feast, and said, Where is he? 12
And there was much murmuring among
the people concerning him: for some said,
He is a good man: others said, Nay; but he
deceiveth the people. 13 Howbeit no man
spake openly of him for fear of the Jews.
14 Now about the midst of the feast Jesus
went up into the temple, and taught. 15
And the Jews marvelled, saying, How
knoweth this man letters, having never
learned? 16 Jesus answered them, and
said, My doctrine is not mine, but his that
sent me. 17 If any man will do his will, he
shall know of the doctrine, whether it be
of God, or whether I speak of myself. 18
He that speaketh of himself seeketh his
own glory: but he that seeketh his glory
that sent him, the same is true, and no
unrighteousness is in him. 19 Did not
Moses give you the law, and yet none of
you keepeth the law? Why go ye about to
kill me? 20 The people answered and said,
Thou hast a devil: who goeth about to kill
thee? 21 Jesus answered and said unto
them, I have done one work, and ye all
marvel. 22 Moses therefore gave unto you
circumcision; (not because it is of Moses,
but of the fathers;) and ye on the sabbath
day circumcise a man. 23 If a man on the
sabbath day receive circumcision, that the
law of Moses should not be broken; are ye
angry at me, because I have made a man
every whit whole on the sabbath day? 24
Judge not according to the appearance,
but judge righteous judgment. 25 Then
said some of them of Jerusalem, Is not this
he, whom they seek to kill? 26 But, lo, he
speaketh boldly, and they say nothing
unto him. Do the rulers know indeed that
this is the very Christ? 27 Howbeit we
know this man whence he is: but when
Christ cometh, no man knoweth whence
he is. 28 Then cried Jesus in the temple as
he taught, saying, Ye both know me, and
ye know whence I am: and I am not come
of myself, but he that sent me is true,
whom ye know not. 29 But I know him:
for I am from him, and he hath sent me.
30 Then they sought to take him: but no
man laid hands on him, because his hour
was not yet come. 31 And many of the
people believed on him, and said, When
Christ cometh, will he do more miracles
than these which this man hath done? 32
The Pharisees heard that the people
murmured such things concerning him;
and the Pharisees and the chief priests
sent officers to take him. 33 Then said
Jesus unto them, Yet a little while am I
with you, and then I go unto him that sent
me. 34 Ye shall seek me, and shall not find
me: and where I am, thither ye cannot
come. 35 Then said the Jews among
themselves, Whither will he go, that we
shall not find him? will he go unto the
dispersed among the Gentiles, and teach
the Gentiles? 36 What manner of saying is
this that he said, Ye shall seek me, and
shall not find me: and where I am, thither**

ye cannot come? 37 In the last day, that great day of the feast, Jesus stood and cried, saying, If any man thirst, let him come unto me, and drink. 38 He that believeth on me, as the scripture hath said, out of his belly shall flow rivers of living water. 39 (But this spake he of the Spirit, which they that believe on him should receive: for the Holy Ghost was not yet given; because that Jesus was not yet glorified.) 40 Many of the people therefore, when they heard this saying, said, Of a truth this is the Prophet. 41 Others said, This is the Christ. But some said, Shall Christ come out of Galilee? 42 Hath not the scripture said, That Christ cometh of the seed of David, and out of the town of Bethlehem, where David was? 43 So there was a division among the people because of him. 44 And some of them would have taken him; but no man laid hands on him. 45 Then came the officers to the chief priests and Pharisees; and they said unto them, Why have ye not brought him? 46 The officers answered, Never man spake like this man. 47 Then answered them the Pharisees, Are ye also deceived? 48 Have any of the rulers or of the Pharisees believed on him? 49 But this people who knoweth not the law are cursed. 50 Nicodemus saith unto them, (he that came to Jesus by night, being one of them,) 51 Doth our law judge any man, before it hear him, and know what he doeth? 52 They answered and said unto him, Art thou also of Galilee? Search, and look: for out of Galilee ariseth no prophet. 53 And every man went unto his own house.

Actions of Jesus divided the Jews. Some believed his miracles proved him to be Christ or one of the prophets. Others disregarded his wonders and decided he deceived the people. Even his own brothers considered him a fraud. Their main reason for rejecting him seemed to rest on his willingness to heal on the Sabbath. To show how inconsistent their argument appeared, he reminded them they circumcise on the Sabbath. Priests on the Sabbath offer sacrifices. Both violate the law if you insist that no work shall be done on the Sabbath. I restored a man's ability to walk on the Sabbath to show God's compassion. You desire to kill me for benefiting the man on the Sabbath. Is your judgment righteous? If you do what I say, you would know that what I teach comes from God. It improves life and extends to you eternal life. Moses gave you the law and circumcision, but none of you keep the law, yet you wish to kill me for not keeping Moses' law. Exercise honest judgment.

Some who gathered in Jerusalem for the feast knew their leaders intended to kill Jesus, and they couldn't understand why they allowed him to teach in the temple without arresting him. They questioned if the rulers knew he was Christ. Many people believed him to be Christ. Jesus pleaded with the people to believe on him while they could, for he must continue with them only a little while. After that they might seek him, but not find him.

John noted again that some knew he was **the Prophet** Moses promised. Showing Jesus fulfilled this prophecy continues to be the thread running throughout John's gospel. (1:21,25;4:25;6:14;7:40) God placed his complete truth in Jesus' mouth, and Jesus spoke all God's truth to the people. (15:15) Those who accepted God's truth as Jesus spoke it continued as God's people, but those who rejected his truth severed themselves from among God's people as Moses promised. (8:44-47; Act.3:22-23)

Excuses for rejecting Jesus included: 1) They knew his parents; 2) He came from Galilee, and God promised no prophet from Galilee; 3) We can't understand what he means; and 4) None of our rulers or Pharisees believe on him. How do you vote? with God or unbelievers? (Mk.1:15)

John

8:1 Jesus went unto the mount of Olives. 2 And early in the morning he came again into the temple, and all the people came unto him; and he sat down, and taught them. 3 And the scribes and Pharisees brought unto him a woman taken in adultery; and when they had set her in the midst, 4 They say unto him, Master, this woman was taken in adultery, in the very act. 5 Now Moses in the law commanded us, that such should be stoned: but what sayest thou? 6 This they said, tempting him, that they might have to accuse him. But Jesus stooped down, and with his finger wrote on the ground, as though he heard them not. 7 So when they continued asking him, he lifted up himself, and said unto them, He that is without sin among you, let him first cast a stone at her. 8 And again he stooped down, and wrote on the ground. 9 And they which heard it, being convicted by their own conscience, went out one by one, beginning at the eldest, even unto the last: and Jesus was left alone, and the woman standing in the midst. 10 When Jesus had lifted up himself, and saw none but the woman, he said unto her, Woman, where are those thine accusers? hath no man condemned thee? 11 She said, No man, Lord. And Jesus said unto her, Neither do I condemn thee: go, and sin no more. 12 Then spake Jesus again unto them, saying, I am the light of the world: he that followeth me shall not walk in darkness, but shall have the light of life. 13 The Pharisees therefore said unto him, Thou bearest record of thyself; thy record is not true. 14 Jesus answered and said unto them, Though I bear record of myself, yet my record is true: for I know whence I came, and whither I go; but ye cannot tell whence I come, and whither I go. 15 Ye judge after the flesh; I judge no man. 16 And yet if I judge, my judgment is true: for I am not alone, but I and the Father that sent me. 17 It is also written in your law, that the testimony of two men is true. 18 I am one that bear witness of myself, and the Father that sent me beareth witness of me. 19 Then said they unto him, Where is thy Father? Jesus answered, Ye neither know me, nor my Father: if ye had known me, ye should have known my Father also. 20 These words spake Jesus in the treasury, as he taught in the temple: and no man laid hands on him; for his hour was not yet come. 21 Then said Jesus again unto them, I go my way, and ye shall seek me, and shall die in your sins: whither I go, ye cannot come. 22 Then said the Jews, Will he kill himself? because he saith, Whither I go, ye cannot come. 23 And he said unto them, Ye are from beneath; I am from above: ye are of this world; I am not of this world. 24 I said therefore unto you, that ye shall die in your sins: for if ye believe not that I am he, ye shall die in your sins. 25 Then said they unto him, Who art thou? And Jesus saith unto them, Even the same that I said unto you from the beginning. 26 I have many things to say and to judge of you: but he that sent me is true; and I speak to the world those things which I have heard of him. 27 They understood not that he spake to them of the Father. 28 Then said Jesus unto them, When ye have lifted up the Son of man, then shall ye know that I am he, and that I do nothing of myself; but as my Father hath taught me, I speak these things. 29 And he that sent me is with me: the Father hath not left me alone; for I do always those things that please him. 30 As he spake these words, many believed on him. 31 Then said Jesus to those Jews which believed on him, If ye continue in my word, then are ye my disciples indeed; 32 And ye shall know the truth, and the truth shall make you free. 33 They answered him, We be Abraham's seed, and were never in bondage to any man:

how sayest thou, Ye shall be made free? 34 Jesus answered them, Verily, verily, I say unto you, Whosoever committeth sin is the servant of sin. 35 And the servant abideth not in the house for ever: but the Son abideth ever. 36 If the Son therefore shall make you free, ye shall be free indeed. 37 I know that ye are Abraham's seed; but ye seek to kill me, because my word hath no place in you. 38 I speak that which I have seen with my Father: and ye do that which ye have seen with your father. 39 They answered and said unto him, Abraham is our father. Jesus saith unto them, If ye were Abraham's children, ye would do the works of Abraham. 40 But now ye seek to kill me, a man that hath told you the truth, which I have heard of God: this did not Abraham. 41 Ye do the deeds of your father. Then said they to him, We be not born of fornication; we have one Father, even God. 42 Jesus said unto them, If God were your Father, ye would love me: for I proceeded forth and came from God; neither came I of myself, but he sent me. 43 Why do ye not understand my speech? even because ye cannot hear my word. 44 Ye are of your father the devil, and the lusts of your father ye will do. He was a murderer from the beginning, and abode not in the truth, because there is no truth in him. When he speaketh a lie, he speaketh of his own: for he is a liar, and the father of it. 45 And because I tell you the truth, ye believe me not. 46 Which of you convinceth me of sin? And if I say the truth, why do ye not believe me? 47 He that is of God heareth God's words: ye therefore hear them not, because ye are not of God. 48 Then answered the Jews, and said unto him, Say we not well that thou art a Samaritan, and hast a devil? 49 Jesus answered, I have not a devil; but I honour my Father, and ye do dishonour me. 50 And I seek not mine own glory: there is one that seeketh and judgeth. 51 Verily, verily, I say unto you, If a man keep my saying, he shall never see death. 52 Then said the Jews unto him, Now we know that thou hast a devil. Abraham is dead, and the prophets; and thou sayest, If a man keep my saying, he shall never taste of death. 53 Art thou greater than our father Abraham, which is dead? and the prophets are dead: whom makest thou thyself? 54 Jesus answered, If I honour myself, my honour is nothing: it is my Father that honoureth me; of whom ye say, that he is your God: 55 Yet ye have not known him; but I know him: and if I should say, I know him not, I shall be a liar like unto you: but I know him, and keep his saying. 56 Your father Abraham rejoiced to see my day: and he saw it, and was glad. 57 Then said the Jews unto him, Thou art not yet fifty years old, and hast thou seen Abraham? 58 Jesus said unto them, Verily, verily, I say unto you, Before Abraham was, I am. 59 Then took they up stones to cast at him: but Jesus hid himself, and went out of the temple, going through the midst of them, and so passed by.

How may we distinguish God's people from Satan's? God's descendants hear and do God's will; Satan's follow the evil path. John recorded numerous examples showing that people considered themselves God's people, but they were Satan's people. Nicodemus confessed Jesus came from God, but rejected Jesus' command to be born again of water and Spirit to enter God's kingdom. Jesus explained to Jerusalem Jews Moses condemned them for not accepting and doing God's truth. Galilean Jews refused to accept Jesus as the water of life though he fed them. Now Jews deny that Jesus existed before Abraham.

Sin claims our lives when we sin. God offers freedom from sin, but that freedom remains open only to those who believe Jesus came to tell us the way of all God's truth. To refuse his words constitutes death.

Luke

7:36 And one of the Pharisees desired him that he would eat with him. And he went into the Pharisee's house, and sat down to meat. 37 And, behold, a woman in the city, which was a sinner, when she knew that Jesus sat at meat in the Pharisee's house, brought an alabaster box of ointment, 38 And stood at his feet behind him weeping, and began to wash his feet with tears, and did wipe them with the hairs of her head, and kissed his feet, and anointed them with the ointment. 39 Now when the Pharisee which had bidden him saw it, he spake within himself, saying, This man, if he were a prophet, would have known who and what manner of woman this is that toucheth him: for she is a sinner. 40 And Jesus answering said unto him, Simon, I have somewhat to say unto thee. And he saith, Master, say on. 41 There was a certain creditor which had two debtors: the one owed five hundred pence, and the other fifty. 42 And when they had nothing to pay, he frankly forgave them both. Tell me therefore, which of them will love him most? 43 Simon answered and said, I suppose that he, to whom he forgave most. And he said unto him, Thou hast rightly judged. 44 And he turned to the woman, and said unto Simon, Seest thou this woman? I entered into thine house, thou gavest me no water for my feet: but she hath washed my feet with tears, and wiped them with the hairs of her head. 45 Thou gavest me no kiss: but this woman since the time I came in hath not ceased to kiss my feet. 46 My head with oil thou didst not anoint: but this woman hath anointed my feet with ointment. 47 Wherefore I say unto thee, Her sins, which are many, are forgiven; for she loved much: but to whom little is forgiven, the same loveth little. 48 And he said unto her, Thy sins are forgiven. 49 And they that sat at meat with him began to say within themselves, Who is this that forgiveth sins also? 50 And he said to the woman, Thy faith hath saved thee; go in peace.

What attributes in man please God? Simon believed devotion to Pharisee strictness demonstrated what gained God's favor. The woman Simon viewed as a sinner pleased God by washing Jesus' feet with her tears and drying them with her hair. Simon considered Jesus a deceiver, but the woman Simon considered a sinner demonstrated her trust in Jesus as one sent from God whom she desired to honor.

Receiving God's messenger and obeying his truth honors God, but looking for flaws in God's heralds dishonors God. Simon found fault with Jesus because he failed to wash before sitting down to eat. Mary, the sinful woman, saw Jesus as one sent to her from God. (See notes on Math.26:6-13; Lk.10:38-42.) She listened intently to his message and understood lowly service to others manifested the love of God. She gladly used what God gave her to comfort God's messenger.

Simon despised Mary. She's a sinner. If Jesus were truly God's prophet, he would know Mary lived sinfully. Mary received Jesus. Simon invited him to eat primarily to prove he wasn't from God. Mary's many sins God forgave; Simon's he retained.

Attitude toward God's ambassadors sets the stage for mercy or condemnation. Simon and Mary lived in the same city, but lived worlds apart. Simon befriended self-righteous men; Mary admitted her sin and looked to God for help and mercy.

Jesus explained God's way. Walk humbly before God, love mercy, and do justice. (Gen.18:19; Math.9:13;12:7)

How shall God explain mercy and love to man? Abundant harvest without thankfullness convinces few. Constant care leaves men with a sense of security without obligation. Relieving him of great debt touches few hearts. A deep sense of guilt relieved prompts some to love God and man.

Simon and Mary portray magnetic opposing poles as to how they saw Jesus. Secure among self-righteous associates, Simon felt free to cast contempt toward Mary and envious disdain toward Jesus whom he rejected as God's prophet. Mary recognized and admitted sin which burdened her. God's truth issuing from Jesus prompted her to seek relief and return to God who relieves heavy hearts and holds out blessings to all who seek him and depart from evil's pathway.

Mary's joy of forgiveness encouraged her to love God much and demonstrate that love to Jesus and others who, as she, experienced the blessings of walking close to God. Simon refused to abandon praise of his fellows to gain honor from heaven. God offered Simon little, because he loved God little. Friendship with man's system abandons friendship with God. Friendship with the world develops unthankfulness, contempt, faultfinding, and a host of related disrespectful deeds. Friendship with God releases one from the self-preserving path to demonstrate kindness to all we meet. We look for good in others, not their faults. The depraved mind fails to recognize good. Darkness within sees blackness without. Only light allows us to behold light in others, even those engulfed by sin. God can bring light to all lives if we trust God's truth which Jesus relayed from God to us.

Jesus carried eternal truth to all Israel during his lifetime. Though Israelites anticipated the promised blessings of God since the time of Abraham, many, yea, most of them failed to recognize those blessings when Jesus explained them. Was it because of sin in their lives or blindness of heart? Did they carry preconceived notions of what God would do for them when the Messiah arrived? If people truly groan because of Satan's path, why do so many shun a life directed of God? Does Satan's path satisfy the fleshly nature? God offers that which satisfies the spirit within and the body, too. Will man ever seek for the way which meets the longing of all our being? Are we only flesh, or are we spirit, too, as God has demonstrated in Jesus?

If God's prophets correctly conveyed his message, all nations and families someday will become so tired of war, hatred, and destruction they shall call on God to relieve them of all the havoc Satan's system heaps on them. Viewing the condition of today's world, deceived and divided by religious doctrines, ruled by godless, power-seeking rulers, plagued by increasingly tenacious diseases, families torn asunder by divorce with children abandoned, and hopelessness nagging the hearts of poor and rich alike in all nations, how long will God wait before he delivers us from our corruption? He waits until we humbly admit we need God to guide our lives.

What value does this incident contain for present-day Christians? Desire to honor God and his truth above society's customs opens to us the door to God's help and abode. Obedience to God's truth coupled with humility respects God and his messenger, Jesus. When Mary first heard Jesus' words, she might have shielded her iniquities, but God's love penetrated her heart, convincing her God cared for her and asked her to repent and return to God. None of us enjoy admitting error, but until we confess we are sinners, God cannot cleanse us. As Mary openly honored Jesus, each of us must make a decision. Shall I admit sin or act as if I'm perfect and have no need of God? If I confess sin, then I must abandon it and serve God. This involves abandoning self to please God. Acting on this choice opens for me an entrance into his kingdom to enjoy its blessings with God's fellowship.

Reader, are you defensive, trying desperately to hide your sins and faults, hoping others will see you as better than you know you are? God knows he made us subject to fault. Why? to help us rely on God who shows mercy to the humble.

Matthew

**15:10 And he called the multitude, and
said unto them, Hear, and understand: 11
Not that which goeth into the mouth
defileth a man; but that which cometh out
of the mouth, this defileth a man. 12 Then
came his disciples, and said unto him,
Knowest thou that the Pharisees were
offended, after they heard this saying? 13
But he answered and said, Every plant,
which my heavenly Father hath not
planted, shall be rooted up. 14 Let them
alone: they be blind leaders of the blind.
And if the blind lead the blind, both shall
fall into the ditch. 15 Then answered
Peter and said unto him, Declare unto us
this parable. 16 And Jesus said, Are ye
also yet without understanding? 17 Do not
ye yet understand, that whatsoever
entereth in at the mouth goeth into the
belly, and is cast out into the draught? 18
But those things which proceed out of the
mouth come forth from the heart; and
they defile the man. 19 For out of the
heart proceed evil thoughts, murders,
adulteries, fornications, thefts, false
witness, blasphemies: 20 These are the
things which defile a man: but to eat with
unwashen hands defileth not a man.**

Outward signs of devotion to God may appear sincere, but what one thinks determines true devotion to God. Pharisees in the time of Jesus maintained many signs of devotion, but their minds retained a steadfast connection with living to satisfy the desires of the flesh. Serving God acceptably requires that one change thought patterns. No longer may we retain a heart set on pleasing the flesh. We must serve God with all our heart and mind. (Deu.6:5;10:12;11:13;16:20; Math.22:37)

Evil imaginations originated the great wickedness in the days of Noah. (Gen.6:5) Moses reiterated God's warning to Israel not to expect peace if they walked in the imagination of their evil hearts. (Deu.12:8; 29:19)

Mark

**7:14 And when he had called all the
people unto him, he said unto them,
Hearken unto me every one of you, and
understand: 15 There is nothing from
without a man, that entering into him can
defile him: but the things which come out
of him, those are they that defile the man.
16 If any man have ears to hear, let him
hear. 17 And when he was entered into
the house from the people, his disciples
asked him concerning the parable. 18 And
he saith unto them, Are ye so without
understanding also? Do ye not perceive,
that whatsoever thing from without
entereth into the man, it cannot defile
him; 19 Because it entereth not into his
heart, but into the belly, and goeth out
into the draught, purging all meats? 20
And he said, That which cometh out of the
man, that defileth the man. 21 For from
within, out of the heart of men, proceed
evil thoughts, adulteries, fornications,
murders, 22 Thefts, covetousness,
wickedness, deceit, lasciviousness, an evil
eye, blasphemy, pride, foolishness: 23 All
these evil things come from within, and
defile the man.**

God sent Jesus into the world to deliver Israel from the continual pattern of evil thinking which Satan teaches his children. If we think evil, we do and speak evil. Jesus explained good thoughts and deeds please and honor God (Phil.4:8), not Satan, who is a liar and the father of lies. (Jno.8:44) Jesus desired his disciples to understand and distinguish between hearts that please God and those that please Satan.

Paul instructed the churches and young ministers to warn against impure thinking. **"Unto the pure all things are pure: but unto them that are defiled and unbelieving is nothing pure; but even their mind and conscience is defiled."** (Tit. 1:15) Jesus came to purify our consciences and actions. Changed minds and thinking produce changed lives.

Matthew

**15:21 Then Jesus went thence, and
departed into the coasts of Tyre and
Sidon. 22 And, behold, a woman of
Canaan came out of the same coasts, and
cried unto him, saying, Have mercy on
me, O Lord, thou Son of David; my
daughter is grievously vexed with a devil.
23 But he answered her not a word. And
his disciples came and besought him,
saying, Send her away; for she crieth
after us. 24 But he answered and said, I
am not sent but unto the lost sheep of the
house of Israel. 25 Then came she and
worshipped him, saying, Lord, help me.
26 But he answered and said, It is not
meet to take the children's bread, and to
cast it to dogs. 27 And she said, Truth,
Lord: yet the dogs eat of the crumbs
which fall from their masters' table. 28
Then Jesus answered and said unto her, O
woman, great is thy faith: be it unto thee
even as thou wilt. And her daughter was
made whole from that very hour.**

Jews in any nation must rejoice to know God brought the Messiah through them, not by any other nation. Even so, when one of another nation pleaded for God's help, Jesus extended his father's blessings to help that person.

What influences God to hear the plea of any person? Surely it isn't because he/she is more righteous than others. Did not God count Abraham righteous because he believed the promises of God? (Gen.15:6; Rom.4:3) This Gentile woman demonstrated her faith in Jesus. Being confident that he could heal her tormented daughter, she disregarded the taunt of being referred to as a "dog". Getting help for her daughter counted more than anything else.

Trusting God to help us overcome provides strength to prevail in the face of all odds. Did not Jonathan, Saul's son, rout a superior Philistine garrison because he believed God blessed Israel to overthrow their overlords? He and his armor bearer

Mark

**7:24 And from thence he arose, and went
into the borders of Tyre and Sidon, and
entered into an house, and would have no
man know it: but he could not be hid. 25
For a certain woman, whose young
daughter had an unclean spirit, heard of
him, and came and fell at his feet: 26 The
woman was a Greek, a Syrophenician by
nation; and she besought him that he
would cast forth the devil out of her
daughter. 27 But Jesus said unto her, Let
the children first be filled: for it is not
meet to take the children's bread, and to
cast it unto the dogs. 28 And she answered
and said unto him, Yes, Lord: yet the dogs
under the table eat of the children's
crumbs. 29 And he said unto her, For this
saying go thy way; the devil is gone out of
thy daughter. 30 And when she was come
to her house, she found the devil gone out,
and her daughter laid upon the bed.**

with God's help prevailed. (1 Sam.14:1-24)

Why has God chosen to count faith as righteousness? If people gained righteousness by keeping deeds of the law of Moses, we earned righteousness, and God became indebted to pay us for our work, and man might glory before God. (Rom.4:4-5) Since before God no amount of work earns salvation, God devised a plan whereby we might become righteous before him. His plan involves faith. If we believe God's promises and act on them, he counts our faith as if we had been righteous before him as he did Abraham. Through faith in Jesus' blood to cleanse us from our sins, God opens the promise to attain righteousness before him. Faith requires action even as Abraham showed when he departed from Ur and journeyed to the land of Canaan which God promised to give to him and to his children. Though nearly ninety years old, he believed God's promise that Sarah would bear him a son, Isaac. Through Isaac, God promised to bless all nations. (Gen.26:4) Do you believe God can bless your life?

Matthew

15:29 And Jesus departed from thence,
and came nigh unto the sea of Galilee; and
went up into a mountain, and sat down
there. 30 And great multitudes came unto
him, having with them those that were
lame, blind, dumb, maimed, and many
others, and cast them down at Jesus' feet;
and he healed them: 31 Insomuch that the
multitude wondered, when they saw the
dumb to speak, the maimed to be whole,
the lame to walk, and the blind to see: and
they glorified the God of Israel. 32 Then
Jesus called his disciples unto him, and
said, I have compassion on the multitude,
because they continue with me now three
days, and have nothing to eat: and I will
not send them away fasting, lest they faint
in the way. 33 And his disciples say unto
him, Whence should we have so much
bread in the wilderness, as to fill so great
a multitude? 34 And Jesus saith unto
them, How many loaves have ye? And
they said, Seven, and a few little fishes. 35
And he commanded the multitude to sit
down on the ground. 36 And he took the
seven loaves and the fishes, and gave
thanks, and brake them, and gave to his
disciples, and the disciples to the
multitude. 37 And they did all eat, and
were filled: and they took up of the
broken meat that was left seven baskets
full. 38 And they that did eat were four
thousand men, beside women and
children. 39 And he sent away the
multitude, and took ship, and came into
the coasts of Magdala.

Isaiah mentioned wonders to astonish people with the coming of Christ: blind eyes see; lame men leap; deaf ears hear; and bound tongues sing. (Is.35:3-6) Matthew's account of these miracles identified many wonders; Mark mentioned only a deaf and speechless person whom he healed, but Luke omitted this incident.

Matthew stated Jesus went to Magdala, but Mark stated he went to Dalmanutha. Since both noted Jesus fed four thousand at this time, I consider them the same event. After Jesus healed the diseased, lame, sightless, speechless, and taught the people the gospel of God's kingdom, the day waned. Rather than send the people away hungry, Jesus showed his compassion by feeding them. Taking seven loaves of bread and a few small fishes, Jesus thanked his Father and distributed to the disciples who served the people. When all had eaten, the disciples gathered the uneaten food.

Healing the afflicted and feeding the people demonstrated God's love for their physical welfare, but teaching them the gospel of God's kingdom supplied them spiritual food. (Rev.21:6:22:2) Our heavenly Father values and provides for our complete being, physical and spiritual.

After people have forgotten God for many years, why has he demonstrated such patience and kindness? The clearest way to explain such love sets it in the realm of parental concern. When a mother or father sees a son or daughter, learning to walk, fall and injure himself/herself, love prompts the parent to comfort and soothe the hurt. God, our heavenly Father, watches over all his children and beholds all our hurts, sorrows, and distresses. Our discomforts God feels, for we are his offspring. He grieves to see Satan's tricks plague by luring us to satisfy physical passion without regard to God's law. Abandoning us to Satan's wiles gives our heavenly Father no pleasure. Only when we refuse to listen to his message and messengers does he allow us to sink into the mire of degradation, hoping we may sometime awaken to understand God still loves us and holds open to us a far better way of life if we submit to his truth. Why will we resist such a loving Father who always seeks the best for us? Has Satan prevailed again by his lies? Has he convinced us God doesn't care? Has he convinced us, like deists, God has abandoned his creation? Satan contradicts every promise of God.

Mark

7:31 And again, departing from the coasts
of Tyre and Sidon, he came unto the sea
of Galilee, through the midst of the coasts
of Decapolis. 32 And they bring unto him
one that was deaf, and had an impediment
in his speech; and they beseech him to put
his hand upon him. 33 And he took him
aside from the multitude, and put his
fingers into his ears, and he spit, and
touched his tongue; 34 And looking up to
heaven, he sighed, and saith unto him,
Ephphatha, that is, Be opened. 35 And
straightway his ears were opened, and the
string of his tongue was loosed, and he
spake plain. 36 And he charged them that
they should tell no man: but the more he
charged them, so much the more a great
deal they published it; 37 And were
beyond measure astonished, saying, He
hath done all things well: he maketh both
the deaf to hear, and the dumb to speak.
8:1 In those days the multitude being very
great, and having nothing to eat, Jesus
called his disciples unto him, and saith
unto them, 2 I have compassion on the
multitude, because they have now been
with me three days, and have nothing to
eat: 3 And if I send them away fasting to
their own houses, they will faint by the
way: for divers of them came from far. 4
And his disciples answered him, From
whence can a man satisfy these men with
bread here in the wilderness? 5 And he
asked them, How many loaves have ye?
And they said, Seven. 6 And he com-
manded the people to sit down on the
ground: and he took the seven loaves, and
gave thanks, and brake, and gave to his
disciples to set before them; and they did
set them before the people. 7 And they
had a few small fishes: and he blessed,
and commanded to set them also before
them. 8 So they did eat, and were filled:
and they took up of the broken meat that
was left seven baskets. 9 And they that
had eaten were about four thousand: and
he sent them away. 10 And straightway he
entered into a ship with his disciples, and
came into the parts of Dalmanutha.

Besides offering more satisfying life on earth now, God promises life after death. Jesus shows us we need not believe that once we make a mess of our lives we must continue to suffer all the tragedies associated therewith. Returning to our heavenly Father as the prodigal son, confessing our errors, and abandoning them, God restores hope, a deliverance from the agonies we brought on ourselves, and fellowship with our heavenly Father. As children sometimes want to free themselves from parents, but later appreciate and seek closer ties, we draw near to God because of his love.

Does God's willingness to receive us sound like good news? Does it appeal to us? Are all people convinced the message from God can be trusted? When a person finds himself/herself in such straits as Satan drives us, why do we continue to search for good in Satan's refuse? It might be compared to people preferring to eat from the garbage dump rather than to come to a well-provided feast. Does God honestly mean he withholds no good thing from us? (Ps.84:11) Is it true that God's statutes give us only good? (Deu.6:24) Will obeying Jesus' commands secure for us an abundant life? (Jno.7:17;10:10) Peter instructed that loving life and seeing good days comes only by eschewing evil and seeking and ensuing peace. (1 Pet.3:10-11) Do our own experiences confirm this? Will treating others kindly usually bring us kindness? Does hating and revenging ourselves result in like bitterness from others? Do our experiences corroborate Jesus' doctrine? If they do, why are we so willing to listen to Satan's advice? Consideration of others' needs, being spiritual in nature, produces blessings to the one who shows mercy as well as to the one receiving mercy. Showing friendship brings friendship. (Prov.18:24) From experience we know this, but still we resist.

Matthew

16:1 The Pharisees also with the Sadducees came, and tempting desired him that he would shew them a sign from heaven. 2 He answered and said unto them, When it is evening, ye say, It will be fair weather: for the sky is red. 3 And in the morning, It will be foul weather to day: for the sky is red and lowring. O ye hypocrites, ye can discern the face of the sky; but can ye not discern the signs of the times? 4 A wicked and adulterous generation seeketh after a sign; and there shall no sign be given unto it, but the sign of the prophet Jonas. And he left them, and departed. 5 And when his disciples were come to the other side, they had forgotten to take bread. 6 Then Jesus said unto them, Take heed and beware of the leaven of the Pharisees and of the Sadducees. 7 And they reasoned among themselves, saying, It is because we have taken no bread. 8 Which when Jesus perceived, he said unto them, O ye of little faith, why reason ye among yourselves, because ye have brought no bread? 9 Do ye not yet understand, neither remember the five loaves of the five thousand, and how many baskets ye took up? 10 Neither the seven loaves of the four thousand, and how many baskets ye took up? 11 How is it that ye do not understand that I spake it not to you concerning bread, that ye should beware of the leaven of the Pharisees and of the Sadducees? 12 Then understood they how that he bade them not beware of the leaven of bread, but of the doctrine of the Pharisees and of the Sadducees.

Mark

8:11 And the Pharisees came forth, and began to question with him, seeking of him a sign from heaven, tempting him. 12 And he sighed deeply in his spirit, and saith, Why doth this generation seek after a sign? verily I say unto you, There shall no sign be given unto this generation. 13 And he left them, and entering into the ship again departed to the other side. 14 Now the disciples had forgotten to take bread, neither had they in the ship with them more than one loaf. 15 And he charged them, saying, Take heed, beware of the leaven of the Pharisees, and of the leaven of Herod. 16 And they reasoned among themselves, saying, It is because we have no bread. 17 And when Jesus knew it, he saith unto them, Why reason ye, because ye have no bread? perceive ye not yet, neither understand? have ye your heart yet hardened? 18 Having eyes, see ye not? and having ears, hear ye not? and do ye not remember? 19 When I brake the five loaves among five thousand, how many baskets full of fragments took ye up? They say unto him, Twelve. 20 And when the seven among four thousand, how many baskets full of fragments took ye up? And they said, Seven. 21 And he said unto them, How is it that ye do not understand?

Token religion Satan holds before mankind as a means to allow people to live after the flesh and at the same time feel they know God. Pharisees and Sadducees fell prey to this deception. If they appeared religious and performed ceremonies God commanded, they believed it pleased God. Satan claims unclean thoughts or overlooking the plight of poor, aged parents, or strangers affects not one's relationship to God. He desires that we perform his rights and sacrifices, and he will forgive our shortcomings. Jesus advised his people God looks on the heart of a person. If one's heart feels sorrow for the aged, down-trodden, poor, strangers, etc., then he will do what he can to help relieve their suffering. God desires of us mercy, not sacrifice. (Math.9:13;12:7)

Is it any wonder that John the Baptist, Jesus, and his apostles came preaching baptism and repentance, for the kingdom of God nears? (Math.3:2;4:17;10:7) Satan deceives us by his lies and steals God's joy.

Luke

12:1 In the mean time, when there were gathered together an innumerable multitude of people, insomuch that they trode one upon another, he began to say unto his disciples first of all, Beware ye of the leaven of the Pharisees, which is hypocrisy. 2 For there is nothing covered, that shall not be revealed; neither hid, that shall not be known. 3 Therefore whatsoever ye have spoken in darkness shall be heard in the light; and that which ye have spoken in the ear in closets shall be proclaimed upon the housetops.

Leaven of the Pharisees and Herod overlooked the appeal of Moses' law, prophets, and psalms which entreated them to turn their hearts to God. How could God's kingdom spread peace over the earth if those who peopled his kingdom lived as those who populated Satan's kingdom? Peace between individuals and nations originates in the minds of men and women, not in outward signs of pompous ceremonies which elevate the person for a short time during the ceremony, but allows one to return to the old path of disregard of others to achieve his own interests in life? Indeed, if God's kingdom benefits men more than Satan's, there must be a change of goals from self-interest to concern for the needs of those about us. God's kingdom instills brotherly love, Satan's self-love.

Hard hearts plagued the disciples even while they walked with the Master. Dare we think that our hearts may escape this problem? What is a hard heart? For the apostles, it involved not understanding the truth Jesus conveyed to them. Pharisees, Sadducees, and Herod retained hard hearts which disregarded the truth of God and plodded on in the scheme of Satan's lifestyle.

Did the Jews truly not discern that John the Baptist, Jesus, and his disciples preached the kingdom of God, or were they feigning ignorance? They knew how to interpret signs

Luke

12:54 And he said also to the people, When ye see a cloud rise out of the west, straightway ye say, There cometh a shower; and so it is. 55 And when ye see the south wind blow, ye say, There will be heat; and it cometh to pass. 56 Ye hypocrites, ye can discern the face of the sky and of the earth; but how is it that ye do not discern this time? 57 Yea, and why even of yourselves judge ye not what is right?

of the sky, but claimed not to realize God sent Jesus to return them to God and the path of truth. Jesus suggested they spoke the truth about him in secret, but denied him in public. In time, their hypocrisy shall be known. You deny me to the people because you are jealous, desiring to retain control of the people. Your wickedness God will reprove and make known to all peoples, and they will abandon your hypocrisy.

Many present-day religious guides portray deceived minds. Honest people refuse to accept such corrupt religion which allows people to practice homosexual deviancy, but some ministers convince people God allows these deeds which God stated emphatically he hates. (Lev.20:13; Deu.23:17) Can such teaching be anything but hypocrisy as well as Satan's lie?

Unless men and women resign our hearts to God and his will, God shall abandon us to our own depravity. Paul wrote that when people push God from their minds, God gives them up to work all manner of depravity and to receive the reward of their own godless deeds. (Rom.1:18-32) We look at the Soviet Union and behold how casting God aside brought that system and its people to ruin. If we in the United Sates of America remove God from our hearts, shall we not plunge to the depths of Satan's pit? Or do we believe we are naturally superior, and we shall never see want. Many ancient capitals believed Satan's lie, and God desolated them forever. (Jer. ch. 50; Na. ch. 2)

Matthew

16:13 When Jesus came into the coasts of Caesarea Philippi, he asked his disciples, saying, Whom do men say that I the Son of man am? 14 And they said, Some say that thou art John the Baptist: some, Elias; and others, Jeremias, or one of the prophets. 15 He saith unto them, But whom say ye that I am? 16 And Simon Peter answered and said, Thou art the Christ, the Son of the living God. 17 And Jesus answered and said unto him, Blessed art thou, Simon Barjona: for flesh and blood hath not revealed it unto thee, but my Father which is in heaven. 18 And I say also unto thee, That thou art Peter, and upon this rock I will build my church; and the gates of hell shall not prevail against it. 19 And I will give unto thee the keys of the kingdom of heaven: and whatsoever thou shalt bind on earth shall be bound in heaven: and whatsoever thou shalt loose on earth shall be loosed in heaven. 20 Then charged he his disciples that they should tell no man that he was Jesus the Christ. 21 From that time forth began Jesus to shew unto his disciples, how that he must go unto Jerusalem, and suffer many things of the elders and chief priests and scribes, and be killed, and be raised again the third day. 22 Then Peter took him, and began to rebuke him, saying, Be it far from thee, Lord: this shall not be unto thee. 23 But he turned, and said unto Peter, Get thee behind me, Satan: thou art an offence unto me: for thou savourest not the things that be of God, but those that be of men.

Who was Jesus? In his lifetime this question generated much discussion. Was he a prophet, the Messiah, God's Son, or just another man? Only those who examine the truth of God with a genuine determination to know and believe God will arrive at the conclusion that he fulfilled all the prophecies and must be the Messiah, the Son of God. Only God reveals this truth.

Mark

8:22 And he cometh to Bethsaida; and they bring a blind man unto him, and besought him to touch him. 23 And he took the blind man by the hand, and led him out of the town; and when he had spit on his eyes, and put his hands upon him, he asked him if he saw ought. 24 And he looked up, and said, I see men as trees, walking. 25 After that he put his hands again upon his eyes, and made him look up: and he was restored, and saw every man clearly. 26 And he sent him away to his house, saying, Neither go into the town, nor tell it to any in the town. 27 And Jesus went out, and his disciples, into the towns of Caesarea Philippi: and by the way he asked his disciples, saying unto them, Whom do men say that I am? 28 And they answered, John the Baptist: but some say, Elias; and others, One of the prophets. 29 And he saith unto them, But whom say ye that I am? And Peter answereth and saith unto him, Thou art the Christ. 30 And he charged them that they should tell no man of him. 31 And he began to teach them, that the Son of man must suffer many things, and be rejected of the elders, and of the chief priests, and scribes, and be killed, and after three days rise again. 32 And he spake that saying openly. And Peter took him, and began to rebuke him. 33 But when he had turned about and looked on his disciples, he rebuked Peter, saying, Get thee behind me, Satan: for thou savourest not the things that be of God, but the things that be of men.

Belief in Jesus as the Christ results from a cooperation of man and God. Beginning with God sending Jesus, and apostles recording all the evidences, each person looks at the evidence. If each finds the facts presented sound and thinks about them, God reveals the truth so each person believes it. Refusing to hear or examine and think about the evidence produces unbelief.

Luke

9:18 And it came to pass, as he was alone praying, his disciples were with him: and he asked them, saying, Whom say the people that I am? 19 They answering said, John the Baptist; but some say, Elias; and others say, that one of the old prophets is risen again. 20 He said unto them, But whom say ye that I am? Peter answering said, The Christ of God. 21 And he straitly charged them, and commanded them to tell no man that thing; 22 Saying, The Son of man must suffer many things, and be rejected of the elders and chief priests and scribes, and be slain, and be raised the third day.

Common people who heard and saw Jesus believed him to be a prophet, John the Baptist, Elijah, or some other prophet of centuries long ago. What really concerned Jesus lay in how his apostles perceived him. All three synoptic gospels noted Peter's reply. You are the Christ, the Son of the living God.

Matthew alone recorded that Jesus blessed Peter for his confession and confirmed that Peter alone had not come to that conclusion. God revealed it to Peter. The truth Peter spoke stands as the foundation of the church or kingdom of God on earth. All who enter the everlasting kingdom of God must confess Jesus to be Christ, God's Son. This becomes the key which admits or excludes all who seek shelter within God's dominion.

Why did Jesus instruct his disciples to withhold this information from the people until God raised him from the dead? For Jews who conceived of the return of David's reign as a kingdom of civil authority, they may have proclaimed him king as they sought to do. (Jno.6:15) God's plan included no throne for Jesus on earth or in the city of Jerusalem, only one in heaven at God's right hand. (Ps.110:1-7; Act.3:21)

God's kingdom corresponds not to the kingdoms of this world. (Jno.18:36) Though God determines Jesus shall be King of kings and Lord of lords, he sits on David's throne in heaven and shall remain there until all his enemies submit. (Ps.110:1; Act.2:34,35;3:21) When all enemies fall, then God sends Jesus to gather his people, and Jesus shall return the kingdom to the Father. (1 Cor.15:24-28) Not understanding God's plan, even Peter resisted, and attempted to persuade Jesus that he should not go to Jerusalem to suffer and die. (Math.16:22)

Today many who seek the kingdom of God view it as a kingdom of this world, not a heavenly one. They, as Peter, desire to see the day when Jesus returns to this earth to set up his kingdom to reign in Jerusalem. If Jesus remains as our only high priest and mediator, he cannot be a priest on earth. (Heb.8:4) If this plan were implemented, who will intercede to God for us when we sin? Not allowed of God to serve as priest on earth, Jesus cannot plead to his Father for our weaknesses.

Why not submit to God's plan for his kingdom? As Jesus sits on David's throne in heaven, he becomes both king and priest on his throne. (Zech.6:13) Following God's plan, Jesus rules all nations and intercedes as priest at the same time. Suppose Jesus ruled in Jerusalem. Think of the time and money involved for a person to come before Christ to plead for mercy. Expense alone would force the poor to lose contact with their high priest. Submitting to God's plan, Jesus awaits rich and poor alike night or day.

Jeremiah penned a prophecy which forever forbids Jesus to rule as king in Jerusalem. He promised that no descendant of Coniah (Jeconias, Math.1:11) shall reign in Jerusalem and prosper. (Jer.22:30) How can Jesus reign, subdue enemies, and not prosper? He reigns in heaven, not on earth.

All who anticipate Jesus to set up his throne in Jerusalem to reign believe one of Satan's lies. God's king and kingdom is not of this earth. (Jno.18:36) Why will people refuse God's truth and believe a lie? Why be an offense to Jesus, like Peter?

Matthew

16:24 Then said Jesus unto his disciples, If any man will come after me, let him deny himself, and take up his cross, and follow me. 25 For whosoever will save his life shall lose it: and whosoever will lose his life for my sake shall find it. 26 For what is a man profited, if he shall gain the whole world, and lose his own soul? or what shall a man give in exchange for his soul? 27 For the Son of man shall come in the glory of his Father with his angels; and then he shall reward every man according to his works. 28 Verily I say unto you, There be some standing here, which shall not taste of death, till they see the Son of man coming in his kingdom.

God requires all who desire to enter his kingdom to make a choice between living as children of this world or as children of God. This decision involves determining which path rewards you with what you value most. If living to fulfill the desires of the flesh appeals to you the most, then God's kingdom promises you little. Should you seek more to find peace and enjoy a fuller life, God's system holds out to you the most rewarding way.

Jesus taught his followers that every person who seeks him must bear a cross. If that involves losing one's life, he must determine conclusively to sacrifice his life rather than abandon the truth of God. Suppose you choose to live as the children of this world which results in your accumulating such a mass of wealth as all the world could supply, but left you without hope of eternal security after death. Is this world's goods so valuable you prefer to sacrifice eternal life for a few short years of glory on earth? The opposite choice involves foregoing pleasures, satisfying to the fleshly appetites, to gain eternal life. Each person must make this choice. We cannot serve two masters. We either submit to God's or Satan's life style and rewards. Many believe Satan's lie--you can have both.

Mark

8:34 And when he had called the people unto him with his disciples also, he said unto them, Whosoever will come after me, let him deny himself, and take up his cross, and follow me. 35 For whosoever will save his life shall lose it; but whosoever shall lose his life for my sake and the gospel's, the same shall save it. 36 For what shall it profit a man, if he shall gain the whole world, and lose his own soul? 37 Or what shall a man give in exchange for his soul? 38 Whosoever therefore shall be ashamed of me and of my words in this adulterous and sinful generation; of him also shall the Son of man be ashamed, when he cometh in the glory of his Father with the holy angels. 9:1 And he said unto them, Verily I say unto you, That there be some of them that stand here, which shall not taste of death, till they have seen the kingdom of God come with power.

Most of us know what it's like to be ashamed to associate with some person or group of people. Those who relish the life of gambling, drinking, dancing, sexual immorality, etc. usually show discomfort if their associates see them with those who choose to please God. Christians also show embarrassment when their friends see them associating with the ungodly. Once you know the will of God, are you embarrassed to gather with certain people? Jesus taught that if you or I find ourselves ashamed of him or his gospel when with our friends, he shall show embarrassment to acknowledge you or me before his Father and his holy angels in heaven.

Once Pharisees and priests in Jerusalem determined to cast from the synagogue all who confessed Jesus to be the Messiah, many who had flocked to Jesus, refused to admit any association with him. For example, after Jesus gave sight to the man born blind, the former blind man's parents refused to admit any knowledge of how their

Luke

9:23 And he said to them all, If any man
will come after me, let him deny himself,
and take up his cross daily, and follow me.
24 For whosoever will save his life shall
lose it: but whosoever will lose his life for
my sake, the same shall save it. 25 For
what is a man advantaged, if he gain the
whole world, and lose himself, or be cast
away? 26 For whosoever shall be ashamed
of me and of my words, of him shall the
Son of man be ashamed, when he shall
come in his own glory, and in his Father's,
and of the holy angels. 27 But I tell you of
a truth, there be some standing here,
which shall not taste of death, till they see
the kingdom of God.

son received his sight. They feared being excluded from the synagogue and from their Jewish friends. (Jno.9:13-23) God casts out all who deny his Son Jesus.

From the preaching of John the Baptist to the crucifixion and resurrection of Jesus, people, rulers, and even Jesus' disciples desired to know when to expect the kingdom of heaven. Luke noted that Pharisees demanded of Jesus when the kingdom of God would come. (Lk.17:20) Some expected God's kingdom to appear immediately. (Lk.19:11) Even after God raised Jesus from the dead, the apostles asked him if he would restore the kingdom to Israel. (Act.1:6) To satisfy this anticipation of God's kingdom, Jesus informed his audience that some who stood listening to him should not die before the arrival of God's kingdom.

How any person could misconstrue this plain statement might astonish us. Notwithstanding, most Jews today continue to expect the coming of the Messiah and the restoration of David's reign over Israel. They aren't alone in this blindness. Such groups as the Jehovah's Witnesses contend God's kingdom delayed its arrival until 1914 A.D. Methuselah, the oldest recorded man, would be only a young man compared to the age of those who continued to live from Jesus' day until 1914 A.D. How can any person or group of people affirm such an irrational position? Either Jesus established God's kingdom before the end of the first century A.D., or John the Baptist, Jesus, and the apostles lied.

Does God's word inform us when Jesus gave power to God's kingdom? Yes. Why must some suppose that an issue so important remains secret? **"Ye shall receive power, after the Holy Ghost is come upon you."** (Act.1:8) They received the Holy Ghost in about two weeks. (Act.2:4)

Do any of the epistles to churches indicate people had entered the kingdom of God? Consider these records. **"Who hath delivered us from the power of darkness, and hath translated us into the kingdom of his dear Son:"** (Col.1:13) People reside either in God's kingdom or Satan's. If Jesus translated some into God's kingdom, they left Satan's domain and entered God's. Who are the "us" in this verse? Paul included himself and those in the church at Colosse. God translated them into the kingdom of God's dear Son. **"I John, who also am your brother, and companion in tribulation, and in the kingdom and patience of Jesus Christ, was in the isle that is called Patmos, for the word of God, and for the testimony of Jesus Christ."** (Rev.1:9) John, the apostle of Jesus Christ, claimed he rested in the kingdom of Jesus. Did he misstate his situation? No, he testified that what he wrote shows the true message of God. (Rev.22:8)

Does God inform us when his kingdom came? Two apostles and the churches to whom they addressed state clearly that both they and those to whom they wrote God had translated into his kingdom. That means it began during the first century when the apostles received the Holy Spirit. (Act.2:4) It began demonstrating power on Pentecost in 33 A.D. Those who obeyed entered it that day. Jesus ruled as king that day.

Matthew

17:1 And after six days Jesus taketh Peter,
James, and John his brother, and
bringeth them up into an high mountain
apart, 2 And was transfigured before
them: and his face did shine as the sun,
and his raiment was white as the light. 3
And, behold, there appeared unto them
Moses and Elias talking with him. 4 Then
answered Peter, and said unto Jesus,
Lord, it is good for us to be here: if thou
wilt, let us make here three tabernacles;
one for thee, and one for Moses, and one
for Elias. 5 While he yet spake, behold, a
bright cloud overshadowed them: and
behold a voice out of the cloud, which
said, This is my beloved Son, in whom I
am well pleased; hear ye him. 6 And when
the disciples heard it, they fell on their
face, and were sore afraid. 7 And Jesus
came and touched them, and said, Arise,
and be not afraid. 8 And when they had
lifted up their eyes, they saw no man, save
Jesus only. 9 And as they came down from
the mountain, Jesus charged them, saying,
Tell the vision to no man, until the Son of
man be risen again from the dead. 10 And
his disciples asked him, saying, Why then
say the scribes that Elias must first come?
11 And Jesus answered and said unto
them, Elias truly shall first come, and
restore all things. 12 But I say unto you,
That Elias is come already, and they knew
him not, but have done unto him
whatsoever they listed. Likewise shall also
the Son of man suffer of them. 13 Then
the disciples understood that he spake
unto them of John the Baptist.

On the mount of transfiguration, Peter, James, and John witnessed Jesus glorified with Moses and Elijah. Peter suggested they construct three tabernacles: one for Moses, one for Elijah, and one for Jesus. God spoke from a bright cloud and instructed them to hear Jesus, God's beloved Son. Jesus tells you all truth. (Jno.15:15)

Seeing Elijah prompted the apostles to ask

Mark

9:2 And after six days Jesus taketh with
him Peter, and James, and John, and
leadeth them up into an high mountain
apart by themselves: and he was
transfigured before them. 3 And his
raiment became shining, exceeding white
as snow; so as no fuller on earth can white
them. 4 And there appeared unto them
Elias with Moses: and they were talking
with Jesus. 5 And Peter answered and
said to Jesus, Master, it is good for us to
be here: and let us make three tab-
ernacles; one for thee, and one for Moses,
and one for Elias. 6 For he wist not what
to say; for they were sore afraid. 7 And
there was a cloud that overshadowed
them: and a voice came out of the cloud,
saying, This is my beloved Son: hear him.
8 And suddenly, when they had looked
round about, they saw no man any more,
save Jesus only with themselves. 9 And as
they came down from the mountain, he
charged them that they should tell no man
what things they had seen, till the Son of
man were risen from the dead. 10 And
they kept that saying with themselves,
questioning one with another what the
rising from the dead should mean. 11 And
they asked him, saying, Why say the
scribes that Elias must first come? 12 And
he answered and told them, Elias verily
cometh first, and restoreth all things; and
how it is written of the Son of man, that
he must suffer many things, and be set at
nought. 13 But I say unto you, That Elias
is indeed come, and they have done unto
him whatsoever they listed, as it is written
of him.

why scribes taught Elijah must precede Christ's coming. Elijah shall restore Israel to God, but Elijah came, and they didn't recognize him and put him to death. John the Baptist was Elijah. (Mal.4:5-6) Leaders of Israel shall slay me the same way. Satan's lies blinded Jewish eyes and hearts so they could not recognize God's kingdom.

Luke

9:28 And it came to pass about an eight days after these sayings, he took Peter and John and James, and went up into a mountain to pray. 29 And as he prayed, the fashion of his countenance was altered, and his raiment was white and glistering. 30 And, behold, there talked with him two men, which were Moses and Elias: 31 Who appeared in glory, and spake of his decease which he should accomplish at Jerusalem. 32 But Peter and they that were with him were heavy with sleep: and when they were awake, they saw his glory, and the two men that stood with him. 33 And it came to pass, as they departed from him, Peter said unto Jesus, Master, it is good for us to be here: and let us make three tabernacles; one for thee, and one for Moses, and one for Elias: not knowing what he said. 34 While he thus spake, there came a cloud, and overshadowed them: and they feared as they entered into the cloud. 35 And there came a voice out of the cloud, saying, This is my beloved Son: hear him. 36 And when the voice was past, Jesus was found alone. And they kept it close, and told no man in those days any of those things which they had seen.

In the transfiguration, Jesus resembled angels who brought God's messages to men. (Dan.10:6; Heb.1:7) Only Luke recorded the topic of Moses and Elijah as they visited with Jesus concerning his death to be accomplished at Jerusalem. Since Peter rejected Jesus' words that he must go to Jerusalem and be delivered to death, Moses and Elijah, talking about the same event, should convince the apostles that Christ's death accomplished God's plan. They must reconcile their hopes according to God's plan for his Son. Hear Jesus for God sends him to deliver all God's truth to men today. (Deu. 18:15-19; Heb.1:1-3)

Luke noted that Jesus prayed as Moses and Elijah appeared. Neither Matthew nor Mark recorded his praying at that time. In order to prepare himself for the ordeal of suffering on the cross, Jesus must have called often to his Father to strengthen him against that day. Moses and Elijah also appeared to encourage him to face the coming trials.

God acknowledged Jesus as his Son who also pleased him. The Father confessed Jesus before John the Baptist and those present at his baptism. (Math.3:17) Here he testifies before Peter, James, and John that Jesus is his Son in whom he is well pleased. Shortly before his apprehension by his enemies, God spoke again to Jesus in presence of an audience in Jerusalem that God would soon glorify Jesus. (Jno.12:28)

What significance are we to see in God's confessing Jesus audibly before men? Is it an example for men? Does it indicate three-way fellowship of God, Jesus, and man? Can men fellowship with God without confessing Jesus is God's Son? Does Jesus confess us to the Father when we are baptized in the name of the Father, and the Son, and the Holy Spirit? Does Jesus testify to the Father that he is well pleased with us when we face up to the difficult trials we must endure as the Father did Jesus when he willingly journeyed to Jerusalem to be rejected by the elders, to be condemned to death, and to suffer the agony on the cross? When John wrote of the fellowship with the Father and Son available to us, was confessing the Father and Son to our peers part of that fellowship? (1 Jno.1:3) Jesus remarked, **"Whosoever therefore shall confess me before men, him will I confess also before my Father which is in heaven. But whosoever shall deny me before men, him will I also deny before my Father which is in heaven."** (Math.10:32-33) Introduce Jesus to your friends, and Jesus shall introduce you to his Father. Deny him to your friends, and Jesus shall deny you and me before his Father. If we believe Jesus' statement we will stand up for him to our friends.

Matthew

17:14 And when they were come to the multitude, there came to him a certain man, kneeling down to him, and saying, 15 Lord, have mercy on my son: for he is lunatick, and sore vexed: for ofttimes he falleth into the fire, and oft into the water. 16 And I brought him to thy disciples, and they could not cure him. 17 Then Jesus answered and said, O faithless and perverse generation, how long shall I be with you? how long shall I suffer you? bring him hither to me. 18 And Jesus rebuked the devil; and he departed out of him: and the child was cured from that very hour. 19 Then came the disciples to Jesus apart, and said, Why could not we cast him out? 20 And Jesus said unto them, Because of your unbelief: for verily I say unto you, If ye have faith as a grain of mustard seed, ye shall say unto this mountain, Remove hence to yonder place; and it shall remove; and nothing shall be impossible unto you. 21 Howbeit this kind goeth not out but by prayer and fasting.

Matthew's account of the apostles' failure to heal the lunatic son contains less detail than Mark's, which often occurs. Apostles expected to cast out the child's devil, but failed. Jesus attributed their lack of success to their lack of faith. Do we experience failure in God's eyes for our lack of faith in his promises? Has not our heavenly Father promised that no temptation shall overtake us which will be too powerful for us to withstand? (1 Cor.10:13) We, like the apostles, fail the temptation tests daily perhaps because we trust in ourselves more than in God's power. May we all concentrate on trusting all God's truth that our lives may be blessed and God glorified. (2 Cor.1:9; 1 Tim.6:17)

When the father of this child saw his son released from Satan's domination, he must have realized how God helped his belief. God desires to strengthen our belief, too. (Eph.3:16; Col.1:11)

Mark

9:14 And when he came to his disciples, he saw a great multitude about them, and the scribes questioning with them. 15 And straightway all the people, when they beheld him, were greatly amazed, and running to him saluted him. 16 And he asked the scribes, What question ye with them? 17 And one of the multitude answered and said, Master, I have brought unto thee my son, which hath a dumb spirit; 18 And wheresoever he taketh him, he teareth him: and he foameth, and gnasheth with his teeth, and pineth away: and I spake to thy disciples that they should cast him out; and they could not. 19 He answereth him, and saith, O faithless generation, how long shall I be with you? how long shall I suffer you? bring him unto me. 20 And they brought him unto him: and when he saw him, straightway the spirit tare him; and he fell on the ground, and wallowed foaming. 21 And he asked his father, How long is it ago since this came unto him? And he said, Of a child. 22 And ofttimes it hath cast him into the fire, and into the waters, to destroy him: but if thou canst do any thing, have compassion on us, and help us. 23 Jesus said unto him, If thou canst believe, all things are possible to him that believeth. 24 And straightway the father of the child cried out, and said with tears, Lord, I believe; help thou mine unbelief. 25 When Jesus saw that the people came running together, he rebuked the foul spirit, saying unto him, Thou dumb and deaf spirit, I charge thee, come out of him, and enter no more into him. 26 And the spirit cried, and rent him sore, and came out of him: and he was as one dead; insomuch that many said, He is dead. 27 But Jesus took him by the hand, and lifted him up; and he arose. 28 And when he was come into the house, his disciples asked him privately, Why could not we cast him out? 29 And he said unto

them, This kind can come forth by nothing, but by prayer and fasting.

When the apostles inquired of Jesus why they failed to cast out the devil, he explained that kind removes only by fasting and prayer. When we deprive ourselves for the misfortunes of others and call on the Father for help, God works wonders. Relying on ourselves to accomplish God's work results in disappointments. We need always to keep before our eyes that we with God prevail, but by ourselves we fail. When we rely on God for help to meet life's problems, we won't falter in personal problems and temptations as the apostles did here and as Peter when he denied Jesus before those who insisted he followed Jesus. God is our present helper in every situation if we call on his help. Let us not be faithless, but believing in the words of God's Son, Jesus, who has explained the whole truth of our heavenly Father. Our lives produce the light of God if we face the devil and his wiles as David when he, with trust in God, met mighty Goliath. (1 Sam. 17:45) Our Father gladly helps us.

True faith in God provides us with confidence that God abides at our side in every situation. With him, nothing becomes impossible, and we fearlessly face men and tasks with assurance that God will help overcome whether it's with temptations of flesh or oppositions by unbelievers. Trials aren't dreaded, for God secures the outcome to his glory and to our benefit. With this outlook on life, why are we faithless? "**My brethren, count it all joy when ye fall into divers temptations; knowing this, that the trying of your faith worketh patience.**" (Ja.1:2-3) Let each of us show our heavenly Father that we are children of faith that his name may be glorified in the land of the living. Only by faith shall we, as God's soldiers, vanquish the children of darkness and spread the kingdom of light over all the earth. (Dan.7:27) God's kingdom shall prevail when we believe and obey.

Luke

9:37 And it came to pass, that on the next
day, when they were come down from the
hill, much people met him. 38 And,
behold, a man of the company cried out,
saying, Master, I beseech thee, look upon
my son: for he is mine only child. 39 And,
lo, a spirit taketh him, and he suddenly
crieth out; and it teareth him that he
foameth again, and bruising him hardly
departeth from him. 40 And I besought
thy disciples to cast him out; and they
could not. 41 And Jesus answering said, O
faithless and perverse generation, how
long shall I be with you, and suffer you?
Bring thy son hither. 42 And as he was yet
a coming, the devil threw him down, and
tare him. And Jesus rebuked the unclean
spirit, and healed the child, and delivered
him again to his father.

How shall we regard the inclusion or exclusion of details by gospel writers? Only Luke mentioned that Satan tormented the man's only son. Matthew omitted how he frothed, and Satan bruised, and tore the child. Mark included most of the details. Why did Mark and Luke provide these details, but Matthew recorded the basic facts of the narrative? Did each writer include such information as supported the purpose of his gospel and omitted the parts that failed to meet his goals? Might the audience of one writer have needed more information than another? Did God so direct each writer to include parts, but omit other parts so each reader in ages to come might read all the accounts? Even the length of scroll may have helped determine what information to include and omit. After nearly 2000 years, all the purposes of each writer may prove impossible for us to ascertain. Even so, the general scope of each author seems to convey an overall theme which runs throughout each gospel. Discovering each theme provides us with insight into the needs of each audience. God has seen fit to record four accounts of his Son's deeds.

Matthew

17:22 And while they abode in Galilee, Jesus said unto them, The Son of man shall be betrayed into the hands of men: 23 And they shall kill him, and the third day he shall be raised again. And they were exceeding sorry. 24 And when they were come to Capernaum, they that received tribute money came to Peter, and said, Doth not your master pay tribute? 25 He saith, Yes. And when he was come into the house, Jesus prevented him, saying, What thinkest thou, Simon? of whom do the kings of the earth take custom or tribute? of their own children, or of strangers? 26 Peter saith unto him, Of strangers. Jesus saith unto him, Then are the children free. 27 Notwithstanding, lest we should offend them, go thou to the sea, and cast an hook, and take up the fish that first cometh up; and when thou hast opened his mouth, thou shalt find a piece of money: that take, and give unto them for me and thee.

Mark

9:30 And they departed thence, and passed through Galilee; and he would not that any man should know it. 31 For he taught his disciples, and said unto them, The Son of man is delivered into the hands of men, and they shall kill him; and after that he is killed, he shall rise the third day. 32 But they understood not that saying, and were afraid to ask him.

Luke

9:43 And they were all amazed at the mighty power of God. But while they wondered every one at all things which Jesus did, he said unto his disciples, 44 Let these sayings sink down into your ears: for the Son of man shall be delivered into the hands of men. 45 But they understood not this saying, and it was hid from them, that they perceived it not: and they feared to ask him of that saying.

Unlike others, Jesus knew the time and manner of his death. He first compared his decease to Jonah. As Jonah dwelt three days in the whale's belly, death must swallow him three days. (Math.12:40). In Cesarea, he explained clearly to his disciples he must go to Jerusalem, suffer much from the elders, chief priests, scribes, and be killed, only to rise again the third day. (Math.16:20) Here, he reiterated and confirmed that same message.

Why did Jesus repeat this message to his followers? He tried to prepare them for this upsetting event that would shake their faith. They perceived him to be Christ, God's anointed, who reestablished David's throne, but how could his death accomplish what they thought their law foretold of him? This example of what the disciples believed hindered them from grasping the truth of God. Today our expectations often stand in our way of understanding the truth of God. For example, many anticipate that Jesus shall return to earth and set up his kingdom in the city of Jerusalem and rule from there. Clinging to this theory blocks our understanding of God's kingdom. His kingdom, being spiritual, God decrees that Jesus rules from his throne in heaven beside the throne of his Father. (Ps.110:1-7; Act.3:21) It took the death of Jesus to correct the apostles' conception of God's kingdom. Why do some persist in holding to the apostles' incorrect concept even now? If Jesus' own words fail to sway our thinking, will it require the day of eternal judgment to convince us that our cherished plan for God's kingdom opposes God's? Do we hold so dearly our plan for God's kingdom that we would ask God to alter his eternal plan to comply with our expectations? Let us submit to God's plan, for God will not change his eternal plan to please us. We must abide by his plan if we honor God and Jesus.

Matthew

18:1 At the same time came the disciples unto Jesus, saying, Who is the greatest in the kingdom of heaven? 2 And Jesus called a little child unto him, and set him in the midst of them, 3 And said, Verily I say unto you, Except ye be converted, and become as little children, ye shall not enter into the kingdom of heaven. 4 Whosoever therefore shall humble himself as this little child, the same is greatest in the kingdom of heaven. 5 And whoso shall receive one such little child in my name receiveth me. 6 But whoso shall offend one of these little ones which believe in me, it were better for him that a millstone were hanged about his neck, and that he were drowned in the depth of the sea.

Man's goals conflict with God's. (Ja.4:5) Even when men serve God, our natural tendency runs counter to God's. The disciples walked with Jesus and listened to his message for three years, but they still harbored the goal to be greater than others when Jesus established his kingdom.

If the apostles struggled to reconcile their desire to be greatest with God's will to serve, show love, and humility, should we be aghast when we recognize the same evil desire stalking

Mark

9:33 And he came to Capernaum: and being in the house he asked them, What was it that ye disputed among yourselves by the way? 34 But they held their peace: for by the way they had disputed among themselves, who should be the greatest. 35 And he sat down, and called the twelve, and saith unto them, If any man desire to be first, the same shall be last of all, and servant of all. 36 And he took a child, and set him in the midst of them: and when he had taken him in his arms, he said unto them, 37 Whosoever shall receive one of such children in my name, receiveth me: and whosoever shall receive me, receiveth not me, but him that sent me.

us?

God knows how to deliver men from Satan's snares. Taking a small, innocent child and setting him before the apostles, Jesus informed them that unless they converted their desire to be greatest to become like the child before them, they could not enter God's kingdom.

Man's pride offends God who endows each of us with assets and abilities with which to glorify him who created us, but we think we are great by our own power. (Prov.6:16-17)

Luke

9:46 Then there arose a reasoning among them, which of them should be greatest. 47 And Jesus, perceiving the thought of their heart, took a child, and set him by him, 48 And said unto them, Whosoever shall receive this child in my name receiveth me: and whosoever shall receive me receiveth him that sent me: for he that is least among you all, the same shall be great.

Satan defiles thinking. We see ourselves above our peers. Faith in God's truth delivers us from Satan's deceptions. Serving other's needs squelches Satan's corruption that drives us to dishonor one another and God who endowed us with abilities to honor God. Being convinced God blesses those who serve doesn't shield us from later incursions of Satan. He departed from Jesus only for a season after Jesus thwarted his devices during his forty days in the wilderness. (Lk.4:13) History reveals many a churchman whom Satan deceived to seek lordship over God's flock. Constant prayer, vigilance, and faith in God's truth releases us from Satan's system which seeks self-aspirations rather than service to others. Test God's plan. Serving humbles proud hearts and increases joy.

Matthew

**18:7 Woe unto the world because of
offences! for it must needs be that
offences come; but woe to that man by
whom the offence cometh! 8 Wherefore if
thy hand or thy foot offend thee, cut them
off, and cast them from thee: it is better
for thee to enter into life halt or maimed,
rather than having two hands or two feet
to be cast into everlasting fire. 9 And if
thine eye offend thee, pluck it out, and
cast it from thee: it is better for thee to
enter into life with one eye, rather than
having two eyes to be cast into hell fire. 10
Take heed that ye despise not one of these
little ones; for I say unto you, That in
heaven their angels do always behold the
face of my Father which is in heaven. 11
For the Son of man is come to save that
which was lost. 12 How think ye? if a man
have an hundred sheep, and one of them
be gone astray, doth he not leave the
ninety and nine, and goeth into the
mountains, and seeketh that which is gone
astray? 13 And if so be that he find it,
verily I say unto you, he rejoiceth more of
that sheep, than of the ninety and nine
which went not astray. 14 Even so it is not
the will of your Father which is in heaven,
that one of these little ones should perish.**

Mark

**9:38 And John answered him, saying,
Master, we saw one casting out devils in
thy name, and he followeth not us: and we
forbad him, because he followeth not us.
39 But Jesus said, Forbid him not: for
there is no man which shall do a miracle
in my name, that can lightly speak evil of
me. 40 For he that is not against us is on
our part. 41 For whosoever shall give you
a cup of water to drink in my name,
because ye belong to Christ, verily I say
unto you, he shall not lose his reward. 42
And whosoever shall offend one of these
little ones that believe in me, it is better
for him that a millstone were hanged
about his neck, and he were cast into the
sea. 43 And if thy hand offend thee, cut it
off: it is better for thee to enter into life
maimed, than having two hands to go into
hell, into the fire that never shall be
quenched: 44 Where their worm dieth
not, and the fire is not quenched. 45 And
if thy foot offend thee, cut it off: it is
better for thee to enter halt into life, than
having two feet to be cast into hell, into
the fire that never shall be quenched: 46
Where their worm dieth not, and the fire
is not quenched. 47 And if thine eye
offend thee, pluck it out: it is better for
thee to enter into the kingdom of God
with one eye, than having two eyes to be
cast into hell fire: 48 Where their worm
dieth not, and the fire is not quenched. 49
For every one shall be salted with fire,
and every sacrifice shall be salted with
salt. 50 Salt is good: but if the salt have
lost his saltness, wherewith will ye season
it? Have salt in yourselves, and have
peace one with another.**

Great sorrow in this life and anguish of eternal hell awaits every person who offends one for whom Christ died. Therefore, any goal of mine which casts a stumbling block in another's road I must abandon if I value eternal life, or if I hope to escape torment in hell. Parable of amputating a hand, foot, or plucking out an eye illustrates the seriousness of offense to one of God's children. Few consider cutting off a hand or foot or plucking out an eye because of the resulting serious handicap. Even so, God and his Son advise us that losing an important body part is preferable to offending one of God's children. Anyone who offends one of God's children shall languish in hell's fire unless he corrects his error. Angels who watch over the Father's children ever appear before God to report all misdeeds. Jesus, the faithful Shepherd, seeks to save all God's lost sheep, leaving none abandoned. Offenses will come, but let me not be charged with the offense. God's love motivating me helps me show kindness, not hate.

Luke

9:49 And John answered and said, Master, we saw one casting out devils in thy name; and we forbad him, because he followeth not with us. 50 And Jesus said unto him, Forbid him not: for he that is not against us is for us.

Rebuke sin, but don't offend. Forgive sins against yourself, but don't cause another to fall.

John probably discouraged the good deeds of the one he rebuked for casting out devils. If someone performs a beneficial act, don't become jealous, rather commend him and thank God.

When God created man, he made him good, but our desires of the mind and flesh drive us to forget others. Do we consider how our words and deeds affect those with whom we associate? Potentially, we possess the wherewith to brighten or darken the lives of every person we meet. God asks that I consider the welfare of every person and treat him/her as I wish they might treat me. This isn't an impossible task, nor is it an unpleasant one. Taking time to lift another in turn lifts me. We know this, but we attempt to justify ourselves for disregarding others. We can't take time to speak to every person or help everyone we meet who wishes to have our attention. This is true, but do we use the opportunities we have? God desires us to be considerate and to use the time he gives to provide welfare for others. He has provided us with time and situation. Do I choose to use both to please him who created me, or do I disregard his wishes and continue right on with my own activities? Considering the rewards offered, I am reminded that I probably receive far more benefits than I give by submitting to the requests of my heavenly Father.

Mark stressed the woe awaiting those who offend God's children. Torment and anguish in an ever-burning hell where no respite relieves suffering and no hope of escaping its

Luke

17:1 Then said he unto the disciples, It is impossible but that offences will come: but woe unto him, through whom they come! 2 It were better for him that a millstone were hanged about his neck, and he cast into the sea, than that he should offend one of these little ones.

14:34 Salt is good: but if the salt have lost his savour, wherewith shall it be seasoned? 35 It is neither fit for the land, nor yet for the dunghill; but men cast it out. He that hath ears to hear, let him hear.

agony awaits all who offend in this life.

All of us experience the natural tendency to show contempt or hate. Jesus tells us plainly that if we persist in following this lifestyle, God shall certainly cast us into that everlasting punishment designed for the devil and all who continue in his ways. Far better shall it be for us to lose an eye, hand, foot, or leg and suffer the hardships associated with that loss than to offend and abide in torment forever.

Salt seasons and preserves. God expects of his children acts which flavor life with benefits for people, not just a religion of church-going people. If we lose that spicing ability God provides, we become the salt which has lost its seasoning ability. As men discard useless spices, so God informs us discretely that we are useless to him in bringing blessings to mankind when we fail to demonstrate the light-giving effect of God's truth. Unless we give heed to the words of Jesus, we may think we please the Father in heaven when, in truth, we only deceive ourselves. Let God's truth sink down into our hearts and show that we do listen to the words of his Son who is God's last messenger to us. Glorify God and his Son Jesus by demonstrating God's light.

Leaders have appeared since God sent Jesus, claiming they are God-sent to lead people to God, but their words and deeds conform not to truth. Receive them not.

Matthew

18:15 Moreover if thy brother shall trespass against thee, go and tell him his fault between thee and him alone: if he shall hear thee, thou hast gained thy brother. 16 But if he will not hear thee, then take with thee one or two more, that in the mouth of two or three witnesses every word may be established. 17 And if he shall neglect to hear them, tell it unto the church: but if he neglect to hear the church, let him be unto thee as an heathen man and a publican. 18 Verily I say unto you, Whatsoever ye shall bind on earth shall be bound in heaven: and whatsoever ye shall loose on earth shall be loosed in heaven. 19 Again I say unto you, That if two of you shall agree on earth as touching any thing that they shall ask, it shall be done for them of my Father which is in heaven. 20 For where two or three are gathered together in my name, there am I in the midst of them. 21 Then came Peter to him, and said, Lord, how oft shall my brother sin against me, and I forgive him? till seven times? 22 Jesus saith unto him, I say not unto thee, Until seven times: but, Until seventy times seven. 23 Therefore is the kingdom of heaven likened unto a certain king, which would take account of his servants. 24 And when he had begun to reckon, one was brought unto him, which owed him ten thousand talents. 25 But forasmuch as he had not to pay, his lord commanded him to be sold, and his wife, and children, and all that he had, and payment to be made. 26 The servant therefore fell down, and worshipped him, saying, Lord, have patience with me, and I will pay thee all. 27 Then the lord of that servant was moved with compassion, and loosed him, and forgave him the debt. 28 But the same servant went out, and found one of his fellowservants, which owed him an hundred pence: and he laid hands on him, and took him by the throat, saying, Pay me that thou owest. 29 And his fellowservant fell down at his feet, and besought him, saying, Have patience with me, and I will pay thee all. 30 And he would not: but went and cast him into prison, till he should pay the debt. 31 So when his fellowservants saw what was done, they were very sorry, and came and told unto their lord all that was done. 32 Then his lord, after that he had called him, said unto him, O thou wicked servant, I forgave thee all that debt, because thou desiredst me: 33 Shouldest not thou also have had compassion on thy fellowservant, even as I had pity on thee? 34 And his lord was wroth, and delivered him to the tormentors, till he should pay all that was due unto him. 35 So likewise shall my heavenly Father do also unto you, if ye from your hearts forgive not every one his brother their trespasses.

When we call on God for mercy for all our injuries to others and transgressions against the truth of God, he requires of us a forgiving attitude toward all who sin against us. Peter and the other apostles considered this a high cost when Jesus first taught this commandment of God, but when they came to realize how it opened avenues of friendships closed by injustices, they realized God's way stood far above Satan's which perpetuated hostilities and hatred.

Jesus utilized a parable to help his disciples understand God's truth about forgiving one another. Two servants each owed a creditor, one a great debt, but the other one quite small. When the lender demanded payment, the one owing $18,500,000 pleaded for time to pay. Realizing he could never pay such a debt, the lender canceled the whole debt. This same servant had a creditor who owed him $5.00, but when he could not pay, he cast him into prison until he paid. His lord, hearing of his injustice, cast him into torment. When God forgives us, he asks us to forgive others, or he will require us to pay for our sins.

Luke

**17:3 Take heed to yourselves: If thy
brother trespass against thee, rebuke him;
and if he repent, forgive him. 4 And if he
trespass against thee seven times in a day,
and seven times in a day turn again to
thee, saying, I repent; thou shalt forgive
him. 5 And the apostles said unto the
Lord, Increase our faith. 6 And the Lord
said, If ye had faith as a grain of mustard
seed, ye might say unto this sycamine tree,
Be thou plucked up by the root, and be
thou planted in the sea; and it should obey
you. 7 But which of you, having a servant
plowing or feeding cattle, will say unto
him by and by, when he is come from the
field, Go and sit down to meat? 8 And will
not rather say unto him, Make ready
wherewith I may sup, and gird thyself,
and serve me, till I have eaten and
drunken; and afterward thou shalt eat
and drink? 9 Doth he thank that servant
because he did the things that were
commanded him? I trow not. 10 So
likewise ye, when ye shall have done all
those things which are commanded you,
say, We are unprofitable servants: we
have done that which was our duty to do.**

Peter and the other apostles questioned if they had faith sufficient to keep this command of Jesus to forgive each time a brother or sister asked forgiveness, regardless of how often they plead for mercy. Jesus assured the apostles that if they possessed even a minute bit of faith, it equaled all that was necessary to uproot trees and cast them into the sea. We, too, may wonder if we can muster faith to execute this command of Jesus, but he assures us also that our faith in him will suffice if we desire to keep the Father's commands.

Will God thank us for showing mercy? Does a master thank a servant for doing his bidding? No, it is his responsibility. God will not thank us for showing mercy. Doing the Father's will with all our heart, soul, and body produces blessings for each of us who submit to the Father's will. Can there be any question how God instructs us to handle sin by another Christian? First, talk to the brother or sister, trying to settle the dispute peacefully. If you are rebuffed, take one or two witnesses to establish a settling effect. Should the matter still not resolve, take the matter before the assembly. If the transgressor refuses to listen to the total assembly, it indicates faith in God's truth and mercy has disappeared from the person at least for the present. Let him/her be regarded by the assembly as a foreigner to the truth of God.

Peace on earth among men can rule the earth if we are willing to submit to the wisdom of our Father in heaven. He knows what's within man and what melts the heart of stone. When we submit to the truth of God, he will see to it that truth and peace replaces the hatred and warfare that has engulfed the main activities of mankind all through the ages. Rest assured, Jesus will rule until he ends all the ravages of the Evil One who drives us against one another to fulfill the desires of our minds and flesh and to forget the decencies and kindness which our fathers and mothers have taught us while we were growing up, but which we seem to forget as grownups.

When we refuse to forgive one another, how does this affect other Christians and unbelievers? In the parable of Jesus, they were sorry and showed their lord. Our activities show a pronounced influence on other children of God. If we sin, others sorrow. They call on God, asking him to somehow change our minds to submit to the laws of the kingdom of God. Those outside the church usually blaspheme God, saying that God's children act no better than infidels and unbelievers. Some claim they are more righteous than God's people, even though they claim no influence of God in their lives.

Apostles submitted to Jesus' instructions to forgive. When all Christians forgive, God's peace reigns in us.

Matthew

19:1 And it came to pass, that when Jesus had finished these sayings, he departed from Galilee, and came into the coasts of Judaea beyond Jordan;

Though Matthew, Mark, and Luke omit how often Jesus traveled between Galilee and Jerusalem, John indicates Jesus probably made that trek for each of the three major feasts and perhaps at other times also. All four gospels note Jesus journeyed to Jerusalem for the last Passover before his crucifixion. Luke's wording appears to indicate Jesus headed to Jerusalem to be received up into glory after his death. Going through Samaria sometimes shortened the trip.

Because of hostilities between Samaritans and Jews, Samaritans tended to reject Jesus. James and John chafed at this rejection and asked Jesus if they could call fire down on the exasperating Samaritans. Apostle's attitude demonstrated hatred, not mercy. Jesus responded he came to save men's lives, not to destroy them. They proceeded to another Samaritan city.

In another Samaritan village ten lepers called to Jesus for mercy. He instructed them to go show themselves to the Jewish priests as Moses taught. This might have offended Samaritans, but the ten headed toward the priests. As they went, God cleansed each of his leprosy. Only one, a Samaritan, returned to thank Jesus for his mercy and to glorify God. Though Luke didn't say the nine were Jews, he suggested it. Why didn't they return to thank Jesus for God's mercy and honor God? It's unfortunate that we often forget to thank God for all his wonderful blessings which he so abundantly bestows on us.

Why did Luke pick incidents that portrayed Samaritans and Syrians as respectable people as he did this leper and the Samaritan who helped the man who fell among thieves? (Lk.10:30) Luke seems to have chosen these incidents to gain respect for strangers from God's covenant. Did Luke

Mark

10:1 And he arose from thence, and cometh into the coasts of Judaea by the farther side of Jordan: and the people resort unto him again; and, as he was wont, he taught them again.

write to those whose forefathers wandered far from God's blessings bestowed on his faithful children? God loves all his children and sent Jesus to offer to all peoples salvation and the blessings promised to Abraham. We need to have faith in God and his promises through Jesus. Had not God promised to bless all nations through Abraham's seed? (Gen.12:3; Gal.3:14-16) Had not Isaiah and Micah indicated God's house must be exalted above nations, and all nations would flow unto it? God would teach all nations his ways and judge among nations. Then nations would cease war and learn peace. (Is.2:2-4; Mi.4:1-2) Showing how the Samaritan leper asked for God's mercy and Jesus healed his leprosy testifies that God desires to bless all peoples through his Son. This Samaritan's return to glorify God shows that God sent Jesus to heal Satan's hurts to people of all races. (Is.61:1-3; Lk.4:18-19)

As we visualize that Jesus embodied God on earth (Math.1:23; Is.7:14;9:6-6), we understand God's longing to heal the sorrows Satan heaps on mankind. By convincing us that living to please ourselves and to satisfy the desires of the mind and flesh brings life, Satan's deceives. God's messenger, Jesus, corrects all the deceptions of the Evil One by explaining to us the whole truth of our heavenly Father. God's instructions direct us to follow that which results in our good at all times if we have faith enough to submit to God's truth. (Deu.6:24; Ps.84:11) No nation had laws as righteous as those God provided Israel. (Deu.4:7-8) Jesus fulfilled their law, demonstrating how mercy shown to all peoples blesses the giver of mercy as well as the receiver. Obeying God's truth Jesus taught, we honor and glorify God.

Luke

9:51 And it came to pass, when the time was come that he should be received up, he stedfastly set his face to go to Jerusalem, 52 And sent messengers before his face: and they went, and entered into a village of the Samaritans, to make ready for him. 53 And they did not receive him, because his face was as though he would go to Jerusalem. 54 And when his disciples James and John saw this, they said, Lord, wilt thou that we command fire to come down from heaven, and consume them, even as Elias did? 55 But he turned, and rebuked them, and said, Ye know not what manner of spirit ye are of. 56 For the Son of man is not come to destroy men's lives, but to save them. And they went to another village.

Living to please ourselves casts the shadows of gloom over all who follow Satan's and his children's deceptions. God calls to all peoples, saying, life and peace comes only from doing the will of our Creator. He alone knows the nature of man. Only God advises us how to enjoy life and experience peace. War and heartaches follow all who tread the path of Satan and his children. Hear Jesus, "**I am come that they might have life, and that they might have it more abundantly.**" (Jno.10:10) Paul restated the same message. "**Godliness is profitable unto all things, having promise of the life that now is, and of that which is to come.**" (1 Tim.4:8) "**This is a faithful saying, and these things I will that thou affirm constantly, that they which have believed in God might be careful to maintain good works. These things are good and profitable unto men.**" (Tit.3:8) Peter exhorted, "**For he that will love life, and see good days, let him refrain his tongue from evil, and his lips that they speak no guile: Let him eschew evil, and do good; let him seek peace, and ensue it. For the eyes of the Lord are over the righteous, and his ears are open unto**

Luke

17:11 And it came to pass, as he went to Jerusalem, that he passed through the midst of Samaria and Galilee. 12 And as he entered into a certain village, there met him ten men that were lepers, which stood afar off: 13 And they lifted up their voices, and said, Jesus, Master, have mercy on us. 14 And when he saw them, he said unto them, Go shew yourselves unto the priests. And it came to pass, that, as they went, they were cleansed. 15 And one of them, when he saw that he was healed, turned back, and with a loud voice glorified God, 16 And fell down on his face at his feet, giving him thanks: and he was a Samaritan. 17 And Jesus answering said, Were there not ten cleansed? but where are the nine? 18 There are not found that returned to give glory to God, save this stranger. 19 And he said unto him, Arise, go thy way: thy faith hath made thee whole.

their prayers: but the face of the Lord is against them that do evil." (1 Pet.3:10-12; see Ps.34:12-16.)

Before God, what is true religion? James answered, "**If any man among you seem to be religious, and bridleth not his tongue, but deceiveth his own heart, this man's religion is vain. Pure religion and undefiled before God and the Father is this, To visit the fatherless and widows in their affliction, and to keep himself unspotted from the world.**" (Ja.1:26-27) A good life, one which brings true enjoyment, originates only from following the truth of the living God. Though Satan contradicts this message, all who follow his advice suffer untold hardships and agonies in life's activities whether it's in family, business, recreation, or social pursuits. Submitting to God's truth directs us to avoid the pitfalls Satan places in the paths of men. When all God's children believe and do truth, peace rules between nations, families, and friends. Are you experiencing God's good life?

Matthew

19:2 And great multitudes followed him; and he healed them there. 3 The Pharisees also came unto him, tempting him, and saying unto him, Is it lawful for a man to put away his wife for every cause? 4 And he answered and said unto them, Have ye not read, that he which made them at the beginning made them male and female, 5 And said, For this cause shall a man leave father and mother, and shall cleave to his wife: and they twain shall be one flesh? 6 Wherefore they are no more twain, but one flesh. What therefore God hath joined together, let not man put asunder.

What is God's truth concerning marriage, divorce, and remarriage? Let's not attempt to change God's law on these matters to justify our deeds. In creation, God made male and female. When we choose to marry, a man and woman are to leave parents and join together to form their own home. This family union God ordained from creation. (Gen.2:24; Math.19:4-6; Mk.10:6-9) No man or woman possesses the right to split the bond created by the union of a man and woman and cemented together by our heavenly Father. (Math.19:6; Mk.10:9) Husband and wife are one flesh. This union forms the foundation for society.

Why did Moses allow divorce and remarriage? (Deu.24:1-4) Moses led a rebellious and hardhearted generation of Jews from Egypt. (Deu.9:6-7,23-24) Because they hardened their hearts in unbelief, God allowed divorce and remarriage, but only because of uncleanness. (Deu.24:1)

Why did Jesus teach Jews during his personal ministry they were allowed to divorce and remarry on grounds of fornication? Jesus explained to his people the intent of their law. Most of his generation proved to be as unbelieving and hardhearted as their forefathers whom Moses taught. They, as our society today, rejected God's design and chose to live to satisfy the desires of the flesh and mind.

Mark

10:2 And the Pharisees came to him, and asked him, Is it lawful for a man to put away his wife? tempting him. 3 And he answered and said unto them, What did Moses command you? 4 And they said, Moses suffered to write a bill of divorcement, and to put her away. 5 And Jesus answered and said unto them, For the hardness of your heart he wrote you this precept. 6 But from the beginning of the creation God made them male and female. 7 For this cause shall a man leave his father and mother, and cleave to his wife; 8 And they twain shall be one flesh: so then they are no more twain, but one flesh. 9 What therefore God hath joined together, let not man put asunder.

(Math.5:31-32;19:9) When the Jews transgressed their law of marriage and divorce, they committed adultery and violated the seventh commandment of God. (Ex.20:16)

Why did Mark and Luke omit Jesus teaching divorce and remarriage for fornication? Mark and Luke addressed Gentile believers who had turned to God through Jesus. Their hearts rested on God and his truth. Not being rebellious and hardhearted, divorce and remarriage didn't apply to them. Since Matthew wrote to Jews to convince them Jesus was indeed Christ, he needed to teach their law on marriage, divorce, and remarriage. Had Matthew omitted this part of Jewish law, Jews certainly would have rejected Jesus' message to them. Jesus testified he came not to destroy their law, but to fulfill it. (Math.5:17) What Matthew recorded Jesus teaching on the subject of marriage, divorce, and remarriage fulfilled what God allowed through Moses.

Letters to the churches after Christ's resurrection do not allow divorce and remarriage to another companion unless death separated the companionship.

"The woman which hath an husband is bound by the law to her husband so long as he liveth; but if the husband be dead,

she is loosed from the law of her husband. So then if, while her husband liveth, she be married to another man, she shall be called an adulteress: but if her husband be dead, she is free from that law; so that she is no adulteress, though she be married to another man." (Rom.7:2-3) **"Unto the married I command, yet not I, but the Lord, Let not the wife depart from her husband: but and if she depart, let her remain unmarried, or be reconciled to her husband: and let not the husband put away his wife."** (1 Cor.7:10-11) **"The wife is bound by the law as long as her husband liveth; but if her husband be dead, she is at liberty to be married to whom she will; only in the Lord."** (1 Cor.7:39)

Jewish priests lived by the law of marriage God ordained in creation. (Lev. 21:1-7; Ezek.44:22) Their law differed from the profane Jew's law. (Deu.24:1-4) Since Christians are holy to God, we live by God's creation decree on marriage, divorce, and remarriage. We are the true priesthood of God today. **"Ye also, as lively stones, are built up a spiritual house, an holy priesthood, to offer up spiritual sacrifices, acceptable to God by Jesus Christ....But ye are a chosen generation, a royal priesthood, an holy nation, a peculiar people; that ye should shew forth the praises of him who hath called you out of darkness into his marvelous light."** (1 Pet.2:5,9)

If we believe Jesus and the apostles communicated God's truth on marriage, divorce, and remarriage in the letters to the churches, we will abide by God's creation decree. A man and his wife God joined together as one flesh for life. In God's sight, only death severs the bond between a husband and wife. To divorce and remarry another before our first mate dies proves we are hardhearted toward the companion God has given us. Furthermore, we violate our pledge: "Till death separates us." Present practice of divorcing at will destroys society and dishonors God.

God hates divorce. (Mal.2:14-16) In his eyes, we deal treacherously with one another by divorcing. God instructs his children to love their own wives and husbands. (Eph. 5:22-33) This makes us a godly seed. (Mal. 2:15) Don't become adulterers or adulteresses. Live courteously with the companion God gives you.

God never withholds any good thing from those who love him and walk uprightly. (Ps. 84:11) For children given to a union of marriage, what good comes from a husband or wife divorcing and remarrying some other person? Scars linger all during lifetime for children who see their parents divorce. They feel they caused the breakup of their home. The two people they love most can't get along. They are torn between two households. They ask why can't Mother and Daddy get back together and live happily?

Lingering thoughts of a man and woman about their first marriage often cause difficulties after remarriage to another companion. One man often complained his second wife asked if she was a better wife than his first. This continual goading so annoyed him that nearly every time I went to work with him he mentioned the problem. If remarriage appeals so much to this generation, is Satan promoting this concept? Does he today manipulate a husband and wife to distrust one another and bring divorce to thwart the law of God as he did in the beginning? His advice proved to be the undoing of the race then and continues to do so today. Christian, believe God's truth, not Satan's lie on divorce and remarriage. Satan's lie will cost you your mansion in heaven.

Will men and women someday submit to God's law on marriage? Yes, God promises Christ shall reign until he destroys Satan's works. (1 Cor.15:25-26) Husbands and wives, apply God's remedy to resolve conflicts. Talk about differences and forgive.

Matthew

19:7 They say unto him, Why did Moses then command to give a writing of divorcement, and to put her away? 8 He saith unto them, Moses because of the hardness of your hearts suffered you to put away your wives: but from the beginning it was not so. 9 And I say unto you, Whosoever shall put away his wife, except it be for fornication, and shall marry another, committeth adultery: and whoso marrieth her which is put away doth commit adultery. 10 His disciples say unto him, If the case of the man be so with his wife, it is not good to marry. 11 But he said unto them, All men cannot receive this saying, save they to whom it is given. 12 For there are some eunuchs, which were so born from their mother's womb: and there are some eunuchs, which were made eunuchs of men: and there be eunuchs, which have made themselves eunuchs for the kingdom of heaven's sake. He that is able to receive it, let him receive it.

Permanency of marriage those not subject to God's law refuse to accept. God understands our nature better than we understand ourselves. Only those who have submitted to rebirth and enter God's kingdom submit to God's system. Paul explained this to Corinthians. **"The natural man receiveth not the things of the Spirit of God: for they are foolishness unto him: neither can he know them, because they are spiritually discerned."** (1 Cor.2:14) Why do Satan's children balk at God's truth and refuse to submit to God? **"Because the carnal mind is enmity against God: for it is not subject to the law of God, neither indeed can be. So then they that are in the flesh cannot please God."** (Rom.8:7-8) For one to enter into God's kingdom, he must radically modify his thinking from pleasing himself to submitting to the will of God that God may be glorified. Without this conversion, no person pleases God.

Mark

10:10 And in the house his disciples asked him again of the same matter. 11 And he saith unto them, Whosoever shall put away his wife, and marry another, committeth adultery against her. 12 And if a woman shall put away her husband, and be married to another, she committeth adultery.

Mark's gospel omits divorce on grounds of fornication because he addressed Gentile Christians who had abandoned Satan's kingdom with its rebellion against God's laws. Moses' law never applied to them. God eliminated the hardness of their hearts when they believed Jesus to be God's Son and died to this world with Jesus in baptism. (Rom.6:3-6) Having a new birth, the old man who followed Satan's rebellion against God died, and he now lives unto God. He gladly receives the truth of God because it brings greater joy to life than Satan's deceptions. A different companion won't increase happiness. Divorce and remarriage to another adds woes.

Considering the hurts accompanying a husband and wife who divorce, how can any person argue that divorce and remarriage to another benefit those involved? Children born to the union carry the scars of the broken home with them all their lives. Children reared in a broken home generally view marriage as lasting only a short time. They, too, divorce and remarry. Families become so confused that children find it difficult to know who are their real mother and father. In this age children reared in shattered homes hold a false view of marriage. There is no real commitment for life. Other relatives and friends must readjust their relationship to the new union. Governments must modify laws, and God sorrows that his children abandon the good he gives them. Indeed, God's marriage plan benefits men and women. Satan's lies curse individuals, families, nations, and they call God a liar as Satan did when he deceived Eve.

Luke

16:14 And the Pharisees also, who were covetous, heard all these things: and they derided him. 15 And he said unto them, Ye are they which justify yourselves before men; but God knoweth your hearts: for that which is highly esteemed among men is abomination in the sight of God. 16 The law and the prophets were until John: since that time the kingdom of God is preached, and every man presseth into it. 17 And it is easier for heaven and earth to pass, than one tittle of the law to fail. 18 Whosoever putteth away his wife, and marrieth another, committeth adultery: and whosoever marrieth her that is put away from her husband committeth adultery.

Luke's gospel clearly shows that he wrote to Theophilus, whose name translated, means one who loves God or is a friend of God. (Lk.1:3) Luke included no mention of the Jewish law allowing divorce and remarriage to another for fornication.

The sole justification for Christians to divorce and remarry another rests on Matthew's gospel. Considering that his narrative from beginning to end appeals to Jewish readers, one must ask if Matthew included permission to divorce and remarry another applied to unbelieving Jews. It did not include Christian Jews and Gentiles. If it included Gentile Christians, then God granted them more leniency than they possessed before they entered the kingdom of God. Do you ask how this could be? God never issued a law to Gentiles permitting them to divorce and remarry another. That law God gave to Jews alone and only because they retained hard hearts. One wonders why letters written to Jew or Gentile churches never mentioned that God allowed them to divorce and remarry another. Apostles did forbid this practice.

Matthew recorded Jesus explaining to Jews the true meaning of their law from God. Moses allowed divorce and remarriage only for fornication. Moses used the terms "uncleanness" and "defiled" interchangeably. (Deu.24:1-4) One becomes defiled by living as another's husband or wife. He or she may not return to the former companion. Ezekiel mentioned how an ungodly man might defile his neighbor's wife. Moses included a procedure to determine if a woman had been defiled by lying with another man. (Num.5:11-31) If a husband discovered his wife defiled herself with another man, then he could apply the law to divorce his wife because she "defiled" herself by fornication as Jesus explained. (Math.5:31-32;19:9) Even Jews committed adultery when they divorced and married another for any other reason.

Before God instituted the law of Moses and gave it to Israel, no man or woman had a God-given right to divorce and marry another. Once Jesus' death sealed the new covenant, no person, Jew or Gentile, had a God-given right to divorce and marry another. God's law at creation once again became the law for marriage. God joins a man and woman together for life, and no person can rightly claim that God has granted him or her a just right to divorce and marry another because their partner committed fornication. Jesus' death made the Old Testament law of Moses obsolete. (Heb.8:13;9:15-16;10:9)

Many do not realize they use the Old Testament law to justify divorce and remarriage to another. If we are justified by the law of Moses, we are fallen from grace. (Gal.5:4) Neither Jesus, the apostles, nor God allows divorce and remarriage to another for any person after Jesus died on the cross and God raised him from the dead. To divorce and remarry another places one's eternal destiny in peril. God does permit a person to divorce and remain unmarried or be reconciled to the companion God first gave him/her. (1 Cor.7:10-11) Let all God's children submit to God's truth rather than do whatsoever is right in our own eyes.

Matthew

19:13 Then were there brought unto him little children, that he should put his hands on them, and pray: and the disciples rebuked them. 14 But Jesus said, Suffer little children, and forbid them not, to come unto me: for of such is the kingdom of heaven. 15 And he laid his hands on them, and departed thence.

One's attitude prepares him to enter or reject God's kingdom. Small children exemplify the attitude characterizing those who enter the kingdom of heaven. Humble and devoid of pride, small children obey parents. Proud and obstinate minds regard God's plan of life lowly and beneath them. They refuse to submit to God.

The disciples needed nurturing on the attitude that pleases our Father in heaven. Paying attention to small children seemed unimportant to them. They envisioned God's kingdom as adults who jostled for positions of honor rather than that of service. To modify this misconception, Jesus explained that small children demonstrate the attitude of those who gladly receive the kingdom of God which subdues and blesses every family on earth. Permit little children to come to me. Those devoid of the attributes of small

Mark

10:13 And they brought young children to him, that he should touch them: and his disciples rebuked those that brought them. 14 But when Jesus saw it, he was much displeased, and said unto them, Suffer the little children to come unto me, and forbid them not: for of such is the kingdom of God. 15 Verily I say unto you, Whosoever shall not receive the kingdom of God as a little child, he shall not enter therein. 16 And he took them up in his arms, put his hands upon them, and blessed them.

children shall not enter God's kingdom. They cling tenaciously to Satan's plan of life. He entreats men to be wise, not humble, to search for that which appeals to the eye, not to satisfy the inner craving of the spirit within. Glory among peers meets Satan's children's strivings.

Small children seek to please mother and father. God searches for grownups who look to God for guidance and do all to please and honor him.

Is it any wonder that God devised a plan to convert men's self-gratifying goals of life to honor others and God? Men and women alike must die to Satan and self. Unless this spiritual death occurs, newness of life eludes them. They become deceived. Old patterns of Satan's system merely trans-

Luke

18:15 And they brought unto him also infants, that he would touch them: but when his disciples saw it, they rebuked them. 16 But Jesus called them unto him, and said, Suffer little children to come unto me, and forbid them not: for of such is the kingdom of God. 17 Verily I say unto you, Whosoever shall not receive the kingdom of God as a little child shall in no wise enter therein.

pose. They believe they entered God's glorious kingdom, but nothing changed. Bitterness continues to darken their minds and lives because others fail to honor their great achievements. They regard not the Father in heaven who provided them with their abilities. They disregard him and believe it's by their wisdom and prowess they excel. Self-ambition continues to propel their lives to disregard the feelings and needs of the less fortunate whom God places among men to show the need for kindness and friendship. Lack of concern for these humble lives deprives us of warmth which ultimately produces within us contempt for others and emptiness within our hearts. Vain goals drive our lives. Satan manipulates us to believe his lies, and then we suffer for trusting Satan's lies. Our only hope of escape is in Jesus.

Matthew

**19:16 And, behold, one came
and said unto him, Good
Master, what good thing shall I
do, that I may have eternal
life? 17 And he said unto him,
Why callest thou me good?
there is none good but one, that
is, God: but if thou wilt enter
into life, keep the com-
mandments. 18 He saith unto
him, Which? Jesus said, Thou
shalt do no murder, Thou shalt
not commit adultery, Thou
shalt not steal, Thou shalt not
bear false witness, 19 Honour
thy father and thy mother:
and, Thou shalt love thy
neighbour as thyself. 20 The
young man saith unto him, All
these things have I kept from
my youth up: what lack I yet?
21 Jesus said unto him, If thou
wilt be perfect, go and sell that
thou hast, and give to the poor,
and thou shalt have treasure in
heaven: and come and follow
me. 22 But when the young
man heard that saying, he went
away sorrowful: for he had
great possessions. 23 Then said
Jesus unto his disciples, Verily
I say unto you, That a rich man
shall hardly enter into the
kingdom of heaven. 24 And
again I say unto you, It is
easier for a camel to go
through the eye of a needle,
than for a rich man to enter
into the kingdom of God. 25
When his disciples heard it,
they were exceedingly amazed,
saying, Who then can be
saved? 26 But Jesus beheld
them, and said unto them,
With men this is impossible;
but with God all things are
possible.**

Covetousness, violating the tenth commandment, barred the young man from God's kingdom. Being unwilling to distribute his wealth to relieve the wants of those who needed cursed him.

Mark

**10:17 And when he was gone
forth into the way, there came
one running, and kneeled to
him, and asked him, Good
Master, what shall I do that I
may inherit eternal life? 18
And Jesus said unto him, Why
callest thou me good? there is
none good but one, that is,
God. 19 Thou knowest the
commandments, Do not com-
mit adultery, Do not kill, Do
not steal, Do not bear false
witness, Defraud not, Honour
thy father and mother. 20 And
he answered and said unto
him, Master, all these have I
observed from my youth. 21
Then Jesus beholding him
loved him, and said unto him,
One thing thou lackest: go thy
way, sell whatsoever thou hast,
and give to the poor, and thou
shalt have treasure in heaven:
and come, take up the cross,
and follow me. 22 And he was
sad at that saying, and went
away grieved: for he had great
possessions. 23 And Jesus
looked round about, and saith
unto his disciples, How hardly
shall they that have riches
enter into the kingdom of God!
24 And the disciples were
astonished at his words. But
Jesus answereth again, and
saith unto them, Children, how
hard is it for them that trust in
riches to enter into the
kingdom of God! 25 It is easier
for a camel to go through the
eye of a needle, than for a rich
man to enter into the kingdom
of God. 26 And they were
astonished out of measure,
saying among themselves, Who
then can be saved? 27 And
Jesus looking upon them saith,
With men it is impossible, but
not with God: for with God all
things are possible.**

Covetousness includes desire to keep what I now possess. He

Luke

**18:18 And a certain ruler
asked him, saying, Good
Master, what shall I do to
inherit eternal life? 19 And
Jesus said unto him, Why
callest thou me good? none is
good, save one, that is, God. 20
Thou knowest the com-
mandments, Do not commit
adultery, Do not kill, Do not
steal, Do not bear false witness,
Honour thy father and thy
mother. 21 And he said, All
these have I kept from my
youth up. 22 Now when Jesus
heard these things, he said unto
him, Yet lackest thou one
thing: sell all that thou hast,
and distribute unto the poor,
and thou shalt have treasure in
heaven: and come, follow me.
23 And when he heard this, he
was very sorrowful: for he was
very rich. 24 And when Jesus
saw that he was very
sorrowful, he said, How hardly
shall they that have riches
enter into the kingdom of God!
25 For it is easier for a camel
to go through a needle's eye,
than for a rich man to enter
into the kingdom of God. 26
And they that heard it said,
Who then can be saved? 27
And he said, The things which
are impossible with men are
possible with God.**

cherished his wealth more than God's kingdom.

Apostles staggered at Jesus' comment. Those who trust in riches hardly enter into God's kingdom. If we covet material wealth above treasure in heaven, we, too, exclude ourselves from the heavenly realm. We must be willing to sacrifice everything God entrusts to our stewardship to gain heaven, or we forfeit our mansion there. God and Satan tell us how to use wealth. Our choice determines our destiny. Therefore choose wisely.

Matthew

19:27 Then answered Peter and said unto him, Behold, we have forsaken all, and followed thee; what shall we have therefore? 28 And Jesus said unto them, Verily I say unto you, That ye which have followed me, in the regeneration when the Son of man shall sit in the throne of his glory, ye also shall sit upon twelve thrones, judging the twelve tribes of Israel. 29 And every one that hath forsaken houses, or brethren, or sisters, or father, or mother, or wife, or children, or lands, for my name's sake, shall receive an hundredfold, and shall inherit everlasting life. 30 But many that are first shall be last; and the last shall be first.

What blessings await all who sacrifice self-interests to please our Father above? To Abraham, God promised to bless all families in every nation. (Gen.12:3;18:18) Abandoning personal interests to benefit others and to honor God, magnifies life's enjoyment. Others open their homes, their beauties, and their God-given blessings for you to rejoice with them. Besides these earthly honors, God opens his everlasting abode in heaven for each person who glorifies him among men by doing what he asked. Sharing God's truth with others, God shares his heavenly treasures with us. Paul amplified this message, "**All things are yours.**" (1 Cor. 3:21-23)

Mark

10:28 Then Peter began to say unto him, Lo, we have left all, and have followed thee. 29 And Jesus answered and said, Verily I say unto you, There is no man that hath left house, or brethren, or sisters, or father, or mother, or wife, or children, or lands, for my sake, and the gospel's, 30 But he shall receive an hundredfold now in this time, houses, and brethren, and sisters, and mothers, and children, and lands, with persecutions; and in the world to come eternal life. 31 But many that are first shall be last; and the last first.

God promised Christ to rule on David's throne forever. Matthew stressed this truth. It included blessings for the apostles. They rule on twelve thrones to judge the twelve tribes of Israel. Later, Jesus promised all who overcome Satan's deceptions and serve God faithfully rule the nations with him. (Rev.2:26-27; 3:21;5:10) God's promises include eternal life as opposed to eternal punishment of fire in hell for the disobedient. (Mk.9:38-50) Jesus demonstrated that those who serve are greatest in God's kingdom (Jno.13:13-17); but served are least in his kingdom.

Luke

18:28 Then Peter said, Lo, we have left all, and followed thee. 29 And he said unto them, Verily I say unto you, There is no man that hath left house, or parents, or brethren, or wife, or children, for the kingdom of God's sake, 30 Who shall not receive manifold more in this present time, and in the world to come life everlasting.

Do these ideas bless individuals, families, and nations? Yes, they encourage good actions in people who believe them. Satan's self-seeking goals prompt evil attitudes and deeds among his children. (Ja.4:1-17) Satan convinces his followers there is no life beyond the grave. Live to get all this life offers. It's a life without hope: no promises and no rewards to those who forgo satisfying their desires to consider other's needs. Satan's children feel a vacuum gnawing at their lives. This emptiness drives them to seek some way to satisfy this longing to feed the spiritual need of genuine love. They think it comes only by satisfying the wants of the body. They seldom, if ever, realize this searching originates from the need to walk with our heavenly Father, by being subject to his will, not serving self. God fulfills his promise to satisfy all our needs.

Matthew

20:1 For the kingdom of heaven is like unto a man that is an householder, which went out early in the morning to hire labourers into his vineyard. 2 And when he had agreed with the labourers for a penny a day, he sent them into his vineyard. 3 And he went out about the third hour, and saw others standing idle in the marketplace, 4 And said unto them; Go ye also into the vineyard, and whatsoever is right I will give you. And they went their way. 5 Again he went out about the sixth and ninth hour, and did likewise. 6 And about the eleventh hour he went out, and found others standing idle, and saith unto them, Why stand ye here all the day idle? 7 They say unto him, Because no man hath hired us. He saith unto them, Go ye also into the vineyard; and whatsoever is right, that shall ye receive. 8 So when even was come, the lord of the vineyard saith unto his steward, Call the labourers, and give them their hire, beginning from the last unto the first. 9 And when they came that were hired about the eleventh hour, they received every man a penny. 10 But when the first came, they supposed that they should have received more; and they likewise received every man a penny. 11 And when they had received it, they murmured against the goodman of the house, 12 Saying, These last have wrought but one hour, and thou hast made them equal unto us, which have borne the burden and heat of the day. 13 But he answered one of them, and said, Friend, I do thee no wrong: didst not thou agree with me for a penny? 14 Take that thine is, and go thy way: I will give unto this last, even as unto thee. 15 Is it not lawful for me to do what I will with mine own? Is thine eye evil, because I am good? 16 So the last shall be first, and the first last: for many be called, but few chosen.

Jesus answered Peter's question about their reward for abandoning all to serve Jesus. God does not regard how long or how great a service one performs to determine his reward. Faith in God's truth determines whether God gives us an inheritance. If how great or length of service determined our inheritance, it depends on works, not grace. We don't earn heaven. It's God's gift for faith in his truth. **"Even the righteousness of God which is by faith of Jesus Christ unto all and upon all them that believe: for there is no difference: for all have sinned, and come short of the glory of God."** (Rom.3:22-23) **"If Abraham were justified by works, he hath whereof to glory; but not before God. For what saith the scripture: Abraham believed God, and it was counted unto him for righteousness. Now to him that worketh is the reward not reckoned of grace, but of debt."** (Rom.4:1-4)

Do God's commands benefit those who do them? As obedience to God's commands changes us from his enemies to his friends, it promotes better relationships between family members, neighborhoods, cities, states, nations, and within ourselves. Disregarding truth Jesus taught destroys relationships and defiles our consciences. God made us social beings. Keeping God's laws smoothes relationships. Pleasing ourselves alienates. We become mere ravaging beasts, destroying civilizations, social structures, bringing misery to ourselves and others.

Our heavenly Father teaches us how to enjoy this life and inherit the eternal glory with all the righteous who ever lived. His commands produce good for us and those with whom we associate. No good thing does God ever withhold from us. (Deu.6:24; Ps.84:11; Jno.10:10) We need to repent and believe the gospel. (Mk.1:15) Do we really believe God offers us every good thing life can possibly give us?

Matthew

20:17 And Jesus going up to Jerusalem took the twelve disciples apart in the way, and said unto them, 18 Behold, we go up to Jerusalem; and the Son of man shall be betrayed unto the chief priests and unto the scribes, and they shall condemn him to death, 19 And shall deliver him to the Gentiles to mock, and to scourge, and to crucify him: and the third day he shall rise again.

Preparing the apostles against the events soon to transpire in Jerusalem, Jesus separated from the multitude. Then he explained to the twelve how one of them would betray him to the chief priests and scribes who would condemn him to death by crucifixion. Gentiles would take, mock, spit on, scourge, and ultimately kill him, but he would triumph over death the third day. Earlier Peter refused to accept this. (Math.16:21-22; Mk.8:31-32;9:31-32) Even now as they approached Jerusalem, minds of the apostles had not reconciled what Jesus taught with what they anticipated. Today our minds are often rejecting certain truth Jesus taught. Only by continued meditation and prayer to God for understanding will God grant us a fuller comprehension of God's plan which he shall bring to pass.

Mark

10:32 And they were in the way going up to Jerusalem; and Jesus went before them: and they were amazed; and as they followed, they were afraid. And he took again the twelve, and began to tell them what things should happen unto him, 33 Saying, Behold, we go up to Jerusalem; and the Son of man shall be delivered unto the chief priests, and unto the scribes; and they shall condemn him to death, and shall deliver him to the Gentiles: 34 And they shall mock him, and shall scourge him, and shall spit upon him, and shall kill him: and the third day he shall rise again.

As long as we determine to have God's plan conform to our wishes, God withholds his truth from us. Isaiah explained this to Jews of his age. **"For my thoughts are not your thoughts, neither are your ways my ways, saith the Lord. For as the heavens are higher than the earth, so are my ways higher than your ways, and my thoughts than your thoughts."** (Is.55:8-9) Paul wrote, **"We speak the wisdom of God in a mystery, even the hidden wisdom; which God ordained before the world unto our glory: which none of the princes of this world knew: for had they known**

Luke

18:31 Then he took unto him the twelve, and said unto them, Behold, we go up to Jerusalem, and all things that are written by the prophets concerning the Son of man shall be accomplished. 32 For he shall be delivered unto the Gentiles, and shall be mocked, and spitefully entreated, and spitted on: 33 And they shall scourge him, and put him to death: and the third day he shall rise again. 34 And they understood none of these things: and this saying was hid from them, neither knew they the things which were spoken.

it, they would not have crucified the Lord of Glory." (1 Cor.2:7-8) Much of the confusion obstructing Christian unity today originates with so many attempting to force God's word to conform to our preconceived plans which conform not to what God has ordained for his kingdom and glory. Determining to have Jesus return to earth and set up his throne in the ancient city of Jerusalem where he shall rule counters God's will. We have not submitted to God's plan that the church contains the fullness of God's kingdom on earth. Jesus rules at God's right hand until he subdues all his enemies, including death. (Ps.110:1; 1 Cor.15:24-26)

Matthew

20:20 Then came to him the mother of Zebedee's children with her sons, worshipping him, and desiring a certain thing of him. 21 And he said unto her, What wilt thou? She saith unto him, Grant that these my two sons may sit, the one on thy right hand, and the other on the left, in thy kingdom. 22 But Jesus answered and said, Ye know not what ye ask. Are ye able to drink of the cup that I shall drink of, and to be baptized with the baptism that I am baptized with? They say unto him, We are able. 23 And he saith unto them, Ye shall drink indeed of my cup, and be baptized with the baptism that I am baptized with: but to sit on my right hand, and on my left, is not mine to give, but it shall be given to them for whom it is prepared of my Father. 24 And when the ten heard it, they were moved with indignation against the two brethren.

Selfish desires generated contentions among the disciples. Desiring supreme positions of honor in the approaching kingdom precipitated ill will even among those whom Jesus had taught the mysteries of God's kingdom. Is it any wonder that God instructs us to abandon Satan's system? **"I beseech you therefore, brethren, by the mercies**

Mark

10:35 And James and John, the sons of Zebedee, come unto him, saying, Master, we would that thou shouldest do for us whatsoever we shall desire. 36 And he said unto them, What would ye that I should do for you? 37 They said unto him, Grant unto us that we may sit, one on thy right hand, and the other on thy left hand, in thy glory. 38 But Jesus said unto them, Ye know not what ye ask: can ye drink of the cup that I drink of? and be baptized with the baptism that I am baptized with? 39 And they said unto him, We can. And Jesus said unto them, Ye shall indeed drink of the cup that I drink of; and with the baptism that I am baptized withal shall ye be baptized: 40 But to sit on my right hand and on my left hand is not mine to give; but it shall be given to them for whom it is prepared. 41 And when the ten heard it, they began to be much displeased with James and John.

of God, that ye present your bodies a living sacrifice, holy, acceptable unto God, which is your reasonable service. And be not conformed to this world: but be transformed by the renewing of your mind, that ye may prove what is the good and

Luke

22:24 And there was also a strife among them, which of them should be accounted the greatest.

acceptable, and perfect, will of God. For I say, through the grace given unto me, to every man that is among you, not to think of himself more highly than he ought to think; but to think soberly, according as God hath dealt to every man the measure of faith." (Rom.12:1-3) **"Let nothing be done through strife or vain glory; but in lowliness of mind let each esteem other better than themselves."** (Phil.2:4)

It's a lifelong task for each of us to learn how to incorporate God's attitude into every activity of our lives. The nearer we approach this goal, the greater benefits God gives us.

As we gain a more comprehensive submission to God's truth, we can see why it became necessary for God to send Jesus into this world to explain to men steeped in Satan's system how God's plan for life differs from that of the Evil One. Living to please the flesh conflicts with the spirit, and living according to the spirit strikes against the interests of the flesh. Being contrary one to the other, we determine to submit to God or we are not his children. (Rom.8:9) Do we believe Satan or God?

Matthew

20:25 But Jesus called
them unto him, and said,
Ye know that the princes
of the Gentiles exercise
dominion over them, and
they that are great exer-
cise authority upon them.
26 But it shall not be so
among you: but whoso-
ever will be great among
you, let him be your
minister; 27 And whoso-
ever will be chief among
you, let him be your
servant: 28 Even as the
Son of man came not to be
ministered unto, but to
minister, and to give his
life a ransom for many.

God organizes his kingdom differently from kingdoms of this world. Civil rulers occupy high positions of authority. They decree laws which the people must obey or suffer for disobedience. People serve the rulers who wear the exquisite clothing, occupy the grand houses, circulate among the elite, and usually command the greatest wealth. Rulers are the VIP (very important people). God desires his kingdom to operate on different principles. The greatest in God's realm become the servants of the most. They ask, not command; help, not demand others to serve God, not themselves. They consider each individual equal to themselves. They are brethren of equal status. They understand God grants abil-

Mark

10:42 But Jesus called
them to him, and saith
unto them, Ye know that
they which are accounted
to rule over the Gentiles
exercise lordship over
them; and their great ones
exercise authority upon
them. 43 But so shall it not
be among you: but who-
soever will be great among
you, shall be your min-
ister: 44 And whosoever of
you will be the chiefest,
shall be servant of all. 45
For even the Son of man
came not to be ministered
unto, but to minister, and
to give his life a ransom for
many.

ities to each person for the good of all. Whether one swings the hammer or directs the workers, makes no difference. God sets each person in his dominion as he wills and endows each with abilities necessary to accomplish God's work. We function as a body. Eyes, nose, feet, arms, legs, head, mouth, ears, or whatever part, each has its particular function. Thus is God's kingdom. **"For as we have many members in one body, and all members have not the same office: So we being many, are one body in Christ, and every one members one of another."** (Rom.12:4-5) When we, as members of God's house, learn to function as God designed, then God's kingdom shall benefit all.

Luke

22:25 And he said unto
them, The kings of the
Gentiles exercise lordship
over them; and they that
exercise authority upon
them are called bene-
factors. 26 But ye shall not
be so: but he that is
greatest among you, let
him be as the younger; and
he that is chief, as he that
doth serve. 27 For whether
is greater, he that sitteth at
meat, or he that serveth? is
not he that sitteth at meat?
but I am among you as he
that serveth. 28 Ye are
they which have continued
with me in my temp-
tations. 29 And I appoint
unto you a kingdom, as my
Father hath appointed
unto me;

Unfortunately, church leaders have controlled the church as if it resembled an earthly kingdom. Leaders decreed laws to govern their assemblies, threatened members with expulsion for noncompliance, often punishing them with death when other means failed to bring submission, and elevated themselves to rule as kings over God's heritage. Such harsh treatment of God's sheep have caused them to flee from their hireling shepherds who care nothing for the welfare of the flock. This godless system continues to divide the church and dishonor God. Jesus allows Satan's tares to grow with the wheat until harvest.

Matthew

20:29 And as they departed from Jericho, a great multitude followed him. 30 And, behold, two blind men sitting by the way side, when they heard that Jesus passed by, cried out, saying, Have mercy on us, O Lord, thou Son of David. 31 And the multitude rebuked them, because they should hold their peace: but they cried the more, saying, Have mercy on us, O Lord, thou Son of David. 32 And Jesus stood still, and called them, and said, What will ye that I shall do unto you? 33 They say unto him, Lord, that our eyes may be opened. 34 So Jesus had compassion on them, and touched their eyes: and immediately their eyes received sight, and they followed him.

Some days before the Passover Jesus came to Jericho. Matthew stated two blind men asked for his mercy. Mark and Luke recorded that one pleaded for his sight. Mark alone named Bartimaeus as the one who spoke. Personalizing his message suggests Mark's audience may have known Bartimaeus who addressed Jesus as the son of David. God promised to restore David's throne. Bartimaeus trusted Jesus came to fulfill God's promise to David. Though the multitude tried

Mark

10:46 And they came to Jericho: and as he went out of Jericho with his disciples and a great number of people, blind Bartimaeus, the son of Timaeus, sat by the highway side begging. 47 And when he heard that it was Jesus of Nazareth, he began to cry out, and say, Jesus, thou Son of David, have mercy on me. 48 And many charged him that he should hold his peace: but he cried the more a great deal, Thou Son of David, have mercy on me. 49 And Jesus stood still, and commanded him to be called. And they call the blind man, saying unto him, Be of good comfort, rise; he calleth thee. 50 And he, casting away his garment, rose, and came to Jesus. 51 And Jesus answered and said unto him, What wilt thou that I should do unto thee? The blind man said unto him, Lord, that I might receive my sight. 52 And Jesus said unto him, Go thy way; thy faith hath made thee whole. And immediately he received his sight, and followed Jesus in the way.

to silence Bartimaeus, he believed Jesus would supply his request if he could get his attention. Jesus showed compassion on Bartimaeus and his companion.

Luke

18:35 And it came to pass, that as he was come nigh unto Jericho, a certain blind man sat by the way side begging: 36 And hearing the multitude pass by, he asked what it meant. 37 And they told him, that Jesus of Nazareth passeth by. 38 And he cried, saying, Jesus, thou Son of David, have mercy on me. 39 And they which went before rebuked him, that he should hold his peace: but he cried so much the more, Thou Son of David, have mercy on me. 40 And Jesus stood, and commanded him to be brought unto him: and when he was come near, he asked him, 41 Saying, What wilt thou that I shall do unto thee? And he said, Lord, that I may receive my sight. 42 And Jesus said unto him, Receive thy sight: thy faith hath saved thee. 43 And immediately he received his sight, and followed him, glorifying God: and all the people, when they saw it, gave praise unto God.

Example of Bartimaeus benefits us if we recognize a need and call on Jesus to supply our need.. Bartimaeus expected Jesus to care and provide his need. James encourages us to present our requests to God through Jesus. (Ja.4:1-3) God wants us to call on him. (Phil.4:6-7)

Luke

19:1 And Jesus entered and passed through Jericho. 2 And, behold, there was a man named Zacchaeus, which was the chief among the publicans, and he was rich. 3 And he sought to see Jesus who he was; and could not for the press, because he was little of stature. 4 And he ran before, and climbed up into a sycomore tree to see him: for he was to pass that way. 5 And when Jesus came to the place, he looked up, and saw him, and said unto him, Zacchaeus, make haste, and come down; for to day I must abide at thy house. 6 And he made haste, and came down, and received him joyfully. 7 And when they saw it, they all murmured, saying, That he was gone to be guest with a man that is a sinner. 8 And Zacchaeus stood, and said unto the Lord; Behold, Lord, the half of my goods I give to the poor; and if I have taken any thing from any man by false accusation, I restore him fourfold. 9 And Jesus said unto him, This day is salvation come to this house, forsomuch as he also is a son of Abraham. 10 For the Son of man is come to seek and to save that which was lost.

Did Zacchaeus' heart make an about face the day he met Jesus face to face? Did he change from one disobedient to God to the obedient? Was his mind which had been alienated to God turned to the heart of his heavenly Father as Luke's central theme indicates? (Lk.1:16-17; Mal.4:5-6)

Many of God's wayward children may feel he/she has sunk so deeply in sin God can no longer help him/her, or he doesn't care about me any longer. This may have permeated Zaccheus' thinking. As one encounters daily conflicts of life, many, yea, most of us recognize how we failed to do what was right before God. In time, our attitude slowly drifts from desiring to live to please God. Then an attitude of I make so many blunders, how could God ever forgive me begins to creep into one's mind. As time passes, hopelessness turns to despair and we give up trying to please God. Even Zacchaeus, a son of Abraham, struggled with this problem. This attitude may have led him to accept the Jewish-hated employment of a tax-collector for the Romans.

The day Zacchaeus met Jesus face to face, and Jesus called him to come down from the sycamore tree, he realized God did still love and care for him, even when Jesus knew his occupation and perhaps his sins. Jesus was even willing to dine with Zacchaeus in his house. How could God's Son accept Zacchaeus when he embarrassed his own nation to work as a publican? His tendency to cheat his own people by fraud to get rich had alienated him from his own people, but God still cared for him and desired him to return to God. This realization prompted Zacchaeus to want to make amends for all his wrongs. Why? because hope again filled his heart, knowing God still loved him in spite of all his sins.

Christians and all who read about Zacchaeus ought to realize that God sent his only begotten Son to deliver all his children from despair of thinking there remains no more hope for me after all the things I've done against God's commands and hurt other people. God sent Jesus into this world because he loves all his children and desires to give us all a complete life on earth and a hope of dwelling with our heavenly Father when we pass from this world. Jesus came to seek and save sinners, not the righteous. (Mk.2:17) Repenting and trusting in his blood to cleanse our sins pleases our heavenly Father, and he will not charge us with sin when we err. Isn't our heavenly Father gracious and merciful? Surely we ought to love him with all our heart and praise him to others.

What breaks down our resistance to God and transforms our minds from trying to put God out of our minds to a desire to draw close to our heavenly Father? (Rom.1:24-28) For Zacchaeus it centered on Jesus' love, not on his miracles, nor on what Jesus taught in the synagogue or by the sea side. Jesus spoke to Zacchaeus words that proved Zacchaeus was not just another person. He knew Zacchaeus by name, not by occupation nor by his ancestry. Jesus provided Zacchaeus with an opportunity to serve by saying he must abide in Zacchaeus' house that day. These words penetrated Zacchaeus' feelings. Jesus cared about him, disregarding everything he'd done to offend his nation and God. Zacchaeus perceived Jesus' affection, much as a parent affectionately and sympathetically demonstrates love and cares for a hurt child.

Paul, writing to Thessalonians, expressed how he entered their city, not with guile, flattering words, covetousness, nor seeking glory from them. Paul imparted himself to them, not just his teaching. He labored among them day and night because he considered them dear persons. (1 Thes.2:13-14) Even after persecution drove Paul from their city, Paul continued to care about their welfare. (1 Thes.2:17-20) Paul learned this loving attitude from Jesus. Though Paul had consented to Stephen's stoning, beat and imprisoned Christians, tried to force them to blaspheme God and Christ, Jesus showed Paul he cared about Paul. (Act.26:9-18) Jesus didn't reproach Paul for his previous obstinacy, but showed God cared for him.

When Zacchaeus detected Jesus' genuine care for him, it melted all bitterness and self-seeking which had motivated Zacchaeus. From that time Zacchaeus wanted to change himself to honor God. Perceiving God's love manifested in Jesus, it lodged in his soul and developed love for God within Zacchaeus. Love in God begets love in man.

Once God banishes ill will from our hearts, it doesn't mean we shall never find Satan utilizing life's difficulties to reinfect our hearts with bitterness. God still loves us even when we falter and let hatred drive us to mistreat another of God's children whether that person obeys or disobeys God. If we repent and demonstrate God's caring, God will never charge us with sin because we trust in Jesus' blood for the cleansing of our offenses. (Rom.3:22-26;4:6-8; Ps.32:1-2)

What Jesus did for Zacchaeus in revamping his mind, God's record of his only begotten Son continues to do to help all God's children overcome life's frustrations, disappointments, and hurts. Parents, family, children, friends, etc. may disregard what affects us, but God cares so much he gladly gave his only begotten Son to demonstrate his love. (Jno.3:16) God first loved us, and then we grasp that love to love all God's children. (1 Jno.3:14;4:7-11) God's way reaches beyond our comprehension at times, but it never fails, still hoping it will melt the hatred that builds up in our minds and spills over into ill will toward others. Yes, Jesus demonstrated God dwelling among men in a physical sense. (Is.7:14;8:8,10; Math.1:23) Spiritually, Jesus presents Emmanuel (God with us) when he dwells daily in our hearts by faith in the words he spoke and demonstrated. (Act.1:1)

Luke appears to be the only gospel writer who specifically referred to Malachi's prophecy that John the Baptist's and Jesus' coming would turn the hearts of the fathers to their children and the hearts of the children to their fathers. If this failed to transpire, God promised to smite the earth with a curse. Seeing how fathers and children today show such alienation toward one another, is God cursing the land with severe hurricanes, tornadic winds, droughts, fire storms, destroying forests and crops, blights of Africanized honey bees, fire ants, and the host of destructive events? Was not this that God spoke to Moses, promising blessings for obedience, but curses of drought, sword, disease, and wild beasts to humble them when they abandoned God's commands? (Lev.26:14-39) When God promises to curse in our age, don't regard disasters as normal. Let us repent and submit to God.

John

9:1 And as Jesus passed by, he saw a man which was blind from his birth. 2 And his disciples asked him, saying, Master, who did sin, this man, or his parents, that he was born blind? 3 Jesus answered, Neither hath this man sinned, nor his parents: but that the works of God should be made manifest in him. 4 I must work the works of him that sent me, while it is day: the night cometh, when no man can work. 5 As long as I am in the world, I am the light of the world. 6 When he had thus spoken, he spat on the ground, and made clay of the spittle, and he anointed the eyes of the blind man with the clay, 7 And said unto him, Go, wash in the pool of Siloam, (which is by interpretation, Sent.) He went his way therefore, and washed, and came seeing. 8 The neighbours therefore, and they which before had seen him that he was blind, said, Is not this he that sat and begged? 9 Some said, This is he: others said, He is like him: but he said, I am he. 10 Therefore said they unto him, How were thine eyes opened? 11 He answered and said, A man that is called Jesus made clay, and anointed mine eyes, and said unto me, Go to the pool of Siloam, and wash: and I went and washed, and I received sight. 12 Then said they unto him, Where is he? He said, I know not. 13 They brought to the Pharisees him that aforetime was blind. 14 And it was the sabbath day when Jesus made the clay, and opened his eyes. 15 Then again the Pharisees also asked him how he had received his sight. He said unto them, He put clay upon mine eyes, and I washed, and do see. 16 Therefore said some of the Pharisees, This man is not of God, because he keepeth not the sabbath day. Others said, How can a man that is a sinner do such miracles? And there was a division among them. 17 They say unto the blind man again, What sayest thou of him, that he hath opened thine eyes? He said, He is a prophet. 18 But the Jews did not believe concerning him, that he had been blind, and received his sight, until they called the parents of him that had received his sight. 19 And they asked them, saying, Is this your son, who ye say was born blind? how then doth he now see? 20 His parents answered them and said, We know that this is our son, and that he was born blind: 21 But by what means he now seeth, we know not; or who hath opened his eyes, we know not: he is of age; ask him: he shall speak for himself. 22 These words spake his parents, because they feared the Jews: for the Jews had agreed already, that if any man did confess that he was Christ, he should be put out of the synagogue. 23 Therefore said his parents, He is of age; ask him.

Jews doubted Jesus gave sight to a blind man. After they inquired into the matter, they could not deny he had indeed given sight to one born blind. Not being able to prove Jesus only appeared to have performed a wonder, they changed their approach and tried to convince the man that Jesus sinned by giving him his sight on the Sabbath. He replied that he knew two things. He had been born blind, and now he could see. Jesus must be of God, otherwise God would not have empowered him with the ability to give sight to the blind. He must be a prophet of God. Next, Jews tried to break the testimony of the blind man's parents. They admitted their son was born blind. They didn't know how he gained sight. Ask him. Being thwarted in every area, the Jews resorted to denying access to the synagogue to every person who confessed Jesus to be Christ.

Why would honest people restrict others from trying to know God especially when they claimed to be spiritual leaders? One might think they recognized defeat and simply desired to prove they possessed power to punish.

24 Then again called they the man that was blind, and said unto him, Give God the praise: we know that this man is a sinner. 25 He answered and said, Whether he be a sinner or no, I know not: one thing I know, that, whereas I was blind, now I see. 26 Then said they to him again, What did he to thee? how opened he thine eyes? 27 He answered them, I have told you already, and ye did not hear: wherefore would ye hear it again? will ye also be his disciples? 28 Then they reviled him, and said, Thou art his disciple; but we are Moses' disciples. 29 We know that God spake unto Moses: as for this fellow, we know not from whence he is. 30 The man answered and said unto them, Why herein is a marvellous thing, that ye know not from whence he is, and yet he hath opened mine eyes. 31 Now we know that God heareth not sinners: but if any man be a worshipper of God, and doeth his will, him he heareth. 32 Since the world began was it not heard that any man opened the eyes of one that was born blind. 33 If this man were not of God, he could do nothing. 34 They answered and said unto him, Thou wast altogether born in sins, and dost thou teach us? And they cast him out. 35 Jesus heard that they had cast him out; and when he had found him, he said unto him, Dost thou believe on the Son of God? 36 He answered and said, Who is he, Lord, that I might believe on him? 37 And Jesus said unto him, Thou hast both seen him, and it is he that talketh with thee. 38 And he said, Lord, I believe. And he worshipped him. 39 And Jesus said, For judgment I am come into this world, that they which see not might see; and that they which see might be made blind. 40 And some of the Pharisees which were with him heard these words, and said unto him, Are we blind also? 41 Jesus said unto them, If ye were blind, ye should have no sin: but now ye say, We see; therefore your sin remaineth.

God seeks honest people who aren't ashamed to confess him before those of this world. This man born blind knew Jesus must be from God. He confessed it to leaders of his own nation though they reviled him for his belief. When they failed to break down his confidence in Jesus and God, they called him a sinner. You were born in sin [a statement which Jesus had corrected in his own disciples]. (Jno.9:2-3) Satan utilizes every power of his children to coerce people of God to abandon their trust in truth, but this man born blind knew truth when he saw it. He would not let his mother, father, high-ranking leaders, or anyone dissuade him from truth.

After hearing that Pharisees deprived the former blind man from the right to assemble with his people in the synagogue to worship God, Jesus found him and asked him if he believed in the Son of God. He desired to know who he was. Jesus confessed that he was God's Son. The former blind man confessed he believed Jesus to be God's Son. He would do the will of God as he himself had explained to the Pharisees.

Does this incident provide reliable evidence that Jesus came from God as his Son? Does it also encourage God's children to face up to ridicule from Satan's fold? Truly, God asks his children to be strong. Meet the fiery weapons of Satan's ranks. They know the evidence proves Jesus is God's Son. They fear to oppose their peers and confess and do truth. They prefer to submit to the pressures of this world rather than suffer with those few who determine to show forth the praises of their Creator and supplier of every good.

Why did Jews believe God spoke through Moses? How did Moses convince Jews God spoke through him? Jews in Moses' day questioned that God spoke only through Moses. Miracles Moses performed convinced Jews God spoke by Moses. (Num. 12:2-13) Why were miracles insufficient to prove God spoke through Jesus?

John

10:1 Verily, verily, I say unto you, He that
entereth not by the door into the
sheepfold, but climbeth up some other
way, the same is a thief and a robber. 2
But he that entereth in by the door is the
shepherd of the sheep. 3 To him the
porter openeth; and the sheep hear his
voice: and he calleth his own sheep by
name, and leadeth them out. 4 And when
he putteth forth his own sheep, he goeth
before them, and the sheep follow him:
for they know his voice. 5 And a stranger
will they not follow, but will flee from
him: for they know not the voice of
strangers. 6 This parable spake Jesus unto
them: but they understood not what
things they were which he spake unto
them. 7 Then said Jesus unto them again,
Verily, verily, I say unto you, I am the
door of the sheep. 8 All that ever came
before me are thieves and robbers: but
the sheep did not hear them. 9 I am the
door: by me if any man enter in, he shall
be saved, and shall go in and out, and find
pasture. 10 The thief cometh not, but for
to steal, and to kill, and to destroy: I am
come that they might have life, and that
they might have it more abundantly. 11 I
am the good shepherd: the good shepherd
giveth his life for the sheep. 12 But he that
is an hireling, and not the shepherd,
whose own the sheep are not, seeth the
wolf coming, and leaveth the sheep, and
fleeth: and the wolf catcheth them, and
scattereth the sheep. 13 The hireling
fleeth, because he is an hireling, and
careth not for the sheep. 14 I am the good
shepherd, and know my sheep, and am
known of mine. 15 As the Father knoweth
me, even so know I the Father: and I lay
down my life for the sheep. 16 And other
sheep I have, which are not of this fold:
them also I must bring, and they shall
hear my voice; and there shall be one fold,
and one shepherd. 17 Therefore doth my
Father love me, because I lay down my
life, that I might take it again. 18 No man
taketh it from me, but I lay it down of
myself. I have power to lay it down, and I
have power to take it again. This
commandment have I received of my
Father. 19 There was a division therefore
again among the Jews for these sayings.
20 And many of them said, He hath a
devil, and is mad; why hear ye him? 21
Others said, These are not the words of
him that hath a devil. Can a devil open the
eyes of the blind?

People seek their own kind. Jesus looked for those who loved God. People who love God flocked to Jesus to hear a message from God who also draws near to those who draw near to him. (2 Chr.15:2; Ja.4:8) True children of God recognized Jesus as genuine. His miracles and words vibrated their hearts. They understood his message because they meditated on it, and God opened their hearts to comprehend. Satan's children perceived Jesus as an impostor. Neither his wonders nor his words impressed them. Hence Jesus employed the parable of sheep and shepherd to illustrate how God's people understood Jesus as sheep detect their own shepherd's voice, but flee from strangers. As a true shepherd of God's sheep, he voluntarily sacrificed his life for the welfare of God's people. (See Ezek.34:1-31.)

As Jesus' personal ministry polarized God's people and Satan's, today some grasp the gospel of the kingdom of God, but others reject it, preferring the things offered in this life to those God offers. Jesus provides a far more abundant life here and eternal life hereafter. Those seeking God obey God's truth Jesus taught. They who know only elements of this life turn deaf ears to Jesus. Their master is Satan, and his voice they recognize and follow. Why some claim they follow Jesus as the true shepherd, but refuse to hear and do what he taught mystifies me. They cling tenaciously to creeds and doctrines of men, not God.

**22 And it was at Jerusalem the feast of the
dedication, and it was winter. 23 And
Jesus walked in the temple in Solomon's
porch. 24 Then came the Jews round
about him, and said unto him, How long
dost thou make us to doubt? If thou be the
Christ, tell us plainly. 25 Jesus answered
them, I told you, and ye believed not: the
works that I do in my Father's name, they
bear witness of me. 26 But ye believe not,
because ye are not of my sheep, as I said
unto you. 27 My sheep hear my voice, and
I know them, and they follow me: 28 And
I give unto them eternal life; and they
shall never perish, neither shall any man
pluck them out of my hand. 29 My
Father, which gave them me, is greater
than all; and no man is able to pluck them
out of my Father's hand. 30 I and my
Father are one. 31 Then the Jews took up
stones again to stone him. 32 Jesus
answered them, Many good works have I
shewed you from my Father; for which of
those works do ye stone me? 33 The Jews
answered him, saying, For a good work
we stone thee not; but for blasphemy; and
because that thou, being a man, makest
thyself God. 34 Jesus answered them, Is it
not written in your law, I said, Ye are
gods? 35 If he called them gods, unto
whom the word of God came, and the
scripture cannot be broken; 36 Say ye of
him, whom the Father hath sanctified,
and sent into the world, Thou
blasphemest; because I said, I am the Son
of God? 37 If I do not the works of my
Father, believe me not. 38 But if I do,
though ye believe not me, believe the
works: that ye may know, and believe,
that the Father is in me, and I in him. 39
Therefore they sought again to take him:
but he escaped out of their hand, 40 And
went away again beyond Jordan into the
place where John at first baptized; and
there he abode. 41 And many resorted
unto him, and said, John did no miracle:
but all things that John spake of this man
were true. 42 And many believed on him
there.**

Jesus demonstrated genuine care for all his people. Though many viewed him as a bigot and a blasphemer, he continued to plead with them to think objectively. You reject what I teach, but surely the wonders God empowers me to perform ought to impress you. You don't deny that I restored useless limbs, gave sight to the blind, raised the dead, and numerous other wonders. Do these count for nothing in your eyes? What made your fathers trust that God sent Moses? Was it not the miracles he showed? Are the miracles God gives to me any less impressive than those of Moses? Moses explained to your fathers that I must come and speak all the truth of God to you. Furthermore, he instructed you that if you refused to hear me, God promised to sever you from among his people. Now you claim you trust Moses who wrote of me, but you disregard what God has given me to show and tell you. Are you not severing yourselves from God by rejecting my truth which God has given me to tell you? They continued to stumble over the idea he claimed to be God's Son. Jesus reminded them their law called men gods because God gave his word to them. (Ps.82:6) God gave his word to Jesus. He, therefore, even by their own law, rightfully called himself God's Son. They didn't see it that way. He deserved death because he made himself God when he was only a man.

John recorded the evidence for every generation to evaluate. Are we any less blind than those Jews? Do Jesus' miracles and his message of love prove him to be God's Son? Does his message improve the lives of those who do it? (Jno.7:17) If all the evidence supports Jesus' claim to be God's Son, why do we allow Satan's tactics to turn us from God's eternal plan of salvation? Do we really find Satan's followers that formidable?

John

11:1 Now a certain man was sick, named Lazarus, of Bethany, the town of Mary and her sister Martha. 2 (It was that Mary which anointed the Lord with ointment, and wiped his feet with her hair, whose brother Lazarus was sick.) 3 Therefore his sisters sent unto him, saying, Lord, behold, he whom thou lovest is sick. 4 When Jesus heard that, he said, This sickness is not unto death, but for the glory of God, that the Son of God might be glorified thereby. 5 Now Jesus loved Martha, and her sister, and Lazarus. 6 When he had heard therefore that he was sick, he abode two days still in the same place where he was. 7 Then after that saith he to his disciples, Let us go into Judaea again. 8 His disciples say unto him, Master, the Jews of late sought to stone thee; and goest thou thither again? 9 Jesus answered, Are there not twelve hours in the day? If any man walk in the day, he stumbleth not, because he seeth the light of this world. 10 But if a man walk in the night, he stumbleth, because there is no light in him. 11 These things said he: and after that he saith unto them, Our friend Lazarus sleepeth; but I go, that I may awake him out of sleep. 12 Then said his disciples, Lord, if he sleep, he shall do well. 13 Howbeit Jesus spake of his death: but they thought that he had spoken of taking of rest in sleep. 14 Then said Jesus unto them plainly, Lazarus is dead. 15 And I am glad for your sakes that I was not there, to the intent ye may believe; nevertheless let us go unto him. 16 Then said Thomas, which is called Didymus, unto his fellowdisciples, Let us also go, that we may die with him. 17 Then when Jesus came, he found that he had lain in the grave four days already. 18 Now Bethany was nigh unto Jerusalem, about fifteen furlongs off: 19 And many of the Jews came to Martha and Mary, to comfort them concerning their brother. 20 Then Martha, as soon as she heard that Jesus was coming, went and met him: but Mary sat still in the house. 21 Then said Martha unto Jesus, Lord, if thou hadst been here, my brother had not died. 22 But I know, that even now, whatsoever thou wilt ask of God, God will give it thee. 23 Jesus saith unto her, Thy brother shall rise again. 24 Martha saith unto him, I know that he shall rise again in the resurrection at the last day. 25 Jesus said unto her, I am the resurrection, and the life: he that believeth in me, though he were dead, yet shall he live: 26 And whosoever liveth and believeth in me shall never die. Believest thou this? 27 She saith unto him, Yea, Lord: I believe that thou art the Christ, the Son of God, which should come into the world. 28 And when she had so said, she went her way, and called Mary her sister secretly, saying, The Master is come, and calleth for thee. 29 As soon as she heard that, she arose quickly, and came unto him. 30 Now Jesus was not yet come into the town, but was in that place where Martha met him. 31 The Jews then which were with her in the house, and comforted her, when they saw Mary, that she rose up hastily and went out, followed her, saying, She goeth unto the grave to weep there. 32 Then when Mary was come where Jesus was, and saw him, she fell down at his feet, saying unto him, Lord, if thou hadst been here, my brother had not died. 33 When Jesus therefore saw her weeping, and the Jews also weeping which came with her, he groaned in the spirit, and was troubled, 34 And said, Where have ye laid him? They said unto him, Lord, come and see. 35 Jesus wept. 36 Then said the Jews, Behold how he loved him! 37 And some of them said, Could not this man, which opened the eyes of the blind, have caused that even this man should not have died? 38 Jesus therefore again groaning in himself cometh to the grave. It was a cave, and a

stone lay upon it. 39 Jesus said, Take ye away the stone. Martha, the sister of him that was dead, saith unto him, Lord, by this time he stinketh: for he hath been dead four days. 40 Jesus saith unto her, Said I not unto thee, that, if thou wouldest believe, thou shouldest see the glory of God? 41 Then they took away the stone from the place where the dead was laid. And Jesus lifted up his eyes, and said, Father, I thank thee that thou hast heard me. 42 And I knew that thou hearest me always: but because of the people which stand by I said it, that they may believe that thou hast sent me. 43 And when he thus had spoken, he cried with a loud voice, Lazarus, come forth. 44 And he that was dead came forth, bound hand and foot with graveclothes: and his face was bound about with a napkin. Jesus saith unto them, Loose him, and let him go. 45 Then many of the Jews which came to Mary, and had seen the things which Jesus did, believed on him.

Had you and I stood among those who witnessed Jesus come to the grave of Lazarus and saw him call him from the grave, would it have convinced us that God sent Jesus? No person today has power to call one who has died from the grave. Only a few God-sent prophets and his Son ever astonished the living with such deeds. Martha and Mary believed Jesus could do anything if he called on God's help. Many of the Jews who saw Jesus resurrect Lazarus believed that Jesus had to be God's messenger. Some beheld that wonder and refused to believe Jesus to be the Christ.

Jesus promised God would raise him from the dead on the third day. Three days he lay in the tomb, but God refused to allow his body to decay. Jesus triumphed over the grave to show all individuals, families, and nations that there is life beyond the grave. Our loved ones whom we sorrow to see buried will rise again. We, too, must come to the shadow of death. Our loved ones will carry our bodies to the grave and leave them. Those who believe in Jesus as the Son of God know all who have lived will rise from the dead. (Jno.5:26-29) They understand that when God sends his angels to announce that great resurrection judgment time follows. Those who have ordered their lives as God directed because they trust Jesus to be God's Son will rise to meet Jesus in the sky to go meet the heavenly Father face to face and share the glorious mansions with him and the redeemed of all ages. Resurrection for those who rejected Jesus as God's Son must face God and Jesus, too. Theirs will be a sad day. They will hear Jesus pronounce doom. You despised me while you lived as you pleased on earth, but now you will suffer the agonies of all unbelievers and haters of God and his Son Jesus Christ.

Neither priests nor Pharisees questioned Jesus performed true miracles. They checked them out and found them genuine. Why then did they reject him as Messiah? They claimed Israel was God's people and feared Roman rulers would come and destroy Jerusalem and their nation if they followed Jesus as King of the Jews. Envy also played its part in this drama. It's difficult for leaders to see their authority erode. They spent their lives trying to attain a sense of power among their people. They must do what they could to retain their position. Furthermore, they failed to understand that God's kingdom promised relief to people of all nations. From their point of view, David's throne in Jerusalem meant a political re-establishment of the glory Israel once held among nations. Jesus taught God planned a spiritual kingdom which did not meet their expectations of a nation ruled, like David, from Jerusalem by the Messiah.

Why do people today reject Jesus as God's Son and still view God's kingdom as a nation among nations, rather than as a spiritual empire which governs nations? Many factors interfere, but a great factor is their preference in an earthly kingdom in Judah.

John

11:46 But some of them went their ways to the Pharisees, and told them what things Jesus had done. 47 Then gathered the chief priests and the Pharisees a council, and said, What do we? for this man doeth many miracles. 48 If we let him thus alone, all men will believe on him: and the Romans shall come and take away both our place and nation. 49 And one of them, named Caiaphas, being the high priest that same year, said unto them, Ye know nothing at all, 50 Nor consider that it is expedient for us, that one man should die for the people, and that the whole nation perish not. 51 And this spake he not of himself: but being high priest that year, he prophesied that Jesus should die for that nation; 52 And not for that nation only, but that also he should gather together in one the children of God that were scattered abroad. 53 Then from that day forth they took counsel together for to put him to death. 54 Jesus therefore walked no more openly among the Jews; but went thence unto a country near to the wilderness, into a city called Ephraim, and there continued with his disciples. 55 And the Jews' passover was nigh at hand: and many went out of the country up to Jerusalem before the passover, to purify themselves. 56 Then sought they for Jesus, and spake among themselves, as they stood in the temple, What think ye, that he will not come to the feast? 57 Now both the chief priests and the Pharisees had given a commandment, that, if any man knew where he were, he should shew it, that they might take him.

It's much easier for us to visualize and understand the physical rather than the spiritual and to view an idol as God rather than a spiritual God. We, being physical, cherish the parts of this world that satisfy the physical appetites of our being. Even though we understand friendship, kindness, mercy, and gentleness improve relationships between us and others, we like what excites the body. It's our first choice. Only after we reflect on matters, do we begin to consider the spiritual as of equal or greater importance. We live for the present more than for the hereafter. God asks us to consider and to reconcile both parts of our nature. Only then can we experience fullness of life. (Jno.10:10)

Though Matthew, Mark, and Luke note Jesus approached Jerusalem only once, John recorded he came to the city at least three times shortly before the last Passover preceding his crucifixion. He attended the winter feast of dedication during which Jewish leaders threatened to stone him for making himself equal with God. Leaving Jerusalem, Jesus retired beyond Jordan where John the Baptist had baptized. (Jno. 10:22,31-40) Martha and Mary urged him to come restore Lazarus' health, but before Jesus arrived Lazarus died. Then Jesus called him from the grave. (Jno.11:1-46) Leaving Bethany, Jesus and his disciples departed to the city of Ephraim which was some ten miles northeast of Jerusalem. (Jno.11:54) About six days before the Passover, Jesus and his disciples journeyed to Bethany where Martha, Mary, and Lazarus feasted with him and his disciples. (Jno.12:1-11) The next day he rode triumphantly into Jerusalem while the multitude cried hosanna to King Jesus. (Jno. 12:12-13)

Shortly before the Passover, Jews from the surrounding country came to Jerusalem to purify themselves that they might eat the Passover. As they visited among themselves, they asked one another if they expected Jesus to attend the feast. They knew their leaders threatened to stone Jesus and had heard that the council requested that if any knew where Jesus was, they should inform the council. Thus, many questioned if he would attend this Passover. Judas, hearing the council's wish to take Jesus, conceived of a plan to secure money.

Because false teachers circulated among churches, modifying and contradicting God's true record of his Son, God directed two apostles and two companions of apostles to record for all generations and peoples true accounts of Jesus' life, compassion on his people, miracles, truths he taught, how only a few believed and followed him when their leaders rejected him as a deceiver and false prophet, how Jewish leaders deceitfully arrested, tried him, condemned, and crucified him, only to discover God raised him from the dead the third day. (Math. 27:62-66;28:11-15)

Though Jewish elite denied God's Messiah, God accomplished his eternal plan as testified beforehand by O.T. prophets. Unless we today perceive God's overall plan concerning Jesus, many tend to follow erroneous concepts spread among churches today as happened even during days of the apostles and spread after their decease.

Can Christians today ascertain a true concept of God's eternal plan accomplished in Jesus' miraculous birth, glorious miracles, astonishing doctrine, unjust death, and wondrous resurrection. God promised Adam the seed of the woman would bruise the serpent's head, but Satan would bruise his heel. (Gen.3:15) Isaiah explained a virgin giving birth to a son would manifest God dwelling with men, accomplishing God's promise to Adam. Matthew's and Luke's gospels testify God chose Mary, a virgin, to bear God's only begotten Son. (Math.1:18-25; Lk.1:26-2:20)

Jesus' authoritative doctrine, morally uplifting, and blessing those who do what he taught, converts hearts from serving self to serving God and others. Isaiah and Micah promised God would teach mankind his ways, and all peoples would come to be taught of God. Our warring nature God changes to peaceful deeds. (Is.2:2-4; Mi.4:1-4) We enter God's holy city, spiritual Jerusalem, the church of the living God (Heb. 12:22-24), by being taught of God (Is.54:11-14, Jno.6:44-45), dying to Satan's life style with Christ in water baptism and rising with Jesus to a new life, being born of God's Spirit to a new creature to honor God with good deeds. (Rom.6:1-11; Gal.3:26-27; Col. 2:11-13; Ja.1:18; 1 Pet.1:22-23)

Glorious miracles Jesus performed released men and women from Satan's fetters, relieved suffering, and demonstrated God's power and glory. (Is.61:1-3; Lk.13:16)

God explained Jesus' death paid our debt, the penalty for sin. (Is.53:1-12) From creation God decreed sin's penalty is death. (Gen.2:17; Rom.1:32;6:23) Jesus died on the cross, not for his sins, but for mine and yours. Without Jesus' interceding death every person who sinned must die for his sins. Since life of the flesh is sustained by one's blood, Jesus' shed blood spares each of us from death if we believe in and obey him. (Lev.17:11; Math.26:26-28; Mk.14:22-24; Lk.22:15-20; Rom.6:17-18)

Had God not raised Jesus miraculously from the dead, none of us would have hope of life beyond the grave. (1 Cor.15:12-23) Before creation God promised eternal life (Tit.1:2), but immortality God explains only by the gospel. (2 Tim.1:9-10)

Christ serves as our only mediator to God. (1 Tim.2:5) If God had not called Jesus to heaven to intercede for our sins, asking for God's mercy for our daily sins, God would not forgive us. We must die eternally for our transgressions. (Rom.1:32)

Since God explains his mystery of eternal redemption through the gospel of Christ, why do so many Christians deny certain parts of God's eternal plan? Is it any wonder God gave us four gospels to show us truth? Mark quoted Jesus, saying we must repent and believe God's gospel. Otherwise we affirm God is a liar. (Mk.1:15; 1 Jno.5:10) If you and I dread the thought to stand before God, knowing we claimed God lied in what gospels recorded, now is the time to repent.

Luke

13:6 He spake also this parable: A certain man had a fig tree planted in his vineyard; and he came and sought fruit thereon, and found none. 7 Then said he unto the dresser of his vineyard, Behold, these three years I come seeking fruit on this fig tree, and find none: cut it down; why cumbereth it the ground? 8 And he answering said unto him, Lord, let it alone this year also, till I shall dig about it, and dung it: 9 And if it bear fruit, well: and if not, then after that thou shalt cut it down. 10 And he was teaching in one of the synagogues on the sabbath.

The unproductive fig tree in the vineyard portrays unbelieving Jewish leaders who should be bearing fruits of righteousness to God, but bear no fruit. God determines to destroy the fruitless tree, but Jesus, as the gardener, asked for one more year for God to spare the unproductive tree. During that year Jesus fertilized the tree with the word of God. Next year, if it remains fruitless, then he cuts it down. This parable shows how Jesus intercedes to God for his people. Because of his love for the lost, he pleads to his Father for time that people might repent when they hear the truth of the gospel of the kingdom of heaven.

Jesus loves each person so much he asks God for time that each of us, after hearing of the kindness of God, will repent and return to God. He gives us life and time on earth to repent and return to him. However, if we persist in disobedience, time will run out, and we lose life. (2 Pet.3:9)

Applying this parable to leaders of Israel, one can see that God placed them in his vineyard to produce fruits to God's glory. Rather than honor God, their deeds blighted God's name among Israel and Gentiles. Jesus entreated God to grant them a little time that they may turn from their sin and bring forth righteous fruit, influencing Israel and Gentiles to praise God. Jesus' heart must have grieved when leaders disbelieved him.

Luke

13:11 And, behold, there was a woman which had a spirit of infirmity eighteen years, and was bowed together, and could in no wise lift up herself. 12 And when Jesus saw her, he called her to him, and said unto her, Woman, thou art loosed from thine infirmity. 13 And he laid his hands on her: and immediately she was made straight, and glorified God. 14 And the ruler of the synagogue answered with indignation, because that Jesus had healed on the sabbath day, and said unto the people, There are six days in which men ought to work: in them therefore come and be healed, and not on the sabbath day. 15 The Lord then answered him, and said, Thou hypocrite, doth not each one of you on the sabbath loose his ox or his ass from the stall, and lead him away to watering? 16 And ought not this woman, being a daughter of Abraham, whom Satan hath bound, lo, these eighteen years, be loosed from this bond on the sabbath day? 17 And when he had said these things, all his adversaries were ashamed: and all the people rejoiced for all the glorious things that were done by him.

Ruler of the synagogue, as a spiritual leader, should have had compassion on those who frequented his synagogue, but he didn't. All of us recognize hardness of heart in ourselves, but we must learn to show concern for the welfare of others. If Satan replaces God's love with his base attitudes, we will act as the ruler of the synagogue. Jesus melted the heart of the ruler by showing he allowed more compassion on his ass or ox than he did for the deformed woman whom Jesus healed on the Sabbath.

Jesus refused to judge after the sight of his eyes. Righteousness girdled his loins and faithfulness his reins. (Is.11:1-5) He distinguished clearly between Satan's dark paths and God's light. May Satan blind not our eyes to distinguish day from night.

Luke

13:22 And he went through the cities and villages, teaching, and journeying toward Jerusalem. 23 Then said one unto him, Lord, are there few that be saved? And he said unto them, 24 Strive to enter in at the strait gate: for many, I say unto you, will seek to enter in, and shall not be able. 25 When once the master of the house is risen up, and hath shut to the door, and ye begin to stand without, and to knock at the door, saying, Lord, Lord, open unto us; and he shall answer and say unto you, I know you not whence ye are: 26 Then shall ye begin to say, We have eaten and drunk in thy presence, and thou hast taught in our streets. 27 But he shall say, I tell you, I know you not whence ye are; depart from me, all ye workers of iniquity. 28 There shall be weeping and gnashing of teeth, when ye shall see Abraham, and Isaac, and Jacob, and all the prophets, in the kingdom God, and you yourselves thrust out. 29 And they shall come from the east, and from the west, and from the north, and from the south, and shall sit down in the kingdom of God. 30 And, behold, there are last which shall be first, and there are first which shall be last.

Lord, are there many who enter your kingdom? As Noah entered the ark, and God shut the door to ban those who refused to enter, so this parable shows God opens his kingdom for us, but closes the door and shuts out those who refuse to enter. (Gen.7:7-16) The Hebrew writer quoted from Psalms, saying, "**To day if ye will hear his voice, harden not your hearts, as in the provocation....to whom sware he that they should not enter into his rest.**" (Heb.3:15-18; Ps.95:7-11) Jewish leaders refused to enter the kingdom of heaven and hindered those who would enter. (Math.23:13) Jesus explained that Gentiles choose to enter, but you shall be thrust out because you believe not I am Christ. (Jno.8:24; See p. 89.)

Luke

13:31 The same day there came certain of the Pharisees, saying unto him, Get thee out, and depart hence: for Herod will kill thee. 32 And he said unto them, Go ye, and tell that fox, Behold, I cast out devils, and I do cures to day and to morrow, and the third day I shall be perfected. 33 Nevertheless I must walk to day, and to morrow, and the day following: for it cannot be that a prophet perish out of Jerusalem. 34 O Jerusalem, Jerusalem, which killest the prophets, and stonest them that are sent unto thee; how often would I have gathered thy children together, as a hen doth gather her brood under her wings, and ye would not! 35 Behold, your house is left unto you desolate: and verily I say unto you, Ye shall not see me, until the time come when ye shall say, Blessed is he that cometh in the name of the Lord.

Luke recorded no explanation why Pharisees encouraged Jesus to discontinue his journey to Jerusalem. He regarded their words idle. Herod would not kill him. Jewish leaders devised that plot which they determined to fulfill. Had not Jewish leaders led plots to kill prophets of old? Even Jesus should perish in Jerusalem. Jesus sorrowed over the city. Though you have stoned and killed the prophets God sent you, I would have gathered your children unto God as a hen gathers her brood under her wings for protection, but you refused me. The days come when your Jerusalem shall be desolate. Some day you will be glad to see me and shall bless my name. Unfortunately, now you choose sorrow for yourself by rejecting me and God's truth I have taught you.

God humbles all who spurn the everlasting gospel. He sent Romans to destroy Jerusalem. All nations that forget God reap bitterness. (Ps.9:17; Prov.14:34; Is.60:12) Individually, each of us choose to accept or reject God's only provision to escape Satan's fetters and doom.

Matthew

21:1 And when they drew nigh unto Jerusalem, and were come to Bethphage, unto the mount of Olives, then sent Jesus two disciples, 2 Saying unto them, Go into the village over against you, and straightway ye shall find an ass tied, and a colt with her: loose them, and bring them unto me. 3 And if any man say ought unto you, ye shall say, The Lord hath need of them; and straightway he will send them. 4 All this was done, that it might be fulfilled which was spoken by the prophet, saying, 5 Tell ye the daughter of Sion, Behold, thy King cometh unto thee, meek, and sitting upon an ass, and a colt the foal of an ass. 6 And the disciples went, and did as Jesus commanded them, 7 And brought the ass, and the colt, and put on them their clothes, and they set him thereon. 8 And a very great multitude spread their garments in the way; others cut down branches from the trees, and strawed them in the way. 9 And the multitudes that went before, and that followed, cried, saying, Hosanna to the Son of David: Blessed is he that cometh in the name of the Lord; Hosanna in the highest. 10 And when he was come into Jerusalem, all the city was moved, saying, Who is this? 11 And the multitude said, This is Jesus the prophet of Nazareth of Galilee.

Culmination of Jesus' work neared. He prepared to enter Jerusalem as Zechariah wrote, riding on the foal of an ass. (Zech. 9:9) As the multitude gathered enthusiasm, they spread before him their garments and tree branches much as nations spread out the red carpet to welcome high-ranking dignitaries. They raised their voices, proclaiming the arrival of Jesus of Nazareth. He brings with him the return of the kingdom of our father David. God blesses us by his coming. Jerusalem stirred with excitement with the approach of the procession. Jewish leaders viewed Jesus' triumphant arrival as threatening to them and their nation.

Mark

11:1 And when they came nigh to Jerusalem, unto Bethphage and Bethany, at the mount of Olives, he sendeth forth two of his disciples, 2 And saith unto them, Go your way into the village over against you: and as soon as ye be entered into it, ye shall find a colt tied, whereon never man sat; loose him, and bring him. 3 And if any man say unto you, Why do ye this? say ye that the Lord hath need of him; and straightway he will send him hither. 4 And they went their way, and found the colt tied by the door without in a place where two ways met; and they loose him. 5 And certain of them that stood there said unto them, What do ye, loosing the colt? 6 And they said unto them even as Jesus had commanded: and they let them go. 7 And they brought the colt to Jesus, and cast their garments on him; and he sat upon him. 8 And many spread their garments in the way: and others cut down branches off the trees, and strawed them in the way. 9 And they that went before, and they that followed, cried, saying, Hosanna; Blessed is he that cometh in the name of the Lord: 10 Blessed be the kingdom of our father David, that cometh in the name of the Lord: Hosanna in the highest. 11 And Jesus entered into Jerusalem, and into the temple: and when he had looked round about upon all things, and now the eventide was come, he went out unto Bethany with the twelve.

Pharisees in the multitude encouraged Jesus to moderate the excitement of the people. They couldn't deny the miracle of Lazarus' resurrection, but proclaiming Jesus as the one to restore David's throne in Jerusalem worried them. Jesus' reply undoubtedly added to their anxiety. He replied that if the crowd kept silence, even the rocks along the path must resound the message the people proclaimed. It was futile for them to resist God's plan.

Luke

19:28 And when he had thus spoken, he went before, ascending up to Jerusalem. 29 And it came to pass, when he was come nigh to Bethphage and Bethany, at the mount called the mount of Olives, he sent two of his disciples, 30 Saying, Go ye into the village over against you; in the which at your entering ye shall find a colt tied, whereon yet never man sat: loose him, and bring him hither. 31 And if any man ask you, Why do ye loose him? thus shall ye say unto him, Because the Lord hath need of him. 32 And they that were sent went their way, and found even as he had said unto them. 33 And as they were loosing the colt, the owners thereof said unto them, Why loose ye the colt? 34 And they said, The Lord hath need of him. 35 And they brought him to Jesus: and they cast their garments upon the colt, and they set Jesus thereon. 36 And as he went, they spread their clothes in the way. 37 And when he was come nigh, even now at the descent of the mount of Olives, the whole multitude of the disciples began to rejoice and praise God with a loud voice for all the mighty works that they had seen; 38 Saying, Blessed be the King that cometh in the name of the Lord: peace in heaven, and glory in the highest. 39 And some of the Pharisees from among the multitude said unto him, Master, rebuke thy disciples. 40 And he answered and said unto them, I tell you that, if these should hold their peace, the stones would immediately cry out.

John

12:12 On the next day much people that were come to the feast, when they heard that Jesus was coming to Jerusalem, 13 Took branches of palm trees, and went forth to meet him, and cried, Hosanna: Blessed is the King of Israel that cometh in the name of the Lord. 14 And Jesus, when he had found a young ass, sat thereon; as it is written, 15 Fear not, daughter of Sion: behold, thy King cometh, sitting on an ass's colt. 16 These things understood not his disciples at the first: but when Jesus was glorified, then remembered they that these things were written of him, and that they had done these things unto him. 17 The people therefore that was with him when he called Lazarus out of his grave, and raised him from the dead, bare record. 18 For this cause the people also met him, for that they heard that he had done this miracle. 19 The Pharisees therefore said among themselves, Perceive ye how ye prevail nothing? behold, the world is gone after him.

God will bring the peace which eases mankind's sorrows. Jesus shall reign as king on David's throne in heaven, not in Jerusalem. Neither priests, Pharisees, nor Romans shall defeat God's plan. "**Why do the heathen rage, and the people imagine a vain thing? The kings of the earth set themselves, and the rulers take counsel together, against the Lord, and against his anointed, saying, Let us break their bands asunder, and cast away their cords from us. He that sitteth in the heavens shall laugh: the Lord shall have them in derision. Then shall he speak unto them in his wrath, and vex them in his sore displeasure. Yet have I set my king upon my holy hill of Zion. I will declare the decree: the Lord hath said unto me, Thou art my Son; this day have I begotten thee. Ask of me, and I shall give thee the heathen for thine inheritance, and the uttermost parts of the earth for thy possession. Thou shalt break them with a rod of iron; thou shalt dash them in pieces like a potter's vessel. Be wise now therefore, O ye kings: be instructed, ye judges of the earth. Serve the Lord with fear, and rejoice with trembling.**" (Ps.2:1-11) Unknowingly, Jewish officials tried to defeat God's plan, but failed. Could religious leaders today be resisting God's plan?

Matthew

21:12 And Jesus went into the temple of God, and cast out all them that sold and bought in the temple, and overthrew the tables of the moneychangers, and the seats of them that sold doves, 13 And said unto them, It is written, My house shall be called the house of prayer; but ye have made it a den of thieves. 14 And the blind and the lame came to him in the temple; and he healed them. 15 And when the chief priests and scribes saw the wonderful things that he did, and the children crying in the temple, and saying, Hosanna to the Son of David; they were sore displeased, 16 And said unto him, Hearest thou what these say? And Jesus saith unto them, Yea; have ye never read, Out of the mouth of babes and sucklings thou hast perfected praise? 17 And he left them, and went out of the city into Bethany; and he lodged there.

Matthew compared Jesus' coming to Jerusalem to David's capture of the city, mentioning the lame and blind. Ungodliness prevailed when God's anointed took the city. (Math.21:14; 2 Sam.5:6) God sent Jesus to correct their unjust merchandising in his temple. How could people consider the temple as God's house of praise if evil persisted there? God allowed Jews who lived far from the temple to sell their offerings at home and carry the money to the city where God's house dwelt and there buy sacrifices they needed for worship. (Deu. 14:24-26) Merchants and temple leaders used this law to justify selling the sacrifice objects in the temple. It wasn't the selling of objects for worship that provoked God's displeasure. Merchants charged exorbitant prices for their goods and became thieves. This discredited God and made God's temple a place of injustice. (Is.56:7)

Mark called God's house the house of prayer to all nations, but Matthew omitted the "all nations" which suggests Matthew addressed Jews, but Mark addressed Gentiles.

Mark

11:15 And they come to Jerusalem: and Jesus went into the temple, and began to cast out them that sold and bought in the temple, and overthrew the tables of the moneychangers, and the seats of them that sold doves; 16 And would not suffer that any man should carry any vessel through the temple. 17 And he taught, saying unto them, Is it not written, My house shall be called of all nations the house of prayer? but ye have made it a den of thieves. 18 And the scribes and chief priests heard it, and sought how they might destroy him: for they feared him, because all the people was astonished at his doctrine. 19 And when even was come, he went out of the city.

Children in the temple identified Jesus as David's son which Mark omitted, showing again that Matthew mentioned concepts dear to Jews, but of little interest to Gentiles, Mark's audience. When chief priest inquired why Jesus allowed children to praise him as David's son, he referred to their psalm which stated perfect praise issued from the mouths of babes. (Ps.8:2)

What plan has God to prevent his people from dishonoring his house and name? When God prescribes details which guide men how to build his house and to worship him, what more should we need? Any of us who contracted to have our house built and furnished demand that the contractor adhere to the blueprint and specifications written in the contract. God's covenant with Israel delineated the specifications for his house and how Israel must worship him. All deviations dishonored God.

Christians need to learn that God designed the church and its worship. If we are to please God, we must make its structure and worship comply with God's plan. History shows that Christians, like Jews, have suffered terrible tribulations for departing from God's plan.

In the temple Jesus restored sight and

Luke

19:41 And when he was come near, he
beheld the city, and wept over it, 42
Saying, If thou hadst known, even thou, at
least in this thy day, the things which
belong unto thy peace! but now they are
hid from thine eyes. 43 For the days shall
come upon thee, that thine enemies shall
cast a trench about thee, and compass
thee round, and keep thee in on every
side, 44 And shall lay thee even with the
ground, and thy children within thee; and
they shall not leave in thee one stone upon
another; because thou knewest not the
time of thy visitation. 45 And he went into
the temple, and began to cast out them
that sold therein, and them that bought;
46 Saying unto them, It is written, My
house is the house of prayer: but ye have
made it a den of thieves. 47 And he taught
daily in the temple. But the chief priests
and the scribes and the chief of the people
sought to destroy him, 48 And could not
find what they might do: for all the people
were very attentive to hear him.

healed the lame. Chief priests disregarded how Jesus brought praise to God by helping those Satan bruised. Instead, they found fault and discredited him. Surely, their hearts understood not the love of God for his downtrodden children.

Jesus taught that a person is the child of him whom he obeys though he believes in Jesus. (Jno.8:31-47) Satan lied to Adam and Eve when he informed them they would not die when they ate of the tree of the knowledge of good and evil. Instead, their eyes would be opened to good and evil. When Adam and Eve followed Satan's instructions, they became his children. Today many who trust they are God's faithful children follow the advice of Satan. God told us how to build and worship in his church, but Satan's ministers have changed his way of worship.

Luke informed Theophilus that Jesus sorrowed for Jerusalem as he prepared to enter the city. Like Daniel, Jesus explained God planned to waste the city for transgressing his commandments and rejecting Jesus, God's messenger to it. (Dan.9:24-27; Math.24:1-35) Israel suffered great hardships during Egyptian bondage, days of the judges, and when Assyria and Babylon destroyed their cities, killed multitudes of the people, and exiled survivors as captives. Walls of their cities they demolished, burned their houses, desecrated and finally burned God's holy temple. Thinking of all these disasters, Jesus wept over the city, for God would devastate their whole social system again for their rebellion.

Why would a loving God take such drastic actions against his own people? When God made his covenant with Israel at Sinai, he explained in detail all the blessings he promised Israel if they submitted to his will. Equally explicit, he identified curses which must plague them if they refused to obey. (Lev.26:3-46) These curses canceled every blessing God promised: famine, sword, disease, and wild beasts destroyed their cattle and children, and desolated their cities and sanctuary. Now that multitudes in Israel refused to turn to Jesus as God's faithful messenger to return them to the truth of God, he determined to again implement his curses. Though Jesus sought so desperately to guide his people to return them to the way of God, they closed their ears and hearts to his message. It grieved Jesus to see them spurn God and his truth. Knowing the tribulations to come upon them, Jesus wept. If only they would remember what Moses taught and wrote to guide them, they could prevent all this destruction and agony, but rebellion against God shall reap the disasters he promised in his covenant. They could escape God's promised tribulations only by submitting to God's laws delivered to them by Moses. God even sent John the Baptist, Jesus, and the apostles, pleading with Israel to repent and produce fruits of righteousness, but few repented.

Matthew

21:18 Now in the morning as he returned into the city, he hungered. 19 And when he saw a fig tree in the way, he came to it, and found nothing thereon, but leaves only, and said unto it, Let no fruit grow on thee henceforward for ever. And presently the fig tree withered away. 20 And when the disciples saw it, they marvelled, saying, How soon is the fig tree withered away! 21 Jesus answered and said unto them, Verily I say unto you, If ye have faith, and doubt not, ye shall not only do this which is done to the fig tree, but also if ye shall say unto this mountain, Be thou removed, and be thou cast into the sea; it shall be done. 22 And all things, whatsoever ye shall ask in prayer, believing, ye shall receive.

Mark

11:12 And on the morrow, when they were come from Bethany, he was hungry: 13 And seeing a fig tree afar off having leaves, he came, if haply he might find any thing thereon: and when he came to it, he found nothing but leaves; for the time of figs was not yet. 14 And Jesus answered and said unto it, No man eat fruit of thee hereafter for ever. And his disciples heard it.

11:20 And in the morning, as they passed by, they saw the fig tree dried up from the roots. 21 And Peter calling to remembrance saith unto him, Master, behold, the fig tree which thou cursedst is withered away. 22 And Jesus answering saith unto them, Have faith in God. 23 For verily I say unto you, That whosoever shall say unto this mountain, Be thou removed, and be thou cast into the sea; and shall not doubt in his heart, but shall believe that those things which he saith shall come to pass; he shall have whatsoever he saith. 24 Therefore I say unto you, What things soever ye desire, when ye pray, believe that ye receive them, and ye shall have them. 25 And when ye stand praying, forgive, if ye have ought against any: that your Father also which is in heaven may forgive you your trespasses. 26 But if ye do not forgive, neither will your Father which is in heaven forgive your trespasses.

Jesus' drying up a fig tree on his return from Bethany to the temple illustrated the power God provides to those who ask of him. Having faith strengthens us when we ask reasonable requests and believe God will supply our wishes. God enables us to accomplish feats which appear impossible. (Math.19:26; Phil.4:13)

Mark injects another aspect of prayer. When you pray to the Father in heaven, forgive others who trespass against you, otherwise God will not forgive your sins. If you are unwilling to overlook what others do that irritate you, do you expect the Father of all men to forgive your insults against him? What you ask God to do for you, be willing to do the same for others. Holding a grudge against someone signifies that you still do the works of Satan. Jesus taught that a person is the child of the one whom he follows even if he believes in God and Jesus. (Jno.8:31-47) God seeks people who do the will of God, not Satan.

When we consider prayer as one part of our friendship and fellowship with God, we talk to him as we might a friend, explaining our difficulties and wishes. As we expect a genuine friend to listen, encourage, and help with our trials, we come to share with God those difficulties and joys which affect us. This interaction develops a lasting relationship of trust and confidence that we and God walk together in life, each doing those things which please and help the other.

How can man help God? Since many of God's children no longer listen to him, he calls on his faithful children to help his wayward children see there is a considerable benefit in returning to and walking with our heavenly Father.

Do Satan's children pray to God? Jesus taught they do, but God reacts unfavorably to their prayers for various reasons: 1) If their prayers in public seek men's admiration, God withholds his reward. (Math. 6:5) 2) Satan's children often employ long, repetitive speeches, thinking God listens to them because of their fluency or high-sounding vocabulary. (Math.6:7) God knows what we need even before we present our petitions. Furthermore, our heavenly Father endowed each of us with our ability to speak whether it be with oratory or common language. (Ex.4:11) God cannot be impressed by how well we order our requests. 3) Children of this world sometimes call on God, believing they're better than others. For example, a Pharisee thanked God he was not like other men: extortioners, unjust, adulterers, or as publicans. He fasted twice a week and tithed of all he possessed. Believing God respected his prayer because his righteousness stood above others disqualified his prayer. God sees us for what we really are. Perhaps our actions haven't dishonestly taken other's wealth, but have we desired what God gave someone else? Maybe we haven't committed adultery, but the desire tempted us. Seeking to be just, do we look back on how we treated others and realize certain of our activities lacked justice? Even perceiving that we are better than others blocks God from answering our prayers. (Lk.18:9-14) 4) James noted that entreaties to God to provide us with opportunities to fulfill our fleshly passions disqualifies our petitions before God. (Ja.4:3) If we request God to give us those things which satisfy the desires of the flesh and/or mind, God views us as children of the Evil One, not his offspring. Therefore God turns a deaf ear to our prayers. God seeks for those whose spirits draw near to him, not those whose hearts lust after the world and its vain goals.

How does one seek to please our Father in heaven by prayer and know he will grant our requests? 1) Humility probably stands as the supreme prerequisite. Abandoning pride, as much as we know how, presents a needy spirit or attitude before God. (Math.5:3) It says to our Creator and provider, I'm unworthy of all thou hast given me. My weaknesses and transgressions abound even when I honestly try to do thy will. I often find my mind being ungrateful and wanting more. Father, be merciful to me, a sinner. **"The Lord is nigh unto them that are of a broken heart; and saveth such as be of a contrite spirit."** (Ps.34:18) **"The sacrifices of God are a broken spirit: a broken and contrite heart, O God, thou wilt not despise."** (Ps.51:17) **"I dwell in the high and holy place, with him also that is of a contrite and humble spirit, to revive the spirit of the humble, and to revive the heart of the contrite ones."** (Is.57:15) **"But to this man will I look, even to him that is poor and of a contrite spirit, and trembleth at my word."** (Is.66:2) 2) Isaiah presented a second attitude God honors: one whose mind submits completely to God's will. It says to God that thou has placed me on earth to do thy will, and I am resolved to submit to all thy commandments. I make no exceptions, nor do I reserve any of my personal rights. I intend to make no alterations of thy commandments to please myself. Jesus said, **"Lo, I come to do thy will, O God."** (Heb.10:9) Without these attitudes of humility and submission, do we honestly expect God to take knowledge of our prayers? God granted Hanna her son Samuel when she manifested a humble attitude. (1 Sam.1:9-28) Quoting from Psalms, Peter penned, **"For the eyes of the Lord are over the righteous, and his ears are open unto their prayers: but the face of the Lord is against them that do evil."** (1 Pet.3:12)

Our heavenly Father seeks all his children to call on him in a humble attitude. Petition him for what we need and ask his blessing to fulfill the needs of others, too. (I Tim.3:1-4)

Matthew

**21:23 And when he was come into the
temple, the chief priests and the elders of
the people came unto him as he was
teaching, and said, By what authority
doest thou these things? and who gave
thee this authority? 24 And Jesus
answered and said unto them, I also will
ask you one thing, which if ye tell me, I in
like wise will tell you by what authority I
do these things. 25 The baptism of John,
whence was it? from heaven, or of men?
And they reasoned with themselves,
saying, If we shall say, From heaven; he
will say unto us, Why did ye not then
believe him? 26 But if we shall say, Of
men; we fear the people; for all hold John
as a prophet. 27 And they answered Jesus,
and said, We cannot tell. And he said unto
them, Neither tell I you by what authority
I do these things. 28 But what think ye? A
certain man had two sons; and he came to
the first, and said, Son, go work to day in
my vineyard. 29 He answered and said, I
will not: but afterward he repented, and
went. 30 And he came to the second, and
said likewise. And he answered and said, I
go, sir: and went not. 31 Whether of them
twain did the will of his father? They say
unto him, The first. Jesus saith unto them,
Verily I say unto you, That the publicans
and the harlots go into the kingdom of
God before you. 32 For John came unto
you in the way of righteousness, and ye
believed him not: but the publicans and
the harlots believed him: and ye, when ye
had seen it, repented not afterward, that
ye might believe him.**

Mark

**11:27 And they come again to Jerusalem:
and as he was walking in the temple, there
come to him the chief priests, and the
scribes, and the elders, 28 And say unto
him, By what authority doest thou these
things? and who gave thee this authority
to do these things? 29 And Jesus answered
and said unto them, I will also ask of you
one question, and answer me, and I will
tell you by what authority I do these
things. 30 The baptism of John, was it
from heaven, or of men? answer me. 31
And they reasoned with themselves,
saying, If we shall say, From heaven; he
will say, Why then did ye not believe him?
32 But if we shall say, Of men; they
feared the people: for all men counted
John, that he was a prophet indeed. 33
And they answered and said unto Jesus,
We cannot tell. And Jesus answering saith
unto them, Neither do I tell you by what
authority I do these things.**

Were the priests and elders honest or playing politics when they asked Jesus for his authority to cleanse the temple of merchants? Jesus promised to answer their question if they would answer for him his question. Was the baptism of John the Baptist from man or God? They debated among themselves about how to answer his question. If they replied of man, they feared the people might stone them, for they believed God sent John. If rulers determined that God sent John, they expected Jesus to ask why they refused to submit to his baptism. Therefore they replied they could not tell. Since they refused to answer his question truthfully, he withheld his answer, but taught a parable about two sons which illustrated attitudes of his generation. In the parable the priests and elders portrayed the son who promised to work in the father's vineyard, but didn't go. They agreed to obey God, but rejected the baptism of John. Publicans and harlots signified the son who refused to work in the vineyard, but repented and worked in his father's vineyard. When they listened to John's gospel, they turned from their evil deeds and submitted to John's baptism. Are Christians more like priests or publicans today? Do we obey God or turn from his commands, refusing to submit to Jesus' baptism. Christians who refuse to submit to Jesus' baptism agree with priests. Jesus' baptism is from man, not God.

Luke

20:1 And it came to pass, that on one of
those days, as he taught the people in the
temple, and preached the gospel, the chief
priests and the scribes came upon him
with the elders, 2 And spake unto him,
saying, Tell us, by what authority doest
thou these things? or who is he that gave
thee this authority? 3 And he answered
and said unto them, I will also ask you one
thing; and answer me: 4 The baptism of
John, was it from heaven, or of men? 5
And they reasoned with themselves,
saying, If we shall say, From heaven; he
will say, Why then believed ye him not? 6
But and if we say, Of men; all the people
will stone us: for they be persuaded that
John was a prophet. 7 And they an-
swered, that they could not tell whence it
was. 8 And Jesus said unto them, Neither
tell I you by what authority I do these
things.

Why did only Matthew record the parable of the two sons? If Mark and Luke addressed Gentiles, their main concern rested on helping Gentiles understand John and Jesus preached by the authority of God. Matthew, however, needed to help his Jewish brethren realize that their leaders rebelled against God by refusing John's baptism and by rejecting Jesus as Messiah. John truly called Israel to God's righteousness and prepared them to receive Jesus as the one to restore David's throne. Jesus' words and deeds should convince honest people that God sent him. Only those whose hearts rested on doing their own will could reject John or Jesus. Even today all who hear the gospel must decide whether God sent John and Jesus. Did they speak the truth of God? If we say no, we call God a liar. If we say God sent them, then we must wonder why our age refuses to submit to the truths they proclaimed. Few die to sin with Jesus in baptism to rise with him to a new life. (Rom.6:3-5) In Jesus' parable, which son are we like?

Consider the evidence. Did John and Jesus act and teach by God's authority? John's message of good news to Israel may be summarized by saying that God's kingdom neared. To enter his kingdom when it arrives, you must repent and submit to baptism. John taught that even today there lives among you one whose shoes I'm unworthy to untie. God sent him to usher you into his everlasting kingdom. Keep the righteous deeds of our law. Remember the poor and follow right actions. God's Holy Spirit guided John to identify Jesus as the Lamb of God to remove sins. John even fulfilled the last prophecy of their Scriptures. He demonstrated the spirit of Elijah to return Israel to the living God. (Mal.4:5-6) God sent John. Those who recognized sin in their lives listened to John and knew he came from God, but the self-righteous Pharisees and priests rejected him and his mission to reunite Israel with their God.

Jesus appealed to four witnesses to confirm his truth and prove that God sent him to fulfill all their Scriptures, and he asked his people to consider these four evidences which proved him to be the Messiah: 1) Moses wrote of me. I am the prophet like Moses who speaks all God's truth. God speaks to you through me. (Deu.18:18-19) 2) John testified that I am the one God sent to sit on David's throne. (2 Sam.7:12-14) 3) My miracles prove God sent me as the Messiah. Without God's power, no man can do the wonders I show. 4) Examine your Scriptures, for they testify of me. (Jno.5:32-47) You seek honor of men, not of God. For this reason you will not come to me. (Jno.5:44)

Is recorded evidence insufficient to confirm God sent John as the forerunner and Jesus as the Messiah? Moses stated in their law that in the mouth of two or three witnesses shall every matter be established. (Deu.17:6;19:15; Math.18:16) Are four witnesses sufficient for Christians to believe Jesus is God's Son who must be obeyed?

Matthew

21:33 Hear another parable: There was a certain householder, which planted a vineyard, and hedged it round about, and digged a winepress in it, and built a tower, and let it out to husbandmen, and went into a far country: 34 And when the time of the fruit drew near, he sent his servants to the husbandmen, that they might receive the fruits of it. 35 And the husbandmen took his servants, and beat one, and killed another, and stoned another. 36 Again, he sent other servants more than the first: and they did unto them likewise. 37 But last of all he sent unto them his son, saying, They will reverence my son. 38 But when the husbandmen saw the son, they said among themselves, This is the heir; come, let us kill him, and let us seize on his inheritance. 39 And they caught him, and cast him out of the vineyard, and slew him. 40 When the lord therefore of the vineyard cometh, what will he do unto those husbandmen? 41 They say unto him, He will miserably destroy those wicked men, and will let out his vineyard unto other husbandmen, which shall render him the fruits in their seasons. 42 Jesus saith unto them, Did ye never read in the scriptures, The stone which the builders rejected, the same is become the head of the corner: this is the Lord's doing, and it is marvellous in our eyes? 43 Therefore say I unto you, The kingdom of God shall be taken from you, and given to a nation bringing forth the fruits thereof. 44 And whosoever shall fall on this stone shall be broken: but on whomsoever it shall fall, it will grind him to powder. 45 And when the chief priests and Pharisees had heard his parables, they perceived that he spake of them. 46 But when they sought to lay hands on him, they feared the multitude, because they took him for a prophet.

Mark

12:1 And he began to speak unto them by parables. A certain man planted a vineyard, and set an hedge about it, and digged a place for the winefat, and built a tower, and let it out to husbandmen, and went into a far country. 2 And at the season he sent to the husbandmen a servant, that he might receive from the husbandmen of the fruit of the vineyard. 3 And they caught him, and beat him, and sent him away empty. 4 And again he sent unto them another servant; and at him they cast stones, and wounded him in the head, and sent him away shamefully handled. 5 And again he sent another; and him they killed, and many others; beating some, and killing some. 6 Having yet therefore one son, his wellbeloved, he sent him also last unto them, saying, They will reverence my son. 7 But those husbandmen said among themselves, This is the heir; come, let us kill him, and the inheritance shall be ours. 8 And they took him, and killed him, and cast him out of the vineyard. 9 What shall therefore the lord of the vineyard do? he will come and destroy the husbandmen, and will give the vineyard unto others. 10 And have ye not read this scripture; The stone which the builders rejected is become the head of the corner: 11 This was the Lord's doing, and it is marvellous in our eyes? 12 And they sought to lay hold on him, but feared the people: for they knew that he had spoken the parable against them: and they left him, and went their way.

Identifying parts of Jesus' parable helps us understand its meaning. Vineyard signifies God's people; fruit is righteousness; husbandmen are the leaders of Israel; servants are the prophets; and the son is Jesus. From Moses to John, God sent his prophets, pleading with Israel to return to him. Leaders mistreated and/or killed them. John, God's last messenger before sending his son Jesus, leaders beheaded. Finally, God sent his Son whom they cast out of the vineyard

Luke

20:9 Then began he to speak to the people this parable; A certain man planted a vineyard, and let it forth to husbandmen, and went into a far country for a long time. 10 And at the season he sent a servant to the husbandmen, that they should give him of the fruit of the vineyard: but the husbandmen beat him, and sent him away empty. 11 And again he sent another servant: and they beat him also, and entreated him shamefully, and sent him away empty. 12 And again he sent a third: and they wounded him also, and cast him out. 13 Then said the lord of the vineyard, What shall I do? I will send my beloved son: it may be they will reverence him when they see him. 14 But when the husbandmen saw him, they reasoned among themselves, saying, This is the heir: come, let us kill him, that the inheritance may be ours. 15 So they cast him out of the vineyard, and killed him. What therefore shall the lord of the vineyard do unto them? 16 He shall come and destroy these husbandmen, and shall give the vineyard to others. And when they heard it, they said, God forbid. 17 And he beheld them, and said, What is this then that is written, The stone which the builders rejected, the same is become the head of the corner? 18 Whosoever shall fall upon that stone shall be broken; but on whomsoever it shall fall, it will grind him to powder. 19 And the chief priests and the scribes the same hour sought to lay hands on him; and they feared the people: for they perceived that he had spoken this parable against them.

and hanged on the cross to die. For this offense, God destroyed the leadership of Israel and replaced it with church leaders. Have church leaders encouraged true righteousness? Consider church history during nearly two thousand years. Do we see people and leaders producing the fruits of righteousness of God's vineyard? When new leaders arose to recall men, women, and leaders to the fruits of the kingdom of heaven, how have church leaders treated them? How many have they banished, beaten, ridiculed, debated with and/or burnt at the stake? Is it not the will of God to take the husbandmen of the vineyard of God's church and destroy them for resisting the call to repentance? Was not the Reformation a casting out of the medieval clergy and replacing them with the Protestant husbandmen? How have Protestant clergy fared? Have they resisted the call of God's servants to repentance, turned the back, not listened, beat, banished, flogged, and killed those who called for true righteousness? We see constant decay of righteousness, call to repentance, retaliation, replacing of old unfruitful leaders with new only to start the cycle again. When will there arise faithful leaders who will produce true righteousness God demands of his kingdom? As priests and Pharisees in the days of Jesus desired the fruit for themselves, throughout church history and today churchmen seem to seek a name for themselves by calling their followers by their names rather than call the people of God simply the kingdom of heaven or the church. As leaders of this world fathom that civilization rises and falls in conjunction with the fruits of God's righteousness in his kingdom, hopefully some sound-thinking men will demand the righteousness of God as fruits for the kingdom of heaven. Then shall there be peace on earth and good will toward men.

Present conditions in churches, for the most part, produce only spurious fruits of righteousness. Pomp of rituals and entertainment appeals to man's fleshly interests, abandoning the spirit to starvation. As this darkness gathers, more chaos and hopelessness grips nations. Only the blind fail to see the present state of Christianity. Are we more obedient to Jesus' teaching than the Jews were to Moses' law in Jesus' day? Are we producing fruits of God vineyard?

Luke

**16:1 And he said also unto his disciples,
There was a certain rich man, which had
a steward; and the same was accused unto
him that he had wasted his goods. 2 And
he called him, and said unto him, How is
it that I hear this of thee? give an account
of thy stewardship; for thou mayest be no
longer steward. 3 Then the steward said
within himself, What shall I do? for my
lord taketh away from me the stewardship: I cannot dig; to beg I am ashamed. 4
I am resolved what to do, that, when I am
put out of the stewardship, they may
receive me into their houses. 5 So he
called every one of his lord's debtors unto
him, and said unto the first, How much
owest thou unto my lord? 6 And he said,
An hundred measures of oil. And he said
unto him, Take thy bill, and sit down
quickly, and write fifty. 7 Then said he to
another, And how much owest thou? And
he said, An hundred measures of wheat.
And he said unto him, Take thy bill, and
write fourscore. 8 And the lord commended the unjust steward, because he
had done wisely: for the children of this
world are in their generation wiser than
the children of light. 9 And I say unto you,
Make to yourselves friends of the mammon of unrighteousness; that, when ye
fail, they may receive you into everlasting
habitations. 10 He that is faithful in that
which is least is faithful also in much: and
he that is unjust in the least is unjust also
in much. 11 If therefore ye have not been
faithful in the unrighteous mammon, who
will commit to your trust the true riches?
12 And if ye have not been faithful in that
which is another man's, who shall give
you that which is your own? 13 No servant can serve two masters: for either he
will hate the one, and love the other; or
else he will hold to the one, and despise
the other. Ye cannot serve God and
mammon.**

God entrusts ministers with all the truth of the gospel of God. In it resides the whole truth of the living God. (Deu.18:18; Jno. 15:15; Act.20:27; 1 Pet.5:12) Those who preach and/or teach God's truth find many temptations to dilute it. Worldly minded people resist having to abandon a lifestyle given to gratifying the desires of the mind and flesh. This includes those who reject it. In order to gain respect from ungodly church members and the world, ministers are tempted to soften the truth of God. If they succumb to this temptation, God counts them unfaithful stewards of the grace of God. Paul asked the church in Galatia if he became their enemy because he told them the truth of God. (Gal.4:16) Many Jews believed in Jesus, but when he explained to them that God expected them to be holy like God, they departed from following him. (Jno.8:30-44) Paul admonished Timothy, **"Take heed unto thyself, and unto the doctrine; continue in them: for in doing this thou shalt both save thyself, and them that hear thee."** (1 Tim.4:16) Issues such as women leaders, homosexuals, church organization, and representative assemblies test how ministers function as the stewards of the grace of God today. How any minister of God can promote these concepts mystifies me. Are they good stewards of God? He removes them as his stewards, but the world receives them. The world elevates such ministers to positions of great honor and leadership in their organizations which they call churches. As years pass, those who might be sincerely searching for the complete truth of God hear these God-deposed ministers who proved unjust stewards of God's grace and follow them. They reap loss of eternal life with their ministers.

Sincerely search for God; read and evaluate his truth. Let no minister convince us it is unnecessary to comply with all God's law. Handle that treasure well or God counts us unjust stewards, too. In time, God will replace godless ministers with faithful ones.

Luke

16:14 And the Pharisees also, who were covetous, heard all these things: and they derided him. 15 And he said unto them, Ye are they which justify yourselves before men; but God knoweth your hearts: for that which is highly esteemed among men is abomination in the sight of God. 16 The law and the prophets were until John: since that time the kingdom of God is preached, and every man presseth into it. 17 And it is easier for heaven and earth to pass, than one tittle of the law to fail. 18 Whosoever putteth away his wife, and marrieth another, committeth adultery: and whosoever marrieth her that is put away from her husband committeth adultery. 19 There was a certain rich man, which was clothed in purple and fine linen, and fared sumptuously every day: 20 And there was a certain beggar named Lazarus, which was laid at his gate, full of sores, 21 And desiring to be fed with the crumbs which fell from the rich man's table: moreover the dogs came and licked his sores. 22 And it came to pass, that the beggar died, and was carried by the angels into Abraham's bosom: the rich man also died, and was buried; 23 And in hell he lift up his eyes, being in torments, and seeth Abraham afar off, and Lazarus in his bosom. 24 And he cried and said, Father Abraham, have mercy on me, and send Lazarus, that he may dip the tip of his finger in water, and cool my tongue; for I am tormented in this flame. 25 But Abraham said, Son, remember that thou in thy lifetime receivedst thy good things, and likewise Lazarus evil things: but now he is comforted, and thou art tormented. 26 And beside all this, between us and you there is a great gulf fixed: so that they which would pass from hence to you cannot; neither can they pass to us, that would come from thence. 27 Then he said, I pray thee therefore, father, that thou wouldest send him to my father's house: 28 For I have five brethren; that he may testify unto them, lest they also come into this place of torment. 29 Abraham saith unto him, They have Moses and the prophets; let them hear them. 30 And he said, Nay, father Abraham: but if one went unto them from the dead, they will repent. 31 And he said unto him, If they hear not Moses and the prophets, neither will they be persuaded, though one rose from the dead.

God's law must be obeyed for one to receive God's grace and gain eternal life. He allows no man or group of men to modify his law. Luke considers two precepts of the law of Moses which Pharisees disregarded: 1) Marriage is for life; 2) Show mercy to the poor. Pharisees ignored both. Though they desired to be masters of the law of God, they justified their actions by overlooking God's truth or by changing it. Marriage they canceled for any cause. (Math.19:3) The poor they despised as Luke showed here in the story about Lazarus and the rich man. God requires men to submit to every precept of God with no modifications. Consequences follow for those who do change or blind their eyes to his decrees. In the case of Lazarus and the rich man, the wealthy one suffered torment after death. Having God's law demands we do it. Allowing one to rise from the dead to prompt us to comply with God's truth fails to change our hearts. Has not God raised Jesus from the dead to silence sin in our lives? If we refuse to hear Jesus and his apostles, nothing shall persuade us to submit to God. We shall languish in torment with the rich man, Satan, and his children. (Math.25:41-46)

Revelation records a general church history from apostles to the time God deposes Satan's ministers who infiltrated God's kingdom, modifying God's truth. Revelation's plagues torment those who change God's message and act the part of the unjust steward. (Rev.22:18-19) Ministers and all, submit to our heavenly Father.

John
12:20 And there were certain Greeks
among them that came up to worship at
the feast: 21 The same came therefore to
Philip, which was of Bethsaida of Galilee,
and desired him, saying, Sir, we would see
Jesus. 22 Philip cometh and telleth
Andrew: and again Andrew and Philip
tell Jesus. 23 And Jesus answered them,
saying, The hour is come, that the Son of
man should be glorified. 24 Verily, verily,
I say unto you, Except a corn of wheat fall
into the ground and die, it abideth alone:
but if it die, it bringeth forth much fruit.
25 He that loveth his life shall lose it; and
he that hateth his life in this world shall
keep it unto life eternal. 26 If any man
serve me, let him follow me; and where I
am, there shall also my servant be: if any
man serve me, him will my Father
honour. 27 Now is my soul troubled; and
what shall I say? Father, save me from
this hour: but for this cause came I unto
this hour. 28 Father, glorify thy name.
Then came there a voice from heaven,
saying, I have both glorified it, and will
glorify it again. 29 The people therefore,
that stood by, and heard it, said that it
thundered: others said, An angel spake to
him. 30 Jesus answered and said, This
voice came not because of me, but for
your sakes. 31 Now is the judgment of this
world: now shall the prince of this world
be cast out. 32 And I, if I be lifted up from
the earth, will draw all men unto me. 33
This he said, signifying what death he
should die. 34 The people answered him,
We have heard out of the law that Christ
abideth for ever: and how sayest thou,
The Son of man must be lifted up? who is
this Son of man? 35 Then Jesus said unto
them, Yet a little while is the light with
you. Walk while ye have the light, lest
darkness come upon you: for he that
walketh in darkness knoweth not whither
he goeth. 36 While ye have light, believe in
the light, that ye may be the children of
light. These things spake Jesus, and
departed, and did hide himself from them.
37 But though he had done so many
miracles before them, yet they believed
not on him: 38 That the saying of Esaias
the prophet might be fulfilled, which he
spake, Lord, who hath believed our
report? and to whom hath the arm of the
Lord been revealed?

Multitudes followed Jesus, but few believed him. To show that God extended the hope of eternal life to other nations, John mentioned that Greeks came to see Jesus. When the disciples told Jesus, he replied that time had come for God to glorify him, and God also should be glorified. How was this to be accomplished? Jesus must shatter Satan's power over the race by triumphing over death. He taught a parable of the grain of wheat to illustrate this truth. Unless the life in the grain dies, new life cannot be supplied to many new grains. Through Jesus' death and resurrection, God provides the possibility of a new life to all who believe in Jesus and obey his truths.

Jesus asked God to glorify him that God also be glorified. God spoke to Jesus in the audience of the multitude, saying he had and would continue to glorify Jesus. By dying and God resurrecting him, Jesus becomes King of light to all nations. He crushed Satan's power of darkness over mankind and provided light to all nations.

Why did John enter Philip's name at this point? His gospel would have been just as clear if John had simply recorded that Greeks also came to Jesus. I suggest that since John mentioned Philip in his narrative several times, that John addressed his gospel to people who knew Philip personally, possibly he even labored among them in preaching the gospel. Placing an incidental remark about some mutual friend provides a means of connecting friends and extending friendship. It may have served to add support to Philip's ministry by connecting his name to Jesus' ministry.

John

12:39 Therefore they could not believe, because that Esaias said again, 40 He hath blinded their eyes, and hardened their heart; that they should not see with their eyes, nor understand with their heart, and be converted, and I should heal them. 41 These things said Esaias, when he saw his glory, and spake of him. 42 Nevertheless among the chief rulers also many believed on him; but because of the Pharisees they did not confess him, lest they should be put out of the synagogue: 43 For they loved the praise of men more than the praise of God. 44 Jesus cried and said, He that believeth on me, believeth not on me, but on him that sent me. 45 And he that seeth me seeth him that sent me. 46 I am come a light into the world, that whosoever believeth on me should not abide in darkness. 47 And if any man hear my words, and believe not, I judge him not: for I came not to judge the world, but to save the world. 48 He that rejecteth me, and receiveth not my words, hath one that judgeth him: the word that I have spoken, the same shall judge him in the last day. 49 For I have not spoken of myself; but the Father which sent me, he gave me a commandment, what I should say, and what I should speak. 50 And I know that his commandment is life everlasting: whatsoever I speak therefore, even as the Father said unto me, so I speak.

Spiritual light from God shines only through his truth. (Ps.119:105,130) Jesus spoke all the truth of God. (Jno.15:15) If God's truth frees us from Satan's prison, why did the Jews then and people today shy from the truth of God which Jesus taught? Isaiah encountered the same problem. **"Who hath believed our report? and to whom is the arm of the Lord revealed?"** (Is.53:1) **"Go, and tell this people, Hear ye indeed, but understand not; and see ye indeed, but perceive not. Make the heart of this people fat, and make their ears heavy, and shut their eyes; lest they see with their eyes, and hear with their ears, and understand with their heart, and convert, and be healed."** (Is.6:9-10) Didn't God want Israel to be saved? Yes, but as long as they preferred the praise of man above that of God, their understanding of his truth eluded them. While they or we today choose honor of men, or to please ourselves, God will never open our understanding of his truth. We shall remain in Satan's prison house until the day we die. When we sacrifice our own wills to the will of God then shall he open our insight. We must convert from self to God, otherwise he hides his truth from our eyes and understanding.

Jesus pleaded with his people to walk in the light while they had the light, but they chose darkness. He testified that if they believed on him, they were really believing in God, for he spoke only what God told him. If they rejected God's truth, they chose darkness. In turn, this meant they chose Satan's prison rather than God's freedom; they cherished death instead of everlasting life; they held to confusion in place of peace, and they preferred hatred rather than love and good will.

When we consider the alternatives, it seems inconceivable that even we today make these irrational choices that the Jews made in Isaiah's and Jesus' days. Surely, we ought to see more clearly than they the alternatives.

Are we to profit from history? Reading through the Old Testament, we see Jews suffered terribly when they abandoned the commands of God, but prospered greatly when they obeyed his will. Do we refuse to believe that, **"Righteousness exalteth a nation: but sin is a reproach to any people?"** (Prov.14:34) Will America fall before we learn this lesson? (Ps.9:17)

Today is the day to repent and return to God's truth which Jesus taught. Continuing in pleasing ourselves in how we worship God will end in total chaos.

Matthew

22:1 And Jesus answered and spake unto them again by parables, and said, 2 The kingdom of heaven is like unto a certain king, which made a marriage for his son, 3 And sent forth his servants to call them that were bidden to the wedding: and they would not come. 4 Again, he sent forth other servants, saying, Tell them which are bidden, Behold, I have prepared my dinner: my oxen and my fatlings are killed, and all things are ready: come unto the marriage. 5 But they made light of it, and went their ways, one to his farm, another to his merchandise: 6 And the remnant took his servants, and entreated them spitefully, and slew them. 7 But when the king heard thereof, he was wroth: and he sent forth his armies, and destroyed those murderers, and burned up their city. 8 Then saith he to his servants, The wedding is ready, but they which were bidden were not worthy. 9 Go ye therefore into the highways, and as many as ye shall find, bid to the marriage. 10 So those servants went out into the highways, and gathered together all as many as they found, both bad and good: and the wedding was furnished with guests. 11 And when the king came in to see the guests, he saw there a man which had not on a wedding garment: 12 And he saith unto him, Friend, how camest thou in hither not having a wedding garment? And he was speechless. 13 Then said the king to the servants, Bind him hand and foot, and take him away, and cast him into outer darkness; there shall be weeping and gnashing of teeth. 14 For many are called, but few are chosen.

Parables of the marriage feast and vineyard confirm Daniel's and Jesus' promise to destroy Jerusalem with its worship. (Dan. 9:24-27; Math.21:33-46; Mk.12:7-12; Lk. 20:9-19) God often sent his prophets to call Jews to his marriage feast, but they refused to attend. Now God calls Gentiles.

Luke

14:1 And it came to pass, as he went into the house of one of the chief Pharisees to eat bread on the sabbath day, that they watched him. 2 And, behold, there was a certain man before him which had the dropsy. 3 And Jesus answering spake unto the lawyers and Pharisees, saying, Is it lawful to heal on the sabbath day? 4 And they held their peace. And he took him, and healed him, and let him go; 5 And answered them, saying, Which of you shall have an ass or an ox fallen into a pit, and will not straightway pull him out on the sabbath day? 6 And they could not answer him again to these things. 7 And he put forth a parable to those which were bidden, when he marked how they chose out the chief rooms; saying unto them, 8 When thou art bidden of any man to a wedding, sit not down in the highest room; lest a more honourable man than thou be bidden of him; 9 And he that bade thee and him come and say to thee, Give this man place; and thou begin with shame to take the lowest room. 10 But when thou art bidden, go and sit down in the lowest room; that when he that bade thee cometh, he may say unto thee, Friend, go up higher: then shalt thou have worship in the presence of them that sit at meat with thee. 11 For whosoever exalteth himself shall be abased; and he that humbleth himself shall be exalted. 12 Then said he also to him that bade him, When thou makest a dinner or a supper, call not thy friends, nor thy brethren, neither thy kinsmen, nor thy rich neighbours; lest they also bid thee again, and a recompence be made thee. 13 But when thou makest a feast, call the poor, the maimed, the lame, the blind: 14 And thou shalt be blessed; for they cannot recompense thee: for thou shalt be recompensed at the resurrection of the just. 15 And when one of them that sat at meat with him heard these things, he said unto

him, Blessed is he that shall eat bread in the kingdom of God. 16 Then said he unto him, A certain man made a great supper, and bade many: 17 And sent his servant at supper time to say to them that were bidden, Come; for all things are now ready. 18 And they all with one consent began to make excuse. The first said unto him, I have bought a piece of ground, and I must needs go and see it: I pray thee have me excused. 19 And another said, I have bought five yoke of oxen, and I go to prove them: I pray thee have me excused. 20 And another said, I have married a wife, and therefore I cannot come. 21 So that servant came, and shewed his lord these things. Then the master of the house being angry said to his servant, Go out quickly into the streets and lanes of the city, and bring in hither the poor, and the maimed, and the halt, and the blind. 22 And the servant said, Lord, it is done as thou hast commanded, and yet there is room. 23 And the lord said unto the servant, Go out into the highways and hedges, and compel them to come in, that my house may be filled. 24 For I say unto you, That none of those men which were bidden shall taste of my supper. 25 And there went great multitudes with him: and he turned, and said unto them, 26 If any man come to me, and hate not his father, and mother, and wife, and children, and brethren, and sisters, yea, and his own life also, he cannot be my disciple. 27 And whosoever doth not bear his cross, and come after me, cannot be my disciple. 28 For which of you, intending to build a tower, sitteth not down first, and counteth the cost, whether he have sufficient to finish it? 29 Lest haply, after he hath laid the foundation, and is not able to finish it, all that behold it begin to mock him, 30 Saying, This man began to build, and was not able to finish. 31 Or what king, going to make war against another king, sitteth not down first, and consulteth whether he be able with ten thousand to meet him that cometh against him with twenty thousand? 32 Or else, while the other is yet a great way off, he sendeth an ambassage, and desireth conditions of peace. 33 So likewise, whosoever he be of you that forsaketh not all that he hath, he cannot be my disciple. 34 Salt is good: but if the salt have lost his savour, wherewith shall it be seasoned? 35 It is neither fit for the land, nor yet for the dunghill; but men cast it out. He that hath ears to hear, let him hear.

Few attended God's Son's marriage feast, but one attending arrived without a marriage garment, signifying he obeyed not God's gospel. God cast him into outer darkness.

What is God's marriage feast? Jesus is the bridegroom of the church, his bride. (Jno. 3:29; Eph.5:23-32; Rev.21:2-10) God invites Jews and Gentiles to enjoy blessings of his kingdom, the church. (Math.16:18-19) Jews and Gentiles disregard or make light of God's invitation to his Son's marriage. Those who attend his feast enter God's kingdom of heaven.

Revelation identifies a second disdain of God's marriage feast after which God destroys Babylon the Great, the corrupt church, Gentile rebel city, which followed the example of Jewish rebellion. (Rev.17:1-18)

God calls every person to his Son's marriage, but not many attend. Would we ignore an invitation to dine with the President of the U.S.A.? Why then do we treat the greatest King so lightly? Are we so attached to this life we don't care?

Jesus requires all to make a genuine commitment. He illustrated this with three parables: 1) Family members must take second place in God's kingdom; 2) Don't consider building a house without first determining the expected cost; 3) Kings consider the enemy's strength before going to battle. **"No man can serve two masters:....Ye cannot serve God and mammon."** (Math.6:24)

Matthew

22:15 Then went the Pharisees, and took counsel how they might entangle him in his talk. 16 And they sent out unto him their disciples with the Herodians, saying, Master, we know that thou art true, and teachest the way of God in truth, neither carest thou for any man: for thou regardest not the person of men. 17 Tell us therefore, What thinkest thou? Is it lawful to give tribute unto Caesar, or not? 18 But Jesus perceived their wickedness, and said, Why tempt ye me, ye hypocrites? 19 Shew me the tribute money. And they brought unto him a penny. 20 And he saith unto them, Whose is this image and superscription? 21 They say unto him, Caesar's. Then saith he unto them, Render therefore unto Caesar the things which are Caesar's; and unto God the things that are God's. 22 When they had heard these words, they marvelled, and left him, and went their way.

Each gospel writer included situations which helped his intended audience understand the nature of God's kingdom. Those entering the kingdom of heaven needed to understand its relationship to nations and empires. Are those in God's kingdom to submit to civil rulers? Do Christians honor civil rulers for their positions in government? Shall Christians pay taxes to support governments when they disregard God's laws? Such questions need genuine God-given answers, particularly in the case of Theophilus whom Luke addressed. Gospels note that Pharisees approached Jesus on this matter, hoping to hear Jesus issue statements which violated Roman law and make him subject to the governor's penalty.

What responsibility do Christians have to civil rulers? Jesus taught that some matters belong to civil rulers and others to God's kingdom. Taxes, honor, punishing offenders, and submission all belong to civil rulers. Apostles reminded churches of God's order to obey kings and all rulers. (Rom.13:1-8)

Mark

12:13 And they send unto him certain of the Pharisees and of the Herodians, to catch him in his words. 14 And when they were come, they say unto him, Master, we know that thou art true, and carest for no man: for thou regardest not the person of men, but teachest the way of God in truth: Is it lawful to give tribute to Caesar, or not? 15 Shall we give, or shall we not give? But he, knowing their hypocrisy, said unto them, Why tempt ye me? bring me a penny, that I may see it. 16 And they brought it. And he saith unto them, Whose is this image and superscription? And they said unto him, Caesar's. 17 And Jesus answering said unto them, Render to Caesar the things that are Caesar's, and to God the things that are God's. And they marvelled at him.

"Let every soul be subject unto the higher powers. For there is no power but of God: the powers that be are ordained of God. Whosoever therefore resisteth the power, resisteth the ordinance of God: and they that resist shall receive to themselves damnation. For rulers are not a terror to good works, but to the evil. Wilt thou then not be afraid of the power? do that which is good, and thou shalt have praise of the same. For he is the minister of God to thee for good. But if thou do that which is evil, be afraid; for he beareth not the sword in vain: for he is the minister of God, a revenger to execute wrath upon him that doeth evil. Wherefore ye must needs be subject, not only for wrath, but also for conscience sake. For for this cause pay ye tribute also: for they are God's ministers, attending continually upon this very thing. Render therefore to all their dues: tribute to whom tribute is due; custom to whom custom; honour to whom honour." (Rom. 13:1-7) Understanding God's system, we must submit to civil rulers to escape punishment and to preserve a good conscience.

Luke

20:20 And they watched him, and sent forth spies, which should feign themselves just men, that they might take hold of his words, that so they might deliver him unto the power and authority of the governor. 21 And they asked him, saying, Master, we know that thou sayest and teachest rightly, neither acceptest thou the person of any, but teachest the way of God truly: 22 Is it lawful for us to give tribute unto Caesar, or no? 23 But he perceived their craftiness, and said unto them, Why tempt ye me? 24 Shew me a penny. Whose image and superscription hath it? They answered and said, Caesar's. 25 And he said unto them, Render therefore unto Caesar the things which be Caesar's, and unto God the things which be God's. 26 And they could not take hold of his words before the people: and they marvelled at his answer, and held their peace.

Once God's people understand civil rulers are God's revengers of unrighteousness, we see that civil and religious leaders complement, not conflict with each other. Civil rulers compliment or punish actions regulated by the second through the ninth commandments. Church leaders deal with the first and tenth commandments, or violations of serving God and loving our neighbor. Civil rulers punish physically; churchmen correct the heart and mind.

When the Pharisees claimed Jesus showed no respect to any man, they failed to perceive Jesus taught minds and aimed to correct hearts. Before God, all minds and hearts are equal. Before the civil law all men must be commended or punished equally. One's level of prosperity or social standing should not alter his degree of guilt or innocence. Since all men, women, and children are created in God's image, each should be respected as God's child. Jesus honored all people. Evil and dishonest minds and hearts he exposed. He encouraged every person to love his neighbor and enemy by treating them as he wished to be treated. (Math.7:12) When we reach for this goal, we, too, honor all people, but show no special respect to our friends when they violate civil law and/or their own consciences by not loving others.

Pharisees accused Jesus of respecting no person. It was their minds and hearts that could not distinguish between respect and favoritism. Satan's system functions on favoritism; God's on respect. Satan's children favor those who favor them. God's children honor every person, but show not favoritism. We seek to help everyone understand he/she is important, that each feels respected, regardless of age, race, wealth, social status, formal education, intelligence, etc. God's system elevates each person; Satan's treads down.

Even when all nations and peoples enter God's kingdom, civil rulers shall continue to revenge evil and commend good. Churchmen during the Middle Ages failed to grasp this separation of powers Jesus taught. They often exercised physical force and punished physically. Countless lives perished wrongly because they transgressed church ordinances. Imprisonment, sword, or burning at the stake in addition to excommunication appeared to them proper means to compel their subjects to submit to church ordinances. Such violence God has not authorized for churchmen to exercise. This falls in the realm of civil rulers.

During the days when Israel operated under a theocracy, judges and kings exercised both civil and religious revenge, but they often punished those who served God faithfully. God's wisdom now separates the two spheres of dominion. When each realm abides by God's system of punishment and commendation, peace prevails, and neither infringes on the other's God-given duty.

Let each person who considers himself or herself be conscience bound to obey their rulers. This respects God and Jesus.

Matthew

22:23 The same day came to him the Sadducees, which say that there is no resurrection, and asked him, 24 Saying, Master, Moses said, If a man die, having no children, his brother shall marry his wife, and raise up seed unto his brother. 25 Now there were with us seven brethren: and the first, when he had married a wife, deceased, and, having no issue, left his wife unto his brother: 26 Likewise the second also, and the third, unto the seventh. 27 And last of all the woman died also. 28 Therefore in the resurrection whose wife shall she be of the seven? for they all had her. 29 Jesus answered and said unto them, Ye do err, not knowing the scriptures, nor the power of God. 30 For in the resurrection they neither marry, nor are given in marriage, but are as the angels of God in heaven. 31 But as touching the resurrection of the dead, have ye not read that which was spoken unto you by God, saying, 32 I am the God of Abraham, and the God of Isaac, and the God of Jacob? God is not the God of the dead, but of the living. 33 And when the multitude heard this, they were astonished at his doctrine.

Doctrine of the resurrection divided Jews into sects: Pharisees and Sadducees. Paul met this issue when Jews accused him before the council. (Act.23:6-8) He noted that Pharisees expected a resurrection of the dead, but Sadducees denied the resurrection. (Act.24:15) God promised Jewish fathers a resurrection. (Act.26:6) In fact, God promised eternal life before creation. (Tit.1:2-3), but manifested it by raising Jesus from the dead. (1 Cor.15:20-21) Sadducees faltered on the resurrection on two accounts: 1) They didn't know their own Scriptures; 2) They didn't trust the power of God. Jesus silenced their opposition by showing that God served as God to Abraham, Isaac, and Jacob even in Moses' days. He serves as God of the living, not the dead.

Mark

12:18 Then come unto him the Sadducees, which say there is no resurrection; and they asked him, saying, 19 Master, Moses wrote unto us, If a man's brother die, and leave his wife behind him, and leave no children, that his brother should take his wife, and raise up seed unto his brother. 20 Now there were seven brethren: and the first took a wife, and dying left no seed. 21 And the second took her, and died, neither left he any seed: and the third likewise. 22 And the seven had her, and left no seed: last of all the woman died also. 23 In the resurrection therefore, when they shall rise, whose wife shall she be of them? for the seven had her to wife. 24 And Jesus answering said unto them, Do ye not therefore err, because ye know not the scriptures, neither the power of God? 25 For when they shall rise from the dead, they neither marry, nor are given in marriage; but are as the angels which are in heaven. 26 And as touching the dead, that they rise: have ye not read in the book of Moses, how in the bush God spake unto him, saying, I am the God of Abraham, and the God of Isaac, and the God of Jacob? 27 He is not the God of the dead, but the God of the living: ye therefore do greatly err.

Therefore Abraham, Isaac, and Jacob are living, and not dead as Sadducees supposed. Jesus' answer astonished the people. Unbelievers today stagger on the doctrine of the resurrection for the same two reasons.

Among those who consider themselves Christians today exists a group who teach that only a very small group shall be raised from the dead. They continue the philosophy of the Sadducees. To foster their belief, they publish their own version of the Bible, but even their own book carries the same message: there shall be a general resurrection of all who have lived. God will require all to account for life's deeds when God raises all who have died. (Jno.5:25-29)

Luke

20:27 Then came to him certain of the Sadducees, which deny that there is any resurrection; and they asked him, 28 Saying, Master, Moses wrote unto us, If any man's brother die, having a wife, and he die without children, that his brother should take his wife, and raise up seed unto his brother. 29 There were therefore seven brethren: and the first took a wife, and died without children. 30 And the second took her to wife, and he died childless. 31 And the third took her; and in like manner the seven also: and they left no children, and died. 32 Last of all the woman died also. 33 Therefore in the resurrection whose wife of them is she? for seven had her to wife. 34 And Jesus answering said unto them, The children of this world marry, and are given in marriage: 35 But they which shall be accounted worthy to obtain that world, and the resurrection from the dead, neither marry, nor are given in marriage: 36 Neither can they die any more: for they are equal unto the angels; and are the children of God, being the children of the resurrection. 37 Now that the dead are raised, even Moses shewed at the bush, when he calleth the Lord the God of Abraham, and the God of Isaac, and the God of Jacob. 38 For he is not a God of the dead, but of the living: for all live unto him.

Sadducees knew not their own Scriptures nor the power of God to call all people from the grave. If people cling to God, why can't they take him at his word? If he is God, the Creator of heaven and earth and all that is in them, why question his ability to call a halt to everything he created? Is it impossible for him to cancel the power of the Evil One who introduced death into the world by convincing man that disobedience to God will not result in death? In God's truth there is no clearer message than that Jesus shall overcome and destroy every work of the devil and that death shall be destroyed. Every person having lived shall rise from the dead. Afterward, God authorizes Jesus to call each person to give account of how he used life with its blessings. (1 Cor.15:52-55; 2 Cor. 5:10-11; 1 Thes.4:15-17; Heb.2:27) In a sense, the parable of talents may be applied to resurrection and judgment. God entrusts each of us with life, and each must give account of how we use God's talents which he has given to us. If we gain the abundant life of which Jesus promised, we use life as God decreed, but if we use not the talent of life well, God will hold us accountable for misuse of his gift. Therefore, the talent of life is not for us to use as we please. God demands we use it to glorify him. (Ps.12:4)

Those who gladly anticipate meeting their Creator know they have used life to benefit others, but they who dread to face God in judgment know well they squandered the gift of God. They wish to remove from their minds the awful thought of having to face God for unproductive and ungodly lives. To put this out of our minds is to act like the Sadducees who, by denying the resurrection, manifested to all that they were ignorant of the Scriptures and the power of God.

A segment of our society attempts to remove the threat of accountability in judgment by saying they don't believe there is a God. This is not new. Three thousand years ago the psalmist recorded, "**The fool hath said in his heart, There is no God. They are corrupt, they have done abominable works, there is none that doeth good.**" (Ps.14:1) What profit does one gain by claiming that a rose is not a rose, that there is no such thing as color, that a cow is not a cow? It only shows one's ignorance to deny truth and fact. Denying a resurrection of all who ever lived equates to a criminal who thinks he shall never have to pay for his crimes. Day of retribution will come. Our denying this truth shall not change God's promise. He will judge each of us as to how we used life, obediently or disobediently.

Matthew

**22:34 But when the Pharisees had heard
that he had put the Sadducees to silence,
they were gathered together. 35 Then one
of them, which was a lawyer, asked him a
question, tempting him, and saying, 36
Master, which is the great commandment
in the law? 37 Jesus said unto him, Thou
shalt love the Lord thy God with all thy
heart, and with all thy soul, and with all
thy mind. 38 This is the first and great
commandment. 39 And the second is like
unto it, Thou shalt love thy neighbour as
thyself. 40 On these two commandments
hang all the law and the prophets.**

How one conducts himself/herself in relation to God and others determines his/her quality of life. Since the first commandment asks that we love God with all our heart, mind, and soul, if one lives in such a way that God dwells with and in him/her, a good relationship with God follows. Similarly, when a person shows kindness and respect to and with every person with whom he/she contacts, there will always continue a pleasant quality of life with each. An abundant life results. If, however, our relationship with God continues to be denial of or a hiding from God, misery follows. Equally dissatisfying are associations with others when there exists a continual complaining, displeasure, or annoyance. Realizing this, is it any wonder that God has identified loving God and man as the two greatest commandments? Listen to Peter on this matter. "**For he that will love life, and see good days, let him refrain his tongue from evil, and his lips that they speak no guile.**" (1 Pet.3:10) Good life begins and continues by obeying God's commands. When the lawyer agreed with Jesus' comment, Jesus remarked that he was not far from the kingdom of God.

Though I may be convinced that loving God and man are the two greatest commands, without showing this love, I remain outside God's kingdom and the abundant life which obeying these two commands brings.

Mark

**12:28 And one of the scribes came, and
having heard them reasoning together,
and perceiving that he had answered
them well, asked him, Which is the first
commandment of all? 29 And Jesus
answered him, The first of all the
commandments is, Hear, O Israel; The
Lord our God is one Lord: 30 And thou
shalt love the Lord thy God with all thy
heart, and with all thy soul, and with all
thy mind, and with all thy strength: this is
the first commandment. 31 And the
second is like, namely this, Thou shalt love
thy neighbour as thyself. There is none
other commandment greater than these.
32 And the scribe said unto him, Well,
Master, thou hast said the truth: for there
is one God; and there is none other but
he: 33 And to love him with all the heart,
and with all the understanding, and with
all the soul, and with all the strength, and
to love his neighbour as himself, is more
than all whole burnt offerings and
sacrifices. 34 And when Jesus saw that he
answered discreetly, he said unto him,
Thou art not far from the kingdom of
God. And no man after that durst ask him
any question.**

For what reason did one offer sacrifices under the law of Moses? Was it not to atone for offenses? (Lev.6:5; Math.5:23) The scribe understood that if one loved God so he neither offended God nor man, no sacrifice should be needed. Which is better: to refrain from offending or to correct a wrong? Do I find it easier to confess that I mistreated a person or to prevent injuring the person? Personally, I find it more difficult to apologize for transgression than to do the kind deed in the beginning. Most people prefer not having to correct wrongs. If keeping God's commands will deliver me from the weakness to transgress the interests of another person for which I must make amends to honor God, then I should ask God for wisdom and strength not to offend.

Luke

10:25 And, behold, a certain lawyer stood
up, and tempted him, saying, Master,
what shall I do to inherit eternal life? 26
He said unto him, What is written in the
law? how readest thou? 27 And he
answering said, Thou shalt love the Lord
thy God with all thy heart, and with all
thy soul, and with all thy strength, and
with all thy mind; and thy neighbour as
thyself. 28 And he said unto him, Thou
hast answered right: this do, and thou
shalt live. 29 But he, willing to justify
himself, said unto Jesus, And who is my
neighbour? 30 And Jesus answering said,
A certain man went down from Jerusalem
to Jericho, and fell among thieves, which
stripped him of his raiment, and wounded
him, and departed, leaving him half dead.
31 And by chance there came down a
certain priest that way: and when he saw
him, he passed by on the other side. 32
And likewise a Levite, when he was at the
place, came and looked on him, and
passed by on the other side. 33 But a
certain Samaritan, as he journeyed, came
where he was: and when he saw him, he
had compassion on him, 34 And went to
him, and bound up his wounds, pouring in
oil and wine, and set him on his own
beast, and brought him to an inn, and
took care of him. 35 And on the morrow
when he departed, he took out two pence,
and gave them to the host, and said unto
him, Take care of him; and whatsoever
thou spendest more, when I come again, I
will repay thee. 36 Which now of these
three, thinkest thou, was neighbour unto
him that fell among the thieves? 37 And
he said, He that shewed mercy on him.
Then said Jesus unto him, Go, and do
thou likewise.

Luke's gospel states that the lawyer asked how he might gain eternal life. Jesus asked how he read the law. He replied that loving God with his whole being and loving one's neighbor as himself produced eternal life. Jesus agreed. If you do this, you shall have eternal life.

To justify himself, the lawyer asked who was his neighbor. Using a story, Jesus related a situation where a man traveling from Jerusalem to Jericho fell among thieves who wounded him, took his goods, and left him half dead. A priest passing that way saw the half-dead man and passed on. Not long thereafter, a Levite came by and beheld the man's condition, but went on his way without giving help. Afterward a Samaritan approached and, seeing the plight of the man, showed compassion by treating his wounds, setting him on his own beast, and took him to an inn where he paid the innkeeper to care for the wounded man. Before leaving, the Samaritan promised to pay any additional cost to care for the injured man, when he returned. Jesus asked the lawyer which man acted as a neighbor? It was he who showed mercy replied the lawyer. If you do likewise to those needing help, you will be a neighbor.

Christians, are we more like the priest, Levite, or Samaritan? To love God and man, we must extend help to those who need. Levites and priests had taught the concept of love your neighbor as yourself for 1500 years, but they failed to practice it. Moses addressed the command to love one's neighbor as himself primarily to the priests and Levites to teach to Israel. (Lev.19:18) That's wisdom of the just, and Luke's theme is to turn the disobedient to the wisdom of the just. (Lk.1:17)

You and I inherit eternal life by showing the compassion and love of the Samaritan to our neighbors. If we sincerely desire eternal life, let's pray to our heavenly Father for strength to demonstrate the compassion and love Jesus taught the lawyer. God will show us compassion by granting us that eternal life which he promised before creation. (Tit.1:2) Do we believe Jesus' words are God's promises? If we do, then seek eternal life by showing God's children mercy.

Matthew

22:41 While the Pharisees were gathered together, Jesus asked them, 42 Saying, What think ye of Christ? whose son is he? They say unto him, The Son of David. 43 He saith unto them, How then doth David in spirit call him Lord, saying, 44 The LORD said unto my Lord, Sit thou on my right hand, till I make thine enemies thy footstool? 45 If David then call him Lord, how is he his son? 46 And no man was able to answer him a word, neither durst any man from that day forth ask him any more questions.

Lord means king. How could David refer to Christ as his king when Jews looked to David as a great king? From the Jews' viewpoint, there was no answer. From God's perspective, the answer was simple. David ruled as a civil king; Christ reigns as spiritual King. David's dominion extended from Egypt to Euphrates River as God promised Israel. (Gen.15:18) Christ, being King of kings, and Prince of kings on earth, rules above every king on earth, including David. (1 Tim.6:15; Rev.19:16) The dominions of David and Christ lie in different realms. Therefore, David could call Christ his Lord. Jesus' laws govern every king on earth, but not all submit. (Heb.2:8)

Mark

12:35 And Jesus answered and said, while he taught in the temple, How say the scribes that Christ is the Son of David? 36 For David himself said by the Holy Ghost, The LORD said to my Lord, Sit thou on my right hand, till I make thine enemies thy footstool. 37 David therefore himself calleth him Lord; and whence is he then his son? And the common people heard him gladly.

Addressing strangers, Mark emphasized that even David, Israel's great king, referred to Christ as David's Lord, suggesting civil rulers should submit to Christ. Common people listened to what Jesus taught. Mark may have written for common people among the Romans.

David penned this prophecy about Christ to show his own standing as compared to that of Christ and to indicate where Christ's throne rested. (Ps.110:1) Christ (anointed Lord) shall sit at the right hand of the Lord (God) until God subdues all Christ's enemies. From this psalm, it should be clear that Jesus rules from heaven, not on earth, until all his enemies bow to him. Jews then and many today anticipate an earthly throne in Jerusalem for Christ. We need to believe God's way.

Is it proper for a father to

Luke

20:39 Then certain of the scribes answering said, Master, thou hast well said. 40 And after that they durst not ask him any question at all. 41 And he said unto them, How say they that Christ is David's son? 42 And David himself saith in the book of Psalms, The LORD said unto my Lord, Sit thou on my right hand, 43 Till I make thine enemies thy footstool. 44 David therefore calleth him Lord, how is he then his son?

call his son lord? Yet David called his son Lord. This mystified the scribes. They believed David spoke by the inspiration of God's Spirit. Without events in the New Testament no person could have understood how this might happen. On the day of Pentecost in Acts chapter two, Peter explained. God raised up Jesus from the dead to sit on David's throne. God had made Jesus both Lord and Christ. (Act.2:34-36) Peter and John explained the heavens must retain Jesus until the restoration of all things. (Act. 3:21) Jesus now sits on David's throne at the right hand of the Majesty on high to serve as our high priest and king. (Zech.6:12-13; Heb.1:3) Is it unwise for Christians to perpetuate the Jewish error that Christ shall reign in Jerusalem? God says he reigns in heaven.

Matthew

23:1 Then spake Jesus to the multitude, and to his disciples, 2 Saying, The scribes and the Pharisees sit in Moses' seat: 3 All therefore whatsoever they bid you observe, that observe and do; but do not ye after their works: for they say, and do not. 4 For they bind heavy burdens and grievous to be borne, and lay them on men's shoulders; but they themselves will not move them with one of their fingers. 5 But all their works they do for to be seen of men: they make broad their phylacteries, and enlarge the borders of their garments, 6 And love the uppermost rooms at feasts, and the chief seats in the synagogues, 7 And greetings in the markets, and to be called of men, Rabbi, Rabbi. 8 But be not ye called Rabbi: for one is your Master, even Christ; and all ye are brethren. 9 And call no man your father upon the earth: for one is your Father, which is in heaven. 10 Neither be ye called masters: for one is your Master, even Christ. 11 But he that is greatest among you shall be your servant. 12 And whosoever shall exalt himself shall be abased; and he that shall humble himself shall be exalted.

Mark

12:38 And he said unto them in his doctrine, Beware of the scribes, which love to go in long clothing, and love salutations in the marketplaces, 39 And the chief seats in the synagogues, and the uppermost rooms at feasts: 40 Which devour widows' houses, and for a pretense make long prayers: these shall receive greater damnation.

Luke

20:45 Then in the audience of all the people he said unto his disciples, 46 Beware of the scribes, which desire to walk in long robes, and love greetings in the markets, and the highest seats in the synagogues, and the chief rooms at feasts; 47 Which devour widows' houses, and for a shew make long prayers: the same shall receive greater damnation.

Those who know not God rely on outward show to make themselves appear great. Satan influenced Jewish leaders to use pomp to gain respect of those who noticed their piety. Long robes, high-sounding titles, sitting in chief places at feasts and in the synagogues gained them the respect they desired from their peers and the people. God looks at the inward person of the spirit and sees what man often overlooks. Is it the high and mighty that generate lasting friendships or the humble? Genuine kindness and mercy proceeds not from the one who puts on an air of greatness. God sent Jesus to awaken men and women to mercy generated by concern for the well-being of others. Compassion reaches into the soul; pomp reaches the eye.

One would think Christian ministers could escape Satan's fraudulent paths, but we are in his power when we rely not on God's word to strengthen us. (Eph.3:16)

Satan drives us to dishonor one another just as the priest and Levite did. We observe with admiration those who pose as ministers of Jesus, wearing long robes or special clothing to distinguish them as the clergy. They desire special religious titles as Father, Holy Father, Reverend, Right Reverend, Holy Lord, Doctor, etc. These special greetings appeal to them. It sets them above the common people or laity. How can we reconcile these distinguishing garbs and titles with Jesus' message from our heavenly Father?

Christian leaders must be brethren, not lords of God's flock; be servants, not served. If we are Christians, we should be like Christ, not rule as lords over God's heritage as Gentile rulers. (1 Pet.5:1-3) Are we as blind as Jewish leaders: teachers, but not doers? None of us can show kindness to every person, but we must use the opportunities God gives us.

Matthew

23:13 But woe unto you, scribes and Pharisees, hypocrites! for ye shut up the kingdom of heaven against men: for ye neither go in yourselves, neither suffer ye them that are entering to go in. 14 Woe unto you, scribes and Pharisees, hypocrites! for ye devour widows' houses, and for a pretence make long prayer: therefore ye shall receive the greater damnation. 15 Woe unto you, scribes and Pharisees, hypocrites! for ye compass sea and land to make one proselyte, and when he is made, ye make him twofold more the child of hell than yourselves. 16 Woe unto you, ye blind guides, which say, Whosoever shall swear by the temple, it is nothing; but whosoever shall swear by the gold of the temple, he is a debtor! 17 Ye fools and blind: for whether is greater, the gold, or the temple that sanctifieth the gold? 18 And, Whosoever shall swear by the altar, it is nothing; but whosoever sweareth by the gift that is upon it, he is guilty. 19 Ye fools and blind: for whether is greater, the gift, or the altar that sanctifieth the gift? 20 Whoso therefore shall swear by the altar, sweareth by it, and by all things thereon. 21 And whoso shall swear by the temple, sweareth by it, and by him that dwelleth therein. 22 And he that shall swear by heaven, sweareth by the throne of God, and by him that sitteth thereon. 23 Woe unto you, scribes and Pharisees, hypocrites! for ye pay tithe of mint and anise and cummin, and have omitted the weightier matters of the law, judgment, mercy, and faith: these ought ye to have done, and not to leave the other undone. 24 Ye blind guides, which strain at a gnat, and swallow a camel. 25 Woe unto you, scribes and Pharisees, hypocrites! for ye make clean the outside of the cup and of the platter, but within they are full of extortion and excess. 26 Thou blind Pharisee, cleanse first that which is within the cup and platter, that the outside of them may be clean also. 27 Woe unto you, scribes and Pharisees, hypocrites! for ye are like unto whited sepulchres, which indeed appear beautiful outward, but are within full of dead men's bones, and of all uncleanness. 28 Even so ye also outwardly appear righteous unto men, but within ye are full of hypocrisy and iniquity. 29 Woe unto you, scribes and Pharisees, hypocrites! because ye build the tombs of the prophets, and garnish the sepulchres of the righteous, 30 And say, If we had been in the days of our fathers, we would not have been partakers with them in the blood of the prophets. 31 Wherefore ye be witnesses unto yourselves, that ye are the children of them which killed the prophets. 32 Fill ye up then the measure of your fathers. 33 Ye serpents, ye generation of vipers, how can ye escape the damnation of hell?

Religious leaders in Jesus' day knew not God. They barred entrance into God's kingdom by denying the truth Jesus spoke and discouraged others from listening to Jesus. They claimed he wasn't from God. (Jno.9:16), that he cast out devils by Satan's power (Math.12:24), by saying that they didn't know his origin (Jno.9:30), and by threatening to exclude from the synagogue those who accepted Jesus as Christ. (Jno.9: 22) Their tactics dissuaded many from obeying God's truth Jesus taught. (Ja.3:1)

Scribes and Pharisees persuaded widows to give all they possessed to them, then they used the proceeds for personal gratification. They zealously proselyted others to submit to their godless doctrines, making converts more sinful than they were before listening to their leaders. Scribes and Pharisees glorified physical appearance and wealth in place of encouraging spiritual well-being. They substituted favoritism for God's judgment, mercy, and faith. They practiced the arts of the Evil One and knew not the God of heaven who respects not man's person. Rather than demonstrating faith in

Luke

**11:37 And as he spake, a certain Pharisee
besought him to dine with him: and he
went in, and sat down to meat. 38 And
when the Pharisee saw it, he marvelled
that he had not first washed before
dinner. 39 And the Lord said unto him,
Now do ye Pharisees make clean the
outside of the cup and the platter; but
your inward part is full of ravening and
wickedness. 40 Ye fools, did not he that
made that which is without make that
which is within also? 41 But rather give
alms of such things as ye have; and,
behold, all things are clean unto you. 42
But woe unto you, Pharisees! for ye tithe
mint and rue and all manner of herbs,
and pass over judgment and the love of
God: these ought ye to have done, and not
to leave the other undone. 43 Woe unto
you, Pharisees! for ye love the uppermost
seats in the synagogues, and greetings in
the markets. 44 Woe unto you, scribes and
Pharisees, hypocrites! for ye are as graves
which appear not, and the men that walk
over them are not aware of them. 45 Then
answered one of the lawyers, and said
unto him, Master, thus saying thou
reproachest us also. 46 And he said, Woe
unto you also, ye lawyers! for ye lade men
with burdens grievous to be borne, and ye
yourselves touch not the burdens with one
of your fingers. 47 Woe unto you! for ye
build the sepulchres of the prophets, and
your fathers killed them. 48 Truly ye bear
witness that ye allow the deeds of your
fathers: for they indeed killed them, and
ye build their sepulchres.**

God's truth spoken by Jesus, they made their own rules. For mercy they talked of kindness, helping the unfortunate, but provided little help for the needy. They could not forgive offenses. They adorned the visible body well, but permitted the inward being to languish in hatred, envy, bitterness, lust, and other deeds that darken men's lives. They bemoaned how their forefathers persecuted and killed God's prophets and claimed they would not have participated in slaying God's prophets and messengers. In fact, they belittled and killed John the Baptist and proceeded to do the same to Jesus, God's greatest prophet.

Does Christianity today groan under godless leaders as did Israel in the first century A.D.? Do present-day Christian leaders shut up the kingdom of heaven to those who would enter by denying the need to submit to all God's truth which Jesus taught? For example, among us many deny the need of faith and/or baptism. Catholic and some Protestant leaders affirm christening at birth as an appropriate substitute for baptism even without faith within the heart of the infant. Others stress faith in their creeds, but deny true burial-in-water baptism as the last step to rebirth. These man-made doctrines close the gates which gain entrance into God's kingdom. Did not Jesus inform Nicodemus that he needed to be born again of water and Spirit to enter the kingdom of God? (Jno.3:3,5,7) Notorious instances of TV evangelists who fleece widows, aged, and poor of their livelihood to glorify themselves, run rampant. They represent only a small fraction of a wider cancerous blight, cursing our age. People trust these benighted and spiritually blind leaders. Converts practice the examples of their leaders. Their proselytes become twofold children of Satan. Some Christian leaders condone a go-to-church religion that allows ungodly men and women to participate in every sin: covenant-breakers, homosexuals, adulterers, thieves, extortioners, drunkards, you name it. These hypocrites occupy the pews, listen to their ministers, and continue to live ungodly day after day, yet expect to dwell with God in heaven. Do we care little about how we dishonor our heavenly Father?

If we call God our heavenly Father, honor him by submitting to his laws of obedience and wholesome conduct as Malachi pleaded with his generation. (Mal.1:6)

Matthew

23:34 Wherefore, behold, I send unto you prophets, and wise men, and scribes: and some of them ye shall kill and crucify; and some of them shall ye scourge in your synagogues, and persecute them from city to city: 35 That upon you may come all the righteous blood shed upon the earth, from the blood of righteous Abel unto the blood of Zacharias son of Barachias, whom ye slew between the temple and the altar. 36 Verily I say unto you, All these things shall come upon this generation.

Israel's rebellion against the truth of God influenced them to persecute God's ancient messengers, John the Baptist, and Jesus. Their obstinance would not stop with crucifying Jesus. After his resurrection, Jesus commissioned the apostles and others to speak to Israel and Gentiles the hope of the gospel of the kingdom of heaven. Some of these messengers Israel and Gentiles would seek to destroy because they preached to them to abandon the way of Satan and return to the living God.

This rebellion and persecution has not ended to this day. Even after Jesus subdues the nations, the book of ***Revelation*** explains that a time will come when Satan's forces of wickedness shall revamp themselves and attempt to overthrow the Lordship of Jesus. (Rev.20:7-9)

Since this great struggle between the forces of good and evil must continue, each of us needs to examine carefully his position. Am I one of the rebels or one of the true servants of Jesus? It's evident that many who believe they serve Jesus are, in fact, opposing him. (Math.7:22-23) Before Jesus met Paul on the road to Damascus, Paul believed he was right when he persecuted, bound, delivered to prison God's people, and consented to the stoning of Stephen. (Act.7:58;22:3-5) One either serves Jesus or persecutes him and his people. (Act.9:4) May God open our eyes to serve, not destroy God's faithful ministers.

Luke

11:49 Therefore also said the wisdom of God, I will send them prophets and apostles, and some of them they shall slay and persecute: 50 That the blood of all the prophets, which was shed from the foundation of the world, may be required of this generation; 51 From the blood of Abel unto the blood of Zacharias, which perished between the altar and the temple: verily I say unto you, It shall be required of this generation. 52 Woe unto you, lawyers! for ye have taken away the key of knowledge: ye entered not in yourselves, and them that were entering in ye hindered. 53 And as he said these things unto them, the scribes and the Pharisees began to urge him vehemently, and to provoke him to speak of many things: 54 Laying wait for him, and seeking to catch something out of his mouth, that they might accuse him.

Though many then and today honestly believe they do the will of God, others know they transgress God's will. Many scribes, Pharisees, and lawyers knew Jesus spoke the truth of God, but they did not choose to abandon their way of life. I have met religious leaders who knew they did not practice the will of God, but they refused to repent and obey the gospel of God. It's heartbreaking to see this, but what is worse, they continue to lead others away from Jesus and God. I often ask myself why people persist in rebellion when they know the end will ruin them. Satan offers a way of life too appealing for them to abandon. They can't understand how much more satisfying life could be if they would submit to God. Jesus promises abundant life on earth and eternal life with God and his children hereafter. (Jno.10:10; 1 Pet.1:4)

God charged persecutors in Jesus' day with the blood of all God's prophets from creation. Offenses of the ungodly continue to build against God's people. (Rev.18:24) Will we be offended or faithfully serve God?

Mark

12:41 And Jesus sat over against the
treasury, and beheld how the people cast
money into the treasury: and many that
were rich cast in much. 42 And there
came a certain poor widow, and she threw
in two mites, which make a farthing. 43
And he called unto him his disciples, and
saith unto them, Verily I say unto you,
That this poor widow hath cast more in,
than all they which have cast into the
treasury: 44 For all they did cast in of
their abundance; but she of her want did
cast in all that she had, even all her living.

How does God look at our giving? The rich often contribute much, but the poor give little. Does God evaluate man's giving as we do, or does his evaluation rest on other criteria?

While in the temple, Jesus observed those who gave. Rich men cast considerable sums into God's coffer, but a poor widow tossed very little into the treasury. Jesus commented that the widow cast more into the service of God than all the rich combined. Her two mites, in God's evaluation, outweighed all the rich contributions. How could this be true? The widow gave all she had, all her living, to God. The wealthy, though they gave much, loaned God only a small part of their living. Thus, God evaluates our giving in relation to what he has given us, but man's evaluation considers only what one gives, regardless of how much he possesses. Paul explained to Corinthians giving as God sees it. After a person gives himself to God and his people, **"If there be first a willing mind, it is accepted according to that a man hath, and not according to that he hath not."** (2 Cor.8:12) God considers giving in light of what we have. A $100 of a hundred million is a small gift; one dollar out of two God considers a large gift. Can we learn God's standard of giving and willingly contribute according to how well he shares with us? **"It is more blessed to give than to receive."**

Luke

21:1 And he looked up, and saw the rich
men casting their gifts into the treasury. 2
And he saw also a certain poor widow
casting in thither two mites. 3 And he
said, Of a truth I say unto you, that this
poor widow hath cast in more than they
all: 4 For all these have of their
abundance cast in unto the offerings of
God: but she of her penury hath cast in all
the living that she had.

When a person cheerfully purposes in his mind and ungrudgingly gives, it pleases God who counts it as righteousness. Those whose poverty is relieved glorify God. (2 Cor.9:12)

During the thirty-nine years I taught in public schools, it became evident that how one contributed to help the poor made a big difference in how the needy received help. When the unfortunate perceive help arrives from reluctant contributors, they resent it deeply. Barrier between the haves and have-nots widens. When the needy realize others contribute because they care, the barrier diminishes. Similarly, how one gives to God determines how God receives it. God shows his people truth in every activity of life. If we believe him, our lives and the lives of those about us glow with greater joy.

As I realize more fully how God's truth improves the quality of life for those who live as God instructs, I try to visualize what a glorious day it will be when God's truth transforms every family on earth. Much of the sorrows engulfing the race will pass, and those who enter the kingdom of God will enjoy the abundant life. (Jno.10:10)

Comparing man's standards which are based on Satan's platform of selfishness with God's system which he bases on helping others, why haven't more people abandoned Satan? God provides laws which produce only that which is good for us. Satan's advice brings only emptiness, and sand in our teeth. If we will obey, God will give us a better life. Whose promise can we trust, Satan's or God's?

Matthew

23:37 O Jerusalem, Jerusalem, thou that killest the prophets, and stonest them which are sent unto thee, how often would I have gathered thy children together, even as a hen gathereth her chickens under her wings, and ye would not! 38 Behold, your house is left unto you desolate. 39 For I say unto you, Ye shall not see me henceforth, till ye shall say, Blessed is he that cometh in the name of the Lord.

Though Jesus taught and performed so many wonders in the city of Jerusalem, few in the city believed him to be the Messiah and even fewer obeyed what he taught. Jesus must have sorrowed much to see his own people spurn the invitation to enter the kingdom of God which their fathers awaited so long. As the prophets of old spoke of cities as mothers and the people within as her children, Jesus employed the parable to explain how the city of Jerusalem must experience the destruction mentioned by Daniel the prophet because it rejected the Messiah and his message to them from God. When this destruction came, those within the city could not escape except for the few who recognized the impending carnage which Daniel and Jesus taught, believed Jesus, and fled the city. Truly, Jerusalem lay

Luke

13:34 O Jerusalem, Jerusalem, which killest the prophets, and stonest them that are sent unto thee; how often would I have gathered thy children together, as a hen doth gather her brood under her wings, and ye would not! 35 Behold, your house is left unto you desolate: and verily I say unto you, Ye shall not see me, until the time come when ye shall say, Blessed is he that cometh in the name of the Lord.

desolate after the Roman army exercised its wrath on the city for its rebellion.

As parents grieve to see their children abandon their instructions and suffer hardships, Jesus sorrowed for Jerusalem and its impending destruction. He had taught his people the truth from the heavenly Father, but they refused it. Now they must suffer for their rebellion, but Jesus took no joy in seeing his people suffer.

Peace ensues those who submit to the council of God. Devastation awaits those who reject God and his commands. (Prov.14:34) Jerusalem turned from John the Baptist and the words of Jesus. Both spoke only God's truth. They were God's messengers to Israel, seeking repentance. Israel killed both. Now peace departed from their glorious city of Jerusalem. In the

Luke

19:41 And when he was come near, he beheld the city, and wept over it, 42 Saying, If thou hadst known, even thou, at least in this thy day, the things which belong unto thy peace! but now they are hid from thine eyes. 43 For the days shall come upon thee, that thine enemies shall cast a trench about thee, and compass thee round, and keep thee in on every side, 44 And shall lay thee even with the ground, and thy children within thee; and they shall not leave in thee one stone upon another; because thou knewest not the time of thy visitation.

eyes of Jewish leaders, they expected no problems. They anticipated only good.

Does God continue to bless nations and civilizations for obeying his commands, but destroy them for transgressing his precepts? Historians note that civilizations have risen and collapsed since the dawn of history. If this is true, is it a natural sequence of events, or is this from the hand of God because his children violate his rules which elevate obedient peoples, but destroy the disobedient? If God changed his way of correcting his children, how could we understand his disciplining? Did not God affirm he changes not? God does rule in man's kingdoms.

Jesus referred to Daniel's prophecy of Jerusalem's destruction after Babylon destroyed the city and carried away captives. I include a brief recount of Daniel's prophecy. Daniel himself survived the Babylonian assault on Jerusalem. He and three other Jewish captives the Babylonians trained in Babylonian wisdom and language. (Dan.1:1-4) They refused the dainty food of the king and continued to serve God as best they could in captivity. (Dan.1:4-16) God gave them knowledge and skill in learning and wisdom, but he provided Daniel with special understanding in visions and dreams. (Dan.1:17) He explained two dreams to King Nebuchadnezzar (Dan.2:1-45;4:4-27) and one vision to King Belshazzar. (Dan.5:1-29) Besides explaining dreams and visions to Babylonian kings, God gave Daniel four visions and explained them to him. (Dan.7:1-28;8:1-27;9:1-27; 10:1-12:13) All the visions Daniel recorded explained the rise and fall of kings, nations, and empires, but they impacted God's people.

Like God's other prophets, Daniel explained what would happen and how much time the vision covered. The most unusual feature of Daniel's visions dealt with his setting a starting time from which to begin his prophecies. Daniel recorded the time for Christ's coming, his death, and Jerusalem's desolation by Rome. Please examine this prophecy Gabriel explained to Daniel. "**Seventy weeks are determined upon thy people and upon thy holy city, to finish the transgression, and to make an end of sins, and to make reconciliation for iniquity, and to bring in everlasting righteousness, and to seal up the vision and prophecy, and to anoint the most Holy. 25 Know therefore and understand, that from the going forth of the commandment to restore and to build Jerusalem unto the Messiah the Prince shall be seven weeks, and threescore and two weeks: the street shall be built again, and the wall, even in troublous times. 26 And after threescore and two weeks shall Messiah be cut off, but not for himself: and the people of the prince that shall come shall destroy the city and the sanctuary; and the end thereof shall be with a flood, and unto the end of the war desolations are determined. 27 And he shall confirm the covenant with many for one week: and in the midst of the week he shall cause the sacrifice and the oblation to cease, and for the overspreading of abominations he shall make it desolate, even until the consummation, and that determined shall be poured upon the desolate.**" (Dan.9:24-27)

The first part of this prophecy covered "seventy weeks" or 490 years, using a day to signify a year. During the 490 years from the command to rebuild Jerusalem, God would accomplish seven events: 1) finish transgression; 2) make an end of sins; 3) make reconciliation for iniquity; 4) bring in everlasting righteousness; 5) seal up the vision and prophecy; 6) anoint the most Holy; and 7) bring the Messiah to Israel. King Artaxerxes commissioned Ezra to return to Jerusalem and teach Israel God's statutes and judgments. (Ez.7:1-28) The king sent Ezra to reestablish the Jewish system in 457 B.C. Christ would appear "sixty-nine weeks" or 483 years after the command to restore Jerusalem. Ussher placed Jesus' baptism at 26 A.D. which was 483 years after Ezra returned to teach God's law.

In the second part of Daniel's prophecy, Gabriel explained 62 weeks or 434 years. During this time, the holy city would be destroyed and the Messiah be cut off. Between 33 A.D. at Jesus' death, and 476 A.D. Jerusalem would be destroyed and Christ would be cut off from the church by the great falling away Paul explained. Both desolations resulted from disobedience. (2 Thes.2:3-12; see **Triumph of Three Cities**, p. 39.) God does continue to correct sin today as he always has. (Mal.4:4-6)

Matthew

24:1 And Jesus went out, and departed from the temple: and his disciples came to him for to shew him the buildings of the temple. 2 And Jesus said unto them, See ye not all these things? verily I say unto you, There shall not be left here one stone upon another, that shall not be thrown down. 3 And as he sat upon the mount of Olives, the disciples came unto him privately, saying, Tell us, when shall these things be? and what shall be the sign of thy coming, and of the end of the world?

Grandeur of the temple prompted the disciples to comment on its beauty. Jesus responded by explaining that all its beauty must be destroyed. In private, four disciples asked Jesus when this catastrophe must come. What sign indicates the approaching desolation of God's temple? Matthew added two additional, but related questions: 1) What will be the sign of thy coming: and 2) What sign will inform us of the end of the world? These last two questions continue to intrigue us even today.

Matthew answered when Jerusalem would be destroyed in verses one through thirty-five. He recorded Jesus' answer to the question about the sign of his coming from 24:36-

Mark

13:1 And as he went out of the temple, one of his disciples saith unto him, Master, see what manner of stones and what buildings are here! 2 And Jesus answering said unto him, Seest thou these great buildings? there shall not be left one stone upon another, that shall not be thrown down. 3 And as he sat upon the mount of Olives over against the temple, Peter and James and John and Andrew asked him privately, 4 Tell us, when shall these things be? and what shall be the sign when all these things shall be fulfilled?

25:13. Their question about the end of the world he answered in 25:14-46. If one realizes that Matthew recorded three questions and their answers, but Mark and Luke recorded only one, it may help to understand what each gospel means. How each writer recorded the apostles' questions and Jesus' answers may provide clues to identify the audience of each writer.

Is there a reason for the different questions? One person might need all three questions answered, but others might desire the answers for only one. Audience needs affect content.

Having known how God blessed and cursed his people through the ages, Jews might show more

Luke

21:5 And as some spake of the temple, how it was adorned with goodly stones and gifts, he said, 6 As for these things which ye behold, the days will come, in the which there shall not be left one stone upon another, that shall not be thrown down. 7 And they asked him, saying, Master, but when shall these things be? and what sign will there be when these things shall come to pass?

interest in when Jesus would come and when to expect the end of the world. Gentiles' interest might rest more in Jesus' ability to explain when and by whom Jerusalem would be destroyed. Interest and need of the audience dictated what each writer included in his gospel. Since Jesus taught and did so many wonders, it became impossible for each writer to include everything Jesus did and taught. Matthew answered unbelieving Jews' needs; Mark addressed believing Roman needs; Luke answered a believing Syrian ruler's needs, answering his need to confirm truth; and John emphasized how Jesus fulfilled Moses' prophecy about **the Prophet** to be like Moses by delivering all God's truth to Israel. All who rejected God's words which **the Prophet** spoke God would require it of them by severing them from his people. (Act.3:23)

Matthew

24:4 And Jesus answered and said unto them, Take heed that no man deceive you. 5 For many shall come in my name, saying, I am Christ; and shall deceive many. 6 And ye shall hear of wars and rumours of wars: see that ye be not troubled: for all these things must come to pass, but the end is not yet. 7 For nation shall rise against nation, and kingdom against kingdom: and there shall be famines, and pestilences, and earthquakes, in divers places. 8 All these are the beginning of sorrows. 9 Then shall they deliver you up to be afflicted, and shall kill you: and ye shall be hated of all nations for my name's sake. 10 And then shall many be offended, and shall betray one another, and shall hate one another. 11 And many false prophets shall rise, and shall deceive many. 12 And because iniquity shall abound, the love of many shall wax cold. 13 But he that shall endure unto the end, the same shall be saved. 14 And this gospel of the kingdom shall be preached in all the world for a witness unto all nations; and then shall the end come.

Deceivers, famines, earthquakes, wars, betrayals, and persecutions all precede the fall of Jerusalem, but the

Mark

13:5 And Jesus answering them began to say, Take heed lest any man deceive you: 6 For many shall come in my name, saying, I am Christ; and shall deceive many. 7 And when ye shall hear of wars and rumours of wars, be ye not troubled: for such things must needs be; but the end shall not be yet. 8 For nation shall rise against nation, and kingdom against kingdom: and there shall be earthquakes in divers places, and there shall be famines and troubles: these are the beginnings of sorrows. 9 But take heed to yourselves: for they shall deliver you up to councils; and in the synagogues ye shall be beaten: and ye shall be brought before rulers and kings for my sake, for a testimony against them. 10 And the gospel must first be published among all nations.

gospel of the kingdom of God shall be preached among nations, and then you may expect Jerusalem's destruction to near. Some of you shall be killed and many of you hated before the fall of the city. When the gospel reaches all peoples, Jerusalem's end comes.

One might wonder why Jesus related the time of Jerusalem's desolation to the persecutions and hardships

Luke

21:8 And he said, Take heed that ye be not deceived: for many shall come in my name, saying, I am Christ; and the time draweth near: go ye not therefore after them. 9 But when ye shall hear of wars and commotions, be not terrified: for these things must first come to pass; but the end is not by and by. 10 Then said he unto them, Nation shall rise against nation, and kingdom against kingdom: 11 And great earthquakes shall be in divers places, and famines, and pestilences; and fearful sights and great signs shall there be from heaven. 12 But before all these, they shall lay their hands on you, and persecute you, delivering you up to the synagogues, and into prisons, being brought before kings and rulers for my name's sake. 13 And it shall turn to you for a testimony. 14 Settle it therefore in your hearts, not to meditate before what ye shall answer:

which the apostles and brethren must face. Continuing faithful to God and Christ even during all the offenses brought believing Jews in Judah more stress than nearly all other hardships. Jesus emphasized the need for faithfulness to God's truth to the end to gain eternal life. God requires faithfulness by all.

Matthew

24:15 When ye therefore shall see the abomination of desolation, spoken of by Daniel the prophet, stand in the holy place, (whoso readeth, let him understand:) 16 Then let them which be in Judaea flee into the mountains: 17 Let him which is on the housetop not come down to take any thing out of his house: 18 Neither let him which is in the field return back to take his clothes. 19 And woe unto them that are with child, and to them that give suck in those days! 20 But pray ye that your flight be not in the winter, neither on the sabbath day: 21 For then shall be great tribulation, such as was not since the beginning of the world to this time, no, nor ever shall be.

Recognize events before Jerusalem's destruction, or you will not escape. When Roman armies lay siege, you must flee for your lives. Do not gather your belongings. If you're in the field, enter not the city. Those with child or young children will have a more difficult time. Ask God that you do not have to flee on the Sabbath or during winter. That will make your escape more difficult. Only Matthew told Jews to pray they flee not on the Sabbath.

All nations hear the gospel before Jerusalem falls. Testify before kings and councils as the Spirit guides you. Don't worry about what to say. God shall guide you at that time.

Mark

13:11 But when they shall lead you, and deliver you up, take no thought beforehand what ye shall speak, neither do ye premeditate: but whatsoever shall be given you in that hour, that speak ye: for it is not ye that speak, but the Holy Ghost. 12 Now the brother shall betray the brother to death, and the father the son; and children shall rise up against their parents, and shall cause them to be put to death. 13 And ye shall be hated of all men for my name's sake: but he that shall endure unto the end, the same shall be saved. 14 But when ye shall see the abomination of desolation, spoken of by Daniel the prophet, standing where it ought not, (let him that readeth understand,) then let them that be in Judaea flee to the mountains: 15 And let him that is on the housetop not go down into the house, neither enter therein, to take any thing out of his house: 16 And let him that is in the field not turn back again for to take up his garment. 17 But woe to them that are with child, and to them that give suck in those days! 18 And pray ye that your flight be not in the winter. 19 For in those days shall be affliction, such as was not from the beginning of the creation which God created unto this time, neither shall be.

Because of the difficulties many Christians will grow

Luke

21:15 For I will give you a mouth and wisdom, which all your adversaries shall not be able to gainsay nor resist. 16 And ye shall be betrayed both by parents, and brethren, and kinsfolks, and friends; and some of you shall they cause to be put to death. 17 And ye shall be hated of all men for my name's sake. 18 But there shall not an hair of your head perish. 19 In your patience possess ye your souls. 20 And when ye shall see Jerusalem compassed with armies, then know that the desolation thereof is nigh. 21 Then let them which are in Judaea flee to the mountains; and let them which are in the midst of it depart out; and let not them that are in the countries enter thereinto. 22 For these be the days of vengeance, that all things which are written may be fulfilled. 23 But woe unto them that are with child, and to them that give suck, in those days! for there shall be great distress in the land, and wrath upon this people.

cold and turn from God. You must endure to the end if you are to reap eternal life. Pray to the Father for strength to overcome all these afflictions. God loves you and will help you through every problem if you abide in his faith. Take courage, for God promises to be with you even during all your tribulations. He will never leave you alone.

Deceivers shall abound during this time of tribulation.

Matthew

24:22 And except those days should be shortened, there should no flesh be saved: but for the elect's sake those days shall be shortened. 23 Then if any man shall say unto you, Lo, here is Christ, or there; believe it not. 24 For there shall arise false Christs, and false prophets, and shall shew great signs and wonders; insomuch that, if it were possible, they shall deceive the very elect. 25 Behold, I have told you before. 26 Wherefore if they shall say unto you, Behold, he is in the desert; go not forth: behold, he is in the secret chambers; believe it not. 27 For as the lightning cometh out of the east, and shineth even unto the west; so shall also the coming of the Son of man be. 28 For wheresoever the carcase is, there will the eagles be gathered together.

Satan's children shall spread the message that you may find Christ if you go to the desert or to some secret place. Believe them not. They only trouble you. When I come to punish Jerusalem for turning from the truth of God, all shall see me. I lead the Roman army to Jerusalem. They are my sword to curse Jerusalem for disobeying the Father in heaven. Remember what I explained to you before it comes to pass. Trust what I have told you. Let not Satan unsettle you. Even if deceivers show some wonder, trust not their message. If you trust these deceivers you enter Jerusalem rather than

Mark

13:20 And except that the Lord had shortened those days, no flesh should be saved: but for the elect's sake, whom he hath chosen, he hath shortened the days. 21 And then if any man shall say to you, Lo, here is Christ; or, lo, he is there; believe him not: 22 For false Christs and false prophets shall rise, and shall shew signs and wonders, to seduce, if it were possible, even the elect. 23 But take ye heed: behold, I have foretold you all things.

flee as I tell you. They say Christ is in the city. Don't believe them or you will lose your life with the unbelievers.

How long will the trials of Jerusalem's destruction last? It will continue until the city and temple lay desolate and without inhabitant. You should pray to the Father to shorten those days of trials, otherwise, none of you shall survive. When I return to bring God's vengeance on the city, it shall not be in secret. As the lightning shines from the east to the west for all to see, so my coming shall become visible to all. Nevertheless, only those who believe God sent me shall escape the great tribulations. Only they will trust that I have told you all these things before they come to pass. (See Ps.17:13-14.) As the Roman army lays siege to the city of Jerusalem, these temple buildings, houses, and walls fall and turn to ruins. People die by the sword, famine, and disease. Some shall

Luke

21:24 And they shall fall by the edge of the sword, and shall be led away captive into all nations: and Jerusalem shall be trodden down of the Gentiles, until the times of the Gentiles be fulfilled.

eat their own children in the siege. Those who survive, the Roman soldiers shall carry away into all nations. They shall not return to their beloved city, for it shall lie desolate. Gentiles trample the city under foot for many years--until the time when God allows the Gentiles to desecrate it no more. (See p.242.)

Jesus spoke these warnings in 33 A.D., but it was not until 70 A.D. that Titus destroyed the city and captivated those who survived.

God warns his faithful of impending disaster that they may escape. (Am.3:7) In the case of Jerusalem, Daniel and Jesus foretold God's faithful what to expect and what to do to escape the danger by fleeing when the signs matched what Jesus explained to them.

Though Jerusalem's tribulation seems beyond imagination, those who reject Jesus' words shall suffer much greater agony when this world draws to a close. A worse catastrophe awaits all who are unprepared.

Seeing how how God forewarned saints to flee Jerusalem before its destruction, we must understand he warns all to flee the world's end lest we suffer eternally.

Matthew

**24:29 Immediately after the tribulation of
those days shall the sun be darkened, and
the moon shall not give her light, and the
stars shall fall from heaven, and the
powers of the heavens shall be shaken: 30
And then shall appear the sign of the Son
of man in heaven: and then shall all the
tribes of the earth mourn, and they shall
see the Son of man coming in the clouds of
heaven with power and great glory. 31
And he shall send his angels with a great
sound of a trumpet, and they shall gather
together his elect from the four winds,
from one end of heaven to the other. 32
Now learn a parable of the fig tree; When
his branch is yet tender, and putteth forth
leaves, ye know that summer is nigh: 33
So likewise ye, when ye shall see all these
things, know that it is near, even at the
doors. 34 Verily I say unto you, This
generation shall not pass, till all these
things be fulfilled. 35 Heaven and earth
shall pass away, but my words shall not
pass away.**

Mark

**13:24 But in those days, after that
tribulation, the sun shall be darkened, and
the moon shall not give her light, 25 And
the stars of heaven shall fall, and the
powers that are in heaven shall be shaken.
26 And then shall they see the Son of man
coming in the clouds with great power
and glory. 27 And then shall he send his
angels, and shall gather together his elect
from the four winds, from the uttermost
part of the earth to the uttermost part of
heaven. 28 Now learn a parable of the fig
tree; When her branch is yet tender, and
putteth forth leaves, ye know that summer
is near: 29 So ye in like manner, when ye
shall see these things come to pass, know
that it is nigh, even at the doors. 30 Verily
I say unto you, that this generation shall
not pass, till all these things be done. 31
Heaven and earth shall pass away: but my
words shall not pass away.**

Continuing to teach his disciples by parable, Jesus explained the collapse of Jewish authority resulting from the destruction of Jerusalem. Those once recognized as leaders resembled the sun, stars, and constellations: they gave light to the people. When their authority ceased, darkness spread over the land. Jewish leaders such as priests no longer guided the people. This darkness, though spiritual and political, produced great confusion for the populace. Similar to revolutions, massive earthquakes, devastating windstorms, and tidal waves, confusion followed. This vacuum must be replaced by some form of authority to guide the people. Jesus explained that the sign of the Son of man rises to replace that of the Mosaical priest system. His authority in religion shall supersede that of Moses. Jesus not only is the Son of God, he now rises as the Sun of righteousness. (Mal.4:2) Many have misunderstood Jesus' message to his disciples on this point. They conceive of this as explaining the end of time when Jesus returns to close this whole world. Note that Jesus informed his disciples his generation would not pass away before what he had just explained to them shall come to pass. (Math.24:34) All that generation died, but Jesus has not returned to end this world. Therefore, we must consider some other way to understand the message he presented to his followers.

Please consider similar messages recorded by God's ancient prophets which applied to both Jews and Gentiles. When God came to punish Babylon by the armies of Medes and Persians, Isaiah called it the day of the Lord. (Is.13:1,9,17,19) **"For the stars of heaven and the constellations thereof shall not give their light: the sun shall be darkened in his going forth, and the moon shall not cause her light to shine."** (Is.13:10)

"Therefore I will shake the heavens, and the earth shall remove out of her place, in

the wrath of the LORD of hosts, and in the day of his fierce anger." (Is.13:13)

Idumea reaped similar destruction. God spoke through Isaiah saying, **"Come near, ye nations, to hear; and hearken, ye people: let the earth hear, and all that is therein; the world, and all things that come forth of it. 2 For the indignation of the LORD is upon all nations, and his fury upon all their armies: he hath utterly destroyed them, he hath delivered them to the slaughter. 3 Their slain also shall be cast out, and their stink shall come up out of their carcases, and the mountains shall be melted with their blood. 4 And all the host of heaven shall be dissolved, and the heavens shall be rolled together as a scroll: and all their host shall fall down, as the leaf falleth off from the vine, and as a falling fig from the fig tree. 5 For my sword shall be bathed in heaven: behold, it shall come down upon Idumea, and upon the people of my curse, to judgment."** (Is.34:1-5)

Pharaoh, king of Egypt, heard God's curse from Ezekiel. **"And when I shall put thee out, I will cover the heaven, and make the stars thereof dark; I will cover the sun with a cloud, and the moon shall not give her light. 8 All the bright lights of heaven will I make dark over thee, and set darkness upon thy land, saith the Lord GOD."** (Ezek.32:7-8)

Isaiah recorded this proverb against the king of Babylon **"Thy pomp is brought down to the grave, and the noise of thy viols: the worm is spread under thee, and the worms cover thee. 12 How art thou fallen from heaven, O Lucifer, son of the morning! how art thou cut down to the ground, which didst weaken the nations! 13 For thou hast said in thine heart, I will ascend into heaven, I will exalt my throne above the stars of God: I will sit also upon the mount of the congregation, in the sides of the north: 14 I will ascend above the heights of the clouds; I will be like the**

Luke

21: 25 And there shall be signs in the sun, and in the moon, and in the stars; and upon the earth distress of nations, with perplexity; the sea and the waves roaring; 26 Men's hearts failing them for fear, and for looking after those things which are coming on the earth: for the powers of heaven shall be shaken. 27 And then shall they see the Son of man coming in a cloud with power and great glory. 28 And when these things begin to come to pass, then look up, and lift up your heads; for your redemption draweth nigh. 29 And he spake to them a parable; Behold the fig tree, and all the trees; 30 When they now shoot forth, ye see and know of your own selves that summer is now nigh at hand. 31 So likewise ye, when ye see these things come to pass, know ye that the kingdom of God is nigh at hand. 32 Verily I say unto you, This generation shall not pass away, till all be fulfilled. 33 Heaven and earth shall pass away: but my words shall not pass away.

most High. 15 Yet thou shalt be brought down to hell, to the sides of the pit." (Is.14:11-15)

Using clearer terms, Jeremiah wrote, **"Though Babylon should mount up to heaven, and though she should fortify the height of her strength, yet from me shall spoilers come unto her, saith the LORD."** (Jer.51:53)

Prophets' parable-like language use sun, moon, stars, and constellations to signify rulers. When a nation crushes another nation and removes its rulers, the prophets portray this by saying the heavens are darkened: the sun fails to shine; moon gives no light; and stars are not seen. Jesus used this parable to show Rome would demolished Judah and removed her rulers. (See **Triumph of Three Cities**, pp. 60-96.) Jesus explained that Moses' system must be replaced by God's new system which opens salvation to all nations on equal terms. Then Jesus reigns.

Matthew

24:36 But of that day and hour knoweth no man, no, not the angels of heaven, but my Father only. 37 But as the days of Noe were, so shall also the coming of the Son of man be. 38 For as in the days that were before the flood they were eating and drinking, marrying and giving in marriage, until the day that Noe entered into the ark, 39 And knew not until the flood came, and took them all away; so shall also the coming of the Son of man be. 40 Then shall two be in the field; the one shall be taken, and the other left. 41 Two women shall be grinding at the mill; the one shall be taken, and the other left.

Mark

13:32 But of that day and that hour knoweth no man, no, not the angels which are in heaven, neither the Son, but the Father.

God gave Jesus no specific time for Jerusalem's collapse and for the rulers to lose their authority after which the power of Jesus as King of kings must begin to subdue the nations. Though his authority actually began on Pentecost, 33 A.D., when Jesus ascended to the Father in heaven, it seemed to many Jews that Christianity remained only a small segment of the Jewish system. Not until Jerusalem's destruction when Christianity continued to grow did it become evident that Christianity was a distinct system itself.

When Titus and the Roman army lay siege to Jerusalem, then the Jews realized that God's wrath rested on them. As in the days of Noah when he and his family entered the ark, and the flood waters descended on those outside the ark, then the unbelievers knew their time had arrived. It was too late to enter the ark. Even so it was for Jerusalem. Christians fled the city as Jesus instructed, but unbelievers remained to be destroyed or taken captive.

Jews in Jerusalem continued their daily activities until the fatal day arrived for the Roman army to lay siege to the city. If two men worked in the field, one a believer in Jesus as the Messiah, and the other an unbeliever, the believer fled to the mountains as the Roman army approached, but the unbeliever retired to the city expecting safety therein. If two women were grinding at the mill, one an unbeliever and the other a Christian, the Christian recognized the sign of destruction and departed from the city, but the unbeliever remained to her sorrow. God grants safety to his children when they listen to his instructions. (Is.3:10-11)

Eternal life and eternal death function much the same way that God separated believers and unbelievers in the city of Jerusalem at its desolation by Rome. Individuals who listen to the message of the gospel and realize that sin in their lives condemns them to eternal destruction often repent and obey the gospel, but many who hear the truth of the gospel contend that a just God would never condemn people to eternal hell. They disbelieve God's truth. When the time of death or judgment arrives, and they hear the words proclaimed by Jesus, "**Depart from me, ye cursed, into everlasting fire, prepared for the devil and his angels,**" (Math.25:41) it will be too late to escape doom. It's wiser to listen to God than to listen to the devil ridicule the truth of God. Adam and Eve erred in the Garden when they disbelieved God's message, "**Ye shall surely die,**" if ye eat or touch the fruit of the tree of the knowledge of good and evil. (Gen.2:17) They believed Satan, who contradicted God, claiming God knows you won't die. Your eyes will be enlightened to know good and evil. (Gen. 3:5)

Parents warn their children today to avoid being addicted to cocaine, but when their friends comment on how good it makes them feel, they set aside the wisdom of their elders and find themselves hooked. Pharisees demanded of Jesus when to expect the kingdom of God, Those who demand show

Luke

17:20 And when he was demanded of the Pharisees, when the kingdom of God should come, he answered them and said, The kingdom of God cometh not with observation: 21 Neither shall they say, Lo here! or, lo there! for, behold, the kingdom of God is within you. 22 And he said unto the disciples, The days will come, when ye shall desire to see one of the days of the Son of man, and ye shall not see it. 23 And they shall say to you, See here; or, see there: go not after them, nor follow them. 24 For as the lightning, that lighteneth out of the one part under heaven, shineth unto the other part under heaven; so shall also the Son of man be in his day. 25 But first must he suffer many things, and be rejected of this generation. 26 And as it was in the days of Noe, so shall it be also in the days of the Son of man. 27 They did eat, they drank, they married wives, they were given in marriage, until the day that Noe entered into the ark, and the flood came, and destroyed them all. 28 Likewise also as it was in the days of Lot; they did eat, they drank, they bought, they sold, they planted, they builded; 29 But the same day that Lot went out of Sodom it rained fire and brimstone from heaven, and destroyed them all. 30 Even thus shall it be in the day when the Son of man is revealed. 31 In that day, he which shall be upon the housetop, and his stuff in the house, let him not come down to take it away: and he that is in the field, let him likewise not return back. 32 Remember Lot's wife. 33 Whosoever shall seek to save his life shall lose it; and whosoever shall lose his life shall preserve it. 34 I tell you, in that night there shall be two men in one bed; the one shall be taken, and the other shall be left. 35 Two women shall be grinding together; the one shall be taken, and the other left. 36 Two men shall be in the field; the one shall be taken, and the other left. 37 And they answered and said unto him, Where, Lord? And he said unto them, Wheresoever the body is, thither will the eagles be gathered together.

little respect for others. Pharisees seemed to conceive of God's kingdom as something which could be seen with the physical eye. Jesus explained that the kingdom of God resides inside a person and does not appear as other kingdoms. To say God's kingdom exists here or there and one must go to it physically presents a misconception of the kingdom of heaven. Being within people carries the idea that it rules from within, not by officers who force compliance with the laws of the dominion. God grants us the ability to control our lives instead of having the world, friends, drugs, sin, or Satan dictate what each of us shall choose to do. (Prov.16:32) This is part of the freedom Jesus gives us. (Jno.8:31-32). We are free to live, but not free to indulge in sinful lusts. (Gal.5:13) God frees us from the bondage of sin. (Jno.8:34; Rom.6:18) Pharisees and those who follow the nature of this world wished to live to satisfy the base desires of the flesh and will do so until apprehended by the law or until death. God asks us to free ourselves from this bondage. (1 Pet.2:16) Live free. Live abundant, spirit-satisfying life, not lustful lives. (Jno.10:10; 1 Tim.4:8;6:6,18-19; Tit.3:8) Experience peace and goodwill.

If the Pharisees and people of our age truly sought the kingdom of God, demanding something of God ought not to be a reasonable attitude. Even if we respect our fellow sojourners on earth, we don't demand. We might request or entreat, but not demand which conveys an air of superiority or even pride. God looks for humble attitudes within his people. Without this feeling of need, one rarely turns to God. True life remains beyond their grasp.

Jesus foretold his disciples God's temple in Jerusalem must be destroyed. In its place God erects a spiritual temple, the church.

Matthew

24:42 Watch therefore: for ye know not what hour your Lord doth come. 43 But know this, that if the goodman of the house had known in what watch the thief would come, he would have watched, and would not have suffered his house to be broken up. 44 Therefore be ye also ready: for in such an hour as ye think not the Son of man cometh. 45 Who then is a faithful and wise servant, whom his lord hath made ruler over his household, to give them meat in due season? 46 Blessed is that servant, whom his lord when he cometh shall find so doing. 47 Verily I say unto you, That he shall make him ruler over all his goods. 48 But and if that evil servant shall say in his heart, My lord delayeth his coming; 49 And shall begin to smite his fellowservants, and to eat and drink with the drunken; 50 The lord of that servant shall come in a day when he looketh not for him, and in an hour that he is not aware of, 51 And shall cut him asunder, and appoint him his portion with the hypocrites: there shall be weeping and gnashing of teeth.

Throughout Old Testament times God's people started out zealously, but as time lapsed, they began to neglect the instructions of

Mark

13:33 Take ye heed, watch and pray: for ye know not when the time is. 34 For the Son of man is as a man taking a far journey, who left his house, and gave authority to his servants, and to every man his work, and commanded the porter to watch. 35 Watch ye therefore: for ye know not when the master of the house cometh, at even, or at midnight, or at the cockcrowing, or in the morning: 36 Lest coming suddenly he find you sleeping. 37 And what I say unto you I say unto all, Watch.

God. Jesus understood that his followers would respond similarly. He has given us a complete catalog of all the will of God. It is not a matter of not knowing what God wants of us. (Rom.10:6-10) Do we have faith and endurance to complete our walk with our heavenly Father? Jesus ascended to heaven and gave us instruction on how to keep his house. When he returns, will he find each of us performing the activities he assigned us? Even in our short lifetime most of us know some who have returned to live godless lives. Jesus instructs us to pray to the Father that we not become stewards who abandon the master's charge. Otherwise, we shall not escape all the trials God

Luke

21:34 And take heed to yourselves, lest at any time your hearts be overcharged with surfeiting, and drunkenness, and cares of this life, and so that day come upon you unawares. 35 For as a snare shall it come on all them that dwell on the face of the whole earth. 36 Watch ye therefore, and pray always, that ye may be accounted worthy to escape all these things that shall come to pass, and to stand before the Son of man. 37 And in the day time he was teaching in the temple; and at night he went out, and abode in the mount that is called the mount of Olives. 38 And all the people came early in the morning to him in the temple, for to hear him.

assigns to the faithless.

As one attempts to encourage the faithless to repent and return to serve God and his Son Jesus, some respond, saying they intend to correct their lives some day, but like Felix, the convenient season never presents itself. (Act.24:25) Years roll on until the interest in God's way of righteousness fades from their lives, or they pass on to the eternal abode without God. He rewards only faithfulness to the end. Light emanates from God. We must use God's light now. (Jno.1:

Matthew

25:1 Then shall the kingdom of heaven be likened unto ten virgins, which took their lamps, and went forth to meet the bridegroom. 2 And five of them were wise, and five were foolish. 3 They that were foolish took their lamps, and took no oil with them: 4 But the wise took oil in their vessels with their lamps. 5 While the bridegroom tarried, they all slumbered and slept. 6 And at midnight there was a cry made, Behold, the bridegroom cometh; go ye out to meet him. 7 Then all those virgins arose, and trimmed their lamps. 8 And the foolish said unto the wise, Give us of your oil; for our lamps are gone out. 9 But the wise answered, saying, Not so; lest there be not enough for us and you: but go ye rather to them that sell, and buy for yourselves. 10 And while they went to buy, the bridegroom came; and they that were ready went in with him to the marriage: and the door was shut. 11 Afterward came also the other virgins, saying, Lord, Lord, open to us. 12 But he answered and said, Verily I say unto you, I know you not. 13 Watch therefore, for ye know neither the day nor the hour wherein the Son of man cometh.

4-9) Those who do the will of God reflect the light of God in their lives that others in darkness may behold the light of God and desire to have God's light in themselves. (Math.5:14-16)

Parable of ten virgins indicates some of God's people never allow God's light to be extinguished from their lives, and God allows them to enter his rest. Others fail to emit God's light all their lives, and when the time to enter his rest arrives, God and Jesus shut them out. Jesus instructs all to be prepared for his coming at all times lest he come when we are unprepared. Satan and his children use every possible means to persuade God's children to abandon God.

God requires faithfulness at all times.

Luke

12:37 Blessed are those servants, whom the lord when he cometh shall find watching: verily I say unto you, that he shall gird himself, and make them to sit down to meat, and will come forth and serve them. 38 And if he shall come in the second watch, or come in the third watch, and find them so, blessed are those servants. 39 And this know, that if the goodman of the house had known what hour the thief would come, he would have watched, and not have suffered his house to be broken through. 40 Be ye therefore ready also: for the Son of man cometh at an hour when ye think not. 41 Then Peter said unto him, Lord, speakest thou this parable unto us, or even to all? 42 And the Lord said, Who then is that faithful and wise steward, whom his lord shall make ruler over his household, to give them their portion of meat in due season? 43 Blessed is that servant, whom his lord when he cometh shall find so doing. 44 Of a truth I say unto you, that he will make him ruler over all that he hath. 45 But and if that servant say in his heart, My lord delayeth his coming; and shall begin to beat the menservants and maidens, and to eat and drink, and to be drunken; 46 The lord of that servant will come in a day when he looketh not for him, and at an hour when he is not aware, and will cut him in sunder, and will appoint him his portion with the unbelievers. 47 And that servant, which knew his lord's will, and prepared not himself, neither did according to his will, shall be beaten with many stripes. 48 But he that knew not, and did commit things worthy of stripes, shall be beaten with few stripes. For unto whomsoever much is given, of him shall be much required: and to whom men have committed much, of him they will ask the more.

Honor him with all our love and strength.

Matthew

25:14 For the kingdom of heaven is as a man travelling into a far country, who called his own servants, and delivered unto them his goods. 15 And unto one he gave five talents, to another two, and to another one; to every man according to his several ability; and straightway took his journey. 16 Then he that had received the five talents went and traded with the same, and made them other five talents. 17 And likewise he that had received two, he also gained other two. 18 But he that had received one went and digged in the earth, and hid his lord's money. 19 After a long time the lord of those servants cometh, and reckoneth with them. 20 And so he that had received five talents came and brought other five talents, saying, Lord, thou deliveredst unto me five talents: behold, I have gained beside them five talents more. 21 His lord said unto him, Well done, thou good and faithful servant: thou hast been faithful over a few things, I will make thee ruler over many things: enter thou into the joy of thy lord. 22 He also that had received two talents came and said, Lord, thou deliveredst unto me two talents: behold, I have gained two other talents beside them. 23 His lord said unto him, Well done, good and faithful servant; thou hast been faithful over a few things, I will make thee ruler over many things: enter thou into the joy of thy lord. 24 Then he which had received the one talent came and said, Lord, I knew thee that thou art an hard man, reaping where thou hast not sown, and gathering where thou hast not strawed: 25 And I was afraid, and went and hid thy talent in the earth: lo, there thou hast that is thine. 26 His lord answered and said unto him, Thou wicked and slothful servant, thou knewest that I reap where I sowed not, and gather where I have not strawed: 27 Thou oughtest therefore to have put my money to the exchangers, and then at my coming I should have received mine own with usury. 28 Take therefore the talent from him, and give it unto him which hath ten talents. 29 For unto every one that hath shall be given, and he shall have abundance: but from him that hath not shall be taken away even that which he hath. 30 And cast ye the unprofitable servant into outer darkness: there shall be weeping and gnashing of teeth.

This parable resembles one recorded by Luke. (19:11-27) Both parables portray Jesus as a householder who prepares to travel into a far country for a long time. To have his house cared for during his absence, he assigned his servants tasks to perform. Each servant received treasure to invest. Some had greater responsibilities than others. During the householder's absence, most of the servants used their goods well, but one in each parable feared his lord and hid his gift. Upon the lord's return, he called his servants to evaluate how well each used his master's property. The householder complimented the servants who used the goods well, but condemned the slothful servants. The lord gave the responsible servants greater positions, but the irresponsible lost what their lord gave them and received punishment.

Jesus' parables depict how God's kingdom functions. 1. Jesus blesses each believer with certain abilities for which he must give account. 2. Jesus needed to go to God before receiving his kingdom. (Dan.7:13-14) 3. Jesus will return to have every person give account of his service in the last day. (Jno.5:25-29) 4. Those who have used God's kingdom's riches wisely reign with Christ. (Rev.2:26-27;3:21;5:10) 5. Unproductive servants he strips of their wealth and dishonors with punishment. 6. Those who refuse to submit to King Jesus he destroys. This first referred to Jews who claimed citizenship within God's kingdom, but it includes Gentiles after Jesus' resurrection.

Luke

19:11 And as they heard these things, he
added and spake a parable, because he
was nigh to Jerusalem, and because they
thought that the kingdom of God should
immediately appear. 12 He said therefore,
A certain nobleman went into a far
country to receive for himself a kingdom,
and to return. 13 And he called his ten
servants, and delivered them ten pounds,
and said unto them, Occupy till I come. 14
But his citizens hated him, and sent a
message after him, saying, We will not
have this man to reign over us. 15 And it
came to pass, that when he was returned,
having received the kingdom, then he
commanded these servants to be called
unto him, to whom he had given the
money, that he might know how much
every man had gained by trading. 16 Then
came the first, saying, Lord, thy pound
hath gained ten pounds. 17 And he said
unto him, Well, thou good servant:
because thou hast been faithful in a very
little, have thou authority over ten cities.
18 And the second came, saying, Lord, thy
pound hath gained five pounds. 19 And he
said likewise to him, Be thou also over five
cities. 20 And another came, saying, Lord,
behold, here is thy pound, which I have
kept laid up in a napkin: 21 For I feared
thee, because thou art an austere man:
thou takest up that thou layedst not down,
and reapest that thou didst not sow. 22
And he saith unto him, Out of thine own
mouth will I judge thee, thou wicked
servant. Thou knewest that I was an
austere man, taking up that I laid not
down, and reaping that I did not sow: 23
Wherefore then gavest not thou my
money into the bank, that at my coming I
might have required mine own with
usury? 24 And he said unto them that
stood by, Take from him the pound, and
give it to him that hath ten pounds. 25
(And they said unto him, Lord, he hath
ten pounds.) 26 For I say unto you, That
unto every one which hath shall be given;
and from him that hath not, even that he
hath shall be taken away from him. 27
But those mine enemies, which would not
that I should reign over them, bring
hither, and slay them before me.

Every knee shall bow to King Jesus. (Rom.14:11)

Luke's theme of turning the disobedient to the just's wisdom resurfaces. Foreseeing coming accountability, the wise prepare, but the unwise never prepare to give account. (Prov.1:17; Is.56:9-12)

Synoptic gospels indicate Jesus approached Jerusalem only for this Passover. John recorded Jesus left Jerusalem at least twice after coming to Jerusalem. After the feast of dedication, Jesus and disciples crossed Jordan near where John the Baptist baptized. (Jno.10:22,40) At Lazarus' death, Jesus and disciples came to Bethany where he called Lazarus from the grave. (Jno.11:1-53) When the Jewish council determined they must eliminate Jesus or the whole world would turn to him, Jesus departed for Ephraim, a city some ten miles northeast of Jerusalem. (Jno.11:55) Six days before the Passover Jesus approached Bethany where Martha, Mary and Lazarus feasted with Jesus and his disciples. (Jno.12:1-11) The next day Jesus entered Jerusalem as the multitude rejoiced, crying hosanna to King Jesus. (Jno.12:12-15)

After the council determined to kill Jesus on pretext of saving Jerusalem and Judah from Roman retaliation, they commanded Israelites to inform them of Jesus' whereabouts. No one responded until Judas conceived the plan of betraying Jesus for thirty pieces of silver. (Zech.11:12; Math. 26:14-16; Lk.22:2-6) At heart, Judas remained a thief all the while he occupied the role of an apostle. (Jno.6:70-71;12:4-6) Unless we prepare our hearts to honor God, Satan discovers ways to make us hypocrites before God and his Son. We must remove Satan's goals from our minds to please God.

Matthew

**25:31 When the Son of man shall come in
his glory, and all the holy angels with him,
then shall he sit upon the throne of his
glory: 32 And before him shall be
gathered all nations: and he shall separate
them one from another, as a shepherd
divideth his sheep from the goats: 33 And
he shall set the sheep on his right hand,
but the goats on the left. 34 Then shall the
King say unto them on his right hand,
Come, ye blessed of my Father, inherit the
kingdom prepared for you from the
foundation of the world: 35 For I was an
hungred, and ye gave me meat: I was
thirsty, and ye gave me drink: I was a
stranger, and ye took me in: 36 Naked,
and ye clothed me: I was sick, and ye
visited me: I was in prison, and ye came
unto me. 37 Then shall the righteous
answer him, saying, Lord, when saw we
thee an hungred, and fed thee? or thirsty,
and gave thee drink? 38 When saw we
thee a stranger, and took thee in? or
naked, and clothed thee? 39 Or when saw
we thee sick, or in prison, and came unto
thee? 40 And the King shall answer and
say unto them, Verily I say unto you,
Inasmuch as ye have done it unto one of
the least of these my brethren, ye have
done it unto me. 41 Then shall he say also
unto them on the left hand, Depart from
me, ye cursed, into everlasting fire,
prepared for the devil and his angels: 42
For I was an hungred, and ye gave me no
meat: I was thirsty, and ye gave me no
drink: 43 I was a stranger, and ye took me
not in: naked, and ye clothed me not: sick,
and in prison, and ye visited me not. 44
Then shall they also answer him, saying,
Lord, when saw we thee an hungred, or
athirst, or a stranger, or naked, or sick, or
in prison, and did not minister unto thee?
45 Then shall he answer them, saying,
Verily I say unto you, Inasmuch as ye did
it not to one of the least of these, ye did it
not to me. 46 And these shall go away into
everlasting punishment: but the righteous
into life eternal.**

This judgment scene conveys the same message as the parable of the householder who traveled into a far country, leaving his servants in charge of his house. Jesus provides each of us with the task of showing compassion to others while he resides in heaven with his Father. When he returns to reckon with each of us individually as to how well we cared for those in his kingdom on earth, he rewards us with heaven for obedience, but he rewards with everlasting torment with the devil and his angels if we have not showed love to one another. Many times Jesus informed us that each of us must be responsible to him for how we live, how we deal with one another, how we work for others, how we obey or disobey our rulers, and how we have walked before God.

Parable of the judgment scene reinforces the same idea of responsibility, but specifies duties to the children of God. Providing for the needs of God's children such as food, clothing, drink, shelter, and visiting them during sickness or while in prison amounts to serving Jesus. If we believe that whatever we do to one of God's children we actually do this to Jesus and God, it changes the whole way we consider how we treat others. Serving others as if we do these things to Jesus and God somehow improves our zeal if we truly love God.

Viewing our children, parents, the sick, needy, old or young as seeing Jesus, and how we relate to others as how we relate to Jesus tends to make us live more circumspectly. It has the effect of helping us see that God resides in each of us. We feel more inclined to serve rather than be served, to help rather than ask for help, to give rather than to receive, to comfort rather than hurt, to honor one another that God may honor us in that final day when God rewards his faithful. When discouraged, call on God's help to view the promised goal, not the hardships we face. What we see influences our zeal.

Matthew

26:1 And it came to pass, when Jesus had finished all these sayings, he said unto his disciples, 2 Ye know that after two days is the feast of the passover, and the Son of man is betrayed to be crucified. 3 Then assembled together the chief priests, and the scribes, and the elders of the people, unto the palace of the high priest, who was called Caiaphas, 4 And consulted that they might take Jesus by subtilty, and kill him. 5 But they said, Not on the feast day, lest there be an uproar among the people.

Jesus prepared his disciples for his death, and rulers counseled to take Jesus to kill him. Two days before the Passover all the forces converged in Jerusalem to cast the die for the most formidable event in the history of mankind since creation. Rulers believed they must destroy Jesus, or their nation would perish. Jesus knew that unless he suffered death on the cross, no person could be saved. God's plan to defeat the deception of Satan will prevail. Jesus' disciples still had not understood why Jesus must suffer death to bring God's kingdom into being. In all this confusion, the disciples continued to follow him, but tried to reconcile Jesus' words with what they expected.

Mark

14:1 After two days was the feast of the passover, and of unleavened bread: and the chief priests and the scribes sought how they might take him by craft, and put him to death. 2 But they said, Not on the feast day, lest there be an uproar of the people.

Jewish rulers knew they wrestled with a very delicate problem. How could they arrest Jesus and dispose of him without riling the populous? Jesus understood that Judas who coveted money would succumb to the temptation and betray him to the rulers while he retired to the garden to pray for strength to endure the trials and afflictions to come. People who proclaimed Jesus to be the son of David to restore David's throne looked for Jesus to introduce the kingdom of God. How could all these aspirations culminate? God works in the kingdoms of men to bring to fruition his plans even when men believe they direct their own affairs without God. (Prov. 21:1; Is.10:5-19) Wouldn't life be wonderful if men submitted to God? Why are we so proud that we think we accomplish all by our own wisdom and strength? Our Creator continues to control our actions to accomplish his plans. If we resist God's plan, we add difficulties to ourselves.

Luke

22:1 Now the feast of unleavened bread drew nigh, which is called the Passover. 2 And the chief priests and scribes sought how they might kill him; for they feared the people.

Consider how Mark and Luke identify features of the Passover, but Matthew simply refers to it as the feast of the Passover. Mark and Luke wrote to people who knew little about the Passover, but Matthew addressed Jews who participated in the feast each year and knew its details. Mark and Luke explained that during the Passover, Jews ate unleavened bread. These small clues may help identify recipients of the gospels.

Though it would seem all the rulers consented to destroy Jesus, Joseph, one of the counselors, refused to consent to killing him. (Lk. 23:50-53) What can one or two do when the majority choose to do evil? This question you and I must answer because we face this almost daily when we work beside those who live by the rule of the archenemy of all men, Satan. If someone like David who alone faced Goliath won't take the initiative to reverse the challenges of the Evil One, will we ever see Satan's plans ruined? We need to ask God for faith and strength to prevail.

Matthew

26:14 Then one of the twelve, called Judas Iscariot, went unto the chief priests, 15 And said unto them, What will ye give me, and I will deliver him unto you? And they covenanted with him for thirty pieces of silver. 16 And from that time he sought opportunity to betray him.

Satan can drive a person to do every evil deed. Once a person gives that Serpent a place in his thinking, there will be no depth too low and no action too diabolic. The devil destroys families, friendships, partnerships, businesses, cities, nations, yes, and any covenant or promise when he finds a place in the lives of one or more involved. Yet Satan holds out promises to us of such great things he makes it seem as though he hands us the world on a platter. Deception identifies his plans. To Eve he promised wisdom and to open her eyes to see all the possibilities of life, all this without the threat of death. He approached Judas with an evil scheme. Judas, if you will but give Jesus into the hands of the rulers, they will reward you handsomely. Don't worry, the people will refuse to allow the rulers to do any dreadful thing to Jesus. Common people desired Jesus to be king of Israel. Let God complete his plan his way, not in our way. Whatever it was that convinced Judas to betray his friend, it must have appealed to him and opened dreams of amazing possibilities. However, his pleasant vision changed abruptly when the rulers condemned Jesus to death for blasphemy and persuaded the multitude to unite, calling for Jesus to be crucified. Then Judas repented and took the thirty pieces of silver which he once cherished so much and threw them down at the priests' feet, confessing he had betrayed innocent blood. Then he proceeded to hang himself. Even his body split open when it crashed against the rocks. (Math.27:3-5; Act.1:18) Deceptive promises offered by the devil leave only destructive trials of bitterness, heartaches, and death. Why do we listen to him when we see all the havoc he has brought to so many whom nearly all of us see so frequently?

When the apostles penned letters to the churches, they admonished brethren not to give place in their minds and lives to the devil. (Eph.4:27; 2 Cor.2:11; Ja.4:7; 1 Pet.5:8-9) Satan walks among us as a roaring lion, seeking prey to devour. We escape Satan's wiles only by resisting steadfastly his alluring bait.

How does one give Satan a foothold in his life? Satan first approaches us with a desire natural to the flesh. If it appeals strongly to us, and when we think on the temptation, we give Satan a place within us. Lust, anger, riches, and excitement become Satan's doorways to control our lives.

How do I avoid Satan? Think on those things that are good, honest, wholesome, and what God teaches us. (Phil.4:4-8) God pleads for his children to abandon Satan's thought patterns. If we contemplate his ways we open a way for him to lead us to do things we know are detrimental to us and others. Ask for God's help to resist Satan's allurements.

Mark

14:10 And Judas Iscariot, one of the twelve, went unto the chief priests, to betray him unto them. 11 And when they heard it, they were glad, and promised to give him money. And he sought how he might conveniently betray him.

Luke

22:3 Then entered Satan into Judas surnamed Iscariot, being of the number of the twelve. 4 And he went his way, and communed with the chief priests and captains, how he might betray him unto them. 5 And they were glad, and covenanted to give him money. 6 And he promised, and sought opportunity to betray him unto them in the absence of the multitude.

Matthew

26:6 Now when Jesus was in Bethany, in the house of Simon the leper, 7 There came unto him a woman having an alabaster box of very precious ointment, and poured it on his head, as he sat at meat. 8 But when his disciples saw it, they had indignation, saying, To what purpose is this waste? 9 For this ointment might have been sold for much, and given to the poor. 10 When Jesus understood it, he said unto them, Why trouble ye the woman? for she hath wrought a good work upon me. 11 For ye have the poor always with you; but me ye have not always. 12 For in that she hath poured this ointment on my body, she did it for my burial. 13 Verily I say unto you, Wheresoever this gospel shall be preached in the whole world, there shall also this, that this woman hath done, be told for a memorial of her.

Evaluating five gospel accounts, Simon, Martha, Mary, Lazarus, and Judas seem to be members of one family who viewed Jesus differently. Family members are Simon (father), Martha and Mary (daughters), and Lazarus and Judas (sons). Simon, a Pharisee leper, invited Jesus to eat with him, but withheld from him common guest courtesies. Martha busied herself in food preparation, but fretted because Mary sat, listening to Jesus teach about God's kingdom. Lazarus and Judas shared in the meal, but Judas chided Mary for wasting precious ointment on Jesus. Jesus loved each member, but he needed to modify attitudes and deeds for each to enjoy fullness of life. Only Martha and Mary expressed trust in Jesus as God's Son. Though Jesus raised Simon's son, Lazarus, from the dead, he told himself Jesus could not be God's prophet, or he wouldn't allow sinful Mary to touch him. Mary showed her love for Jesus by anointing him with precious ointment. Judas, the only Judaean apostle, opened the door to Satan by considering money more valuable than Jesus. At a crucial time Satan entered into Judas' heart and influenced him to offer to betray Jesus for thirty pieces of silver to the Jewish leaders who planned to put him to death. Lazarus' view of Jesus gospels omit.

Mark

14:3 And being in Bethany in the house of Simon the leper, as he sat at meat, there came a woman having an alabaster box of ointment of spikenard very precious; and she brake the box, and poured it on his head. 4 And there were some that had indignation within themselves, and said, Why was this waste of the ointment made? 5 For it might have been sold for more than three hundred pence, and have been given to the poor. And they murmured against her. 6 And Jesus said, Let her alone; why trouble ye her? she hath wrought a good work on me. 7 For ye have the poor with you always, and whensoever ye will ye may do them good: but me ye have not always. 8 She hath done what she could: she is come aforehand to anoint my body to the burying. 9 Verily I say unto you, Wheresoever this gospel shall be preached throughout the whole world, this also that she hath done shall be spoken of for a memorial of her.

Jesus taught the parable of two debtors to correct Simon's bitter view of him. If two debtors, one owing 500 days' wages and the other five days' wages, each owed the same lender, if the lender canceled both debts which will love him more? Simon replied that the one who owed him more. Jesus agreed and explained that Simon considered Mary a sinner. Her sins are forgiven because she loved much, but Simon's sins were retained because he showed little love, even to those he invited to be his guests.

Some questioned Jesus' power to forgive sins, but didn't Moses' law offer forgiveness of sins to the one who sinned ignorantly and offered appropriate sacrifices? (Lev.5:1-16) Even Pharaoh admitted his sin to Moses and asked Moses to forgive his sin. (Ex.10:16-17) God authorized Jesus' power on earth to forgive sins, and he proved it by healing a palsied man. (Mk.2:1-12) God's promise to forgive sins is a main foundation of Christianity. Do we trust Jesus' power to forgive our sins and to cleanse our consciences of offense as God promised by Jeremiah? (Jer.31:31-34) Because God forgives we must forgive.

Luke

7:36 And one of the Pharisees desired him that he would eat with him. And he went into the Pharisee's house, and sat down to meat. 37 And, behold, a woman in the city, which was a sinner, when she knew that Jesus sat at meat in the Pharisee's house, brought an alabaster box of ointment, 38 And stood at his feet behind him weeping, and began to wash his feet with tears, and did wipe them with the hairs of her head, and kissed his feet, and anointed them with the ointment. 39 Now when the Pharisee which had bidden him saw it, he spake within himself, saying, This man, if he were a prophet, would have known who and what manner of woman this is that toucheth him: for she is a sinner. 40 And Jesus answering said unto him, Simon, I have somewhat to say unto thee. And he saith, Master, say on. 41 There was a certain creditor which had two debtors: the one owed five hundred pence, and the other fifty. 42 And when they had nothing to pay, he frankly forgave them both. Tell me therefore, which of them will love him most? 43 Simon answered and said, I suppose that he, to whom he forgave most. And he said unto him, Thou hast rightly judged. 44 And he turned to the woman, and said unto Simon, Seest thou this woman? I entered into thine house, thou gavest me no water for my feet: but she hath washed my feet with tears, and wiped them with the hairs of her head. 45 Thou gavest me no kiss: but this woman since the time I came in hath not ceased to kiss my feet. 46 My head with oil thou didst not anoint: but this woman hath anointed my feet with ointment. 47 Wherefore I say unto thee, Her sins, which are many, are forgiven; for she loved much: but to whom little is forgiven, the same loveth little. 48 And he said unto her, Thy sins are forgiven. 49 And they that sat at meat with him began to say within themselves, Who is this that forgiveth sins also? 50 And he said to the woman, Thy faith hath saved thee; go in peace.

Luke

10:38 Now it came to pass, as they went, that he entered into a certain village: and a certain woman named Martha received him into her house. 39 And she had a sister called Mary, which also sat at Jesus' feet, and heard his word. 40 But Martha was cumbered about much serving, and came to him, and said, Lord, dost thou not care that my sister hath left me to serve alone? bid her therefore that she help me. 41 And Jesus answered and said unto her, Martha, Martha, thou art careful and troubled about many things: 42 But one thing is needful: and Mary hath chosen that good part, which shall not be taken away from her.

John

12:1 Then Jesus six days before the passover came to Bethany, where Lazarus was which had been dead, whom he raised from the dead. 2 There they made him a supper; and Martha served: but Lazarus was one of them that sat at the table with him. 3 Then took Mary a pound of ointment of spikenard, very costly, and anointed the feet of Jesus, and wiped his feet with her hair: and the house was filled with the odour of the ointment. 4 Then saith one of his disciples, Judas Iscariot, Simon's son, which should betray him, 5 Why was not this ointment sold for three hundred pence, and given to the poor? 6 This he said, not that he cared for the poor; but because he was a thief, and had the bag, and bare what was put therein. 7 Then said Jesus, Let her alone: against the day of my burying hath she kept this. 8 For the poor always ye have with you; but me ye have not always. 9 Much people of the Jews therefore knew that he was there: and they came not for Jesus' sake only, but that they might see Lazarus also, whom he had raised from the dead. 10 But the chief priests consulted that they might put Lazarus also to death; 11 Because that by reason of him many of the Jews went away, and believed on Jesus.

Satan divides families, but God reconciles. (See Table 2: Simon's House p.304.)

Luke

18:1 And he spake a parable unto them to this end, that men ought always to pray, and not to faint; 2 Saying, There was in a city a judge, which feared not God, neither regarded man: 3 And there was a widow in that city; and she came unto him, saying, Avenge me of mine adversary. 4 And he would not for a while: but afterward he said within himself, Though I fear not God, nor regard man; 5 Yet because this widow troubleth me, I will avenge her, lest by her continual coming she weary me. 6 And the Lord said, Hear what the unjust judge saith. 7 And shall not God avenge his own elect, which cry day and night unto him, though he bear long with them? 8 I tell you that he will avenge them speedily. Nevertheless when the Son of man cometh, shall he find faith on the earth? 9 And he spake this parable unto certain which trusted in themselves that they were righteous, and despised others: 10 Two men went up into the temple to pray; the one a Pharisee, and the other a publican. 11 The Pharisee stood and prayed thus with himself, God, I thank thee, that I am not as other men are, extortioners, unjust, adulterers, or even as this publican. 12 I fast twice in the week, I give tithes of all that I possess. 13 And the publican, standing afar off, would not lift up so much as his eyes unto heaven, but smote upon his breast, saying, God be merciful to me a sinner. 14 I tell you, this man went down to his house justified rather than the other: for every one that exalteth himself shall be abased; and he that humbleth himself shall be exalted.

Why do people pray to God? Most commonly, they ask for help with a pressing problem. In the case of the widow in Jesus' parable, someone tormented her. She called on the judge to avenge or punish the troublemaker. Though the judge himself feared not God and disregarded others, he performed the responsibility of a judge to prevent the widow from continually harassing him. From this parable Jesus drew this observation: God will respond to his children who show faith to ask him for help. Though God faithfully helps his children, when Jesus returns from heaven, will he find the children of God faithfully calling on God to help in their time of distress? Do we really think God listens to our requests and grants our wishes? Do we approach his throne of mercy often to thank and ask petitions of him? May God help us grow in faith to trust his promises.

Why did God justify the publican, but reject the Pharisee? Humility seems to be the clue. "**What doth the Lord require of thee, but to do justly, and to love mercy, and to walk humbly with thy God**? (Mi. 6:8) Where had the Pharisee faltered? Was he humble before God, or did he trust in his own righteousness? True, he attempted to live justly and even showed mercy in tithing, but where was his humility? Pride in men and women offends God. (Prov.6:16-18) Is there any ability you and I possess God has not granted us? Are there any material blessings God has not graciously given us? This being true, why are we prone to exalt ourselves? God desires we recognize him and all his works of mercy in what he provides us. (See Deu.8:7-18.) Instead, all too often we think about how great we are in accomplishments and wealth. Do we regard God in our daily activities?

The Pharisee remarked, God, I thank thee I am not like other men. The publican pleaded, God, have mercy on me, a sinner. In our own associations with others which attitude turns us off and which one tends to gain our respect? Do we think God is any more pleased with the person who displays a proud attitude than are we? It's the humble or poor spirit within us that God sees as respectable before him. Understanding this, approach God in a humble spirit, and he will bless us as he pleases.

Matthew

26:14 Then one of the twelve, called Judas Iscariot, went unto the chief priests, 15 And said unto them, What will ye give me, and I will deliver him unto you? And they covenanted with him for thirty pieces of silver. 16 And from that time he sought opportunity to betray him.

Mark

14:10 And Judas Iscariot, one of the twelve, went unto the chief priests, to betray him unto them. 11 And when they heard it, they were glad, and promised to give him money. And he sought how he might conveniently betray him.

Luke

22:3 Then entered Satan into Judas surnamed Iscariot, being of the number of the twelve. 4 And he went his way, and communed with the chief priests and captains, how he might betray him unto them. 5 And they were glad, and covenanted to give him money. 6 And he promised, and sought opportunity to betray him unto them in the absence of the multitude.

Satan can drive a person to do every evil deed. Once a person gives that Serpent a place in his thinking, there will be no depth too low and no action too diabolic. The devil destroys families, friendships, partnerships, businesses, cities, nations, yes, and any covenant or promise when he finds a place in the lives of one or more involved. Yet Satan holds out promises to us of such great things he makes it seem as though he hands us the world on a platter. Deception and lies identify his plans. To Eve he promised wisdom and to open her eyes to see all the possibilities of life, all this without the threat of death. He approached Judas with an evil scheme. Judas, if you will but give Jesus into the hands of the rulers, they will reward you handsomely. Don't worry, the people will refuse to allow the rulers to do any dreadful thing to Jesus. Common people desired Jesus to be king of Israel. Let God complete his plan his way, not in our way. Whatever it was that convinced Judas to betray his friend, it must have appealed to him and opened dreams of amazing possibilities. However, his pleasant vision vanished abruptly when the rulers condemned Jesus to death for blasphemy and persuaded the multitude to unite, calling for Jesus to be crucified. Then Judas repented and took the thirty pieces of silver which he once cherished so much and threw them down at the priests' feet, confessing he had betrayed innocent blood. Then he proceeded to hang himself. Even his body split open when it crashed against the rocks. (Math.27:3-5; Act.1:18) Deceptive promises offered by the devil leave only destructive trials of bitterness, heartaches, and death. Why do we listen to him when we see all the havoc he has brought to so many whom nearly all of us see so frequently.

When the apostle penned letters to the churches, they admonished brethren not to give place in their minds and lives to the devil. (Eph.4:27; 2 Cor.2:11; Ja.4:7; 1 Pet.5:8-9) Satan walks among us as a roaring lion, seeking prey to devour. We escape Satan's wiles only by resisting steadfastly his alluring bait.

How does one give Satan a foothold in his life? Satan first approaches us with a desire natural to the flesh. If it appeals strongly to us, and when we think on the temptation, we give Satan a place within us. Lust, anger, riches, and excitement become Satan's doorways to control our lives.

How do I avoid Satan? Think on those things that are good, honest, wholesome, and what God teaches us. (Phil.4:4-8) God pleads for his children to abandon Satan's thought patterns. If we contemplate his ways we open a way for him to lead us to do things we know are detrimental to us and others. Ask for God's help to resist Satan' allurements.

Did Judas have a choice to betray Jesus or not to betray him? If God planned Christ's sacrificial death from creation, could Judas escape from his God-ordained task of betraying Jesus to the Jewish council? Don't the Scriptures speak of God's eternal plan of redemption? If not Judas, then another must have sold Jesus to his enemies.

It's true God's eternal plan to redeem all obedient believers required Christ's unjust death that Christ's righteous blood should serve as an atonement for every person who sins. (Is.53:1-12; Dan.9:24; Eph.3:11) Without Jesus taking our place in death, every person must die for his own sins, because God's penalty for sin (transgression of God's law) is death. (Gen.2:17; Ezek.18:4; Rom. 1:32;6:23; 1 Jno.3:4) Jesus knew shortly after Herod imprisoned John the Baptist who would betray him. (Math.26:21; Jno.6:70-71)

Does this mean Judas could not prevent himself from betraying Jesus? Paul discussed a similar point where Egypt's Pharaoh served in God's hand to force an issue which resulted in Israel's release from Egyptian bondage. God purposely selected Pharaoh to rule over Egypt when God began to fulfill his promise to Abraham that in the fourth generation, God would punish Israel's oppressor and return Israel to take the land God previously gave Canaan's descendants, but deprived them of that land when their sins prevailed. (Gen.15:3-16; Rom.9:17-23) Did God force Pharaoh against his will to harden his heart, refusing to release Israel, or did God choose to elevate a wicked, hard-hearted, self-determined man to rule Egypt? Being self-willed, he would refuse to submit to God's request to release Israel that God may punish Egypt for all the wickedness they heaped on Israelites while they held them in bondage. Knowing Pharaoh's obstinacy and refusal to submit to any power other than his own will, Pharaoh would deny Israel's freedom while God demonstrated his power that ultimately persuaded Egyptians that Israel's God would impoverish and destroy them if Pharaoh refused to bow to God's plan. Thus God's power and glory manifested itself to Egypt and all surrounding nations, and they greatly feared him for centuries. (Josh.2: 9-11; 1 Sam.4:5-9)

Was Judas wicked at heart before Jesus chose him as an apostle, and did he listen to all Jesus' God-given message, see all his healing and raising the dead, but refused to repent and believe the gospel? Yes, Jesus knew Judas' heart the day he named him an apostle. He knew Judas would betray him, fulfilling God's eternal plan. It was Judas' choice to continue living with a bitter, covetous heart. Jesus chose him because he was evil-hearted. God always selects the person who is self-directed to fit the part God needs to act the evil drama of life.

God chose Jesus because he retained a heart to please and honor his heavenly Father, disregarding all the taunts of his countrymen, brothers, Pharisees, and others who considered him a challenge to their cherished status in their society. (Heb. 10:7,9; Ps.40:4-10) Like Judas, God gave Jesus complete freedom to choose his course of life. Weighing the rewards, for the obedient and disobedient, Jesus chose to submit completely to his heavenly Father's will.

As Pharaoh, Judas, and Jesus chose, God fitted each for the events they served to accomplish his goals. You and I also act the hero or villain in God's drama of real life. Our condition of mind and heart determines which role God offers us. Pure in heart and submissive to God's will we play the admirable roles, but the obstinate and self-willed act the evil roles. If you hate the role you play, repent, and God will offer you a more respectable part as he did Saul of Tarsus who first persecuted Christians, but when he repented, God gave him an honorable role. When Jesus taught, **"Blessed are the meek: for they shall inherit the earth,"** he identified those whom God elevates in his kingdom to serve in honorable roles.

Matthew

**26:17 Now the first day of the feast of
unleavened bread the disciples came to
Jesus, saying unto him, Where wilt thou
that we prepare for thee to eat the
passover? 18 And he said, Go into the city
to such a man, and say unto him, The
Master saith, My time is at hand; I will
keep the passover at thy house with my
disciples. 19 And the disciples did as Jesus
had appointed them; and they made ready
the passover. 20 Now when the even was
come, he sat down with the twelve. 21
And as they did eat, he said, Verily I say
unto you, that one of you shall betray me.
22 And they were exceeding sorrowful,
and began every one of them to say unto
him, Lord, is it I? 23 And he answered
and said, He that dippeth his hand with
me in the dish, the same shall betray me.
24 The Son of man goeth as it is written of
him: but woe unto that man by whom the
Son of man is betrayed! it had been good
for that man if he had not been born. 25
Then Judas, which betrayed him,
answered and said, Master, is it I? He said
unto him, Thou hast said.**

As Moses instructed Israel, Jesus and his disciples assembled in the place where God placed his name to eat the Passover. (Deu.12:5-7;16:1-8) The lamb they killed on the fourteenth day of their first month, Abib. (Ex.12:18-20;13:3-7) As Jesus and his disciples feasted, Jesus remarked that one of the twelve would betray him. Each seemed to sorrow that such must happen, and each asked if he would be the guilty one. When Judas asked if he would betray Jesus, he replied that Judas would. In addition, Jesus pronounced a woe on Judas, saying it would have been better for him not to have been born if he betrayed Jesus.

In a sense, every person who obeys Jesus to believe and be baptized to become a child of God and then turns back to live as the world betrays Jesus and receives a woe like

Mark

**14:12 And the first day of unleavened
bread, when they killed the passover, his
disciples said unto him, Where wilt thou
that we go and prepare that thou mayest
eat the passover? 13 And he sendeth forth
two of his disciples, and saith unto them,
Go ye into the city, and there shall meet
you a man bearing a pitcher of water:
follow him. 14 And wheresoever he shall
go in, say ye to the goodman of the house,
The Master saith, Where is the guestchamber, where I shall eat the passover
with my disciples? 15 And he will shew
you a large upper room furnished and
prepared: there make ready for us. 16
And his disciples went forth, and came
into the city, and found as he had said
unto them: and they made ready the
passover. 17 And in the evening he cometh
with the twelve. 18 And as they sat and
did eat, Jesus said, Verily I say unto you,
One of you which eateth with me shall
betray me. 19 And they began to be
sorrowful, and to say unto him one by
one, Is it I? and another said, Is it I? 20
And he answered and said unto them, It is
one of the twelve, that dippeth with me in
the dish. 21 The Son of man indeed goeth,
as it is written of him: but woe to that
man by whom the Son of man is betrayed!
good were it for that man if he had never
been born.**

Judas. (Gal.3:1; Jude 11-13) A new birth requires one to be faithful to God. I suppose each of us faces numerous times in life when we ask ourselves which role we really chose to play in life. We are tempted to follow the easy path as most, but Jesus and God ask for brave men and women who willingly sacrifice their own wishes in life to honor them. Though Judas followed Jesus with his body, his will never fully resigned to what Jesus taught. If one never fully commits himself/herself to the service of God, Satan will appear at such a time when his way appeals, and we shall fall.

Luke

22:7 Then came the day of unleavened bread, when the passover must be killed. 8 And he sent Peter and John, saying, Go and prepare us the passover, that we may eat. 9 And they said unto him, Where wilt thou that we prepare? 10 And he said unto them, Behold, when ye are entered into the city, there shall a man meet you, bearing a pitcher of water; follow him into the house where he entereth in. 11 And ye shall say unto the goodman of the house, The Master saith unto thee, Where is the guestchamber, where I shall eat the passover with my disciples? 12 And he shall shew you a large upper room furnished: there make ready. 13 And they went, and found as he had said unto them: and they made ready the passover. 14 And when the hour was come, he sat down, and the twelve apostles with him. 15 And he said unto them, With desire I have desired to eat this passover with you before I suffer: 16 For I say unto you, I will not any more eat thereof, until it be fulfilled in the kingdom of God. 17 And he took the cup, and gave thanks, and said, Take this, and divide it among yourselves: 18 For I say unto you, I will not drink of the fruit of the vine, until the kingdom of God shall come.

John

13:1 Now before the feast of the passover, when Jesus knew that his hour was come that he should depart out of this world unto the Father, having loved his own which were in the world, he loved them unto the end. 2 And supper being ended, the devil having now put into the heart of Judas Iscariot, Simon's son, to betray him; 3 Jesus knowing that the Father had given all things into his hands, and that he was come from God, and went to God; 4 He riseth from supper, and laid aside his garments; and took a towel, and girded himself. 5 After that he poureth water into a bason, and began to wash the disciples' feet, and to wipe them with the towel wherewith he was girded. 6 Then cometh he to Simon Peter: and Peter saith unto him, Lord, dost thou wash my feet? 7 Jesus answered and said unto him, What I do thou knowest not now; but thou shalt know hereafter. 8 Peter saith unto him, Thou shalt never wash my feet. Jesus answered him, If I wash thee not, thou hast no part with me. 9 Simon Peter saith unto him, Lord, not my feet only, but also my hands and my head. 10 Jesus saith to him, He that is washed needeth not save to wash his feet, but is clean every whit: and ye are clean, but not all. 11 For he knew who should betray him; therefore said he, Ye are not all clean. 12 So after he had washed their feet, and had taken his garments, and was set down again, he said unto them, Know ye what I have done to you? 13 Ye call me Master and Lord: and ye say well; for so I am. 14 If I then, your Lord and Master, have washed your feet; ye also ought to wash one another's feet. 15 For I have given you an example, that ye should do as I have done to you.

Before the next Passover, the kingdom of God arrived. Then Jesus and his disciples ate and drank of the Lord's supper in the kingdom of God.

During the feast, Jesus reemphasized that each person in the kingdom of God must serve one another. He washed the apostles' feet to solidly stress this concept. If we today please God and Jesus, we will serve one another, not wish to be served as the world desires it. God instructed Jesus to teach and demonstrate that serving willingly rewards the doer with a sense of worthwhileness which is missing from the lives of those who ask to be served. Let each of us seek this serving attitude in life. It is one of the rewards God gives his children for submitting to his will and seeking the best for others above ourselves. God always seeks the best for each of us. (Deu.6:24)

Matthew

26:26 And as they were eating, Jesus took bread, and blessed it, and brake it, and gave it to the disciples, and said, Take, eat; this is my body. 27 And he took the cup, and gave thanks, and gave it to them, saying, Drink ye all of it; 28 For this is my blood of the new testament, which is shed for many for the remission of sins. 29 But I say unto you, I will not drink henceforth of this fruit of the vine, until that day when I drink it new with you in my Father's kingdom. 30 And when they had sung an hymn, they went out into the mount of Olives.

Emblems of bread and juice of the fruit of the vine signify respectively the body and blood of Jesus in the Lord's supper. Broken bread indicates his body broken on the cross, and the fruit of the vine portrays his blood by which he sealed the covenant of the new testament. (Heb.9:11-28) Jesus asked his disciples when partaking of the Lord's supper to think about his body on the cross and his blood shed to reconcile us to the living God. (1 Cor.11:17-30) These remind us of his death until he returns from heaven at the appointed time.

As Christians eat the Lord's supper, Jesus eats and drinks with us if our hearts ponder the meaning of his sacrifice for our sins. Unless we realize that each of us is guilty of sin and worthy of death because of sin, we are not participating in the Lord's supper with Jesus and his brethren. (Rom.1:32; 5:12;6:16,21-25;7:5;8:13) God asks each of us for our hearts to be on the meaning of what we do to glorify his name. We may find ourselves participating in taking the emblems, but without contemplating their significance before God and his beloved Son. God so loves each of us that he willingly gave his only begotten Son to pay the penalty for our sins that we do not have to be separated from God eternally for our transgressions. (Jno.3:16)

Mark

14:22 And as they did eat, Jesus took bread, and blessed, and brake it, and gave to them, and said, Take, eat: this is my body. 23 And he took the cup, and when he had given thanks, he gave it to them: and they all drank of it. 24 And he said unto them, This is my blood of the new testament, which is shed for many. 25 Verily I say unto you, I will drink no more of the fruit of the vine, until that day that I drink it new in the kingdom of God. 26 And when they had sung an hymn, they went out into the mount of Olives.

Because we are worthy of death for our sins, Jesus, by the will of God, suffered death on the cross to pay the penalty of death due each of us. Since blood contains the life of the flesh, shedding his blood denotes giving his life. (Lev.17:11) God determined that blood of another on the altar might pay the penalty of death for the one who sinned. With this decree in mind, God determined to have his only begotten Son who remained without sin suffer the agony of death for all who have sinned. (Heb.4:15; 1 Pet.2:22) Therefore we are justified before God by the blood of Jesus and no longer subject to eternal death for our sins if we trust in Jesus' blood to shelter us from the wrath of God. This isn't a license to sin after we believe, or we shall die spiritually. (Rom.5:9;8:13)

The blood of the Passover lamb illustrated the need for Christ's death. When God sent the destroyer to slay all the firstborn in Egypt, any house which lacked the blood of the Passover lamb on the lintel and side posts of the door, the destroyer took the life of the firstborn. God instructed Israelites how to spare their firstborn by sprinkling the Passover lamb's blood around their doorways. (Ex.12:18-30) When Christ returns from heaven, all who have not been washed in Christ's blood and remained in Christ, he shall destroy. (Math.25:41-46)

It's unfortunate that many Christians deny the need of Christ's blood to cleanse sin.

Luke

22:19 And he took bread, and gave thanks, and brake it, and gave unto them, saying, This is my body which is given for you: this do in remembrance of me. 20 Likewise also the cup after supper, saying, This cup is the new testament in my blood, which is shed for you. 21 But, behold, the hand of him that betrayeth me is with me on the table. 22 And truly the Son of man goeth, as it was determined: but woe unto that man by whom he is betrayed! 23 And they began to inquire among themselves, which of them it was that should do this thing. 24 And there was also a strife among them, which of them should be accounted the greatest. 25 And he said unto them, The kings of the Gentiles exercise lordship over them; and they that exercise authority upon them are called benefactors. 26 But ye shall not be so: but he that is greatest among you, let him be as the younger; and he that is chief, as he that doth serve. 27 For whether is greater, he that sitteth at meat, or he that serveth? is not he that sitteth at meat? but I am among you as he that serveth. 28 Ye are they which have continued with me in my temptations. 29 And I appoint unto you a kingdom, as my Father hath appointed unto me; 30 That ye may eat and drink at my table in my kingdom, and sit on thrones judging the twelve tribes of Israel.

Even during the last supper together, desire to occupy the chief position in the kingdom of God plagued the apostles. Again Jesus reminded them how Gentile rulers held authority over the people, but God's kingdom rules differently. If you seek the chief position among your brethren in God's dominion, you must become the servant of all. Then Jesus appointed them the right to eat and drink at his table as God appointed him King of kings in the kingdom of heaven.

John

13:16 Verily, verily, I say unto you, The servant is not greater than his lord; neither he that is sent greater than he that sent him. 17 If ye know these things, happy are ye if ye do them. 18 I speak not of you all: I know whom I have chosen: but that the scripture may be fulfilled, He that eateth bread with me hath lifted up his heel against me. 19 Now I tell you before it come, that, when it is come to pass, ye may believe that I am he. 20 Verily, verily, I say unto you, He that receiveth whomsoever I send receiveth me; and he that receiveth me receiveth him that sent me. 21 When Jesus had thus said, he was troubled in spirit, and testified, and said, Verily, verily, I say unto you, that one of you shall betray me. 22 Then the disciples looked one on another, doubting of whom he spake. 23 Now there was leaning on Jesus' bosom one of his disciples, whom Jesus loved. 24 Simon Peter therefore beckoned to him, that he should ask who it should be of whom he spake.

That the apostles might believe him to be Christ, he referred to their Scriptures, noting that he would be betrayed by one who ate with him. By helping them to know the prophecy, they would trust him.

Receiving one whom Jesus sends to teach the gospel of God means that one receives Jesus. Conversely, by rejecting one who preaches the good news of the kingdom of heaven one rejects Jesus and the heavenly Father who sent him. Though the apostles had experienced rejection by their own people during their ministry with Jesus, after his death, Jews and Gentiles alike would often reject their message. Some would even vent their anger on them. Even today receiving or rejecting one who preaches the word of God's kingdom signifies that a person receives or rejects God. Knowing this it is wise to examine carefully ministers' exhortation to return to God.

Matthew

26:31 Then saith Jesus unto them, All ye shall be offended because of me this night: for it is written, I will smite the shepherd, and the sheep of the flock shall be scattered abroad. 32 But after I am risen again, I will go before you into Galilee. 33 Peter answered and said unto him, Though all men shall be offended because of thee, yet will I never be offended. 34 Jesus said unto him, Verily I say unto thee, That this night, before the cock crow, thou shalt deny me thrice. 35 Peter said unto him, Though I should die with thee, yet will I not deny thee. Likewise also said all the disciples.

A notable weakness of mankind pleases Satan greatly. We think we can withstand temptations all by ourselves and remain unstained. Peter and all the apostles fell prey to this folly. Each of them stated confidently that he would not deny Jesus in any situation. Those about us at the time all too often control our actions. When with God's people, we believe we're strong for God, but when we assemble with unbelievers, we question our position and become intimidated. Peter followed Jesus at a distance when the mob arrested him. In the midst of those who wished to destroy Jesus, Peter alone yielded. When accused of being one of Jesus' disciples, Peter denied it three times. Is it any wonder that Paul cautioned the Corinthians, "**Do not be deceived: Bad company ruins good morals?**" (1 Cor. 15:33; RSV) Solomon admonished, "**Make no friendship with an angry man; and with a furious man thou shalt not go: Lest thou learn his ways, and get a snare to thy soul.**" (Prov.22:24) We need to ponder well Peter's feebleness while he assembled with the destroyers of the Lord Jesus Christ. We could succumb to frailty, too. Even the strength of youth enters temptations when with wrong crowds. Don't offer Satan an opportunity to lead you into temptation by the pride of false stability.

Mark

14:27 And Jesus saith unto them, All ye shall be offended because of me this night: for it is written, I will smite the shepherd, and the sheep shall be scattered. 28 But after that I am risen, I will go before you into Galilee. 29 But Peter said unto him, Although all shall be offended, yet will not I. 30 And Jesus saith unto him, Verily I say unto thee, That this day, even in this night, before the cock crow twice, thou shalt deny me thrice. 31 But he spake the more vehemently, If I should die with thee, I will not deny thee in any wise. Likewise also said they all.

Consider Jesus' mercy. After Jesus told the disciples they would all deny him before morning, and they claimed they would not, Jesus encouraged them to meet him in Galilee after he rose from the dead. Though you deny me before the multitude, I still love you. I will meet you in Galilee as we walked together before the rulers condemned me to death.

Are we forgiving when we feel our friends slight us? We ought to realize Jesus embodied the compassion of our heavenly Father who observes how prone we are to fickleness. God holds out his hand to receive us as friends again even when we deny his Son. Would you and I benefit from such a friend who overlooks our faltering ways and remains our devoted friend? If we believe in the blood of Jesus and its power to sustain us when we fall, God counts our faith as righteousness. (Rom.3:24-28)

Witnessing such a forgiving spirit in Jesus, we need to embody this attitude in ourselves. Does holding a grudge benefit my life? How am I uplifted by harboring hatred? Is bitterness that which sweetens life? When a husband, wife, or child irritates me, will reminding him/her of the offense improve family relationships? By experience we have learned that overlooking faults in others eases inter-personal frictions. By example, God encourages forgiveness.

Luke

**22:31 And the Lord said, Simon, Simon,
behold, Satan hath desired to have you,
that he may sift you as wheat: 32 But I
have prayed for thee, that thy faith fail
not: and when thou art converted,
strengthen thy brethren. 33 And he said
unto him, Lord, I am ready to go with
thee, both into prison, and to death. 34
And he said, I tell thee, Peter, the cock
shall not crow this day, before that thou
shalt thrice deny that thou knowest me. 35
And he said unto them, When I sent you
without purse, and scrip, and shoes,
lacked ye any thing? And they said,
Nothing. 36 Then said he unto them, But
now, he that hath a purse, let him take it,
and likewise his scrip: and he that hath no
sword, let him sell his garment, and buy
one. 37 For I say unto you, that this that is
written must yet be accomplished in me,
And he was reckoned among the transgressors: for the things concerning me
have an end. 38 And they said, Lord,
behold, here are two swords. And he said
unto them, It is enough.**

After the Jewish rulers delivered Jesus to the governor to be crucified, there shall be a change in the preparations you need to make as you go preaching the gospel. You have not needed extra clothing or food because your audiences provided these. Now you will need to prepare as you preach. Your relatives and friends shall view you as strangers and will not provide for you. As I am regarded among transgressors, even as the Scripture says, so you will be regarded. (Is.53:12) Therefore make provisions for your journeys. Take money, extra clothing, and whatever you will need. I send you to those who know you not. Many will hear you gladly, but those who receive not your words will hate you, delivering you to governors, councils, kings, and persecuting you. Let not these things astonish you. They rejected me, and they will treat you the same.

John

**13:25 He then lying on Jesus' breast saith
unto him, Lord, who is it? 26 Jesus
answered, He it is, to whom I shall give a
sop, when I have dipped it. And when he
had dipped the sop, he gave it to Judas
Iscariot, the son of Simon. 27 And after
the sop Satan entered into him. Then said
Jesus unto him, That thou doest, do
quickly. 28 Now no man at the table knew
for what intent he spake this unto him. 29
For some of them thought, because Judas
had the bag, that Jesus had said unto him,
Buy those things that we have need of
against the feast; or, that he should give
something to the poor. 30 He then having
received the sop went immediately out:
and it was night. 31 Therefore, when he
was gone out, Jesus said, Now is the Son
of man glorified, and God is glorified in
him. 32 If God be glorified in him, God
shall also glorify him in himself, and shall
straightway glorify him. 33 Little children, yet a little while I am with you. Ye
shall seek me: and as I said unto the Jews,
Whither I go, ye cannot come; so now I
say to you. 34 A new commandment I give
unto you, That ye love one another; as I
have loved you, that ye also love one
another. 35 By this shall all men know
that ye are my disciples, if ye have love
one to another. 36 Simon Peter said unto
him, Lord, whither goest thou? Jesus
answered him, Whither I go, thou canst
not follow me now; but thou shalt follow
me afterwards. 37 Peter said unto him,
Lord, why cannot I follow thee now? I
will lay down my life for thy sake. 38
Jesus answered him, Wilt thou lay down
thy life for my sake? Verily, verily, I say
unto thee, The cock shall not crow, till
thou hast denied me thrice.**

Continuing to prepare his disciples for coming events, Jesus informed them they would soon not see him. Their hearts would grieve and fear grip them, but after his resurrection, he would meet them again.

John

14:1 Let not your heart be troubled: ye
believe in God, believe also in me. 2 In my
Father's house are many mansions: if it
were not so, I would have told you. I go to
prepare a place for you. 3 And if I go and
prepare a place for you, I will come again,
and receive you unto myself; that where I
am, there ye may be also. 4 And whither I
go ye know, and the way ye know. 5
Thomas saith unto him, Lord, we know
not whither thou goest; and how can we
know the way? 6 Jesus saith unto him, I
am the way, the truth, and the life: no
man cometh unto the Father, but by me. 7
If ye had known me, ye should have
known my Father also: and from hence-
forth ye know him, and have seen him. 8
Philip saith unto him, Lord, shew us the
Father, and it sufficeth us. 9 Jesus saith
unto him, Have I been so long time with
you, and yet hast thou not known me,
Philip? he that hath seen me hath seen the
Father; and how sayest thou then, Shew
us the Father? 10 Believest thou not that I
am in the Father, and the Father in me?
the words that I speak unto you I speak
not of myself: but the Father that dwell-
eth in me, he doeth the works. 11 Believe
me that I am in the Father, and the Father
in me: or else believe me for the very
works' sake. 12 Verily, verily, I say unto
you, He that believeth on me, the works
that I do shall he do also; and greater
works than these shall he do; because I go
unto my Father. 13 And whatsoever ye
shall ask in my name, that will I do, that
the Father may be glorified in the Son. 14
If ye shall ask any thing in my name, I
will do it. 15 If ye love me, keep my com-
mandments. 16 And I will pray the
Father, and he shall give you another
Comforter, that he may abide with you
for ever; 17 Even the Spirit of truth;
whom the world cannot receive, because it
seeth him not, neither knoweth him: but
ye know him; for he dwelleth with you,
and shall be in you.

Time for Jesus to leave the disciples neared. Jesus encouraged them to believe in him as they did the Father. He assured them God's house contains many mansions, as the temple housed many quarters for priests and Levites. (Ezek.42:13-14) Though Jesus must leave them, he goes to prepare a place for them in God's house. He expected them to know he returned to God and that they knew no person could go to God except through him, for he alone is the way to God. He spoke all God's truth, and dispensed eternal life from God. Philip asked for Jesus to show them the Father, but Jesus remarked that if you have seen me, you have seen the Father. We work so closely together that if you have seen me, you have seen God. If you believe in me, you will be able to do everything I've done and more because I return to God. This glorifies the Father. When I'm gone, you may ask anything of me, and I will supply your requests. If you really love me, you will keep my commands, then God will give you his Spirit to comfort you forever, and God's Spirit shall abide with you forever. Those of the world cannot have the Holy Spirit because they don't know his ways. The Spirit has been with you as you preached and healed. Now he shall dwell in you. God provides great blessings for his people. (1 Cor.2:14)

Could any person do greater works than those Jesus performed? It would seem such is impossible, but Jesus promised his disciples they could accomplish greater works than he did when the Father's Spirit came to them. Healing all manner of physical ailments amazed his audiences, but his disciples will be able to heal the spirits of people in every nation. Jesus visited primarily Jewish people, but taking the true gospel of God to every nation, they reached far more than Jesus in his personal ministry. As apostles healed spiritual blights with gospel they exceeded Jesus' body healing.

John

14:18 I will not leave you comfortless: I will come to you. 19 Yet a little while, and the world seeth me no more; but ye see me: because I live, ye shall live also. 20 At that day ye shall know that I am in my Father, and ye in me, and I in you. 21 He that hath my commandments, and keepeth them, he it is that loveth me: and he that loveth me shall be loved of my Father, and I will love him, and will manifest myself to him. 22 Judas saith unto him, not Iscariot, Lord, how is it that thou wilt manifest thyself unto us, and not unto the world? 23 Jesus answered and said unto him, If a man love me, he will keep my words: and my Father will love him, and we will come unto him, and make our abode with him. 24 He that loveth me not keepeth not my sayings: and the word which ye hear is not mine, but the Father's which sent me. 25 These things have I spoken unto you, being yet present with you. 26 But the Comforter, which is the Holy Ghost, whom the Father will send in my name, he shall teach you all things, and bring all things to your remembrance, whatsoever I have said unto you. 27 Peace I leave with you, my peace I give unto you: not as the world giveth, give I unto you. Let not your heart be troubled, neither let it be afraid. 28 Ye have heard how I said unto you, I go away, and come again unto you. If ye loved me, ye would rejoice, because I said, I go unto the Father: for my Father is greater than I. 29 And now I have told you before it come to pass, that, when it is come to pass, ye might believe. 30 Hereafter I will not talk much with you: for the prince of this world cometh, and hath nothing in me. 31 But that the world may know that I love the Father; and as the Father gave me commandment, even so I do. Arise, let us go hence.

How can Jesus and his Father come and manifest themselves to the disciples, and the world not see them? Obedience to the truth of God determines whether one loves and sees the Father, Son, and Spirit and determines if they dwell with a person. Though God desires to dwell with all his children, sin separates man from God. (Is.59:1-2) Even receiving God's peace rests on whether one keeps the words of Jesus which he brought down to us from the Father. If you desire the eternal life which Jesus provides, you must obey his words.

Judas, not the betrayer, asked Jesus how he could show himself to the apostles, but not to the world. Since the apostles heard and kept the commands of Jesus, he promised to show himself to them, but worldly people who refused to obey the Father's truth could not see him, neither could they know the Spirit nor the Father.

Why did Jesus speak these things then? They had walked together for three years and had bonded together as friends. Hearing him say he must leave caused them sorrow. Promising to return to them with the Father and Spirit encouraged them and gave them peace of mind. They must experience tribulation in this world, but peace within themselves comes from the Father. Having explained these ideas to them before his crucifixion and burial helped them to believe him to be the Messiah.

If we desire God's love, continued presence of God's Son and Spirit, peace of God in the midst of a troubled world, the comfort of knowing God dwells with and keeps us, we can assure these only by one means. We must obey the words Jesus spoke. Otherwise, we are of the world, and God, Jesus, and the Spirit will not come and abide with us. These are the words God gave to Jesus to deliver to mankind. Let each of us trust God and his promises as we would our best friend, for he will not tell us a lie. If you and I genuinely want God, Jesus, and God's Spirit to dwell with us each day, we will keep all God's commandments Jesus brought to us from our heavenly Father.

John

**15:1 I am the true vine, and my Father is
the husbandman. 2 Every branch in me
that beareth not fruit he taketh away: and
every branch that beareth fruit, he
purgeth it, that it may bring forth more
fruit. 3 Now ye are clean through the
word which I have spoken unto you. 4
Abide in me, and I in you. As the branch
cannot bear fruit of itself, except it abide
in the vine; no more can ye, except ye
abide in me. 5 I am the vine, ye are the
branches: He that abideth in me, and I in
him, the same bringeth forth much fruit:
for without me ye can do nothing. 6 If a
man abide not in me, he is cast forth as a
branch, and is withered; and men gather
them, and cast them into the fire, and they
are burned. 7 If ye abide in me, and my
words abide in you, ye shall ask what ye
will, and it shall be done unto you. 8
Herein is my Father glorified, that ye bear
much fruit; so shall ye be my disciples. 9
As the Father hath loved me, so have I
loved you: continue ye in my love. 10 If ye
keep my commandments, ye shall abide in
my love; even as I have kept my Father's
commandments, and abide in his love. 11
These things have I spoken unto you, that
my joy might remain in you, and that
your joy might be full. 12 This is my
commandment, That ye love one another,
as I have loved you. 13 Greater love hath
no man than this, that a man lay down his
life for his friends. 14 Ye are my friends,
if ye do whatsoever I command you. 15
Henceforth I call you not servants; for the
servant knoweth not what his lord doeth:
but I have called you friends; for all
things that I have heard of my Father I
have made known unto you. 16 Ye have
not chosen me, but I have chosen you, and
ordained you, that ye should go and bring
forth fruit, and that your fruit should
remain: that whatsoever ye shall ask of
the Father in my name, he may give it
you.**

Like Moses, Jesus explained all God's truth to his disciples. It requires a person to continue loving and obeying all God's commands. Doing this produces fruitful lives and joy in the believer and in God. This friendship with God and Jesus opens the communication whereby we may call on our heavenly Father in Jesus' name for help in every situation and know he will respond as any good friend.

Failure to abide in God's love, Jesus, and God's truth loses all God's promises. Jesus likened our need to abide in Jesus and God's love to branches on a plant. Unproductive branches a gardener cuts off and burns. God made Jesus the plant, and each person a branch. If we produce no fruit to God, he, as a gardener, clips us from the plant of Christ and destroys us. If this is God's truth, why do some teach a Christian cannot so sin as to be lost. This concept conflicts with what Jesus taught.

God designed his commands to produce true joy in the heart of the believer. He assures us that abundant life and joy fills the lives of those who keep the commandments of his Father. Contrast this with Satan's message which claims to produce a joyful life by forgetting God's words. Which precepts produce a more joyful life? When a person follows the advice of the Evil One, he does those things which please himself and disregards the feelings of others. Does obeying God's truth result in a full life or an empty life with many sorrows and regrets? What about submitting to the truth Jesus taught? Does it result in a more satisfying life, one which produces joy and self-fulfillment? Satisfaction of any undertaking or product is what we expect when we pay money. If it fails to produce the promised results, we feel cheated and wish to have our money refunded. Does Satan's or God's instruction bring true satisfaction? Satan's brings sorrow; God's produces joy. If we seek true joy, submit to God's truth.

John

15:17 These things I command you, that
ye love one another. 18 If the world hate
you, ye know that it hated me before it
hated you. 19 If ye were of the world, the
world would love his own: but because ye
are not of the world, but I have chosen
you out of the world, therefore the world
hateth you. 20 Remember the word that I
said unto you, The servant is not greater
than his lord. If they have persecuted me,
they will also persecute you; if they have
kept my saying, they will keep yours also.
21 But all these things will they do unto
you for my name's sake, because they
know not him that sent me. 22 If I had not
come and spoken unto them, they had not
had sin: but now they have no cloke for
their sin. 23 He that hateth me hateth my
Father also. 24 If I had not done among
them the works which none other man
did, they had not had sin: but now have
they both seen and hated both me and my
Father. 25 But this cometh to pass, that
the word might be fulfilled that is written
in their law, They hated me without a
cause. 26 But when the Comforter is
come, whom I will send unto you from the
Father, even the Spirit of truth, which
proceedeth from the Father, he shall
testify of me: 27 And ye also shall bear
witness, because ye have been with me
from the beginning.

Spiritual warfare looms between the world which follows Satan's precepts and Christians who adhere to God's truth as Jesus taught. The world loves its own, and God loves his faithful children. With such contradicting life styles, God's children must expect intense opposition which existed during Old Testament days and continued to harass Jesus and his disciples.

By loving one another, Jesus, God, and we form a strong community, the kingdom of God, which shall some day conquer the foe led by Satan. Jesus, the apostles, and we unite to explain to Satan's deceived that their lives of sin darken and leave their lives empty. Jesus' miracles proved beyond all contradiction he proceeded from the heavenly Father. What he taught contained God's complete truth. Rejecting that truth leaves the world no excuse for sin, but Satan and his followers ridicule, harass, persecute, and kill those who abandon their system. They hope to prevent others from escaping their camp.

What reason can the world proclaim to hate Jesus and God's light? Did not Jesus help Satan's followers by healing their sicknesses, restoring arms and legs, and raising their dead loved ones? Did he cheat, hate, deceive, or kill any of them? If not, why did they hate him, and why do they hate his followers? Do you know any person who likes to be told he does evil? Even when the world knows its deeds produce sorrow to themselves and others, they hate to hear they do evil. Refusing to admit wrong in order to save face hinders multitudes from abandoning sin. God pleads that confessing sin relieves many agonies of life. How many of us struggle with a smiting conscience that drags us down day after day? When we can bear it no longer, we share with the wronged our sin. We are relieved. Life looks brighter. We wonder why we hesitated so long to make things right. God's way alone provides life.

Jesus promised to send the Holy Spirit from the Father to comfort his disciples after he departed. What benefits would the Spirit provide them? He would testify of Jesus. Since Jesus alone opens the way to eternal life, and since Jesus commissioned apostles to preach this message of hope to all nations, they needed help to convince their hearers that Jesus proceeded from God. God's Spirit empowered them to perform wonders to convince those who listened that Jesus came from God. The Spirit also brought all truth to their remembrance. Our heavenly Father makes provision for every need the apostles and we may encounter.

John

16:1 These things have I spoken unto you, that ye should not be offended. 2 They shall put you out of the synagogues: yea, the time cometh, that whosoever killeth you will think that he doeth God service. 3 And these things will they do unto you, because they have not known the Father, nor me. 4 But these things have I told you, that when the time shall come, ye may remember that I told you of them. And these things I said not unto you at the beginning, because I was with you. 5 But now I go my way to him that sent me; and none of you asketh me, Whither goest thou? 6 But because I have said these things unto you, sorrow hath filled your heart. 7 Nevertheless I tell you the truth; It is expedient for you that I go away: for if I go not away, the Comforter will not come unto you; but if I depart, I will send him unto you. 8 And when he is come, he will reprove the world of sin, and of righteousness, and of judgment: 9 Of sin, because they believe not on me; 10 Of righteousness, because I go to my Father, and ye see me no more; 11 Of judgment, because the prince of this world is judged. 12 I have yet many things to say unto you, but ye cannot bear them now. 13 Howbeit when he, the Spirit of truth, is come, he will guide you into all truth: for he shall not speak of himself; but whatsoever he shall hear, that shall he speak: and he will shew you things to come. 14 He shall glorify me: for he shall receive of mine, and shall shew it unto you. 15 All things that the Father hath are mine: therefore said I, that he shall take of mine, and shall shew it unto you.

How easy it is when we are offended to turn from God! It seems to be a reaction common to the world that when a friend offends us to abandon them. Jesus understood this reaction. Therefore he explained to his apostles that they must be thrust from the synagogues, beaten, and killed because they testify to the world of its sinful ways. Had not the Jews hated Jesus? Did they not contemplate killing him for telling the truth that their ways angered God? Were not their forefathers during the days of the prophets those who stoned the messengers of God? If the people treated Jesus indecently, do you think they shall forbear hating you, too? Jesus had not dwelt on this topic much, but now that he returned to the Father, he explained coming events. He hoped that knowing the trial he must endure, it would not be offensive to them when the world mistreated them for attempting to give eternal life to the world. (Ps.119:23,78,87, 95,110,141)

During my short lifetime, I have observed brethren who became offended when they tried to help others know the way of God, but were rejected. Often they gave up and eventually turned away from God and Jesus. Only those who endure unto the end inherit eternal life. (Math.10:22;24:13)

Sorrow filled the hearts of the apostles when Jesus informed them of his departure and the difficulties they must endure. However, he reemphasized that he would dispatch God's Spirit to guide, help, and comfort them after his departure. All the Holy Spirit's work shall be to glorify Jesus and his kingdom. By assisting and dwelling in God's children, the Spirit strengthens us to remain faithful to Jesus. (Eph.3:16; Col.1:9-11) Jesus' dominion grows and defeats Satan's wiles. With God and Jesus working together with us we shall triumph.

As Jesus closed this part of his farewell discourse, he reminded them that he had overcome the world. Starting shortly after John baptized Jesus, Satan made his first bid to subject Jesus to his plan. In each of the three temptations, Jesus met his persuasions with instructions from the Scriptures. Satan then enlisted Jewish leaders to counter Jesus' efforts to help Israel. Eventually, Satan utilized Peter to persuade him what he taught

John

**16:16 A little while, and ye shall not see
me: and again, a little while, and ye shall
see me, because I go to the Father. 17
Then said some of his disciples among
themselves, What is this that he saith unto
us, A little while, and ye shall not see me:
and again, a little while, and ye shall see
me: and, Because I go to the Father? 18
They said therefore, What is this that he
saith, A little while? we cannot tell what
he saith. 19 Now Jesus knew that they
were desirous to ask him, and said unto
them, Do ye inquire among yourselves of
that I said, A little while, and ye shall not
see me: and again, a little while, and ye
shall see me? 20 Verily, verily, I say unto
you, That ye shall weep and lament, but
the world shall rejoice: and ye shall be
sorrowful, but your sorrow shall be
turned into joy. 21 A woman when she is
in travail hath sorrow, because her hour
is come: but as soon as she is delivered of
the child, she remembereth no more the
anguish, for joy that a man is born into
the world. 22 And ye now therefore have
sorrow: but I will see you again, and your
heart shall rejoice, and your joy no man
taketh from you. 23 And in that day ye
shall ask me nothing. Verily, verily, I say
unto you, Whatsoever ye shall ask the
Father in my name, he will give it you. 24
Hitherto have ye asked nothing in my
name: ask, and ye shall receive, that your
joy may be full. 25 These things have I
spoken unto you in proverbs: but the time
cometh, when I shall no more speak unto
you in proverbs, but I shall shew you
plainly of the Father. 26 At that day ye
shall ask in my name: and I say not unto
you, that I will pray the Father for you:
27 For the Father himself loveth you,
because ye have loved me, and have
believed that I came out from God. 28 I
came forth from the Father, and am come
into the world: again, I leave the world,
and go to the Father. 29 His disciples said
unto him, Lo, now speakest thou plainly,
and speakest no proverb. 30 Now are we
sure that thou knowest all things, and
needest not that any man should ask thee:
by this we believe that thou camest forth
from God. 31 Jesus answered them, Do ye
now believe? 32 Behold, the hour cometh,
yea, is now come, that ye shall be
scattered, every man to his own, and shall
leave me alone: and yet I am not alone,
because the Father is with me. 33 These
things I have spoken unto you, that in me
ye might have peace. In the world ye shall
have tribulation: but be of good cheer; I
have overcome the world.**

should not be. Even Judas' betrayal attempted to alter God's plan. When Pilate judged Jesus unworthy of death, he reversed his own decision because the mob demanded his death. Jesus overcame every tactic of the Evil One to defeat his work. Jesus reminded his apostles that he had overcome, and they must understand they fought a death struggle against Satan. They must not grow weak-hearted. They fought for God's kingdom, they shall overcome.

Within hours Jesus must die on the cross. It seemed then to the disciples Satan had won. Three days later Jesus rose from the dead, showing Jesus defeated all Satan's work. The apostles saw him alive again. They rejoiced. After forty days, Jesus ascended to his Father. The world killed Jesus and rejoiced, but the disciples sorrowed. After his resurrection, the world mourned, but the apostles rejoiced. They who witnessed his ascension rejoiced again, knowing God's plan was unfolding as he planned, and he would complete his plan. Resurrection and ascension of Jesus destroys Satan's hold on mankind. God shall sever Satan's hold over mankind, and deliver his people from death. Even by overcoming death Jesus destroys Satan's work. (1 Cor. 15:26) Records of Jesus' birth, life, death, resurrection, and ascension encourages faith.

John

17:1 These words spake Jesus, and lifted up his eyes to heaven, and said, Father, the hour is come; glorify thy Son, that thy Son also may glorify thee: 2 As thou hast given him power over all flesh, that he should give eternal life to as many as thou hast given him. 3 And this is life eternal, that they might know thee the only true God, and Jesus Christ, whom thou hast sent. 4 I have glorified thee on the earth: I have finished the work which thou gavest me to do. 5 And now, O Father, glorify thou me with thine own self with the glory which I had with thee before the world was. 6 I have manifested thy name unto the men which thou gavest me out of the world: thine they were, and thou gavest them me; and they have kept thy word. 7 Now they have known that all things whatsoever thou hast given me are of thee. 8 For I have given unto them the words which thou gavest me; and they have received them, and have known surely that I came out from thee, and they have believed that thou didst send me. 9 I pray for them: I pray not for the world, but for them which thou hast given me; for they are thine. 10 And all mine are thine, and thine are mine; and I am glorified in them. 11 And now I am no more in the world, but these are in the world, and I come to thee. Holy Father, keep through thine own name those whom thou hast given me, that they may be one, as we are. 12 While I was with them in the world, I kept them in thy name: those that thou gavest me I have kept, and none of them is lost, but the son of perdition; that the scripture might be fulfilled. 13 And now come I to thee; and these things I speak in the world, that they might have my joy fulfilled in themselves. 14 I have given them thy word; and the world hath hated them, because they are not of the world, even as I am not of the world. 15 I pray not that thou shouldest take them out of the world, but that thou shouldest keep them from the evil. 16 They are not of the world, even as I am not of the world. 17 Sanctify them through thy truth: thy word is truth. 18 As thou hast sent me into the world, even so have I also sent them into the world. 19 And for their sakes I sanctify myself, that they also might be sanctified through the truth. 20 Neither pray I for these alone, but for them also which shall believe on me through their word; 21 That they all may be one; as thou, Father, art in me, and I in thee, that they also may be one in us: that the world may believe that thou hast sent me. 22 And the glory which thou gavest me I have given them; that they may be one, even as we are one: 23 I in them, and thou in me, that they may be made perfect in one; and that the world may know that thou hast sent me, and hast loved them, as thou hast loved me. 24 Father, I will that they also, whom thou hast given me, be with me where I am; that they may behold my glory, which thou hast given me: for thou lovedst me before the foundation of the world. 25 O righteous Father, the world hath not known thee: but I have known thee, and these have known that thou hast sent me. 26 And I have declared unto them thy name, and will declare it: that the love wherewith thou hast loved me may be in them, and I in them.

Transition of God's truth from the Father to Jesus and from Jesus to the apostles stands out here. God sent Jesus into the world with the whole truth of God which will change the course of men's lives if they will do as God instructs. From Adam's and Eve's transgression in the Garden, Satan has directed men's lives to seek that which produced self-gratification and exaltation with little regard for how their goals affect others. Center of God's message to man Jesus explained is loving God and man as a person loves himself. If we will try God's plan, we will become convinced that it surpasses Satan's system as light benefits man more than darkness. God sent Jesus into the world with the whole truth of God. (Deu.18:18-19; Jno.15:15) The apostles received God's truth which sanctified them from the world. (Jno.17:6,17-19) In turn, the apostles Jesus charged with the responsibility of preaching the complete truth of God to the world (Jno.17:8) that the world might be sanctified through the word which the apostles spoke. (Jno.17:20) If the apostles faithfully discharged their responsibility, God could unite himself, Jesus, the apostles, and all who receive and do the truth which they taught. (Jno.17:21) Such unity glorifies God. His unity supersedes Satan's division, anarchy, war, hatred, and all his evil deeds.

It's obedience to God's system of truth that severs man from Satan's system. None of man's efforts to gain unity shall produce enduring unity unless it is based on God's system of treating others as we desire to be treated. From shortly after Noah's flood, men have sought unity without God. They even tried to build a city and tower to prevent being scattered over the face of the earth. God knew their plan could not succeed based, as it was, on Satan's system. (Gen.11:1-9) Look at our cities today. They are torn apart by economic, race, gang, family, and poverty strife, all of which originate from doing the will of the Evil One. God instructs us that city and nation chaos shall not subside as long as men and women are deceived by Satan to search for selfish goals. Even when it looks like such anarchy as so recently devastated Los Angeles has been mollified by court justice, it won't last. Why? because the majority of the people have cast God's truth aside. Unity proceeds from God and doing his truth. Casting his truth aside brings only the dark side of man into focus.

Is there any hope that this civil chaos shall ever improve? Yes, review the state of Europe before the fall of the Roman Empire which served to unite most of Europe and the Middle East. While Christianity prompted many to depress their base motives, a peace never known to society prevailed. As the influence of God's truth faded from the daily activities of those within the Empire, chaos spread, finally causing the Empire to collapse. Darkness of Satan spread over the area once ruled by the Empire. Degradation mounted until even cities and highways which once knit the Empire vanished. That age of darkness continued for over a 1000 years, until some sane men began to return to God's truth. Slowly, but surely, God's light dawned on Europe. Men improved their morals and associations with one another. The land produced abundant food, and villages began to grow. Travel once again became safe enough to go from village to village. As men began to respect one another, civilization spread and cities and trade developed.

Why do we see the downward cycle again? Is it not associated with a departure from God's principles of love God and man as we love ourselves? Unity, whether it's in religion or society proceeds only from submitting to God's principles. When we depart from his truth, we bring confusion on ourselves. Will we never be convinced of this truth?

Jesus is God's messenger to us. He tells us if we want life abundantly, keep the will of our Father in heaven. (Jno.10:10) If we turn from God's words, we seek death. Satan shall enslave us until we return to the Father by the words which he has given to Jesus to help us overcome the way of the Evil One. Jesus explained to his people, **"And ye will not come to me, that ye might have life."** (Jno.5:40) Will we come to him and gain that life from God? or will we continue our obstinacy and see civilization collapse again? Challenging God's system defeats us. Submitting to his way exalts nations, families and each of us individually. Helping others helps us; hurting others ruins us.

Matthew

26:36 Then cometh Jesus with them unto a place called Gethsemane, and saith unto the disciples, Sit ye here, while I go and pray yonder. 37 And he took with him Peter and the two sons of Zebedee, and began to be sorrowful and very heavy. 38 Then saith he unto them, My soul is exceeding sorrowful, even unto death: tarry ye here, and watch with me. 39 And he went a little further, and fell on his face, and prayed, saying, O my Father, if it be possible, let this cup pass from me: nevertheless not as I will, but as thou wilt. 40 And he cometh unto the disciples, and findeth them asleep, and saith unto Peter, What, could ye not watch with me one hour? 41 Watch and pray, that ye enter not into temptation: the spirit indeed is willing, but the flesh is weak. 42 He went away again the second time, and prayed, saying, O my Father, if this cup may not pass away from me, except I drink it, thy will be done. 43 And he came and found them asleep again: for their eyes were heavy. 44 And he left them, and went away again, and prayed the third time, saying the same words. 45 Then cometh he to his disciples, and saith unto them, Sleep on now, and take your rest: behold, the hour is at hand, and the Son of man is betrayed into the hands of sinners. 46 Rise, let us be going: behold, he is at hand that doth betray me.

Even Jesus feared the trials and agonies of death. (Heb.5:7) When he departed from the city, ascended Olivet, and entered the garden, Jesus prayed earnestly that his Father might remove from him the cross if it were possible for his Father to do so and still accomplish his plan, designed from creation of the world, to save men. Three times he pleaded for his Father to remove the cross from him, but when Judas approached with the mob, God had strengthened him to face the situation. Though man may fail us, God shall not fail.

Mark

14:32 And they came to a place which was named Gethsemane: and he saith to his disciples, Sit ye here, while I shall pray. 33 And he taketh with him Peter and James and John, and began to be sore amazed, and to be very heavy; 34 And saith unto them, My soul is exceeding sorrowful unto death: tarry ye here, and watch. 35 And he went forward a little, and fell on the ground, and prayed that, if it were possible, the hour might pass from him. 36 And he said, Abba, Father, all things are possible unto thee; take away this cup from me: nevertheless not what I will, but what thou wilt. 37 And he cometh, and findeth them sleeping, and saith unto Peter, Simon, sleepest thou? couldest not thou watch one hour? 38 Watch ye and pray, lest ye enter into temptation. The spirit truly is ready, but the flesh is weak. 39 And again he went away, and prayed, and spake the same words. 40 And when he returned, he found them asleep again, (for their eyes were heavy,) neither wist they what to answer him. 41 And he cometh the third time, and saith unto them, Sleep on now, and take your rest: it is enough, the hour is come; behold, the Son of man is betrayed into the hands of sinners. 42 Rise up, let us go; lo, he that betrayeth me is at hand.

(Deu.31:6; 1 Chr.28:20)

Jesus encouraged his closest disciples to watch and pray with him. Three times they slept as Jesus prayed. Judas led the band who laid hands on Jesus to take him before the council. Disciples slightly resisted, but abandoned Jesus to his enemy. Once so determined they would never be ashamed to stand and to die with him, now in the face of the actual situation, they did not fulfill their promise. God alone provides that strength when the devil lures us into sin. Why worry? God will complete his plan for all his children. God and Jesus do ask of us to continue faithfully to love and obey them.

Luke

22:39 And he came out, and went, as he was wont, to the mount of Olives; and his disciples also followed him. 40 And when he was at the place, he said unto them, Pray that ye enter not into temptation. 41 And he was withdrawn from them about a stone's cast, and kneeled down, and prayed, 42 Saying, Father, if thou be willing, remove this cup from me: nevertheless not my will, but thine, be done. 43 And there appeared an angel unto him from heaven, strengthening him. 44 And being in an agony he prayed more earnestly: and his sweat was as it were great drops of blood falling down to the ground. 45 And when he rose up from prayer, and was come to his disciples, he found them sleeping for sorrow, 46 And said unto them, Why sleep ye? rise and pray, lest ye enter into temptation.

Why did Luke alone record that God sent his angel to strengthen Jesus? Even at the beginning of his gospel, he noted that God sent Gabriel to Zacharius and to Mary. (Lk. 1:13,19,26,30,35) Angels announced Jesus' birth to the shepherds. (Lk.2:10,13) It might seem that Theophilus needed confirmation that God did in fact dispatch his angels to communicate to some of his people. Even so, God never intended for his people to worship angels. (Col.2:18) (Consult the Hebrew letter for a comparison of Jesus and angels. Heb.1:4-2:18)

How did Judas know he could lead the council's officers and their followers to the garden and expect to find Jesus there? John penned that Jesus customarily retired to the garden with his disciples. Expecting Jesus to conform to his usual pattern, Judas assured the council that he could lead them to Jesus while the multitude retired from him. Trusting Judas' promise, they dispatched their guards to follow Judas and arrest Jesus. All the disciples abandoned Jesus in the hour of his need. Confidence in ourselves falters, but God strengthens us.

John

18:1 When Jesus had spoken these words, he went forth with his disciples over the brook Cedron, where was a garden, into the which he entered, and his disciples.

If you and I are to benefit from the weaknesses of the apostles, we need to evaluate their self-confidence that they would never forsake Jesus and their failure at the critical moment. Paul once cautioned the church at Corinth, "**Wherefore let him that thinketh he standeth take heed lest he fall. There hath no temptation taken you but such as is common to man: but God is faithful, who will not suffer you to be tempted above that ye are able; but will with the temptation also make a way to escape, that ye may be able to bear it.**" (1 Cor.10:12-13) Confidence of their determination and power to stand faithfully with Jesus in every trial proved disastrous to them when Judas approached with the officers. Considering their weakness, we need to ask ourselves what caused the faint-heartedness at the crucial time? Was it the lack of prayer, confidence in themselves, or some other group of factors? Paul admonished Corinthians not to trust their strength against Satan's devices. Put your trust in God. Self-assurance to withstand Satan should rest in God, not our own confidence. Paul's comment is a general exhortation to churches everywhere, (Rom.5:6; 1 Cor.1:2) Satan proved from the day of man's fall he can outwit us. We must put our trust in God's power, or Satan will certainly defeat our most cherished confidence. As Jesus called on his heavenly Father for strength to vanquish the devil and escape his carefully designed plans, we need to call on God to provide us with power to prevent Satan from leading us into sin. God strengthened Jesus his only begotten Son, and he promises to strengthen all his children who trust his promises. (Eph.3:16; Col.1:9-11) Do we have faith to experience God's promise? He won't fail us in our time of need.

Matthew

26:47 And while he yet spake, lo, Judas, one of the twelve, came, and with him a great multitude with swords and staves, from the chief priests and elders of the people. 48 Now he that betrayed him gave them a sign, saying, Whomsoever I shall kiss, that same is he: hold him fast. 49 And forthwith he came to Jesus, and said, Hail, master; and kissed him. 50 And Jesus said unto him, Friend, wherefore art thou come? Then came they, and laid hands on Jesus, and took him. 51 And, behold, one of them which were with Jesus stretched out his hand, and drew his sword, and struck a servant of the high priest's, and smote off his ear. 52 Then said Jesus unto him, Put up again thy sword into his place: for all they that take the sword shall perish with the sword. 53 Thinkest thou that I cannot now pray to my Father, and he shall presently give me more than twelve legions of angels? 54 But how then shall the scriptures be fulfilled, that thus it must be? 55 In that same hour said Jesus to the multitudes, Are ye come out as against a thief with swords and staves for to take me? I sat daily with you teaching in the temple, and ye laid no hold on me. 56 But all this was done, that the scriptures of the prophets might be fulfilled. Then all the disciples forsook him, and fled.

Being confident that his Father controlled all things in the universe and that what was taking shape with Judas' leading the mob to take him, Jesus faced his foe with complete confidence. He submitted to arrest. Peter resisted, drew a sword, and cut off the ear of the high priest's servant. Jesus rebuked Peter, telling him that if you live by the sword, you shall die by it. Then he healed Malchus' ear. If each of us realized our Father in heaven watches over us and makes every event turn out for our good, we would be more calm and worry less. Trust our heavenly Father's care as Jesus did in trials.

Mark

14:43 And immediately, while he yet spake, cometh Judas, one of the twelve, and with him a great multitude with swords and staves, from the chief priests and the scribes and the elders. 44 And he that betrayed him had given them a token, saying, Whomsoever I shall kiss, that same is he; take him, and lead him away safely. 45 And as soon as he was come, he goeth straightway to him, and saith, Master, master; and kissed him. 46 And they laid their hands on him, and took him. 47 And one of them that stood by drew a sword, and smote a servant of the high priest, and cut off his ear. 48 And Jesus answered and said unto them, Are ye come out, as against a thief, with swords and with staves to take me? 49 I was daily with you in the temple teaching, and ye took me not: but the scriptures must be fulfilled. 50 And they all forsook him, and fled. 51 And there followed him a certain young man, having a linen cloth cast about his naked body; and the young men laid hold on him: 52 And he left the linen cloth, and fled from them naked.

Only Mark's gospel indicates that anyone but the apostles came to the garden with Jesus that fateful night. Mark noted that a young man followed Jesus and observed how Judas led the officers to arrest Jesus. As they took Jesus, some of the young men laid hands on this young man, but he fled, leaving his garment in their hands. If this young man was Mark, he probably included this in his narrative as strong evidence to his readers that he himself witnessed this event. Placing personal references this way helped his audience better relate to the event, especially if they knew Mark personally. Thus, three gospel writers watched as the officers bound Jesus and led him away to stand before the Jewish council. Their records are firsthand evidences, not simple stories they had heard. Faithful children of God believe all the evidences in gospels.

Luke

22:47 And while he yet spake, behold a multitude, and he that was called Judas, one of the twelve, went before them, and drew near unto Jesus to kiss him. 48 But Jesus said unto him, Judas, betrayest thou the Son of man with a kiss? 49 When they which were about him saw what would follow, they said unto him, Lord, shall we smite with the sword? 50 And one of them smote the servant of the high priest, and cut off his right ear. 51 And Jesus answered and said, Suffer ye thus far. And he touched his ear, and healed him. 52 Then Jesus said unto the chief priests, and captains of the temple, and the elders, which were come to him, Be ye come out, as against a thief, with swords and staves? 53 When I was daily with you in the temple, ye stretched forth no hands against me: but this is your hour, and the power of darkness.

Luke added words of Jesus not mentioned by other gospels. Jesus remarked to the leaders of the mob. "**This is your hour, and the power of darkness.**" You laid no hands on me while I taught in the temple, but in the darkness of night, like a thief, you take me. He might as well have said that they hid their evil deed by darkness.

Jesus taught his followers to do good even to their enemies. (Lk.6:27,35) As the officers arrested him, Jesus guided his own actions by what he taught. After Peter cut off Malchus' ear, Jesus healed his ear, showing God's goodness even to those who hated his only begotten Son. When Luke penned Acts, he stated that Jesus went about doing good. (Act.10:38) God desires that we follow the example of his Son, going about doing good even when others are mistreating us. (1 Pet.2:21-23) Then we are the children of our heavenly Father, following his example and his Son's. Their names are glorified by our lives which is the Father's will. (Eph.1:6,12,14;3:21; See Job 9:22.) I must remind myself that my actions glorify God.

John

18:2 And Judas also, which betrayed him, knew the place: for Jesus ofttimes resorted thither with his disciples. 3 Judas then, having received a band of men and officers from the chief priests and Pharisees, cometh thither with lanterns and torches and weapons. 4 Jesus therefore, knowing all things that should come upon him, went forth, and said unto them, Whom seek ye? 5 They answered him, Jesus of Nazareth. Jesus saith unto them, I am he. And Judas also, which betrayed him, stood with them. 6 As soon then as he had said unto them, I am he, they went backward, and fell to the ground. 7 Then asked he them again, Whom seek ye? And they said, Jesus of Nazareth. 8 Jesus answered, I have told you that I am he: if therefore ye seek me, let these go their way: 9 That the saying might be fulfilled, which he spake, Of them which thou gavest me have I lost none. 10 Then Simon Peter having a sword drew it, and smote the high priest's servant, and cut off his right ear. The servant's name was Malchus. 11 Then said Jesus unto Peter, Put up thy sword into the sheath: the cup which my Father hath given me, shall I not drink it?

The apostle John knew the high priest personally and probably knew Malchus also. (Jno.18:15) Including Malchus' name as a personal note indicates that John's audience also may have known him. I hope Malchus might have thought how Jesus showed him good even when he came to arrest him. This might have influenced him to repent and obey the gospel.

Jesus knew the events to follow. God designed these deeds and inspired the prophets to foretell and record them long before they came to pass. (Is.53:1-12) Our God declares the end from the beginning, explaining what shall come. (Is.46:10) Does Jesus' confidence in his Father inspire you and me to stand in the face of great trials?

Matthew

**26:57 And they that had laid hold on
Jesus led him away to Caiaphas the high
priest, where the scribes and the elders
were assembled. 58 But Peter followed
him afar off unto the high priest's palace,
and went in, and sat with the servants, to
see the end. 59 Now the chief priests, and
elders, and all the council, sought false
witness against Jesus, to put him to death;
60 But found none: yea, though many
false witnesses came, yet found they none.
At the last came two false witnesses, 61
And said, This fellow said, I am able to
destroy the temple of God, and to build it
in three days. 62 And the high priest
arose, and said unto him, Answerest thou
nothing? what is it which these witness
against thee? 63 But Jesus held his peace.
And the high priest answered and said
unto him, I adjure thee by the living God,
that thou tell us whether thou be the
Christ, the Son of God. 64 Jesus saith unto
him, Thou hast said: nevertheless I say
unto you, Hereafter shall ye see the Son of
man sitting on the right hand of power,
and coming in the clouds of heaven. 65
Then the high priest rent his clothes,
saying, He hath spoken blasphemy; what
further need have we of witnesses?
behold, now ye have heard his blasphemy.
66 What think ye? They answered and
said, He is guilty of death. 67 Then did
they spit in his face, and buffeted him;
and others smote him with the palms of
their hands, 68 Saying, Prophesy unto us,
thou Christ, Who is he that smote thee?**

Mark

**14:53 And they led Jesus away to the high
priest: and with him were assembled all
the chief priests and the elders and the
scribes. 54 And Peter followed him afar
off, even into the palace of the high priest:
and he sat with the servants, and warmed
himself at the fire. 55 And the chief priests
and all the council sought for witness
against Jesus to put him to death; and
found none. 56 For many bare false
witness against him, but their witness
agreed not together. 57 And there arose
certain, and bare false witness against
him, saying, 58 We heard him say, I will
destroy this temple that is made with
hands, and within three days I will build
another made without hands. 59 But
neither so did their witness agree
together. 60 And the high priest stood up
in the midst, and asked Jesus, saying,
Answerest thou nothing? what is it which
these witness against thee? 61 But he held
his peace, and answered nothing. Again
the high priest asked him, and said unto
him, Art thou the Christ, the Son of the
Blessed? 62 And Jesus said, I am: and ye
shall see the Son of man sitting on the
right hand of power, and coming in the
clouds of heaven. 63 Then the high priest
rent his clothes, and saith, What need we
any further witnesses? 64 Ye have heard
the blasphemy: what think ye? And they
all condemned him to be guilty of death.
65 And some began to spit on him, and to
cover his face, and to buffet him, and to
say unto him, Prophesy: and the servants
did strike him with the palms of their
hands.**

Why did the high priest contend Jesus blasphemed when he admitted he was Christ, the Son of God? Jews called God their Father. (Jno.8:41) That made them sons of God. God informed David that David's son to reign after him would be God's son and God would be his father. (2 Sam.7:12-14; 1 Chr.28:4-6) This applied first to Solomon and later to Christ. Priests knew Christ must be the son of David; therefore, he had to be a man. When their own Scriptures made such clear statements, why did they condemn him? Jesus commented that they refused to believe Moses' writings, how could they believe Jesus? (Jno.5:43-47) They desired the praise of their comrades rather than God's praise. When people reject truth, God confounds their understanding. (Math.11:25)

Luke

22:54 Then took they him, and led him, and brought him into the high priest's house. And Peter followed afar off.
22:63 And the men that held Jesus mocked him, and smote him. 64 And when they had blindfolded him, they struck him on the face, and asked him, saying, Prophesy, who is it that smote thee? 65 And many other things blasphemously spake they against him. 66 And as soon as it was day, the elders of the people and the chief priests and the scribes came together, and led him into their council, saying, 67 Art thou the Christ? tell us. And he said unto them, If I tell you, ye will not believe: 68 And if I also ask you, ye will not answer me, nor let me go. 69 Hereafter shall the Son of man sit on the right hand of the power of God. 70 Then said they all, Art thou then the Son of God? And he said unto them, Ye say that I am. 71 And they said, What need we any further witness? for we ourselves have heard of his own mouth.

When Jesus came before the Jewish council that condemned him to death for blasphemy, was it a genuine trial or mockery? Had they not previously determined to kill Jesus? Even before they offered Judas money to betray him they planned to kill Jesus. What drove the Jewish leaders to condemn a man who benefited the people, taught the truth of God, had John's testimony that he was the lamb of God, fulfilled all the Old Testament prophecies, and sought no position of power among them? Even Pilate could see the Jews delivered Jesus to him for envy. (Math.27:18; Mk.15:10) Satan sets every obstacle imaginable before people to prevent them from returning to God. Satan determines he must not lose hold in people's minds and lives. If people turn to God, he loses his power over them. Satan's children desire to retain power also. Will we never realize God closes our understanding when we reject God's truth? (1 Cor.1:27-29)

John

18:12 Then the band and the captain and officers of the Jews took Jesus, and bound him, 13 And led him away to Annas first; for he was father in law to Caiaphas, which was the high priest that same year. 14 Now Caiaphas was he, which gave counsel to the Jews, that it was expedient that one man should die for the people. 15 And Simon Peter followed Jesus, and so did another disciple: that disciple was known unto the high priest, and went in with Jesus into the palace of the high priest. 16 But Peter stood at the door without. Then went out that other disciple, which was known unto the high priest, and spake unto her that kept the door, and brought in Peter.

The apostle John seems to have been the one who introduced Peter into the priest's palace. (Jno.21:20-24) What purpose might John have had in mind to gain entrance for Peter? Did he think he and Peter together might influence the council to release Jesus? It didn't turn out that way. The group who gathered to condemn Jesus squelched any enthusiasm Peter had to encourage Jesus. What of John who also assembled there? How did his faith fare? Did the crowd intimidate him also?

Angry groups of people are unreasonable. When a mood of confidence in a plan prevails, there exists minimal opportunity for one, two, or many to change the intent of the gathering. I've seen debates where few, if any, minds changed as the result of the discussion. In Ephesus, when the enraged crowd assembled and cried praise to Diana, Paul couldn't preach Christ to them. (Act. 19:23-41) The people were riled by Demetrius who fretted because Paul contended there were no gods made with hands. He lost market for his trade in idols. When one threatens another's vested interests, he finds intense opposition. Jewish leaders felt Jesus challenged the positions of authority, and they would do anything to stop him.

Matthew

26:69 Now Peter sat without in the palace: and a damsel came unto him, saying, Thou also wast with Jesus of Galilee. 70 But he denied before them all, saying, I know not what thou sayest. 71 And when he was gone out into the porch, another maid saw him, and said unto them that were there, This fellow was also with Jesus of Nazareth. 72 And again he denied with an oath, I do not know the man. 73 And after a while came unto him they that stood by, and said to Peter, Surely thou also art one of them; for thy speech bewrayeth thee. 74 Then began he to curse and to swear, saying, I know not the man. And immediately the cock crew. 75 And Peter remembered the word of Jesus, which said unto him, Before the cock crow, thou shalt deny me thrice. And he went out, and wept bitterly.

Attention shifted to Peter while he assembled with those gathered at the high priest's palace. They supported the priest's position that Jesus must die to preserve the Jewish nation and people. Peter probably seemed a stranger to their camp, and they eyed him cautiously. After a while the maid who kept the door confronted Peter, suggesting he was a follower of Jesus. Peter assured her she must be mistaken. Probably feeling somewhat uncomfortable, Peter retired to the porch where another maid pointed him out as one who accompanied Jesus of Nazareth. Again he denied. By this time others watched and listened to Peter and concluded he had to be Jesus' disciple. His speech showed it. Annoyed, Peter cursed and sware he did not follow Jesus. At that moment a cock's crow cut Peter to the heart. He had denied Jesus.

Guilt feelings bear heavily on one who has let down a close friend. What do you do when you hurt one so close to you? Peter wept bitterly as he left the priest's palace to be alone. How could it happen when he was so determined to defend Jesus?

Mark

14:66 And as Peter was beneath in the palace, there cometh one of the maids of the high priest: 67 And when she saw Peter warming himself, she looked upon him, and said, And thou also wast with Jesus of Nazareth. 68 But he denied, saying, I know not, neither understand I what thou sayest. And he went out into the porch; and the cock crew. 69 And a maid saw him again, and began to say to them that stood by, This is one of them. 70 And he denied it again. And a little after, they that stood by said again to Peter, Surely thou art one of them: for thou art a Galilaean, and thy speech agreeth thereto. 71 But he began to curse and to swear, saying, I know not this man of whom ye speak. 72 And the second time the cock crew. And Peter called to mind the word that Jesus said unto him, Before the cock crow twice, thou shalt deny me thrice. And when he thought thereon, he wept.

Sin produces sorrow in the lives of those who sin and to those sinned against. Peter hurt within, but how do you suppose Jesus felt when Peter cursed and swore that he didn't even know Jesus? Most of us remember quite vividly how much it cut us when a friend shunned us. The hurt lingered and when we attempted to turn our attention to something else, remembering the snubbing renewed the hurt. Even if we tried to convince ourselves the person didn't intentionally ignore us, it continued to haunt us. Maybe the person did intend to sever the friendship. Then we ask ourselves what I have done wrong?

We need to discern clearly that Satan's action patterns divide and destroy friendships, families, organizations, and nearly any form of unity. Conversely, God's system heals hurts and restores friendships, families, organizations, unity, and heals the bitterness associated with transgression. We know how to restore friendships with kindness, but why do we reject God's perfect way?

Luke

22:55 And when they had kindled a fire in the midst of the hall, and were set down together, Peter sat down among them. 56 But a certain maid beheld him as he sat by the fire, and earnestly looked upon him, and said, This man was also with him. 57 And he denied him, saying, Woman, I know him not. 58 And after a little while another saw him, and said, Thou art also of them. And Peter said, Man, I am not. 59 And about the space of one hour after another confidently affirmed, saying, Of a truth this fellow also was with him: for he is a Galilaean. 60 And Peter said, Man, I know not what thou sayest. And immediately, while he yet spake, the cock crew. 61 And the Lord turned, and looked upon Peter. And Peter remembered the word of the Lord, how he had said unto him, Before the cock crow, thou shalt deny me thrice. 62 And Peter went out, and wept bitterly.

While the council proceeded, Jesus and Peter could see one another. When those who favored the council's actions identified Peter as one of Jesus' disciples, Peter denied it three times. Jesus looked at Peter, and their eyes met. At that moment the cock crowed. Peter suddenly realized what he had done. He had denied the Christ before men. Departing in tears, he wept alone. His conscience smote him. How could he have denied Jesus before unbelievers?

How does Satan lead people into traps to entangle us in situations which we hate? Even the apostle Paul remarked that he did those things which he would never allow because of sin which dwelt in him. (Rom. 7:7-25) Satan utilizes our weaknesses to defeat our best intentions. Is there any way a person can prevent being drawn into such situations? Jesus advised Peter to pray that he enter not into temptation. If we believe God's promises and ask for his help, we can overcome Satan's snares. God desires to help us defeat Satan, but we resist God.

John

18:17 Then saith the damsel that kept the door unto Peter, Art not thou also one of this man's disciples? He saith, I am not. 18 And the servants and officers stood there, who had made a fire of coals; for it was cold: and they warmed themselves: and Peter stood with them, and warmed himself. 19 The high priest then asked Jesus of his disciples, and of his doctrine. 20 Jesus answered him, I spake openly to the world; I ever taught in the synagogue, and in the temple, whither the Jews always resort; and in secret have I said nothing. 21 Why askest thou me? ask them which heard me, what I have said unto them: behold, they know what I said. 22 And when he had thus spoken, one of the officers which stood by struck Jesus with the palm of his hand, saying, Answerest thou the high priest so? 23 Jesus answered him, If I have spoken evil, bear witness of the evil: but if well, why smitest thou me? 24 Now Annas had sent him bound unto Caiaphas the high priest. 25 And Simon Peter stood and warmed himself. They said therefore unto him, Art not thou also one of his disciples? He denied it, and said, I am not. 26 One of the servants of the high priest, being his kinsman whose ear Peter cut off, saith, Did not I see thee in the garden with him? 27 Peter then denied again: and immediately the cock crew.

John, knowing the high priest and those closely associated with him, more accurately identified those about him. He called Malchus by name, and identified his relationship as a servant of the high priest. Even Malchus' kinsman appeared in his record. The maid who first accused Peter of being one of Jesus' disciples, John called the keeper of the door. These first-hand records introduce readers to a better insight into the incidents mentioned. God desired those who read about his Son to know the people who accused him.

Matthew

27:1 When the morning was come, all the chief priests and elders of the people took counsel against Jesus to put him to death: 2 And when they had bound him, they led him away, and delivered him to Pontius Pilate the governor. 3 Then Judas, which had betrayed him, when he saw that he was condemned, repented himself, and brought again the thirty pieces of silver to the chief priests and elders, 4 Saying, I have sinned in that I have betrayed the innocent blood. And they said, What is that to us? see thou to that. 5 And he cast down the pieces of silver in the temple, and departed, and went and hanged himself. 6 And the chief priests took the silver pieces, and said, It is not lawful for to put them into the treasury, because it is the price of blood. 7 And they took counsel, and bought with them the potter's field, to bury strangers in. 8 Wherefore that field was called, The field of blood, unto this day. 9 Then was fulfilled that which was spoken by Jeremy the prophet, saying, And they took the thirty pieces of silver, the price of him that was valued, whom they of the children of Israel did value; 10 And gave them for the potter's field, as the Lord appointed me. 11 And Jesus stood before the governor: and the governor asked him, saying, Art thou the King of the Jews? And Jesus said unto him, Thou sayest. 12 And when he was accused of the chief priests and elders, he answered nothing.

Mark

15:1 And straightway in the morning the chief priests held a consultation with the elders and scribes and the whole council, and bound Jesus, and carried him away, and delivered him to Pilate. 2 And Pilate asked him, Art thou the King of the Jews? And he answering said unto him, Thou sayest it. 3 And the chief priests accused him of many things: but he answered nothing.

When Judas saw the council condemned Jesus to death, his desire for money vanished. Realizing he had betrayed an innocent friend to death haunted him. Repenting, he approached the priests and elders and confessed he had sinned in delivering Jesus to them, for Jesus committed no transgression worthy of death. Casting the thirty pieces of silver down before them relieved no sense of guilt. His remorse didn't generate any sympathy in the priests and elders. It meant nothing to them. They appeared unaffected by his deep sorrow. Sin so callused their hearts they cared nothing for how others grieved. Desiring to be blameless legally, they refused to put the blood money into the treasury, so they bought a potter's field as a place to bury strangers, fulfilling a prophecy of Zechariah, noting the thirty pieces of silver with which they valued Christ they used to purchase a field from the potter. (Zech.11:10-13)

Binding Jesus as a common criminal, the council delivered him to Pilate and accused him of grave violations of their law. Jesus replied to none of their accusations. Pilate asked him if he admitted to being King of the Jews. Even when he knew that death awaited him if he confessed that he was, Jesus answered Pilate that he was Christ. Jesus felt duty bound to tell the truth of God regardless of the cost. (1 Tim.6:13)

Few times do all four gospel writers record the same event, and it's possible from comparing these records to gain insight into the writer's viewpoint and the needs of his audience. Why did Matthew alone tell about Judas repenting and the council buying the burying field with the thirty pieces of silver? Did his readers have knowledge of Zechariah's prophecy? Matthew recorded many correlations of events in Jesus' life with their prophets, suggesting he wrote to Jews. Even details of their law against blood money being brought to the Lord's treasury he recorded for his Jewish audience.

Luke

23:1 And the whole multitude of them arose, and led him unto Pilate. 2 And they began to accuse him, saying, We found this fellow perverting the nation, and forbidding to give tribute to Caesar, saying that he himself is Christ a King. 3 And Pilate asked him, saying, Art thou the King of the Jews? And he answered him and said, Thou sayest it.

Pharisees once asked Jesus if it was lawful to give tribute to Caesar. He answered by asking whose face appeared on the money. They replied it was Caesar's. Then give Caesar what belongs to him and to God what belongs to God. (Math.22:15-22; Mk.12:13-17; Lk.20:19-26) They knew Jesus did not teach it violated the Jew's system to pay tax to Gentiles. All through Jewish history, when Israel transgressed their covenant with God, he delivered them into the hands of Gentile nations to subdue and tax them.

Why would the Jews accuse Jesus of proclaiming himself as King? By claiming to be King, they suggested Jesus elevated his kingdom as a rebellion against the Roman Empire. If they could convince Roman leaders of this, Rome would be forced to destroy Jesus. This conflict, however, was only imaginary, for God's kingdom supports good civil rulers and attempts to improve those who rule well. God shows that exercising fair and just judgment government benefits all who attempt to live law-abiding lives. In fact, God himself ordained civil governments to punish ungodly living and to praise those who live justly. (Rom.13:1-7; 1 Pet.2:13-14) Jewish leaders understood the relationship of God's dominion and civil rulers and couldn't justify condemning Jesus as a king who vaunted himself against the Roman government. Jesus explained his kingdom was not of this world. (Jno.18:36) God's kingdom enhances civil government. When individuals and parties use religion to justify civil violence, they blaspheme God who ordained civil rulers. (Rom.13:1-7)

John

18:28 Then led they Jesus from Caiaphas unto the hall of judgment: and it was early; and they themselves went not into the judgment hall, lest they should be defiled; but that they might eat the passover. 29 Pilate then went out unto them, and said, What accusation bring ye against this man? 30 They answered and said unto him, If he were not a malefactor, we would not have delivered him up unto thee. 31 Then said Pilate unto them, Take ye him, and judge him according to your law. The Jews therefore said unto him, It is not lawful for us to put any man to death: 32 That the saying of Jesus might be fulfilled, which he spake, signifying what death he should die. 33 Then Pilate entered into the judgment hall again, and called Jesus, and said unto him, Art thou the King of the Jews? 34 Jesus answered him, Sayest thou this thing of thyself, or did others tell it thee of me? 35 Pilate answered, Am I a Jew? Thine own nation and the chief priests have delivered thee unto me: what hast thou done?

Notice how the Jewish leaders considered eating the Passover feast more important than destroying an innocent man. They clamored for the death of Jesus who had not violated Moses' law, but they were willing to commit murder to preserve their positions. To them, eating the Passover physically clean superseded violating their conscience and Moses' law against judging unjustly. It's strange how men use religion to cloak their real motives. As long as they looked respectable to others, it didn't matter how God viewed their deeds or how wicked their thoughts may be. Jesus explained that God looks at the heart of man. If you think evil thoughts, you violate the tenth commandment. What a person thinks determines how he lives. Think evil; you do evil. Think good; you do good. We understand what Jesus taught is correct, but we love evil ideas.

Matthew

27:13 Then said Pilate unto him, Hearest thou not how many things they witness against thee? 14 And he answered him to never a word; insomuch that the governor marvelled greatly. 15 Now at that feast the governor was wont to release unto the people a prisoner, whom they would. 16 And they had then a notable prisoner, called Barabbas. 17 Therefore when they were gathered together, Pilate said unto them, Whom will ye that I release unto you? Barabbas, or Jesus which is called Christ? 18 For he knew that for envy they had delivered him. 19 When he was set down on the judgment seat, his wife sent unto him, saying, Have thou nothing to do with that just man: for I have suffered many things this day in a dream because of him. 20 But the chief priests and elders persuaded the multitude that they should ask Barabbas, and destroy Jesus. 21 The governor answered and said unto them, Whether of the twain will ye that I release unto you? They said, Barabbas.

Solomon wrote, **"The kings' heart is in the hand of the Lord, as the rivers of water: he turneth it whithersoever he will."** (Prov.21:1) God directed Pilate to accomplish God's will. Pilate's wife sent him a message not to condemn Jesus because she suffered from a terrible dream because of him. Pilate tried to maneuver the Jews to release Jesus at the Passover, but God's plan required Jesus die to provide for all men a means to attain forgiveness of sins and a new beginning of life for those who sorrowed for all the wrongs they had done. By refusing to condemn Jesus, Pilate judged honestly, yet God's obstinate people condemned their own Messiah. Peter reminded them of their actions, but tried to encourage them to repent. You denied Jesus before Pilate and chose a murderer be given you, but you did it ignorantly because you didn't understand your own prophets. (Act.3:12-26) When we reject truth, we lose understanding.

Mark

15:4 And Pilate asked him again, saying, Answerest thou nothing? behold how many things they witness against thee. 5 But Jesus yet answered nothing; so that Pilate marvelled. 6 Now at that feast he released unto them one prisoner, whomsoever they desired. 7 And there was one named Barabbas, which lay bound with them that had made insurrection with him, who had committed murder in the insurrection. 8 And the multitude crying aloud began to desire him to do as he had ever done unto them. 9 But Pilate answered them, saying, Will ye that I release unto you the King of the Jews? 10 For he knew that the chief priests had delivered him for envy. 11 But the chief priests moved the people, that he should rather release Barabbas unto them. 12 And Pilate answered and said again unto them, What will ye then that I shall do unto him whom ye call the King of the Jews?

Evil deeds return to haunt the guilty. Less than two months after the Jews cried for Pilate to crucify Jesus, Peter cast these words to them. **"The God of our fathers, hath glorified his Son Jesus; whom ye delivered up, and denied him in the presence of Pilate, when he was determined to let him go. But ye denied the Holy One and the Just, and desired a murderer to be granted unto you; and killed the Prince of life, whom God hath raised from the dead."** (Act.3:14) How did the priests and leaders react to Peter's accusation? His words grieved them so much they cast him and John into prison. Two evils won't make a right. Don't fight against God. It's far better to confess guilt rather than to try to deny or cover it. The people knew Peter spoke truth. How did the common people react to Peter's words? Many repented and obeyed the message he delivered to them from God. May each of us act honestly before our heavenly Father.

Luke

23:4 Then said Pilate to the chief priests and to the people, I find no fault in this man. 5 And they were the more fierce, saying, He stirreth up the people, teaching throughout all Jewry, beginning from Galilee to this place. 6 When Pilate heard of Galilee, he asked whether the man were a Galilaean. 7 And as soon as he knew that he belonged unto Herod's jurisdiction, he sent him to Herod, who himself also was at Jerusalem at that time. 8 And when Herod saw Jesus, he was exceeding glad: for he was desirous to see him of a long season, because he had heard many things of him; and he hoped to have seen some miracle done by him. 9 Then he questioned with him in many words; but he answered him nothing. 10 And the chief priests and scribes stood and vehemently accused him. 11 And Herod with his men of war set him at nought, and mocked him, and arrayed him in a gorgeous robe, and sent him again to Pilate.

Determined to have their own way, priests and elders accused Jesus more angrily, claiming he incited trouble from Galilee to Jerusalem. Pilate sent Jesus to Herod to rid himself of the situation, but after Herod ridiculed Jesus, he returned him to Pilate. How could Pilate do justice and still maintain order among the Jews whose frenzy seemed to be mounting? Did his wife's words echo in his mind? How could he have nothing to do with Jesus when Jewish rulers demanded that he crucify Jesus? It's a sad state of affairs when people place their rulers in such contradicting situations. Are rulers to uphold justice or cave in to popular demands? At this very time our President, to gain support of a small segment of our society, proposes to legalize sodomy. May God have mercy on us and our leaders to recognize and abandon such corruption before God destroys our nation. We all know wickedness destroys civilization.

John

18:36 Jesus answered, My kingdom is not of this world: if my kingdom were of this world, then would my servants fight, that I should not be delivered to the Jews: but now is my kingdom not from hence. 37 Pilate therefore said unto him, Art thou a king then? Jesus answered, Thou sayest that I am a king. To this end was I born, and for this cause came I into the world, that I should bear witness unto the truth. Every one that is of the truth heareth my voice. 38 Pilate saith unto him, What is truth? And when he had said this, he went out again unto the Jews, and saith unto them, I find in him no fault at all. 39 But ye have a custom, that I should release unto you one at the passover: will ye therefore that I release unto you the King of the Jews? 40 Then cried they all again, saying, Not this man, but Barabbas. Now Barabbas was a robber.

Heart of John's gospel centers on the whole truth of God which Jesus, **the prophet** like unto Moses, spoke to the people. God's truth emphasized here states that Jesus was born to be King. His kingdom differs from other kingdoms. His servants use not swords and manmade weapons to conquer. They wield the sword of the Spirit to convince men of sin. (2 Cor.10:4-5) Being convicted, we repent and become born anew of water and Spirit to become the children of the living God. (Jno.3:3,5,7) Doing this we enter the kingdom of heaven. When Jesus mentioned he witnessed to the truth of God, Pilate asked what is truth? In his present situation, Pilate probably questioned if truth existed. God and his commands show truth.

If we sincerely search for truth, listen to Jesus. Obey his commands, for he spoke God's complete truth and sent the Holy Spirit to guide his ministers to record that truth for people of every generation to have and obey. God has not left us to wander in darkness and doubt. Are we willing to submit to truth and do it? Being self-willed ruins us.

Matthew

27:22 Pilate saith unto them, What shall I do then with Jesus which is called Christ? They all say unto him, Let him be crucified. 23 And the governor said, Why, what evil hath he done? But they cried out the more, saying, Let him be crucified. 24 When Pilate saw that he could prevail nothing, but that rather a tumult was made, he took water, and washed his hands before the multitude, saying, I am innocent of the blood of this just person: see ye to it. 25 Then answered all the people, and said, His blood be on us, and on our children. 26 Then released he Barabbas unto them: and when he had scourged Jesus, he delivered him to be crucified.

Mark

15:13 And they cried out again, Crucify him. 14 Then Pilate said unto them, Why, what evil hath he done? And they cried out the more exceedingly, Crucify him. 15 And so Pilate, willing to content the people, released Barabbas unto them, and delivered Jesus, when he had scourged him, to be crucified.

Pilate knew Jesus committed no crime. He testified to the mob that he found no offense in Jesus, but they riled more, creating such a stink he feared they might start a riot. To signify he could not justly condemn Jesus to death, he washed his hands before the priests and said he found Jesus to be innocent. They must bear the ignominy of this great miscarriage of justice. They replied that his blood shall be on us and our children. Less than sixty days later the high priests complained that the apostles brought Jesus' blood on them by preaching Jesus and the resurrection of the dead. (Act.5:28) They were murderers! Why should they complain when they were charged with their sin? Soon they would kill Stephen for calling them murderers. (Act.7:52) Sin leads one into deeper transgression. Unless the race understands Satan destroys lives, including our own, God cannot help us escape Satan's evil ways. Guilt will haunt us all our days, and peace within and without shall elude us. O that each of us would listen to God's call and examine it honestly. Without Jesus' cleansing blood, we shall never realize the peace the angels announced at his birth.

Having the four gospels to review, you and I are able to examine the evidence. Sadducees, those who rejected the resurrection, stood as chief priests. If there is no resurrection, what had they to lose by killing Jesus? They would never have to stand before God to account for his murder. Furthermore, Jesus taught there was a resurrection and judgment to follow for every deed of each person. They must destroy him, or people would abandon their belief. Pharisees, on the other hand, believed in a resurrection, but Jesus condemned their lives for hypocrisy. They had to kill Jesus to save face with the people. Their system of righteousness must remain. Followers of both the Sadducees and Pharisees supported their leaders.

Only those whose hearts desired to draw close to God had no reason to kill Jesus. They knew what he taught came from the Father above. They chose to please God at all cost. They listened to Jesus with intense interest that they might know the God of Abraham, Isaac, and Jacob.

How do you see Jesus? Was he an impostor, troublemaker, self-seeker, liar, or some other plague to society? All honest inquirers who examine the record of the four gospels must concede Jesus is God's Son. The doctrine of loving God and others as we love ourselves does improve human relationships. Desire to serve rather than being served produces a more satisfying life. Knowing we must account for how we use the life God gives teaches accountability which we respect. Two Jewish comments disturbed Pilate: 1) Jesus made himself the Son of God. 2) If you let this man go, you are not Caesar's friend. How could Pilate

Luke

23:12 And the same day Pilate and Herod were made friends together: for before they were at enmity between themselves. 13 And Pilate, when he had called together the chief priests and the rulers and the people, 14 Said unto them, Ye have brought this man unto me, as one that perverteth the people: and, behold, I, having examined him before you, have found no fault in this man touching those things whereof ye accuse him: 15 No, nor yet Herod: for I sent you to him; and, lo, nothing worthy of death is done unto him. 16 I will therefore chastise him, and release him. 17 (For of necessity he must release one unto them at the feast.) 18 And they cried out all at once, saying, Away with this man, and release unto us Barabbas: 19 (Who for a certain sedition made in the city, and for murder, was cast into prison.) 20 Pilate therefore, willing to release Jesus, spake again to them. 21 But they cried, saying, Crucify him, crucify him. 22 And he said unto them the third time, Why, what evil hath he done? I have found no cause of death in him: I will therefore chastise him, and let him go. 23 And they were instant with loud voices, requiring that he might be crucified. And the voices of them and of the chief priests prevailed. 24 And Pilate gave sentence that it should be as they required. 25 And he released unto them him that for sedition and murder was cast into prison, whom they had desired; but he delivered Jesus to their will.

kill God's Son? Yet, how could he release Jesus if he were a king to oppose Caesar? Pilate must judge. Satan places people in difficult straits. We lose every way. How many times have Satan's deceptive tricks trapped you, making you lose either way you went? God stands ready to deliver us from Satan's snares, but we must learn to rely on his wisdom rather than to think we can solve our own problems.

John

19:1 Then Pilate therefore took Jesus, and scourged him. 2 And the soldiers platted a crown of thorns, and put it on his head, and they put on him a purple robe, 3 And said, Hail, King of the Jews! and they smote him with their hands. 4 Pilate therefore went forth again, and saith unto them, Behold, I bring him forth to you, that ye may know that I find no fault in him. 5 Then came Jesus forth, wearing the crown of thorns, and the purple robe. And Pilate saith unto them, Behold the man! 6 When the chief priests therefore and officers saw him, they cried out, saying, Crucify him, crucify him. Pilate saith unto them, Take ye him, and crucify him: for I find no fault in him. 7 The Jews answered him, We have a law, and by our law he ought to die, because he made himself the Son of God. 8 When Pilate therefore heard that saying, he was the more afraid; 9 And went again into the judgment hall, and saith unto Jesus, Whence art thou? But Jesus gave him no answer. 10 Then saith Pilate unto him, Speakest thou not unto me? knowest thou not that I have power to crucify thee, and have power to release thee? 11 Jesus answered, Thou couldest have no power at all against me, except it were given thee from above: therefore he that delivered me unto thee hath the greater sin. 12 And from thenceforth Pilate sought to release him: but the Jews cried out, saying, If thou let this man go, thou art not Caesar's friend: whosoever maketh himself a king speaketh against Caesar. 13 When Pilate therefore heard that saying, he brought Jesus forth, and sat down in the judgment seat in a place that is called the Pavement, but in the Hebrew, Gabbatha. 14 And it was the preparation of the passover, and about the sixth hour: and he saith unto the Jews, Behold your King! 15 But they cried out, Away with him, away with him, crucify him. Pilate saith unto them, Shall I crucify your King? The chief priests answered, We have no king but Caesar. 16 Then delivered he him therefore unto them to be crucified. And they took Jesus, and led him away.

Let us learn to rely on God's help when Satan backs us into tight situations.

Matthew

27:27 Then the soldiers of the governor took Jesus into the common hall, and gathered unto him the whole band of soldiers. 28 And they stripped him, and put on him a scarlet robe. 29 And when they had platted a crown of thorns, they put it upon his head, and a reed in his right hand: and they bowed the knee before him, and mocked him, saying, Hail, King of the Jews! 30 And they spit upon him, and took the reed, and smote him on the head. 31 And after that they had mocked him, they took the robe off from him, and put his own raiment on him, and led him away to crucify him. 32 And as they came out, they found a man of Cyrene, Simon by name: him they compelled to bear his cross. 33 And when they were come unto a place called Golgotha, that is to say, a place of a skull, 34 They gave him vinegar to drink mingled with gall: and when he had tasted thereof, he would not drink. 35 And they crucified him, and parted his garments, casting lots: that it might be fulfilled which was spoken by the prophet, They parted my garments among them, and upon my vesture did they cast lots. 36 And sitting down they watched him there; 37 And set up over his head his accusation written, THIS IS JESUS THE KING OF THE JEWS. 38 Then were there two thieves crucified with him, one on the right hand, and another on the left. 39 And they that passed by reviled him, wagging their heads, 40 And saying, Thou that destroyest the temple, and buildest it in three days, save thyself. If thou be the Son of God, come down from the cross.

Mark

15:16 And the soldiers led him away into the hall, called Praetorium; and they call together the whole band. 17 And they clothed him with purple, and platted a crown of thorns, and put it about his head, 18 And began to salute him, Hail, King of the Jews! 19 And they smote him on the head with a reed, and did spit upon him, and bowing their knees worshipped him. 20 And when they had mocked him, they took off the purple from him, and put his own clothes on him, and led him out to crucify him. 21 And they compel one Simon a Cyrenian, who passed by, coming out of the country, the father of Alexander and Rufus, to bear his cross. 22 And they bring him unto the place Golgotha, which is, being interpreted, The place of a skull. 23 And they gave him to drink wine mingled with myrrh: but he received it not. 24 And when they had crucified him, they parted his garments, casting lots upon them, what every man should take. 25 And it was the third hour, and they crucified him. 26 And the superscription of his accusation was written over, THE KING OF THE JEWS. 27 And with him they crucify two thieves; the one on his right hand, and the other on his left. 28 And the scripture was fulfilled, which saith, And he was numbered with the transgressors. 29 And they that passed by railed on him, wagging their heads, and saying, Ah, thou that destroyest the temple, and buildest it in three days, 30 Save thyself, and come down from the cross.

Scourged, buffeted, slapped, and spat on, Jesus endured all these revilings at the hands of Pilate's soldiers. Then they compelled Simon of Cyrene to carry Jesus' cross to Golgotha where they crucified Jesus between two thieves. The soldiers cast lots to determine which of Jesus' garments each might receive for a souvenir. Bystanders then railed on Jesus, saying, he who would destroy the temple of God and rebuild it in three days should now save himself if he is God's Son. Jesus' followers grieved and helplessly watched, bewildered. Pilatc prepared an inscription in three languages and placed it above Jesus' head on the cross. Jewish rulers objected to Pilate's sign's

Luke

23:26 And as they led him away, they laid hold upon one Simon, a Cyrenian, coming out of the country, and on him they laid the cross, that he might bear it after Jesus. 27 And there followed him a great company of people, and of women, which also bewailed and lamented him. 28 But Jesus turning unto them said, Daughters of Jerusalem, weep not for me, but weep for yourselves, and for your children. 29 For, behold, the days are coming, in the which they shall say, Blessed are the barren, and the wombs that never bare, and the paps which never gave suck. 30 Then shall they begin to say to the mountains, Fall on us; and to the hills, Cover us. 31 For if they do these things in a green tree, what shall be done in the dry? 32 And there were also two other, malefactors, led with him to be put to death. 33 And when they were come to the place, which is called Calvary, there they crucified him, and the malefactors, one on the right hand, and the other on the left. 34 Then said Jesus, Father, forgive them; for they know not what they do. And they parted his raiment, and cast lots. 35 And the people stood beholding. And the rulers also with them derided him, saying, He saved others; let him save himself, if he be Christ, the chosen of God. 36 And the soldiers also mocked him, coming to him, and offering him vinegar, 37 And saying, If thou be the king of the Jews, save thyself. 38 And a superscription also was written over him in letters of Greek, and Latin, and Hebrew, THIS IS THE KING OF THE JEWS.

John

19:17 And he bearing his cross went forth into a place called the place of a skull, which is called in the Hebrew Golgotha: 18 Where they crucified him, and two other with him, on either side one, and Jesus in the midst. 19 And Pilate wrote a title, and put it on the cross. And the writing was, JESUS OF NAZARETH THE KING OF THE JEWS. 20 This title then read many of the Jews: for the place where Jesus was crucified was nigh to the city: and it was written in Hebrew, and Greek, and Latin. 21 Then said the chief priests of the Jews to Pilate, Write not, The King of the Jews; but that he said, I am King of the Jews. 22 Pilate answered, What I have written I have written. 23 Then the soldiers, when they had crucified Jesus, took his garments, and made four parts, to every soldier a part; and also his coat: now the coat was without seam, woven from the top throughout. 24 They said therefore among themselves, Let us not rend it, but cast lots for it, whose it shall be: that the scripture might be fulfilled, which saith, They parted my raiment among them, and for my vesture they did cast lots. These things therefore the soldiers did.

words, but he refused to change the wording. Leaders also cast fiery words at Jesus to display their contempt.

As Jesus looked down from the cross at the various faces, he spoke to the women who wailed at the sight they beheld. He instructed them not to weep for him. They needed to weep for themselves and their children. Days were coming when Jerusalem shall be laid waste. Hardships shall overwhelm its inhabitants and their children. At that time they would wish for relief, but it shall not arrive. If leaders have treated me so badly, what shall they do to you? Ezekiel expresses God's concern. **"Have I any pleasure at all that the wicked should die? saith the Lord God? and not that he should return from his ways, and live?"** (Ezek.18:23)

Rulers believed they had eliminated a great problem by putting Jesus to death. To emphasize their contempt for Jesus, they taunted him, saying if he were God's Son he would come down from the cross. They still saw only the visible. Being God's Son, he must die on the cross to fulfill God's plan.

Matthew

27:41 Likewise also the chief priests mocking him, with the scribes and elders, said, 42 He saved others; himself he cannot save. If he be the King of Israel, let him now come down from the cross, and we will believe him. 43 He trusted in God; let him deliver him now, if he will have him: for he said, I am the Son of God. 44 The thieves also, which were crucified with him, cast the same in his teeth. 45 Now from the sixth hour there was darkness over all the land unto the ninth hour. 46 And about the ninth hour Jesus cried with a loud voice, saying, Eli, Eli, lama sabachthani? that is to say, My God, my God, why hast thou forsaken me? 47 Some of them that stood there, when they heard that, said, This man calleth for Elias. 48 And straightway one of them ran, and took a spunge, and filled it with vinegar, and put it on a reed, and gave him to drink. 49 The rest said, Let be, let us see whether Elias will come to save him. 50 Jesus, when he had cried again with a loud voice, yielded up the ghost. 51 And, behold, the veil of the temple was rent in twain from the top to the bottom; and the earth did quake, and the rocks rent; 52 And the graves were opened; and many bodies of the saints which slept arose, 53 And came out of the graves after his resurrection, and went into the holy city, and appeared unto many.

For six hours Jesus hung on the cross. Chief priests ridiculed him because he claimed to be God's Son. They chided, asking why God didn't come and save him from the cross if he was God's Son. He saved others, but he couldn't save himself. One of the thieves added his voice of contempt, but the other rebuked him, saying that they were punished justly for their deeds, but Jesus unjustly. He asked Jesus to remember him when he came into his kingdom. Jesus granted him paradise that day.

Mark

15:31 Likewise also the chief priests mocking said among themselves with the scribes, He saved others; himself he cannot save. 32 Let Christ the King of Israel descend now from the cross, that we may see and believe. And they that were crucified with him reviled him. 33 And when the sixth hour was come, there was darkness over the whole land until the ninth hour. 34 And at the ninth hour Jesus cried with a loud voice, saying, Eloi, Eloi, lama sabachthani? which is, being interpreted, My God, my God, why hast thou forsaken me? 35 And some of them that stood by, when they heard it, said, Behold, he calleth Elias. 36 And one ran and filled a spunge full of vinegar, and put it on a reed, and gave him to drink, saying, Let alone; let us see whether Elias will come to take him down. 37 And Jesus cried with a loud voice, and gave up the ghost. 38 And the veil of the temple was rent in twain from the top to the bottom.

Looking on his followers, Jesus charged John to care for his mother. In agony, Jesus cried to his Father, asking why he had forsaken him. One bystander attempted to help Jesus by offering him vinegar which he refused. As blood oozed from his wounded hands and feet, Jesus' strength waned. For three hours, from noon to three o'clock, darkness covered the sky. Jesus cried with a loud voice as his spirit departed. Some thought Jesus called on Elijah to come for him. As he died, a great earthquake shook the land, splitting the rocks, ripping the temple veil from top to bottom, and opening graves of the saints. Matthew noted that some of the bodies of the saints arose after Jesus' resurrection, entered Jerusalem, and appeared to many. The centurion remarked that surely these signs prove Jesus must be the Son of God. God beheld the death of his only begotten Son and demonstrated his concern and the significance of Jesus' death by tearing the temple veil.

Luke

**23:39 And one of the malefactors which
were hanged railed on him, saying, If thou
be Christ, save thyself and us. 40 But the
other answering rebuked him, saying,
Dost not thou fear God, seeing thou art in
the same condemnation? 41 And we
indeed justly; for we receive the due
reward of our deeds: but this man hath
done nothing amiss. 42 And he said unto
Jesus, Lord, remember me when thou
comest into thy kingdom. 43 And Jesus
said unto him, Verily I say unto thee, To
day shalt thou be with me in paradise. 44
And it was about the sixth hour, and there
was a darkness over all the earth until the
ninth hour. 45 And the sun was darkened,
and the veil of the temple was rent in the
midst. 46 And when Jesus had cried with
a loud voice, he said, Father, into thy
hands I commend my spirit: and having
said thus, he gave up the ghost.**

Considering the hateful attitudes manifested that day, how shall God change the minds of men to honor his Son Jesus? Perhaps we catch a glimpse from the thief who remarked that he and his fellow thief received just punishment for their taking the property God had given others. Until men perceive their deeds are unjust and that they receive just punishment for wrongdoing, attitudes will not mend. The thief confessed his sins and asked Jesus for mercy which Jesus granted. If we can humble ourselves to admit to ourselves and to God that we are unworthy of all his goodness and mercy, this attitude change pleases God. He knows he made us frail and subject to sin. All he asks of us is to abandon our mighty views of ourselves. Realize how prone we are to do wrong. Change our minds to honor God rather than ourselves. Change of attitude becomes a prerequisite to rebirth. God's kingdom welcomes those who abandon the attitude of Satan and his children. They die spiritually with Christ in baptism and rise with him to a new life. (Rom.6:1-14)

John

**19:25 Now there stood by the cross of
Jesus his mother, and his mother's sister,
Mary the wife of Cleophas, and Mary
Magdalene. 26 When Jesus therefore saw
his mother, and the disciple standing by,
whom he loved, he saith unto his mother,
Woman, behold thy son! 27 Then saith he
to the disciple, Behold thy mother! And
from that hour that disciple took her unto
his own home. 28 After this, Jesus
knowing that all things were now
accomplished, that the scripture might be
fulfilled, saith, I thirst. 29 Now there was
set a vessel full of vinegar: and they filled
a spunge with vinegar, and put it upon
hyssop, and put it to his mouth. 30 When
Jesus therefore had received the vinegar,
he said, It is finished: and he bowed his
head, and gave up the ghost.**

When we rise from the watery grave of baptism with Jesus, a new attitude manifests itself in all our actions. We desire to benefit others, not to cast down, belittle, cheat, lie, or destroy. We visualize each individual as God's child, some obedient, others disobedient. With love and respect, perhaps even the rebellious will desire to return and honor our Father in heaven. As one catches a glimpse of the light of life, it gives him hope that he, too, can find a better life which God provides to those who love him and his children. It's love, not hate, that generates enthusiasm for God. Jesus manifested this love to the daughters of Jerusalem and for his own mother even while his blood trickled down his arms and feet as he hung on the cross. Thinking of the welfare of others, that's God's love manifested in men's lives. God first loved us by sending Jesus to deliver us from the bondage of the Evil One. Jesus showed it by suffering the penalty for our sins. He was bruised for our iniquities, not his. God asks us to demonstrate this love in our lives. If we set our affections on things above, Jesus lives in us, and God is glorified by our lives as Jesus glorified God.

Matthew

27:54 Now when the centurion, and they that were with him, watching Jesus, saw the earthquake, and those things that were done, they feared greatly, saying, Truly this was the Son of God. 55 And many women were there beholding afar off, which followed Jesus from Galilee, ministering unto him: 56 Among which was Mary Magdalene, and Mary the mother of James and Joses, and the mother of Zebedee's children. 57 When the even was come, there came a rich man of Arimathaea, named Joseph, who also himself was Jesus' disciple: 58 He went to Pilate, and begged the body of Jesus. Then Pilate commanded the body to be delivered. 59 And when Joseph had taken the body, he wrapped it in a clean linen cloth, 60 And laid it in his own new tomb, which he had hewn out in the rock: and he rolled a great stone to the door of the sepulchre, and departed. 61 And there was Mary Magdalene, and the other Mary, sitting over against the sepulchre. 62 Now the next day, that followed the day of the preparation, the chief priests and Pharisees came together unto Pilate, 63 Saying, Sir, we remember that that deceiver said, while he was yet alive, After three days I will rise again. 64 Command therefore that the sepulchre be made sure until the third day, lest his disciples come by night, and steal him away, and say unto the people, He is risen from the dead: so the last error shall be worse than the first. 65 Pilate said unto them, Ye have a watch: go your way, make it as sure as ye can. 66 So they went, and made the sepulchre sure, sealing the stone, and setting a watch.

Mark

15:39 And when the centurion, which stood over against him, saw that he so cried out, and gave up the ghost, he said, Truly this man was the Son of God. 40 There were also women looking on afar off: among whom was Mary Magdalene, and Mary the mother of James the less and of Joses, and Salome; 41 (Who also, when he was in Galilee, followed him, and ministered unto him;) and many other women which came up with him unto Jerusalem. 42 And now when the even was come, because it was the preparation, that is, the day before the sabbath, 43 Joseph of Arimathaea, an honourable counsellor, which also waited for the kingdom of God, came, and went in boldly unto Pilate, and craved the body of Jesus. 44 And Pilate marvelled if he were already dead: and calling unto him the centurion, he asked him whether he had been any while dead. 45 And when he knew it of the centurion, he gave the body to Joseph. 46 And he bought fine linen, and took him down, and wrapped him in the linen, and laid him in a sepulchre which was hewn out of a rock, and rolled a stone unto the door of the sepulchre. 47 And Mary Magdalene and Mary the mother of Joses beheld where he was laid.

Gospel writers record convincing evidence to show Jesus truly died. When Joseph asked Pilate for Jesus' body, Pilate called the centurion to confirm Jesus had died. Soldiers pierced his side which revealed blood and water, solid evidence Jesus' body had already begun to decompose. Joseph and Nicodemus wound his body in linen, preserved it with spices, and buried it in Joseph's own tomb. Jewish leaders approached Pilate with the recommendation that the tomb be sealed and a watch be set at the tomb for three days to prevent his disciples from stealing his body and claiming he was yet alive. There can be no mistake. Centurion, soldiers, Joseph, Nicodemus, Pilate, and Jewish rulers were convinced Jesus actually died. God directed his scribes to record firm evidence, proving Jesus died and rose again.

God's prophets foretold Jesus' death, burial, and resurrection: They pierced my

Luke

23:47 Now when the centurion saw what was done, he glorified God, saying, Certainly this was a righteous man. 48 And all the people that came together to that sight, beholding the things which were done, smote their breasts, and returned. 49 And all his acquaintance, and the women that followed him from Galilee, stood afar off, beholding these things. 50 And, behold, there was a man named Joseph, a counsellor; and he was a good man, and a just: 51 (The same had not consented to the counsel and deed of them;) he was of Arimathaea, a city of the Jews: who also himself waited for the kingdom of God. 52 This man went unto Pilate, and begged the body of Jesus. 53 And he took it down, and wrapped it in linen, and laid it in a sepulchre that was hewn in stone, wherein never man before was laid. 54 And that day was the preparation, and the sabbath drew on. 55 And the women also, which came with him from Galilee, followed after, and beheld the sepulchre, and how his body was laid. 56 And they returned, and prepared spices and ointments; and rested the sabbath day according to the commandment.

John

19:31 The Jews therefore, because it was the preparation, that the bodies should not remain upon the cross on the sabbath day, (for that sabbath day was an high day,) besought Pilate that their legs might be broken, and that they might be taken away. 32 Then came the soldiers, and brake the legs of the first, and of the other which was crucified with him. 33 But when they came to Jesus, and saw that he was dead already, they brake not his legs: 34 But one of the soldiers with a spear pierced his side, and forthwith came there out blood and water. 35 And he that saw it bare record, and his record is true: and he knoweth that he saith true, that ye might believe. 36 For these things were done, that the scripture should be fulfilled, A bone of him shall not be broken. 37 And again another scripture saith, They shall look on him whom they pierced. 38 And after this Joseph of Arimathaea, being a disciple of Jesus, but secretly for fear of the Jews, besought Pilate that he might take away the body of Jesus: and Pilate gave him leave. He came therefore, and took the body of Jesus. 39 And there came also Nicodemus, which at the first came to Jesus by night, and brought a mixture of myrrh and aloes, about an hundred pound weight. 40 Then took they the body of Jesus, and wound it in linen clothes with the spices, as the manner of the Jews is to bury. 41 Now in the place where he was crucified there was a garden; and in the garden a new sepulchre, wherein was never man yet laid. 42 There laid they Jesus therefore because of the Jews' preparation day; for the sepulchre was nigh at hand.

hands and feet. (Ps.22:16) They looked on him whom they pierced. (Zech.12:10) None of his bones should be broken. (Ps.34:20) He made his grave with the wicked and with the rich in his death. (Is.53:9) Thou shalt not leave my soul in hell. (Ps.16:10) Luke confirmed to Theophilus that not all Jewish leaders approved the council's decision to put Jesus to death. Joseph and Nicodemus, who had assembled with the council when they decided to destroy Jesus, disapproved. They demonstrated their regret by taking his body from the cross, preparing it for burial, and burying it in Joseph's own new tomb.

With all this evidence, some present-day skeptics affirm Jesus didn't die. They call God and all who testified to Jesus' death liars. Either those who affirm Jesus didn't really die have not examined the evidence or they blind their eyes to facts. Jesus did die, and God returned to him to life.

Matthew

**28:1 In the end of the sabbath, as it began
to dawn toward the first day of the week,
came Mary Magdalene and the other
Mary to see the sepulchre. 2 And, behold,
there was a great earthquake: for the
angel of the Lord descended from heaven,
and came and rolled back the stone from
the door, and sat upon it. 3 His
countenance was like lightning, and his
raiment white as snow: 4 And for fear of
him the keepers did shake, and became as
dead men. 5 And the angel answered and
said unto the women, Fear not ye: for I
know that ye seek Jesus, which was
crucified. 6 He is not here: for he is risen,
as he said. Come, see the place where the
Lord lay. 7 And go quickly, and tell his
disciples that he is risen from the dead;
and, behold, he goeth before you into
Galilee; there shall ye see him: lo, I have
told you. 8 And they departed quickly
from the sepulchre with fear and great
joy; and did run to bring his disciples
word.**

Jesus is risen from the dead! These words amazed Mary as she approached the tomb in that first day of the week following the Passover. She and the other Mary trembled because of the angel and the earthquake which accompanied the angel's appearance. He directed them to hurry and spread the good news of Jesus' resurrection to his disciples and Peter. Jesus shall meet you in Galilee as he has said. Both Marys trembled and hurried to where the disciples assembled.

Terror must have struck the soldiers who kept the sepulchre at the time of the earthquake and the angel's coming. Even the stone removed from the tomb's entrance. They had tried to perform their responsibility faithfully, but what could they do against God, an earthquake, and an angel? They fled from the scene quickly and reported the incident to the chief priests. Assembling, the priests counseled to have the soldiers to tell

Mark

**16:1 And when the sabbath was past,
Mary Magdalene, and Mary the mother
of James, and Salome, had bought sweet
spices, that they might come and anoint
him. 2 And very early in the morning the
first day of the week, they came unto the
sepulchre at the rising of the sun. 3 And
they said among themselves, Who shall
roll us away the stone from the door of
the sepulchre? 4 And when they looked,
they saw that the stone was rolled away:
for it was very great. 5 And entering into
the sepulchre, they saw a young man
sitting on the right side, clothed in a long
white garment; and they were affrighted.
6 And he saith unto them, Be not
affrighted: Ye seek Jesus of Nazareth,
which was crucified: he is risen; he is not
here: behold the place where they laid
him. 7 But go your way, tell his disciples
and Peter that he goeth before you into
Galilee: there shall ye see him, as he said
unto you. 8 And they went out quickly,
and fled from the sepulchre; for they
trembled and were amazed: neither said
they any thing to any man; for they were
afraid.**

their superiors Jesus' disciples came by night and stole him away as we slept. Since sleeping on duty meant death, the priests gave them much money and promised to persuade the governor not to prosecute them if trouble ensued. The soldiers agreed. This transaction was commonly reported among the Jews.

How could Sadducees who claimed there is no resurrection and no such thing as an angel reconcile this happening with their belief? Would they discount the soldiers' testimony as they had rejected Jesus' and the writings of Moses? They could not find Jesus' body to disprove the soldiers' statements. How could they continue to believe a lie? Jesus answered these questions by saying they valued the praise of their associates more than they loved God.

Luke

24:1 Now upon the first day of the week, very early in the morning, they came unto the sepulchre, bringing the spices which they had prepared, and certain others with them. 2 And they found the stone rolled away from the sepulchre. 3 And they entered in, and found not the body of the Lord Jesus. 4 And it came to pass, as they were much perplexed thereabout, behold, two men stood by them in shining garments: 5 And as they were afraid, and bowed down their faces to the earth, they said unto them, Why seek ye the living among the dead? 6 He is not here, but is risen: remember how he spake unto you when he was yet in Galilee, 7 Saying, The Son of man must be delivered into the hands of sinful men, and be crucified, and the third day rise again. 8 And they remembered his words, 9 And returned from the sepulchre, and told all these things unto the eleven, and to all the rest. 10 It was Mary Magdalene, and Joanna, and Mary the mother of James, and other women that were with them, which told these things unto the apostles. 11 And their words seemed to them as idle tales, and they believed them not. 12 Then arose Peter, and ran unto the sepulchre; and stooping down, he beheld the linen clothes laid by themselves, and departed, wondering in himself at that which was come to pass.

John

20:1 The first day of the week cometh Mary Magdalene early, when it was yet dark, unto the sepulchre, and seeth the stone taken away from the sepulchre. 2 Then she runneth, and cometh to Simon Peter, and to the other disciple, whom Jesus loved, and saith unto them, They have taken away the Lord out of the sepulchre, and we know not where they have laid him. 3 Peter therefore went forth, and that other disciple, and came to the sepulchre. 4 So they ran both together: and the other disciple did outrun Peter, and came first to the sepulchre. 5 And he stooping down, and looking in, saw the linen clothes lying; yet went he not in. 6 Then cometh Simon Peter following him, and went into the sepulchre, and seeth the linen clothes lie, 7 And the napkin, that was about his head, not lying with the linen clothes, but wrapped together in a place by itself. 8 Then went in also that other disciple, which came first to the sepulchre, and he saw, and believed. 9 For as yet they knew not the scripture, that he must rise again from the dead. 10 Then the disciples went away again unto their own home.

When the women explained to the disciples how the angel rolled the stone from the tomb and informed them that Jesus had risen from the dead, even apostles disbelieved. Finally, Peter and John ran to the sepulchre and found it empty except for the linen which Joseph and Nicodemus had wound around Jesus. This really shocked Peter and John. Maybe he has risen from the dead as he promised.

As Peter and John reported their find to the rest, their disbelief began to change to belief that God had raised Jesus from the dead. How were they to reconcile their expectations of God's kingdom with what happened? Though Jesus tried to change their view of God's kingdom, his words hadn't altered their concept of the kingdom.

When we see how the apostles wrestled with the problem of harmonizing their plans for God's kingdom with what Jesus taught, we need not be too surprised when we experience a similar challenge. Even the parables of Jesus only compared God's kingdom to familiar situations. Apostles needed to consider the similarities to gain understanding of the kingdom of heaven. Without God's help even we may never arrive at a clear concept of God's kingdom. Ask for God's guidance to understand his truth then do what it commands.

Matthew

**28:9 And as they went to tell his disciples,
behold, Jesus met them, saying, All hail.
And they came and held him by the feet,
and worshipped him. 10 Then said Jesus
unto them, Be not afraid: go tell my
brethren that they go into Galilee, and
there shall they see me. 11 Now when they
were going, behold, some of the watch
came into the city, and shewed unto the
chief priests all the things that were done.
12 And when they were assembled with
the elders, and had taken counsel, they
gave large money unto the soldiers, 13
Saying, Say ye, His disciples came by
night, and stole him away while we slept.
14 And if this come to the governor's ears,
we will persuade him, and secure you. 15
So they took the money, and did as they
were taught: and this saying is commonly
reported among the Jews until this day.**

Mark

**16:9 Now when Jesus was risen early the
first day of the week, he appeared first to
Mary Magdalene, out of whom he had
cast seven devils. 10 And she went and
told them that had been with him, as they
mourned and wept. 11 And they, when
they had heard that he was alive, and had
been seen of her, believed not. 12 After
that he appeared in another form unto
two of them, as they walked, and went
into the country. 13 And they went and
told it unto the residue: neither believed
they them. 14 Afterward he appeared
unto the eleven as they sat at meat, and
upbraided them with their unbelief and
hardness of heart, because they believed
not them which had seen him after he was
risen.**

Coordinating all four gospels, this seems to be the order of events after Jesus' resurrection. The women arrived at the sepulchre at about dawn as an earthquake shook the area and as the angel rolled back the tomb's stone, opening the tomb. An angel informed them that Jesus had risen from the dead, and they should go tell the apostles. Hurrying to spread the good news, they informed the apostles. Peter and John ran to the grave with Mary Magdalene following. John arrived first, but Peter entered first. They saw the burial clothes lying where Jesus had been lying. Peter and John returned to the city, but Mary tarried at the tomb. Jesus appeared to her and told her to instruct his brethren, the apostles, to meet him in Galilee. She then ran to the apostles, telling them she had seen Jesus alive, but they didn't believe her.

While Mary shared the joy with the apostles, the keepers of the sepulchre hurried to the chief priests to tell them what transpired. The Jews' council assembled and decided to silence the report by paying the soldiers to claim that Jesus' disciples stole his body while they slept. However, they could not silence the fact that Jesus arose from the dead. News of his resurrection and the council's plan to keep his resurrection secret spread in the city. Even with the soldiers confirming that Jesus rose from the dead, Sadducees disbelieved.

Disciples of Jesus disbelieved Mary when she told them she had seen and touched Jesus. Though he had taught them repeatedly he must go to Jerusalem to be betrayed, killed, and rise from the dead the third day, they seemed not to understand. Their minds rejected the idea that Jesus must die and rise again. Even after Jesus appeared to other disciples, the eleven continued to disbelieve until Jesus met with them and rebuked their unbelief.

We today ought not to be too harsh with those who continue to reject some of the truths recorded in the word of God. There's one thing certain. When people die or continue to live until he returns, they most certainly shall believe his resurrection, but it will be too late to benefit them, for God allows only one lifetime to believe him. Let all who fear standing before God in judgment prepare while you can.

Luke

**24:13 And, behold, two of them went that
same day to a village called Emmaus,
which was from Jerusalem about
threescore furlongs. 14 And they talked
together of all these things which had
happened. 15 And it came to pass, that,
while they communed together and
reasoned, Jesus himself drew near, and
went with them. 16 But their eyes were
holden that they should not know him. 17
And he said unto them, What manner of
communications are these that ye have
one to another, as ye walk, and are sad?
18 And the one of them, whose name was
Cleopas, answering said unto him, Art
thou only a stranger in Jerusalem, and
hast not known the things which are come
to pass there in these days? 19 And he said
unto them, What things? And they said
unto him, Concerning Jesus of Nazareth,
which was a prophet mighty in deed and
word before God and all the people: 20
And how the chief priests and our rulers
delivered him to be condemned to death,
and have crucified him. 21 But we trusted
that it had been he which should have
redeemed Israel: and beside all this, to
day is the third day since these things
were done. 22 Yea, and certain women
also of our company made us astonished,
which were early at the sepulchre; 23 And
when they found not his body, they came,
saying, that they had also seen a vision of
angels, which said that he was alive. 24
And certain of them which were with us
went to the sepulchre, and found it even
so as the women had said: but him they
saw not.**

All four gospels provide abundant evidence to prove to those with honest minds that Jesus truly was God's Son and that Jews condemned him to death, but God raised him from the dead. All who choose to disbelieve the record God has given of his Son call God a liar. (1 Jno.5:10) Disobedient Christians cause much disbelief.

John

**20:11 But Mary stood without at the
sepulchre weeping: and as she wept, she
stooped down, and looked into the
sepulchre, 12 And seeth two angels in
white sitting, the one at the head, and the
other at the feet, where the body of Jesus
had lain. 13 And they say unto her,
Woman, why weepest thou? She saith
unto them, Because they have taken away
my Lord, and I know not where they have
laid him. 14 And when she had thus said,
she turned herself back, and saw Jesus
standing, and knew not that it was Jesus.
15 Jesus saith unto her, Woman, why
weepest thou? whom seekest thou? She,
supposing him to be the gardener, saith
unto him, Sir, if thou have borne him
hence, tell me where thou hast laid him,
and I will take him away. 16 Jesus saith
unto her, Mary. She turned herself, and
saith unto him, Rabboni; which is to say,
Master. 17 Jesus saith unto her, Touch me
not; for I am not yet ascended to my
Father: but go to my brethren, and say
unto them, I ascend unto my Father, and
your Father; and to my God, and your
God. 18 Mary Magdalene came and told
the disciples that she had seen the Lord,
and that he had spoken these things unto
her.**

Luke's account of how Jesus appeared to the two traveling to Emmaus illustrates God's mercy. Understanding the hardness of the disciples' minds against God's plan, he provided several opportunities to prove to them Jesus did rise from the dead. Though Cleopas and his companion trusted that Jesus would redeem Israel, they, too, were unable to reconcile his crucifixion with what they expected Christ to do. As they discussed Mary's news of his resurrection and Peter's and John's visit to the sepulchre, Jesus met with and explained the Scriptures to them. When Jesus revealed himself, they believed Jesus and their Scriptures. Do we believe God's truth?

Luke

24:25 Then he said unto them, O fools, and slow of heart to believe all that the prophets have spoken: 26 Ought not Christ to have suffered these things, and to enter into his glory? 27 And beginning at Moses and all the prophets, he expounded unto them in all the scriptures the things concerning himself. 28 And they drew nigh unto the village, whither they went: and he made as though he would have gone further. 29 But they constrained him, saying, Abide with us: for it is toward evening, and the day is far spent. And he went in to tarry with them. 30 And it came to pass, as he sat at meat with them, he took bread, and blessed it, and brake, and gave to them. 31 And their eyes were opened, and they knew him; and he vanished out of their sight. 32 And they said one to another, Did not our heart burn within us, while he talked with us by the way, and while he opened to us the scriptures? 33 And they rose up the same hour, and returned to Jerusalem, and found the eleven gathered together, and them that were with them, 34 Saying, The Lord is risen indeed, and hath appeared to Simon. 35 And they told what things were done in the way, and how he was known of them in breaking of bread. 36 And as they thus spake, Jesus himself stood in the midst of them, and saith unto them, Peace be unto you. 37 But they were terrified and affrighted, and supposed that they had seen a spirit. 38 And he said unto them, Why are ye troubled? and why do thoughts arise in your hearts? 39 Behold my hands and my feet, that it is I myself: handle me, and see; for a spirit hath not flesh and bones, as ye see me have. 40 And when he had thus spoken, he shewed them his hands and his feet.

Convincing his disciples that Jesus truly had risen from the grave took many sightings and reviewing the Scriptures. However, by late during the resurrection day

John

20:19 Then the same day at evening, being the first day of the week, when the doors were shut where the disciples were assembled for fear of the Jews, came Jesus and stood in the midst, and saith unto them, Peace be unto you. 20 And when he had so said, he shewed unto them his hands and his side. Then were the disciples glad, when they saw the Lord.

most of them had seen Jesus, his pierced hands, feet, and side. These evidences convinced them that he was Jesus and that the prophets of old had foretold all these events which should happen long before his birth. Once Jesus convinced his disciples he had risen from the dead, he could return to the right hand of his Father and to the glory God gave him before creation.

As I reviewed all these evidences, It inspired me to see how completely the gospel writers related the evidences of his life, teaching, betrayal, unjust judgment, being reviled, crucifixion, death, and resurrection. Even the soldiers and council could not refute the evidences. They devised lies to continue to deceive the people and persuade them not to believe in Jesus as the Son of God.

What will it take to convince people of every nation that Jesus offers the only way to find peace in this world? He fulfilled the promise made to Abraham that in his descendent all people of the world should be blessed. After 2000 years, only a small part of the world trusts in God's redemption plan, and where is promised peace? Present trends indicate the percentage of world population who believe in Jesus as Christ decreases. Is unbelief caused by lack of preaching God's truth, sin, or a combination of both? Jesus shall conquer by his truth. He shall sit at God's right hand until he has put down all rebellion against his Father. (1 Cor.15:25-28) If you and I refuse to submit to God's truth, Jesus will subdue by force. Why defy God and suffer his wrath?

Luke

24:41 And while they yet believed not for joy, and wondered, he said unto them, Have ye here any meat? 42 And they gave him a piece of a broiled fish, and of an honeycomb. 43 And he took it, and did eat before them. 44 And he said unto them, These are the words which I spake unto you, while I was yet with you, that all things must be fulfilled, which were written in the law of Moses, and in the prophets, and in the psalms, concerning me. 45 Then opened he their understanding, that they might understand the scriptures, 46 And said unto them, Thus it is written, and thus it behoved Christ to suffer, and to rise from the dead the third day: 47 And that repentance and remission of sins should be preached in his name among all nations, beginning at Jerusalem. 48 And ye are witnesses of these things.

Eating food before the disciples and recalling how he fulfilled the prophecies of the Scriptures, Jesus convinced the disciples he was the Christ, the Son of God, raised from the dead. Does God need to unveil minds today for people to understand his truth? Paul instructed Timothy he does. **"Consider what I say; and the Lord give thee understanding in all things."**(2 Tim.2:7) Unless one truly meditates on the truth of God, desiring to grasp God's truth, God will not open his mind to perceive his message. Our own wisdom fails to grasp the truth of God. God alone opens understanding. If it were otherwise, only the wise would fathom the message of God. Utilizing this plan, God defeats the wise who so often trust in their wisdom. He hides his truth from them and reveals it unto babes, those who put their trust in God, not in themselves. **"I thank thee, O Father, Lord of heaven and earth, because thou hast hid these things from the wise and prudent, and hast revealed them unto babes."** (Math.11:25)

John

20:21 Then said Jesus to them again, Peace be unto you: as my Father hath sent me, even so send I you. 22 And when he had said this, he breathed on them, and saith unto them, Receive ye the Holy Ghost: 23 Whose soever sins ye remit, they are remitted unto them; and whose soever sins ye retain, they are retained. 24 But Thomas, one of the twelve, called Didymus, was not with them when Jesus came. 25 The other disciples therefore said unto him, We have seen the Lord. But he said unto them, Except I shall see in his hands the print of the nails, and put my finger into the print of the nails, and thrust my hand into his side, I will not believe. 26 And after eight days again his disciples were within, and Thomas with them: then came Jesus, the doors being shut, and stood in the midst, and said, Peace be unto you. 27 Then saith he to Thomas, Reach hither thy finger, and behold my hands; and reach hither thy hand, and thrust it into my side: and be not faithless, but believing. 28 And Thomas answered and said unto him, My Lord and my God. 29 Jesus saith unto him, Thomas, because thou hast seen me, thou hast believed: blessed are they that have not seen, and yet have believed. 30 And many other signs truly did Jesus in the presence of his disciples, which are not written in this book: 31 But these are written, that ye might believe that Jesus is the Christ, the Son of God; and that believing ye might have life through his name.

Does the evidence recorded by the gospel writers convince you? Do his miracles, deeds, fulfilling the Scriptures, the testimony of John the Baptist, the testimony of all God's prophets, and the truths Jesus himself spoke suffice to prove Jesus came from God and showed to us God's true plan of life? If so, obey it. Surely so many witnesses didn't lie. Let all ministers believe all God's truth.

Matthew

28:16 Then the eleven disciples went away into Galilee, into a mountain where Jesus had appointed them. 17 And when they saw him, they worshipped him: but some doubted.

Twice in Jerusalem Jesus showed himself to the disciples as a group. Now five of them assembled on one of the mountains of Galilee. While there, Peter decided he wanted to go fishing. John, Thomas, and Nathanael chose to accompany him. That night they caught nothing, but as morning dawned, Jesus called to them from the shore, asking if they had caught fish. They answered they hadn't. He directed them to cast their net on the right side of the boat. They did and netted such a large catch they couldn't draw in the net. John commented that Jesus stood on the shore. Peter quickly clothed himself and plunged into the sea of Tiberias and swam ashore while the others came by boat. Jesus had prepared breakfast of bread and fish. They drew their catch of a hundred fifty-three large fish ashore without tearing the net. Jesus invited them to dine with him. All the disciples knew that it was Jesus who ate with them. This was the third time Jesus appeared to them after he arose.

As they visited, Jesus asked Peter if he loved him more than the fish he had just snared. Peter replied, "Lord, you know I love you." Three times Jesus asked Peter the same question. Twice Jesus asked him to feed his sheep, meaning he should use his time to teach the truth of God to God's children. It becomes far more important to supply the spiritual food for those hungering for the bread of life than to cast nets into the sea to catch food for the body.

Jesus informed Peter that in his later life, men would bind him and take him where he preferred not to go, denoting how he must die to glorify God in his death. Even this encouraged Peter to follow him. Peter asked Jesus what would happen to John. He

John

**21:1 After these things Jesus shewed
himself again to the disciples at the sea of
Tiberias; and on this wise shewed he
himself. 2 There were together Simon
Peter, and Thomas called Didymus, and
Nathanael of Cana in Galilee, and the sons
of Zebedee, and two other of his disciples.
3 Simon Peter saith unto them, I go a
fishing. They say unto him, We also go
with thee. They went forth, and entered
into a ship immediately; and that night
they caught nothing. 4 But when the
morning was now come, Jesus stood on
the shore: but the disciples knew not that
it was Jesus. 5 Then Jesus saith unto
them, Children, have ye any meat? They
answered him, No. 6 And he said unto
them, Cast the net on the right side of the
ship, and ye shall find. They cast
therefore, and now they were not able to
draw it for the multitude of fishes. 7
Therefore that disciple whom Jesus loved
saith unto Peter, It is the Lord. Now when
Simon Peter heard that it was the Lord,
he girt his fisher's coat unto him, (for he
was naked,) and did cast himself into the
sea. 8 And the other disciples came in a
little ship; (for they were not far from
land, but as it were two hundred cubits,)
dragging the net with fishes. 9 As soon
then as they were come to land, they saw
a fire of coals there, and fish laid thereon,
and bread. 10 Jesus saith unto them,
Bring of the fish which ye have now
caught. 11 Simon Peter went up, and
drew the net to land full of great fishes, an
hundred and fifty and three: and for all
there were so many, yet was not the net
broken. 12 Jesus saith unto them, Come
and dine. And none of the disciples durst
ask him, Who art thou? knowing that it
was the Lord. 13 Jesus then cometh, and
taketh bread, and giveth them, and fish
likewise. 14 This is now the third time
that Jesus shewed himself to his disciples,
after that he was risen from the dead. 15**

**So when they had dined, Jesus saith to
Simon Peter, Simon, son of Jonas, lovest
thou me more than these? He saith unto
him, Yea, Lord; thou knowest that I love
thee. He saith unto him, Feed my lambs.
16 He saith to him again the second time,
Simon, son of Jonas, lovest thou me? He
saith unto him, Yea, Lord; thou knowest
that I love thee. He saith unto him, Feed
my sheep. 17 He saith unto him the third
time, Simon, son of Jonas, lovest thou me?
Peter was grieved because he said unto
him the third time, Lovest thou me? And
he said unto him, Lord, thou knowest all
things; thou knowest that I love thee.
Jesus saith unto him, Feed my sheep. 18
Verily, verily, I say unto thee, When thou
wast young, thou girdedst thyself, and
walkedst whither thou wouldest: but
when thou shalt be old, thou shalt stretch
forth thy hands, and another shall gird
thee, and carry thee whither thou
wouldest not. 19 This spake he, signifying
by what death he should glorify God. And
when he had spoken this, he saith unto
him, Follow me. 20 Then Peter, turning
about, seeth the disciple whom Jesus loved
following; which also leaned on his breast
at supper, and said, Lord, which is he that
betrayeth thee? 21 Peter seeing him saith
to Jesus, Lord, and what shall this man
do? 22 Jesus saith unto him, If I will that
he tarry till I come, what is that to thee?
follow thou me. 23 Then went this saying
abroad among the brethren, that that
disciple should not die: yet Jesus said not
unto him, He shall not die; but, If I will
that he tarry till I come, what is that to
thee? 24 This is the disciple which
testifieth of these things, and wrote these
things: and we know that his testimony is
true. 25 And there are also many other
things which Jesus did, the which, if they
should be written every one, I suppose
that even the world itself could not
contain the books that should be written.
Amen.**

replied that if he chose to permit John to live until Jesus returned, it was not any of Peter's business. Some understood this to mean John would never die, but that wasn't what Jesus meant.

John who wrote this gospel identified himself by saying he was the one Jesus loved. It was he that lay on Jesus' breast during the last supper and asked Jesus who would betray him. Having witnessed all the things recorded in his gospel, he affirmed that all things written therein were true. He hadn't recorded everything he saw and heard Jesus say and do, but he picked what he wrote so that those who read his gospel might have abundant evidence to determine for themselves whether Jesus fulfilled the role of the Messiah as foretold by the ancient prophets. Had John penned everything Jesus did and taught, the whole world might not be large enough to contain the books.

As you examine John's gospel, does it prove to you Jesus' actions and doctrine show he fulfilled the prophecy of Moses that God would raise up a **Prophet** like Moses? Did God speak through the mouth of Jesus all his will? Did he show that those who rejected the doctrine Jesus taught that God cut them off from the blessings God promised to Israel? Did Jesus grant to those who received his words that they should inherit all the blessings God promised to those who obeyed his truth? Were his miracles sufficient to warrant one to trust that Jesus performed those wonders only by the power of God? Could his foes refute any of his wonders or prove God did not raise him from the dead? If one lived as Jesus instructed would it truly benefit his life and provide an abundant life on earth? Did he set forth a clear expectation of what blessings God awarded his faithful children after the resurrection? What curses did Jesus say awaited the rebellious? If you believe the evidence abundantly sufficient to prove Jesus fulfilled and spoke all God's truth, will you obey all God's truth to walk with God?

Matthew

28:18 And Jesus came and spake unto them, saying, All power is given unto me in heaven and in earth. 19 Go ye therefore, and teach all nations, baptizing them in the name of the Father, and of the Son, and of the Holy Ghost: 20 Teaching them to observe all things whatsoever I have commanded you: and, lo, I am with you alway, even unto the end of the world. Amen.

As God commissioned Jesus to come into the land of Israel to teach the will of the Father and show all his wonders, Jesus sent his apostles into all the world to teach all nations how to die to Satan's evil manner of life and bitterness and baptize believers to begin that new life. Once each person experiences the new birth, teach them to do all the truth of God which Jesus explained to the apostles.

Their mission to deliver people from Satan's kingdom and translate them into the kingdom of God did not leave them without God's presence. As God worked with Jesus to show Israel the new covenant promised by the prophets, God shall go with you wherever you go to show all peoples the living God. You will work with God to bring good tidings to all peoples and nations.

Matthew and Mark leave the impression that Jesus

Mark

16:15 And he said unto them, Go ye into all the world, and preach the gospel to every creature. 16 He that believeth and is baptized shall be saved; but he that believeth not shall be damned. 17 And these signs shall follow them that believe; In my name shall they cast out devils; they shall speak with new tongues; 18 They shall take up serpents; and if they drink any deadly thing, it shall not hurt them; they shall lay hands on the sick, and they shall recover. 19 So then after the Lord had spoken unto them, he was received up into heaven, and sat on the right hand of God. 20 And they went forth, and preached every where, the Lord working with them, and confirming the word with signs following. Amen.

continued in Galilee until his ascension, but Luke shows that Jesus led the apostles from Jerusalem up to Bethany where he ascended up to his Father. However, Luke omitted Jesus meeting the apostles in Galilee after his resurrection. Each gospel writer included those events which fulfilled the goals they had in mind when they recorded their gospels.

From creation God desired to dwell with men, but men, believing Satan's lies, severed that relationship.

Luke

24:49 And, behold, I send the promise of my Father upon you: but tarry ye in the city of Jerusalem, until ye be endued with power from on high. 50 And he led them out as far as to Bethany, and he lifted up his hands, and blessed them. 51 And it came to pass, while he blessed them, he was parted from them, and carried up into heaven. 52 And they worshipped him, and returned to Jerusalem with great joy: 53 And were continually in the temple, praising and blessing God. Amen.

Apostles spread God's truth, showing how God and man may walk together again if we will believe God's truth, not Satan's lies. God now speaks to us through Jesus whom he raised from the dead. (Heb.1:1-2) The apostles spread the news and means of how God and men may walk together again. Guided by God's Spirit, apostles demonstrated and taught how people come to dwell with God in heaven if we will walk with him while on earth.

Apostles remained in Jerusalem until the Spirit empowered them on Pentecost. As they waited his coming, they praised God for his love and mercy extended to them through his Son Jesus. You, too, can enjoy the presence of God with you each day.

Viewpoints
Table 2: Simon's House

Mt.26:6-13	Mk.14:3-9	Lk.7:36-48	Lk.10:38-42	Jn.11:1-5	Jn.12:1-5
1. Bethany	Bethany	city	village	Bethany	Bethany
2. Simon's house	Simon's house	Simon's house	Martha's house	Martha served	
3. leper	leper	Pharisee			
4. alabaster box	alabaster box	alabaster box			
5. precious ointment	spikenard ointment	ointment		ointment	spikenard ointment
6. on head	on head	on feet		on feet	on feet
7.		wipe with hair		wipe with hair	wipe with hair
8. woman	woman	woman: sinner	Mary: sister	Mary and Martha	Martha served
9.				Lazarus: brother	Lazarus raised
11.					Judas: Simon's son 12:4; 13:2,6
12. for burial	for burial				for burial
13.		Simon: no courtesy	Mary: good part	Lazarus: brother, sick	Lazarus raised
14.		Mary's sins forgiven			
15.Disciples complained	some complained	Simon complained	Martha complained	sisters complained	Judas complained

Questions:

1. Are these people all in one family?
2. Are there one, two, or four incidents?
3. Why did Matthew and Mark say she anointed head, but Luke and John, feet?
4. Does the context determine purpose and where Jesus was anointed?
5. Why do Matthew, Mark, and John place the incident near Jesus' death, but Luke in the middle of Jesus' ministry?
6. Why doesn't Luke tell us this happened in Judaea?
7. Did Jesus cleanse Simon's leprosy? Why? Why not?
8. Does author's purpose determine where Jesus was anointed?